Global Practices of Corporate
Social Responsibility

Samuel O. Idowu • Walter Leal Filho
Editors

Global Practices of Corporate Social Responsibility

 Springer

Editors
Samuel O. Idowu
London Metropolitan University
London Metropolitan Business School
84 Moorgate
London, EC2M 6SQ
UK
s.idowu@londonmet.ac.uk

Professor Walter Leal Filho
Hamburg University of Applied Sciences
Research and Transfer Centre
"Applications of Life Sciences"
Lohbruegger Kirchstraße 65
21033 Hamburg
Germany
walter.leal@haw-hamburg.de

ISBN 978-3-540-68812-9   e-ISBN 978-3-540-68815-0

Library of Congress Control Number: 2008931165

Cover design: WMX Design GmbH, Heidelberg, Germany

Printed on acid-free paper

9 8 7 6 5 4 3 2 1

springer.com

*This book is dedicated to all those who
are genuinely striving to be socially responsible
wherever they are on planet Earth.*

Foreword

That the issue of corporate social responsibility (CSR) has moved up the corporate agenda in recent years cannot be doubted, but given the emerging evidence on such critical issues as climate change, one would have expected that. Although many companies address environmental and other issues of social concern, they rarely do so in such a way that satisfies all groups. While being kind to the environment can produce bottom line benefits, difficult choices often need to be made and financial return is not always consistent with environmental imperatives. The CSR agenda, like most other areas of business activity, is not easy to deliver upon, and this is as true for universities as it is for corporations.

There have been periods in the past when the environment was a dominant issue, but time elapsed and the issue became less prominent. For those looking to be let off the CSR hook, I do not see this happening in the future. The growing scientific consensus on the likely devastating impact of global warming, the development of major funds which will only invest in socially responsible companies and the increasing weight given to social and environmental factors in the construction of risk indices are amongst the compelling reasons for this.

So if this issue is on the corporate radar and seems likely to stay there, practitioners need to search for answers. Restricting this search to the local area is unlikely to be good enough. This is why this book is so timely. By providing a comprehensive account of how organizations in over 20 different countries approach the issue of corporate social responsibility, the reader is able to contrast the differing interpretations of the concept and the practice of CSR. I am sure you will find much here of value, and to the extent that the lessons learned produce more socially responsible behaviours the benefits will be enjoyed by us all.

Vice Chancellor & Chief Executive   Brian Roper
London Metropolitan University
London, UK

Preface

The idea for this book was conceived when it was realized that, after more than two decades of a general acceptance of the concept of *corporate social responsibility*, a gap exists in the market for a book which readers would find both useful and informative on how corporate entities in different political settings, economic contexts and cultural circumstances around the world understand, perceive and are indeed practicing the field of *social responsibility*. The need for a book that contains a first-hand account by experienced researchers and leading academics from the six continents and that addresses important issues and expectations of modern stakeholders, justifies the publication of a book of this sort. It explores in detail those actions which corporate entities in different countries consider socially responsible behaviour, especially when there is still no standard definition of what CSR means or entails and bearing in mind that the field is still evolving. This book provides information on how corporate entities (both profit seeking and not-for profit) in nineteen independent nations around the world are striving to demonstrate that being socially responsible in whatever they do is now part of normal business practice.

Each chapter was written with the sole objective of satisfying the information needs of modern stakeholders, practitioners, researchers, legislators, international organizations, governments, tomorrow's business managers (students) and all those who are enthusiastic about the field of CSR and its latest developments. It is hoped that this first attempt at codifying in one book the international experiences of twenty-first century corporate entities around the globe will further enhance our readers' understanding of what CSR is all about, how corporate entities are absorbing its principles in their day-to-day business and how it is developing around the world.

Samuel O. Idowu, Walter Leal Filho   Winter 2008

Acknowledgements

We thank a lot of our friends and colleagues whose names are far too numerous to mention for helping us either directly or indirectly towards making the publication of this book a reality. Samuel O. wants to thank the following individuals; Michael A. Idowu, Elizabeth A. A. Lawal, Olufunmilola O. Idowu, Christopher Hutchinson, Eric Woodin, Richard Norrie, Denis Haffner, Andrea Dunhill, Fred Smith, Kojo Menyah, Timothy Cleary, Berna Kirkulak, Habib Rahman, Kerstin Sahlin, Celine Louche, Royston Gustavson, Jennifer J. Griffin, Roger Palmer, Jeremy Moon, Philip Burns, Edward Akintaro, Brian Towler, Bode Akinwande, Samuel Ogunlaja, David Ogunlaja, Michael Soda, Timothy Ogunyale, Getachew Zergaw, Roger Alderman, Louise Slater, Anthony Brabazon and David Crowther. And also his very special thanks are due to his darling daughters: Rachael T., Mary T. and Abigail O. who have shared with him both the pleasures and travails of co-editing a book of international standing like this one! Finally, he wants to thank his Vice Chancellor, Brian Roper who has supported all his CSR projects and the Deputy Director of London Metropolitan Business School; Bob Morgan who has played a silent but unique role in some aspects of the book.

Walter Leal wants to thank Franziska Mannke, Paulina Pawlak, Ralf Behrens and Christopher Maas for their inputs and for organizing the RENEW Fair, the CSR Study and the Hamburg CSR Conference in the autumn of 2007, which have provided useful insights into current practices in the field.

We both want to thank two colleagues at Springer in Heidelberg, Germany; Dr. Martina Bihn for facilitating the initial process and our publishing editor Dr. Niels Peter Thomas who has been very helpful and cooperative during entire process of coordinating the efforts of our contributors spread across the globe and in the publication of the book.

We have taken all possible steps to ensure that the facts presented in this book are error free however; infallibility is a trait that is totally beyond humanity. We therefore wish to register our sincere apologies for any act of omission or error that may appear anywhere in the book, no harm was intended to anyone, after all we are only trying to be socially responsible!

Finally, we take this opportunity to extend our sincere condolences to one of our colleagues – Professor Olukunle Iyanda, of the University of Botswana, Gaborone, Botswana who was unable to contribute a chapter on the practice of CSR in Botswana following the sudden death of his wife, Omotola, at the critical time of his preparation for the project.

Contents

List of Contributors

Professor Konstantinos G. Aravossis is a Lecturer in the School of Mechanical Engineering in Section of Industrial Management and Operational Research, NTU Athens. He has completed many scientific projects and publications in his research interest areas and was president of the Greek Association of Environmental Protection Companies (2001–2006). His academic interests are Environmental Management, Environmental Economics, Investment Assessment, and Technology Economics.

Dr S. Burak Arzova is an associate professor of accounting at the Faculty of Economics and Administrative Sciences, Marmara University, Istanbul, Turkey.

Dr. Mariana Lima Bandeira is a Professor and Researcher at the Universidad Andina Simón Bolívar, Ecuador. Her research interests include human behaviour in organisations; social responsibility and qualitative methodology.

Ataur Belal obtained his Ph.D. and MBA from Sheffield University Management School and Cardiff Business School respectively. He is now working as a Lecturer at Aston Business School, Aston University, UK. His principal research interest is in the area of corporate social reporting. His articles appeared in academic journals such as Accounting, Auditing and Accountability Journal, Environmental Politics, Sustainable Development and Corporate Social Responsibility, and Environmental Management.

Claudia Bustamante is a professor in the engineering college at the University of Sonora, Mexico. She holds a Masters degree from the Monterrey Institute of Technology and Higher Education. She is the statistical advisor to the Sustainable Development Group.

Dr. Javier Esquer holds a doctoral degree from the University of Massachusetts, Lowell in the field of Cleaner Production and Pollution Prevention. He is a professor in sustainability issues at the University of Sonora, Mexico. His recent work aims at promoting Environmental Management Systems.

Dr Patricia Everaert is currently an assistant professor at Ghent University. She finished her Ph.D. on target costing in 1999. She has published several international articles in the area of target costing, outsourcing and time-driven Activity-based Costing. One of her current research interests is in CSR reporting.

Pauline Göthberg, Licentiate of Economics, from the Department of Business studies, Uppsala University. Pauline has studied CSR on a corporate level, more specifically, she has examined the conditions for social projects to be organized and established in multinational corporations. Currently, Pauline is working as a project manager with a brief to establish a new research institute at MID Sweden University.

Maria Grafström holds a Ph.D. in Business Studies from Uppsala University. Her main research interest concerns the relationship between media and corporations, how media participate in creating suitable conditions to flourish corporations. More specifically, she has studied the development and organization of business newspapers, content, and production of business news, and how management models, such as CSR, get attention in the media. She has been teaching on courses in management, organization, and market strategy at the undergraduate level.

Dr. Jennifer J. Griffin is an Associate Professor of Strategic Management & Public Policy at The George Washington University, Washington DC, USA. She is the Program Director, Global Stakeholder Strategies at George Washington Institute of Corporate Responsibility. She has contributed papers to several high quality academic journals.

Hande Gürdağ is a research assistant at the Department of Political Science and International Relations, Ufuk University Ankara, Turkey.

Dr Royston Gustavson lectures in the School of Management, Marketing, and International Business, The Australian National University, in business ethics, corporate sustainability, and corporate strategy. His primary area of research is corporate governance, especially the role of governance in ethics and sustainability. He has an MBA with Distinction from the Melbourne Business School, a Ph.D. from The University of Melbourne, is a Fellow of the Australian Institute of Company Directors, and an Associate Fellow of the Australian Institute of Management.

Ralph Hamann is senior researcher at the University of Cape Town Environmental Evaluation Unit (EEU), an independent, self-funded research, training, and consulting unit. He is an Extraordinary Associate Professor at the Sustainability Institute at Stellenbosch University. With a Ph.D. from the University of East Anglia (UK), he has worked with and consulted to a range of public and private sector organisations and has working experience in Africa, Europe, and Asia. He is on the editorial board of *Environment: Linking Science and Policy for Sustainable Development* and he has guest edited two special journal editions on CSR related issues, both of which were the result of international research conferences he organised.

Professor (Dr) Laurence Eberhard Harribey holds the Chair in *"Sustainable Development & Global Responsibility of organisations"* at Bordeaux School of Management. She is the coordinator for the implication of BEM in the GRLI (Global Responsible Leadership Initiative). She began her career as the Secretary General of an International NGO and worked for ten years at the European level before beginning a career as a researcher in European Politics. Her current research work focuses on Globally Responsible Leaders' Education for one part and on the analysis of the public and private networks confrontation in the emergence of a European framework on Corporate Social Responsibility and Sustainable Development for the other part.

Peter Hills is Professor and Director of the Centre of Urban Planning and Environmental Management, at the University of Hong Kong in the People's Republic of China.

Elizabeth Hogan holds two Master of Arts degrees in Natural Resources & Sustainable Development and International Relations. Elizabeth has recently completed a training programme with the Camara de Industrias de Costa Rica in San Pedro, where she focused on environmental standards for Costa Rican businesses. Much of her graduate and thesis research has focused on corporate environmental responsibility, particularly as it pertains to climate change and international development.

Marie d'Huart is a lawyer in international law, with a Master's degree in science and environmental management. She worked in the European institutions, in Canada, Peru, Maghreb and South Africa, mainly on the environmental management of industrial projects. She founded CAP Conseil in 2003, a company which specialises in sustainable development and social responsibility. She is an expert in social and environmental indicators and standards, such as AA1000, SA 8000, ISO 14001, GRI, Global Compact and the soon to become effective: ISO 26000. From Brazil to China, CAP Conseil provides research and pragmatic advice to both private and public sector organisations.

Dr. Wesley Johnston is Professor of Marketing at Georgia State University. Johnston received his Ph.D. at University of Pittsburgh. He has published several articles in *Journal of Consumer Research*, *Journal of International Business Studies*, *Journal of Marketing*, and *Journal of the Academy of Marketing Science*, among others. His research interests include application of behavioral sciences to marketing in the areas of customer relationship management and strategic account programs, as well as network dynamics and relationship strategies, especially in sales force management.

Luc Van Liedekerke is professor of business ethics at the Universities of Leuven and Antwerp. He is director of the Centre for Economics and Ethics (KULeuven) and of the Centre for Ethics (University Antwerp). He is also chairman of the register committee of Ethibel/Stock at Stake (Brussels), an organization specialized in ethical screening of companies. He studied philosophy and economics both at the KULeuven and holds a Ph.D. in philosophy and an M.Sc. in Economics. He has published among other things Explorations in financial ethics, Peeters, Leuven, (2000) and Business en Ethiek: spelregels voor ethisch ondernemen, Lannoo, (2002). He teaches regularly at business schools in Belgium and abroad. He is also the organizer of an annual chair in business ethics with lectures at the universities of Leuven and Antwerpen and held the Rector Dhanis chair at the University of Antwerp. He was recently elected as president of the European Business Ethics Network (EBEN), a network organization that brings together business ethics scholars as well as business people with around 1,000 members, present in 37 countries.

Dr. Adam Lindgreen is Professor of Strategic Marketing at Hull University Business School. He has published in *Business Horizons, Industrial Marketing Management, Journal of Business Ethics, Journal of Business and Industrial Marketing*, and *Psychology & Marketing*, among other journals. His research interests include business and industrial marketing, consumer behaviour, relationship and value management, experiential marketing, and corporate social responsibility. He serves on the board of many journals and has guest edited *British Food Journal, Entrepreneurship and Regional Development, Journal of Business Ethics, Journal of Business & Industrial Marketing*, and *Supply Chain Management*.

Lassi Linnanen is a professor at the Department of Energy and Environmental Management, Lappeenranta University of Technology, Lappeenranta, Finland.

Céline Louche is an Assistant Professor at Vlerick Leuven Gent Management School. She teaches and researches in the area of Corporate Social Responsibility (CSR). She obtained her Ph.D. in 2004 on the institutionalisation of socially responsible investment (SRI) at the Rotterdam Erasmus University (The Netherlands) for which she obtained the FIR Finance & Sustainability Prize award for the best European Ph.D. thesis in 2005. She also worked for five years as a Sustainability Analyst for SRI at the Dutch Sustainability Research institute. In her work, she explores the way processes of change take place. Her major research interest is the construction of the CSR field with a special focus on SRI and stakeholders processes. She is member of the Academic Board of the European Academy of Business in Society, the scientific committee of the International Network for Research on Organisations and Sustainable Development, and the SRI advisory committee of Dexia Asset Management.

Vasily Lubinin obtained his Bachelor's degree in management from Moscow State University. He also obtained his M.Sc. in Accounting and Business from Aston University, UK. He is now working in JSC Unified Energy Systems of Russia Settlements Centre as a head of treasury department.

Amina Marin is professor in occupational issues at the University of Sonora, Mexico. She holds a doctoral degree in cleaner production and pollution prevention and she is participating in sustainability projects in Maquiladora industries.

Dr. Nora Munguía holds a doctoral degree from the University of Massachusetts Lowell in the field of Cleaner Production and Pollution Prevention. She is professor/researcher in sustainability issues at the University of Sonora, Mexico. Her most recent work involves cleaner production and pollution prevention in Sonoran industries.

Peggy Moschou is a Mechanical Engineer. Her academic interests are in CSR and Performance Measurement.

Olatoye Ojo, Ph.D., is a Senior Lecturer in Estate Management at Obafemi Awolowo University, Ile-Ife, Nigeria. He also currently serves as Chairman, Project Implementation Committee of the University and by virtue of this position, belongs to some other committees of the University.

He is a Fellow of The Nigerian Institution of Estate Surveyors and Valuers and a Registered Estate Surveyor and Valuer by Estate Surveyors and Valuers Registration Board of Nigeria. Before entering academia, he was the Managing Partner of Olatoye Ojo & Co – a real estate consulting outfit with head office at Ibadan and branches in major cities of Nigeria. He has served as – Pioneer Chairman. He currently serves as Chairman/Editor-In-Chief of The Estate Surveyor and Valuer (the Institution's professional journal); moderator of professional examinations of The Nigerian Institution of Estate Surveyors and Valuers and External Examiner, Federal University of Technology, Minna. He has also served as Member, Education and Joint CPD Committees of The Estate Surveyors and Valuers Registration Board of Nigeria.

Olatoye Ojo has published several articles in reputable national and international journals in the areas of housing, housing finance, property development and management and investment analysis. He has attended many national and international conferences and has presented papers in such fora.

Virgilio Panapanaan is a post-doctoral research fellow at the Laboratory for Environmental Economics and Management, Lappeenranta University of Technology, Lappeenranta, Finland.

Nikolaos A. Panayiotou is a Lecturer in the School of Mechanical Engineering in NTU Athens, Section of Industrial Management and Operational Research. He has experience in BPR projects both in the public and the private sector. His academic interests are Business Process Reengineering, Business Process Improvement, Performance Measurement and IT-enabling technology.

Dr. Fernando López Parra, Ph.D. in Administration is an independent consultant, Coordinator of the Ph.D. program in Administration at the Universidad Andina Simón Bolívar, Ecuador. He is also a professor and researcher in the same institution.

Paulina S. Pawlak holds an M.Sc. degree in Environmental Engineering and an MBA in Technology Management. She researches Corporate Sustainability as a Business Case and as a source of Competitive Advantage.

Dirk Le Roy is Founder and Managing Director of SUSTENUTO, a private strategic consultancy specialised in Corporate Social Responsibility (CSR) and Sustainable Development (SD). Dirk has been educated as bio-engineer and followed the executive MBA at the Vlerick Leuven Gent Management School where he received "De Buck & Co Award". He supports large companies in developing CSR into their strategies, facilitates CSR learning networks in cooperation with employer federations such as regional Chambers of Commerce and SME-federations, supports policy formulations on the subject and is widely connected to CSR research conducted in business schools, as member of the MC of RESPONSE – a global research project funded by the EC. Dirk has executed a significant number of policy studies for regional and national governments, the European Commission and the World Bank.

Ans Rossy has a Master of Social Science (Netherlands) and a post-graduate diploma in Cross-Sector Partnerships (UK). She has a broad international experience with corporate and NGO's of which she spent 7 years in Portugal. In Belgium, she was a year-long Editor-in-chief of the e-magazine on CSR 'Alter Business News' in Belgium. In 2003–2004, Ans worked as SD-expert for the Regional Brussels government in a tri-partite partnership. In 2005–2006, Ans worked for the Interdepartmental Commission on Sustainable Development (ICDO/CIDD) for the Belgian federal government. She was responsible for the Secretariat of the federal interdepartmental working group on CSR, which developed, in a participatory process with a variety of stakeholders, a Belgian framework on CSR.

Dr Aly Salama completed a 4-year degree in Accounting (Excellent with Honour) in 1990 and then went on to pursue his M.Sc. in auditor independence at the Faculty of Commerce at Suez Canal University (SCU) in Egypt. During 1990–1996, he was an instructor in Accounting at SCU. During 1996–1999, he was an assistant lecturer in accounting at SCU. He obtained his M.Phil./ Ph.D. from the University of Nottingham. After the successful completion of his doctorate, he was awarded a postdoctoral fellowship from the ESRC, which had been held at the Nottingham University Business School. In 2004, he joined the University of Sunderland as a senior lecturer in Accounting and Finance. Now, he is a lecturer in Accounting at the University of Durham Business School.

Dr. Valérie Swaen is Assistant Professor of Marketing at the Université catholique de Louvain and was previously with the IESEG School of Management. Her doctoral research examined consumer perceptions and reactions to corporate citizenship activities in terms of consumer trust, commitment, and loyalty. She has published papers in *Journal of Business Ethics*, *Recherche et Applications en Marketing, Revue Française du Marketing*, and *Corporate Reputation Review*, among other journals.

Prof. Dr. R. Şeminur Topal is a Professor at Yildiz Technical University, Istanbul Turkey. She has published over 140 publications to her name and worked for several national and international organizations.

Dr Luis Velázquez is an internationally recognized professor/researcher in sustainability issues. He is the founder and Director of the Sustainable Development Group at the University of Sonora. He holds a doctoral degree in the major of Cleaner

Production and Pollution Prevention from the University of Massachusetts, Lowell, USA.

Ben Vivari lectures at The George Washington University School of Business, Washington DC.

Richard Welford is an Associate Professor in the Centre of Urban Planning and Environmental Management at the University of Hong Kong and a Director of CSR, Asia.

Karolina Windell holds a Ph.D. from the Department of Business studies, Uppsala University. Her primary research interest concerns the spread and construction of new ideas about management, more specifically her research focuses on the emergence of the idea CSR, which is a topic dealt with in her thesis as well as in other publications. In addition, she has been studying the relationship between media and other organizations and how this influences news production. She has been teaching undergraduates in market strategy, management, and CSR.

Professor Dr. Mustaffa Mohamed Zain is a Deputy Vice Chancellor at the University Teknologi MARA Malaysia in Selangor, Malaysia.

Andrea Ing Zavala is professor in sustainability issues at the University of Sonora, Mexico. She has a Masters degree in cleaner production and pollution prevention. She is the coordinator for the "Toward a Sustainable University: ISO 14001" project at the same institution.

Global Practices of CSR in Context

Samuel O. Idowu and Walter Leal Filho

Events around the world over the last few decades have emphasised the need for corporate entities, their stakeholders, governments and international organizations to take the issue of corporate social responsibility seriously. Incidents such as the explosion at Union Carbide in Bhopal, India in 1984, the oil spillage at Prince William Sound, Alaska USA in 1989, a few corporate scandals; for example the Mirror Group UK 1991, Bank of Credit and Commerce International (BCCI) 1991 UK, Polly Peck 1992 UK, Enron USA 2001, World Com USA 2002, Parmalat Italy 2003 remain fresh and indelible in our minds. Other issues such as climate change and global warming, human rights abuses, terrorism and the globalization of the world economy also affect how corporate entities conduct their operational practices. These operational practices consequently impinge on how corporate entities perceive their responsibilities to societies; and in turn societies' expectations from corporate entities have increased.

The issue of CSR is a topical one in every country around the world today (although the importance attached to it may differ in each country), not because CSR is a soft issue but because it is an issue that touches different aspects which are important and of concern to us all. A transnational organization for example; may be faced with differing aspects of CSR in different countries of operation. What falls under the umbrella of CSR in one country may perhaps be of little or no significance in another. Issues such as poverty, inability to service and repay international debt, illiteracy, HIV/AIDS, the absence of clean running water and electricity, fraud, bribery and corruption are social ills typical of the underdeveloped world whilst other issues such as global warming, terrorism, money laundering, corporate and individual philanthropy, CO_2 emissions reduction might be issues that affect all nations but are publicized by the more industrialized ones. The impact of these social problems, will differ from country to country and some of the consequences are CSR related which require CSR related solutions.

Many years ago, corporate entities were 'only' expected by societies to provide goods and services, provide employment, pay corporate taxes, maximize the wealth of the providers of capital regardless of whose interests or feelings were injured during the course of doing so and conform to the basic rules of society. In addition to all these, as a result of some of the events and issues noted above, they are now expected to be socially responsible. Being socially responsible simply requires a corporate entity to behave well in all its dealings and put in place appropriate measures which would help to reduce the adverse impact of its actions on both the environment and its stakeholders. An entity that fails to demonstrate responsibility in its actions, may not survive beyond the short term, it is therefore in the best interest of those corporations which aspire to survive and prosper to behave responsibly. The field of CSR has several challenges and opportunities. It has been argued by some commentators, researchers and advocates of the field of CSR that several benefits could be derived by an entity if it were perceived by its stakeholders and the general public as being socially responsible. The following are a few of the benefits often cited:

- Improvement in its shareholder value
- Increased customer loyalty
- Ability to form beneficial strategic alliances
- Ability to attract motivated and committed workforce
- Sympathetic media at critical times
- Ability to attract top class employees from top class universities
- Tax incentives given by tax authorities

Corporate entities around the world have realized that modern stakeholders are no longer naïve instead they are sophisticated, educated, well informed and above all, they know what is best for them. They will not hesitate to take whatever actions are deemed responsible and legitimate to request corporate entities to produce what is needed. In the United Kingdom for example, stakeholders' increasing requests for information from companies on their CSR activities appear to be the main driving force behind the issuing of CSR reports by UK companies. These companies have realized that providing information to 'all and sundry' on their CSR activities is a good method of achieving positive public relations. Several other benefits flow from this action, for example customers will continue to be loyal, equity investors will be happy to invest, donors will continue to donate generously, loan creditors and suppliers would happily take credit risks, there will be nothing for the non-governmental organizations (NGOs) and their members to complain or protest about and several other requirements of modern stakeholders and the environment would have been met. Everyone will be happy! Effective CSR is now at the forefront of what modern corporate entities crave, they aspire to implement CSR initiatives which portray them as being socially responsible in all the actions they take, visible results of these initiatives go a very long way to placate and satisfy all stakeholders.

This book – the *Global Practices of Corporate Social Responsibility* is an attempt to codify in a single document, international evidence of the CSR actions of corporate entities which are already actively practicing or in the process of formalizing their practices in different countries. How are corporate entities in these countries dealing with those issues which relate to CSR? How are they practicing CSR? Which issues fall under the umbrella of CSR in each of these countries? Who are the players in the field of CSR? Why have corporate entities suddenly become more moral or ethical? Why is everyone embracing CSR? Our readers will find some answers to these questions either directly or indirectly from the 21 chapters of this book. The articles in each chapter suggest that being socially responsible by modern corporate entities is no longer an option; it is now a moral and business requirement. The consequences of not being so are serious for the entity concerned, its stakeholders and the environment it operates in.

To assist in the reading of papers in the book contributors have adopted different approaches in describing how corporate entities in their chosen countries are practicing CSR. Contributors have variously titled their chapters in order to reflect how corporate entities largely view CSR in each particular country, it is hoped that this action demonstrates to our readers the uniqueness of each chapter.

The first chapter for example argues that CSR means different things to different people. This will perhaps explain why the approaches adopted in a particular country will be determined by several factors including the social and economic problems it faces at any point in time which require CSR related solutions. Having accepted that CSR is practiced differently across the world, the question, is, how is CSR practiced in the People's Republic of China, Egypt, Costa Rica, Russia, Australia or any of the remaining participating countries featured in the book? The answer is to be found by looking at the results which contributors to the book have reached in their studies of CSR practices in these countries'.

The participating counties in the project have been divided into five parts. Countries have been grouped together geographically. Part I – Europe, Part II – East Asia, Part III – The Americas, Part IV – Middle East & Africa and Part V – Australasia.

In the first chapter entitled "Practicing Corporate Social Responsibility in the United Kingdom" *Samuel O Idowu* argues that CSR has been practiced in the UK for well over 200 years: before and during the Industrial Revolution. The UK government has played a part in globalizing the practice of CSR, which now appears to be part of normal business practice in the UK, 81% of the FTSE 100 companies are now actively practicing CSR and this action has now permeated to a larger number of smaller UK companies, non-profit seeking entities are also making it apparent that they too are CSR conscious. The Archbishop of Canterbury, Dr Rowan Williams, in his 2007 Christmas message, enjoins all Christians wherever they are to do all they can to protect the environment.

In the second chapter "*CSR Global Practices: France*" Laurence Eberhard Harribey argues that the progress France has made in the field of CSR has some legal connotations, there are many significant legal texts in France on the application of CSR. By the middle of the first decade of the 21st century 400 French companies had joined the United Nations Global Compact Initiatives. The skepticism in Europe about the idea of morality in business and the historic perception of the relationships between the state and companies could explain why France has opted for the legal route in encouraging its companies to be CSR conscious, this author argues.

Walter Leal Filho and Paulina Pawlak in Chap. 3 on "*An overview of CSR practices in corporate Germany*" argue that as a result of the ambiguity in the use of the term CSR and the absence of an internationally recognized definition of the

term, some German companies perceive CSR as simply about corporate philanthropy, whilst other commentators in the field in the country recognize that corporate entities of whatever shape have some environmental responsibility towards
society. They also argue that CSR is practiced in Germany from two dimensions –
Internal and External which is in line with the European Commission's perception
of the field of CSR.

Virgilio Panapanaan and Lassi Linnanen in "*An exploratory study of the social
dimension of corporate responsibility in Finland*" examine the role of corporate
responsibility in Finland using a four stage roadmap to illustrate how Finnish companies are managing their responsibilities. They argue that business transparency
is innate in Finnish culture and provides a positive impetus which enables Finnish
companies to comfortably practice the field in Finland and elsewhere in the world.

Karolina Windell, Maria Grafstrom and Pauline Gothberg in "*The practice of
CSR in Sweden*" argue that CSR has a long history in Sweden but the debate has
only emerged during the last few decades. They argue that Swedish corporations
started practicing some form of CSR between the mid seventeenth century and mid
nineteenth century when they played a prominent role in the local community. The
Swedish discourse on CSR changed during the last 20 years because stakeholders
continue to urge corporations to take on a greater responsibility in the contributions
they make to societies.

Celine Louche et al. in "*Understanding the CSR landscape in Belgium*" argue
that CSR is a recently adopted concept in Belgium. It became popular in the mid
1990s. Belgium has also taken a legal route towards the adoption of its practice,
the field in the country is argued by these authors to offer great disparities and
diversities.

Nikolaos Panayiotou, Konstantinos Aravosis and Peggy Moschou in "*Contents
of corporate social responsibility reports of companies in Greece*" argue that the
necessity to make positive contributions to society has suddenly become apparent to
Greek companies over the last few decades. These companies have opted to use their
CSR reports as a vehicle to propagate the positive contributions they are making to
societies around the world. The results of the authors' extensive study of Greek
companies are found in Chap. 7.

Ataur Rahman Belal and Vasily Lubinin in "*Corporate social disclosures in
Russia*" argue that the literature depicts corporate social disclosures in Russia as
an under researched area. The authors studied the annual reports of twenty large
Russian companies and note that 90% of companies disclose employee related information, 85% of companies disclose information about the environment and 55%
of companies made ethical disclosures, and even then the quality of the information
disclosed is generally poor for two reasons, the lack of external verification and the
lack of completeness.

Richard Welford and Peter Hills in the chapter on "*Corporate social responsibility in China*" argue that CSR in a Chinese context is still driven in the main
by the leading Western brands and those of a few locally often Hong Kong based
companies that have a brand and image to protect. However, the government is
now also promoting CSR as the private sector's contribution to the 'harmonious

society'. Supply chain pressure and local government initiatives are now encouraging domestic companies to adopt environmental and social initiatives. Three key areas for CSR in China, which include the environment, labour and supply chain issues are explored. Obstacles to the adoption of CSR are also examined along with the policies the government are using to try to encourage further good CSR practices.

Mustaffa Mohammed Zain et al. in Chap. 10 argue that the pressure placed on businesses to behave responsibly has heightened interests in corporate donations. The chapter considers the determinants of corporate donations made by 774 Malaysian Plcs using agency and stakeholder theories.

In Chap. 11, *Jennifer Griffin and Ben Vivari,* in their attempt to provide information on CSR practices in the United States of America examine three topics on why USA firms participate in CSR, how they participate in the field and how they report on their CSR activities. These two authors also argue that the practice of CSR in the USA is still evolving and accelerating at an uneven pace across different industries within the country.

In a second chapter for the USA on a snapshot of corporate practices of the field in the USA, *Adam Lindgreen, Valerie Swaen and Wesley J. Johnston* argue that despite the popularity of the field of CSR with its theoretical underpinnings having been a frequent subject of debate and research studies, evidence suggests that the theory of the field may not be in alignment with its practice. They argue that this argue may act as an impediment to a good understanding of the field and its development. Lindgreen et al. in an attempt to address this problem examine the actual CSR practices of five different stakeholder groups in the United States.

Luis Velazquez et al. in Chap. 13 argue that CSR is a concept which encourages firms to recognize their social, environmental and economic impacts on the environment and society. They argue that the benefits of CSR in Mexico appear to have been blurred by the absence and inaccessibility of information which perhaps has contributed to the reason why CSR is still not generally known in Mexico.

Elizabeth Hogan in Chap. 14 examines the differences in the way domestic businesses and subsidiaries of large multinational corporations operating in Costa Rica perceive CSR. Elizabeth argues that domestic businesses view CSR in terms of the Central American Free Trade Agreement (CAFTA) legislation and the anticipated effects it will have on smaller businesses. The chapter also explores the motivations of a few Costa Rican's MNCs involvement in CSR and the lessons domestic businesses can learn from these MNCs CSR practices.

Mariana Lima Bandeira and Fernando Lopez Parra in Chap. 15 argue that the initial attitude of Brazilians about CSR was that it was not an issue. This view has now changed as a result of the country's social problems and the sustainability discourse. They argue that in Brazil CSR is now under construction.

In Chap. 16 *Aly Salama* in "*A study of social responsibility disclosure practices of Egyptian companies*" examines Egyptian companies' internet social reporting with the aim of establishing whether these companies' disclosures recognize the community as an important stakeholder group. Salama notes the existence of some good practices in companies operating in the Telecommunications and construction industries, but he also notes that the social disclosure practices of companies outside these two industries are inadequate and well below the expectations of the community of stakeholder groups.

Seminur Topal and Hande Gurdag in the first of two chapters from Turkey argue that CSR was introduced into Turkey during the presidency of Atarturk in an attempt to meet the needs of the NGOs and to accelerate the process of modernization using several Western ideologies. The chapter goes on to provide information about CSR practices of a few companies in the country.

Chapter 18 *by Burak S Arzova* on *CSR in Turkey* provides a detailed account of the contributions a few local and international companies make to the practice of CSR in Turkey. The chapter argues that CSR has thrived in Turkey following a series of earthquakes especially the one that occurred in 1999. CSR in Turkey is still not widely practiced. The chapter argues that the practice of CSR in corporate Turkey is basically philanthropic with some environmental actions such as planting of trees etc. The author suggests that some government legislations on CSR might further popularize the practice as Turkey prepares its next application for EU membership.

Olatoye Ojo in Chap. 19 on "*CSR activities as a vehicle for economic development in Nigeria*" argues that the development of a nation's economy is a joint venture between its government, citizenry and corporate entities; whilst they are all behaving responsibly. In an attempt to establish how CSR is practiced in Nigeria in order to achieve this objective of economic development, Olatoye Ojo studied how corporate entities in eight sectors of the Nigerian economy (six from profit seeking and two from not for profit (NFPOs)) are practicing CSR and provides the results of his study in this chapter.

In the 20th chapter, *CSR in South Africa:On the role of history, the government and local context, Ralph Hamann* argues that the country's complex and painful history has significant implications on how CSR is understood and implemented by corporate entities and stakeholders. On the one hand, big business has been implicated in human rights abuses committed under apartheid; on the other, the history of apartheid gave rise to early manifestations of voluntary initiatives to contribute to government policy changes and social development. The chapter also argues that in a country like South Africa, CSR cannot be defined purely as voluntary initiatives as in other places. There are no clear distinctions or divisions between voluntary business actions and state-led interventions, it finally concurs that many conventional approaches used to assess or even rank CSR performance are relatively superficial in terms of the interactions between companies and their socio-economic and natural environments.

In the final chapter on the *Practices and Experiences of CSR in Australia, Royston Gustavson* takes the view that CSR in Australia is a recent phenomenon, because most of the current formal frameworks and supporting networks did not exist a decade ago. Royston argues that Australia is a wealthy country with extensive government social support, including universal health care. Combined, this has resulted in a slow move to corporate social responsibility on the part of most organisations, although the best, such as Westpac and BHP Billiton, are world leaders in their industries. Legal obligations and investor expectations make financial performance paramount, and two recent government enquiries have recommended against amending the *Corporations Act* to require CSR. The move towards CSR is being primarily driven by refocusing it as risk management (such as the recent changes to the Australian Stock Exchange Corporate Governance Principles), and the long-term view taken by the ever-increasing influence of institutional investors.

The news of the consensus reached at the Bali Conference, Indonesia on Climate Change of December 2007 by the 187 countries present at the conference is a step in the right direction, it confirms that governments around the world are concerned about the future of our planet and are ready to take appropriate measures to alleviate the problems which global warming is manifesting in different parts of the world.

It is hoped that our readers will find the articles from around the world in this book - the *Global Practices of CSR* – (the first in a series of books on Corporate Social Responsibility, Sustainability and Sustainable Developments) useful. We all owe it to the coming generations to ensure that planet *Earth* is not damaged for them! Professionals' Perspectives of CSR which is the next book in the series; will provide information about CSR experiences of different professions and how these professionals have absorbed CSR's idea into what they do in their various professional callings.

Part I
Europe

Chapter 1
The United Kingdom of Great Britain and Northern Ireland

Samuel O. Idowu

Abstract History suggests that the field of corporate social responsibility (CSR) has been practiced in the UK for well over two hundred years. Albeit, those actions that are tantamount to the activities now referred to as social responsibility were not previously so described. CSR is a relatively modern term used for all those corporate actions that now fall under its ambit. The UK – a widely acknowledged world leader in the field – has played a pivotal role in recent corporate activities/actions in the field. This chapter explores how UK corporate entities (both profit-seeking and not-for-profit) have been practicing CSR over the last few decades. The paper also discusses the roles that the UK governments have assumed at different times in the field of CSR in the past few centuries. The literature provides a wealth of good-quality studies covering different aspects of CSR by researchers both in the UK and across the world, and this chapter refers to some of these excellent studies. The following questions need to be answered in order to fully understand how the field has developed over its history: What has brought about the recent revival or resurgence of interests in CSR since the 1980s? Why have corporate entities across the globe suddenly realized that CSR is a concept that must be warmly embraced if they wished to compete successfully and survive in modern markets? Why are all these entities ensuring that their stakeholders are aware of all their activities in the field? Answers to these and similar questions can be found not just in the UK chapter but throughout the book. To put it simply, doing 'good' is now perceived by all as being trendy and rewarding: if not immediately, then certainly in the longer term. Adam Smith (1776) in his book '*The Wealth of Nations*' said that "It is not from the benevolence of the butcher, the brewer, or the baker, that we expect our dinner, but from their regard to their own interest. We address ourselves not to their humanity but to their self-love, and never talk to them of our necessities but of their advantage." Some large UK firms have argued that 'doing good is good for business', which perhaps sums it all up. However, the actions of '*The Abolitionists*' from the 1780s up until 1833 show that altruistic CSR in the UK has a very long history.

S. O. Idowu and W. L. Filho (eds.), *Global Practices of Corporate Social Responsibility*   11
© Springer-Verlag Berlin Heidelberg 2009

1.1 Introduction

The notion that British corporate entities should behave responsibly can be traced back several centuries. It was the Portuguese that started the slaving of Africans in 1440 Rawley and Behrendt (2005); by 1562 England had joined in the socially irresponsible trade through Sir John Hawkins (Du Bois 1896). By the 1760s, slavery and the treatment of African slaves had become a social issue in Great Britain. By the late 1780s, Sir William Wilberforce and two of his other parliamentary colleagues, Thomas Clarkson and Granville Sharp, had formed the 'social activists group' of their time – '*The Abolitionists*' as they were then called! This pressure group they formed campaigned peacefully (*responsibly*) for 35 years for the abolition of slave trade. The powerful federation of *planters, merchants, manufacturers*, and *ship owners* understandably put up a rearguard resistance against the efforts of these social activists through their actions in both the Houses of Commons and Lords. Finally, on the 25th of March 1807 the Abolition of Slave Trade Act was passed. The Act made it illegal for British ships to carry slaves and for British companies to trade in slaves. In effect, the Act could be interpreted as a legal mandate that forced British corporate entities, including the church, to behave in a socially responsible manner in respect of the trade in human beings and all related activities. However, the trade continued despite the 1807 Act until another Act: the Slavery Abolition Act 1833; even then the Tory government of Robert Peel had to pay compensation to the slave owners. The value of the compensation depended on the number of slaves owned. It was claimed that the then Bishop of Exeter, Dr Henry Phillpotts, was paid £12,700 for 665 slaves, an average of about £19 per slave.

During the Industrial Revolution of 1750–1830, several British industrialists and entrepreneurs had indirectly practiced some aspects of corporate social responsibility (CSR) as we know it today. For example, the entrepreneur Richard Arkwright had identified that employees were 'human assets' who should be treated responsibly in order to get the best work performance from them. Arkwright was the first industrialist to build low-cost houses near his factories for his employees in Derby in 1775. Arkwright had embarked on what in today's terms would be perceived as being socially responsible by providing these homes either rent free or at nominal rents, as pointed out by Crowther (2002), and this took place even in the eighteenth century when making a profit was the single objective of a business enterprise. There was also Titus Salt, the Yorkshire wool baron, who Cook (2003) describes as 'a pioneer of caring capitalism who should really be described as 'the pioneer of modern environmentalism'. In 1848, in an attempt 'to make a difference' in the lives of the residents of Bradford town, which was then described as the most polluted town in Britain, he relocated his woolen mill in Saltaire, outside Bradford town centre. Over a 20-year period, Salt created a model community for his staff in which every home had running water. Cook (2003) recites the social responsibility behaviour of Joseph Rowntree, the sweet manufacturer and famous philanthropist, who in 1904 built 'Rowntree Village' in York for his employees with houses centred around a community hall. In 1906, Rowntree set up a pensions fund for his staff, in 1916 he established a profit-sharing scheme for his employees, and in 1918 he introduced staff holidays. All these acts of social responsibility were revolutionary at the time.

Maltby (2004), in her study of the historical antecedents of CSR reporting in the UK, argues that the assumption that CSR reporting in the UK is a recent phenomenon is incorrect. She notes that CSR reporting had been practiced proactively by several UK manufacturing companies; for example, there is evidence of such reporting by Sheffield steelmakers since the earlier part of the 1900s.

Cook (2003) argues that the UK National Insurance Act of 1911 introduced by Herbert H. Asquith's Liberal Government, which compelled firms to make contributions for unemployment and sickness benefits for all their staff, was the first recorded direct intervention by the state in this aspect of CSR anywhere in the world. History, therefore, indicates that the UK has contributed its fair share in the development of the practice of CSR.

1.2 Different Perceptions of What CSR Entails

It is widely acknowledged that modern corporations have some social responsibility towards society; even the most adamant opponents of CSR agree with this assertion. There is, however, a different perception of what this responsibility entails, which in effect suggests that there are different paradigms of CSR. On the one hand there are some supporters of CSR who believe and argue fervently that an entity's social responsibility is a single one, which is that the entity must increase its profits whilst staying within the rules of the game. To argue otherwise, they say is preaching pure and unadulterated *socialism*; after all businesses are not established for eleemosynary purposes (Friedman 1962, 1970). On the other hand, Elkington (1997) in his triple bottom line reporting argues that the social responsibility of a business entity is three-fold: to create *Economic value* by being profitable; to create *Ecological value*, which is to engage in activities that are beneficial to the natural environment; and to create *Social value*, which is to engage in activities that are beneficial to life and the community. Carroll and Buchholtz (2003) have extended this idea and argue that the social responsibility of a business organization is fourfold. This responsibility, they argue, can be expressed either as a *pyramid* or in terms of an *equation*. When expressed as an *equation*, it is the sum total of four different responsibilities: *Economic responsibilities* (*ECR*) (which is to make a profit) plus *Legal responsibilities* (*LGR*) (to obey the law) plus *Ethical responsibilities* (*ETR*) (to do what is right, fair, and just at all times) plus *Philanthropic responsibilities* (*PHR*) (to be a good corporate citizen).

When the arguments of these researchers are expressed mathematically, three equations emanate:

Friedman (1962, 1970):
$$CSR = Profit$$

Elkington (1997):
$$CSR = ECV + ECLV + SOCV$$

Carroll and Buchholtz (2003):

$$CSR = ECR + LGR + ETR + PHR$$

When Carroll and Buchholtz's (2003) proposition is expressed in terms of a pyramid, it results in an entity's ECR at the base and its PHR at the top. The entity's CSR is therefore depicted in a hierarchical form in the order of ECR, LGR, ETR, and PHR.

Friedman (1962, 1970), Elkington (1997), and Carroll and Buchholtz (2003) all agree that making a profit is a social responsibility of a business entity and that this is one of the objectives of any profit-seeking concern. A not-for-profit corporate entity either has no social responsibility or has a different set of CSRs according to Friedman (1962, 1970). Interestingly, all but Friedman (1962, 1970) agree that there is more to CSR than just profit seeking. CSR covers a wide spectrum of other activities that seek to make life a lot better for stakeholders, societies, and the environment.

This chapter is structured as follows: a review of the literature on CSR; a discussion of three organizations that are promoting CSR in the UK; an examination of the roles the UK governments have played in CSR either directly or indirectly since 1970s; an exploration the motivation behind corporate entities' involvement in CSR in the UK; a consideration of the question of how UK firms demonstrate that they are CSR conscious, including an exploration of the contents of CSR reports of a few UK companies; and finally a review of the future of CSR in the UK with some concluding remarks on the chapter.

1.3 Literature Review

The field of knowledge that encompasses what amounts to socially responsible actions has been variously described in the literature and elsewhere as *corporate social responsibility, corporate citizenship, corporate philanthropy, corporate community involvement, corporate giving, community relations, community affairs, community development, corporate responsibility, global citizenship, and corporate societal marketing*. Kotler and Lee (2005) stated simply that CSR was about '*doing good*'. Kakabadse et al. (2005) also argue that people within and outside the field of CSR promote and defend different interpretations of what it is and refer to it as what they believe is closest to the cause that is of interest to them. This explains why Crowther and Rayman-Bacchus (2004) argue that CSR means different things to different people and why Moon (2004) suggests that CSR is a difficult concept to pin down since it overlaps with other concepts such as corporate citizenship, sustainable business, environmental responsibility, the triple bottom line, social and environmental accountability, business ethics, and corporate accountability. This consequently explains why Carroll (1991), Jones (1995, 1999), McWilliams and Siegel (2001), and Idowu and Papasolomou (2007) have all argued that there is still no generally acceptable definition of CSR; it remains to be seen whether there will ever be one. The field touches an infinitely wide aspect of human existence. To a

Table 1.1 Definitions of CSR – by researchers and organizations promoting the field

Author	Definition
WBCSD[a] (1999)	CSR is the ethical behaviour of a company towards society; management acting responsibly in its relationship with other stakeholders who have a legitimate interest in the business, and it is the commitment by business to behave ethically and contribute to economic development while improving the quality of life of the workforce and their families as well as the local community and society at large.
Bloom and Gundlach (2001)	The obligations of the firm to its stakeholders – people and groups who can affect or who are affected by corporate policies and practices. These obligations go beyond legal requirements and the company's duties to its shareholders. The fulfillment of these obligations is intended to minimize any harm and maximize the long-run beneficial impact of the firm on society.
McWilliams and Siegel (2001)	CSR are actions that appear to further some social good, beyond the interests of the firm and that which is required by law.
Jackson (2003)	CSR is the overall relationship of the corporation with all its stakeholders. . . . Elements of corporate social responsibility include investment in community outreach, employee relations, creation and maintenance of employment, environmental responsibility, human rights, and financial performance.
Crowther and Rayman-Bacchus (2004)	CSR is concerned with what is – or should be – the relationship between the global corporation, government of countries, and individual citizens.
The European Union (2004)	CSR is a concept whereby companies integrate social and environmental concerns in their business operations and in their interaction with their stakeholders on a voluntary basis.
Kotler and Lee (2005)	CSR is a commitment to improve community well-being through discretionary business practices and contributions of corporate resources.

[a]WBCSD stands for World Business Council for Sustainable Development.

large extent, involvement in CSR-related activities by a corporate entity is still voluntary in the UK. Idowu and Towler (2004) have suggested that one reason some UK firms practice CSR is to reduce the need for government legislation in the area, but Henderson (2001) argues that promoting CSR could lead to undesirable regulation of business activities.

In addition to eliciting the range of definitions that have been applied to CSR, this chapter also seeks to explore how UK corporate entities, both profit-seeking and not-for-profit, practice the field of CSR. In order to present a logical argument on this process, this chapter will review how the field is described or promoted and how it is defined by the entity in question. Archie Carroll (1999) has led the way, tracing the evolution of CSR definitional construct for the period between the 1950s and 1990s. Carroll (1999) suggests that Howard R. Bowen should be given the title the "Father of Corporate Social Responsibility" simply because 'it is easy to see how his book marks the modern serious discussion on the field of CSR'. Carroll (1999) identified 20 definitions of CSR, and Kakabadse et al. (2005) identified nine definitions covering a period of 50 years between 1953 and 2003. These more recent definitions of CSR have been complied. In Table 1.1 a further list is provided.

This author holds the view that CSR is about businesses putting the interests of others before their own. CSR is about being concerned with the welfare of all of an entity's stakeholders, whether primary or secondary – everyone who would be affected either directly or indirectly by its actions including its competitors. CSR is about decency in the conduct of the affairs of the entity with all its stakeholders including the natural environment. It is about the old religious moral doctrine of 'love thy neighbour as thyself'. The belief that economic and social goals must always conflict is laid to rest by the principles encompassed in CSR, and that argument can no longer apply in the twenty-first century. CSR advocates that economic and social goals must co-exist; they must run alongside each other for an entity to survive and prosper in modern markets.

Despite the fact that CSR has been variously defined, all these recent definitions have a common theme: they all state that modern businesses must recognize the economic, social, and environmental impacts of their operations/actions on both their stakeholders and the natural environment, or requires them to minimize the adverse effects and maximize the consequential benefits of their actions on stakeholders and the environment.

1.4 Organizations Promoting CSR in the UK

Several organizations are promoting the field of CSR in the UK and around the world. The following organizations have played a significant role in encouraging best practice in the UK.

1.4.1 Business in the Community (BitC)

Business in the Community (BitC) is a movement in the UK of some 700 member companies. It was set up in 1982 by the then Conservative government's Secretary of State for the Environment, Tom King (now Lord King), against a backdrop of high levels of unemployment and urban rioting in the UK. It was an attempt to directly involve businesses in finding lasting solutions to some social problems of the time and it has continued to play this role within the UK and beyond. BitC states on its website that its purpose is to inspire, challenge, engage, and support businesses to continually improve their positive impact on society through the five stated principles:

- Inspiration
- Integrity
- Integration
- Innovation
- Impact

The aim was not driven by pure altruism but because it was the right thing to do from a business perspective. BitC believes from its origin that "healthy back streets make for healthy high streets" and it engages in a series of programmes including annual awards for excellence, Cares, The Prince's Seeing is Believing, and Corporate Responsibility (CR) Index.

1.4.2 FTSE4Good Indices

FTSE4Good Index Series is a set of benchmark and tradable indices on the London Stock Exchange. The indices can be used for investment, research, reference, and benchmarking and is similar to the Dow Jones Sustainability Index in New York. The index was launched in 2001 with the main objective of meeting the information needs of socially responsible investors who seek to:

- Invest in companies that demonstrate good standards in corporate responsibility
- Actively encourage companies to be more responsible
- Minimalize the social, ethical, and environmental risks within their portfolios
- Capitalize on the benefits of good corporate responsibility
- Avoid investing in traditionally excluded socially responsible investment sectors, for example, tobacco, defence, and nuclear power

In an attempt to encourage financial institutions to improve on their CSR performance through the use of the FTSE4Good index, some large fund managers in London are building CSR league tables and assessing the lending record of banks. Most large to medium sized UK Plcs are now included in the Index.

1.4.3 The ACCA Best Practices for Sustainability Reporting

The Association of Chartered Certified Accountants (ACCA) (a UK-based professional accountancy body), one of the largest professional accountancy bodies in the world, launched the 'ACCA Sustainability Reporting Awards' in 1990. The ACCA website states that the aim of the awards is 'to promote greater transparency in the reporting of organizations' social and environmental impacts' and the objective is 'to identify and reward innovative attempts to communicate corporate performance but not the performance itself'. Those judging how the performance is reported use three criteria:

- Completeness
- Credibility
- Communication

The awards operate in more than 20 countries in Europe, Africa, North America, and Asia. Companies in the following countries appear to have benefited in winning the awards: Hong Kong, UK, Ireland, Singapore, Pakistan, Australia, New Zealand, Malaysia, Sri Lanka, South Africa, Canada, and the USA. Several awards are given to companies in different countries each year.

1.5 The Role of UK Governments Since the 1970s

UK governments have been involved in different aspects of the field of CSR either directly or indirectly. Moon (2004) notes that the two ostensibly very different governments of Thatcher (Conservative, 1979–1991) and Blair (Labour 1997–2007) have helped the growth and institutionalization of CSR in the UK. Idowu and Towler (2004) argue that initially it was the rights of employees that were first recognized as needing government attention. Acts of Parliament have been passed including the Equal Pay Act 1970, Health and Safety at Work Act 1974, Sex Discrimination Act 1975, and Race Relation Act 1976. Because of the influences of the European Union (EU), it has become necessary for the UK government to take cognizance of EU Directives and issue parliamentary Acts such as the Disability Discrimination Act 1995, Data Protection Act 1998, Human Rights Act 1998, and Public Information Act 1998, just to mention a few. All these were concerted attempts by the government to ensure that employees had legal protection during employment, as they have been generally perceived as the weaker of the two sides in an employer/employee relationship.

During the Thatcher era of the 1980s, the UK experienced several social and economic problems that manifested themselves in terms of high unemployment, inner city riots, high inflation, and high interest rates. The government believed that it had no choice but to indirectly delegate the task of finding solutions to some of these social and economic problems to the business community by encouraging them to be CSR conscious (Moon and Richardson 1985). The Thatcher years were noted for encouraging a more *laissez faire* attitude to certain social issues; citizens/families were encouraged to be more independent and self reliant. People were assisted to buy their council homes, social security benefits were drastically reduced, school fees for overseas students were charged at full cost, some nationalized industries were privatized, and state-funded institutions were left to market forces. Some would argue that the approach appears to have worked because some of the then prevailing social and economic problems have gradually disappeared.

At the start of the new millennium, the Labour government of Tony Blair was very keen to ensure that UK companies take the matter of CSR very seriously. The government appointed the world's first Minister for CSR, Dr Kim Howells, in March 2000. The working brief was to ensure that UK companies, especially the FTSE 350 listed companies, take a lead in adopting and reporting their CSR activities. As a result of the government's keen interest in CSR, Departments in Whitehall and devolved Administrations in Northern Ireland, Scotland, and Wales have major on-going programmes that engage business in a wide range of issues such as promoting the business case and celebrating achievements, regeneration and skills development, codes of practice and joint actions, reporting and labelling, modernizing government and dialogue with business, strengthening international collaboration, engaging a wider range of businesses in CSR, especially smaller businesses, improving coherence of government actions and consultation with business and other groups and promoting business case for tackling literacy and numeracy weaknesses, and investment in deprived areas (DTI 2001). The following have been appointed as ministers of CSR between March 2000 and the time of writing: Rt. Hon. Kim Howells, Douglas Alexander, Stephen Timms, Malcolm Wicks, Nigel Griffiths, Barry Gardiner, Margaret Hodge, and Stephen Timms (second time post holder).

In March 2004, in an attempt to continue to portray itself as an enthusiastic advocate of CSR, the government issued a consultative document, *Corporate Social Responsibility – A Draft International Strategic Framework*. In the document, the government asserts that it has an ambitious vision for CSR, which involves UK businesses in 'taking account of their economic, social and environmental impacts and acting to address the key sustainable development challenges based on their core competences wherever they operate – locally, regionally or internationally' (DTI 2004). Other similar documents include *Shows Promise: But Must Try Harder* (Sustainable Development Commission 2004) and *Achieving A Better Quality of Life* (Department of Environment, Food and Rural Affairs, DEFRA 2002). In DEFRA's 2002 document, 15 Headline Indicators and 56 key issues and impacts that need to be taken into account in relation to each of the sustainable development objectives were identified.

In 2001, the government launched a CSR-dedicated website, www.societyand-business.gov.uk, to promote debate on CSR and set out its own role in creating the necessary frameworks for the field to thrive in the UK. CSR.gov.uk reports that all Government Departments now produce Sustainable Development Plans setting out their contribution and commitments towards the government's Sustainable Goals.

As part of its attempts to popularize the field, the government issued an update to its strategy for advancing its CSR vision in May 2004, which it hopes, will facilitate the following objectives:

- Promote business activities that bring simultaneous economic, social, and environmental benefits.
- Work in partnership with the private sector, community bodies, unions, consumers, and other stakeholders.
- Encourage innovative approaches and continuing development and application of best practice.
- Ensure there are decent minimum levels of performance in areas such as health and safety, the environment, and equal opportunities.
- Encourage increased awareness, open constructive dialogue, and trust.
- Create a policy framework that encourages and enables responsible behaviour by business.

A statement was included in the Update from the then Chancellor of the Exchequer (now the Prime Minister), Gordon Brown, who writes:

> Today, CSR goes beyond the old philanthropy of the past – donating money to good causes at the end of the financial year – and is instead an all year round responsibility that companies accept for the environment around them, for the best working practices, for their engagement in local communities and for their recognition that brand names depend not only on quality, price and uniqueness but on how, cumulatively they interact with companies' workforce, community and environment. Now we need to move towards a challenging measure of corporate responsibility, where we judge results not just by the input but by its outcome: the difference we make to the world in which we live, and the contribution we make to poverty reduction (Department of Trade and Industry 2004, p. 2).

This is a powerful statement that confirms that Gordon Brown's administration will continue to take the issue of CSR both in the UK and internationally seriously.

Internationally, the UK government has played and continues to play a leading role in the field. It is a prominent supporter of the Global Compact. At the Johannesburg World Summit on Sustainable Development in 2002, it pledged to promote corporate responsibility and sustainability. It also takes a lead in encouraging UK corporate entities to strategize the reduction of greenhouse effects and debt relief for the poorer nations of the world. Moon (2004) notes in a survey of European business leaders that UK businesses are regarded as keener on CSR matters than their European counterparts, which may be a result of the government's initiatives.

Figure 1.1 is an organization chart of the major players in the field of CSR in the UK. From the diagram, it can be seen that the government indirectly plays a mediation role between the stakeholders on one hand and corporate entities on the other. The government has taken a view that whilst CSR cannot be imposed through regulation, nevertheless, the regulatory and market framework can support businesses' engagement in CSR. This may explain why the government in its response to the independent Company Law Review of 1998–2001 incorporated guidance to companies on how to report the impact of their performance and on the duties of Directors with regard to social and environmental issues.

Several UK-based charitable organizations are actively involved in different aspects of CSR. Organizations such as Oxfam, Green Peace, Amnesty International, Friends of the Earth, Sight Saver International, Leprosy Mission, and

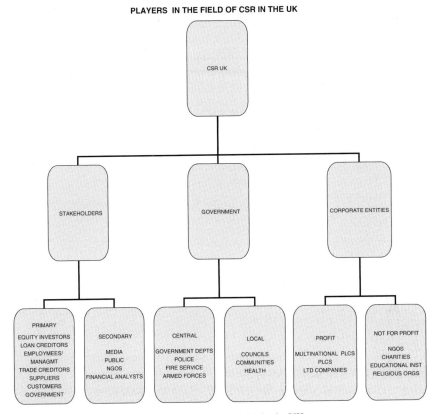

Fig. 1.1 Organization chart of players in the field of CSR in the UK

Voluntary Service Overseas (VSO) engage in several of the issues that fall under the umbrella of CSR, and for several decades they have also practiced and continue to practice what Lantos (2001) calls *altruistic CSR and philanthropic CSR* in their various activities both in the UK and around the world, in particular in the poorer areas.

1.6 Motivation for Issuing CSR Reports by UK Companies

It is perhaps appropriate at this point once again to remember Adam Smith's (1776) argument that 'the butcher and the others do not set out to meet their customers' requirements merely because of their deep love for those customers who buy from them but because of the butcher's etc self-love'. Adam Smith's (1776) statement was one of the driving forces behind an empirical study that was carried out in 2005 by this author with the objective of establishing the motivation behind corporate entities' involvement in CSR activities in the UK. Letters were sent to either

Table 1.2 Company categories

Provided explanations	Sent CSR report	Sent annual report	Referred us to their website
Abbey National[a]	Centrica	Jarvis	AstraZeneca[a]
AstraZeneca[a]	Costain	Northern Foods	Bradford and Bingley[a]
Balfour Beatty	Friends Provident[a]	Investec	Centrica[a]
Bradford and Bingley	British Airways[a]		Friends Provident[a]
British Airways[a]	mmO2[a]		Tesco[a]
British Gas Group[a]	Royal Bank of Scotland[a]		
British Telecommunications[a]	Tesco[a]		
International Power	3i Group[a]		
Marks and Spencer[a]			
National Grid Transco[a]			
Tesco[a]			
3i Group[a]			

Note: [a]FTSE 100 companies.

the company secretary or finance director of 40 UK companies that were known to issue CSR reports. These companies were chosen from two sectors of the capital market – 20 companies from FTSE 100 and 20 companies outside FTSE 100. As it was uncertain who was in charge of CSR, the company secretary or finance director was asked to pass the letter on to the responsible officer if CSR were to fall outside their domain. The letter explained the objective of the study: to "explain in as much detail as possible the reasons why the entity followed a strategy of issuing information on its CSR activities".

The study revealed that all respondent companies now have a member of the board responsible for CSR matters. It also revealed that these companies now have in post a CSR manager (most of them females). The respondents did not identify whether these companies now have a CSR department and if so how many staff were employed to work solely on CSR matters.

The replies received were in different forms. Some companies provided the required direct responses to the questions posed; some sent either their latest CSR reports or annual reports that contained a section on their CSR activities; and some referred us to their websites stating that the required information could be found there. Table 1.2 identifies companies in these different categories.

Since the completion of the study a few changes have taken place. Abbey National is now no longer an FTSE 100 company because it was taken over by a Spanish company whose shares are quoted on the Madrid Stock Exchange. Bradford and Bingley has been demoted from the FTSE 100 companies, and International Power has now been promoted to the FTSE 100 companies. mmO2 has changed its name to O_2 and is now no longer an FTSE 100 company, as it has also been bought over by a Spanish company. National Grid Transco has changed its name to National Grid.

The following general impression emanates from the study:

Forty-five percent of the FTSE 100 respondent companies began issuing CSR reports in 2000 or shortly after, which coincides with the year Tony Blair's Labour government first appointed a Minister for CSR.

Before presenting the findings from this study, it is worth noting a few factors that have underpinned the respondent companies' stated motivation for their involvement in CSR and its related activities. Some of these are the industry in which the particular company operates, the tradition embedded in its history, and the culture its management had been exposed to in the past.

The industry in which a company operates plays a significant role vis-à-vis how its stakeholders, including pressure groups, perceive that company. If a company operating in a particular industry with a high incidence of waste emission fails to disclose its positive contributions to the "common good", it exposes itself to criticisms and other sanctions by activists and other interest groups.

A respondent company argued that it started out as a Quaker family business and, like many similar businesses of this type, its founder believed that it had a role in society over and above that of delivering profits. It therefore saw CSR as a way of carrying forward their founder's perceived tradition.

Another company states that its senior managers came from a culture that strives to strike a balance between the needs of its shareholders and that of other stakeholders. The field of CSR fits in perfectly well with meeting that objective.

1.6.1 A Summary of the Reasons for Reporting CSR Cited by Respondent Companies

- To inform stakeholders of their contributions to social betterment – 100% of respondents gave this reason
- To provide a more rounded picture of what they are doing in response to NGOs' criticism that companies in the industry they operate in are not doing enough for the environment – 10% of respondent companies cited this
- To meet best practice in company reporting – 50% of respondents gave this reason
- To derive CSR's positive public relations benefits – 10% cited this
- To satisfy disclosure requirements of major shareholders (institutional investors) – 10% cited this
- To ensure that employees are aligned to the company's CSR targets – 5% cited this
- To demonstrate an open management style – 30% cited this
- To reflect the importance attached to CSR by the company – 10% cited this
- To align with the request of the government that all FTSE 350 companies should report on the social and environmental impacts of their activities – 5% cited this;

- To demonstrate to stakeholders that non-financial matters are also important – 20% cited this
- In response to questionnaires often completed for tenders and for government departments – 5% cited this
- To strengthen its corporate reputation, core values, and corporate conscience – 5% cited this
- To use CSR as an impetus to challenge its existing practices and focus on introducing rigorous processes in what it does – 5% cited this
- To supplement its annual report because it believes the two will provide a comprehensive review of its economic, social and, environmental performance – 5% cited this
- To continue with its philosophy of setting the pace in the industry it operates – 5% cited this
- To inform its readers on how its approach to CSR is developing, the successes it has made, and the challenges it still faces – 5% cited this
- To convey to the world at large that it has a role in society over and above that of delivering profits – 5% cited this
- To explain to its readers how the company governs itself internally, how it works to satisfy its customers' needs to the highest level of excellence, how it looks after its employees, how it works to earn the support of its shareholders, and how it responds to the wider expectations that society has of it as a modern business enterprise – 5% cited this

The above reasons have been summarized in Table 1.3.

1.6.2 CSR in UK Universities – a Group of Not-for-profit Corporate Entities

CSR falls within the domain of both profit-seeking and not-for-profit corporate entities. Universities in the UK operate as non-profit-seeking corporate entities. In a recent study, Idowu (2008) investigated the issues that UK higher education institutions consider to be their CSR. Letters were sent to 121 heads of UK universities asking them to specify what they see as the roles of their universities in CSR. Twenty-four universities (19.83%) responded. The following is a summary of the information the respondents gave:

(a) To encourage Widening Participation (WP) – WP is a philosophy used in the UK in an attempt to encourage prospective students from traditional non-university-attending families, ethnic minorities, and adult learners to go on to higher education
(b) To develop and communicate performance on sustainable development – a requirement of the Higher Education Partnership for Sustainability (HEPS)
(c) To make a positive contribution to national and international university systems of education

Table 1.3 Summary of the reasons for reporting on CSR

Corporate reputation	Stakeholder pressure	Economic performance	Genuine concern	Broad social/cultural
To provide a more rounded picture of the company	To inform stakeholders	To meet best practice in company reporting	To ensure that employees are aligned to company's targets	To demonstrate an open management style
To meet best practice in company reporting	To provide a more rounded picture of the company	To derive CSR's positive public relations benefits	To demonstrate an open management style	To reflect the importance attached to CSR by the company
To derive CSR's positive public relations benefits	To satisfy disclosure requirements of major shareholders	To satisfy disclosure requirements of major shareholders	To reflect the importance attached to CSR by the company	To uphold its core values, to act as corporate conscience
To reflect the importance attached to CSR by the company	To align with the request of the current UK government	To ensure that employees are aligned to company's targets	To demonstrate to stake holders that non-financial issues are also important	To continue the culture that its founder started at the inception of the company
To demonstrate to stakeholders that non-financial issues are also important	In response to questionnaires to be completed for tenders and government departments	In response to questionnaires to be completed for tenders and government departments	To act as an impetus to challenge its existing practices	To demonstrate that its senior managers are from a culture that strives to strike a balance between the needs of its shareholders and that of other stakeholders
To strengthen corporate reputation	To inform its readers how its approach to CSR is developing: the successes it has made and the challenges it still has	To supplement its annual report because it believes the two will provide a comprehensive review of its economic, social and environmental performance	To convey to the world at large that it has a role in society other than delivering profits	To continue with its philosophy of setting the pace in its industry

Source: Idowu, S.O. and Papasolomou, I. (2007), Are the corporate Social Responsibility matters based on good intentions or false pretences? An empirical study of the motivations behind the issuing of CSR reports by UK companies, Corporate Governance: International Journal of Business in Society, Vol. 7, No. 2 pp. 136–147.

(d) To manage the economic, social, and environmental impacts of their activities
(f) To take into account the interests of their stakeholders and act as good citizens
(g) To respond to social needs in terms of education and innovation
(h) To provide a more effective community service
(i) To provide a challenging, inspiring, and supportive environment for students to grow intellectually and as individuals
(j) To sustain and add value to the United Kingdom's culture, economy, and the natural environment
(k) To manage and govern these universities with responsibility and sensitivity

The above, together with the results of the study by Idowu and Papasolomou (2007), suggest that the field of CSR is important to both profit- and non-profit-seeking corporate entities. The manner in which they discharge the challenges of CSR may not necessarily be the same, but these two fundamentally different corporate entities are expected to be socially responsible. One fact that clearly manifests itself is that modern corporate entities can no longer operate reactively; they must be quick to recognize those social and environmental issues that fall within their areas of confine and proactively institute appropriate strategies in other to ensure that they remain good and responsible business citizens.

1.7 How do UK Companies Demonstrate that they are CSR Conscious?

Over the last few years, UK companies, as a result of some of the factors noted above, have taken a conscious decision to ensure that they are perceived by their stakeholders as being socially responsible. They are all aware of the enormous benefits that could be derived from taking this course of action (Idowu and Towler 2004). Each of them has identified those issues that are of concern to society in the industry in which they operate. Most of these organizations are prepared to draw the attention of everyone to all the actions they are taking to demonstrate responsibility.

Large supermarkets including Tesco, Asda, Sainsbury's, and Morrison's retailing clothes, shoes, fruits, and other food items that are imported in to the UK from the less developed parts of the world are aware of the concern that some of these factory and plantation owners treat their employees irresponsibly in terms of paying poor wages, providing abysmal working conditions, making use of child labour, and other unacceptable practices in the industries in which they operate. These retailers are now members of the Fairtrade Labelling Organization (FLO), which ensures that plantation and factory owners avoid or minimize these problems. Davies (2007) argues that the UK is the largest physical market of Fairtrade goods in the world worth £140 million in 2004, with large year-on-year growth (46% in 2003 and 52% in 2004). In line with the sales growth, the number of participant organizations has also grown significantly from less than 20 organizations that signed a Fairtrade licensing agreement in 2000 to nearly 150 organizations in 2006 (Davies 2007). Davies (2007) reminds the readers that the idea of fair trade was conceived in the UK in the 1960s.

A visit to a local branch of Marks and Spencer (a UK-based large retailer of clothes and other household goods) reveals some practice of CSR. The following statements in large prints on the walls of the escalators and other conspicuous places were found in the shop:

There is nothing woolly about our commitment to animal welfare
It's not just our green dyes that won't harm the environment
We wear our clothes out before you buy them

Marks and Spencer's website (2007) (www.marksandspencer.com/com/gp/node/ nsite contains details of the achievements they made in 2006 with regard to some CSR-related issues which affect their operations: for instance, Customers, Environment, Suppliers, Workplace, Investors, and Community. The following were noted:

Salt – We are reducing salt content ahead of industry target.
Environment – We are managing chemical responsibly
Fats – We are leading the field on removing hydrogenated fats.
Durability – Our products are extremely durable.
Recycling – We recycle relentlessly.
Fairtrade – We sell fair-trade tea and coffee in our cafes.
Sustainability – We fish responsibly and protect endangered species such as cod.
Washability – We work hard to ensure that our clothes are easy to clean.
Free Range – We focus on selling and using free-range eggs.
Non-GM – We are the only UK food retailer to sell only non-GM food.
Animal Welfare – We care about animal welfare.

Other UK companies refer to their *philanthropic CSR* activities. Northern Rock (a Building-Society-turned Bank) were eager to say that 16% of their pre-tax profit is donated to charities annually – in 2006, the pre-tax profit was £626.7 million; thus £100.3 million was donated to good causes.

Some companies talk about the percentage reduction they achieved in CO_2 emission or how they have ensured that their supply chains take on board all those CSR-related issues that affect their industry.

A South London church has a bold inscription on one side of their church – "*Global Warming – Let's All Help God to Save His World*". The message that we should all behave responsibly whether we are a corporate body or an individual appears to have been taken everywhere in the UK. The planet Earth must be saved by our collective actions.

1.8 Exploring the Contents of CSR Reports of UK Companies

The last few years have seen an increasing number of UK companies reporting on their CSR activities by issuing annual CSR reports either on a stand-alone basis or embedding the report in their annual reports. In 2002 a MORI

(Market and Opinion Research International) survey notes that in the UK 61% of small and medium sized companies were either involved a great deal or a fair amount in local community matters (DTI 2002). Maignon and Ralston (2002) and Chambers et al. (2003) have both noted an increase of about 150% in FTSE 250 companies reporting on their CSR activities between 2001 and 2003. Idowu and Towler (2004) also note that 80% of FTSE 100 companies were reporting on their CSR activities. As of March 2007, 81% of FTSE 100 companies report on their CSR activities, 5% of FTSE 100 companies have their CSR activities reported on by related organizations, and 14% of these FTSE 100 companies do not report on their CSR activities (Corporate Register.com). SalterBaxter/Context (2004) notes an increase in the number of companies having their CSR reports independently verified. Barclays Bank states in their CSR report that it was externally verified by SGS (an independent provider of management systems certification, environmental report verification, and ethical auditing).

In an attempt to understand the factors that have catalyzed the development of CSR reports, accounting researchers have classified these under four different theoretical perspectives. These are agency theory, legitimacy theory, political economy of accounting theory, and stakeholder theory (Gray et al. 1995, 1996; Guthrie and Parker 1990; Patten 1992; Roberts 1992). However, Vogl (2003) also argues that four factors could be identified as contributing to it but takes a different approach in classifying these factors. The Vogl (2003) factors are tightening regulatory pressures, changing demographics, pressure from NGOs, and the increased necessity for greater transparency.

When reporting on their CSR activities, UK companies adopt two distinct practices. Some companies issue separate CSR reports, whilst others devote a section in their annual reports for providing information on these activities. Idowu and Towler (2004) note that UK CSR reports disclose information about the contributions an entity has made during the year that has just ended under four main perspectives: *environment, community, marketplace, and workplace.*

When reporting under the heading of *Environment*, the reporting entity may state that during the year that has just ended they took all necessary actions to ensure that their activities did not pollute the land, water, or air; they have contributed to conserving natural resources by minimizing the use of non-renewable resources through recycling materials, by using recycled products and packaging, and by minimizing the use of energy; they intend to increase their responses in these areas in future years.

When reporting under the heading of *Community*, the entity could assert that it recognized it had an obligation to play a positive role in its community and may provide information on some of the positive roles it has played in the community during the reporting period. For example, it could report that staff were released during company hours to undertake fund-raising activities for a local charity, that they matched the money raised pound for pound, that they helped a local charity in preventing and alleviating the causes of homelessness, that donations were made for charitable purposes during the reporting period, that computers were donated to local schools, and a host of other community-related actions the company took during the year.

Under the heading of *Marketplace*, the company could report that it has made an agreement with its main suppliers that raw materials be recycled where possible, that the use of child labour is prohibited in the less developed parts of the world where raw materials and other products come from, that it is company policy to invest ethically (Green investments), and other market-related actions the company has taken or intends to take.

Under the heading of *Workplace*, it might be reported that during the reporting period the company took a series of steps to ensure the health and safety of its employees, customers, and its local community and that the company is an equal opportunities employer, stating the number of disabled employees it has, the number of minorities and women in senior management positions, and the number of health and safety training hours provided to employees during the year to ensure that they are not in danger during the course of performing their work roles.

Some of these companies that operate internationally are also keen to talk about the actions they took during the reporting period to help employees and people in these countries with HIV/AIDS as well as how they have provided equipment and other teaching material to schools, provided running water for villages, and donated funds for research in local universities in these countries.

In 2003, Idowu and Towler carried out a comparative study of the contents of CSR reports of UK companies with the main objective of establishing the sort of information these reports disclose to their readers. Thirty companies with registered office in different parts of the UK were asked to send their latest CSR reports by post. The companies contacted were drawn from the following industries: insurance, banking, food retailing and processing, petroleum processing and retailing, sports and entertainment, and construction. The telephone was used as the medium of contact for two reasons: to test whether corporate social responsibility reports are well known by everybody within the company, and to test the ease of obtaining the report by telephone. It was found that some employees did not know what a CSR report was and some offered to send their organizations' annual reports or suggested a more senior individual in the organization who might be able to help us. The research was also designed to highlight what companies in industries with insignificant impact and those with pronounced impact on the environment disclose to their readers, in order to contribute positively to society what companies are doing, and to increase their readers' understanding of the impacts they have on the environment.

Information was received from 60% of the companies contacted; 40% were unwilling to provide the required report, probably because in 2003 reporting on CSR had not yet found its way as an important item on to these companies' corporate agenda. From the information received, it was deduced that UK companies had adopted the use of one of two practices; CSR reports were either issued on a stand-alone basis, or a section of the annual report was devoted for reporting this activity.

The companies studied are The Royal Bank of Scotland, Balfour Beatty, Barclays Bank, Tesco, The Royal Dutch/Shell Group, Northern Rock, Friend Provident, Northern Foods, mm02 (now known as O2), National Grid Transco (now known as National Grid), Safeway (taken over in March 2004 by Morrisons Plc), Manchester

Table 1.4 Companies in each of the two reporting categories

Companies with stand-alone CSR reports	Companies embedding their CSR reports in the annual financial reports
Royal Dutch/Shell Group	Manchester United
Tesco	BG Group
Royal Bank of Scotland	Centrica
Barclays Bank	Northern Foods
Friends Provident	Bradford and Bingley
Balfour Beatty	Kingston Communications
Northern Rocks	Safeway (now part of Morrisons)
	National Grid
	Tullow Oil
	mmO2 (now known as O2)

United, BG Group, Centrica, Bradford and Bingley, Kingston Communications, and Tullow Oil. Table 1.4 classifies companies according to how they publish their CSR reports.

By 2007, some of the companies on the right-hand side of Table 1.4 had moved to the left and have started issuing a separate stand-alone CSR report, whilst continuing to embed an abridged version of the CSR report in their annual report.

The information each of the 17 companies disclosed in the reports provided is capable of being classified either as a combination of altruistic CSR, philanthropic CSR and strategic CSR (Lantos 2001) or as an aspect of each of them. Altruistic CSR and philanthropic CSR are similar, as they relate to the good deeds of an entity in the form of "giving back" time and money voluntarily for the benefit of others – contributing to the common good. Strategic CSR, on the other hand, relates to an entity's fulfillment of its social obligations which then result in that entity and some of its stakeholders benefiting from the act. Table 1.5 provides some of the identifiable differences in these companies' reporting practices at the time the study was carried out. If the study were to be carried out today, it should reveal many improvements from the 2003 study because UK companies are now more confident about this area than they were 4 years ago.

Table 1.5 provides information on areas where there are differences in the reporting practices of the companies at the time of the study.

1.9 The Future of CSR in the UK

The field of CSR has a long history in the UK; several entities – the government, companies, charities, NGOs etc. – appear to have embraced the concept and all that it stands for, and there is considerable activity to promote CSR and to facilitate its growth from strength to strength both in the UK and across the world. The UK is a world-acknowledged leader of the field. The question that this section of Chap. 1

Table 1.5 Differences in companies' reporting practices

Company	Stand-alone CSR	Director responsible for CSR	FTSE4 Good Index	Business in the community Index	Dow Jones Sustainability Index	ISO 14001 Index	Supports named charities?	CSR Report with a theme	Setting annual targets for CSR	Having Web site for CSR
Shell Group	✓	✓	×	✓	×	×	✓	✓	✓	×
Tesco	✓	✓	×	✓	×	×		×	✓	×
Royal Bank of Scotland	✓	✓	×	✓	✓	✓	✓	✓	✓	✓
Barclays Bank	✓	✓	✓	✓	✓	✓	✓	×	✓	✓
Manchester United	×	✓	✓	✓	×	✓	✓	×	✓	×
Friends Provident	✓	✓	✓	✓	×	×	✓	✓	✓	✓
BG Group	×	×	×	×	×	✓	✓	×	✓	×
Centrica	×	✓	✓	✓	✓	✓	✓	×	✓	×
Northern Foods	×	✓	×	✓	×	×	✓	×	✓	×
Bradford and Bingley	×	✓	×	✓	×	×	✓	×	✓	×
Kingston Communications	×	×	✓	✓	×	✓	✓	×	✓	×
Balfour Beatty	✓	✓	×	✓	✓	✓	×	✓	✓	×
Safeway (now Morrisons)	×	✓	✓	×	✓	✓	×	×	✓	✓
National Grid	×	✓	×	✓	×	✓	✓	✓	✓	✓
Tullow Oil	×	×	×	×	×	×	✓	✓	✓	×
mmO2(O2)	×	✓	✓	✓	✓	✓	✓	✓	✓	✓
Northern Rock	✓	✓	✓	✓	×	✓	✓	✓	✓	✓

Source: Idowu, S.O. and Towler, B.A. (2004) A comparative study of the contents of corporate social responsibility reports of UK companies, Management of Environmental Quality: An International Journal, Vol. 15, No. 4, pp. 420–437.

proposes to answer is, *Whether CSR in the UK will continue to have a high profile in the future is debatable* and *Will its profile be still high in the country in 20 or 30 years time?* Probably not, is the author's straight answer! This has been said for various reasons.

It has been suggested by some researchers in the field that CSR might be dead in the UK by 2015! The paper *CSR at Crossroads* Ward and Smith (2006) asserts that CSR will have a lower profile by 2015 because it has now become a troublesome term! This author does not necessarily share that view, but for it to survive a lot would have to be done. One of the arguments the Ward and Smith (2006) in their study put forward which they say would bring about its demise 'is the lack of a single agreed definition of CSR and its objectives'. However, it can be argued that the absence of a universal definition of the field is actually its 'charm' – this is why it appeals to everyone across all sectors of an economy and across international borders. It means different things to different people, Crowther and Rayman-Bacchus (2004) have argued. The presence of a single definition would restrict its practice and how it is perceived across different disciplines, which would consequently reduce innovations and developments in the field.

What may be a problem is the way CSR is currently described. The term *Social* in the name of the field may need to be deleted. *Social* does not connote an impression that it is something to be taken seriously! Some researchers and organizations have already taken this on board and simply refer to the field as *Corporate Responsibility*, which, it is proposed, has more gravity and is something to be taken seriously and is a more *businesslike* phrase.

The field of CSR would need to be broken down into its different parts. The term CSR or CR is too wide; each industry or sector would need to come up with a unique term that one can easily associate with a particular sector of an economy. CSR is now big business! There are several organizations that are now specializing in different aspects of the field – as consultants, practitioners, verifiers, auditors, etc., and this will probably continue for a long time.

To suggest that the field CSR or CR would last in perpetuity in the UK or anywhere else would be too simplistic – nothing lasts forever! Dynamism in the corporate scene is a regular occurrence in the developed world, and may result in the displacement of CSR for another concept that becomes more fashionable. What that new 'more fashionable concept' will be and when it would come on to the corporate scene is a six million dollar question, the answer to which this author is not knowledgeable enough to predict.

1.10 Conclusion

As outlined in this chapter, CSR has a long history in the United Kingdom. Some aspects of it had been practiced since the Industrial Revolution, as demonstrated by the actions of some social activists of the time – *The Abolitionists* led by Sir William Wilberforce between 1780 and 1833 played a significant part in bringing about the end of slave trade; and some British industrialists demonstrated that they were socially responsible even at a time CSR meant nothing to everyone! The course of history would vindicate the UK as having contributed its fair share in the developments of modern CSR; this perhaps explains why the UK is a widely acknowledged leader in the field.

What CSR entails is still an ongoing debate by researchers and academics; but everyone acknowledges that corporate entities owe some responsibility to society. There are still a few opponents who are skeptical of its desirability; for instance, Henderson (2001) derides CSR as "global Salvationism" which will do nothing but lead to undesirable regulation of business, raising costs, and diminishing both economic freedom and profits. This confirms that those enormous benefits that are generally perceived could accrue from practicing CSR are still not universally recognized.

The UK governments of Margaret Thatcher and Tony Blair have both contributed to the growth of the field in the UK. To show the seriousness and importance attached to the field of CSR in the UK, it became the first government anywhere in the world to appoint a Minister for CSR. The government continues to encourage and support all legitimate CSR programmes and activities, either nationally or internationally. As a result of the government's lead in CSR in the UK, corporate entities of all shapes and forms (whether profit-seeking or non-profit-seeking) have also taken the issue seriously. Most large UK-based companies now have a member of the board in charge of CSR matters. Several other organizations in the UK are also active in encouraging corporate entities within and outside the Kingdom to behave responsibly; three of them were looked at in the chapter. Most large to medium sized UK companies consider everything that CSR requires of them as a challenge, and many are actively busy practicing CSR to varying degrees as it applies to the industry in which they operate. Several higher education institutions in the UK now run degree courses in CSR and its related disciplines and research studies in the area continue every time. There are still several years of growth and development left in the study and practice of CSR around the world, especially as the debate about climate change continues to intensify here in the UK and elsewhere.

Acknowledgements

The author would like to thank Andrea J. Dunhill of Kingston Business School, UK, for reading the final draft of this paper and Timothy P. Cleary of London Metropolitan Business School, UK, for his Information Technology (IT) assistance.

References

Bloom, P.N. and Gundlach, G.T. (2001), Handbook of Marketing and Society, Thousand Oaks, CA, Sage.

Carroll, A.B. (1991), The pyramid of corporate social responsibility: towards the moral management of organizational stakeholders, *Business Horizons*, Vol. 34, No. 4, pp. 39–48.

Carroll, A.B. (1999), Corporate social responsibility: evolution of a definitional construct, *Business and Society*, Vol. 38, No. 3, pp. 268–295.

Carroll, A.B. and Buchholtz, A.K. (2003), Business and Society: Ethics and Stakeholder Management, South Western Pub. 5th Edition, Cincinnati.

Chambers, E., Chapple, W., Moon, J. and Sullivan, M. (2003), CSR in Asia: a seven country study of CSR website reporting, *Business and Society*, Vol. 44, No. 4, pp. 415–441.

Cook, S. (2003), "Who care wins", *Management Today*, January pp. 40–47, London.

Crowther, D. (2002) A social critique of corporate reporting, Ashgate, Aldershot.

Crowther, D. and Rayman-Bacchus, L. (2004), *Perspectives in Corporate Social Responsibility*, Ashgate, Aldershot.

Davies, I. A. (2007), The eras and participants of fair trade: an industry structure/stakeholder perspective on the growth of the fair trade industry, *Corporate Governance*, Vol. 7, No. 4, pp. 455–470.

Department of Environment, Food and Rural Affairs (DEFRA) (2002), Sustainable Development: Achieving a better quality of life, Defra Publications, March, London.

Department of Trade and Industry (2001), Business and Society: Developing corporate social responsibility in the UK, HMSO, London.

Department of Trade and Industry (2004), Corporate Social Responsibility: A Government update, HMSO, London.

Du Bois, W.E.B. (1896), The Suppression of the African Slave Trade to the USA 1638–1870, Harvard University Press, Cambridge.

Elkington, J. (1997), Cannibals with Forks: The Triple Bottom Line of 21st Century Business, Capstone, Oxford.

European Union, (2004), Euroabstract: Corporate social responsibility, Vol. 42–1, February. European Commission: Directorate-General for Enterprise.

Friedman, M. (1962), Capitalism and Freedom, University of Chicago Press, Chicago, IL.

Friedman, M. (1970), The social responsibility of business is to increase its profits, *The New York Times Magazine,* September 13: 33, 122–126.

Gray, R., Kouhy, R., and Levers, S. (1995), Corporate Social and environmental reporting: a review of the literature and a longitudinal study of UK disclosure, *Accounting, Auditing and Accountability Journal*, Vol. 8, No. 2, pp. 47–77.

Gray, R., Owen, D., and Adams, C. (1996), Accounting and Accountability: Changes and Challenges in Corporate Social Environmental Reporting, Prentice Hall, Englewood, Cliffs, NI.

Guthrie, J. and Parker, L. (1990), Corporate social disclosure practice: a comparative international analysis, *Advances in Public Interest Accounting*, Vol. 3, pp. 159–175.

Henderson, D. (2001), Misguided Virtue – False notion of corporate social responsibility, Institute of Economic Affairs, London.

Idowu, S.O. and Towler, B.A. (2004), A comparative study of the contents of corporate social responsibility reports of UK companies, *Management of Environmental Quality: An International Journal*, Vol. 15, No. 4, pp. 420–437.

Idowu, S.O. (2008), An empirical study of what institutions of higher education in the UK consider to be their corporate social responsibility, in Aravossis, K, Brebbia, C.A. and Gomez, N. (Eds.), Environmental Economics and Investment, pp. 263–273, WIT Press, Southampton.

Idowu, S.O. and Papasolomou, I. (2007), Are the corporate Social Responsibility matters based on good intentions or false pretences? An empirical study of the motivations behind the issuing of CSR reports by UK companies, *Corporate Governance: International Journal of Business in Society*, Vol. 7, No. 2, pp. 136–147.

Jackson, P. (2003), Serving Stakeholders, CA Magazine, Toronto, March, pp. 34–36.

Jones, T.M. (1995), Instrumental stakeholder theory: a synthesis of ethics, *The Academy of Management Review*, Vol. 20, No. 2, pp. 404–437.

Jones, T.M. (1999), The institutional determinants of social responsibility, *Journal of Business Ethics*, Vol. 20, No. 2, pp. 163–179.

Kakabadse, N.K., Rozuel, C., and Lee-Davies, L. (2005), Corporate social responsibility and stakeholder approach: a conceptual review, *International Journal of Business Governance and Ethics*, Vol. 1, No. 4, pp. 277–302.

Kotler, P. and Lee, N. (2005), Corporate Responsibility: Doing the Most Good for Your Company and Your Cause, Wiley, Hoboken, New Jersey.

Lantos, G.P. (2001), The boundaries of strategic corporate social responsibility, *Journal of Consumer Marketing*, Vol. 18, No. 7, pp. 595–632.

Maignon, I. and Ralston, D. (2002), Corporate social responsibility in europe and the us: insights from businesses' self-presentations, *Journal of International Business Studies*, Vol. 33, No. 3, pp. 497–514.

Maltby, J. (2004), Hardfields Ltd: its annual general meetings 1903–1939 and their relevance for contemporary corporate social reporting, *The British Accounting Review*, Vol. 36, No. 4, pp. 415–439.

McWilliams, A. and Siegel, D. (2001), Corporate responsibility: a theory of the firm perspective, *The Academy of Management Review*, Vol. 26, No. 1, pp. 117–127.

Moon, J. and Richardson, J.J. (1985), Unemployment in the UK: Politics and Policies, Gower, Aldershot.

Moon, J. (2004), Government as a driver of corporate social responsibility, University of Nottingham, International Centre for Corporate Social Responsibility, Research paper Series No. 20 ISSN 1479–5124.

Patten, D.M. (1992), Intra-industry environmental disclosures in response to the Alaskan oil spill: a note on legitimacy theory, *Accounting, Organisation and Society*, Vol. 17, No. 5, pp. 471–475.

Rawley, J.A. and Behrendt, S.D. (2005), The Transatlantic Slave Trade – A History, revised edition, University of Nebraska Press, Lincoln.

Roberts, C. (1992), Environmental disclosures in corporate annual reports in Western Europe, in Owen, D. (ed.), Green Reporting: *Accountancy and the Challenge of the nineties*, pp. 139–165.

SalterBaxter/Context (2004), Directions 4 – Trends in CSR Reporting 2003–2004 SalterBaxter/ Context: Lsondon.

Smith, A. (1776), The Wealth of Nations, Book 1 Chap. II.

Vogl, A.J. (2003), Does it pay to be good? *Across the Board*, January/February, pp. 16–23.

Ward, H. and Smith, C. (2006), CSR at a Crossroads: Futures for CSR in the UK to 2015, International Institute for Environment and Development (iied), London ISBN 1 84369 628 2.

WBCSD (1999), Corporate social responsibility, World Business Council for Sustainable Development, Geneva.

http://www.marksandspencer.com/gp/node/n site visited on August 3, 2007

http://www.corporateregister.com/charts/FTSE.htm site visited 12 August 2007

Chapter 2
France

Laurence Eberhard Harribey

Abstract By the middle of the first decade of the twenty-first century, almost 400 French companies had joined the United Nations Global Compact. Today there are almost a dozen significant legal texts in existence on the application of corporate social responsibility (CSR) in France. Despite several studies showing that the concept of CSR is intrinsically linked with a more Anglo-American tradition, it seems that CSR is more and more established in France. This chapter first explores the specificity of the French context in regard of CSR. The historic perception of the relationships between state and companies and the European skepticism about the very idea of morality in business explain the important legal framework: the turning point was undoubtedly the law of the 15th May 2001 on the new economic regulations. But anyway, despite the considerable weight of the legal framework and the political dimension of CSR, the corporate practices and attitudes to CSR finally present a great diversity. On the basis of concrete examples, the chapter offers a large panel of corporate strategies distinguishing the voluntary companies from those considering CSR as a constraint and developing defensive strategies. Finally, the chapter puts in evidence some general remarks on the global progress and limits on CSR global practices in France.

2.1 Introduction

By the middle of the first decade of the twenty-first century, almost 400 French companies had joined the United Nations Global Compact, almost a fifth of all participating companies at that time. Since the 2001 economic reform of public procurement contracts, strengthened in 2004, sustainable development criteria have been incorporated into tenders and this has somewhat modified public–private relations in terms of adopting corporate social responsibility (CSR). Lastly, there are almost a dozen significant legal texts in existence on the application of CSR in France. More recently, after the May 2007 presidential elections, the new government introduced an important institutional development with the appointment of a high-ranking Minister, number two in the hierarchy after the Prime Minister, with special responsibility for ecology, sustainable development, and planning. With a high level of corporate participation in the dynamics of CSR, activism on the part of local organizations and local government, and a substantial legal framework to back it up, do these indicators suggest that CSR is well established in France, despite several studies showing that the concept is intrinsically linked with a more Anglo-American tradition? In this chapter we hope to shed some light on the CSR situation in France by describing some of the specific features of the current situation in this country and then highlighting the characteristics of corporate and organizational practices.

2.2 A Specific French Context that Partly Explains the Nature of the Commitment by Economic and Social Actors to CSR

2.2.1 The Lexical Ambiguity of the Expression "Corporate Social Responsibility"

In fact, the term "social" in the expression "corporate social responsibility" poses a lexical and conceptual problem in French. The word "social" as used in the expression in English is commonly translated into French using the same word, whereas in fact "social" in French has a more restricted meaning, as it is limited for the most part to the social dimension of sustainable development. Thus the three dimensions inherent to this notion, "economic efficiency", "social equity", and "control of resources", are not naturally covered by the term "social" in French. Hence, this problem of language can lead to confusion as to the very meaning of "social responsibility". Some analysts even believe that this word is the reason for a strong and threefold resistance to CSR in the French-speaking world: trade unions reject the idea that unilateral private sector standards should govern the social aspects of a company; employers are afraid of having new obligations forced on them, in an area that they believe to be already very restrictive; the State does not accept that principles that have been historically laid down to govern corporate social relations, and which combine legal intervention and collective bargaining under full public scrutiny, should now be challenged (Doucin 2004). Thus the term "societal" would perhaps be more appropriate here, expressing as it does a systemic vision incorporating all three aspects of social responsibility: economic, social, and environmental.

This lexical clarification has more significance than a simple stylistic elegance. It highlights the French notion of relations between economic, social, and political actors, especially with regard to labour relations. This notion is based on two founding principles: firstly, the importance of a clearly established public standard for labour relations, and secondly the fact that social dialogue was historically carried out in a context of negotiations between social partners with no privileges involved, which can happen when decisions are taken unilaterally in the context of the company. There is indeed to some extent a hierarchical opposition between *hard law* and the inferior *soft law* which can only be invoked as an adjunct to the hard law. As a result, CSR in the French context has a fundamentally political dimension, which must in turn have repercussions on the way the French democratic model functions (Rose 2006). As Elizabeth Laville emphasized, creator of Utopies, a consultancy firm specializing in corporate social and environmental responsibility, "France is not necessarily an easy country in which to implement these CSR-related topics, and this for two reasons: first of all because our Catholic culture inclines us towards scepticism, even cynicism, when confronted with those who claim to be doing good and making money at the same time; and second because of our long-established and all-pervading Colbertism we have more confidence in public institutions for resolving problems than in the private sector and businesses" (Laville 2004). This echoes the view of various authors who have shown that the European model of society is based on traditional roles, with the State in charge of *social welfare* (Clough and Shepard 1960; Grahl and Teague 1997). In general, the very idea of morality in business and capitalism leaves observers sceptical to say the least, not to say totally cynical (Vogel 1992): even to the point where a comparative study of the development of CSR in the United States and four European countries concluded that public scepticism can make European companies reluctant to publish data about their voluntary efforts relating to CSR for fear of exposing themselves to public criticism (Maignan and Ralston 2002). This partly explains why there are two aspects to the CSR situation in France: an important legal framework on the one hand, and a strong political dimension on the other.

2.2.2 A Substantial Body of Legislation

The first laws to cover the notions incorporated in CSR, though without this term being explicitly mentioned, appeared in France in the middle of the 1970s with a law on social reporting 1977.[1] Without referring specifically to CSR as such, this law already required that the social reports that were compulsory for companies with more than 300 employees should apply 134 specific measures and indicators, and these reflected notions are now commonly used in relation to CSR. Thus the social report required by this 1977 law opted deliberately for a social vision that focussed entirely on employees and social policies (Igalens and Joras 2002). However, it was mainly after 2000 that the body of legislation began to develop.

The turning point was undoubtedly the law of 15 May 2001 on new economic regulations.[2] With the adoption of this "NRE" law (*loi Nouvelles Régulations Economiques*), which today affects more than 700 listed companies, France was the first country to make it mandatory for listed companies to account for the

---

[1] Décret d'application de la loi sur le bilan social du 12 Juillet 1977.

[2] Loi NRE, 15 May 2001, no. 2001–420.

social and environmental consequences of their activities. When the French Council of State later fixed by decree the information that the business report should contain regarding social responsibility, the legislative arm gave themselves the means to oblige these listed companies to be transparent in their activities. More obligations followed on from this decree in the social and environmental areas: numbers hired, types of contract, information on staff cutback plans, organization and length of the working week, pay scales, health and safety conditions, labour relations and reports on collective agreements, training policy, employment and professional integration of the disabled, community work, these were the main social areas where companies had to account for their actions. With regard to environmental areas, they had to be in a position to notify their consumption of resources and any measures taken to improve energy efficiency such as nuisance control and waste treatment. Reference is made in the legislation to evaluation and certification procedures and it is suggested that an environment management system be put place. On top of this, companies must also justify the way in which they assess the impact of their activities on local development and the local population. They must explain their commitment to their stakeholders, including non-governmental organizations, consumers, educational institutions, and local communities. In fact, this new legal framework was in addition to that of the 1999 directive law concerning territorial planning and sustainable local and regional development (the "LOADT" law – *loi d'Orientation pour l'Aménagement Durable du Territoire*) and was an attempt to reorganize relations between the different local authorities by integrating economic and social actors into the procedure. Local authorities too are becoming subjected more and more to the requirements of sustainable development and new regulations on governance, and as they draw up their own local Agenda 21[3] they will need a higher level of involvement and responsibility from companies in matters of local development Durrieu et al. (2006).

Following on from the NRE law, which to some extent laid down the foundations, more laws were added to complete the CSR legal framework in France; these sometimes echoed decisions taken at European level, especially in relation to environmental aspects.[4] Thus, with regard to controlling major accident hazards, the law of 30 July 2003 ensured that so-called Seveso companies (classified sites) adhere to specific rules regarding prevention, civil responsibility, and victim compensation. More recently, the transposition of the European directive on setting up a system for

---

[3] The Agenda 21 for a sustainable development adopted in the framework of United Nations, the role of the local authorities to develop responsible practices is clear specified in the Chap. 28: "each local authority should enter into a dialogue with its citizens, local organizations and private enterprises, and adopt a local Agenda 21. Through consultation and consensus-building, local authorities would learn from citizens and from local civic community, business and industrial organizations and acquire the information needed for formulating the best strategies" (Agenda 21, Chap. 28, Sect. 1.3). In this sense in France, more and more local authorities adopted a local agenda 21. Some examples are described at the end of this chapter.

[4] We should recall that since the SEA (Single European Act), strengthened by the Maastricht Treaty then the Amsterdam Treaty, European environmental politics have become more and more consolidated and a group of directives are emerging that are gradually being integrated into the different national laws. Thus many French texts are Community law transcribed into French law.

the exchange of emission quotas has resulted in a series of obligations in terms of emission declarations and quota delivery. On another level entirely, we should also highlight the solemnity surrounding the adoption in 2005 of the Environment Charter, a Constitution amendment giving legal force to the major environmental principles. This charter places the right to live in a balanced and healthy environment on the same level as the human and social rights and recommends the precautionary principle although without undermining the possibility of innovation.

Lastly, regarding financial matters, the 19 February 2001 Law on employee savings, like that of 17 July 2001 on the creation of a public pension reserve fund,[5] takes ethical, social, and environmental factors into consideration. Similarly, the Law of financial security, dated 1 August 2003, ensures that listed companies produce a specific report describing the conditions governing the preparation and organization of the work of the board of directors, and internal control procedures put in place by the company in order to protect themselves, again with greater transparency, against different types of risk. Thus, in its website, KLM – Air France insists on the fact that "Pursuant to the French Financial Security Act, the chairman of the board of directors of Air France – KLM is required to deliver a special report to the general shareholders' meeting regarding corporate practices, the status of the internal control procedures implemented by Air France – KLM and the restrictions that Air France – KLM board of directors has placed on the powers granted to the chief executive officer". In the same vein, the introduction of new accounting standards in 2005 has brought changes to the rules on information and financial transparency. Thus the 2005 report of AMF (*Autorité des Marchés Financiers*/French Authority for Financial Markets) analyzing 108 reports of listed companies concluded that corporate governance and internal control by companies were of a higher quality. If the report underlined considerable disparities between companies' disclosures in these areas, these differences were however more pronounced in internal control than in corporate governance, where companies can rely on more familiar, longer standing industry recommendations (AMF 2006).

2.2.3 Public Consultation and Instigating Bodies

A *National Council for sustainable development* bringing together almost 100 representatives from various areas of civil society was created in January 2003. Following on from this, a national sustainable development government strategy was adopted in June 2003, in which the French government declared its objective to be "the development of social and environmental responsibility on the part of companies, with the overall concern of good governance". This declared objective has three parts: to create a common frame of reference at national level in the matter of corporate social and environmental responsibility, and then promote it both nationally and internationally; to encourage companies to adopt a responsible

---

[5] Loi épargne salariale, 19 February 2001, no. 2001–152 and Loi fonds de réserve retraite, 17 July 2001, no. 2001–624.

mode of operation both environmentally and socially; and lastly to develop socially responsible investment. The Regions and other tiers of local government (Departments, Communes, and Commune communities) have been similarly active with their own Agenda 21 sustainable development strategies.

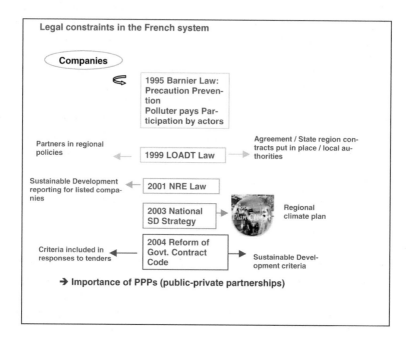

Similarly, in the area of international business relations, a certain number of measures have been put in place in an attempt to influence corporate behaviour. For example, the *French contact point* has been particularly busy: he is responsible for monitoring implementation of the OECD (Organization of Economic Cooperation and Development) leading indicators by multinational companies that are integrating the fundamental principles and rights at work as recognized by the 1998 International Labour Organization (ILO) declaration and the environmental principles in the Rio Declaration, Agenda 21, and the European Union's Aarhus Convention. The contact point has had to apply the public communication procedure on several occasions.

This short retrospective of the legal and institutional background in France shows that CSR is both strongly supported by the law and yet at the same time somewhat scattered across a variety of different rules and regulations. Thus when one tries to analyze corporate practices, it is apparent that while there is certainly considerable weight behind the legal tools that have been put in place, nevertheless, as is the case in other countries, these regulations do nothing to reduce the great diversity not only in corporate practices but also in company attitudes to CSR.

2.2.4 The Emergence in Parallel of Rating Agencies and Mutualized Activities in CSR Awareness and Promotion

There are basically two rating agencies that have emerged in France since the end of the 1990s. The first is the ARESE agency, created in 1997 with support from the *Caisse des Dépôts et de Consignation* (French funding body for public works and housing) and the *Caisses d'Epargne* (savings banks). Its aim was to produce a Social and Environmental Rating for each company based on an econometric procedure, originally intended for fund managers. In 2003, the Vigeo agency, a French public limited company (*Société Anonyme*), took over from ARESE. The agency's board of directors is made up of companies, European trades union organizations, non-governmental organizations (NGOs), and suitably qualified individuals, and they offer sustainable development audits for local authorities, social responsibility audits for companies and organizations, themed studies, and sector-based benchmarking. About 56 projects were completed in 2006, 85% of which were in France, as the group is now active elsewhere in Europe (Belgium and Italy) and also in Morocco since 2004.[6] The agency's auditing activity grew by almost 63% in 2006 compared to 2005, an indication of the growth of this market in France. In socially responsible investment too, Vigeo's turnover increased considerably, showing an annual growth of 56% between 2003 and 2006 and reaching almost 3.2 million euros by the end of 2006.

The second agency, BMJ Ratings, was created from the merger in 2004 of the BMJ sustainable development agency, forerunner in France since 1993 in the field of solicited social ratings, and the Core Ratings agency, thus creating the first European rating agency to cover both social and environmental matters. They offer confidential ratings, and in only 10 years they have built up a client base of over 800 companies.

In parallel with the emergence of rating agencies, a further addition to the CSR landscape was the appearance of mutualized company activities: a certain number of company groups were formed and now play an important role in maintaining the underlying principles of CSR, in promoting CSR awareness, and in encouraging good company practices. Without claiming to produce an exhaustive study, we will look at two types of structured cooperation that are fairly significant today in France. The first are multi-partner groups structured along the same lines as ORSE (*Observatoire sur la Responsabilité Sociétale des Entreprises*), a study centre for corporate social responsibility.[7] ORSE was created in June 2000 on the initiative of major corporations, fund management companies, investment institutions, trade unions, non-governmental associations, and organizations. The aim was to promote a structure for study, exchanges, and permanent monitoring in the field of CSR, sustainable development, and ethical investments. Today ORSE undoubtedly plays a vital role in terms of analyzing practices and assessing the major consequences for companies of issues relevant to CSR.

---

[6] Figures from the Vigeo annual report 2006.

[7] ORSE: www.orse.fr.

Along different lines, a number of associations or employers' groups are flourishing based on the issues surrounding CSR. The association Alliances, for example, whose aim is to help companies improve their performance while still respecting man and the environment, was created in 1994 on a fairly small scale, by three men from companies in northern France more in the spirit of a group of committed managers.[8] The association puts forward the case for CSR, showing it as something company managers should commit to, something that cannot be ignored if their company is to survive, and also as a tremendous opportunity for the future.

2.3 French Companies: Various Strategic Positions on Social and Environmental Responsibility

As we have seen, it is important to consider the specific framework of the French legal and institutional system for a better understanding of CSR in the context of France. The fact still remains, however, that, as in many developed countries, internationalization and shifting power balances between States, companies, and the international civil society combined with new environmental, political, and social challenges are the main factors that account for the transformations that companies are undergoing regarding CSR. Thus, the degree of internationalization, the resulting image problems that must be dealt with, and specific economic features relating to CSR and sustainable development are the main reasons why there is such diversity in practices and strategic positioning on the part of French companies. A European study carried out by Novethic, published in 2002, attempted to analyze the different ways in which sustainable development was integrated into company strategy. It gives some insight into French companies and how involved they were before the NRE Law of 2002 (Novethic 2002). The aim of the study was to measure the link between pressure exerted on the company or the sector by contractual or non-contractual stakeholders and the company's position in relation to sustainable development, in other words the way in which it reacted or did not react to these pressures. Using the methodology of this study and completing it with information from the latest annual reports on sustainable development in businesses, this time in the context of the NRE law, we can show that, unsurprisingly, French companies, just like those in other countries, can be found across the entire range of possible positioning in respect of CSR. They range from companies that are barely inclined to invest, not to say totally resistant to the idea, to those that are fully committed and consider CSR as an essential strategic element: the entire spectrum is there. For the purposes of this work we chose to present just a few glimpses of this panorama. Despite the risk of presenting too generalized a picture, this has the advantage of giving a fairly accurate overall view. Globally we were able to distinguish two major groups of company.

---

[8] Alliances: www.alliances-asso.org.

2.3.1 Voluntarist Companies: From Strategists to Opportunists

The first group is made up of companies that are in one way or another very concerned about CSR and have integrated it in a voluntarist fashion into their strategy. First in this category are companies that we have called "strategists": they have integrated corporate social, and environmental responsibility into their global strategy as a result of both strong pressures and strategic opportunities. The most often quoted French example is Lafarge.

Example of a "strategist" company: Lafarge

World leader in construction materials and cement, internationalized to a high degree particularly in emerging markets and developing countries, Lafarge was one of the first signatories of the Global Compact and one of the first members of the World Business Council for Sustainable Development (WBCSD). The group's activities do have a strong impact on the environment. Accidents in the workplace and the hard working conditions constitute real risks for the company in terms of cost and likewise of image. Since the 1990s, the company has set up an environmental preservation programme, and since 2000 this programme has been based on a conservation partnership with World Wide Fund for Nature (WWF). The two major areas covered by the programme with regard to the environment are the management and rehabilitation of limestone quarries and the use of alternative fuels. Concerning the social aspect of its work, Lafarge has developed a coordinated policy first of all with regard to employees with the aim of drastically reducing the number of accidents in the workplace, improving training, and redeployment when sites are closed. This action extends to local communities in which Lafarge operates, with the company contributing to local development.

While Lafarge is often cited as a company that is concerned about its environmental and social impact, it also makes sustainable development a strategic issue in terms of market opportunities: the group has developed products that use less and less cement thus reducing their environmental impact; it is committed to a policy of waste recycling which also involves their clients. For example, their latest cement works built in Morocco, Titouan II, relies on wind-powered energy which produces 40% of electricity requirements. Lastly, the group has worked with WBCSD to produce offers to help their less creditworthy clients.

There is another type of company: "committed" companies which, unlike the preceding example, experience only low levels of outside pressure as their sector of activity is less exposed (as in the case of banks, for example). The attitude of these companies to environmental and social issues is based more on an extension of the historical values that underlie the company's original goals. In this case, it is a matter of creating a strategic opportunity from this history. Thus these companies will tend to use a more systemic approach to corporate, social, and environmental responsibility by combining exemplary human relations policies with rigorous management in terms of the environment, citizen's actions via sponsorship, and adapting what they offer in terms of products and services. A good example of this type of company is the Caisse d'Epargne group, historically a cooperative banking group founded on humanistic values of popular savings.

Example of a "committed" company: "Groupe Caisse d'Epargne" (CE)

From its inception in 1818, to the Reform Bill of 1999 and right up to the present day, the Groupe Caisse d'Epargne has organized its strategy and operations around one goal: to fulfil missions serving the *General Interest*. These missions can be described as follows: promotion of popular saving; satisfaction of individual, family, and collective needs; participation in local, economic, and social development. Building in this way upon a long-standing tradition of dealing with local actors, CE then decided to favour a different kind of "capital venturing". By placing money under the supervision of a newly created structure, a local development social savings bank *(Caisse Sociale de Développement Local)*, it would then be available to people who did not meet the usual criteria (solvency) required by traditional banking. The main criteria used to assess each venture would be nature of the project, motivation of the person(s) proposing it, and social contribution of the venture. This would be a different approach, going well beyond "venture philanthropy", an approach much closer to the concept of "micro-credit".

Regarding CSR and sustainable development (SD), CE decided, towards the end of 2001, to initiate a test experiment before proceeding further in those fields. Four of CE's local branches were required to implement a self-evaluation process in five areas deemed most important by Headquarters. The selected areas were human resources, relations with customers and suppliers, relations with civil society, corporate governance, and impact on the environment. The results of this self-evaluation process were so encouraging that in July 2002 Headquarters decided that the whole network of local CE (33 branches in France) plus the *Caisse Nationale* would join the initiative, under the supervision of a newly created "National Steering Committee". At the same time, a network of Executives was set up and entrusted with organizing the implementation of CSR and SD in every CE branch.

Last point worth mentioning here is the creation, in 2001, of a *Fondation Caisses d'Epargne pour la Solidarité*. Endowed with 15.2 million euros in capital, it was acknowledged as fulfilling a mission of general public interest (*d'utilité publique*) by the French authorities. The foundation has been assigned three main missions: as a non-profit operation it manages 39 specialized establishments that cater for the needs of 2,500 old, sick, or handicapped residents, with a salaried staff of 1,400; together with public and private partners it also organizes programmes to eradicate illiteracy and dependence (on drugs, alcohol); finally, it is developing a systematic policy of helping with innovative projects that fight different kinds of isolation (psychological, functional, cultural, etc.).

Among the companies that have integrated social and environmental responsibility in a positive fashion, we can distinguish a third sub-category, which we will call "concerned" companies. They are feeling the pressure of sustainable development more and more strongly and therefore feel obliged to integrate the notion gradually, but their approach remains partial, more often than not targeting specific areas that for them represent key market issues. The majority of French companies belong to this category. As an example we have chosen two such companies, Danone and Carrefour.

Carrefour: Member of the Global Compact since 2001, Carrefour, the number two in supermarket distribution, is mainly active in Europe but the group is also increasingly present in South America and Asia, and aims to gain more and more of the market share in the emerging market economies while still retaining client loyalty in Europe. Carrefour's policy in terms of CSR is based on three main areas: the first is product quality and safety, by product traceability and a quality audit system. Thus the Carrefour group openly positions itself against genetically modified foods. The second area is the development since 1995 of a policy to supervise and standardize working conditions within the group and also in their supplier companies. To this end a partnership has been drawn up with the FIDH (*Fédération Internationale des Droits de l'Homme*) to protect human rights. The third area concerns participation in local development and help for small and medium enterprises (SMEs), especially those in their own sector, by setting up a support structure for Carrefour's suppliers in Asia. As well as these current actions, Carrefour has believed since the mid-1990s that the basic movement for responsible consumption represented the groundswell of public opinion and was not simply a popular craze. This idea was strengthened by the fact that a considerable proportion of the group's capital was in the hands of individual shareholders (15%). The group therefore tried to strengthen their product base in two directions: by developing their range of fair trade products and their range of organic products. The strategy they used was to create a range based on the "Carrefour" name rather than risk using pre-existing channels (like Max Havelaar, for example, in France).

Danone: For the Danone group their support for responsible development dates back even earlier, to a speech by Antoine Riboud, managing director and founder in 1972 of the company's dual economic and social project. In 1996, through its environmental charter, the group committed to a more respectful management of the environment from the product design stage through to the recycling of packaging. The group's values, openness, enthusiasm, humanity, and proximity were formalized in 1997 in its code of business conduct (*Principes de Conduite des Affaires*). Since the Danone group became a member of the Global Compact in 2003, it has become involved in a proactive approach towards its suppliers by setting up an evaluation system based on Fundamental Social Principles and incorporating the International Labour Organization (ILO) conventions; this method was generalized from 2006 onwards with the procedure called the *Danone Way*, which encourages subsidiaries to measure their own performance and commit to action plans and progress. The aim is to monitor all suppliers by the end of 2008.

2.3.2 When CSR becomes a Constraint: "Target" and "Entrant" Companies

Many French companies are slowly taking sustainable development into account simply because they have no choice. Rather later than other companies, they are gradually integrating it into their strategic position, and for the larger companies at least, it is now difficult to avoid. Under this heading are, first of all, companies that to some extent constitute "ideal targets" in relation to environmental and social issues. Sustainable development can become a real constraint that companies must nevertheless endure. When this is the case, they will devise avoidance strategies by developing specifically targeted actions according to company type and sector of operation that try to minimize their environmental and social impact. Total is a good illustration of this type of company. The history of this sector and of this company have been plagued by controversy with affairs like the accusations that have lingered since 1992 of complicity with the regime in Burma over the contract to exploit the Yadana gas deposits, the oil spill from the tanker Erika off the Brittany coast in 1999, and also the explosion of the AZF factory near Toulouse. In such cases, strategy will be concentrated on actions that minimize the risk to the company's image and on recovering a degree of credibility over the accusations, as the Total example seems to show.

The SD report by the Total group focuses on two main areas of action. The first concerns environmental management, with a systematic policy of certifying sites, both upstream and downstream from production. As an extension of this activity, the group will concentrate its research and development efforts on renewable energy, wind power, and photovoltaic energy in particular. A corporate foundation dedicated to preserving biodiversity completes this area of activity. The second area of action covers the ethical dimension. An ethics

committee was created in 2001, reinforced by an ethical assessment procedure, carried out by a body from outside the units that make up the group.
Over a 2-year period (2004–2005) a training programme in this ethical procedure has involved almost 2,000 executives from the group and a confidential
whistle blowing system makes it every employee's duty to refer to the ethics
committee in case of practices that do not conform to company ethics. Lastly,
a certain number of actions have been introduced with local communities,
especially in areas where Total's operations are seen as questionable, as in
Burma, for example.

A final category of companies called "entrants" contains a large number of companies, all those that consider that CSR, though not putting them under any pressure,
is nevertheless implicitly becoming the new standard to be adhered to. There are
more and more companies that fall into this category and that are now trying to put
in place what we might call adaptation strategies. These usually consist of a series
of actions that are not properly coordinated with the company's global strategy.

This overview of French companies and their strategic positioning in relation to
environmental and social issues shows again that, as in most developed countries,
there is a fundamental shift: one that seems to be growing towards an increased
awareness of the importance of SD in corporate strategy. This underlying trend,
reinforced by the obligations of the NRE law, has resulted over the last 3 years in a
much higher level of company reporting.

2.3.3 More Widespread Reporting

A study of the mandatory reports[9] required by the NRE law from the last 4 years
seems to show that this reporting obligation is being respected more and more, since
average compliance in 2005 was around 85% compared with 60% in 2002 Alpha
Etudes (2006). So reporting appears to be more generalized and more professional.
The study shows a distinct and continuing improvement in the social information
published by top companies, most of which had set a reporting system in motion
even before the NRE law made it compulsory. Indicators are much more detailed and
relevant, and analysis of the reports suggests that there are advantages in extending
mandatory reporting across the longer term.

The same study shows that the topics on which most information is provided are,
firstly, those that relate to what is already well known about the companies, referring directly to management variables (staff numbers, training, health and safety)
and, secondly, elements associated with image or media pressure such as relations

---

[9] This analysis and these figures are taken mainly from "Les informations sociales dans les rapports
2005 des entreprises du CAC40 – Quatrième année d'application de la Loi NRE". ALPHA –
Etudes. Available on internet http://www.alpha-etudes.com/admin/upload/rp060705.pdf.

with stakeholders, social dialogue, and professional equality. The topics that are not covered nearly as well concern the organization and content of work, touching on some of the most significant aspects of the corporate management of social relations, such as employment dynamics, pay, the organization of work, subcontracting and outsourcing, and also restructuring and its potential impact.

One problem seems to be the low level of staff participation at all stages of the reporting process. Only 5 of the 38 companies studied (AXA, Carrefour, Lafarge, Sanofi-Aventis, Schneider Electric) invited a representative from the workforce, a member of the European works council, to contribute to the report. Because of this shortcoming, the authors of the study stress that the social information that is included covers news that grabs media attention rather than the social functioning of the company. The employees as contributors and constituent elements of the company are entirely absent from this representation of the company.

An analysis of the main themes in French company practice regarding social and environmental responsibility will highlight some strengths and weaknesses that we will look at in greater depth in part three.

2.3.4 SMEs–SMIs: These are Still in Early Stages of CSR

In France, as in most European countries, small and medium enterprises and small and medium industries (SME–SMIs) make up the majority of the country's economic fabric. According to INSEE (Institut National des Statistiques et Eétudes economiques) there are almost 930,000 French companies with fewer than 10 employees and 177,000 with between 10 and 250. Hence the vast majority of these SME–SMIs remains unaffected by problems of sustainable development and feels little commitment to corporate social and environmental responsibility. In this respect, therefore, the situation in France appears to be slightly behind that in other European countries. A survey by the European SME Observatory in 2001 of a representative sample of 76,000 European SMEs with fewer than 250 employees showed that while on average half of European companies were already involved in socially responsible actions, barely a third of French companies were active in this way, contrasting with 83% in Finland, for example. However, some regional studies seem to show that there has been some development, at least in awareness. A study carried out in three successive years (2003, 2004, and 2005) on SME–SMI managers in the Ile-de-France area by CROCIS (*Centre Régional d'Observation du Commerce, de l'Industrie et des Services*), part of the CCIP (*Chambre de Commerce et d'Industrie de Paris*), shows a definite increase in awareness of the issues surrounding sustainable development and the role that companies play (Crocis 2006). Another study, in Aquitaine this time, confirms that SME managers are incorporating CSR much more into their strategic planning. This study does show, however, that the perception of sustainable development remains targeted essentially on matters linked with the environment and that few company directors have a systemic vision incorporating all three aspects of the problem (economic, environmental, and social)

(Harribey and Durrieu 2007). There is another interesting point in these two studies: the fact that the younger the company, the more weight the company director places on CSR and the more it is seen as an accelerator of growth and of opportunity, whereas in older companies CSR is seen more as a constraint and an unwelcome but compulsory transition stage. Nevertheless, many initiatives are being developed to stimulate and encourage CSR practices in SME–SMIs. In response to the complaint often made as to the unsuitability of available evaluation tools, which were all originally designed for large companies, other methods have been devised by the Young Executive Centre (*Centre des Jeunes Dirigeants*) such as the "global performance" method or the "company report". A French version of *SME keys* (CSR Europe) has been produced by the Alliances network of companies, and in 2005 the Caisse Nationale des Caisses d'Epargne and Vigeo also created "Cordé", a CSR self-diagnostic tool for SME–SMIs, which is available to the companies themselves. Lastly, the SD 21000 guide produced by AFNOR/AFAQ (*Association Française de Normalisation/Association Française d'Amélioration de la Qualité*) is an excellent reference tool based on a checklist of 34 key points, including environmental, social, and economic responsibility issues and more transversal topics like eco-design and purchasing linked with client supplier relations (AFNOR 2005).

The majority of studies on the involvement of SMEs in CSR tend to show that any such involvement is above all due to the convictions and the willingness of SME–SMI heads, but this situation must change. External constraints will certainly tend to ensure that CSR will become much more widespread in SME–SMIs in future. There are two elements that favour this development: the first comes from the large companies that are supplied by the SME–SMI subcontractors and that are now beginning to insist that their suppliers use socially responsible practices, urging them to conform to codes of conduct and even to auditing and control procedures. The second element comes from public actors via public contracts, which are more and more frequently stipulating SD criteria in their specifications.

2.4 Social and Environmental Responsibility Reflected in a Diversity of Practices

2.4.1 The Widespread Adoption of Ethics Charters and Codes of Conducts

Although studies have shown that historically French companies and European companies in general use codes and charters to a lesser extent than companies in the USA (Langlois and Bodo 1990), in contrast there has been a significant explosion in recent years in the use of corporate codes of conduct, ethics charters, and declarations of values and principles. According to a more recent study on this specific point in 2004 that looked at listed French companies, more than half have drawn up an ethics charter, 49% have a declaration of principles and values, and 38% have a code of conduct (Alpha 2004). A wide variety of topics are covered, but they usually relate to societal issues such as respecting regulations, health, safety, and environmental questions rather than internal issues such as job training and discrimination. Whereas the majority of companies make reference to an international legal text for the basis of their document, very few mention the ILO's fundamental conventions, despite the fact that these are one of the basic references for French law. The fundamental principle that is most often quoted (by 18% of companies) is that relating to the minimum age at which children may work (ILO convention 138) but only 5% mention convention 182 on the worst forms of child labour. While the style of these texts is usually formulaic, listing in formal terms the moral commitments companies intend to make, the way in which these commitments are to be carried out is rarely specified and the structure used to monitor these commitments is, in the vast majority of cases, the company's own governing body. Indeed, only 3% of the companies studied are associated with an outside control body. These charters and codes appear to have a primarily internal function for the company; they are tools of self-defence and self-protection rather than communication (Orse 2003).

Lastly, these documents are rarely legally enforceable on trading partners and particularly on subcontractors, so companies run the risk of relieving themselves of responsibility for these commitments if they are not aware of the actions of their subcontractors. There are some notable exceptions, however: Carrefour, for example, which imposes contractual obligations on its trading partners to respect the ILO fundamental conventions, or Thomson, which insists that its ethics charter be applied to its entire supply chain and demands that suppliers conform to Thomson's own codes of conduct.

2.4.2 From Charters to Practice: French Companies fall Behind in the Battle Against Discrimination

No sooner had 2007 been declared the European Year of Equal Opportunities, than France was ostracized last March after a survey[10] published by BIT (Bureau International du Travail) revealed that only 11% of employers in France offered candidates truly equal opportunities (Husson-Traore, 2007). And yet this question of professional diversity and equality forms an integral part of reporting frames of reference, especially in the context of the NRE law. However, this BIT survey does to some extent confirm what an earlier study by the Vigeo agency, carried out at the request of ORSE, had already revealed. This European study put France in seventh position out of the 17 countries studied with a rate of company commitment of 47.5%, a considerable distance behind countries like Finland (56.3%) and the United Kingdom (Vigeo 2006).[11] Nevertheless, there are some

---

[10] Survey carried out between the end of 2005 and mid-2006 on four major urban areas in France concerning job offers requiring minimum qualifications in hotel-restauration, sales, commerce, services to companies or local authorities, human services, transport, construction, secretarial, health and social welfare.

[11] Press release by ORSE and Vigeo 15 March 2006, www.vigeogroup.com.

remarkable initiatives in certain sectors. To illustrate this, here are some examples (IGAS 2004): Adecco, a company supplying temporary staffing services and which therefore regularly faces discriminatory requests from their client companies, carried out an anti-discrimination programme in 90 of the largest companies in France, a programme supported by the European Union in the context of the Equal Initiative. Another experiment was carried out by Eiffage-Construction, the leading construction company in France, which had a problem with staff recruitment. In this company, where foreign workers make up two-thirds of the 15,000-strong workforce, a programme was introduced guaranteeing equal treatment both at the recruitment stage and throughout their workers' professional careers. More recently, in 2005, SRF, a market leader in telephony, introduced a support programme to train and then employ disadvantaged young people called *"le passeport ingénieurs télécoms"* (passport to telephone engineering), which was set up in collaboration with government. This programme has already helped almost 150 school leavers from among 30 sensitive urban areas in France to find suitable training and a place in an engineering school. A hundred or so tutors, all SRF employees, have guided them. In 2006, this initiative was extended when other companies such as Alcatel, Ericsson, Nokia, and Siemens joined SRF, and the programme has now reached over 400 young people.

In the same spirit, some companies try to develop specific action promoting diversity. For example, the automobile group PSA Peugeot Citroën is setting up a programme composed of three points: firstly, ensuring equal access to employment and career development; secondly, ensuring equality in career development for older employees, the disabled, and foreign nationals; and thirdly, supporting associations promoting the mobility of people in social difficulty. Thus, an agreement was signed in 2004 on diversity and social cohesion with all the labour unions. In 2005, PSA Peugeot Citroën tried out anonymous CVs in collaboration with the Observatory of discrimination in the hiring process.

2.4.3 French Companies: Some Excellent Efforts but Still Mixed Results in Terms of Responsible Practice at International Level

Companies that work at an international level often have the finger pointed at them because of their international practices. Relocation and sub-contracting can indeed lead to contradictions in terms of their claims to support sustainable development: job losses in the Northern Hemisphere and dubious working conditions in the South, especially around the question of child labour in those countries where the national law provides inadequate protection. These are all risks that companies may encounter, and their practices are very carefully monitored by the NGOs. Thus many companies have decided to develop specific programmes in order to guarantee responsible practices at the international level. The increase in the number of international agreements being drawn up is a clear illustration of this. For example, the automobile group PSA Peugeot Citroën has declared its commitment to promote respect for human rights in all the countries in which it operates using a framework agreement ratified by all the trade union organizations of the countries that have sites with more than 500 employees (i.e., 33 signatories from 10 countries). As well as the "rights at work" dimension, international companies are becoming more and more involved with local communities. This may involve funding development actions, like EDF (*Electricité de France*) has done with its programme against poverty which provides the poorest sections of the community with access to electricity; or it may be supporting major causes like Orange Cameroon which has launched a programme to take on HIV-positive employees and is also supporting an AIDS prevention programme.

While framework agreements clearly show great transparency, the same cannot be said for the fight against corruption. Studies by Novethic and by Vigeo in the last 2 years show that almost 80% of CAC40 companies are lagging behind with regards to transparency in their policies to fight corruption; however, since the risk to their reputations is high in this respect, those that do act tend not to talk about what they are doing. And when they do, like Total, Thalès, EADES, Alcatel, EDF, France Telecom, Bouygues, and also Lafarge, they mainly tend to use a very declamatory style. Hence on the Bouygues website we can see this following declaration: "We have seen our business in turmoil during the 1990s and we do not want to be subject to any illegality... In Africa, if corruption by the authorities is too forceful and we are unable to impose our own basic rules of operation, then we will leave."[12] And yet a study by Transparence International France and EthiFinance in 2006 would appear to show that prevention against the risk of corruption is increasing in the major French groups, a risk that apparently none of them can escape entirely. According to the study, 24 companies compared with 17 the previous year, say that they are affected by this problem (Ethifinance and Transparence International 2006).

2.4.4 Partnership between Companies and NGOs are More Numerous and More Structured

For several years now, we have witnessed considerable development in relations between NGOs and companies. It is true that recent laws regarding sponsorship have given rise in the last 3 years to a multiplication of philanthropic actions, and company foundations have flourished. Over and above this phenomenon, however, there has also been a growth in strategic partnerships which has radically readjusted the type of relations between NGOs and companies. Historically, relations between these two groups have always tended towards the conflictual; however, in a partnership context they get on well together. A recent report by ORSE declared that "strategic partnerships help create real alliances between organizations. They are linked by their core business, which includes exchanges of know-how and

---

[12] http://www.bouygues.fr/fr/developpement/groupe_dd.asp.

expertise, work in common, striving in the same direction and building long-lasting and sustainable relationships" (Orse 2005). If we look again at the Carrefour example mentioned above, we can understand the strategic dimension of the Carrefour/FIDH (*Fédération internationale des Droits de l'Homme*/International federation of Human Rights) partnership. By setting up in countries in which working conditions are questionable, and revealing such vulnerability in risking their corporate image, this partnership will give Carrefour a form of credibility in terms of human rights in areas where showing respect for a law that does not even exist, or only at a very low level, would be largely inadequate. In the same sector and with the same intention, Casino has entered into a partnership with Amnesty International who has agreed to accompany the company in their ethical process and assist them in drawing up an ethics charter aimed at their suppliers. In another area of activity, the partnership between Lafarge, a company with a strong impact on the environment, and WWF, protector of the environment, is also understandable in terms of strategy. An even more targeted partnership is that between Suez, leader in environmental management and water treatment, and ESSOR, a French NGO specializing in providing support for local development projects, especially in Brazil. This partnership has enabled Suez to take advantage of the NGO as mediator in the Manaus region while promising to reduce water and sanitation problems. Lastly, in the field of tourism, we can highlight the partnership begun in 2001 between the ACCOR group, a heavyweight in the hotel industry, and ECPAT, an international network of organizations fighting to combat the problem of sex tourism and the sexual exploitation of children (Verger and White 2004)[13].

2.4.5 The Recent Emergence of Responsible Savings and Changes that are Tending to Follow the Anglo-American Model

Socially responsible investment (SRI) has developed in France rather later than in Anglo-American countries. The first mutual fund, *Faim et Développement* (Hunger and Development) dates back to the beginning of the 1980s and was on the initiative of the *Comité Catholique contre la Faim* (CCFD/Catholic Committee against Hunger) together with a banking sector cooperative in the shape of the *Crédit Coopératif*. At the same time, the first common ethical investment fund was born, initiated by a religious order that had the idea of offering investors and individuals alike a means of investing on the stock market in funds that respected man's place in the economy. The 1990s were to be significant for the development of more and more initiatives which followed the example of the ethical solidarity investment fund called *Insertion/Emploi* (Insertion/Employment), launched in 1994 on the initiative of the *Caisse des Dépôts et Consignations* (CDC), the *Caisses d'Epargne*, and a trade Union – the CFDT. In 1997 FINANSOL was created which aimed to

---

[13] Most of these examples are mentioned in a footnote in the ORSE report. See also Verger, O., White, G. "Les partenariats Entreprise/ONG dans le cadre de démarches sociétales, premiers éléments d'analyse", June 2004, IMS.

guarantee the transparency and solidarity of savings products. There were 3 such funds by the end of the 1980s and this increased to 7 in 1997 then to 42 in 2001 and 59 in 2002 with the arrival of the heavyweights from the banking sector like Crédit Agricole, Société Générale, and BNP Paribas. It would seem that 2002 was to mark a turning point, with some key events that would change the shape of SRI: as Eric Loiselet (2003) pointed out, the setting up of the CIES (*Comité Intersyndical pour l'Epargne Salariale*) (Inter-union employee savings committee), the transformation of the ARESE agency into Vigeo which led to a diversification in the supply of information and rating, and also the setting up of the *Conseil de surveillance du fonds de réserve des retraites* (Council to monitor pension reserve funds) were to stimulate the growth of SRI (Loiselet 2003). The CIES, created in January 2002 by four union organizations (CFDT (*Confédération Française du Travail*), CGC (*Confédération Générale des Cadres*), CFTC (*Confédération Française des Travailleurs Chrétiens*), and CGT (*Confédération Générale des Travailleurs*)) would encourage a process of standardization and introduce control procedures based on criteria that take into account in particular the reality of a socially responsible process. With the action of the CIES and the impact of legislation covering employee savings and pension funds, SRI is now moving away from confidentiality. Ten times more money was invested in socially responsible savings funds in 2003 than in 1998. These were still fairly modest amounts, however, as they represented less than 2% of the total in mutual funds. In many respects one might wonder whether the impact of the media attention did not exceed their true significance in the economy. Nevertheless, this growth continued. Novethic recently made public the latest results from a study of SRI in 2006 (Novethic 2007). According to Novethic, the total outstanding SRI[14] held by French residents at the end of 2006 was 16.6 billion euros, 63% of which was by institutional investors. Thus the growth in SRI seems to be due to institutional investors, some of whom are moving gradually towards a real commitment to SRI. At the end of 2006, again according to the Novethic study, SRI in dedicated funds for French institutional investors reached 5.6 billion euros, compared with 1.7 billion at the end of 2005. Amounts of employee savings have also increased compared to 2006, from 1.3 to 2.8 billion euros (+118%). This latest study shows, according to Novethic, that France is becoming much less of an outsider in the international SRI landscape: "The French SRI market is tending to align with the Anglo-American and northern European model, with the majority of institutional investors involved in pensions being more and more aware of the long-term issues and of integrating environmental, social and governance criteria into their fund management".

2.4.6 The Role of Local Authorities becomes More Significant

Changes that have occurred in the French administrative landscape as a result of decentralization legislation and State regional development policies and in

---

[14] In terms of demand, and not of offers present in France.

conjunction with regional and structural European policies have in turn altered local actor networks and relations between local authorities and other economic and social actors. At the same time, local authorities confirm that they too want to promote SD in their areas. The vital role of local authorities had already been mentioned at the time of the Rio Summit in 1992 and was clearly confirmed at the Johannesburg World Summit on Sustainable Development in 2002 with the principle "Think globally, Act locally". The advent of a strong local economy, which can produce wealth and jobs by relying on local resources without overlooking solidarity and responsible development, becomes a major asset. For this reason local authorities are more and more often developing local policies that are in line with sustainable development. In 1997, the ministry responsible for the environment with the Urban Affairs Department launched an appeal for suggestions with a view to developing local Agenda 21 projects. Forty-five projects were selected, all with mainly environmental goals. A second appeal in 2000 around the time of the LOADT law (Law concerning territorial development and planning) broadened the scope of the projects to include principles of social equity, and improvements in working conditions and participation. AFNOR/AFAQ (French Standardization Association) has produced a guide, called SD2100, specifically for local authorities AFNOR (2005).

Today, more towns, urban areas, and commune communities than ever before are committing themselves to Agenda 21. The innovative experience by the Dunkerque urban area in Northern France is an interesting example here. The area was seriously affected by the industrial crisis and weakened by unemployment, so the authorities suggested an entirely integrated development strategy bringing together economic development, promotion of a social life that would allow both individuals and the community to find fulfilment, valorization of the environment, and improvements in the quality of life. Through these Agenda 21 projects, the local authorities tried to encourage companies to become more involved in local development. In the same way as Lyon and Bordeaux had done, they developed a participative procedure which involved the chambers of commerce, socio-professionals, and companies, and what is more, this was done in a formalized manner by producing an economic development plan.

Local authorities can also influence company behaviour via public procurement contracts. The recent reform of the public contract Code stipulates in article 14 that "the public contract conditions laid down in the specifications may include promoting the employment of people experiencing difficulties in finding work, fighting unemployment or protection of the environment". Authorities are applying this principle more and more regularly and hence they do have an influence on companies, especially the SME–SMIs which, in replying to offers to tender, are therefore obliged to include criteria related to their own social and environmental responsibility. Similarly, local authorities also demonstrate social and environmental responsibility by the example of their own actions when they make public purchases. France has adopted a national Plan of action for sustainable public purchasing, the aim being to make France one of the most committed countries in Europe in terms of social and environmental responsibility in the context of public purchasing by 2009. In order to mutualize their experiences and structure their procedural channels accordingly, in 2005 local authorities created networks around public expenditure and sustainable development. At the end of 2006, the "ethical public purchasing" network, for example, organized by *Cités Unies France*, included more than 200 local authorities.[15]

2.5 Conclusion

As we come to the end of this panorama of CSR practices in France, we can conclude that, as in many other countries, the increasing awareness of sustainable development in the decision-making processes in companies and local authorities alike is a trend that is likely to become more generalized in future. All organizations, public or private, are making an effort to adapt their practices in line with greater social and environmental responsibility. Only a few years ago, France in many respects could be considered as being relatively backward in this area. Today, however, when we take the experience gained by the largest international companies during the reporting process and as they integrated CSR into their company strategy, and then consider the legal and partenarial frameworks set up by public authorities, we see that these measures have clearly had an impact on this fundamental transformation. As Professor Jean Jacques Rosé notes, "France came fairly late to CSR, but she is making up for it now" (Rose 2006). In conclusion, France is a good illustration of what a dual approach to organizational social responsibility can be, conceived as a redefinition of relations between political, economic, and social actors. The most important feature is indeed this association of an ever more stringent standardizing framework (following the example of the NRE law or the reform of public contracts) with actions in a partenarial framework by forums or multi-party institutions (in particular mutualization of practices, public/private partnerships, and NGO/Company partnerships).

References

AFNOR (2005), *Guide Agenda 21*, www.sd2100.org
Alpha-Etudes (2004), Chartes éthiques et codes de conduite: état des lieux d'un nouvel enjeu social.
Alpha – Etudes (2006), Les informations sociales dans les rapports 2005 des entreprises du CAC40 – Quatrième année d'application de la Loi NRE.
AMF (2006), AMF 2005 Report on Corporate Governance and Internal Control.
Clough, Shepard B., Philanthropy and the Welfare State in Europe, *Political Science Quarterly*, 37: 87–93. 1960.
CROCIS (2006), *Le développement durable dans les PME-PMI franciliennes, 2003–2004–2005*.
Doucin M., "Il existe une doctrine française de la responsabilité sociale des entreprises", *Droits fondamentaux*, no. 4, January–December 2004.

---

[15] Voir www.achatsresponsables.com/.

Durrieu F., Harribey L., Pesme J. O., "PME et Développement durable du territoire", *Cahiers de Recherche BEM,* 2006, www.bordeaux-bs.edu

EthiFinance et Transparence-International (France), Deuxième étude sur la prévention de la corruption dans les grandes entreprises françaises, Paris, June 2006.

Grahl J., & Teague P., Is the European Social Model Fragmenting? *New Political Economy, 2(3): 405–426, 1997.*

Harribey L., Durrieu F. (2007), Panorama 2006 de la sensibilité des entreprises au développement durable et à la responsabilité sociétale, *Cahiers de Recherche CEREBEM.*

Husson-Traore A.C. (2007), Entrepreneurs: mobilisation contre les discriminations.

Igalens I., Joras M., *La responsabilité sociale de l'entreprise,* Paris, Editions d'Organisation, 2002.

IGAS (2004), Rapport sur la Responsabilité sociale des entreprises, Inspection Générale des Affaires sociales, Ministère de l'emploi, du travail et de la cohésion sociale, Paris, March.

Langlois Catherine C., & Bodo B. Schlegelmich (1990), "Do corporate Codes of Ethics Reflect National Character? Evidence from Europe and the United States, *Journal of International Business Studies,* 21(4) 519–539.

Laville E., (2004), Créer de la valeur avec le développement durable, in Férone G., Debas D., Genin A-S., *Ce que développement durable veut dire,* Paris, Editons d'Organisation & ENSAM, p. 254.

Loiselet E., (2003), Investissement Socialement Responsable: l'âge de la Diffusion, *L'Economie politique,* no. 18, April, 62–73.

Maignan I., Ralston D., Corporate Social Responsibility in Europe and the US: Insights from Businesses' self-presentations, *Journal of International Business Studies,* 33, 3, (Third quarter 2002): 497–514.

Novethic, *Entreprises et Développement Durable: impacts stratégiques,* 2002.

Novethic (2007), Etat et perspectives du marché insitutionnel français – Sixième enquête annuelle. disponible sur, www.novethic.fr

Orse (2003), La déontologie, ce qui va changer dans l'entreprise, Cahiers de l'ORSE.

Orse (2005), Partenariat stratégiques ONG/Entretprises -Rapport de mission remis au Ministre de la Jeunesse, des Sports et de la Vie Associative, Paris.

Rose J.J. (2006) "La France est venue tardivement à la RSE mais elle va vite", *JDN Management.*

Verger O., White G. (2004), Les partenariats Entreprise/ONG dans le cadre de démarches sociétales, premiers éléments d'analyse, Paris, June, IMS.

Vigeo & ORSE (2006), Press release 15 March, www.vigeogroup.com

Vogel D. (1992) The Globalization of Business Ethics: Why America remains Distinctive, *California Management Review,* Fall: 30–49.

Chapter 3
Federal Republic of Germany

Walter Leal Filho and Paulina S. Pawlak

Abstract This chapter outlines some trends in corporate social responsibility (CSR) in Germany. It does so by first of all offering an overview of the subject of CSR as it is perceived in Germany, followed by a description of trends relating to the scope of CSR and analyzing it from a perspective of German companies. Finally, we provide some examples of CSR initiatives being pursued by a sample of German companies and outline some possible future CSR frameworks.

3.1 Sustainability in German Companies: The Changing Role of Business in Society

For many years, the prevailing outlook on the role of business in society could be summarized with the following words of Milton Friedman: "there is one and only one social responsibility of business – (...) to increase its profits" (Friedman 1970). At the beginning of the twenty-first century, the main objective of an enterprise still revolves around the bottom line. There are, however, broader aspects that businesses now have to consider. The changing context within which companies operate, shaped by environmental and globalization forces, affects the way that the role of business is perceived. Multinational companies are expected to conduct business ethically, no matter where they operate. The pressure to clean up the corporate act is largely amplified by the fast-growing socially responsible investment (SRI) movement that raises the importance of good social and environmental performance. Scrutiny of the public opinion, enhanced by ubiquitous media, forces companies to acknowledge the growing expectations that government activists, NGOs, consumers, and many other stakeholders have of them. Therefore, companies are confronted with the challenge to recognize and fulfil their environmental and social responsibilities.

At the heart of this challenge lie the notions of corporate sustainability, corporate social responsibility (CSR) – which has already been extensively discussed elsewhere on this book – and corporate citizenship (CC), to name a few. Although all these concepts refer to the role of business in society, they differ significantly in their scope, which gives rise to confusion. This becomes apparent when studying corporate reports on the topic. Companies communicate their commitment to sustainable development, CSR, CC, social responsibility and many more, often confusing the reader with the abundance of terms. Ambiguity pertains with regard to boundaries and relationships between the terms. In order to gain more clarity, this chapter will also look at some of the influential political actors (mostly from Germany and the European Union (EU)), which shape the way companies understand their responsibilities with regard to environment and society. Further to that, this chapter will analyze how companies perceive their responsibilities from a German context.

3.2 Corporate Social Responsibility from a German Perspective

Corporate strategies for sustainable development have, for some time now, been acknowledged as an emerging field (Banerjee 2001, 2002). Bansal and Roth (2000) have analyzed how companies adopt green policies, under what Hart (1995) defines as a natural-resource-based view, in line with what Christoff (1996) describes as "ecological modernization".

Doppelt (2003) has listed the various challenges that need to be met in leading such complex change processes as part of what Gladwin et al. (1995) see as a paradigm change. Naturally, corporate social responsibility strategies need to consider the interest of the various stakeholders (Sharma and Starik 2004) and need to be supported by a sense of ethics (Christensen et al. 2007).

Still from an international perspective, when discussing the social and ethical role of business, organizations tend to refer to the term CSR. As most readers already know and as referred to elsewhere in this book, CSR has been incorporated as an international goal in the action plan of the World Summit on Sustainable Development, held in Johannesburg in 2002. A new feature is perhaps the fact that, albeit not widely known, the issue was also on the agenda at the G8 Summit in Heiligendamm, Germany, held in the summer of 2007 (G8 Summit 2007). With the amount of publicity and attention it now receives, CSR has without doubt become one of the buzzword of our times.

The experience gathered by the authors in respect of the perception of CSR in Germany is that there is a lot of ambiguity with regard to the term, as no internationally recognized definition is widely used in the country. Some experts – or companies – take a view that CSR is nothing more than philanthropic engagement of a company. Others perceive the term in a much broader sense, acknowledging that business has responsibilities within the environment it operates in. Given a number of different interpretations, definitions coined by the renowned international initiatives (often of political character), with an emphasis on Germany, will be discussed in this section.

The World Business Council for Sustainable Development (WBCSD) states that "Corporate Social Responsibility is the continuing commitment by business to behave ethically and contribute to economic development while improving the quality of life of the workforce and their families as well as of the local community and society at large". Reference to business case of CSR is the central assertion of WBCSD's approach (WBCSD 2007).

The definition of the European Commission (EC) goes a step further in defining that, through CSR, "(…) companies integrate social and environmental concerns in their business operations and in their interaction with their stakeholders on a voluntary basis" (European Commission 2001). The scope of CSR therefore embraces both social and environmental issues, in spite of the misleading term "corporate social responsibility". The definition also highlights the voluntary character of the engagement as well as importance of communication with stakeholders. Furthermore, activities within CSR are said to vary from business to business. For this reason, no concrete legislation enforcing social responsibility on companies is presently envisaged at the European level. It is worthwhile to note that the definition of EC has been officially acclaimed by the German Government (Franz and Pretschker 2007).

Launched by the EC, the European Multi-stakeholder Forum on CSR provides a platform for discussions on the topic among business representatives, nongovernmental organizations (NGOs), scientists, etc., and this is being widely used by German companies. The Forum's work has led to the conclusion that companies should "identify what items are pertinent with regard to the company's vision and specific objectives, the risks and opportunities associated with its environmental and social footprint and the views of relevant stakeholders" (Loew 2005).

In Germany, there is the impression that more concrete guidelines on social responsibility could be expected from the International Standardization Organization (ISO). The reason for this is because ISO is well respected in the country and has taken up the goal to create an international guidance document to assist organizations of all kinds in implementing the tools for corporate sustainability. Although the final outcomes are to be made public in 2009, it has been preliminarily accepted that organizations have a "social responsibility (…) for the impacts of its decisions and activities (including products and services) on society and the environment, through transparent and ethical behaviour that:

- Is consistent with sustainable development and the welfare of the society
- Takes into account the expectations of stakeholders
- Is in compliance with applicable law and consistent with international norms of behaviour
- Is integrated throughout the organization" (Hager 2007)

Such a formulation adds a new aspect of CSR – at least in a German perspective – namely, acknowledgement of existing international norms. These could comprise ILO Norms, OECD Guidelines for Multinational Companies, or Principles of Global Compact, to name a few.

Last but not least, "CSR Germany" (www.csrgermany.de/), a portal created by the Confederation of German Employers' Associations (BDA) and the Federation of German Industries (BDI) is also worth mentioning as a prime example of institutional support to CSR efforts in the country. It conveys the view that CSR includes three dimensions: sustainable development, economy, and society and environment. In terms of practical implementation of CSR, an individual approach of companies is advocated and the idea of "one-size-fits-all" solutions is discarded as such. It is highlighted that interpretation of CSR is very much dependent on the business sector, type of markets where the company is present, as well as the specific needs of the stakeholders. Imposing legally binding specifications on how to implement CSR is therefore discouraged at least in Germany, since it is seen as potentially detrimental to innovativeness and creativity in the field. Instead, general recommendations are advocated that will provide a rough orientation for companies on how to engage in society and the environment (CSR Germany 2007).

Summing up, the following characteristics of CSR – as perceived by German companies – may be listed as follows:

- CSR is a company's contribution to *sustainable development.*
- CSR embraces *social* and *environmental* responsibility.[1]
- A dialogue with the *stakeholders* is embedded in CSR.
- CSR is a voluntary engagement and *no legal enforcement* is to be anticipated.
- CSR is *company specific* and its implementation will vary from organization to organization.

3.3 Scope of Corporate Social Responsibility in German Enterprises

An element that cannot be ignored in the debate on CSR in Germany is the fact that a key role is played by the German Ministry of Environment (BMU), an organization whose remit has been instrumental to general sustainability management. As the Ministry of Environment, it provides the legal framework upon which industrial activities take place and industry operates.

Having dealt with the basic aspects of CSR and its level of understanding by German companies, it may at this stage be helpful to analyze a further important element of CSR in Germany, namely the scope of CSR activities in the country. Typical activity areas that can be aggregated under the umbrella term of "CSR in Germany" are described here – which are much in line with what the European Commission (EC) defines as internal and external dimensions of CSR:

- *Internal:*
  - Human resources management
  - Health and safety at work
  - Adaptation to change (business restructuring)
  - Management of environmental impacts and natural resources

---

[1] Some organizations stipulate for including economic responsibility in CSR.

Table 3.1 Activity areas of CSR in Germany (BMU 2006)

	Vision and strategy	
	Environmental dimension of CSR	Social dimension of CSR
Governance and management systems	Communication with internal and external stakeholders	
	Environmental management	Management of the social areas
Core business processes	Operational environmental protection	Interests of the employees
	Environment protection in the supply chain	Working conditions and human rights in the supply chain
	Integrated product policy	Protection of the consumer and consumer interests
Local environment/ communities	Participation in designing the policy framework (lobbying etc.), anticorruption	
	Corporate citizenship: giving, sponsoring, volunteering, cause-related marketing, etc.	

- *External:*

  o Local communities
  o Business partners, suppliers, and consumers
  o Human rights
  o Global environmental concerns (European Commission 2001)

While the internal dimension reflects the aspects that stem directly from business operation, external dimension pertains more to local communities and issues "outside" of the company. It is, however, a feature of CSR in Germany that both dimensions are regarded as intertwined. This means that in the mindset of most German enterprises, internal dimensions are regarded as priorities, but without neglect to the external dimensions, which are important to business operations and to a company's image.

The BMU differentiates between aspects related to core business processes and the engagement in local communities as well as governance and management system area. Governance can be understood here as a system of management of the organization that includes aspects as vision, strategy, and communication with stakeholders (MBU 2006). According to BMU, core business processes have a wider scope than the internal dimension in the EC's classification. The overview of CSR activity areas is summarized in Table 3.1.

3.4 Corporate Social Responsibility versus Corporate Sustainability

So far, most considerations on this chapter have addressed CSR in a German context, without necessarily defining corporate sustainability, CC, or other similar terms.

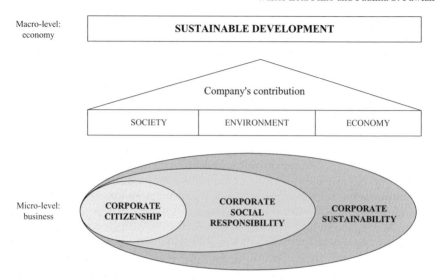

Fig. 3.1 Corporate Citizenship, Corporate Social Responsibility, and Corporate Sustainability and their relationship to sustainable development (adopted after Loew et al. 2004)

Despite the fact that some definitions have been presented elsewhere on this book, it may be helpful to take a look at the implication of these definitions from a German perspective. In Germany, it is fair to say that CSR is largely congruent with corporate sustainability, which can be – in simple words – interpreted as an enterprise's sustainability management (Rat für Nachhaltige Entwicklung 2006).

However, it has to be highlighted that CSR as such does not – at least at present – fully embrace economic responsibility, one of the three dimensions of sustainability. Hence, CSR is in principle a sub-component of corporate sustainability. CC describes a company's commitment within its direct environment – in communities in which it operates. Typical activities of CC will include corporate giving and sponsoring.

The relationship between all the terms is summarized in Fig. 3.1. It can be seen that CC is a component of CSR, the latter addressing wider issues of society and environment. If economic dimension is integrated, corporate sustainability, that is company's contribution to sustainable development, as seen at the macro-level perspective, comes to light.

3.5 Corporate Responsibility from a Company's Perspective and Some CSR Practices in Germany

Although the theory discussed in the earlier sections of this chapter drew a distinction between corporate sustainability and corporate social responsibility, for corporate practice in Germany, the difference – as also seen elsewhere – appears irrelevant

(Loew and Braun 2006). Companies talk either about CS or CSR, often using these terms interchangeably. There are of course differences in interpretations, and this state of affairs is also seen in Germany. Some companies see their role in society solely to be philanthropy. Many companies address their impacts on both environment and society, whilst others discuss their business in all three dimensions of sustainable development. Whereas the first approach is by no means complete, the latter two will in practical terms address similar issues. Whether economic responsibility is also a relevant perspective for a company to address is unquestionable. Economic responsibility is a component of corporate sustainability and, together with environmental and social commitment, comprises a comprehensive picture of a company's role in society. It may be assumed, however, that financial dimension has been at the top of the agenda ever since private enterprise came to existence. There are already well-developed organizational "tools" that deal with economic performance. Financial institutions, commercial law, and shareholders have forced companies to publish reliable and transparent financial information on development of business for many years now. For this reason, companies address the financial side of business in any case; therefore, in practice, CSR and corporate sustainability can be treated equal.

Many German companies talk about CSR in a way that implies that they are also concerned with sustainability, i.e., they refer to CSR implicitly meaning that it means corporate sustainability, incorporating all three dimensions of sustainable development.

In order to make the principles and practices outlined on this chapter a little more concrete, some examples of CSR practices will be provided on this section. This list of examples is by no means comprehensive, nor does it have the ambition to be complete. Rather, its sole purpose is to illustrate some of the activities going on on the ground and to offer readers an overview of the diversity of CSR practices in the country.

A first step in the description of trends in Germany may be taken by considering a ranking produced every 2 years by the German Institute of Ecological Economics (IÖW) and the NGO "Future e.V.". The ranking samples 150 large German enterprises and assesses the extent to which they pursue their corporate responsibilities and transparency. According to the ranking, whose results are summarized in Table 3.2, the top 10 reports are not dominated by companies from any single sector. Rather, enterprises engaged in areas as varied as the chemical industry, banking, or even publishing are investing substantial efforts in pursuing CSR – a number of which under the heading of sustainable development.

One first example of CSR practice in Germany can be taken from the chemical industry. The chemical company Bayer has produced the integrated concept "Bayer Climate Program" across the whole business, in the context of which it intends to reduce the CO_2 emissions deriving from its operations. In addition, the company intends to, as part of its CSR concept, seek new solutions that can assist moves towards greater environmental protection and in addressing the challenges of climate change.

A further example comes from BMW, a company representing the automobile sector. With the opening of the "LoveLIFE" prevention centre for the youth in

Table 3.2 Top 10 sustainability reports by German Companies (2007)

Rank/company	Field of work
Otto	Catalogue sales
RWE	Energy
BASF	Chemicals
KarstadtQuelle	Consumer products
WestLB	Banking
Wacker Chemie	Chemicals
Bayer	Chemicals
Axel Springer	Publisher
Volkswagen	Car manufacturer
BMW	Car manufacturer

Source: Modified from http://www.ranking-nachhaltigkeitsberichte.de/

South Africa, the BMW Group provides a contribution to the social-political problems posed by AIDS in developing countries. BMW has set up and supports an institutional setting, namely the LoveLife Trust, which opened a Centre in November 2007 in Knysna, South Africa.

From the banking sector, the pursuit for corporate responsibility is an important part of the work of Commerzbank, one of the country's largest banks. The varied degree of engagement of Commerzbank in CSR issues involves areas such as societal commitments, well-being of workers, and the integration of economic-ecological considerations in the decision-making process.

Lufthansa, one of the country's largest companies and a prime example of the aviation sector, is also committed to CSR, both within the framework of the activities performed by the aviation units and by its subsidiaries. For example, the company "LSG Sky Chefs", which provides catering for airlines, pursues the strategy of integrating resource conservation and innovative environmental technologies. At the Cologne airport for example, the company has installed two innovative heat pump energy systems, which provide both cheap and environmentally friendly heat for the large catering building. In addition, a mobile "heat-battery", a heat saving device, is employed. Trucks transports compressed heat obtained from power stations and other production units to a central "heat container" placed at the LSG Sky Chefs building in Cologne. The heat is then used to warm up the building.

The food sector, represented by the company Dr. Oetker, is also engaged in CSR affairs. The company produces not only an award-winning sustainability report, but has also expanded its activities in the social field by engaging in initiatives related to balanced diets and nutrition.

The postal service, represented by "Deutsche Post World Net" is a further example of a German company's commitment to CSR. The CSR approach of the company is based on the four-pillar principle, namely, Environment, People, Society, and Capital. From an ecological perspective, the aim of the company is to upkeep is economic success by ensuring the ecological soundness of its operations.

It also defends the view that responsibility is needed in tackling the challenges of globalization by seeking solutions applicable to local contexts together with partners from the political and social fields.

A common feature of the examples here outlined is that the emphasis given to CSR practices is much in line with a company's core business. In addition, companies engaged in CSR activities actively promote what they do, thereby using CSR as a complementary marketing tool. Furthermore, CSR practices in German companies – especially in sectors such as foodstuff, aviation, or the car industry – are associated with many technological developments and innovation. Here it seems that companies that have a technological edge are interested to use that in support of CSR initiatives, a concept which may be replicated elsewhere. Finally, a common feature of the examples here provided is that they are from medium- and large-sized companies. At the small and medium enterprise (SME) level, examples of CSR practices do exist, but they are seldom documented and –with a few exceptions – are hardly ever disseminated to large audiences.

3.6 Conclusions

This chapter has outlined the thinking behind CSR practices in Germany and described how this reflects into current practice. It has also provided an overview of the institutional framework available to support CSR initiatives in the country both from the private sector (for example, the CSR home page of the Conference of German Industries) and the public sector (such as the work of the German Federal Environment Ministry).

From a critical perspective, CSR practices in Germany – and indeed elsewhere – influenced by a number of internal and external factors that make the business-political nexus might be addressed (Crane and Matter 2003). The influence of the so-called Rhenish Capitalism based on networks and interlocking networks affecting ownership, governance, influence, policy, status, and accountability cannot be ignored.

In the face of the current globalization process where economies and financial markets are closely linked, as well as bearing in mind a very dynamic industrial climate characterized by elements such as restructuring, relocation, and subcontracting, German companies seem to be aware of the fact that the social and ethical role of enterprises has come under increasing scrutiny and many have taken action to address this issue.

The sample of concrete examples taken from German companies from various sectors and compiled in this chapter illustrates the wide scope of works and CSR initiatives taking place in the country. They describe the good practices specific to the operational sectors in each company and also illustrate the interplay of the actors involved in planning, implementing, and evaluating the practices concerned. On the basis of the background research performed in the preparation of this chapter, and on the evidences found in the analysis of CSR practices in German companies, there seem to be a few areas that have been emphasized and that will no doubt be the focus of more activities:

1. Awareness-raising and best practice exchange
2. Support to multi-stakeholder initiatives
3. Consumer information and transparency
4. Education
5. New, innovative technologies

The provided examples also seem to indicate a future trend, namely the ever-closer association of CSR initiatives with technological developments, an approach that may be useful in other countries.

References

Banerjee, S.B. (2001), "Corporate environmental strategies and actions", Management Decision, Vol 39 (1), pp. 36–44.

Banerjee, S.B. (2002), "Organisational strategies for sustainable development: developing a research agenda for the new millennium", Australian Journal of Management, Vol 27 (Special Issue), pp. 105–117.

Bansal, P. and Roth, K. (2000), "Why companies go green: A model of ecological responsiveness", Academy of Management Journal, Vol 43 (4), pp. 717–736.

Bundesministerium für Umwelt, Naturschutz und Reaktorsicherheit (2006), "Corporate Social Responsibility, Eine Orientierung aus Umweltsicht".

Christensen, L.J., Peirce, E., Hartman, L.P., Hoffman, W.M., and Carrier, J. (2007), "Ethics, CSR, and Sustainability Education in the Financial Times Top 50 Global Business Schools: Baseline Data and Future Research Directions", Journal of Business Ethics, Vol 73 (4), pp. 347–368.

Christoff, P. (1996), "Ecological Modernisation, Ecological Modernities", Environmental Politics, Vol 5 (3), pp. 476–500.

CSR Germany website (2007), accessed August 2007, [http://www.csrgermany.de].

Crane, A. and Matten, D. (2003), Business Ethics. Oxford University Press, Oxford.

Doppelt, B. (2003), Leading Change toward Sustainability: A Change-Management Guide for Business, Government and Civil Society, Greenleaf Publishing Limited, Sheffield, UK.

European Commission (2001), "Promoting a European Framework for Corporate Social Responsibility", Green Paper.

Franz, P. and Pretschker, U. (2007), "Die Diskussion über CSR aus der Perspektive zweier Bundesressorts", DIN Mitteilungen, July 2007.

Friedman, M. (1970), "The Social Responsibility of business is to increase its profits", New York Times.

G8 Summit website (2007), accessed September 2007, [http://www.g-8.de].

Gladwin, T.N., Kennelly, J.J., and Krause, T.-S. (1995), "Shifting Paradigms for Sustainable Development: Implications for Management Theory and Research", Academy of Management Review, Vol 20 (4), pp. 874–907.

Hager, R. (2007), "Geselschaftliche Verantwortung von Organisationen, Das ISO-Norm Projekt ISO 26000", DIN Mitteilungen, July 2007.

Hart, S.L. (1995), "A natural-resource-based view of the firm", The Academy of Management Review, Vol 20 (4), pp. 986–1014.

Loew, T., Ankele, K., Braun, S., Clausen, J. (2004), Bedeutung der internationalen CSR-Diskussion fur Nachhaltigkeit und die sich daraus ergebenden Anforderungen an Unternehemn. Endericht an das Bundesministerium fur Umwelt, Naturschutz und Reakorsicherheit Berlin.

Loew, T. and Braun, S. (2006), "Organisatorische Umsetzung von CSR: Von Umwelt-managment zur Sustainable Corporate Governance", future e.V. and Institute4Sustainability, [www.4sustainability.org].

Loew, T. (2005), CSR in der Supply Chain: Herausforderungen und Anstzpunkte fur Unternehmen. Vorbereitungspapier fur den 5. Multistakeholderworkshop zu CSR (gefordert durch das Bundesministerium fur Umwelt, Naturschutz und Reaktor-sicherheit) Discussion Paper 4 Sustainability, Berlin.

Rat für Nachhaltige Entwicklung (2006), "Corporate Responsibility in a Globalised World – A German Profile of Corporate Social Responsibility", Recommendations of the German Council for Sustainable Development.

Sharma, S. and Starik, M. (2004), "Stakeholders, the environment and society: multiple perspectives, emerging consensus", in Sharma, S. and Starik, M. (Ed.), Stakeholders, the environment, and society, Edward Elgar, Cheltenham, UK; Northampton, MA, pp. 1–22.

WBCSD website (2007), accessed September 2007, [http://www.wbcsd.org].

Chapter 4
Finland

Virgilio Panapanaan and Lassi Linnanen

Abstract This paper focuses on corporate social responsibility (CSR) of proactive companies that seriously recognize the importance of CSR and its management inside and outside the company. This is an exploration and learning from the experience of Finnish companies, as well as other actors interested or involved in shaping the course of CSR both locally and globally.

The results of the exploration provide insightful information and descriptions of a roadmap useful in learning and understanding the role CSR in Finnish companies. The roadmap starts with variations of CSR concepts and framing CSR within the corporate responsibility concept. Other roadmap indicators are globalization, stakeholders, and pursuit of sustainable development as the main drivers of CSR, as well as employees, suppliers, community, and customers as key management areas of CSR. The roadmap also indicates the importance of Finnish culture, which has a positive influence on the views, thinking, and management practices of CSR issues, thus making it easy to discuss and understand CSR in businesses.

The experience of selected Finnish companies in implementing CSR policies in the supply chain presents a concrete proactive step in advancing socially responsible practices with suppliers both locally and globally. Despite the problems and complexities, particularly in the global supply chain, managing CSR for Finnish companies presents new opportunities and challenges that are expected to intensify in the near future. The proactive stance of Finnish companies towards CSR is complemented by the active supporting role of important societal actors such as the government and non-governmental organizations (NGOs). These actors embark on various promotional efforts and campaigns, thus making CSR a well-acknowledged concept among Finnish companies and strengthening the synergistic learning of CSR within the Finnish businesses and communities.

4.1 Introduction: An Exploratory Study of the Social Dimension of Corporate Responsibility in Finland

During the last decade, a growing number of companies worldwide have acknowledged the importance of corporate social responsibility (CSR) in doing business (Cramer 2003). Today, CSR is an important item on the corporate boardroom agenda for many companies worldwide (Grayson and Hodges 2004). Many companies around the world, including many of the largest multinationals, have voluntarily decided to start examining their social behaviors, articulating the types of commitment they want to make, and issuing CSR reports putting this commitment in black and white for the world to see Hollender (2003).

In Finland, there are many indications that CSR is increasingly becoming an important source of values in both the private and public sectors. Many Finnish companies, particularly the big ones, are in the forefront of taking CSR initiatives. Government's support for CSR is also visible, while NGOs and other interest groups (e.g., the church, labor organizations, and consumer associations) are also busy campaigning for various CSR issues. The issue of globalization has also put Finland on the track of CSR developments because many Finnish companies operate in the global market today. As a member of the European Union (EU), Finland is inevitably influenced by the initiatives, plans, directives, and programs designed to uphold and promote CSR (e.g., the Green Paper 2001, Communication Concerning CSR 2003, Multi-stakeholder Forum, etc.).

Behind this new and modern era of CSR thinking in Finland are a number of questions that are important in a welfare state: for example, how recent layoffs in Finnish companies have both been defended and strongly criticized using corporate responsibility arguments (Haavisto (2004). What is the significance of CSR when the Finnish welfare state has implicitly covered CSR fundamentals? Good economic growth has enabled Finland to build a welfare state characterized by some social basics such as social rights, basic social security for all, a reasonable standard of social security, and a commitment to equality between different regions and population groups (NCSD 2000). Even so, there are arguments justifying why the newly revived thinking about CSR is becoming important in Finland. The changing structure of Finnish society, changing workplace situation, ageing workforce, and globalizing Finnish companies are among issues that are at the forefront of CSR discussions.

The objective of this chapter is to explore and learn more about CSR as a newly revived business concept and an important aspect of corporate sustainability (other than the economic and environmental sustainability) for Finnish companies. The focus is on the experience and management practices of some Finnish companies, as well as on the important actors who are interested and involved in CSR issues and development in Finland. It also focuses on how Finnish culture affects CSR views, thinking, and management perspective.

The chapter is organized in such a way that some consideration is first provided in order to briefly clarify and qualify its scope. The key findings, which are the important aspects of CSR in Finland, are presented thematically on the basis of the development of the study. It started with a general roadmapping of CSR in

Finnish companies (Theme 1). Based on the roadmap, some important issues have emerged and therefore were taken into consideration for further and separate investigations. Finnish culture (Theme 2) and supply chain management (Theme 3) issues are among those highlighted as important aspects of CSR study in Finland. This is followed by an investigation of the role of the government and NGOs (Theme 4) in promoting CSR in Finland. A conclusion follows the presentation of the different themes.

4.2 Some Considerations

This chapter was written on the basis of the idea that corporate responsibility is categorized into three distinct yet related responsibilities. Chronologically, these responsibilities are economic responsibility, environmental responsibility, and social responsibility (Davis 2001). The concept of corporate responsibility is also ascribed to Hart's (1997) fabrics of sustainability and Elkington's (1998) triple bottom line, and the Confederation of Finnish Industries and Employers' (2001) corporate responsibility pillars.

The social responsibility of companies was the main focus of this research. CSR for our purposes primarily refers to social entities (i.e., the people) inside and outside the company to which the responsibility is addressed, directed, and acted upon. Social issues refer to those social basics revolving around human rights, freedom of association, child labor, ethics, respect and quality of life in the workplace, as well as the surrounding communities. Thus, this chapter takes a simplistic perspective of focusing only on the core social aspects of corporate responsibility, referred to as *corporate social responsibility*. It is therefore emphasized at the outset that the chapter discusses social responsibility of companies as the other dimension of corporate responsibility and sustainability other than economic and environmental. The term CSR is used consistently throughout the chapter to mean social issues in a given company.

Information and data presented in this chapter were generally taken from two sources. First, (primary sources) it utilizes data from interviews in selected companies, government institutions, NGOs, business fora, and other informants. Secondly (secondary sources), it also utilizes data taken from written documents, such as company reports (e.g., sustainability reports, annual reports, etc.), company magazines and other printed information (brochures, working papers, and internal communications), and online (Internet) information. Information, reviews, and feedbacks gathered by peers from various organizations such as the academe, policy research organizations, and industrial organizations complement the study.

Thirteen selected Finnish companies are featured in this chapter and it should be understood that statements or descriptions about any particular company or companies used in are exclusive only for them and not necessarily true to all Finnish companies in general. In the same manner, any reference to a company or companies either in a statement, examples, or quotations, should be taken as a reference to any of the 13 companies or all of them. The study also uses 3 main government agencies and 14 NGOs in Finland.

Generally, this chapter focuses intensively on the positive aspects of CSR in Finnish companies. The intention was not to take a critical look at the role of companies in Finnish society, but to gain a first-hand insight about their experiences and relate to the positive contribution that CSR makes to business performance. The chapter takes a practical view of CSR in Finland and highlights how companies address and manage CSR internally and externally. A critical analysis of what Finnish companies are leaving undone with regard to CSR would provide some balance to this paper.

4.3 Important Aspects of CSR in Finland

This chapter discusses the main findings from a study about the experience of Finnish companies as they focus their attention, allocate resources, and implement CSR programs. The presentation of four different themes is based on the development of the study that started from a roadmapping study. From the roadmap, cultural issues and supply chain issues emerged as important aspects of CSR in Finland, hence, the proceeding themes on the influence of national culture on CSR and implementing CSR policy in the supply chain. Additionally, the roles of the government and NGOs were seen as another important aspect of CSR in Finland: hence the separate theme for it. The four themes are:

Theme 1: Road-mapping of CSR in Finnish companies
Theme 2: The influence of national culture on CSR
Theme 3: Implementing CSR policy in the supply chain
Theme 4: The roles of the government and NGOs in promoting CSR

4.3.1 CSR Roadmap in Finnish Companies

This section gives a general picture (or roadmap) of CSR as it is defined, managed, and practiced in selected Finnish companies. The derived roadmap did not give an exact definition of CSR, but instead reveals various *concepts* ascribed to be a part of, if not actually CSR (Table 4.1). Despite the variations, some generally favored conceptual connotations of CSR relate to compliance with laws and regulations, integral to all operations of a company, hinged on environmental responsibilities, important aspect of globalization, and inherent to the Finnish way of thinking, culture, and a long tradition of good, clean business practice.

CSR is not considered a totally new concept but instead a recurring issue in Finland. Intrinsically, CSR is considered a part of the economic progression and industrialization of Finland, which became more pronounced after World War II. CSR was even thought as an ingrained idea right from the conception of the Finnish welfare state. Such thinking sprang from the development of the welfare state, thereby

Table 4.1 Some Finnish concepts relating to CSR

CSR is compliance with strict Finnish laws and regulations.

CSR is integral to all operations of the company and is attached to environmental responsibility.

CSR is a global phenomenon.

CSR is a Finnish way of thinking (to be responsible and behave ethically) based on Northern Europeans' high regard for morality.

CSR is a matter of commonsense and of doing what is right and good for the people; hence, a social policy statement is unnecessary.

CSR is somewhere in the core values and principles of the company. Finns are not fond of writing and paperwork when something is self-evident. CSR is rather a matter of values such as transparency, openness, and trust.

CSR is a recurring concept thrown back by developing countries. It was an issue in Finland 40 or 50 years ago.

Pursuing CSR is not a problem in Finland, but it is one in the developing countries.

CSR relates to corporate citizenship wherein the company is legitimized by the community for its involvement and participation.

CSR is a matter of dialogue and communication, and also of doing what is right within the company's capabilities and means.

making it an inherent value carried through the various stages of the country's societal development. A strong reminder of this historical connotation of CSR is in the past, when companies were the centers of communities and villages providing services such as schools, churches, and support to the community development.

Most companies, more or less, share the same view and opinion that CSR is best understood when framed in the concept of corporate responsibility. Corporate responsibility pertains to incorporating economic, environmental, and social aspects in balance with the motive of realizing sustainability inside a company. These companies have been paying great attention to their corporate responsibility because they believe that dealing and acting on it is a precondition to success and long-term profitability. In this era of rapid globalization, quick-changing consumer mentality, and stakeholders' communication demands, these companies believe that corporate responsibility should be managed seriously because it strongly affects a company's image and reputation. According to these companies, taking some responsibility is a way of controlling this image and the associated risks, thereby strengthening their corporate and brand reputations.

Framing CSR under the concept of corporate responsibility supports some of the earlier studies and advocates that are closely in agreement with the concept. Enderle and Tavis (1998) called it the new balanced concept of the company: that is, balancing the corporate economic, environmental, and social responsibilities. Culpeper (1998) suggested that corporate responsibility evolves through five stages: financial, economic, environmental, social, and political, although he claimed that it is a very loose chronology. But the point still holds true that corporate responsibility typically encompasses economic, environmental, and social aspects. Others studies on corporate responsibility abound, and confirm that the three dimensions of corporate responsibility are in turn the essence of corporate sustainability performance (e.g., van Marrewijk and Hardjono 2003; Clarke 2001).

Globalization, laws and regulations, stakeholders, and the challenge of sustainable development are the identified major drivers of CSR for most of the companies selected for this report. Being in a global market and having worldwide business operations, the increasing demands of different stakeholders for greater social responsibility drive the companies to adopt new policies and strategies ensuring compliance with acceptable global CSR standards. The long pursuit of sustainable development is also seen as a driver of CSR, heeding the general view that sustainability at the corporate level is also defined by socially responsible practices.

The main areas for managing CSR issues are typically focused on employees, community involvement, suppliers, and customers. CSR management, and practices towards employees, suppliers, community, and customers are well-defined locally, based generally on established socially responsible behavior which is typically founded in compliance with the Finnish laws and regulations, good corporate values, and upright business attitude and ethics affected by the national culture.

Employees' issues and management are well established in most companies, and most policies supporting the welfare of employees are in place and available. Although there are wide arrays of employee-related issues, it was observed that some issues (e.g., child labor and forced labor) appeared irrelevant to Finnish companies. This is primarily because such practices do not exist anymore or are unthinkable in any Finnish company or society. However, these irrelevant issues are believed to be very relevant when Finnish companies operate in another country, particularly in developing countries where laws and regulations are different, culture varies, and standards are different compared to Finnish standards. Community involvement has a limited emphasis for most companies. Locally, the most common forms of involvement are support for educational activities and research, child and youth development, and small amounts of grants, donations, and sponsorship. In other countries, community involvement takes different forms depending on the host country's circumstances. On the other hand, traditional suppliers' relations are well-organized in Finnish companies. However, when CSR questions are raised in the supply chain, both the companies and the suppliers do not have ready answers and often lack information. Thus, managing CSR in the supply chain is now considered to require some changes in the purchasing requirements, information, and communications. This is a new challenge for Finnish companies and their suppliers locally and globally. Lastly, customer issues pertinent to CSR are, to some extent, connected with environmental issues, because of the view that products have more inherent environmental aspects than social aspects. Customer issues are hard to isolate from environmental issues, although tracing back the production of goods reveals strong arguments (e.g., child labor, forced labor, human rights, etc.), which are important in CSR management. This issue, however, is not the focus of this chapter. A contingent framework for managing CSR is drawn highlighting these important CSR areas as well as respective issues and management activities (Fig. 4.1).

The contingent framework starts with the assessment of social risks that a company is likely to face. The four main areas of assessment are employees, suppliers, community involvement, and customers. These are considered important areas although the degree of importance may vary depending on the nature of a company's

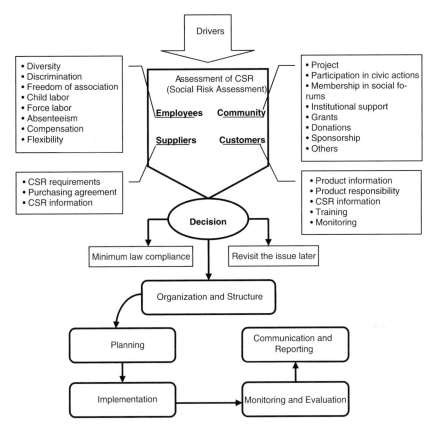

Fig. 4.1 Contingent framework for managing CSR

business. The framework is not a total prescription that all the areas can be dealt with all at the same time. A company may consider addressing one area at a time or starting with the most relevant issues at hand. By checking all the parameters set for each area, an assessment leads to a decision making as to whether a company will proceed with the management of these CSR issues, comply with the minimum scope of the laws, or consider the issue later. An important aspect of this framework is when a top management decision is taken to address CSR issues. This means that management processes of organizing, planning and implementing strategies, communicating, monitoring, and evaluating of CSR activities are to be established accordingly. As such, resource allocation is another consideration for management.

The current approach to CSR by the companies involved in this chapter is considered as both progressive and proactive. Because CSR presents new management challenges, the cited Finnish companies are starting to find ways to organize or structuralize it within the current system. The question most companies ask is – what is the management of CSR like? At the time of the interviews for roadmapping, managing the issue was more of an ad hoc or bolt-on approach or in a haphazard fashion. For instance, some of them deal with CSR narrowly as a personnel management issue or combine it with environmental management issues. Some reasons that explain this haphazard management approach can be attributed to the apparent variation in concepts, effects of Finnish culture, and the impact of different drivers. Furthermore, it can be attributed to some worries that companies are not sure whether or not they are addressing CSR correctly due to absence of information, lack of relevant experience and some administrative problems. Even so, most of the managers in the companies interviewed have positively indicated that they are in the process of finding the appropriate structure and organization for managing CSR progressively and effectively and that it would not take long (probably within a year or so) to realize it. On the basis of the aforementioned roadmap and identified management areas, an initial contingent framework for CSR is drawn up reflecting the current practices and prospects for management strategies. Such a framework reflects the general CSR elements and possible management approach that could serve as a generic guide in streamlining and managing CSR systematically in any given company.

4.3.2 Finnish Culture and CSR

Interestingly, some distinct aspects of Finnish culture also influence the views and management of CSR. From roadmapping study (Theme 1), some similar concepts with CSR are reflective of the Finnish culture and attitude. The assumption that CSR has long been a part of the Finnish culture and business practices is very strong. Hence most CSR principles are, not surprisingly, often taken for granted because it is a self-evident mindset for the Finns. Strongly put, CSR thinking has been in Finland for a long time and that going back to or putting into writing the litany of good, responsible business practices is unlikely to be favored by the Finns. Hence, such a strong cultural bearing was taken as a separate theme of interest (Theme 2).

This section discusses the observed Finnish culture that is not really a stereotype, but more or less like indicators of a likely manifestation when CSR is thought of and practiced. Descriptions of each cultural attribute may be inadequate, but the main idea of why such a cultural attribute is considered is due to the strong bearing and reflection on the notions of CSR. Similarly, these cultural attributes are not exhaustive, but instead are the most frequently identified or cited in a list of initial observations and confirmed from interviews, previous studies, and information given by various sources.

4.3.2.1 Culture of Strong Compliance to Laws and Regulations

Finland is known to be a country of people characterized by rigor and a structured lifestyle (Tixier 1996). Rules shape the behavior and are well internalized despite the liberal nature of Finnish society. Finns generally like that which conforms, is structured, and controlled (Tixier 1996). This characteristic is reflected very much in the Finnish business world. Regulation of companies or industries in Finland is known to be fairly rigid so that companies must diligently comply because non-compliance is heavily penalized (Alvesalo and Tombs 2000).

It is a common claim of Finnish managers and those in business that they generally operate their companies in compliance with laws and regulations. These include compliance with the Finnish Companies Act and other specified laws on taxation, financial reporting, bankruptcies, register of companies, etc. For example, the success of the tax policy in Finland depends on maintaining a culture of positive corporate taxation or tax compliance (Expat-Finland 2002). Although it is claimed by many companies that Finnish taxation is one of the highest in the world, it is generally seen as beneficial in building a society. Similarly, both at the individual and corporate level, paying taxes is best regarded as compliance with the law and that tax evasion is not only illegal but also immoral. Undoubtedly, the government's reputation for strict penalties for tax evasion has played a significant role in establishing this culture of compliance.

Implementing CSR in business therefore is positively enhanced by this strong culture of compliance. Looking at its very essence, CSR is based on the internalization of laws, regulations, standards, policies, and agreements. The claim that companies should do more than comply is good but, still, it starts from a well-founded basis of compliance.

Companies in Finland are also bound to comply with other regulations both locally and internationally, such as those imposed by the Confederation of Finnish Industries, labor organizations, and the EU. Adherence to international codes (e.g., human rights, rights of the child, etc.) is well internalized in most Finnish companies. With this upright stance on laws and regulations, the adoption of CSR practices is obviously favorable. This also demonstrates how companies in Finland fulfill their legal responsibilities that correspond with society's expectation to see them meet their economic duties within the framework of legal requirements. Although self-regulation or voluntary compliance is preferred by most companies (Broadhurst 2000), Finnish companies still make a strong effort to comply with national laws and international codes.

A problem can arise when such a culture of adherence to the law is tested in other countries with different laws and regulations. The experience of some managers in their operations overseas suggests that a typical Finnish way of handling CSR issues is compliance with the local law combined with other flexible measures and a proactive stance to do more than comply. It may be easier said than done, but such a culture of strong compliance becomes a dilemma when practiced in other countries with different corporate laws and ethics and where universal (or multicultural) norms of compliance may be hard to find. Likewise, a negative aspect of this culture of compliance is that it could be inhibitory to pursue flexible approaches of CSR or it could be a strong alibi for some companies to define (e.g., just pay taxes regularly) social responsibility narrowly. Moreover, if self-regulation is viewed by many companies as a better option to exercise greater flexibility, then this may be rather difficult to achieve because of the limitations set by too many compliance requirements.

4.3.2.2 Strong Stance on Morality

In most companies, it is a common stance that Finns behave responsibly and ethically on the basis of the Northern European high regard for morality (Tixier 1996).
It is difficult to make a concrete qualification of the exact description of this Northern European morality, however, Tixier (1996) provides a good characterization of
such a stance on morality. According to Tixier (1996), it can be rooted in the social
solidarity that most Nordic societies have developed in conjunction with ideologies
of social democracy perpetuating in several forms, a puritanical moralistic tradition and inherited religious values (i.e., Lutheran Protestant or Evangelical). These
puritanical ways are more or less encapsulated in the following values or norms:

1. Social solidarity
2. Respect for discipline and modesty
3. Respect for one another and harmony
4. Egalitarianism
5. Work ethics, uprightness, honesty, and good citizenship
6. Integrity in business and loyalty
7. Professionalism

All these values reflect the virtues of CSR directly or indirectly. Generally, these
values are inherently set in the minds of most Finns in business, particularly managers. These values are reflected in the practices of the companies selected for this
chapter. For these companies, therefore, it is rather easy to understand and communicate CSR thinking. Thus, the claim of most Finnish managers in the selected
companies that that their companies have been acting and behaving ethically in dealing with their employees, customers, business partners, and the community around
them is true because such a moral attitude is expected of them.

According to Maignan (2001), such a moral stance supports the fulfillment of
an ethical responsibility required from companies, that is, to abide by established
norms defining appropriate behavior. Because CSR is based on business ethics, it
is clear that moral obligations of the corporations are actually a reflection of their
own constituencies' morals, attitude, and behavior. Hence, co-opting these morals
in CSR management makes it easier to adopt appropriate practices.

Although considered good virtues, it can also be argued that negative points could
be ascribed to this moral attitude. Such moral thinking may be overrated and confor-
mity may not necessarily be true, or may be compromised in practice, because of the
changing nature of business, peoples' thinking, and the agenda of competitiveness.
Likewise, such a moral attitude could be a lag factor if adjustment in a non-Finnish
environment is called for.

4.3.2.3 Strong Emphasis on Common Knowledge (Self-evidence) and Trust

Managers in Finnish companies involved in this report typically claim that some aspects of CSR have been self-evident in knowledge and practice for a long time. This

is particularly true with respect to employees' welfare and customer relations. The thinking that Finland has already done much in the area of social welfare apparently explains such an attitude. Indeed, many of the corporate executives and managers strongly assert that being a socially responsible company is already part of their ideology or a self-evident business practice.

As discussed in the roadmapping theme, CSR is somewhere in the core values and principles of the company. Many Finnish managers claim that these values are self-evident in their daily business life. For example, corporate values such as respect for employees, trust, and openness are common themes for many companies. On the basis of these values and principles, a company builds its code of conduct, either general or specific in scope, which is in turn used as a claim reference that CSR, in a broad sense, is sufficiently taken care of. The effect of this strong emphasis on common knowledge and trust is favorable in terms of laying the basic principles and social policy in a company.

It can be observed that an offshoot of this self-evident thinking is a trait that many Finns can identify with. That is to say that when a matter is self-evident, Finns tend not to write so much on it but rely more on trust. "*It is merely that Finns are not fond of writing and paper work when something is already self-evident. It's a matter of values such as openness and trust.*" This can be attributed to the claim that Finland is traditionally a country with an oral culture, where confidence or trust is conveyed by one's word. The verbal accord is honored and such reciprocal reliability facilitates transactions. In business, people talk more freely than they write (Tixier 1996). This is also the reason why some foreign business people or expatriates are rather fascinated when dealing with Finnish business people where words are honored and respected more than a piece of paper. Tixier's statement captured this essence very well, to quote; "*many things are said among Finns that foreigners have no chance of hearing.*"

One problem concerning this strong emphasis on common or self-evident knowledge and practice is that it can be a potential source of misunderstanding and may cause some issues to be overlooked. This self-evident thinking also leads to decisions being less discussed and quickly put into action but with mistakes occasionally being made (Tixier 1996). Likewise, the laxity in attitude towards writing and formalizing papers poses some problems relevant to document requirements (e.g., auditing for compliance, settling complaints and disputes, etc.).

Furthermore, since CSR does promote greater dialogue and communication, many Finns would find this cumbersome because of the typical claim that Finns lack the skills in high-context communication. This is to say that communication techniques such as public relations, marketing, and hyping are some things that Finns are not known for.

4.3.2.4 Positive Attitude towards Globalization

Globalization is considered by most Finnish managers as one of the main drivers of CSR. This was strongly emphasized in the roadmapping study. This is particularly obvious for some big Finnish companies (e.g., Nokia, UPM-Kymmene, and Wärtsilä) that are very global. These leading companies believe that signals from the global market are important in their efforts to maintain competitiveness and reputation.

CSR being a global phenomenon is easy to communicate with many Finnish managers and executives who strikingly have a very strong positive stance on globalization. Iloniemi's report (1998) confirms this positive attitude of Finnish company executives towards globalization issues. According to Iloniemi (1999), as much as 93% of company executives surveyed consider globalization as an extremely important factor for successful business in the future.

The effect of this positive thinking towards globalization is favorable in the development of CSR in companies involved in this study. Such global thinking finds these Finnish companies supporting and promoting global CSR initiatives (e.g., Global Compact, Sullivan Principles, and SA8000). However, such an attitude may be overrated as well, in the sense that it is hard to know how it really is in practice. It could be that it is too easy to acknowledge and present a positive attitude towards global issues like CSR, but in reality it may be slow in Finland. This could be attributed to the alleged Finnish conservatism and slowness in commercial relations (Tixier 1996), which may also be relevant when it comes to adopting a value-based or soft-management approach like CSR. Although there is a common notion that Finns are quick to adopt the latest technology and engineering, the challenge of CSR's soft nature would find the technocratic Finns lagging and facing some difficulties.

4.3.2.5 Culture of Good Governance and Intolerance to Corruption

Good governance is highly esteemed in Finland making it a strong point in the country's public or state governance (Ministry of Finance 2004). Public or state principles of good governance practiced in Finland can be summarized into four administrative principles, which are (1) the principle of equality, (2) the principle of objectivity, (3) the principle of proportionality, and (4) the principle that any action must be appropriate for its purpose (Koskinen 2003). These principles are found in the Finnish legislation. As such, these principles serve as a strong foundation of avoiding crime or bad governance or bad politics (e.g., corruption, bribery).

Similarly, corporate governance is generally an esteemed culture that many Finnish companies' top management sees as crucial and of prime importance in business management and sustainability. Typically, the corporate accounting and securities markets laws, as well as the rules of the Helsinki Stock Exchange, contain regulations concerning the governance and disclosure practices of listed Finnish companies. Other than that, corporate governance is generally referred to as based on sound principles and high ethical standards that comply with the Finnish

Companies Act,[1] Chamber of Commerce, and Federations of Finnish Industry and Employers.

This corporate governance practice is primarily based on compelling legislation and self-regulation; however, this was recently complemented by some new recommendations of the Helsinki Stock Exchange (HEX Plc.), the Central Chamber of Commerce (CCC) of Finland, and the Confederation of Finnish Industries (EK) in December 2003. The goal of the recommendations is to harmonize the practices of listed companies, improve transparency of their operations, harmonize the information given to shareholders, and improve the quality of disclosure. This will help increase local and international investors' interest in listed Finnish companies and promote trust in the functioning of the securities markets (HEX Plc, CCC, TT 2003).

Having such rigid and crafted support mechanisms to ensure good governance, it is not surprising that one barely reads or hears of grave scandals in Finnish political or business conduct. Relating this culture of good governance to CSR, a recent study conducted by Juholin (2004) concluded that sound corporate governance (leadership and efficiency) is one of the prominent supporting forces behind CSR. Likewise, the practice of this culture of good governance is very much a reflection of the strong Finnish culture of honesty, ethicality, and a strong stance on morality framed in rigid values as indicated earlier.

Corruption is a very important issue when discussing governance and Finland is well known to be ranked number one on the list of least corrupt countries in the world for five consecutive years from 2000 to 2004 as indicated by Transparency International's Corruption Perception Index (CPI) survey. (Transparency International 2000, 2001, 2002, 2003, 2004). According to Brady (2002), corruption in Finland is almost nonexistent and that Transparency International found virtually no corruption in the country from 2000 to 2004.

Corruption connotes a strong negative impression among Finns in business conduct. Most business people agree that such a practice is intolerable and, as in many countries, it is punishable by law in Finland. This is a serious matter for many Finnish companies and they admit that they are beset with this issue when doing business in other countries where corruption is prevalent.

As noted earlier, in international ratings of corruption Finland has enjoyed high esteem for a number of years. Koskinen (2003) discussed this and offered a few possible explanations for this phenomenon, including egalitarianism (no class distinction), good governance, transparency and openness, and collective decision making. Although Koskinen (2003) and Tiihonen (2003) cited those reasons for honesty specifically among civil servants, many Finns not in public service would agree with the same line of reasoning.

---

[1] The regulations on protection of minority shareholders and exercise of the rights of ownership and possession are embedded in the Companies Act. In other words, the law includes detailed compelling regulations on the right to vote, obtain information and submit proposals as well as general meetings of shareholders. The Companies Act also provides for non-discriminating treatment of shareholders.

Finnish intolerance towards corruption in business dealing is a reflection of the legendary uprightness of Finnish managers that makes them reliable in business (Tixier 1996). This can also be ascribed to the Finns' principle of behaving morally and ethically as discussed earlier. Likewise, most Finns consider honesty an important virtue, which is also carried through in their places of work and in companies. This anti-corruption value of the Finns is, therefore, a plus factor that enhances the practice of CSR.

One problem with this culture of intolerance towards corruption, however, is that it could create a potential dilemma for Finns in the global market in terms of competition, for example, in export preference and in investment or project biddings. It is hard to know, although it is likely, whether other non-Finnish multinational companies engage in *"under-the-table deals"* in other counties in order to get market share, business protection, or investment approval. In such conditions, the question is how these Finnish companies tackle these sensitive issues of corruption, bribery, and other under-the-table business practices, which are beyond the observation of this chapter.

4.3.2.6 Little Finland Thinking

Geographically Finland is big, but for most Finns Finland is a small country when it comes to business. This is due in part to the fact that it has barely 5 million people and business centers are basically concentrated in the major cities and/or industrial areas. This setting makes business networking easy and business people are close and familiar with each other. For example, it is a common lament for many Finns in business that whenever there is a meeting, seminar, or conference, it is like a family gathering where familiar faces and business acquaintances are present.

This "Little Finland" thinking influences CSR in terms of easy communication and sharing of information, easy organization, and networking. To a greater extent, this thinking is true as reflected by the fast development and progress of CSR in Finland among various groups particularly in business, government, and NGOs. Since the advent of CSR, a quick mobilization of business leaders was observed, thereby putting the CSR agenda in different business agendas of various industries and sectors. For example, the Confederation of Finnish Industries organized its member industries and promoted an agreed corporate responsibility principles and guidelines. Because of the closeness and Little Finland thinking, organization was easier, and hence the fast emergence of various CSR networks such as the Finnish Ethical Forum, Finnish Business and Society, FinnWatch, etc.

On the other hand, being small, easily recognized, and well connected make it easy to notice bad practice or scandals relating to CSR (e.g., discrimination) or other issues important to a business reputation (e.g., corruption, support to unethical activities, etc). For a Finn in general, *"losing face in business once is the end of it, and it is very hard to get back and regain the same image once it is destroyed."* Thus, in a small business setting, a name or image is very sacred for Finns, and hence this in a way serves as a positive stimulus to support CSR in many ways. In the same manner, being a small and well-ordered country like Finland as indicated by Transparency International's research, corruption among officials and politicians is less likely to flourish just as losing face is like losing everything in Finnish general culture.

Manifestations of these cultural attributes correlate well and typically support the principles of CSR. Thus, understanding these cultural attributes contextually gives a clue as to why and how management, decisions, and strategies pertaining to CSR issues in Finnish business are, to a great extent, easier and readily accepted by the Finns. However, these cultural attributes plus other Finnish traits (e.g., slowness in adopting soft management approaches, lacking skills in communication and public relations) are, to some extent, potential loopholes or lag factors in the development of CSR. For example, the culture of compliance can be inhibitory to flexible CSR, and the moralist stance can be a lag factor if adjustment in a non-Finnish environment or situation is called for. Also, the problem of a strong emphasis on common or self-evident knowledge and practice can be a potential source of miscommunication problems.

It is important that these cultural attributes be understood contextually and that they have an enhancing effect on the views and management of CSR. With such cultural attributes, it is therefore easy and favorable to adopt, communicate, and manage CSR issues in the Finnish environment. Although with some limitations observed, the cultural attributes are generally indicators of the positive attitude of the Finns in such a strong welfare state, thus implicating a positive prospect for CSR in Finland.

4.3.3 CSR in the Supply Chain

Another important aspect of the CSR roadmap was the implementation of CSR policies and strategies in the supply chain. This was the focus of Theme 3, highlighting a good case of proactive and progressive CSR management in the supply chain. On the basis of the experience, it was positively acknowledged that implementing CSR policies and strategies in the supply chain is favorable although associated with some problems and challenges. For this theme, experiences of five companies are presented because they were the only ones that have started implementing CSR policies in their supply chains at the time of collecting data and information for this study. These companies are Kesko, Nokia, UPM Kymmene, Virke, and Danisco-Finland.

The motivations of the five companies to implement CSR in their supply chains are generally anchored in the increasing importance of the issue and their desire to be consistent and progressive with their CSR programs. Since the five companies involved in this report have started working on various CSR issues internally, taking it to external stakeholders (like the suppliers) is just another way to extend their CSR activities further since they believe that CSR should not stay in the company's premises. This desire for consistency and the belief that CSR makes business sense should then be impacting the whole business process including supply chains.

Globalization in itself poses a motivating factor for the five companies to tackle CSR issues in their supply chain because it imposes certain requirements on companies, governments, local authorities, and individual people alike. Since the companies find themselves as players of the globalization process, they know that they are being evaluated (for example, by the media and active NGOs) about their CSR conduct in their supply chain. They consider this a new challenge in doing business globally.

Despite the claim that Finnish companies are typically socially responsible and ethical in their global operations, it is still hard to validate such a claim because of the lack of information and monitoring mechanism. It is also hard to validate because of the complex nature of the supply chain processes. Nevertheless, the process of globalization is seen as an opportunity to set examples of promoting socially responsible business.

The positive impact CSR will have on their image and reputation also motivates Finnish companies to be concerned about CSR issues in their supply chain. This positive impact is seen as an important motivating factor. All the managers of the five companies agreed that they cannot ignore the irresponsible activities in their supply chain (e.g., human rights violation issues or corruption, abuses, etc.). They believe that legal liabilities that could result from suppliers' irresponsible behaviors could affect their products and image (reputation) and therefore should not be tolerated. Hence, internalizing CSR and working with suppliers is an opportunity to improve their reputations.

Another motivating factor that is well acknowledged by the five companies is the role of the government and other social actors, such as the Finnish Ethical Forum, Finnish Business and Society, and the EU, in providing an impetus for taking a stronger and greater responsibility towards people and society at large. It is still an ongoing debate as to whether the government should take a role in promoting CSR or not; however, it is typically argued by the companies that it is just sensible for the government to take a role because regulations are considered vital for business success. Nevertheless, despite their positive stance to forging partnerships with the government and other social actors, they have emphasized the importance of voluntary implementation of CSR.

A striking motivation that is probably unique to Finnish business in general is cultural in nature. The essential culture of observing proper ethics in business, high regards on morality, egalitarianism, respect, fairness, trust, and honesty are some ideals that most Finns share in business. In a way, such a culture motivates them to make it known to their suppliers that the Finnish way of doing business is based on fundamental ideals and virtues that can be built and developed over time. This cultural aspect of CSR in Finnish companies (as discussed in Sect. 4.3.2) suggests that typical Finnish attitudes and cultural bearings play an important role in business dealings. Strong Finnish intolerance of corruption and bribery was also mentioned in the study. Given these ideals and business attitude, Finnish business executives are motivated and proud to be labeled with these virtues when dealing with their partners in the supply chain.

The above-mentioned motivations to manage CSR in the supply chain, although varying in terms of importance, are generally acknowledged by the companies. Most of these motivations are commonly linked to doing what is believed to contribute to image building, or indirectly to profitability measures. It is also an observation that these motivations were not clearly linked to the pursuit of sustainability *per se* in these companies. However, all of them believe that creating CSR in the supply chain is part of achieving some levels of sustainability.

Some of the most common problems encountered by the companies are in any of the following areas: long and complex supply chain; problem when dealing with multi-products; differences in laws, industry standards, culture, and values; communication problems and difficulties in setting concrete targets.

4.3.3.1 Problem with Long and Complex Supply Chain

This is one of the major problems rendering it difficult to conduct CSR dialogues and implement CSR policies with the suppliers. All the companies lament that it is hard for them to draw the supply chain boundary and they are often faced with the problem of how far down the supply chain should companies track CSR. This is further complicated by the presence of subcontractors in the chain. These subcontractors in turn have their own subcontractors who are often hard to see in the chain. Another problem in relation to this is how to ensure that the suppliers would carry out the same CSR policies with their subsuppliers.

4.3.3.2 Problem When Dealing with Multi-products

This is a problem because companies are dealing with hundreds or thousands of products coming from dozens of countries worldwide as typified by Kesko. It is almost impossible to know the CSR-related issues attached to these products. Are these products, if coming from developing countries, made by people whose human rights were violated? Are these products produced by exploiting children and women's labor in a poor country? These are some of the crucial issues that the companies ask when addressing their CSR concerns as they buy their products globally. This problem is further complicated by the way the products are bought (from fairs, exhibitions, lots, e-commerce, etc.), wherein it is difficult to trace the source and attributes of the products. In such cases, other supply chain actors dealing with these products, such as retailers, agents, distributors, sourcing organizations, etc., are unaware of social information regarding the various products they are distributing.

4.3.3.3 Differences in Laws, Industry Standards, Culture, and Values

The effort made by companies to persuade their suppliers to adopt the CSR agenda is also very much affected by the prevailing laws and standards of the country where a company's subsidiary is or where the products are bought from. This is exemplified in UPM-Kymmene, which has experienced hardships in carrying out dialogues with various suppliers because of the differences in laws, standards, cultural understanding, and values. It is often a difficult task to communicate with a diverse group of suppliers coming from different backgrounds. Because of these variations, these companies face many challenges as to how to deal with these issues in a proactive way or how to practice flexibility in relation to their CSR policies.

4.3.3.4 Communication Problems

Often, companies face problems when communicating with their suppliers due to several factors, such as different understanding of CSR, language barriers, cultural orientations, and value judgment. Companies argued that their initial communication with their suppliers on the CSR agenda was faced with many questions in terms definitions and understanding. Questions like "What do you mean by human rights?", "What should be considered as bad in child labor?" and several other sensitive issues were raised, which required both sides to reach a common understanding. Typically for Kesko and Nokia, they are faced with the challenge of communicating with thousands of personnel and suppliers worldwide. For UPM-Kymmene, the concern is also in carrying out effective dialogues with their diverse group of suppliers. The companies, however, acknowledged that most of the communication problems were observed at the beginning of the process when they started a dialogue with their suppliers.

4.3.3.5 Difficulty in Setting Targets

This problem arises when different suppliers agree to follow the CSR policies of their customer companies, but because of the complexity of the supply chain, it is difficult to set performance targets. CSR is still developing and indicators and measurements are still underdeveloped, and hence this problem.

Despite these problems with CSR, the five companies share some similar view that CSR can still be managed in the supply chain. The companies also agree that it is only by acting and taking on the process that solutions to the problems can be found. In that sense, all of them have developed and operationalized some CSR management strategies in their respective supply chains. Although there are many variations, the CSR management strategies taken by these companies are typical and consist of the following progression: (1) evaluating or refocusing on corporate values and principles; (2) making and internalizing new commitments; (3) framing CSR policy for the supply chain; (4) setting codes of conduct and/or adopting social accountability standards; and (5) controlling the implementation and these strategies.

1. Evaluating or Refocusing Corporate Values and Principles

It was clearly noted during the interview that all the companies have serious internal discussions of corporate values. It is a common practice for these companies to define and write down the values that they would like to be identified with. Although some are expressed specifically or broadly, these values have a strong meaning for companies' managers and employees, thus, affecting the companies' goal-setting and decision-making processes.

Typically, corporate values are well communicated to the employees and most managers emphasize the influence of values on the business operation in practice. Since external pressures are increasing particularly with the rise in stakeholders expectations, these values are subject to regular check and revision if necessary in order to reflect the current demands of the stakeholders.

Communicating corporate values to stakeholders has become a common practice for companies. Communicating corporate values with the suppliers has also become important since the new value on "*respecting individuals or people and responsibility*" has become a popular theme for many Finnish companies in recent years.

Such values as respect for people are the essence of CSR; hence, human rights, children's rights, discrimination, employees' welfare, etc. are common parameters of many CSR indicators (e.g., GRI guidelines). Relevant to this point is the notion that corporate values, according to Morsing and Thyssen (2003), provide the background for any concept of CSR, which is why we see values as a fundamental part of the discussion.

Values are the starting point for going through the basics of CSR (Loh 2002; Crosbie 2002; and Confederation of Finnish Industries and Employers 2001). Companies share the same stance just as they typically communicate these values with their employees, customers, suppliers, or the company's stakeholders in general. They believe that these values need to be communicated and should serve as the basis of a sound relationship with their own people and business partners. Likewise, Linnanen (1998) concluded that value bases seem essential in adapting a sustainable behavior. When implementing CSR policies in the supply chain, a company's starting point is to open up and lay out its values to the suppliers and explain the reason why it is important to internalize such values in its supply relationship.

There are at least two important points about these values raised during the discussions with CSR Managers of Finnish companies. First, corporate values are changed or reoriented in some cases, or a new one is created to fit the current needs regarding the way companies feel about CSR in relation to their suppliers, their customers, and society in general. Second, these corporate values, after being communicated and recognized by the suppliers, are maintained in the supply chain.

2. Making and Internalizing a Commitment

All the companies agreed that an important success factor in promoting the CSR agenda is the supply chain; this is a company's commitment (particularly top management commitment) in order to manage corporate responsibility in general and the supply chain in particular. The following are some of the commitments noted by companies involved in this study.

Commitment to uphold corporate responsibility in general. As discussed earlier, corporate responsibility in general is the overriding principle that all companies acknowledge and agree to manage in various aspects of their operations, including the supply chain.

Commitment to have dialogues and partnerships with suppliers for a more ethical and socially responsible supply relationship. Bringing the message to and implementing CSR in the supply chain is best attained through dialogues and partnerships. Dialogues and partnerships should typically be based on trust and the willingness to share responsibility by both sides.

Commitment to provide support in the process of change. This is important when suppliers are incapable of complying with the CSR requirements or make the necessary changes. Although compliance by suppliers may vary in implementation, support from the company should be a proactive commitment.

Commitment to adopt codes, standards, and international declarations. This is a basic commitment of companies although varying in approaches and the tools employed. The goal here is to adhere to socially responsible trading or purchasing codes, employ acceptable standards, and respect international declarations (e.g., The UN Declarations on Human Rights).

Commitment to be open and transparent. This is an important commitment that ensures the building of trust and a steady supply relationship between the two sides. This commitment is characterized by both the company and suppliers' willingness to provide information and reports relevant to their CSR management.

Generally, these commitments are reflected in companies' practical implementation of strategies that are discussed in a later part of this chapter. It is important to highlight at this point that these commitments underpinned the motivation of companies to share and manage CSR issues with their suppliers. Although the commitments of suppliers in return are difficult to gauge and vary to a great extent, our participating companies acknowledged that differences need to be accommodated and continually checked for alignment with CSR values based on shared responsibility for the value chain success.

These commitments when internalized and carried through with suppliers create a sense of assurance that a company is serious in putting the CSR agenda in place and willing to take the responsibility concomitant with it. On top of these commitments is the importance of top management to approve CSR plans and strategies.

3. Framing CSR Policy for the Supply Chain

Four companies involved for this report have formally written their approved-by-the-Board CSR policies, while the fifth company (Virke) has taken a different view about writing its CSR policy. Although varying in format and structure, those policies are basically similar in substance (for example, CSR parameters per Global Reporting Initiatives (GRI) guidelines and CFIE Corporate Responsibility guide booklet). For Virke, its general corporate responsibility framework is considered adequate enough to serve as a guiding principle to cover the company's stance on social responsibility, and therefore writing a CSR policy statement for the sake of formality is viewed as unnecessary or inappropriate. Virke's further argument for

Table 4.2 CSR policy articulated for the supply chain

Company	CSR policy articulated for the supply chain
Kesko (trading and marketing)	Implement ethical princile for product purchasing
Nokia (telecommunication)	Close partnership with suppliers and maintenance of Codes of Conduct
UPM-Kymmene (paper and wood products)	The company complies with international, national, and local rules and regulations, as well as international agreements. The company engages supply chain stakeholders through communication and dialogue conducted with integrity, fairness, and confidentiality
Virke (clothing manufacturing)	Purchase materials only from reliable European manufacturers so that the safety and quality is guaranteed in the end product. Favors suppliers that meet Virke's product safety standards
Danisco-Finland (food ingredients)	Dialogue with suppliers (as external stakeholders) on CSR issues; and understanding and building CSR issues into every component of the value chain

doing so is based on their strict quality and guarantee requirements imposed on its suppliers. Nevertheless, Virke does subscribe to the principles of CSR, compliance with regulations, as well as observance of applicable international laws and standards.

It is hard to point out, unless clearly stated during the interviews or in the written documents provided, the CSR policies specified directly for the supply chain. Going through all the CSR policies, it is easy to say that those policies are generally applicable to the supply chain. To check this problem, the CSR policies of the five companies were examined thoroughly and the policies specified or directly articulated for the supply chain were extracted as shown in Table 4.2.

On the basis of the above streamlined policies, it can be construed that it is basic for a company to first enter into a dialogue with its suppliers and then agree on either codes of conduct or ethical trading principles. The problem that is typically observed here is that the understanding, interpretation, and compliance of the suppliers are difficult to gauge. It is sometimes difficult to know how the suppliers react to the policies and to know the impacts of those policies because of the varying nature and culture of the suppliers and their capacity to comply.

How policies are maintained in the supply chain is also an important question. Companies' responses to this question vary slightly depending on the approaches that each company has taken. For example, Kesko maintains its policy by linking it to an auditable social accountability standard like SA8000, and since Kesko employs third-party auditors, the policies are conscientiously checked as stipulated in its socially responsible trading principles. Other examples are observed in Nokia and UPM-Kymmene, where CSR policies are clearly reflected and emphasized in their Codes of Conduct. For all these companies, however, a dialogue with suppliers is considered the basic way to maintain and check the compliance of suppliers with their policies.

4. Setting Codes of Conduct and/or Adopting Social Accountability Standard

Rules of conduct in every civilized society exist for the benefit of society at large and in order to give freedom to individual members to go about their legitimate business within the bounds of behavior accepted and observed by their fellows (Royal Statistical Society 1993).

At the corporate level, codes of conduct are a set of rules to be observed in business. It is an embodiment of the defined rules of behavior that are perceived as good virtues and accepted by people inside and outside the corporation and they indicate the ethical and moral stance of a company. With the increasing attention to CSR, many companies nowadays have started to require suppliers to comply with the company's codes of conduct or social accountability standard (SA8000 as in the case of Kesko).

This section describes the codes of conduct or ethical principles of Kesko, Nokia, and UPM-Kymmene. So far, these three companies have fully developed and publicly available codes of conduct. The other two companies (Virke and Danisco) do not yet have available codes of conduct because of the argument that writing the codes of conduct for formality's sake is considered unnecessary yet. For these two companies, the notion of codes of conduct is inferred in their main corporate responsibility or corporate sustainability principles in general.

Kesko, instead of preparing codes of conduct, has sought another way of presenting its social and ethical profile to its suppliers by the adoption of ethical quality control using the SA8000 standard. Kesko applies the principles based on the United Nations Universal Declaration of Human Rights and Convention on the Rights of the Child and the International Labour Organisation's conventions. The SA8000 standard is more or less based on these conventions. These are particularly applied in its purchases from the developing countries. Kesko strongly promotes the adoption of the standard so that as many suppliers as possible can prove their social reliability by obtaining certification. By mid-2000, over 100 of Kesko's buyers for imported products have participated in the basic training in this standard.

Nokia's codes of conduct cover a wide range of interests and stakeholders reflecting Nokia's values and way of working. It is based on compliance with the highest standards of ethical conduct and appropriate law. The compliance commitment in the codes covers various matters, which include decisions relating to trade, investment, subcontracting, supplying, business development, and other business relationships.

Zeroing in on the codes of conduct pertaining to Nokia's suppliers, the codes infer that Nokia does its best to contract only with suppliers or subcontractors who themselves adhere to international human rights and environmental laws and practices. Nokia commits to monitoring the social and ethical performance of its suppliers and to taking immediate and thorough steps in cases when the ethical performance of its suppliers comes into question.

UPM-Kymmene embodies its codes of conduct in its Ethical Principles, which stipulate the company's responsible business operations based on clear and modern operating principles of trust, openness, initiatives, and highest ethical standard in relation to all external target groups. Interestingly, an offshoot of these Ethical

Principles is guidance written in the company's Basic Ethical Rules in Purchasing and Sales. These basic rules form important guidelines of the company's CSR policy.

The codes of conduct and ethical standard of Kesko, Nokia, and UPM-Kymmene are all publicly available and communicated according to their commitment. However, the challenges for these companies with regard to the implementation of these codes are inevitable. How do the suppliers accept these codes? How strong is its impact on the supply chain? How is its compliance monitored? It is still difficult to get concrete answers to these questions, but the companies are aware of these and have started to address these challenges.

5. Practical Implementation and Control of the above Strategies

This section discusses how the five companies are implementing CSR approaches, means of control, and evaluation in the supply chain. Since most of these activities are currently in progress, it is noted that these approaches are not complete but rather developing. So far, this account is about what was gathered during the interviews and observed to be the main points in proceeding with the suppliers on CSR implementation.

Communication of Corporate Values, CSR Policies, and Codes of Conduct. Generally, communication of corporate values, CSR policies, and codes of conduct starts inside the company. As such, it follows that it should be communicated to external stakeholders like the suppliers. From internal management, and on the basis of the commitment to implement CSR in the supply chain, it opens up a new door specifically for external CSR communication. Such communication takes the form of letters, questionnaires, discussions, and meetings where explicit stipulations of the company's commitments and requirements to its core values, codes of conduct, and CSR policy are emphatically presented. In turn, the suppliers are asked to consider those stipulations as a new aspect of the purchasing terms. This approach is considered the first step that these companies take with their suppliers, particularly the major ones. Such communication implies a change in the purchasing regime for both parties particularly towards evaluating their social performances, as well as a decision to retain or possibly cancel a purchasing contract.

A common problem with this approach is the difficulty in interpreting terms and meanings on how they conduct their business dealings (e.g., interpreting local customs as opposed to the requirements of global standards and guidelines). Another problem lies in a situation when some suppliers do not agree with the codes for some socio-cultural or political reasons. In view of these, the responses of companies are generally geared towards committing to do their best to resolve the problem in line with the codes of conduct, local regulations, and international declarations and standards.

Questionnaires. Out of the five companies, four have started sending questionnaires pertaining to CSR issues particularly to their primary or major suppliers, locally and globally. The questionnaires are typically based on the established CSR guidelines (e.g., GRI and SA8000), as well as on the adoption of international declarations and standards, such as the UN Universal Declaration of Human Rights, UN

Convention on the Rights of the Child and ILO Labour Standards. The questionnaires typically deal with basic human rights and core labor issues. These include, but are not limited to, human rights violations, child labor, forced labor, freedom of association, equal opportunities, wages and benefits, working hours, health and safety, and disciplinary measures.

The common problems often encountered with questionnaires are slow and low rate of response or no response at all, problems in interpreting the various terms in the questionnaires, and problems with the inadequacy and verifiability of the information given in the questionnaires returned.

Evaluating of the questionnaires returned helps the companies to roughly understand the circumstances, problems, and nature of their supplier's social performances. Acting on these problems, a company normally takes a proactive stance in following up the questionnaires. This often leads to other communication approaches in the form of personal discussions, meetings, workshops, and suppliers' day programs.

Personal Discussion with Suppliers. Conducting personal discussions or meetings, particularly between the company's buyers and suppliers is another way of communicating CSR. In this approach, the buyer company presents the CSR policy and gets the suppliers' responses; this method is a lot quicker than sending a questionnaire. With such an approach, a company can learn and discuss about the nature of the business of suppliers and supply chain and its role in improving the suppliers' social performance. Such personal discussions bring issues on the spot and make it easier to resolve problems. Evaluation of the social performance of the suppliers can also be elicited using a reasonably discussed and agreed framework. A problem with this approach, however, is made visible when the suppliers are geographically located in far off places and where cultural factors could act as barriers in discussing sensitive issues.

Workshops and Suppliers' Day Programs. This form of communication is rather formal since workshops and suppliers' day programs require an organized administrative and logistic arrangement on the part of the company. A company typically invites its suppliers to a workshop to tackle CSR policy issues and implementation strategies or to present the plan of a standard implementation. This is very true of Kesko, which has conducted a series of workshops on its ethical purchasing principles based on SA8000. Likewise, a suppliers' day program forms a good platform for discussion and exchange of information on CSR and social performance. It is an occasion when the suppliers gather together (normally hosted by the company) to address different issues and problems pertaining to CSR in their supply chain. Similar to personal discussion, the suppliers' day program yields faster feedback from the suppliers themselves. Nokia and UPM-Kymmene typically conduct this kind of program.

Workshops are also typically attended by another group of people, such as the government, industry associations (e.g., CFIE and industry sectors associations), labor associations, consultants, and other interested parties. As such, it creates a richer exchange of information and feedback from various groups and, therefore, enhances the whole CSR and supply management processes.

Development of Working Conditions. Typically, when a supplier has subscribed to the codes of conduct or social accountability standard and agreed to cooperate with a company, the working conditions of both parties start to develop. Developing working conditions means the imposition of sets of requirements or standards (SA8000) to be complied with and following auditing activities. Working conditions also mean working together to solve problem issues or noncompliance in the requirements and auditing procedures.

Control of activities in this stage varies in levels and emphasis. For example, Nokia gives a 30-day response period to its auditing offer. UPM-Kymmene takes a softer stance based on a pragmatic approach through dialogues and culture building with the suppliers. Virke and Danisco stress the importance of control through a thorough discussion of the requirements and problems. On the other hand, Kesko strongly adheres to full observance of SA8000 requirements and active assistance in solving noncompliances. Likewise, Kesko created its own research team in charge of issues related to CSR (e.g., product quality testing).

The auditing process is an important means of control to ensure that all requirements are met. Auditing is typically conducted by company's own audit team or independent third-party auditors. Typically, an audit is focused on factory facilities, working conditions, workers, personnel, and management systems. Auditing takes place on various levels depending on the circumstances, nature of the supply chain, and the desired result by a company.

Auditing is typically carried out by skilled and trained staff. Depending on the audit criteria set by the auditors, an audit can also be limited or exhaustive. A limited audit is one that focuses only on the main issues specified by a company (e.g., on main products, labor issues, etc.). An exhaustive audit follows a routine of checking all the set criteria and is sometimes an iterative process (e.g. checking into the HR file and documentation system, doing a walk-through in all areas of the company or factory, interviewing some personnel, etc.). The results of the audit are evaluated and serve as the point of various control decisions.

Guarantee for Social Performance and Long-term Partnership. When a supplier agrees to comply with the company's CSR policies and when auditing has become established in the working conditions, the company and the suppliers begin forging or renewing a contract guaranteeing the expected social performance. Such a guarantee serves as proof of social responsibility being shared by both parties and the commitment to make it work in time. Therefore, such a guarantee implies a good working relationship for a long period of time.

For the SA8000 standard as employed by Kesko, the guarantee is a certification granted by an accredited SA8000 certifier. This certificate is proof that an audit has been conducted and all the standard requirements are satisfied. Part of the routine to be checked regularly with this guarantee is the provision of reports and other documents such as evaluation report form for audit activities, compliance and noncompliance report, risk analysis report, and a certificate for SA8000 (as in the case of Kesko). Meetings are also part of the routine to update on the progress made, solve new problems, and discuss emerging issues.

Controlling the supply chain for CSR issues is still difficult to gauge because of the company's claim that they are still in the development process. However, given the time and efforts that the companies have invested and reflecting on the approaches that they have implemented, they are progressing fairly well and learning the different measures. Managing CSR in the supply chain indeed requires serious and mutual learning between the different actors in the supply chain. Finally, the apparent benefits of implementing CSR in the supply chain are, but not limited to, streamlined supply chain, identified risks and problems, enhanced supplier relationship, and improved brand image and reputation.

4.3.4 Roles of Government and NGOs

The active roles of the government and NGOs in promoting CSR in Finnish companies have brought Finnish CSR to a more robust level of cooperation and partnership, social development, and international recognition. These important groups (also called stakeholders) play important roles in the development of CSR in the country and even internationally. Typically, they are able to organize coalitions or networks by which they put forward the CSR agenda to companies for consideration.

In general, the Finnish government can be considered very active and well motivated in promoting CSR as a whole, both at the national and international level. One strong argument for such an active stance of the Finnish government is based on the view that there is a positive effect on the economy and social development of the country when companies internalize CSR. With active partnerships, not only with companies but also with other actors in society, the government can be applauded for its good examples on formulating progressive social policies, building human capital, and engaging civil society that help promote CSR in Finnish companies.

Typically, the role of the Finnish government in relation to CSR is more on setting policies or guidelines, information dissemination, encouragement, and support (e.g., for dialogues between different parties and support for SMEs, etc.). Other roles take the form of coordination (e.g., of EU Green Paper, MONIKA, OECD Guidelines), representations (e.g., in forums, meetings, international negotiation of agreements), study and research (e.g., implementing OECD guidelines, ethical investment, and social labeling), and giving advice (consultation). Although it is acknowledged worldwide that the main challenge for many governments is to determine how best to address the realities facing companies today and support socially responsible and sustainable business practices, Finland can be considered to be well ahead and to have progressed well in the practical realization of CSR. Despite the noted progress, the government still faces some challenges as they continue promoting CSR among Finnish companies. The most important challenges identified by the government is in the promotion of CSR in Finnish companies doing business in developing countries, as well as promoting CSR in small and medium-sized companies.

Similarly, many NGOs in Finland are also busy supporting and promoting CSR through various programs, both locally and internationally. Generally, most of them agree that it is important for Finnish companies to internalize CSR because companies are part of a society in which Finns expect them not only to deliver good performance but also to contribute to people's welfare particularly those in the workplace. These NGOs like to see Finnish companies' CSR not just written about and discussed, but also put into practice and in good faith. They believe that Finnish companies can be more competitive while at the same time be recognized as exemplars of good conduct and behavior both locally and internationally. Typically, the roles that these NGOs take in relation to CSR promotion can be any of, but not limited to, giving and sharing information, cooperation and partnership with other groups for social dialogue, networking (e.g., with other local NGOs and EU counterparts), negotiation, lobbying, as well as assisting their own members, clients, and constituencies. Locally, many NGOs find it easy to work on CSR issues, but internationally, especially in developing countries, most of them lament that CSR is entangled in difficulties and troubles. Many of them point to the differences in perspectives, culture and thinking, work environment, and circumstances in other countries as the main reasons for those difficulties. Other common problems encountered by many NGOs are more in the areas of engagement, social dialogues, and trust building in partnerships, as well as promoting CSR among SMEs.

The evolution of different CSR networks, such as the Finnish Ethical Forum (FEF), FinnWatch, and Finnish Business and Society (FiBS), to address CSR issues in Finland and abroad can be described as an accompaniment to the increasing importance of CSR in companies. It can also be articulated that it started from a convergence of common interests among its members. Common interests such as asking and learning about CSR, sharing information and ideas, and prospecting for a change towards perceived public good drove the evolution of these networks. These networks importantly serve as platforms for mapping out common interests and even differences where CSR issues are presented with greater participation of interested parties.

Finally, government's and NGOs' active roles are vital in the development and success of CSR. As for NGOs, the varying intensity of their roles and initiatives depend mainly on the size of an organization, prominence, and focus of interest. Despite some problems, the experience of the Finnish government and Finnish NGOs is a showcase that CSR can be best promoted through soft approaches and sustained and trust-built partnerships. Likewise, the continuous learning, sharing, and exchange of ideas and information through networks have proved to be effective in gaining successful results in CSR locally and internationally.

4.4 Conclusion

In the recent past, the rise and increased attention to CSR in Finland has put companies in the spotlight and created significant interests and/or reactions among different groups in Finnish society. Although considered a concept with various connotations, CSR in its development forms a new aspect of sustainability and the Finnish welfare state.

The insightful information and descriptions in this chapter constitute a useful roadmap important in learning and understanding CSR in Finnish companies. Despite the lack of a concrete definition of CSR, some important roadmap indicators point to the importance of framing CSR within corporate responsibility concept, identification of motivations, and driving forces of CSR, and the explanation of how the current management areas and practices are fitting into the new and modern CSR concept. Driven by globalization, stakeholders, and pursuit of sustainable development, CSR is a rapidly developing concept and practice in the selected companies.

In general, Finnish culture has a positive influence on the views, thinking, and management practices of CSR issues. Such a positive influence of culture therefore makes it easier for business people to discuss and understand CSR because those CSR issues are considered common for Finns and are implicit in the welfare state provisions. While there are potential negative spins when such a culture is tested in a different environment, it is important to bear in mind that those cultural characteristics are essential in understanding and learning the Finnish style of approach to CSR.

The experience of managing CSR by Finnish companies both locally and globally, particularly in the supply chain, is a showcase for a proactive response to the emerging CSR challenges. The implementation of CSR policies in the supply chain reflects the companies' commitments and belief that CSR can be managed with the suppliers. The companies' increasing attention to the supply chain is based on the realization that CSR is problematic and can be a serious issue in the global supply chain (compared to local CSR in Finland). Likewise, the supply chain experience stresses the importance of taking initiatives to address CSR issues with the suppliers and forging collaborative working relationships for a better and socially responsible supply chain management.

The proactive stance of Finnish companies on CSR is complemented by the active supporting role of important societal actors such as the government and NGOs. These active actors have exerted pressure through various promotional efforts and campaigns, thus pushing CSR into the mainstream of Finnish companies and strengthening the synergistic learning about CSR within Finnish business circles. The efforts of the government and NGOs to promote CSR support the importance of a multipartite involvement and the emergence of better civil regulations. The drive to learn, exchange experiences, and contribute to CSR discussions and debates have facilitated the evolution of CSR networks in Finland.

Finally, the issues discussed in this chapter adds to the mounting evidence that CSR, in general, has created a new dimension in managing sustainability at the corporate level. This exploration has provided some compelling empirical observations and evidence, as well as direct quotations, that explain nebulous CSR concepts in particular temporal and geographical contexts. There is immense opportunity to utilize this information to learn and gain new useful insights, approaches, and concepts for understanding and managing CSR.

References

Alvesalo, A. and Tombs, S. 2000. Regulating business: the emergence of an economic crime control programme in Finland. Selected Proceedings of the British Criminology Conference Vol. 4, Leicester, July 2000.

Brady, J. 2002. Corruption in Finland – nearly none at all. Virtual Finland. September 2002.

Broadhurst, A.I. 2000. Corporations and the ethics of social responsibility: an emerging regime of expansion and compliance. *Business Ethics: A European Review* Vol. 9, No. 2. Blackwell Publishers Ltd., UK.

Clarke, T. 2001. Balancing the triple bottom line: financial, social and environmental performance. *Journal of General Management* Vol. 26, No. 4, Summer 2001, pp.16–27.

Confederation of Finnish Industries and Employers (CFIE) 2001. Corporate responsibility: a primer brochure. Finland.

Cramer, J. 2003. Learning about corporate social responsibility: The Dutch experience, National Initiative for Sustainable Development (NIDO). IOS Press, The Netherlands.

Crosbie, L. 2002. Taking an effective management approach to supply chain sustainability: an analysis. *Ethical Corporation Magazine*, UK.

Culpeper, R. 1998. The evolution of corporate responsibility: from unbridled markets to mature capitalism. Speech addressed to the Canadian Center for Ethics and Corporate Policy, North South Institute, Toronto, Canada.

Davis, S.L. 2001. Triple bottom line: the social dimension. ConGo Online (www.congo-online.com).

Elkington, J. 1998. Cannibals with forks: the triple bottom line of 21st century business. Capstone Publishing Ltd., Oxford.

Enderle, G. and Tavis, L.A. 1998. A balanced concept of the firm and the measurement of its long-term planning and performance. *Journal of Business Ethics* Vol. 17, No. 11, pp. 1129–1144.

Expat-Finland 2002. Entrepreneurship in Finland: business taxation. www.expat-finland.com (accessed site on September 2002).

Grayson, D. and Hodges, A. 2004. Corporate social opportunity. Greenleaf Publishing, London.

Haavisto, I. 2004. Why should economy care about virtues? Finnish Business and Policy Forum. Helsinki.

Hart, S. 1997. Beyond greening: strategies for sustainable world. *Harvard Business Review*, January/February 1997, pp. 66–76.

HEX Plc, Central Chamber of Commerce of Finland, and Confederation of Finnish Industry and Employers. 2003. Corporate Governance Recommendations for Listed Companies (December 2003).

Hollender, J. 2003. What matter most: corporate values and social responsibility? *California Management Review* Vol. 45, No. 4 (Summer 2003).

Iloniemi, J. 1998. Lecture on the societal responsibility of corporations. The Center for Finnish Business and Policy Studies (EVA), Finland. (www.eva.fi).

Juholin, E. 2004. For business or the good of all? A Finnish approach to corporate social responsibility. Corporate Governance. *International Journal of Business in Society* Vol. 4, Number 3 (March 2004), Emerald Group Publishing Limited, pp. 20–31.

Koskinen, J. 2003. High-level political conference for the signature of the United Nations convention against corruption, 9–11 December 2003, Merida, Mexico. Ministry of Justice, Finland.

Linnanen, L.R. 1998. Essays on environmental value chain management: challenge of sustainable development. Jyväskylä Studies in Computer Science, Economics and Statistics, University of Jyväskylä, Finland.

Loh, C. 2002. How multinationals need to walk the talk? Greening of Industry Network Conference Workshop. June 23–26, 2002, Göteborg, Sweden.

Maignan, I. 2001. Consumer's perception of corporate social responsibilities: a cross-cultural comparison. *Journal of Business Ethics* Vol. 30. Kluwer Academic Publishers, The Netherlands.

Ministry of Finance. 2004. Ministry of Finance, Finland 2004.

Morsing, M. and Thyssen, C. 2003. The case of Denmark – corporate values and social responsibility. Center for Corporate Values and Responsibility, Copenhagen Business School, Denmark.

NCSD 2000. Sustainable Development Report. NCSD, Finland (www.ncsdnetwork.org).

Royal Statistical Society 1993. Code of conduct. (http://www.rss.org.uk/about/conduct.htm), accessed site on February, 2003.

Tiihonen, P. 2003. Good governance and corruption in Finland. Virtual Finland (May 2003).

Tixier, M. 1996. Cultural adjustments required by expatriate managers working in the Nordic countries. *International Journal of Manpower* Vol. 17, No. 6/7, MCB University Press, pp. 19–42.

Transparency International, 2000. Press Release: Corruption Perceptions Index 2000, Berlin.

Transparency International, 2001. Press Release: The Corruption Perceptions Index 2001, Paris.

Transparency International, 2002. Press Release: Corruption Perceptions Index 2002, Berlin.

Transparency International, 2003. PressRelease: Corruption Perceptions Index 2003, London.

Transparency International, 2004. Press Release: Corruption Perceptions Index 2004, London.

van Marrewijk, M. and Hardjono, W. 2003. European corporate sustainability framework for managing complexity and corporate transformation. *Journal for Business Ethics* Vol. 44. Kluwer Academic Publishers. The Netherlands, pp. 121–132.

Chapter 5
Sweden

Karolina Windell, Maria Grafström, and Pauline Göthberg

Abstract Although the idea of social responsibility of business has a long history, the debate over corporate social responsibility has escalated in Sweden during the past few decades under the label of CSR. CSR has become an idea on the corporate agenda in Sweden. This chapter describes how CSR arrived in Sweden and how social responsibility takes its form and translates into practice in Swedish corporations. In order to understand the background of how CSR entered the Swedish business community, the chapter begins by describing social responsibility from a historical perspective and the recent revival of CSR in Sweden. In broad terms, the topic of the social responsibility of business has a long root in different societies around the world. The emergence of the industrial community in Sweden between the mid-seventeenth century and the mid-nineteenth century was a period in which Swedish corporations had played a prominent role in the local community, contributing to the development of several social institutions, including the fire brigade, medical services, and schools. During the last century, the scope of corporate responsibilities was marginalized to that of economic responsibility. However, in the last 20 years, the Swedish discourse on corporate responsibilities has changed in concert with the state of the market and with the division of roles between corporations and the state. As in many other countries, Swedish companies are being criticized by stakeholders and they are being urged to take on greater responsibilities both in Sweden and elsewhere. Hence, during the last few decades, the field of CSR has solidified and taken a better shape both nationally and internationally. The chapter discusses how companies listed in the Swedish stock exchange communicate information on their CSR activities and also examines how three large Swedish corporations practice CSR.

5.1 Introduction

Organizations and individuals propagating the field of corporate social responsibility (CSR) have undergone dramatic developments during the last decade.

S. O. Idowu and W. L. Filho (eds.), *Global Practices of Corporate Social Responsibility*   103
© Springer-Verlag Berlin Heidelberg 2009

Governments, trade associations, business networks, certification and standardization agencies, non-governmental organizations (NGOs), investment banks, universities and business schools, consultancies, and law firms, among others, have aided the advancement of CSR in Sweden. Several efforts have been made to raise the awareness of the idea and to encourage and exert pressure on corporations to enhance their level of social responsibility. CSR standards, frameworks, and guidelines have been issued; reports on corporate misbehaviour have been published; the ranking of socially responsible corporations in league tables has been inaugurated; research on CSR has been amplified; seminars, workshops, and conferences on CSR have been organized; and fora in which both advocates and opponents of the field of CSR can express their views have been arranged. In addition to all these, one could still come up with an endless list of corporate activities in the name of CSR. These developments imply that CSR has become an important item on the corporate agenda in Sweden and elsewhere.

This chapter addresses the practice of CSR in Sweden. It describes how CSR arrived in Sweden and how social responsibility takes its form and translates into practices in Swedish corporations. Developments in the field in Sweden are, however, as in all countries, interrelated with its experiences in other countries.

The chapter departs from previous Swedish research on CSR. Swedish research within the field has increased in the last few years. Researchers have had different theoretical approaches and have understood CSR from diverging empirical angles. Among the recent studies, we find scholars addressing the presentation and expansion of CSR in the media (Buhr and Grafström 2007; Windell 2006), the practice of CSR among Swedish corporation (Frostenson and Borglund 2006; Frostenson and Borglund 2006; Göthberg 2007a, b; Åhlström and Egels-Zandén 2005), the commercialization of CSR by consultants (Windell 2007), the expansion of socially responsible investments (Sjöström 2007), the development of regulations and standardizations (Jutterström 2006; Tamm Hallström, forthcoming), and the popularization of the idea of CSR (Windell 2006).

This chapter is divided into two parts. The first part describes CSR's arrival in Sweden. This part depicts the Swedish discourse on corporate responsibilities and explains how CSR has solidified and taken a better shape both nationally and internationally following different events. The second part of the chapter demonstrates how Swedish corporations have started to address the issue of CSR, both in rhetoric and in practice. A general overview of how Swedish corporations respond to the expectations of CSR is presented, followed by cases studies of three large Swedish corporations.

5.2 The Arrival of CSR in Sweden

Although CSR has come into vogue during the last decade, the notion that businesses should behave responsibly has a long historical root (Carroll 1999; Carroll 2004; De Bakker et al. 2005; Windell 2006). Indeed, in broad terms, the topic of social responsibility of business has a long root in Swedish society. The emergence of the industrial community in Sweden between the mid-seventeenth century and the mid-nineteenth century was a period in which Swedish corporations played a prominent role in the local community, contributing to the development of several social institutions, including the fire brigade, medical services, and schools. These social services evolved within the industrial communities and were provided at the expense of business proprietors and entrepreneurs (Berglund-Lake and Dahlin 1999; Hellspong and Löfgren 1994).

Around 1950, when the Swedish industry flourished, corporations contributed to the development of the Swedish welfare state. Corporations such as the telecommunications company LM Ericsson developed services for their employees such as kindergarten and recreational activities in order to help their staff (Johnson 2006; Stadsbyggnadskontoret 1982). These are examples of activities that contributed positively towards the prosperity of Swedish industries.

By the 1980s, the Swedish welfare state was well established. This meant that the roles and responsibilities between the three largest social sectors – public, private, and civil – had become secluded (De Geer et al. 2003). During this time, the rhetoric within the private sector had changed, as the Anglo-Saxon dominant rhetoric about shareholder value anchored in the Swedish business community (De Geer et al. 2003). The consequences of the shift in rhetoric led to an increasing focus on the return on investments and a dichotomy between the public and the private sector. This meant that corporations had explicitly become engaged in social developments in the country, a role that was originally perceived as that of the Swedish state.

More recently – in the twentieth century – corporations, however, once again started to assume social responsibility by offering their employees health care, free kindergarten, and recreational activities (Göthberg forthcoming; Johnson 2006). During this time, the role and responsibilities of corporations in relation to the public sector became an issue of debate.

At the end of the twentieth century, the debate about the social responsibility of business intensified both internationally as well as in Sweden. Corporate actions that were previously recognized as legitimate became the subject of public scrutiny, and corporations that had been admired were scrutinized and accused of inappropriate behaviour. Even those corporations that were operating within the law were criticized for inappropriate behaviour. Several multinational clothing retailers received negative publicity for overlooking child labour and dangerous machinery in their factories (Arnold and Bowie 2003; Åhlström 2003); Nike became the international media's example of an irresponsible and greedy corporation during the 1990s (Zadek 2004), and in Sweden the clothing company H&M and the furniture company IKEA were accused in the media of using child labour in their contractors' factories in the less developed parts of the world (SVT 2007; Åhlström and Egels-Zandén 2005).

More recently, in the early twenty-first century, corporations such as Enron, WorldCom, Arthur Andersen, and Parmalat were condemned for unethical and, in some cases, illegal behaviour. The overall debate in Sweden about the social

responsibility of business, ethical conduct, and the role of business in society escalated during this period. In particular, the corporate governance scandal in the
insurance company, Skandia, centring on their bonus programs "wealth builder"
and "sharetracker", and the sale of Skandia Asset Management received widespread
attention (Göthberg 2007b)[1].

Critical articles about corporate behaviour were published in Swedish dailies;
governmental representatives published reports on ethical conduct and corporate
responsibility; and on the 5 September 2002, the Swedish government initiated a
commission to evaluate the trust in the Swedish business community and deal with
corporate governance issues (Förtroendekommittén 2004).

In concert with these developments, the anti-globalization protestors in many
parts of the world – including Sweden – began to protest, drawing attention to the
role of business in the global society and raising questions about social responsibility and globalization. The protestors in the anti-globalization movement have
stressed the growing power of western multinational corporations, a position amplified by the increase in the number of these multinational corporations and by
their annual turnovers that have exceeded the GDP of several developing countries
(Horn af Rantzien 2003; Klein 2000). The globalization debate gained momentum
in Paris in 1998 as governments from different parts of the world met to discuss
the Multilateral Agreement on Investments (MAI),[2] which had first been formed by
the governments of the Organization of Economic Co-operation and Development
(OECD) states in 1995 (Svenskt Näringsliv 2002a). The anti-globalization movement was visible not only in Paris but also at the 1999 World Trade Organization
(WTO) summit in Seattle, USA, where protesters blocked the delegates' entrance to
the summit. These protests were merely the first in a series of demonstrations that
occurred in the following years. In 2000, protesters rallied against the meetings of
the IMF and the World Bank in Washington and Prague. In 2001, new protests took
place at the EU summit in Gothenburg – an event that received widespread attention
in the Swedish media. As a consequence of these developments, the Association of
the Swedish Business Community (ASBC) started an information campaign about
the role of Swedish corporations in globalization (Svenskt Näringsliv 2002a, b,
2003, 2004). The purpose of the campaign was twofold: to increase the trust in
Swedish corporations, and to discuss the scope of corporate responsibilities for the
local and global society.

In concert with these developments, the debate over the social responsibility of
business widened and developed in Sweden. The role of business in society accentuated, particularly in relation to globalization and what this meant for businesses
operating in developing countries. The debate included arguments that benefits derived by corporations for outsourcing production to developing countries rendered

---

[1] In 2003 the top management and corporate board of Skandia were accused of lining their pockets
at the expenses of their shareholder. In 2006 two members of the top-management team were found
guilty and condemned to 2 years in prison.

[2] According to the draft introduced in April 1998, the member countries should use the same principles in dealing with foreigner investors that they would be expected to use in any international exchanges: transparency, non-discrimination of foreign investors, and the most-favored-nation clause.

them responsible for their operations and obliged them to contribute towards solving such global social and economic problems as poverty in these developing countries. General ideas about the social responsibility of business were raised more often but now under the label of CSR.

5.3 Governmental Initiatives in Enforcing CSR

Government ministries are important to the business community because of their role as rule makers; by imposing coercive regulations and directives, they set the boarders for corporate business activities. They are also influential through their mobilization and encouragement of other actors in society to advance ideas that have an impact on the business community.

The Swedish government took a broad approach to CSR, having demonstrated its interest in these questions in 2001 when the Ministry of Foreign Affairs launched the national initiative, *Globalt Ansvar* (The Swedish Partnership for Global Responsibility) as a response to the UN Global Compact. The aim of the scheme was to stimulate corporations to assume increased roles in social responsibility (Pagrotsky 2003).

In an open letter to the Swedish business community, published on 6 March 2002, the Foreign Minister, the Minister for Development Assistance, and the Minster for Industry and Trade requested corporations to take an active part in developing a "human globalization" (Lindh et al. 2002). The letter began by addressing the increasing debate on CSR and the role that Swedish corporations had played so far in this development. Thereafter, the ministers argued that the Swedish government needed help from Swedish corporations to improve working conditions, protect the environment, and develop human rights throughout the world. The goal of the Swedish government was to lead the way in economic, environmental, and social sustainable development and to communicate how corporations ought to behave, mediate, help, advice, and present good examples (Ministry for Foreign Affairs 2002). Through Globalt Ansvar, the Swedish government offers businesses the possibility of increasing the visibility of their cooperation, in return for which it expects them to conform to OCED guidelines for multinational corporations and the UN Global Compact.

Globalt Ansvar has since its launch carried out a number of activities such as seminars and workshops in order to draw attention and create a debate about the scope of CSR. So far just a limited number of corporations have decided to join the governmental initiative. In 2007, 18 large state- and private-owned companies were recruited to the project. However, several of the Swedish corporations have instead decided to join the international counterpart, the UN Global Compact (GC).

Another important governmental initiative that triggered the debate about CSR was the establishment of the "Commission of Trust" (*Förtroendekommissionen*) in 2002. As described above, it was launched in order to evaluate the trust for the Swedish business community and to develop guidelines for desirable corporate governance. The initiative was an outcome of several corporate scandals – both internationally and in Sweden. This resulted in a widespread debate about corporate responsibilities, a debate in which Swedish corporations actively participated.

5.4 Criticized Industries Take up the Cudgels for CSR

It is difficult to outline one general argument or a common motive for Swedish companies' revived interest in CSR. However, in Sweden, criticized industries initially took up the cudgels for social responsibility. Corporations that significantly ran the risk of damaging the environment or had production in third-world countries with controversial working conditions often took the lead and started to work on CSR from its outset in Sweden.

These developments are similar to those in other countries. Professor Alyson Warhurst at Warwick Business School in the UK argues that environmental disasters as well as violations against the human rights have contributed to establishing CSR on the corporate agenda (Warhurst 2001). In the 1990s, CSR often addressed issues relating to supply chain management. The focus was on the practices of Western companies operating production facilities in developing countries: the monitoring of child labour, worker exploitation, and dangerous machinery. In the 1990s, several clothing companies, for example, Gap, Nike, and Disney, started to monitor their supply chains after being accused of similar mistreatment and of violating human rights with "sweatshop" factories (Jenkins 2001; Åhlström and Egels-Zandén 2005).

In 1992, the Swedish retail company Electrolux was the target of consumer boycott. As in many other cases of interest, organizations of various kinds organized a campaign of some sort against Electrolux. In the case of Electrolux, Greenpeace dumped refrigerators outside its headquarters in Stockholm in order to draw attention to the debate about the emission of Freon.

In 1997, the aforementioned Swedish clothing company, H&M, was accused of hiring suppliers with bad working conditions and underpaid employees. A few years later, Swedish companies in the extraction industry came under the spotlight. The Swedish companies Atlas Copco and Sandvik were accused of unethical behaviour. Atlas Copco and Sandvik at that time were selling products to companies in the extraction industry: Ashanti Goldfield and Goldfields Ltd in Ghana, which had been accused of environmental damage and human rights violation (SwedWatch 2003). Hence, the unethical behaviour of Atlas Copco and Sandvik towards their employees and customers became a problem for these companies, as the media drew attention to these issues.

As a consequence of the public debate and the negative publicity that companies such as Electrolux, H&M, Atlas Copco, Sandvik, and others had received, they embarked on programs of change not only to improve their own behaviour, but also to put pressure on their suppliers to improve theirs. Hence, the examples of misbehaving Swedish companies served as an impetus for intensifying the responsibility debate within the Swedish business community. As the examples illustrate, much of the discussion centred on the roles of Swedish multinationals operating in developing countries. The CSR discourse in Sweden is in this way significantly tied to globalization and corporate activities in other parts of the world.

The issue of increasing concern for CSR among corporations has taken different dimensions in Sweden during the past few decades, particularly in the form of new methods of communication. Corporations have begun to display information about social concerns on their Web pages, publish social reports in which they account for their social responsibilities, and present their work at CSR conferences and seminars. By communicating their social concerns, corporations are not only responding to pressure groups who are demanding that corporations increase their social responsibility but are also helping to shape CSR into an idea that is worthy of paying attention to. Here, the argument has been that CSR can contribute to an improvement in financial performance. Even though there is no clear evidence that CSR actually leads to increased profits (Margolis and Walsh 2003), the argument that CSR is a business case has been prominent in the Swedish debate (Windell 2006).

In the following section we sketch the development of CSR in the Swedish business community, and thereafter we present how three major Swedish corporations have decided to tackle and deal with CSR-related issues in their industries.

5.5 CSR in Swedish Corporations

Up until the late 1990s, CSR was still not widely practiced by Swedish corporate entities. The number of organizations and individuals that were contributing to the propagation of CSR ideology in Sweden has increased dramatically only in the last decade. In this way, CSR has also become a widespread management idea within the Swedish business community. The number of corporations working with CSR issues in Sweden has radically increased. It is no longer those corporations that have received a bad press coverage as a result of their unethical behaviour that are now actively addressing social responsibility related issues. Instead, the majority of large Swedish companies now work on their social responsibility matters in one way or another. Today, several Swedish corporations produce social reports and employ CSR consultants and verifiers. In fact, the job title "CSR manager" can be found in some large companies in Sweden.

Most corporations listed on the Stockholm Stock Exchange – the Large Cap list (listing the largest companies in Scandinavia except Norway) – are today communicating their social responsibility on their Web pages. In total, 127 companies are listed on the Large Cap, and 82 of them – 65% – explain their social responsibilities on their Web pages in February 2007. These companies use different titles to present their views on questions relating to social and environmental concerns. The most common titles are CSR, corporate responsibility, sustainability, and community involvement.

The companies listed on Large Cap represent five overarching industries: IT and telecommunication, retail, materials, industrial goods, financial services and health care. Initially, it was companies in the extraction (materials) and retail industries that

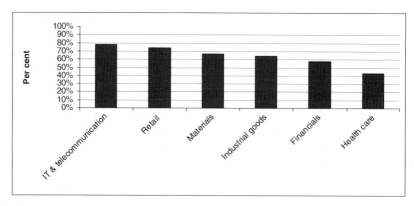

Fig. 5.1 CSR communication in different industries in Scandinavia

started various CSR initiatives in Sweden, but today companies representing several industries have declared that they also are socially responsible. Still, the number of companies within the extraction and the retail industries that communicate information on their social responsibilities are high, but CSR involvement is more popular among companies that operate in the IT and telecommunication industry. Figure 5.1 demonstrates the distribution of corporations that communicate information on social responsibility from different industries.

If Danish and Finnish companies were excluded from the results, in other words by exploring just Swedish companies that are listed on Large Cap, the results will be similar to that depicted above. In total, 70 Swedish companies are listed, and 39 of them (56%) are communicating information on their social responsibilities on their Web pages (See Figure 5.2). In three of the industries, about 60% of the corporations communicate information on their CSR activities. In the health care, however, only 33% of the corporations display their views on social responsibility on their Web pages.

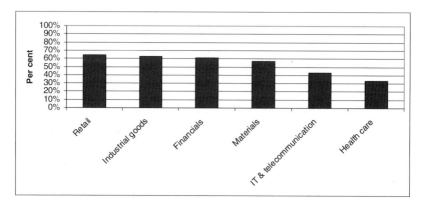

Fig. 5.2 Communicating CSR information by different industries in Sweden

The results also demonstrate that the financial services industry has started to address CSR related issues. This is partly due to increasing interest for investments in ethical funds – Socially Responsible Investments (SRIs). In Sweden, the government has regulated the national pension funds to include social, ethical, and environmental concerns. This action has, in turn, encouraged the development of SRI funds. Since the 1990s, the number of ethical funds has increased. Today, there are 388 ethical funds in Europe (Avanzi SRI Research, 2006) – 67 of them are Swedish (Folksams etikindex 2006). Still, at the time of writing, in 2007, SRIs occupy an insignificant portion of the financial services market, constituting only about 0.5% of the total fund assets in Europe (SiRi Company 2004).

Hence, ethical funds and SRI funds have played a part in bringing CSR to the fore among companies in the financial services sector. Today, these corporations address CSR by focusing on the role they want to play in society. Their approach of presenting social responsibility information relates to how they would like their stakeholders to perceive them in the "good corporate citizenship" race. A cursory look at the Web pages of the largest banks and financial institutions in Sweden would reveal that these companies often address social responsibility in terms of the support they provide to different community involvement projects, in other words in terms of their philanthropic CSR activities. However, there are also several differences among companies in the financial services industry. The investment company Kinnevik, for example, addresses issues such as respectable working conditions at their Swedish offices, equality of opportunities between women and men, bribery, and respecting the law governing restrictive practices (unfair trading). However, on top of their CSR policy – displayed on their Web page – Kinnevik writes: "the primary purpose of Investment in AB Kinnevik is to generate profits to the shareholders." Just as in other European countries, in Sweden there has been ongoing debate about how CSR relates to profits. In particular, critics of CSR have argued that the overarching purpose of any corporation is to look after the interests of its shareholders. This debate is clearly reflected in Kinnevik's CSR policy.

The manner in which corporations in Sweden translate CSR into practices depends both on the ideological perspective held by the top management and on the core business of that corporation. When it comes to the ideological perspective, this revolves around what the top management believes is the role of corporations in a society. Perhaps they might believe that it is only to fulfill the shareholders needs or they could take a view that it is to serve the needs of a larger group of stakeholders. Moreover, corporations with different core businesses also address CSR in diverse ways. Consequently, companies in the retail industry often address CSR from a supply chain management viewpoint, i.e. describing how they secure a more respectable working condition in their suppliers' factories, whereas companies in the financial services industry focus more on how they can contribute positively to the local community.

Most large companies in Sweden that practice CSR have, however, translated CSR into a policy or a code of conduct that describes how the corporation and its employees should behave in a number of different situations. In Sweden, there is no common definition of CSR, which makes it possible for corporations and their top management to interpret and translate CSR into practices that fit the organization. Despite the many different and conflicting definitions of CSR, it has become a popular and widely practiced management ideology in Sweden. A large number of Swedish corporations now not only communicate financial performance but also their CSR activities.

5.6 CSR at the Managerial Level

The questions related to CSR are placed at different departments in the corporations, which also demonstrate that CSR is interpreted rather differently. Out of the 82 companies – listed on Large Cap stock exchange – which communicate social responsibility information, 70 belong to the Swedish stock exchange. Thirty-nine of these 70 companies communicate information about their CSR activities on their Web pages. Out of these 39 companies, 30% have someone employed with either the title of CSR manager or Sustainability manager. For the rest of the companies, the responsibility lies with different departments and managerial levels in the corporations. As Table 5.1 demonstrates, it is rather common that the top management, the human resources department, or the communications department is responsible for these questions. In a few cases, the investor relations department is responsible or a lawyer from the legal department could also be charged with CSR matters. In two cases, the responsibility was divided among different departments, and in two of the corporations we were not able to find one person or department being in charge of CSR matters.

The way corporations decide to organize certain CSR-related matters also says something about how the corporation actually interprets issues on CSR. The distribution of social responsibility actions within a company clearly shows where in the organization its decision-making machinery for CSR resides. A structure of this type makes it less apparent who is responsible for CSR. The results demonstrate that there is no common structure for social responsibility matters within large Swedish corporations.

Table 5.1 CSR at the managerial level

Title/department	Number of corporations
CSR/Sustainability manager	13
Top management	6
Human resources department	5
Communications department	3
Investor relations department	3
Legal department	2
Marketing department	2
Different departments	2
No department	2

In order to obtain a more in-depth picture of the differences in the corporations' practices of CSR in Swedish context, we have provided below three case studies. The next section therefore discusses how three large Swedish corporations representing three different industries – financial services, retail, and construction – operate while practicing corporate social responsibility.

5.7 Three Examples of the Practice of Corporate Social Responsibility in Sweden

Sweden, like many of its counterparts around the world, has not been left behind in the practice CSR. Increasingly, a large number of companies in the country have paid serious attention to CSR and how they communicate information on their activities in the field. In this section we present three Swedish corporate cases in order to illustrate how different industries have chosen to take cognisance of their CSR issues. Each case describes on one hand how these companies communicate information on their CSR activities and on the other outlines their actual activities in the area. The three companies are Hennes & Mauritz (H&M) – a clothing retail company; Skandia – an insurance and savings company; and Skanska – a global construction company. These companies today practice social responsibility in different ways. All of them have also been through different crises when their reputation and responsibility have been severely questioned.

5.7.1 H & M – the Clothing Retail Company

H&M is a clothing company with 60,000 employees and is active in 28 countries around the world. H&M does not own any factories, but production processes of their clothing involve about 2,000 factories with more than 700,000 employees.

H&M is actively creating an image for themselves as a responsible company, and they present their products using the label CSR. It has chosen to use CSR instead of other similar labels and concepts, such as sustainability and corporate citizenship, with the argument that their responsibility includes the social condition in the factories in which their clothes are produced. It defines CSR as a concept that "voluntary integrates social and environmental respect in its business and in its cooperation with stakeholders in order to meet, or surpass, ethical, legal and commercial expectations of the company in the surrounding environment." The definition has several similarities to the definition of the European Commission and states that the social responsibility is formed and reformed in relation to the company's stakeholders.

H&M has chosen to communicate their social responsibility information among other ways through their Website. Interestingly, information about CSR is given as much space as information to investors. From 2007, H&M has decided to align its CSR activities in accordance with the guidelines provided by the Global Reporting

Initiative (GRI) and has developed them together with the textile industry and non-profit organizations.

The company has argued that by including in its strategies actions that recognize and work towards improving peoples' quality of life and caring for the environment will have some positive impacts on their own business and consequently a significant effect on their long-term profitability. One key reason that explains why H&M adopts CSR is the consumers' increased interest about the production of the clothes they and their children wear. Also, CSR issues have become important in recruitment processes, as those in search of work are increasingly asking CSR-related questions.

5.7.2 CSR in Practice – Labour Conditions at Subcontractors' Factories

For H&M, CSR is mainly about the responsibility for labour conditions at the sub-contractors' premises. It does not own any factories itself, but buys these products from subcontractors in low-wage countries, such as China. In total, H&M uses 700 subcontractors around the globe. The production in developing countries, where most of the company's subcontractors are situated, is sometimes criticized for bad labour conditions. To have production in these countries brings with it the risk that these factory owners would have a total disregard for humanity, violate the human rights laws, and commit crimes that are against international labour conventions. Even though H&M's subcontractors have sufficient supply of adult job seekers, there is always a risk that these subcontractors would employ child labour: perhaps because they are cheaper or pay no wages for the child labourers, or provide unsafe machinery and work environment. This is both a risk and a responsibility, says Karolina Dubowicz at H&M's press office (interview, 2 August 2007).

In 1997, H&M started their CSR activities and developed their codes of conduct. The background to this engagement was partly due to the criticisms received by H&M and other similar retailers such as Nike and Disney when they were questioned about the conditions at the factories of their subcontractors. The Swedish Television showed a documentary: "The latest fashion – at what price?" which focused on child labour that existed when subcontractors outsourced production to local subcontractors. Margareta Winberg, the then Minister of Labour in Sweden and Annika Åhnberg, a member of the cabinet, officially declared – as a result of the documentary – that they would boycott the products supplied by H&M; many Swedish customers also followed these ministers' example.

H&M then initiated a range of new activities designed to improve the labour conditions and to counteract the criticisms in the media and among their consumers. Initially it was mostly about working conditions, but today their CSR activities include the environment and union rights. H&M argues that their social responsibility includes making demands on subcontractors to produce their clothes according to existing international regulations. H&M has developed its own set of rules and regulations which subcontractors are obliged to follow.

H&M has collected these rules in the form of a code of conduct, which is based on the code of conduct of United Nations and the ILO conventions. Subcontractors are obliged to follow local regulations and directions as well as H&M's guidelines concerning labour and environmental issues – including that which forbids the use of child labour. Other rules that are part of the guidelines are sufficiently good working conditions such as ventilation, temperature, and lightning, access to toilets, fire security, reasonable working times and salaries, as well as the freedom to be members of recognized unions.

5.7.3 Organization

To investigate how Swedish companies organize their CSR activities – e.g., where does it reside in the company? Who is in charge of CSR matters? – we designed a series of questions that we believed would help us understand how companies were practicing CSR in our country. As noted earlier in this chapter, issues about social responsibility have no obvious residence in Swedish organizations today: sometimes these issues are the responsibility of the communications department, at other times they might be dealt with by the human resources department or even by the CEO.

H&M coordinates its activities at a central level, i.e. at its head office in Stockholm (the capital of Sweden), and there are 10 members of the staff responsible for CSR. The department is independent and its chief is part of the managerial body (a member of the Board) and reports directly to the CEO. The organization of CSR issues shows that they have good support from the top management and that these issues are strategically important to the company. In order to ensure that the code of conduct of the company is followed throughout the production process, H&M has about 60 inspectors and regional coordinators who audit the work. According to H&M, the personnel most often have previous experience of work from different audit agencies, such as Bureau Veritas. The auditing can either be made public or be kept private.

The choice of H&M to organize the audit exercise of their subcontractors by themselves has been criticized as being weak and inadequate. Critics have argued that the process should be done by external, independent inspectors because there is a risk that the factories may make only superficial improvements in order to satisfy the inspectors. H&M's argument for carrying out their own self-audit is that it improves their understanding and enables them to gain insights into the production process and its associated problems.

H&M is a company that communicates, reports, and actively works on its social responsibility. The company follows the already established definitions and regulations, including the ones developed by the European Commission and the Global Reporting Initiative. The responsibility is limited to ensuring that their products are produced under acceptable labour conditions. In this way, H&M has been able to embed CSR into its core business by transforming CSR definitions, motives, and objectives into practice.

5.7.4 Skandia – an Insurance and Savings Company

CSR is also an issue that has gained attention in the financial services industry, in which ethical and environmentally friendly fund investments have become increasingly important. But there is also a range of other social responsibility issues that affect the industry.

Skandia, an insurance and savings company, does business in about 20 countries. Since 2006, Skandia is part of the financial investment group Old Mutual (a UK-based company) and became – with the acquisition – part of its already established CSR policy. Similar to H&M, Skandia has chosen to use the concept of CSR when they present information on their social responsibility. Skandia views CSR as a key factor to success, and a quote from the company perhaps explains this better. Skandia argues "In order to be successful it is important that we in an organised way build social and environmental considerations in our business, and that we live up to, and surpass, the legal obligations that we have towards our stakeholders." (Skandia's policy for responsible business, 7 May 2007). Just as with H&M, Skandia's definition is similar to the generally accepted European Union's definition of the field.

Skandia now communicates information on its social responsibility on their Website by focusing on the societal engagement that is carried out through a foundation and through the department "Ideas for Life". In contrast to H&M, Skandia has no production in low-wages countries. Instead, Skandia's core business is about assessing, purchasing, and packaging different fund managers' products on long-term savings. The two companies' activities on social responsibility therefore differ significantly.

5.7.5 CSR in Practice – to Participate in Creating Societal Development

Skandia's CSR activities are nothing new; rather, its activities are a new start on a work they stopped during the period they were in financial difficulties at the beginning of the twenty-first century. The difficulties they experienced in 2000 meant that they had to suspend the strategically important work initiated by its top management both on their sustainability and CSR. This was suspended in 2001 as a result of a rationalization process that went on at the time. Until then, Skandia had a relatively broad environmental engagement, which was presented in their annual environment report.

Skandia has worked with social responsibility through the department "Ideas for Life". It is working with projects that support children and teenagers – a project they started during the mid-1980s. A foundation is tied to the department that distributes scholarships to different societal projects. The department has project leaders who cooperate with non-profit organizations, foundations, and municipalities and who are responsible for different projects that support children and teenagers. Skandia's employees are allowed to use 2 h of paid time every week to engage with these organizations and their projects.

Hence, since the 1980s Skandia has actively supported children and teenagers. This engagement is also something that Skandia has communicated in different ways. One example is the advertisement movie "Beyond the surface" screened by the Swedish Television and published by Skandia in 1990s. The movie showed a boy standing at one of the main squares in the city centre of Stockholm – a place known for drug peddling. The message of the commercial was to encourage the public to take the responsibility for creating a good childhood for children and teenagers.

Skandia was one of the earliest adopters of some of the principles encompassed in CSR. It has been engaged in CSR-related activities since 1987; thus the company has actively worked with social responsibility long before the concept of CSR became well established in the Swedish business community by the late 1990s. Skandia has promoted themselves as a company that takes part in its communities' social developments. Skandia's reputation was, however, significantly tarnished at the beginning of the new millennium, when the company was experiencing its worst ever crisis. In 2002, the management was accused of cheating their shareholders through their incentive programs "wealth builder" and "share tracker". After 3 years of legal battles, two of their directors were found guilty and sent to prison for 2 years. This scandal resulted in an extensive negative publicity for the company in the Swedish media.

Since Skandia's acquisition by the Old Mutual, it has resumed its work on social responsibility. This time around, in an attempt to improve its public image, Skandia, just like H&M, redefined its CSR activities by focusing their new definition of CSR using some of the key words in the definitions proposed by some international bodies: in the generally accepted conventions and guideline such as the United Nation's Global Compact and the OECD's guidelines for multinational corporations.

Till now, Skandia has mainly engaged in social issues and has understood these as their responsibility. As the old adage says "health is wealth" Skandia can only rely on a healthy society for its savings income; otherwise, its core business will evaporate! It is therefore in the company's best interest to participate in creating a healthy and better society, arguably; this is a relatively broad and vague area of responsibility, but Skandia has chosen to focus on the younger generation.

5.7.5.1 Skanska – a Construction Company

Skandia is a global construction company with business in Europe, USA, and Latin America. Skanska is actively promoting itself as a responsible company. In contrast to H&M and Skandia, it uses the term sustainability for it social responsibility activities instead of CSR. The company defines sustainability according to the commission of Bruntland as a "development which fulfils today's demands without risking future generations' ability to fulfil their demands." The meaning is that the environmental, social, and economic results will balance and thereby contribute to long-term profitability.

Skanska has chosen to use sustainability instead of CSR because they do not believe that their primary responsibility is social in nature. Skanska argues that the social element in CSR is the responsibility of the government of the day, not that of individuals or corporate entities! Skanska believes that its responsibility as a company includes making sure that it provides construction projects that are sustainable.

Skanska communicates information on its responsibility through the home page on the Internet and various brochures it issues. It has chosen to embed its sustainability report as an integral part of the annual report, since the related CSR activities are an integrated part of its core business and something that investors should take part in. According to Peter Gimbe, the chief press officer at Skanska, the company is focusing on sustainability issues because that is what stakeholders expect from Skanska and that is what leads to long-term profitability. In addition, working with sustainability makes it to be an attractive employer.

5.7.6 Sustainability in Practice

To reach a balance between environmental, social, and economic goals for Skanska means significantly different activities in practice in comparison with H&M and Skandia. Skanska argues that its social responsibility is in terms of their construction projects. Employees at Skanska are obliged to follow its code of conduct, which is an internally developed rule book.

The code of conduct is about following national laws in the countries where Skanska operates. In addition, the employees commit themselves to following and respecting the United Nations Declaration on Human Rights and to support a well-functioning dialogue with stakeholders. The code of conduct is also mandatory for Skanska's subcontractors. The code includes guidelines for how employees should treat each other as well as how to handle corruption and bribery and other negative environmental influences.

Skanska works towards four zero-tolerance objectives, which means that the goal is to run the business without financial loss, without environmental disasters, without work place accidents, and without ethical irregularities. In this way, the profit of the company is not allowed to be made at the expense of the environment, work place security, or bribes.

5.7.6.1 Organization

The organization of Skanska's work with responsibility shows that it is an integrated part of its business. Three people are working with sustainability issues and their major task is to develop and update its policies in the area. Their work is a function of the group management, but the chief executive officer (CEO) is not part of the management group as in the case of H&M.

Table 5.2 A summary of the three Swedish companies' CSR practices

	H&M	SKandia	Skanska
Label	CSR	CSR	Sustainable development
Definition	Integrating voluntary environmental and social concerns in all parts of the organization	Integrating voluntary environmental and social concerns in all parts of the organization	Balancing the economic, social, and environmental results
Reporting according to	GRI	Global Compact and OECD	Global Compact and GRI
Motive	Profitability and becoming an attractive employer	Profitability, enhancing the brand, and becoming an attractive employer	Profitability and becoming an attractive employer
Practice	Working conditions at suppliers end, and an environmentally friendly supply chain	Children and youth activities through Ideas for Life	Responsibility for environment and work environment in construction projects
Organization	Top management and decentralized practice.	Top management	Top management and decentralized practice.

The responsibility is spread out on Skanska's 14 core business areas and the task to ensure that the code of conduct is followed lies with the company's management. The four zero visions mentioned earlier are tied to the financial incitements for the management. The system is dependent on employees taking their responsibility and reporting any violation the policy.

5.8 Similar Rhetoric but Fragmented Practices

In this chapter, we have presented how three large Swedish corporations – representing different industries – practice CSR. H&M is a retail company, selling clothes to fashion-conscious and price-sensitive customers. Skanska sells large construction projects all over the world. And Skandia turns to private individuals and corporations with financial services products. Nevertheless, they address CSR in a very similar way, at least at the rhetoric level. They share the common notion that CSR indirectly contributes to increased profitability. However, by taking a closer look at how they actually practice CSR, some significant differences are apparent. H&M and Skanska relate social responsibility to their core business, which of course make their practice very different. H&M addresses working conditions in the supply chain, whereas Skanska works with environmental and social concerns in their construction projects. Skandia, on the other hand, does not connect social responsibility to their core business, but rather argues that they believe their social responsibility revolves round the ability to contribute to social development by helping children to develop and grow.

Table 5.2 displays the differences and the similarities in terms of how the three companies communicate and credibly practice CSR.

There is no common definition of CSR today. Instead, corporations are practicing CSR by what could be termed as "a trial and error" approach, a learning process that involves them developing their social responsibilities in terms of their own ideals, their own core business, and in relation to other companies and stakeholders. Social responsibility is, therefore, a framework of the corporate practices as well as societal expectations.

5.9 Conclusions: CSR Takes Many Forms

The past decade has witnessed a remarkable recognition of CSR in Sweden. In many ways, the contemporary expansion of the idea manifests a long-term debate over the relationship between business and society, one that has waxed in the past decade. Several actor groups with different agendas have involved themselves in this debate. Nevertheless, it is difficult to outline distinctions and similarities in the views on CSR that are held by these actors. Opinions about the meanings of CSR and ways of addressing its associated issues are ambiguous and multiple.

There is no standard definition of CSR in Sweden – its vagueness and ambiguous character has led to varying interpretations of its meaning. Today, Swedish corporations that communicate information and practice CSR are evenly distributed among all industries. Their methods of presenting CSR information are rather similar. Social responsibility is presented as a business case, which enhances the corporate brand and attracts competent personnel. However, in practice CSR takes many forms. Moreover, the CSR debate in Sweden focuses on how corporations behave in other parts of the world, rather than focusing on how they should contribute to the Swedish society.

In Sweden, as in many other countries – large corporations have taken the lead in promoting and developing the concept of social responsibility: primarily, as a consequence of the pressure that has been placed on them by the Swedish government, the media, and different interest groups. CSR is, however, not a nationally isolated idea. CSR is related to Swedish traditions and regulations, but it has also developed alongside global developments. In tandem with the debate about the role of corporations in a global society, the debate has also emerged in Sweden. Moreover, just as the different corporate scandals around the world have catalysed the necessity for the debate about corporate responsibilities, Sweden has not been immune from scandals in its own business community; this has also brought about a debate on CSR in the country. The anti-globalization movement reached Sweden in 2001 when anti-globalization activists rallied in Gothenburg. The Swedish government responded on the UN Global Compact and established its Swedish counterpart – Global Responsibility. These and other events have placed CSR on the agenda of the Swedish business community. By communicating information on their CSR activities, corporations have contributed to shaping and developing ideas about what social responsibilities should entail.

References

Åhlström, J. (2003). A Study of Corporate Adaptation to Pressure for Corporate Social Responsibility – an Idea Network Approach: Stockholm Schools of Economics.

Åhlström, J., & Egels-Zandén, N. (2005). The Processes of Defining Corporate Responsibility: a study of Swedish Garment Retailers' Responsibility. *Business and the Environment*.

Arnold, D. G., & Bowie, N. E. (2003). Sweatshops and Respects for Persons. *Business Ethics Quarterly, 13*(2), 221–242.

Avanzi SRI Research (2006). Green, social and ethical funds in Europe, Review, Milan

Berglund-Lake, H., & Dahlin, B. (1999). *I marknaden under 150 år - Tunadals sågverk 1849–1999*. Sundsvall: SCA Forest and Timber AB.

Buhr, H., & Grafström, M. (2007). The Making of Meaning in Media: the Case of Corporate Social Responsibility in the Financial Times, 1988–2003. In F. den Hond, F. G. A. de Bakker & P. Neergaard (Eds.), *Managing Corporate Social Responsibility in Action: Talking, Doing and Measuring*: Ashgate.

Carroll, A. B. (1999). Corporate Social Responsibility: Evolution of a Definitional Construct. *Business & Society, 38*(3), 268–295.

Carroll, A. B. (2004). Managing Ethically with Global Stakeholders: A Present and Future Challenge. *Academy of Management Executive, 18*(2), 114–119.

De Bakker, F. G. A., Groenewegen, P., & Den Hond, F. (2005). A Bibliometric Analysis of 30 Years of Research and Theory on Corporate Social Responsibility and Corporate Social Performance. *Business & Society, 44*(3), 283–317.

De Geer, H., Borglund, T., & Frostensson, M. (2003). Anglo-Saxification of Swedish Business: Working Paper within the Project "Scandinavian Heritage". *Business Ethics: A European Review, 12*(2), 179.

Frostenson, M. (2006). *Legitimationskontrollen: En studie av etiska värderingars roll i gärnsöverskridane förvärv och fusioner.* Unpublished Doctoral Dissertation, Stockholm School of Economics Stockholm.

Frostenson, M., & Borglund, T. (2006). *Företagens social ansvar och den svenska modellen.* Stockholm: Svenska Institutet för Europapolitiska Studier.

Förtroendekommittén. (2004). *SOU 2004:47 Näringslivet och Förtroendet*: Finansdepartementet.

Göthberg, P. (2007a). Lost in Translation: The Case of Skandia's Ideas for Life. In F. Den Hond, F. G. A. De Bakker & P. Neergaard (Eds.), *Managing Corporate Social Responsibiity in Action: Talking, Doing, and Measuring*: Ashgate.

Göthberg, P. (2007b). *Varför projekt överlever: En studie av Skandias Idéer för livet.* Uppsala University, Uppsala.

Göthberg, P. (forthcoming). *Stabilitetens Dynamik-Skanidas Idéer för livet.* Uppsala University, Uppsala.

Hellspong, M., & Löfgren, O. (1994). *Land och stad: svenska samhällen och livsformer från medeltid till nutid.* Malmö: Gleerup.

Horn af Rantzien, M. (2003). Företagens sociala ansvar – den internationella utvecklingen i ett svenskt perspektiv. In Å. magnusson (Ed.), *Det globala ansvaret – sjutton röster on internationellt företagande och etik.* Stockholm: Ekerlids Förlag.

Jenkins, R. (2001). *Corporate codes of conduct: Self-regulation in a global economy.*

Johnson, A. (2006). *LM-staden – folkhem i förort.* Stocholm: Stockholmia förlag.

Jutterström, M. (2006). *Corporate Social Responsibility: the Supply Side of CSR Standards.* Stockholm: Score.

Klein, N. (2000). *No Logo.* Stockholm: Ordfront Förlag.

Lindh, A., Karlsson, J. O., & Pagrotsky, L. (2002). *Globalt Ansvar: Öppet brev till svenskt näringsliv.* Stockholm: Utrikesdepartementet.

Margolis, J. D., & Walsh, J. P. (2003). Misery Loves Companies Rethinking Social Initiatives by Business. *Administrative Science Quarterly, Vol. 48 (2003)*, 268–305.

Ministry for Foreign Affairs. (2002, 25 September). Företags ansvar.

Pagrotsky, L. (2003). Svenska företag ska vara förebilder. In *Det Globala Ansvaret – sjutton röster om internationellt företagande och etik.* Stockholm: Ekerlids Förlag.

SiRi Company. (2004). Green, Social and Ethical funds in Europe in 2004: SiRi Company

Sjöström, E. (2007). *Facilitators for Socially Responsible Investments: A Study of Hong Kong.* Paper presented at The 10th Conference of the Society for Global Business & Economic Development.

Stadsbyggnadskontoret. (1982). *LM-staden i Midsommarkransen.* Stockholm: Stadbyggnadskontoret.

SwedWatch. (2003). Retrieved 12 september, 2007.

Svenskt Näringsliv. (2002a). Globaliseringsdebatten Argument och positioner (pp. 1–44): Svenskt Näringsliv.

Svenskt Näringsliv. (2002b). PM Näringslivets aktiviteter i samband med FNs toppmöte i Johannesburg. Retrieved 12 April, 2006, Svenskt Näringsliv. (2003).

Soppluncher program för våren 2003.

Svenskt Näringsliv. (2004). The Role of Business in Society: Questions and Answers on the Role of Business in Society.

SVT. (2007). Rena kläder grupp. Retrieved 14 September, 2007, from www.svt.se http://www.sac.se/raw/uinf/siden-sammet.pdf

Tamm Hallström, K. (forthcoming). ISO expands its business into Social Responsibility In M. Boström & C. Garsten (Eds.), *Organizing Transnational Accountability. Mobilization, Tools, and Challenges*. Cheltenham: Edward Elgar.

Warhust, A. and Franklin, K. (2001). Biodiversity conversation, minerals, extraction and developments: Towards a realistic partnership, pp. 183–203 in Bowels, I. A. and Prickett, G. T. (Eds.), Footprints in the jungle: Natural resource industries, infrastructure & Biodiversity converstation, OUP, New York.

Windell, K. (2006). *Corporate Social Responsibility under Construction: Ideas, Translations, and Institutional Change*. Unpublished Doctoral dissertation, Uppsala University, Uppsala.

Windell, K. (2007). The Commercialization of CSR: Consultants Selling Responsibility. In F. Den Hond, F. G. A. De Bakker & P. Neergaard (Eds.), *Managing Corporate Social Responsibility in Action*: Ashgate.

Zadek, S. (2004). The Path to Corporate Responsibility. *Harvard Business Review, 82*, 125-.

Chapter 6
Belgium

Céline Louche, Luc Van Liedekerke, Patricia Everaert, Dirk LeRoy,
Ans Rossy and Marie d'Huart

Abstract Corporate Social Responsibility is a relatively recent concept in Belgium but there has been a significant increase in its awareness since 1995. In May 1997, a legal framework for sustainable development was set up in the country. In April 2006, the government adopted a Reference Framework for CSR which was followed in 2007 by the CSR action plan. In addition to governmental initiatives, the number of actors and fora involved in CSR matters has significantly increased, thus resulting in several CSR initiatives. However, it would be inaccurate to suggest that CSR is a well established concept or a popular practice in corporate Belgium. Indeed, CSR in Belgium offers great disparities and diversities.

Based on multiple sources of information, the paper provides a descriptive and narrative view of CSR in Belgium, gradually leading towards a reflection of its practice in the country towards the end of the paper. After a brief overview of the context for corporate social responsibility in Belgium, the paper investigates the different components that have acted to shape the idea of CSR since the 1970s. Subsequently, it explores how corporate entities in Belgium practice CSR. The chapter concludes by examining the progress that has been made to date in Belgium in the area of corporate social responsibility and its future prospects.

6.1 Introduction: Understanding the CSR landscape in Belgium

The field of Corporate Social Responsibility (CSR) is entering a phase of maturity globally today. The concept has moved beyond its US birthplace (Pasquero, 2005) and has spread all over the world, with an impressive upsurge during the last 10 years (Vogel, 2005). One just has to look at the exponential multiplication of the number of initiatives, platforms and networks, newspaper and journal articles, and events dealing with CSR[1] to appreciate its level of popularity.

---

[1] More than 45 million pages on the World Wide Web address dimensions of corporate social responsibility. Amazon lists 3,066 books on the subject. More than 1,000 corporations have

S. O. Idowu and W. L. Filho (eds.), *Global Practices of Corporate Social Responsibility*   125
© Springer-Verlag Berlin Heidelberg 2009

Although CSR is an internationally accepted concept, its conception and implementation have been through a series of national translation which have resulted in the burgeoning of a variety of practices (Chapple & Moon, 2005; Egri et al., 2004; Maignan & Ferrell, 2001, 2003; Maignan, Ferrell, & Hult, 1999; Maignan & Ralston, 2002). Some authors have argued that the understanding of CSR and the possibilities for CSR actions depend heavily upon prevailing national business systems including social, cultural, political and economic factors within a country (Campbell, 2007; Doh & Guay, 2006; Matten & Moon, 2008, Tempel & Walgenbach, 2007).

This paper explores the dynamics of corporate social responsibility in Belgium. Through an interplay among three interrelated yet separate components – actions (practices), meanings (concepts) and actors (agents) (Zilber, 2002) – CSR in Belgium has not only managed to remain in existence but has also become very important since 1995, leading to new or transformed approaches of business practice. This trend was formalised in March 2006 with the adoption of a governmental Reference Framework for CSR (ICSD,, 2006) and followed in February 2007 by the CSR action plan. Complementing this development was the increase in the number of actors involved in and platforms devoted to CSR. However, it would be overoptimistic to suggest that CSR is a well established concept and a set of standard practices in corporate Belgium. Indeed, CSR in Belgium offers great disparities and diversities.

This chapter provides a descriptive and narrative view on CSR in Belgium, gradually leading towards a reflection of its practice towards the end of the chapter. After a brief overview of the context in which corporate social responsibility operates in Belgium, the paper investigates the different components that have transformed CSR since its advent in the 1970s. Subsequently, the chapter explores how CSR is practiced by Belgian companies. Finally, the chapter concludes by examining the progress which has been made thus far in the area and its future prospects in corporate Belgium.

The paper relies mainly on multiple sources of information – both primary and secondary, including databases on CSR reporting and its performance, existing surveys and studies, as well as using observation-participation through the personal involvements of some of the authors.

6.2 The Belgian Context

Corporate Social Responsibility, as defined by the European Commission,[2] is quite a recent concept in Belgium but it has significantly increased in momentum over the last decade. Although, some early forms of it might have existed much earlier than

developed or signed codes of conduct governing dimensions of their social, environmental and human rights practices, and more than 2,000 firms report on CSR practices.

[2] As defined by the European Commission: 'A concept whereby companies integrate social and environmental concerns in their business operations and in their interaction with their stakeholders on a voluntary basis'. (Commission Green Paper 2001 'Promoting a European Framework for Corporate Social Responsibility', COM(2001) 366 Final).

that, its emergence in the country can be traced back to either the end of the 1980s or beginning 1990s. This development corresponds with the European CSR movement which started to diffuse around this period in Western societies (Habisch, 2005), just after the shift in the values of the 1960s and 1970s (Putnam, 2000). The development of CSR in Europe has been accompanied and stimulated by a general increase in concerns about ethics, heightened awareness of risk and risk management, the growth in media exposure concerning CSR and the rise of the NGOs which have increased the pressure on firms to be more responsible and accountable for the impacts of their actions on the society and environment.

Belgium is a small country with a high population density and with a very specific and unique institutionalised structure. It is a federal state; it is comprised of three communities (Flemish, French and German speaking) and three regions (Flanders, Wallonia and Brussels-Capital). While the Federal Government is responsible for all matters that, for technical and economic reasons, require a uniform national treatment, e.g. control of air pollution from mobile sources, the regions retain most responsibilities with regard to environmental and social policies. For example with regard to the environment, the regions determine objectives and formulate appropriate policy instruments and execute enforcement (O'Brien et al., 2001).

The Belgian business world is made up of a series of large companies and a very high number of SMEs. Some Belgian companies employ thousands of people worldwide, such as Inbev, the world's largest brewery group. However, majority of large companies are subsidiaries of foreign holding groups. SMEs are crucial to the Belgian economy: Belgian SMEs are the most profitable in the EU and Belgium is the only European country where the profitability of SMEs is considerably higher than that of large companies. Approximately 83% of Belgian companies have less than 10 employees and 97% of the companies employ less than 50 people. SMEs account for over 70% of its GDP.

CSR in Belgium is framed within a European and more specifically continental model of welfare state, where social considerations between social partners are anchored in the law, contrary to the Anglo-Saxon model. In these welfare states, governments tend to be heavy handed when dealing with certain issues. This means that the government is inclined to build a (legal) framework for issues such as CSR and sustainability

This is reflected in the legal basis for a sustainable development strategy and process that have been developed by the Federal Government. Belgium is one of the few countries (with Canada, Luxemburg, and Switzerland) with such a legal framework (Mazijn & Gouzee, 2007).

6.3 CSR Development in Belgium: The Institutional Framework

This section presents the Belgian legal framework and the government's perspective with regard to CSR as well as initiatives that have been taken by governmental and non-governmental organisations. CSR is the business contribution to sustainable development. Its development is intimately linked to the concept of sustainability. The institutional setting provides an influential framework for Belgian companies and therefore has a direct impact on the practices of the private sector.

1970: First embryonic form. The year 1970, saw the launch of Febecoop (Fédération belge de l'economie sociale et cooperative), a cooperative gathering of Belgian enterprises aiming at developing and promoting the Social Economy in Belgium. In its own way, Febecoop has been pioneering CSR in Belgium. It should be noted that Belgium has a long history of social economic activities. This has been recently re-emphasised by the government which is actively supporting this sector.[3]

1990's: Institutional embedding of sustainable development. Although the term 'sustainable development' was already present in the Belgian vocabulary in 1990 ('Duurzame Ontwikkeling' in Dutch or 'Développement Durable' in French), its understanding was essentially focusing on the environmental dimension, comparable to many other European countries at that time. A number of environmental legislations and initiatives had started to emerge at the end of the 1980s and the beginning of the 1990's, i.e. Vlarem I (1991), Vlarem II (1995) and Vlarebo (1995) in Flanders, and Bruxelles Environment-IBGE[4] (1989).

In 1997, Belgium set up its *legal framework for sustainable development* through the adoption of the Act of 5 May 1997 on the Co-ordination for Federal Sustainable Development Policy (Martens, 2003). This framework provides an institutional consultation and co-operation process within the different ministries in order to prepare, monitor and assess the federal sustainable development plan that has to be adopted by the federal government every 4 years. The act introduced a Federal plan for sustainable development and a Federal report on sustainable development. Within this framework, the Federal Council for Sustainable Development (FCSD)[5] was established as an advisory body to the federal government on sustainable development policies and as a forum to stimulate the debate amongst the representatives of the civil society. This council was set up in succession to the National Council for Sustainable Development which functioned from 1993. The act also established the Interdepartmental Commission for Sustainable Development (ICSD).[6] This platform consisting of representatives of all Ministers and ministries (called administrations) of the Federal Belgian Government, including representatives (no voting rights) of the three regions and communities is chaired by a government member (responsible for Sustainable Development) and is responsible for the drafting and implementation of the quadrennial federal plan for sustainable development which is discussed and adopted by the federal government. The first plan was adopted in 2000.

The act also commissioned the Federal Planning Bureau (FPB)[7] – a public institution that studies economic, social and environmental policy issues – to coordinate, together with the ICSD secretariat, the writing of this Federal Plan on sustainable

---

[3] For more information: www.socialeconomy.be

[4] Bruxelles Environnement-IBGE (Brussels Institute for Management of the Environment) is the environment and energy administration of the Brussels-Capital Region.

[5] Website: www.frdo-cfdd.be

[6] Website: www.icdo.be

[7] Website: www.plan2004.be

development.[8] The evaluation of the results of this plan is executed by the Task Force Sustainable Development within the BFP, which was created in January 1998.

Next to the governmental developments, were a number of *research organisations and CSR related platforms* created including academic research centres and NGOs and business networks (see appendix). Those platforms are highly influential both at the private and public levels. They are participating in the creation and diffusion of knowledge as well as in opinion forming.

2000: Institutionalisation of the CSR concept. The term Corporate Social Responsibility ('Maatschappelijk Verantwoord Ondernemen' in Dutch or 'Responsabilité Sociétale des Entreprises' in French) started to gain ground in Belgium, both in Flanders and in Wallonia in the late 1990s and the beginning of 2000s. An important factor that has helped with the diffusion of the concept has been the 2-year project called 'The Circle – Enterprise and Sustainable Development' organised by the King Baudouin Foundation (2000–2002). The project consists of monthly meetings between 13 Belgian companies to discuss the implementation of the sustainability concept into business practices. Next to these meetings the foundation also organised a series of conferences, 'The Millennium Conferences', with national and international speakers on very specific themes related to sustainability. The theme of the first conference held in November 1999 was 'Enterprises as model-makers in society'.[9]

The end 1990s–beginning 2000s was also marked with an *increasing and denser CSR network* including business, governmental, trade unions and not-for-profit organisations such as Business and Society Belgium, the Belgian branch of CSR Europe which has corporate members, and the multiplication of CSR initiatives such as Trivisi in 2001, a programme developed under the initiative of the Flemish Minister of Employment and Tourism (see appendix).

In 2001, the *Belgian Social Label*,[10] a voluntary scheme for companies, was approved by the Belgian government. The label offers companies the opportunity to acquire a label, which is granted to products that adopt the eight fundamental ILO conventions in their production processes. The label is granted for a maximum of 3 years by the Ministry of Economic Affairs after the approval of a Committee for Socially Responsible Production (composed of government officials, social partners, consumers and NGO-representatives). The Committee for Socially Responsible Production establishes a programme of control for the companies and monitors its progress on compliance.

The year 2000 was the wake-up call year from *employers' organisations* such as UNIZO[11] in Flanders, the Flemish organisation for the self-employed and SMEs, and the UWE[12] in Wallonia. Between 2003 and 2005 the UNIZO conducted a series of debates on CSR for and within SMEs. More than 300 Flemish SMEs

---

[8] From 2006 on the preparations for the Federal Plan are carried out by the federal administration for Sustainable Development (PODDO) together with the ICSD.

[9] Translated from the Dutch title: Ondernemingen als vormgevers in de samenleving.

[10] Website: www.social-label.be

[11] Unie van Zelfstandige Ondernemers, Website: www.unizo.be

[12] Union Wallonne des Entreprises, Website: www.uwe.be

participated in the project. This led to the publication of a report with best practice and a guideline for SMEs[13] in 2005. Although the project has ended, CSR has remained high on the agenda of UNIZO which tries to stimulate and facilitate its implementation within SMEs. At the same period UWE formed a Sustainable Development Working Group and developed in 2005 a set of 15 indicators to help companies to improve their sustainability performance. The indicators are organised around the three pillars of the sustainable development concept which are economic, social and environmental.[14]

2005: a more integrated approach to CSR. The period around 2005 was marked by a significant new turn and a move towards CSR mainstreaming.[15]

Before 2000 CSR was mainly approached through specific themes: diversity, social audit, the Belgian Social Label, social economy, and corporate governance. These are reflected in the CSR activities of organisations which often have a very particular focus. It was only in 2006, with the Belgian CSR reference framework, that *CSR was redefined in broader terms*:

> *Corporate Social Responsibility is a process in which companies voluntarily strive for improvement on a business as well as societal level by systematically including economic, environmental and social considerations in an integrated and coherent manner in the entire business operations, in which consultation with stakeholders, or interested parties of the company forms part of this process.* (ICSD, 2006)

By 2004, the *government had started to reinforce its support* for CSR by launching two Digital Knowledge Centres, one in Flanders (2004)[16] and one in Wallonia (2006),[17] and also by engaging in a major stakeholder dialogue. On April 28, 2006, the Council of Ministers adopted the *Belgian CSR Reference Framework*[18] which was established by a working group of de ICSD (ICDO/CIDD) through a written consultation process with a variety of Belgian stakeholders from various sectors – business, NGOs, trade unions, academics, etc. They were asked to reflect on the text of the framework and to give the government their thoughts about possible actions to be taken by government to further promote and implement CSR in Belgium. In parallel with the finalization of the CSR Reference Framework, the Interdepartmental Commission for Sustainable Development (ICDO/CIDD) further enhanced the

---

[13] The CSR guideline for SMEs – A socially responsible entrepreneur is a stronger entrepreneur (translated from the Dutch title De MVOGid voor KMOs-Een maatschappelijk verantwoord ondernemer is een sterkere ondernemer"), 2005. This guideline is the outcome of the project 'Tools for SMEs', and initiative of UNIZO-VORMING and Business and Society Belgium led by Commonsense.

[14] The 15 indicators are: (1) research and development, investments, profitability, corporate governance, growth; (2) training, work safety, health and working conditions, evaluation of the competences, quality of the social relationships; (3) energy, waste, and water eco-efficiency, environmental management system, mobility.

[15] A reflection of this change is the number of World Wide Web pages from Belgium mentioning corporate social responsibility. As of August 2007, there were more than 138,000.

[16] Website: www.mvovlaanderen.be

[17] Website: http://rse.wallonie.be

[18] Available at: www.cidd.be/FR/publications/plans_d_actions_spa_cifiques

dialogue with stakeholders in this process and organized a 2-day forum on CSR in April 2006. Based on the input given by the stakeholders, the working group then drafted the *first federal action plan on CSR* which was published on October 25, 2006. Those two documents have been important stimuli in the start of a broad social and national debate on the social responsibility of companies, governments and social actors in Belgium, and have gone even further in setting commitments from the governments in promoting and inspiring CSR in Belgium through 13 concrete actions. Actions range from the public supply chain, investments, to research and dialogue with stakeholders and transparency. Although broadly defined, those actions should lead in the very near future to the creation of new learning networks, information campaigns towards the consumers and the companies, research opportunities, behavioural changes within governmental institutions, as well as new regulations especially with regard to transparency.

Recently, another step has been taken to develop CSR even further, namely education. A number of governmental initiatives have been taken to understand better the needs with regard to CSR education and also to stimulate, support, and improve CSR education.

Government actions

- 1997: legal framework for sustainable development through the adoption of the Act of 5 May 1997.
- From 1997 to end 2006, the FCSD published some 130 advises on climate change, product standards, biodiversity, corporate social responsibilities, natural resources, energy, development cooperation, etc.
- The FPB has published and communicated three federal reports, the first in 1999, the second in 2003 and the third in 2005.
- The government has adopted two sustainable development plans, the 2000–2004 Plan and the 2004–2008 Plan. Now, the preparations for the Plan 2009–2012 have started for an adoption by the federal government in autumn 2008.
- An evaluation of the first federal plan showed that of the 622 measures identified in the plan, 71% had been followed up (mainly concerning energy, transport, ozone and climate), 14% had had no follow up (e.g. measures concerning competences that had been transferred in the meantime to other government levels than the federal ones) and no information was available for the remaining 15%.
- On 28 April 2006 adoption by the Council of Ministers of the Belgian CSR Reference Framework followed by the Federal CSR Action plan on 25 October 2006.

Source: Extracted and adapted from Mazijn & Gouzee (2007)

6.4 What are the Current CSR Practices in Belgium?

What are Belgian companies saying and doing about CSR? In this part, the chapter focuses on companies' CSR business practices. It looks at different aspects of CSR practices and builds on a variety of sources of information. The section initially investigates what companies are saying and doing with regard to CSR. The analysis is based on existing surveys. The second section examines the CSR reporting practices of Belgian listed companies. And the final section explores the CSR performance of the BEL 20 constituents based on the data provided by the social rating organisation Vigeo.

6.4.1 What do They Say and Do?

There is limited data available with regard to CSR practices in Belgium especially from SMEs. Three major studies have recently been carried out. The PASO survey of 2004 investigated the integration of CSR within 600 Flemish organisations from both the profit seeking and non-profit seeking sectors, based on a questionnaire (De Vos et al. 2004). The CSR Barometer from 2005 was based on telephone interviews with 128 companies from the three regions, Flanders, Wallonia and Brussels (Business & Society Belgium, 2005). This survey aimed at measuring the companies' awareness with regard to social and environmental issues. And the last survey, FEB 2007, explored the perception and practices of 250 Belgian companies, small, medium and large enterprises (FEB, 2007). The analysis of these three surveys shows some interesting characteristics of CSR practices in Belgium.

'Yes' to CSR but mixed feelings about its voluntary characteristics. According to the FEB survey (2007), more than 90% of the 250 companies interviewed consider that the purpose of companies goes beyond profit-making and should also include social and environmental aspects (FEB, 2007). This view is shared by companies of all sizes, small, medium and large. But Belgian companies are still far from integrating CSR at the strategic level. Bruggeman et al., (2003) argue that CSR needs to be inscribed in the core strategy of the company in order to achieve consistency and coherence in all the processes of the organisation and go beyond ad hoc projects (Bruggeman et al., 2003). The Paso survey investigates whether or not CSR has become a strategic element by examining the mission and ethical code of companies. Although some may doubt the validity that these elements are aimed at strategic integration, it was at this point that the most spread indicator was found. The results show that only 20% of the Flemish companies have the three CSR pillars – social, economic and environmental – as part of their mission and 29% have adopted an ethical code at the corporate level (De Vos et al., 2004).

The FEB survey (2007) also points out that more than 40% of the respondents believe that companies should not do more than what is prescribed by the law. Only 15% strongly agree that CSR requires going beyond what the law requires. Especially SMEs seems to disagree with the voluntary aspect of CSR (more than 50%).

This highlights a paradox: companies seem to recognise the importance of CSR but do not want to go beyond the law. As argued earlier, the CSR concept is based on the principle of voluntarism and 'beyond the law' (in reference to the European Commission's definition of CSR). This aspect has also been emphasised by the Belgian government in the CSR Reference Framework (ICSD,, 2006).

CSR is a voluntary engagement of companies. It therefore does not simply refer to meeting legal requirements, but precisely to initiatives and actions of companies, groups of companies or sectors, which surpass the applicable regulations. (ICSD,, 2006)

However, it is important to note that many SMEs do extraordinary things every day. Fighting for their place or niche in the market, entrepreneurs are extremely creative and responsive, inventive and risk-taking. The young ones are pushed by highly motivated personnel, increasingly sensitive to sustainable development and aware of the capacity for change that they possess. Here or there, outstanding 'pearls' are found – spin-offs changing their business model, integrating sourcing, energy, mobility, ethical, organic, fair trade, recycling considerations in their daily practices. Especially when they are organised in clusters, they can make scale economies, increasing their competitive advantage. The role of intermediaries and of public impulse at a regional scale is crucial to promoting innovation and increases the attractiveness of this matter.

A few examples: a transport company reviewing its fleet of trucks and modernising the logistics management to reduce traffic and improve the level of occupation both ways, a small company manufacturing and importing from China reusable bags made in environmentally and social-friendly conditions, a chocolate maker who opted for the healing approach of aliments and reviewed all the components of its chocolate to integrate bio and fair trade products, etc.

CSR most favoured domains. Although a more integrated definition of CSR has been adopted by the government (ICSD,, 2006), companies are still not giving equal attention to all aspects of CSR. The PASO study (2004) highlights that companies tend to focus on the 'social' pillar of CSR. In terms of concrete implementation both the PASO and FEB surveys show that companies implement CSR actions on a regular basis but with a strong emphasis on a few themes, namely employees' health and safety, waste recycling, staff training, and work/life balance. In the near future, one may expect an increasing attention to the energy issue. Issues related to human rights, North-South balance or more specifically to developing countries remain marginally addressed. This may be due to the limited exposure of Belgian firms to developing countries, as a large majority of the companies are very small companies. CSR issues addressed by companies are to a great extent sector related, e.g. companies in the chemical sector are more inclined to favour ISO 14000 and environmental measures, whilst those in the retail sector tend to focus on food safety and employee related issues.

Stakeholder dialogue – Communication and stakeholder engagement do not come out as a priority for Belgian companies, regardless of whether they are large or small enterprises. Communication is essentially oral rather than written (FEB, 2007) and CSR reporting remains limited. Reporting is an element of transparency and accountability; these are two key characteristics of CSR.

A majority of the companies do not engage on a regular basis with stakeholders. In case of engagement, the target groups are usually employees and customers (CSR Barometer, 2005 and FEB, 2007). Engaging with not for profit organisations such as environmental and social organisations is almost nonexistent. This lack of or only limited stakeholder dialogue stands in strong contrast to the definition of CSR, stating that companies have responsibilities towards all stakeholders that are directly or indirectly involved with the functioning of the company. Therefore CSR should *'take place in consultation and dialogue with the stakeholders'* (ICSD, 2006).

6.4.1.1 CSR: International Standards

There are more than 500,000 companies in Belgium, among which 149 companies are listed on Euronext Brussels, the only stock market in Belgium (as of December 2006). As of August 2007, 14 Belgian companies have signed the UN Global Compact, 8 are fully following the Global Reporting Initiative (GRI) guideline, 530 have the ISO 14001, 4 the SA8000, 8 are listed on the FTSE4Good Index, and 1 on the Dow Jones World Sustainability Index (see Table 6.1). The PASO survey (2004) shows that although there has been an increasing number of CSR-related organisations and companies' participation rate in CSR projects initiated by companies, still the rate remains below 10% (De Vos et al., 2004). Until now, the Belgian Social Label has also had a very limited implementation. As of 2007, only five products have received the label among which two have an expired date and did not renew the certification. However, the Belgian Social Label has been highly criticised for

Table 6.1 Belgian companies and international CSR commitments

	Initiatives	Number of Belgian companies/ sites involved	Total number of companies involved
Principles and initiatives	UN Global compact	14	2,900
	ETI	0	39
Reporting	GRI (between 2005 and 2007)	8	2,377
	AA1000 Assurance Standard	0	241
Certification/label	SA8000	4	1,315
	ISO 14001	530	887,770 (in 2006)
	EMAS	39 organisations 334 sites	3,725 organisations 5,587 sites
SRI indexes	DJSI World	1	310
	FTS4Good	8	NA
	ASPI	2	118
	Ethibel Excellence Europe	4	175
	Avanzi SRI Euro	4	119

being far from an economic reality, and with limited business relevance, making it difficult to implement.

Those figures support the results of the FEB survey (2007). Companies are aware of the existing international standards and guidelines but a majority are not ready or willing to use/implement them mainly because they lack information, the firms do not perceive a direct relevance for their business and they do not always have the resources (time and financial) to implement them.

Although those results present a rather negative image of Belgian companies with regard to international and widely recognised standards and guidelines, it is important to put them into perspective. First of all, Belgium is essentially made up of small companies and compared to many Anglo-Saxon countries it does not have many multinationals. Tools and guidelines such as UN Global Compact, GRI, SA8000 and many others are primarily addressed to large companies. It is therefore not surprising that a large majority of the Belgian companies do not use and implement them. If one looks at the total number of companies involved in those international standards, Belgium is performing not too badly, especially if one considers the size of the country and the number of large companies compared to other countries. For example, Belgian companies represent 0.5% of the worldwide signatories of the UN Global Compact. The same holds for SRI indexes. The Avanzi SRI Euro index is composed at 3–4% of Belgian companies, which is pretty high when one considers that those indexes only select the best in class stock quoted companies from the major regions of the world.

6.4.2 CSR Reporting

Companies have realized that they need to respond to the stakeholders not only by changing their practices, but also by *reporting* on what kind of actions they take in terms of their corporate social responsibility. Over the last years, we have noticed an increasing number of companies that make some efforts in CSR reporting. Also, in Belgium, the emphasis on CSR reporting has increased in the last 5 years, especially in the larger firms. In this section, we will address how CSR is reported by Belgian companies, look at the contents of CSR reports of Belgian firms and make a few remarks on the extent of CSR reporting in Belgium.

6.4.2.1 Methods of Communicating Information on CSR Activities in Belgian Corporates

The FEB survey (2007) shows that 60% of the companies investigated, communicate CSR matters mainly orally rather than in a written form. Next to oral communication is the issue of paper CSR reports, websites, newsletters and press announcements that are mostly used by large and medium-sized companies although not extensively, while SMEs tend to favour personal communication through direct mailing.

Companies are required by law to provide an *annual report* every year. Annual reports should provide a 'true and fair' view on the activities and financial results of the company. Annual reports are a powerful tool for shaping what is important in the company, and it is also considered as a significant source of accountability, that is publicly available. It is the place where management can include issues that are important for the stakeholders of the firm. The Belgian law with regard to the contents of annual reports does not require any specific information related to CSR issues.[19] The additional CSR reporting in the annual report is voluntary and purely a matter of corporate policy. However, it is interesting that the annual report usually includes more information than this strict minimum. Everaert et al. (2007) studied all annual reports of the listed firms at Euronext, Brussels (Belgium) and found that 60% of the companies disclosed information on CSR related issues in the annual report.

Since 2005 some large Belgian companies have started publishing *stand-alone CSR reports*, addressing only the areas of CSR, and provide it as an appendix to the annual report. Companies prefer to publish it on the same day as the annual report is published and this CSR report follows the same distribution channels as the annual report (freely downloadable or free paper version or version by post mail). For instance, Fortis, one of the largest financial institutions in Belgium, produced a CSR report in 2006, containing 58 pages. This report aims to provide the stakeholders with 'a complete and balanced picture of Fortis's performance in different areas of Corporate Social Responsibility', as mentioned in the Fortis Annual Report.

Content of CSR reporting in Belgium. As mentioned above, there are no legal requirements on CSR reporting in Belgium. However, companies report voluntarily and decide without any regulation on the contents of their CSR reporting. The common standard that is currently surfacing is the Global Reporting Initiative's (GRI). Everaert et al. (2007) used this GRI framework as a coding structure to investigate the content of the 2005 annual report of all 149 Belgian listed firms (Everaert et al., 2007). The results show that most companies (89%) mentioned policies or actions for employees in the pages that dealt with CSR. Examples of issues disclosed include employment diversity, training and education incentives, occupational health and safety investments. Two thirds of the listed companies reported on environmental issues (e.g. waste reduction of materials, energy, water, air pollution). About half of all listed companies reported on product responsibility, dealing with issues such as labeling, customer

---

[19] The minimum content of annual reports consists of financial statements, the audit report and the management discussion and analysis section. "The management discussion & analysis should address the results of the company, both containing the financial and non-financial performance indicators (that might be specific to the company), *including information on environmental and labour practices.*" (art. 96 and 116 W.Venn conform the Fourth European Directive, emphasis added.)

privacy, customer health and safety. Also, half of all the listed companies reported on societal dimensions of CSR, which dealt with community initiatives, anti-corruption, anti-competitive behaviour. Human rights aspects were rarely addressed (in only 5% of the annual reports).

Extent of CSR reporting in Belgium. The extent of CSR reporting has increased in the last 5 years, although there are marked differences in reporting among industries. Utilities (e.g. Electrabel and Fluxis, producers of electricity and gas) and banks (e.g. KBC, Fortis, Nationale bank) are more involved in CSR reporting (either as part of the annual report or as a separate CSR report). For instance, these companies used on average 2,500 words on CSR reporting in the 2005 annual reports (Everaert et al., 2007). Also listed firms in the food and chemicals industries report more extensively than other industries such as pharmaceuticals or electronics. Even within the listed firms, which are all large firms (more than 250 employees), the extent of CSR reporting (measured by the number of words) is correlated with the size of the company. The larger listed firms tend to report more elaborately on CSR than the smaller listed firms (Everaert et al., 2007).

6.4.3 Corporate Social Performance of the BEL20[20] Constituents

Corporate social performance (CSP) is an extension of the theoretical thinking on CSR and measures the firms' concrete CSR actions including policies, programmes and outcomes. Carroll (1999) has defined CSP as 'a business organization's configuration of principles of social responsibility, processes of social responsiveness, and policies, programs, and observable outcomes as they relate to the firm's societal relationships' (Wood, 1991).

Data produced by Vigeo, the French social rating agency founded in 2002 and which took over Stock at Stake of the Belgian social rating agency in 2005, offers insights into the CSP of the major Belgian companies.

Sample description – The Vigeo database contains the ratings of 16 Belgian companies between 1999 and 2006. However, there is no annual rating available for each one of the 16 firms. For the purposes of this analysis, two groups have been constituted: 1999+ and 2006–. The first group consists of the company ratings from 1999. In the absence of a rating for the relevant year, the 2000 rating was used. The second group consists of the company ratings from 2006. In the absence of a rating for a specific year, the rating for 2005 was taken. The 1999+ and 2006– groups are composed of 9 and 16 companies respectively (see Table 6.2). Companies from the sample cover 84% of the BEL20 constituents.

Vigeo's rating model is based on six major themes, namely: Human Resources, Human Rights, Environment, Customers and Suppliers, Community Involvement and Corporate Governance. Note that the theme Human Rights has been added in

---

[20]The BEL20 is the benchmark index of Euronext Brussels. Since March 1, 2007 it contains 19 companies.

Table 6.2 Sample description

Sectors	Number of companies	
	2006−	1999+
Materials	2	1
Food Retail	2	1
Banks	3	3
Financial Services – General	1	1
Utilities	1	1
Telecommunication Services	2	
Pharmaceuticals	1	1
Consumer Durables and Apparel	2	1
Mechanical Components and Equipment	1	
Food, Beverage and Tobacco	1	
Total	16	9

2004. For this reason, this criterion does not appear in the 1999+ data. In total, companies were assessed using 200 criteria.

For each of the themes three levels were looked at:

- Leadership: the role of management in institutionalising each stakeholder criterion into company policy and strategy
- Implementation: the programmes and actions undertaken by the company to put policy and strategy into real practice for each stakeholder criterion.
- Results: the degree, level and consistency of the realisation of policy and strategy and stakeholder satisfaction for each stakeholder criterion supported by quantified performance data.

Each criterion was rated on a scale of 100 points. Each criterion was applied in relation to its sector relevance and was given a weight (from 0 to 3) representing the relative importance of the social responsibility objectives relating to it (Vigeo, August 2007).

Peer theme: companies were also compared to their international sector peers based on a five-point scale: unconcerned, below average, average, advanced and pioneer.

Results: The analysis of the Vigeo data was structured according to three main questions:

1. How do Belgian companies perform on the six themes: Human Resources, Human Rights, Environment, Customers and Suppliers, Community Involvement and Corporate Governance? (see results in Table 6.3)
2. How do Belgian companies perform on the three levels: leadership, implementation and results?
3. How do Belgian companies perform compared to their sector peers on each of the themes? (see results in Table 6.4)

Table 6.3 How do Belgian companies perform on the six themes

	Data group: 2006−				Data group: 1999+			
	Inactive (%)	Reactive (%)	Active (%)	Pro-active (%)	Inactive (%)	Reactive (%)	Active (%)	Pro-active (%)
Human Resources	38	38	25	0	11	67	22	0
Environment	38	56	6	0	0	78	22	0
Customers and Suppliers	25	56	19	0	0	56	44	0
Corporate Governance	13	81	6	0	22	44	33	0
Community Involvement	25	44	31	0	0	67	33	0
Human Rights	19	56	19	6	NA	NA	NA	NA
Total	25	56	19	0	0	78	22	0

For question 1 and 2, a four-scale classification has been used from Inactive to Pro-active based on the Vigeo score. Comparative analyses were possible for questions 1 and 3, but not for question 2 as no data were available for 1999+.

Most of the companies from the sample were classified as re-active or inactive – meaning they received less than 50 points out of 100 – on the six investigated themes as well as on the three levels. Performance of the companies on the six themes tends to be rather similar. Nonetheless, Corporate Governance and Environment issues recorded the lowest performance, while Community Involvement and Human Rights got the highest score. Performance on Human Resources

Table 6.4 How do Belgian companies perform compared with their sector peers on each of the themes?

	Unconcerned (%)	Below average (%)	Average (%)	Advanced (%)	Pioneer (%)
Data group: 2006−					
Human Resources	6	38	25	31	0
Environment	0	38	56	6	0
Customers and Suppliers	6	31	50	13	0
Corporate Governance	13	38	50	0	0
Community Involvement	0	44	31	25	0
Human Rights	13	25	38	25	0
Data group: 1999+					
Human Resources	11	33	33	22	0
Environment	11	33	33	22	0
Customers and Suppliers	0	22	33	44	0
Corporate Governance	0	22	67	11	0
Community Involvement	0	44	56	0	0
Human Rights	NA	NA	NA	NA	NA

was quite dispersed with a large number of companies being reactive and inactive but it was also one the themes with the highest number of companies being active. When looking at the three levels, Customers and Suppliers and Human Rights themes both had very high results in terms of performance – 63% of the companies were classified as active on the results of customers and suppliers with 63% of the companies were classified as pro-active with regard to human rights results – but at the same time it showed a very weak performance on leadership and implementation. Overall the weakest level of the companies investigated was with regard to implementation.

The evolution from 1999+ to 2006− has tended to be negative as more companies fall under the categories of reactive and inactive. Performance on human resources, environment and community involvement have significantly decreased over time.

Compared to their sector peers, Belgian companies had an average score for most of the six themes. In 2006− as well as in 1999+ − three themes recorded the highest percentage of companies in the category 'below average', namely human resources (2006− and 1999+), community involvement (2006−) and environment (1999+). Only one theme, Customers and Suppliers got the highest number of companies in the 'advanced' group in 1999+ but this percentage dropped in 2006−. Although some companies have excellent results in human rights, when compared to their peers they are not above average. For both themes, Human Resources and Human Rights, companies are well distributed between 'below average', 'average' and 'advanced'.

6.4.3.1 Conclusion

From this analysis, we can conclude that the 16 Belgian companies in the sample are all part of the BEL 20, in most cases their score was below average compared with their international sector peers. They do not show any outstanding performance, either negative or positive on any of the six themes investigated. Although there are a couple of pro-active companies, especially in the Banking sector, in general they are characterised as reactive with even a few inactive ones. Moreover, we note a slight deterioration in the corporate social performance of the companies between 1999+ and 2006−.

However, the increasing reactive and inactive categories reflect the relative comparison in the performance of Belgian companies with regards to their sector peers. Overall, sectors represented by the Belgian sample have improved their CSR performance. The negative evolution of Belgian companies does not necessarily mean that Belgian companies are regressing but that they are progressing slower than their sector peers from other countries.

Surprisingly, the data show a high score with regard to Human Rights for most of the companies. This might be explained by the fact that Belgian companies have had limited activities in developing countries although this is changing. It is also interesting to note that the performance of companies on Corporate Governance has been downgraded between 1999+ and 2006 and this was at a time when Belgium published its Corporate Governance Code in 2004. And finally the performance on Human Resources is the most dispersed one out of the six themes with companies ranging equally between advanced and unconcerned. This is not surprising as this is a theme well covered and implemented by all the companies in Belgium. Most of the other themes have very limited data available, making the evaluation and comparison difficult.

6.5 CSR in Belgium: A Multi-faced Landscape

CSR is certainly a living concept in Belgium but its landscape is uneven and moving. One may argue that CSR is not a choice anymore, as a responsible business practice it is becoming an important driver of national and regional competitiveness (Zadek et al., 2005). However the shape it takes and the way it is implemented is open to variation. CSR in Belgium has taken its own specific route, how it will evolve is still uncertain, but it is there and is certainly there to stay.

When one looks back at the origin of CSR, as an (mostly) Anglo-Saxon response from the private sector to a need for the commitment to prevent corporate entities from taking advantage of the absence of regulations to behave irresponsibly towards their weak stakeholders and the environment, or to go further than the search for profit in zones and areas where an extra effort was very much conceivable, one easily understands why Belgian firms do not fit into the original CSR picture.

CSR in Belgium can be characterised as rather 'implicit' – as defined by Matten & Moon (2008), that is, it is embedded in the business–society–government relations within a political system rather than being explicit, that is, driven by the corporations' self interest (Matten et al., 2008). Already by 1997, the legal framework for sustainable development had been put in place to enable an institutionalised structure for a further development of CSR in Belgium. But it was not until recently that CSR is moving towards a Federal approach rather than a regional one. The 2006 CSR Reference Framework which was followed by the CSR Action Plan has brought a whole new dynamism into the CSR landscape in Belgium. Indeed, the three Belgian regions, Flanders, Wallonia and Brussels, have been following different paths with regard to CSR. Flanders has been the most active region launching initiatives and incentives to stimulate CSR, while Wallonia and especially Brussels have been somewhat slower in taking actions. But overall, the government has increasingly adopted CSR policies that will either stimulate or even regulate CSR activities of the corporate actors; although in the implicit form, the government has encouraged the voluntary aspects of CSR. Companies must not only be good citizens through the transparency of their activities and compliance, but they should go beyond this. Companies are expected to contribute to the social change as they are social agents themselves.

Such governmental position and a strong institutional framework may be applauded; nonetheless it may present some risks which may lead to CSR becoming a political battle field rather than an action field for good citizenship. For example the Belgian Social Label has never been successful and perhaps has a very little chance of becoming materialised.

Another Belgian characteristic is the very high density of small and extra-small companies and the limited number of multinationals that can be major drivers for CSR. They can play a vital role as change agents by supporting and inspiring CSR among SMEs. But large companies in Belgium are the exception rather than the rule. SMEs are facing a few hurdles with regard to CSR. Apart from the necessity to inculcate CSR tools and guidelines in everything they do, they are also required address issues which are probably mainly aimed at large companies. This makes it even much more difficult for them to go beyond compliance in a heavily regulated environment making things difficult for them due to the limited resources and the capacity available to do so.

This raises another point, namely the lack of data on CSR practices of Belgian SMEs which is one of the limitations of this paper. Using data from the annual financial and CSR reports of databases like Vigeo made us to concentrate our study on the few largest companies. In order to complete and fully understand the CSR landscape in Belgium, there is an urgent need to know more about the implementation and translation of CSR within SMEs. The data available shows that there are SMEs that have taken exceptional CSR steps. There are also many initiatives that have been put into practice in recent years in Belgium by SMEs. Over the last decade, various public and civil society organisations have tried to address the topic from the SME point of view, for instance these organisations have explained CSR from SMEs' perspectives, presented cases on the best practice, provided platforms to exchange experiences, provided free tools for pre-assessment, mini-audits, translating the international standards and norms into 'light-versions' adapted to their situation and context. More and more press articles, conferences, and research studies by scholars are addressing the implications of CSR to SMEs. But overall SMEs' involvements in the CSR field remain limited to a few groups of SMEs. A lot more actions and support are necessary in order to get a large number of SMEs to action the implementation of CSR policies and make a substantial change towards sustainability.

Overall, it may safe to suggest that CSR practices in Belgium among small and large firms will further spread and diffuse. Governments – both federal and local, and other stakeholders are increasingly exerting pressure and influence on the firms. CSR education is in full development in Belgium especially within universities and business schools. And the business community itself is not only interested in CSR but it is also taking concrete actions and initiatives which one hopes will be generally embraced by all.

Appendix

	Awards prizes	Tools	Initiatives	Research centers	Platforms/ networks	Governmental initiatives
1970						
1987				Centrum Centre for Economy and Ethics, Univ. Leuven	FEBECOOP	
1989						Brussels Environment-IBGE
1990					Flemish Discussion Platform for Sustainable Development	
1991					Ethibel	Law on information and protection for consumers and trade practices forbidding misleading advertising concerning the effects on the environment
1992				Impulse Center Business in Society, Vlerick Leuven Gent Management School		
1993						National Council for Sustainable Development
1995				Centrum for Sustainable Development, Univ. Gent		

Year	Awards prizes	Tools	Initiatives	Research centers	Platforms/networks	Governmental initiatives
1996				Belgian Institute for Governance		
1997				Centre d'Etude du Développement Durable, Free University of Brussels	Kauri Flemish Network for Business Ethics VOSEC	Federal Sustainable Development Policy Federal council for sustainable development Federal Council for Sustainable Development
1998	Best CSR report				Business and Society Belgium	Task Force Sustainable Development First Federal Plan
2000			Circle, King Baudouin Foundation (2000–2002) Trivisi		Network Conscientious Consumption	
2001	Prinses Mathilde Prize	Belgium Social label				
2002	Awards Prizes	Tools	Initiatives Trividend	Research Centers	Platforms Networks	Governmental initiatives Programmed Federal Public Service for Sustainable Development
2003	Plus Prize Enterprise (social economy)		CSR and SME debate (Unizo)		Belsif	Interdepartmental Commission for Sustainable Development Occupational pension law (SRI investment policy)

	Awards prizes	Tools	Initiatives	Research centers	Platforms/ networks	Governmental initiatives
2004		Code of Corporate governance: Code Lippens CSR evaluation indicators, Union Wallone des Enterprises			Digital knowledge center, Flanders	Second Federal Plan
2005	Gender friendly enterprises De Wit vos	Code of Corporate governance: Code Buysse CSR guidelines for SMEs (UNIZO) Guidelines for sustainable working relations (Trade Unions)	VKW Studies	Pôle ReSponsE, HEC Liège		
2006	Vlerick Angels Award The egg of CSR: Best CSR thesis	Guide for NGO-Business partnership Work and Environment (collaboration between three Flemish trade unions: ABVV, ACLVB, ACV) Sustainable Werken	DOEN project (CSR and education) Center for support for Sustainable development Fedis Commission for Sustainable Development	Daniel Janssen Chair in Corporate Social Respiribility, Solvay Business School	Centre of Excellence CSR and SME (Unizo) Digital knowledge center, Wallonia	Forum Days on CSR CSR Reference Framework- CSR Action Plan
2007	Solidaritest					
2008					Social Venture Network	Second Federal Plan

References

Bruggeman, W., Ameels, A., & Scheipers, G. 2003. *Strategisch besturen met de balanced scorecard*. Antwerpen: Maklu.

Business & Society Belgium. 2005. Le baromètre, C. S. R. *Business & Society Belgium Magazine*, Vol. 14: 6–11.

Campbell, J. L. 2007. Why Would Corporations Behave in Socially Responsible Ways? An Institutional Theory of Corporate Social Responsibility. *Academy of management Review*, 32(3): 946–967.

Chapple, W., & Moon, J. 2005. Corporate Social Responsibility (CSR) in Asia: A Seven-Country Study of CSR Web Site Reporting. *Business & Society*, 44(4): 415–441.

De Vos, A., Buyens, D., & Strobbeleir, K. D. 2004. Mainstreaming van maatschappelijk verantwoord ondernemen, *Panel Survey of Organizations in Flandesr (PASO)*. Katholieke Universiteit Leuven

De Vos, A., & Buyens, D. 2004. Mainstreaming van maatschappelijk verantwoord ondernemen, Panel Survey of Organizations in Flanders (PASO), Katholieke Universiteit Leuven and Hoger instiyuut voor de arbeid/Department TEW/Department Sociolgie.

Doh, J. P., & Guay, T. R. 2006. Corporate Social Responsibility, Public Policy, and NGO Activism in Europe and the United States: An Institutional-Stakeholder Perspective. *Journal of Management Studies*, 43(1): 47–73.

Egri, C. P., Ralston, D. A., Milton, L., Naoumova, I., Palmer, I., Ramburuth, P., Wangenheim, F., Fu, P., Hsun Kuo, M., Ansari, M., De la Garcia Carranza, M., Riddle, L., Girson, I., lenkov, D., Dabic, M., Butt, A., Srinivasan, N., Potocan, V. V., Furrer, O., Hallinger, P., Dalgic, T., Thanh, H. V., Richards, M., & Rossi, A. M. 2004. *Managerial Perspectives on Corporate Environmental and Social Responsibilities in 22 Countries*. Paper presented at the Academy of Management Conference Proceedings.

Everaert, P., Bouten, L., Van Liedekerke, L., De Moor, L., & Christiaens, J. 2007. Voluntary Disclosure of Corporate Social Responsibility by Belgian Listed firms: A Content Analysis of Annual Reports, *Working Paper*: Department of Accounting, Faculty of Economics and Business Administration, Ghent University.

FEB 2007. RSE: une dynamique à renforcer. Plutôt qu'à affaiblir! *Focus, n. 17, 10 Mai 2007*. Brussels: Federation of Enterprises in Belgium.

Habisch, A. J. J., Wegner, M., Schmidpeter, R. (Eds.). 2005. *Corporate Social Responsibility Across Europe*. Berlin: Springer.

ICSD. 2006. Reference framework: corporate social responsibility in Belgium.

Maignan, I., & Ferrell, O. C. 2001. Corporate citizenship as a marketing instrument – Concepts, evidence and research directions. *European Journal of Marketing*, 35 (3/4): 457–484.

Maignan, I., & Ferrell, O. C. 2003. Nature of corporate responsibilities: Perspectives from American, French, and German consumers. *Journal of Business Research*, 56 (1): 55–68.

Maignan, I., Ferrell, O. C., & Hult, G. T. 1999. Corporate Citizenship: Cultural Antecedents and Business Benefits. *Journal of the Academy of Marketing Science*, 27(4): 455–470.

Maignan, I., & Ralston, D. A. 2002. Corporate Social Responsibility in Europe and the U.S.: Insights from Businesses' Self-presentations. *Journal of International Business Studies*, 33(3): 497–514.

Martens, B. 2003. A legal framework for a federal sustainable development strategy. Pre-condition for effective sustainable development policy but not sufficient. The Belgian case.

Matten, D., & Moon, J. 2008. Implicit' and 'Explicit' CSR: A Conceptual Framework for comparative understanding of corporate social responsibility. *Academy of Management Review*, April 2008, 33 (2), 404–424.

Matten, D., & Moon, J. Forthcoming. Implicit' and 'Explicit' CSR: A Conceptual Framework for comparative understanding of corporate social responsibility. *Academy of management Review*.

Mazijn, B., & Gouzee, N. 2007. Making sustainable development reality. 10 years of Belgian federal sustainable development strategy: 18. Brussels: Federal Public Planning Service.

O'Brien, P., Carey, D., & Høj, J. 2001. Encouraging Environmentally Sustainable Growth in Belgium, *ECO/WKP (2001)26*: OECD.

Pasquero, J. 2005. La responsabilité sociale de l'entreprise comme objet des sciences de gestion: Un regard historique. In M.-F. Turcotte, & A. Salmon (Eds.), *Responsabilité sociale et environnementale de l'entreprise*: Presses de l'Université du Québec.

Putnam, R. D. 2000. *Bowling Alone: The Collapse and Revival of American Community*. New York: Simon and Schuster.

Tempel, A., & Walgenbach, P. 2007. Global Standardization of Organizational Forms and Management Practices? What New Institutionalism and the Business-Systems Approach Can Learn from Each Other. *Journal of Management Studies*, 44(1): 1–24.

Vigeo 2007. www.vigeo.com.

Vogel, D. 2005. *The Market for Virtue: The Potential and Limits of Corporate Social Responsibility*: Brookings Institution Press.

Wood, D. 1991. Corporate social performance revisited. *Academy of management Review*, 16: 691–718.

Zadek, S., Raynard, P., Oliveira, C., Nascimento, E. D., & Tello, R. 2005. Responsible Competitiveness: Reshaping Global Markets Through Responsible Business Practices, *Research Report*: AccountAbility.

Zilber, T. B. 2002. Institutionalization as interplay between actions, meanings, and actors: the case of a rape crisis center in Israel. *Academy of Management Journal*, 45(1): 234–254.

Chapter 7
Greece: A Comparative Study of CSR Reports

Nikolaos A. Panayiotou, Konstantinos G. Aravossis, and Peggy Moschou

Abstract The last few decades have witnessed an increase in the awareness on the part of corporate entities in Western democracies that they are morally obliged to give something back to the society. To demonstrate that they "care" about people and the environment they operate in, organizations have taken different courses of action. The corporate social responsibility (CSR) reports which are annually published, in addition to the traditional annual financial reports, are considered as one of the vehicles used to demonstrate how caring they have been during the financial period that has just ended and how they intend to continue to be even more proactive in the future. This study examines the adoption of CSR practices and looks at the CSR reports of many companies across different industries in Greece. The CSR disclosures are further classified and the results are analysed and interpreted in order to draw conclusions and to predict the future of CSR in Greece.

7.1 Introduction

The difficulties in defining precisely what corporate social responsibility (CSR) covers are in part reflective of the way in which this topic has developed. For some, it has grown out of community investment or corporate philanthropy with a clear emphasis on social improvements. For others, CSR has a much broader definition and is closely related to, perhaps a surrogate for, the sustainable development agenda launched at the UN Earth Summit in Rio de Janeiro in 1992.

The definitions of CSR can be categorized into three general ones according to three related views (Hancock 2005):

- The sceptic view: The sceptic view takes a cautious position and remains highly critical of CSR. According to this view, the most important purpose and social responsibility of companies are to provide as much wealth as possible to their shareholders, so the notion of CSR distracts them from their purpose of wealth creation and the benefits this has brought to millions of people.

- The utopian view: The utopian view of CSR reflects the idea that companies have a prior duty to anyone touched by their activity, their stakeholders rather than their shareholders, and especially the vulnerable, who may be exploited by the company's operation.
- The realistic view: The realistic view enjoys the greatest acceptance by scientists and practitioners as well. According to this view, CSR is the management of an organization's total impact upon both its immediate stakeholders and upon the society within which it operates. According to this view, CSR is not simply about whatever funds and expertise companies choose to invest in communities to help resolve social problems, but it is about the integrity with which a company governs itself, fulfils its mission, follows its values, engages with its stakeholders, measures its impacts, and reports on its activities.

In the past years, a positive move towards CSR reporting can be identified (Hancock, 2005). Following the recent revelation of corporate scandals in the US and other countries all over the world, it can be seen that there is an urgent need for ensuring a better and more ethical corporate behaviour. There are signs that the Management of companies believe that CSR can be connected with the achievement of improved financial results (Aravosis et al., 2006). A global CEO survey undertaken by PriceWaterhouse Coopers/World Economic Forum found that 70% of chief executives globally agree that CSR is vital to profitability (Fifth Global CEO Survey). In Western Europe, 68% of large companies report what has been coined the triple bottom-line performance (economic, social, and environmental factors) in addition to financial performance, compared with 41% in the United States (PriceWaterHouse Coopers 2002, BSI Global Research Inc. 2002). The Association of Chartered Certified Accountants has called for high-level corporate social and environmental disclosures.

It seems that the large international companies were the first to put trust in CSR. According to a Harris's (year) survey of 800 CEOs in Europe and North America, three out of four international corporations have a corporate reputation measuring system in place. Advocates of CSR reports have put forward some perceived benefits that an organization may derive from its provision (e.g., Crowther, 2003). Typical examples include increased customer loyalty, more supportive communities, the recruitment and retention of more talented employees, improved quality and productivity, and the avoidance of potential reputational risks that may arise from environmental incidents (Idowu and Towler, 2004). However, Cooper (2003) noted that the practical experience of early adopters of CSR reports was mixed. For example, instead of enhancing companies' reputation, CSR reports attracted adverse comments by drawing attention to divergences between the values espoused by the company and its actual behavior.

The rest of the paper analyses the CSR initiatives in Greek companies.

7.2 Research Methodology

We contacted all companies involved with CSR activities that publish CSR reports. In order to identify such companies, we contacted the following CSR organizations:

- Hellenic Network for Corporate Social Responsibility (CSR-Hellas): CSR-Hellas is a business-driven non-profit organization with the mission of promoting the meaning of CSR to both the business community and the social environment. CSR-Hellas has 96 members. It is one of the most active organizations promoting CSR in Greece.
- Centre for Sustainability and Excellence (CSE): The CSE is an advising and leading organization and a Think Tank, with offices in Athens, Brussels, and

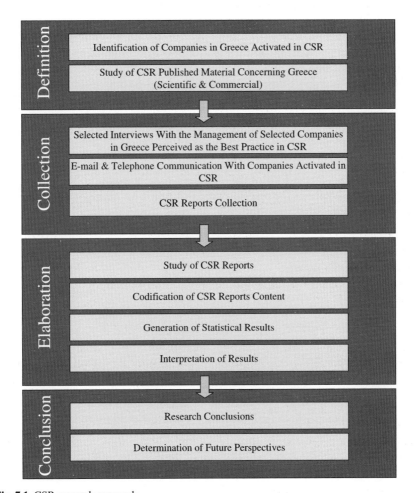

Fig. 7.1 CSR research approach

Dubai, specialized in CSR and sustainable development. Thirty-two members are registered with this organization.

- Eurocharity: Eurocharity is a non-profit company that donates 25% of its annual revenues to charity. It operates a comprehensive CSR directory in Greece. Thirty-five members are registered with Eurocharity.

Moreover, the CSR practices of companies listed in the Athens Stock Exchange were analysed.

Also, we contacted executives of selected companies that had participated in CSR-related conferences in Greece, in order to obtain an in-depth understanding of their CSR initiatives and obtain information concerning their latest CSR reports. As a result, we came into contact with executives from three international companies. The interviews we had worked as pilots and helped us to better understand the CSR reality in Greece.

One hundred and forty-eight companies with registered offices in different parts of Greece were contacted by telephone and/or e-mail in order to obtain information concerning their CSR practices, and 15 of the contacted companies were members of more than one CSR organizations. Our contacts permitted us to identify the companies disclosing CSR information by different methods. Interestingly, some of them offered to send us their organizations' annual reports or suggested putting us through to a more senior individual in the organization who might be able to help us.

In order to understand how the companies contribute positively to societal lives, the research analysis was designed to highlight the companies' disclosures in industries with insignificant impact on the environment, and we received information from 81 companies (about 55% of the organizations contacted).

Figure 7.1 summarizes the research approach followed, highlighting its distinctive phases and its related activities.

7.3 Research Findings

From the information received, it was found that 28 organizations report CSR results in Greece. These organizations have adopted two different ways of reporting CSR activities. Some organizations issue a stand-alone CSR report, while others devote a section in their corporate annual report for CSR activities.

Table 7.1 summarizes the identified methods used by companies for CSR reporting in Greece.

Another classification of the contacted companies was based on the organizational unit that is responsible for CSR issues. Three different practices were identified in Greece:

- A dedicated CSR department responsible for CSR: such a practice shows the importance placed in the CSR processes by the organization. In the case of Greece, 17 companies have a separate CSR department.

Table 7.1 Methods of CSR reporting of companies operating in Greece

Companies with stand-alone CSR reports	BP, Club Hotel Casino Loutraki, Coca-Cola Hellas, Cosmote Germanos, Hitachi, HSBC, Johnson & Johnson, Lloyds TSB, Piraeusbank, S&B, Shell, TIM, TNT, Toshiba, Vodafone, Titan, Athens International Airport, Hellenic Petroleum, Emporiki Bank, Opap, OTE, Friends Provident, Hellenic Exchanges, Italcementi Group
Companies embedding their CSR reports in the annual financial report	Alpha Bank, Siemens, Vivartia

- CSR processes carried out by the public relations department: such a practice implies that CSR is seen as an adjunct of public relations, a function of a company's external relationships, a peripheral activity, not something that needs to be embedded across the organization horizontally and vertically.
- CSR processes are carried out by another executive: similar to the above practice, this may imply that CSR is perceived as a peripheral activity, with small importance, limited to participating in social and economic regeneration initiatives and supporting the work of charities and voluntary bodies.

Table 7.2 presents the companies included in the above three categories.

Table 7.2 Organizational unit responsible for CSR processes

Companies with an independent CSR organizational unit	Companies that make the person in charge of public relations responsible for CSR	Companies that make another executive responsible for CSR
Alpha Bank	Club Hotel Casino Loutraki	Siemens
Cosmote	S&B	Emporiki bank
OPAP	TIM	Athens International Airport
Vodafone	Vivartia	
Piraeusbank	Italcementi Group	
Hitachi	OTE	
Coca-Cola Hellas	Hellenic-Petroleum	
Toshiba	Hellenic Exchanges	
TNT		
Titan		
Shell		
Lloyds TSB		
Johnson & Johnson		
HSBC		
Germanos		
Friends Provident		
BP		

Table 7.3 Classification of companies according to their range of activities

National companies	International companies	
Athens International Airport	Vodafone	Cosmote
TIM Hellas	Piraeus Bank	Titan
Club Hotel Casino Loutraki	Hitachi	Vivartia
Hellenic Exchanges	Toshiba	TNT
	Hellenic-Petroleum	BP
	HSBC	Friends Provident
	Italcementi Group	Shell
	S&B	Siemens
	Coca-Cola 3E	Germanos
	Lloyds TSB	OPAP
	Emporiki Bank	Johnson & Johnson
	OTE	Alpha Bank

The great majority of the companies that issue a CSR report are international companies, as shown in Table 7.3. This first approach shows that the companies that are more active in the field of CSR are those with a wider range of activities. It follows that international companies are more influenced by new trends and also they should demonstrate a good social and environmental behavior in order to be sustainable.

Another classification criterion of the companies was their status of ownership. Two different categories were recognized on the basis of this criterion: private organizations and public organizations. The first category includes all companies in which the majority of the shares belong to private individuals. The second includes all companies in which the majority of the shares belong to the state.

Table 7.4 Classification of companies according to the status of ownership

Private organizations		Organizations with governmental participation
Vodafone	Titan	Athens International Airport
Piraeusbank	Vivartia	Hellenic-Petroleum
Hitachi	TNT	OPAP
Toshiba	BP	
HSBC	Friends Provident	
Italcementi Group	Shell	
S&B	Siemens	
Coca-Cola 3E	Club Hotel Casino Loutraki	
Lloyds TSB	TIM Hellas	
Emporiki Bank	Germanos	
OTE	Johnson & Johnson	
Cosmote	Alpha Bank	
Hellenic Exchanges		

Table 7.5 Sector of operation

Sector of Operation	
Telecommunications	Vodafone, OTE, Cosmote, TIM Hellas, Germanos
Financial Services	Piraeusbank, HSBC, LlyodsTSB, Emporiki Bank, Friends Provident, Alpha Bank, Hellenic Exchanges
Logistics and transportation	Athens International Airport, TNT
Manufacturing	Hitachi, Toshiba, Siemens, Johnson & Johnson
Cement industry	Italcementi Group, Titan
Mining and metals	S&B
Refinery	Hellenic-Petroleum, BP, Shell
Distillery	Coca-Cola 3E
Dairies	Vivartia
Leisure and entertainment	Club Hotel Casino Loutraki
Public agencies	OPAP

Table 7.4 displays the fact that the majority of the organizations are private, which in combination with the above-mentioned facts leads to the conclusion that the companies that are innovative in CSR are those that belong to private individuals, and their activities surpass the borders of Greece. It is a little surprising that there are only three public organizations among those that issue CSR reports. Traditionally, public organizations intent to offer to the public more compared to the private ones. The fact that CSR is not so popular among public organizations may have its roots in the bureaucracy, which leads to slow adoption of new ideas.

Companies were further classified on the basis of their sector of operation. As shown in Table 7.5, companies that publish CSR reports in Greece belong to 11 different sectors: telecommunication, financial services, logistics and transportation, industry, cement industry, mining and metals, refinery, distillery, dairies, leisure and entertainment, and public agencies. Most companies that issue a CSR report belong to the financial services sector. The telecommunications and manufacturing sectors follow.

Our research also shows that the companies that issue CSR reports are big companies in terms of the number of employees they have. It can be seen that

- Eighteen companies have 700–50,000 employees
- Two companies have 50,000–100,000 employees
- Three companies have 100,000–150,000 employees
- Four companies have 150,000 and above employees

For one company (OPAP) we do not have information of its size.

The medium price of the size of companies is: $\mu = \Sigma xi/n \Rightarrow \mu = 73,455$ employees and he mean square deviation is $s = 118,515.62$ employees. The number of employees of the recognized companies is presented in Fig. 7.2.

The CSR reports of the above companies were examined in order to identify the CSR performance measures each company uses. The lack of standards and the fact

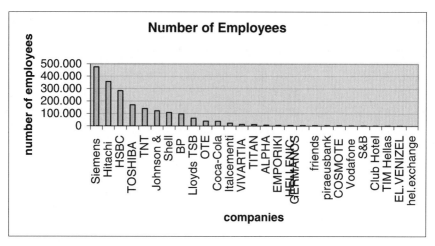

Fig. 7.2 Number of employees in Greek companies that publish CSR reports

that the report has no defined audience but is aimed at the world at large have led to a wide variation in what is reported. In order to overcome this problem, an attempt was made to categorize the CSR behaviour of the companies in Greece according to the categories that were more common among the CSR reports published by the companies. Care was taken to define the categories compatible with those identified in the literature.

The analysis of the results revealed eight distinctive categories of CSR performance measures mostly used (in an informal way) by companies operating in Greece. These categories are

- Economy
- Internal business processes
- Learning and growth
- Environmental impact
- Human resources
- Society
- Market place
- Health and safety

Then by studying each company, CSR performance measures were evaluated for each category. Table 7.6 summarizes the most relevant statistics concerning the performance measures used. It must be noted that these performance measures were not always expressed directly in the report of the companies, but in many cases they were implied in the relevant paragraphs of the CSR reports.

According to the studied companies, the category that seems to be of vital importance is the "environmental impact" of the companies (12 out of 28 companies have more measures in this category than in any other, and the total percentage of indices belonging to this category is 26.4%, which is the largest).

Table 7.6 Number of companies' performance measures in each CSR category

	Economy	Internal business processes	Learning and growth	Environmental impact	Human resources	Society	Market place	Health and safety	Total
Vodafone	4	7	6	16	11	24	11	6	85
Piraeusbank	6	14	7	25	14	6	3	1	76
Athens International Airport	5	0	3	10	13	15	5	9	60
Hitachi	4	2	4	22	5	11	7	3	58
Toshiba	6	1	3	17	7	5	9	2	50
Hellenic-Petroleum	5	0	3	11	13	5	0	12	49
HSBC	5	0	6	18	3	7	2	4	45
Italcementi Group	7	2	4	10	8	6	2	4	43
S&B	0	6	5	11	7	5	0	7	41
Coca-Cola Hellas	0	3	2	16	5	5	5	5	41
Lloyds TSB	6	1	5	10	6	3	4	4	39
Emporiki Bank	2	6	3	9	10	4	3	1	38
OTE	2	1	2	3	5	17	2	6	38
Cosmote	5	2	2	7	6	10	1	1	34
Titan	2	0	5	17	1	6	0	3	34
Vivartia	7	6	2	7	4	3	5	0	34
TNT	6	1	3	7	6	4	2	3	32
BP	1	0	4	10	4	5	1	5	30
Friends Provident	1	1	2	12	5	5	1	0	27
Shell	4	0	4	8	2	3	1	4	26
Siemens	10	0	2	2	2	7	1	1	25
Hellenic Exchanges	0	2	3	0	7	10	0	2	24
Club Hotel Casino Loutraki	4	0	2	0	1	15	1	0	23
TIM	1	0	3	6	0	7	0	0	17
Germanos	1	1	2	3	4	3	2	0	16
OPAP	1	1	3	0	8	1	1	1	16
Johnson & Johnson	1	0	2	0	0	9	0	1	13
Alpha Bank									
Total per category	96	57	92	257	157	201	69	85	1,014
Different performance measures	20	24	12	80	52	57	30	28	303
Percentage (%)	6.60	7.92	3.96	26.40	17.16	18.81	9.90	9.24	

Then follows the category of "society", which was the first category in the number of measures of eight companies. The total percentage of indices belonging to this category is 18.81%.

Three companies have more indices in the category of "human resources", and the total percentage of indices belonging to this category is 17.16%. One company has more indices in the category of "economy", and the total percentage of indices belonging to this category is 6.6% and this category is seventh concerning the total percentage of indices.

Fourth and fifth in terms of the total percentage of indices come from the categories of "market place" and "health and safety" with 9.90% and 9.24%, respectively, of the total indices.

Sixth is the category of "internal business processes" with 7.92%, seventh as mentioned above comes the "economy" with 6.60%, and the last the category of "learning and growth" with 3.96% of the total indices.

The company with more indices in total is Vodafone with 85 indices. Second comes Piraeusbank with 76 indices and third the Athens International Airport with 60 indices.

An important finding of the analysis is the very large number of different performance measures used by the companies disclosing CSR information. More specifically, 303 different performance measures were reported in total. This result implies that there is no clear and consistent approach of CSR performance measurement of the different companies. The existing influences of several international and local organizations by different performance measurement frameworks and initiatives might be a reason for the large number of indices used, which cause confusion to the reader instead of helping him/her to have a clear view and identify what to look for in a 'normal' CSR report.

Below, the two most frequent CSR performance measures for each one of the eight categories are presented, in order to provide a clearer view of the criteria used by companies to assess themselves in CSR in Greece.

7.3.1 Economy

- Total annual revenues (€): Total annual revenues give a good quantitative measure that concerns the shareholders and the society as a whole. A company with large total annual revenues constitutes a powerful company of high potency, which implies that it would be a good investment for the shareholders. As far as the society is concerned, high total annual revenues of a company imply many work positions thereby reducing unemployment and providing the government with more taxes.
- Total sum of taxes of all types paid to the government: This is also a quantitative measure that concerns the society. More taxes would help the government implement its programs for the betterment of the quality of life of the citizens.

7.3.2 Internal Business Processes

- Risk analysis: Risk analysis is a good tool for risk management. It is a qualitative measure that concerns stakeholders such as the employees, employers, and the whole company. With risk analysis, the activities of high risk are detected and then the management of these risks is accomplished. Through this analysis, employee accidents are avoided or minimized and so do loss of products and machinery. Thereby, the risk of accidents, operational costs, and costs of lost working hours are minimized.
- Existing corporate standards for quality management systems: The standards that a company has for its quality management systems is another qualitative index that concerns the whole management of the business and the quality of the products or the services that it offers to the customers. Through adherence to standards, constant quality of the products or the services can be achieved that would lead to systematic and efficient approach of CSR.

7.3.3 Learning and Growth

- Member of national or international organizations specialized in CSR: The involvement of a company in national or international organizations specialized in CSR promotes the learning and growth of the company concerning CSR. A company that follows this practice is better informed in subjects relevant to CSR, and has the opportunity to exchange examples of good practices, ideas, and experiences. This also includes a qualitative measure of the concern for all the stakeholders, as a company well informed in CSR would try to apply the best practices for its stakeholders and would learn from the good and bad practices of others.
- Existence of external auditors: Though the existence of external auditors a company can have an objective assessment of its performance, which is the key to improvement of the quality of the products and services offered and the management systems. This is a qualitative index that could also become quantitative if the percentage of activities and systems audited by external auditors is mentioned and depending on who these auditors are (from which companies, sectors of activity, etc.).

7.3.4 Environmental Impact

- Total water use: The consumption of water should be treated with high concern, as water is a vital ingredient of life. Therefore, the total water use is a quantitative measure that provides us with information about the degree of responsibility a company shows in the protection of the environment.

- Consumption of alternative sources of energy: Use of alternative sources of energy is the key to solving the problem of increasing energy needs of the society, which also minimizes the use of oil that leads to global warming. The use of alternative sources of energy is a quantitative indicator of the environmental concern of a company.

7.3.5 Human Resources

- Total number and rate of employee turnover by age group, gender, and region: A company that tries to treat its employees equally should not make discrimination based on age, gender, or region. Therefore, a good quantitative measure of equal treatment to all employees is the total number and rate of employee turnover by age group, gender, and region.
- Number of employees that attend training programs: Equal treatment should be met also in education. Educational and training programs to all employees improve their skills and qualifications in order to have more opportunities for career growth and better performance at work. The number of employees that attend training programs broken down in terms of the level of education of the employees and by gender is a quantitative index of the degree of care of the company takes in the education of its employees.

7.3.6 Society

- Local donations: An organization should also take care of the local society in order to be sustainable. A popular performance measure related to the interest of companies in local societies, among the companies that issue a CSR report in Greece, is the local donations it makes. This is not only a quantitative index but also a qualitative one, because in the CSR report both the amount of money spent on donations and the content of these donations.
- Number of employees taking part in volunteer programs: The number of employees taking part in volunteer programs is another quantitative measure of the social performance of a company. By promoting volunteer action, a company fosters the spirit of good social performance and the interest about other citizens among its employees.

7.3.7 Market Place

- Number of complaints: The number of complaints is a quantitative measure of the customer satisfaction. Fewer customer complaints about products and services are translated into more successful fulfillment of real customer needs. The

Table 7.7 Summary of CSR findings in Greece

Issues	Findings
Number of companies active in CSR issues in Greece	81
Number of companies found to publish a CSR Report in Greece	28
Number of companies in Greece	More than 800,000
Number of companies listed in the Athens Stock Exchange	310
Most frequent method of CSR reporting	Stand-alone CSR Reports (25/28)
Size of companies	79,031 employees
Scope of operation	International (24/28)
	National (4/28)
Ownership	Private sector (25/28)
	Extended public sector (3/28)
Number of companies with CSR reports listed in Athens Stock Exchange or in other Stock Exchanges	28/28
Dominating industrial sectors	Financial
	Communications
	Petroleum/refinery
	Manufacturing
Recognised CSR categories	Economy
	Internal business processes
	Learning
	Environmental impact
	Human resources
	Society
	Marketplace
	Health and safety
Dominating organisational unit responsible for CSR	CSR Department
	Department of public relations
Number of different performance measures used	303

disclosure of such a measure shows the importance that an organization places on its market.

- Cooperation with suppliers who are reliable and have a good reputation: The reliability of the suppliers and their good reputation is a qualitative as well as a quantitative measure, as it cannot be fully measured with any objective criteria. A reliable supplier is one whose product price matches with the product quality, who is punctual with the supplies, who uses standards for the quality management systems in his business, and who is interested about the CSR performance of his business.

7.3.8 Health and Safety

- Valid and timely information to the society on subjects relevant to health and safety: A CSR-responsible company should care about the health and safety of the society. An index that companies in Greece use for measuring the health and safety of the society is the valid and on-time information to the society on subjects relevant to health and safety. This is a qualitative and quantitative measure, as it indicates not only the quality and the validity of the information provided to the public, but also the number of times prompt information has been provided to the society whereby grave consequences were averted.

- Total number of employee accidents: A very usual measure of health and safety of employees is the total number of employee accidents. This is a quantitative index of the performance of a company in ensuring health and safety of its employees.

Table 7.7 summarizes the results of the study concerning the CSR practice in Greece as revealed by the contents of the CSR Reports of the analysed companies.

7.4 Conclusions

Despite the diversity of the companies and the CSR material selected for investigation, it does seem possible to draw some tentative conclusions about CSR practice in Greece.

First, the penetration of CSR in Greece is definitely small so far, a fact proved by the small number of published CSR reports and the small number of companies participating in organizations active in CSR issues. However, there are indications in the Greek market (identified by personal interviews with CSR experts in Greece) that it will increase in the coming years.

Second, CSR does not appear to be a systematic activity. To the extent that it is not covered by regulations, social disclosure seems to vary in popularity in the subjects to which it gives attention and in terms of the organizations that provide such disclosure.

A third conclusion of the study in Greece concerning CSR is that its adoption by the companies does appear to be related to certain 'demographic' characteristics. In particular, the following trends were found:

- The size of the company plays an important role in its CSR orientation. It is found that large international corporations constitute the majority of the organizations in Greece that publish CSR reports and disclose CSR-related information in a systematic way. The parameter of international operation is considered as very important, revealing that there could be a significant correlation between CSR orientation and the origin of ultimate ownership of the company. This last issues demands further research in the future.
- There is some evidence that the sector of operation affects the degree of CSR adoption. Companies operating in financial services, telecommunications, and the petroleum sector show a much higher penetration rate compared to all the other sectors. It would be very interesting to further examine the reasons for the behaviour of these sectors.

The classification of performance measures used by companies was a very difficult process in our study. The number of the identified performance measures proves the existing degree of complexity and highlights the lack of the following:

- A commonly understood definition (within and across companies)
- A common set of benchmarks to measure the attainment of CSR
- Formal established processes in place to achieve these benchmarks
- A system of internal auditing of the CSR processes
- A system of external verification by accredited bodies

It has to be stated, however, that the fact that companies are beginning to accept that they have to be accountable in some form for their wider impact on society is a significant step. The methodologies behind these social reports may be poor and their terms of reference self-serving for the company, but the commitment is an important one. As the concepts of CSR become more clear and specific, companies will become more sophisticated in their social reporting.

Finally, CSR does not appear to be related to profitability in a documented quantitative way. This finding is not surprising, taking into account the abstract framework of the performance measures.

It is understood that there could be other parameters that might affect the degree of CSR orientation of companies in Greece that cannot be depicted in CSR reports. These include capital intensity (Belkaoui and Karpik, 1989), age of the corporation (Roberts, 1992), and such matters as strategic position, senior executives' attitudes and the existence of a social responsibility committee, or a dedicated organizational unit in CSR.

In sum, our empirical study suggests that CSR in Greece is in its infancy phase. Its adopters are mainly large international companies; however, there are aspects of developments in disclosure practices. Some of the companies seem to believe in CSR concepts, others are just following the best practices, and some appear to use the report as a public relations exercise. CSR reporting needs further improvement, and the information it contains needs to be standardized. Taking into account that there is an increasing number of companies in Greece that are truly concerned about the environment, resources, quality of life, and social matters but are not yet aware of CSR principles, it is believed that the example of CSR reporting by the large and successful companies as well as official encouragement of social responsibility by the Greek Government in the future will lead the way towards a conscious and responsible behaviour of companies operating in Greece.

References

Aravossis K. G., Panyioutu N. A., and Tsousi K. 2006, A Proposed Methodological Framework for the Evaluation of Corporate Social Responsibility *In*: K. Aravossis, C. A. Brebbia, E. Kakaras, & A. G. Kungolos, eds. *Environmental Economics and Investment Assessment*, Southampton UK, WIT Press, pp. 87–95.

Belkaoui A. and Karpik P. G. 1989, Determinants of the Corporate Decision to Disclose Social Information, *Accounting, Auditing & Accountability Journal*, Vol. 2, No. 1, pp. 36–51.

BSI Global Research, Inc. 2002, *Innovation is the Leading Competitive Advantage of Fast Growth Companies*, PriceWaterhouse Coopers "Trendsetter Barometer", 24 June 2002, New York, pp. 1–5.

Cooper B. 2003, *Corporate social responsibility: the Holy Grail?* Chartered Secretary, pp. 12–16.

Crowther D. 2003, Corporate social reporting: genuine action or window dressing?, In: D. Crowther, and L. Rayman-Bacchus, eds. *Perspectives on Corporate Social Responsibility*, Ashgate, Aldershot, pp. 140–160.

Hancock J. 2005, *Investing in Corporate Social Responsibility – A Guide to Best Practice, Business Planning & the UK's Leading Companies.* London: Kogan Page Ltd.

Idowu S. O. and Towler B. A. 2004, A Comparative Study of the Contents of Corporate Social Responsibility Reports of UK Companies, *Management of Environmental Quality: An International Journal*, Vol. 15, No. 4, pp. 420–437.

PriceWaterHouse Coopers 2002, *Uncertain times, Abundant Opportunities*, Fifth Annual PricewaterhouseCoopers Global CEO Survey.

Roberts R. W. 1992, Determinants of Corporate Social Responsibility Disclosure, *Accounting, Organizations and Society*, Vol. 17, No. 6, pp. 595–612.

Chapter 8
Russia: Corporate Social Disclosures

Ataur Rahman Belal & Vasily Lubinin

Abstract This chapter aims to expand the existing CSD literature by providing insights from current Russian CSD practice, which is believed to be an under researched area. The main objective here is to examine the extent of CSD in Russia. For this purpose content analysis of 2004 annual reports of 20 large companies which are listed on the Russian stock exchange was undertaken. The key findings show that 18 (90%) out of the 20 companies included in the study made some social and environmental disclosures. Employee related disclosures are the dominant category with 90% of companies making some form of disclosures in this category. In addition, 85% of companies made some form of environmental disclosures while only 55% of companies made ethical disclosures. According to this study, the quality of disclosure is generally poor due to lack of external verification and lack of completeness. Although it is more likely that in the future, pressures will be brought to bear on Russian companies to engage in more transparent and accountable CSD practice, still very little optimism for improvement can be expressed here. This is mainly due to lack of mandatory requirements for CSD in Russia and also to some extent due to the absence of strong NGOs and other pressure groups who can exert effective pressures on Russian companies to improve their CSD practice.

8.1 Introduction

Corporate social disclosures (CSD) involve external reporting of social, ethical and environmental information by the companies. A recent definition of social accounting and reporting is given below which emphasises the importance of stakeholder accountability as the principal objective of social accounting:

"The preparation and publication of an account is about an organisation's social, environmental, employee, community, customer and other stakeholder interactions and activities and, where possible, the consequences of those interactions and activities. The social account may contain financial information but is more likely to be a combination of quantified non-financial information and descriptive, non-quantified information. The social account may serve a number of purposes but discharge of the organisation's accountability to its stakeholders must be the clearly dominant of those reasons and the basis upon which the social account is judged". (Gray 2000, p. 250)

During the 1980s and early 1990s companies mainly disclosed social and environmental information via their annual reports. However, in recent times companies are increasingly disclosing social and environmental information via separate stand alone reports and websites while the trend of reporting (via annual reports) continues. The phenomenon of increased social and environmental disclosures (via separate reports and website) is not unexpected given the pressures brought to bear on the companies throughout the world for enhanced social and environmental accountability.

The content analysis of social and environmental disclosures made within annual reports has held a long tradition within the CSD literature (Owen 2004). However, prior CSD studies mainly concentrated on Western Developed countries (Belal and Owen 2007). There are only few studies available from the context of developing countries (Belal and Owen 2007) and none, as far as we know, on Russia. The purpose of this chapter is to fill that gap in the literature. The main objective here is to examine the extent of CSD in Russia. This objective will be achieved by undertaking a content analysis of social and environmental disclosures in selected Russian companies' annual reports (see Tables 1 and 2).

Russia is one of the BRICs (Brazil, Russia, India and China) countries which are likely to become a major economic power alongside United States of America by 2050 (Wilson and Purushothaman 2003). With this massive predicted economic growth in Russia the issue of corporate social responsibility and its reporting are becoming very important. Currently, there is a shortage of published academic materials on Russian CSD. This exploratory chapter is motivated by a desire to provide insights on Russian CSD.

The chapter proceeds with a discussion of prior literature on CSD in the second section. Here the focus of discussion will be mainly on developing countries while studies of developed countries will be discussed briefly for the sake of completeness. This is, then, followed by a brief examination of the Russian socio-economic context. The fourth section of the chapter reports the research procedures adopted in this study followed by the presentation of findings in section five. The final section offers discussion and conclusion.

8.2 Prior Studies on CSD

As noted earlier, exploration of corporate motivation via content analysis of social and environmental disclosures within the annual reports has been a dominant research tradition within the CSD literature. In their pursuit of understanding motivations behind social and environmental disclosures researchers have used various theoretical lenses. Prominent amongst those theories are the Political Economy Theory [PET], the stakeholder theory and the legitimacy theory. Most of these studies were conducted from the context of Western developed countries (Belal and Owen 2007). However, there are few descriptive studies which are available from the context of developing countries which are more relevant to the current study and are being discussed in this section. Before that we have briefly reviewed the principal theories used by the previous researchers to examine CSD.

PET argues that social and environmental disclosures need to be analysed in the social and political context in which those disclosures take place. PET enables to widen the analysis in an attempt to 'introduce wider, systemic factors into the interpretation and explanation of the CSD phenomenon' (Gray et al. 1996, p. 47). From the normative perspective, the stakeholder theory argues that corporations should be responsible to all relevant stakeholders irrespective of their power to influence corporate activities. However, using the legitimacy theory researchers found that corporations used CSD as a strategy to negotiate their relationship with powerful stakeholder groups in society. Sadly, these negotiations take place often at the cost of the less powerful stakeholders (Belal 2002; Belal and Owen 2007). These theories are not mutually exclusive. Given the complex nature of CSD, it is argued that the use of multiple theories could help to develop a more robust and richer explanation of CSD practices (Gray et al. 1995b).

CSD studies have grown in size over the last thirty years (Gray 2001). As noted earlier, most of these studies were conducted from the context of the Western developed countries (see for example, Adams et al. 1998; Adams and Kuasirikun 2000; Deegan and Gordon 1996; Deegan et al. 2002; Gray et al. 2001, 1995b; Harte and Owen 1991; Zeghal and Ahmed 1990). It is neither possible nor is it the intention of this chapter to review all of these studies here. Most of the early studies of CSD attempted to determine the extent of disclosure and the factors which explain CSD practices. Such factors include corporate size, industry affiliation, country of origin and profitability. Many studies particularly confirmed the positive relationship between corporate size and CSD indicating that larger organisations are more likely to undertake CSD for the reasons of their political visibility and resources available at their disposal. Although currently there is no conclusive evidence to support the relationship between CSD and profitability, research studies have generally supported the relationships between CSD and industry affiliation and the country of origin.

While most of the above studies were conducted from the context of developed countries few studies are available from the context of developing countries as well (Andrew et al. 1989; Belal 2000, 2001; Singh and Ahuja 1983; Tsang 1998). One of the earliest studies on CSD in developing countries was undertaken by Singh and Ahuja (1983) from an Indian perspective. They studied social disclosures of 40 public sector companies for the year 1975/76. The main findings of the study showed that 40% of the companies made disclosures on various social and environmental matters. Belal's studies (2000, 2001) of social and environmental disclosures in Bangladesh showed that 97% of the companies made some form of employee related disclosures while 90% of the companies made some form of environmental disclosures. His study was based on 30 annual reports of Bangladeshi companies related to the year 1996. Both of Belal's studies conclude that quantity and quality of disclosures were poor. Andrew et al.'s (1989) study from the Malaysian and Singaporean perspective found that only 26% of the companies disclosed social information with employee related disclosures as the main theme. In a longitudinal study of CSD in Singapore over a period of 10 years from 1986 to 1995 Tsang (1998) revealed that out of the 33 companies included in the study 52% made social disclosures. This study also confirmed the popularity of employee category being the highest disclosed category. The above examination shows that content analysis studies of CSD in developing countries mainly concentrated on the Asian economies. There is no such study from the Russian context. It is expected that this study will contribute to the CSD literature by providing a Russian perspective of CSD.

8.3 Russian Socio-Economic Context

As may be seen from the Russian Profile provided in Appendix 1 Russia is one of the fastest growing economies of the world with an economic growth rate of 6.7% and with a per capita income of US$ 12,200. With the fall of the Soviet Union and its communist regimes in the 1990s the current Russian Federation moved from the centrally planned economic system to the principles of market economy. Russia's major part of export earnings come from oil, gas and mineral resources.

In geographic terms Russia is the largest country in the world with an area of 17.07 million square kilometres and a population of 141.38 million which has a nearly 100% literacy rate. Principal social and environmental issues in Russia include HIV/AIDS, human rights, industrial pollution and corruption. Russia is one of the countries of the world which has highest growth rate in HIV infection (https://www.cia.gov/library/publications/the-world-factbook/geos/rs.html, accessed on 10th August, 2007). Human rights have been a major problem and have become worse in recent years. Industrial pollution, particularly air pollution from the heavy industries, appears to be one of the current environmental issues in Russia (https://www.cia.gov/library/publications/the-world-factbook/geos/rs.html, accessed on 10th August, 2007). Corruption is believed to be widespread and in 2006 Corruption Perceptions Index (CPI) prepared by the Transparency International Russia scored only 2.5 out of a possible score of 10 placing it towards the bottom of the list (http://www.transparency.org/policy_research/surveys_indices/cpi, accessed on 10th August, 2007).

With the adoption of market based economic principles Russia privatised most of its state owned enterprises and has undertaken a major liberalisation programme of its corporate and financial sector. Alongside this reform it has also undertaken reforms in its political and legal structure. In spite of these reforms democratic institutions and the establishment of the rule of law are considered to be relatively weak (https://www.cia.gov/library/publications/the-world-factbook/geos/rs.html, accessed on 10th August, 2007). Like these fundamental institutions civil society groups which may exert effective pressures on corporations and government for the betterment of the Russian society are also yet to be developed. In the absence of these institutions it is expected that CSD in Russia will be at a nascent stage. This is confirmed by a global survey of CSD carried out by KPMG which shows that only a handful of companies in Russia are undertaking CSD (KPMG 2005). The KPMG (2005) study citing the source of Perm State Technical University suggested that out of top 100 Russian companies only 5% produced separate social/environmental reports in 2003–2004.

8.4 Research Method

This study is based on 20 large Russian companies' annual reports for the year 2004 as shown in Table 8.1. The companies included in this study range across ten industrial sectors. It includes top Russian industrial sectors, identified by the KPMG (2005) study of CSD, such as oil, non-ferrous and ferrous metals, food and utilities. All of these companies are listed on the Russian Stock Exchange. The selection was ad hoc and was influenced by the availability of the English version of the reports. Collection of annual reports or other data are extremely difficult in Russia. The problem was aggravated by the need for the English version of the reports as most Russian companies publish them in the Russian language. The year

Table 8.1 Particulars of selected Russian companies

Number	Company	Industrial sectors
1	Aeroflot	Transport
2	Alrosa	Mining
3	Avtovaz	Manufacturing
4	Aviacompany Syhoi	Manufacturing
5	Baltika	Food and beverages
6	FosagroAg	Chemical
7	Gaz	Manufacturing
8	Gazprom	Oil and gas
9	Irkutskenergy	Electroenergy
10	Lukoil	Oil and Gas
11	Megafon	Communication
12	Norilsk nickel	Nonferrous metallurgy
13	Novolipetsk stell	Ferrous metallurgy
14	Oskol electric steel works (OEMK)	Ferrous metallurgy
15	Power machines	Manufacturing
16	Severstal	Ferrous metallurgy
17	Svyazinvest	Communication
18	Tatneft	Oil and gas
19	United manufacturing company	Manufacturing
20	Wimm-Billl-Dunn	Food and beverages

2004 was chosen as this was the latest year for which annual reports were available at the time of data collection.

There are several reasons for using annual reports as the basis of this study. Firstly, this is consistent with the previous content analysis studies in the CSD literature. Secondly, annual reports are considered as one of the most important communication medium from the company to the outside world. Most of the companies of this study do not publish separate stand alone social and environmental reports. Therefore, it is most likely that if social and environmental disclosures are made anywhere then that will be within the annual reports. However, we do acknowledge that such disclosures can be made in other mediums such as website, internal reports, brochures and advertisements (Zeghal and Ahmed 1990).

In line with the previous studies content analysis procedures (Krippendorff 1980) have been adopted in this study. This is a widely accepted and applied method in social accounting (Adams et al. 1998; Adams and Kuasirikun 2000; Gray et al. 1995a, b). Content analysis has been defined as, "a technique for gathering data that consists of codifying qualitative information in anecdotal and literary form, into categories in order to derive quantitative scales of varying levels of complexity" (Abbott and Monsen 1979). The amount of disclosures is measured in this study in terms of the proportion of pages and extent of disclosure is determined as a percentage of the companies' disclosing on various social and environmental issues.

Like other methods content analysis has its own limitations. Some authors questioned the reliability of this method (Milne and Chan 1999). However, such reliability has been improved by using the test-retest procedures in this study. One of the principal assumptions in content analysis is that volume of disclosures signifies its importance (Belal 2001). It can be argued that in order to fully understand the significance of disclosures we also need to look at the socio-economic context in which those disclosures take place (Unerman 2000). This is the precise reason why Russian the socio-economic context is considered earlier in this study.

8.5 Results and Analysis

In this section we report the results of our content analysis of annual reports. As we can see from Table 8.2, 18 (90%) out of the 20 companies included in the study made some social and environmental disclosures. Most of these disclosures are located in a separate section on corporate social responsibility. When we look at the volume of disclosures as measured by the number of pages we see that it is very low except for a few companies. In this regard the automobile manufacturer GAZ appears to be the leader with 32 pages of disclosure followed by the oil company LUKOIL (11.5 pages) which are 20% and 13% respectively of the total number of pages in the annual reports (See Table 8.2 below). Two companies, United Manufacturing and Wimm-Billl-Dunn, appear at the bottom of the list with no CSD. Their annual reports contain only the financial statements. The disclosures found in the annual reports were analysed by using three broad categories: employee, ethical and environmental disclosures (See Table 8.2).

Table 8.2 Extent of CSD in Russia

Company	Employee	Ethical	Environmental	No. of Pages
Aeroflot	×	×	×	3.2 (6%)
Alrosa	×	×	×	3 (8%)
Avtovaz	×	×	×	7.5 (9%)
Aviacompany Syhoi	×	×	×	5 (8%)
Baltika	×	×	×	2 (4%)
FosagroAg	×		×	1.1 (2%)
Gaz	×		×	32 (20%)
Gazprom	×	×	×	2 (4%)
Irkutskenergy	×	×	×	2 (4%)
Lukoil	×	×	×	11.5 (13%)
Megafon	×			0 (0%)
Norilsk Nickel	×	×	×	3 (4%)
Novolipetsk Stell	×		×	7 (9%)
OEMK	×		×	3 (6%)
Power Machines	×	×	×	2 (4%)
Severstal	×		×	2.5 (5%)
Svyazinvest	×		×	1.5 (3%)
Tatneft	×	×	×	4 (7%)
United Manufacturing				0 (0%)
Wimm-Billl-Dunn				0 (0%)
Total	18	11	17	

Note: Figures in parentheses indicate percentage of CSD pages as compared to the total number of pages in the annual reports.

8.5.1 Employee Disclosures

This category was defined using the work of Adams et al. (1995). Within this category we captured disclosures on various employee related issues such as employment costs (salaries and wages), employee numbers, employee welfare and training and development. 90% of the companies surveyed made disclosures under this category. In Russia during the period of change in the 1990s declining employment combined with decline in wage levels and outstanding wages was a significant social problem. Most of the companies discussed these issues except the issue of arrears in wages. No companies made a disclosure on this issue of arrears in wages. One possible explanation for this could be that there were no such arrears which would be considered as an achievement over the situation in the recent past in 1990s. Most of the companies reported increase in wages and future programme for further increase. However, such pay rises resulted from redundancies, restructuring and rationalisations as revealed by the following illustrative disclosures:

LUKOIL pursued workforce optimisation in 2004 as part of the restructuring program, initiated in 2002, to raise Company efficiency and capitalization. Modernization of industrial facilities, and reorganisation and withdrawal of non-core subdivisions reduced the number of employees in E & P and refining, while the employee numbers in the Company's expanding retail network increased. The net effect in 2004 was a 2.7% reduction of the LUKOIL workforce. Structural reorganization and wage increases led to 20% increases in the average remuneration per employee (including all payments and bonuses). (Annual Report 2004, LUKOIL, P. 60)

As of January 1, 2005 the Company had 37,565 employees, i.e. a decrease by 460 employees during the reporting year. The average wage per employee was 25,400 Rubbles per month, an increase by 16.1% as compared with the 2003 level. (Annual Report 2004, ALROSA, P. 32)

This trend of balancing the bad news of redundancies with the good news of pay rise was repeated in most of the companies' annual reports.

A number of companies disclosed information about programmes undertaken by the companies which were aimed at the employees' welfare. This information was usually disclosed under the banner of social programmes. Inter alia, such programmes include:

- In-house health care system and resort therapy
- Provision of facilities for leisure, fitness and sports
- Supplementary health and social insurance
- Assistance to workers in improving their living conditions
- Non-repayable financial assistance to staff members
- Support to labour veterans and retired peoples
- Subsidised or free meals on the job

Illustrative disclosures in this sub-category can be provided from the 2004 annual report of OEMK which quantified their expenditures on social programmes as follows:

Table 8.3 Categories of disclosure

Trends of Financing	2003 million Rubles	2004 million Rubles	Deviations
Social installations, including:	90.9	115.4	+24.5
-health, rehabilitation, fitness etc.	*66.5*	*77.1*	*+10.6*
-other	*24.4*	*38.3*	*+13.9*
Collective bargaining agreement and social benefits, including:	21.6	35.2	+13.6
-collective bargaining agreement	*14.7*	*17.1*	*+2.4*
-social benefits	*6.9*	*18.1*	*+11.2*
Other socially-oriented programs	20.4	25.9	+5.5
Total	132.9	176.5	+43.6

(Annual Report 2004, OEMK, P. 41).

As may be seen from the above table, in 2004, the OEMK spent Rb 176.5 million on social programs, including Rb 115.4 million to finance maintenance costs of social facilities, and Rb 35.2 million on payments under the collective bargaining agreement and social benefits. In addition, the company provided financing for other socially-oriented programmes. Preventing and decreasing the incidence of diseases among workers was one of the main achievements of social policies at the OEMK, with 300 workers and 806 children undergoing treatment at the company's rehabilitation centre in 2004. A total of Rb 17.0 million was allocated from profits to finance resort therapy of staff members. Own funds were applied to purchase 1,429 resort vouchers. The preventive medicine centre examined 6,508 patients and accepted 63,028 sick calls. A total of 13,931 x-ray tests were performed. In 2004, the OEMK's fitness centre received more than 6,500 visitors.

Another major theme in the employee related disclosures of the Russian companies included in this study is the investment in human capital in the form of training and development. 75% companies reported in this sub-category. It is expected that companies would invest in the human resources to ensure continued supply of skilled manpower who are able to meet the challenges of changed circumstances in the fast growing economy of Russia. Some representative examples include as follows.

Aeroflot's current professional training and advancement program contributes to increased effectiveness in the performance of job duties, building team work and developing a creative approach to solving the tasks at hand. Employees are trained both at the company's in-house training facility and domestic and foreign training institutions. The company's training facility offers some 200 professional training and advancement programs. In 2004, more than 1,000 training sessions were held, of which 230 were for flight personnel, 140 were for engineering and technical personnel, 317 for cabin attendants and 5,151 were for ground personnel. Also in 2004, more than 10,000 staff from operating units took in-house training. More than 70,000 managers and specialists of the company whose work involves flight safety were either trained or had their certificates extended at the Retraining and Advanced Qualifications Center for air transport managers at the State Technical University for Civil Aviation (MGTU GA) and the Institute for Civil Aviation Industry Managers and Specialists. Professional training was also given to specialists involved in commercial, financial, and legal departments, as well as to employees who sell air tickets and carry out market research. All in all, about 500 employees from 29 different departments enrolled for courses at 34 Russian and foreign training facilities. (Annual Report 2004, AEROFLOT, P. 43)

'Training in the technical skills most required at JSC AVTOVAZ is provided to our employees in the Company's educational institution............ Annually, the above training institutions prepare 1,600 technicians of 15 vocations in the sphere of car manufacturing........ In the course of industrial training and practical training, students are selected for their subsequent employment in the Company. .... In 2004 the Company continued professional development of its personnel. 46,679 employees, including 15,282 managers, technicians and engineers were retrained and gained new skills or improved their qualification'. (Annual Report 2004, AVTOVAZ, P. 73)

8.5.2 Ethical Disclosures

Under this category we captured disclosures related to social/community development and sponsorship and charity activities. 11 out of 20 companies (55%) disclosed information in this category. Under the sub-category of social/community development five companies (25%) made disclosures. In its various areas of operations Lukoil helps in the improvement of social protection standards of local residents in co-operation with the relevant local authorities. For a number of years, the company had been organising summer vacation activities (e.g. study tours and trips to Black Sea Coast) for orphan children. In its pursuit of social development the company specifically focuses on a programme of supporting the indigenous population in the areas of its oil production. Implementation of such programmes requires respect and understanding of the lifestyle and needs of the local community. The company also actively supports the cultural institutions where it operates. Another company Alrosa pays special attention to the socio-economic development of West Yakutia, its main area of operations. The company's commitment in this regard is evident from the following:

The company's objective-oriented programme of regional development covers the following aspects:

- Recreation for children
- Construction, repair and maintenance of facilities, purchase of construction materials
- Organisation of transportation of agricultural produce
- Acquisition of various machinery and equipment, as well as fuel and lubricants
- Development of logistics and supplies for local hunters and fishermen
- Support for indigenous local residents

(Annual Report 2004, Alrosa, P. 34)

Similar commitment of social development was made by the oil and gas company Tatneft:

Being one of the largest taxpayers to the budget of the Republic of Tatarstan, Tatneft is aware of its responsibility towards the society, and implements a series of social programs aimed at improving the living standard in regions of economic activities of the Company. Social investments are made on 16 directions (areas), and in 2004, 110 corporate social projects were registered. (Annual Report 2004, Tetneft, P. 29)

Norilsk Nickel also appears to be committed to the socio-economic development of Norilsk and other regions. In the reporting period of 2004, representative of its Transpolar Branch took part in cultural, sports and recreation events organised at 75 educational institutions of Norilsk and Dudinka, and at 34 infant schools of Norilsk. In support of social stability in the territory, the company, in cooperation with executive authorities and civil society organisations, implemented projects designed to develop culture, arts, mass sports, youth movements, and to address the problems of socially vulnerable population groups (war veterans, disabled people, poor households, orphans etc.). As part of the project for social support to disabled people, traditional assistance was provided to local interest groups of disabled, and to other civil society organisations representing the interests of the vulnerable population.

Irkutskenergo provides financial assistance to socially vulnerable groups in the Irkutsk Region, orphanages and boarding schools, and makes efforts to support disabled children of this region. The company also allocated funds to develop the creative and cultural potential of the region.

The second sub category of ethical disclosures included in this study is corporate sponsorship activities by the Russian companies. Seven companies (35%) disclosed their corporate sponsorship activities. Main sponsorships were in the area of sports, hospital and educational institutions. Some examples of disclosure under this sub-category are provided below:

The company founded charitable foundations Rukhiyat, Miloserdiye. In 2004, Tatneft set up the "Gifted children" foundation. This foundation has been established to support intellectually and technically gifted children and teenagers living in the south-east of Tatarstan. (Annual Report 2004, Tetneft, P. 29)

During 2004, the Baltika Brewery was the general partner of the Russian Soccer Championship...... provided sponsorship assistance to the National Philharmonic Orchestra of Russia by allocating $1 million for the purchase of musical instrument. (Annual Report 2004, Baltika, P. 11)

During the past several years, Gazprom has been carrying out sponsorship and charity activities supporting Russian sports, promoting healthy lifestyle, supporting culture and education, stimulating the development of the scientific and technical sector in the country, protecting environment, rendering assistance to unprotected categories of population, preserving and reviving Russian national values. (Annual Report 2004, Gazprom, P. 51)

8.5.3 Environmental Disclosures

Under this broad category we have examined disclosures related to environmental protection and health and safety. Overall, 17 companies (85%) made environment related disclosures. While most of these companies made disclosure related to the protection of the environment only eight companies (40%) made disclosures on health and safety.

Under environmental protection many companies made extensive disclosures including compliance with ISO 14001. An extract from Gazprom's annual report is given below by way of an illustration:

The main principles underlying Gazprom's environmental activities are the reduction of the adverse effect of its production processes on nature and efficient use of natural resources. In spite of the growing natural gas production and transportation and the large-scale work to reconstruct the UGSS, Gazprom's production facilities maintain a low level of environmental impact or even bring it further down in terms of certain parameters. Gross emissions of Gazprom were reduced by 2.4%. Methane emissions account to some 60% of the total amount of substances getting into the atmosphere. They went down by 7.1% in 2004. (Annual Report 2004, Gazprom, P. 52)

Another large oil company made extensive disclosures on environmental protection. It has clearly stated its environmental commitment in the following terms:

True to its motto of harnessing the power of natural resources for human benefit, LUKOIL accepts responsibility for the environmental impact of its business, and makes efforts to minimise or rectify any damage to the environment, which its business might cause. (Annual Report 2004, Lukoil, P. 54)

In addition to this descriptive disclosure the company (Lukoil) also quantified its environmental impact as follows:

- Polluted Land: 279 hectres [2003: 403 hectres]
- Effluent emissions: 17 million cubic meters [2003: 27 million cubic meters]
- Environmental spending: $285 million [2003: $222 million].

As indicated above 40% of the companies also made disclosures under the sub category of health and safety. For example, Lukoil states:

Labor and industrial safety standards at Lukoil comply with the company's policy document 'Labor and industrial safety and the protection of the environment in the 21st century'.

....

One of the main components of the company's labor and industrial safety system is prevention of industrial accidents and attestation of safety standards in specific jobs (34,000 jobs were attested in 2004). The number of accidents at work declined by 10% compared with 2003. (Annual Report 2004, Lukoil, P. 59)

Similarly, as suggested by the Novolipetsk Stell's annual report, because of considerable efforts on occupational safety issues the company achieved positive results by reducing the incidence of job related accidents.

8.6 Discussion and Conclusion

From the above analysis we see that 90% of the Russian companies included in this study have disclosed information in either employees or ethical or environmental matters within their annual reports. This percentage appears to be high as compared to the Singaporean study by Tsang (1998) where only 52% of the companies disclosed social and environmental information and to the Singaporean and Malaysian study by Andrew et al. (1989) where only 26% of the companies made CSD. There are several reasons for this. Firstly, both of the studies by Tsang (1998) and Andrew et al. (1989) are outdated. The current Russian study reflects more recent developments in CSD globally where companies are increasingly expected to make CSD. Secondly, as a BRICs country and as a result of accelerated economic growth in recent times, Russia and its corporations would be more visible in the international arena giving rise to international expectations of more CSD in line with the increasing global trend of CSD confirmed by the KPMG (2005) study. Finally, questions have been raised about the management and ethical practices of Russian companies in the context of recent corporate governance scandals in Russia. To address these concerns it can be expected that Russian companies would attempt to create, maintain and repair the legitimacy of their relationships with 'key stakeholder groups, in particular the general public and local communities and international business partners' (KPMG 2005, p. 15).

Although we have only examined social and environmental disclosures made within the 2004 annual reports, few companies included in this study have started to publish separate social and environmental reports in recent times. For example, Gazprom, Lukoil and Norilsk Nickel have recently published separate social and environmental reports (http://www.corporateregister.com/search, accessed on 8th October, 2007). Examination of these reports is outside the scope of this study and can be covered in future studies. Future studies also could involve case studies of organisations engaged in extensive CSD by regularly publishing comprehensive separate social and environmental reports. Moreover, future researchers could examine the perceptions of Russian managers and stakeholders towards the emerging phenomenon of CSD in the Russian Federation.

From the reports examined in this study it appears to be that employee related disclosures is the most popular theme (90%) followed by environmental and ethical disclosures. Popularity of employee related disclosures were also confirmed by several previous studies (Andrew et al. 1989; Belal 2000, 2001; Tsang 1998). For example, a slightly higher percentage (97) of Bangladeshi companies made employee related disclosure as revealed by Belal (2001). Emphasis on employee related disclosures is not surprising given the need for skilled manpower in modern Russian Federation. Provision of an efficient workforce will help Russia to capitalise the opportunity arising from the prospect of strong economic growth. Under these circumstances it is expected that companies would attempt to legitimise their relationship with this important stakeholder group – an explanation which is in line with the legitimacy theory argument developed earlier in section two of the paper.

As compared to 90% of the companies making environmental disclosures in the Bangladesh study by Belal (2000) 85% of the companies made environmental disclosures in this study. As discussed in the Russian context section, industrial pollution by heavy industries is a cause of concern for the Russian as well as the international community. Although environmental disclosure is not mandatory in Russia it could be argued that companies are proactively making voluntary environmental disclosures to avoid future regulation in this area. Thus, they are in a position to forestall the regulation in this regard by playing ahead of the game which can be explained with insights from the Political Economy Theory [PET].

Ethical disclosures were the least disclosed category in this study with only 55% of the companies making disclosures in this category. This is much lower than the percentage for ethical disclosures by the Bangladeshi companies (77) and the percentage for ethical disclosures by the Western European companies (86) as shown by Belal (2001) and Adams et al. (1998) respectively. The lower percentage of ethical disclosures by the Russian companies could be due to the fact that although they are contributing to the socio-economic development of Russia they might not be disclosing these important aspects out of modesty. Similarly, in the context of Russian CSD KPMG (2005) study suggests that 'Current CR (Corporate Responsibility) reporting may not yet reflect the level of involvement of companies in CR activities' (P.15). Anecdotal evidence also suggests that Severstal spent an amount of \$50–60 million on socio-economic development projects during the study period but did not disclose it in the annual report.

None of the disclosures analysed in this study were externally verified. It is argued that such independent external verification is necessary to add credibility and increase transparency of the CSD process (O'Dwyer and Owen 2005). Such verification is also required by AA1000 and GRI's Sustainability Reporting Guidelines. Moreover, Sustainability Reporting Guidelines requires disclosures of positive as well as negative aspects of organisational performance (GRI 2006). The reports examined in this study mostly contained positive/good news which further questions the credibility and completeness of the disclosures made. Similar observation was made on Bangladeshi CSD by Belal (2001). In the absence of independent external verification and lack of completeness (due to positive disclosures only) it can be concluded that currently Russian CSD practice is poor in quality. Although it is more likely that in future pressures will be brought to bear on Russian companies to engage in more transparent and accountable CSD practice very little optimism for improvement can be expressed here. This is mainly due to lack of mandatory requirements for CSD in Russia and also to some extent due to the absence of strong NGOs and other pressures groups who can exert effective pressures on Russian companies to improve their CSD practice.

References

Abbott, W. F., & Monsen, R. J. 1979. On the Measurement of Corporate Social Responsibility: Self-reported Disclosures as a Method of Measuring Corporate Social Involvement. *Academy of Management Journal*, 22(3): 501–515.

Adams, C., Hill, W., & Roberts, C. 1998. Corporate Social Reporting Practices in Western Europe: Legitimating Corporate Behaviour? *British Accounting Review*, 30(1): 1–21.

Adams, C., Hills, W. Y., & Roberts, C. B. 1995. Environmental, Employee and Ethical Reporting in Europe. London: Association of Chartered Certified Accountants (ACCA).

Adams, C., & Kuasirikun, N. 2000. A comparative analysis of corporate reporting on ethical issues by UK and German chemical and pharmaceutical companies. *European Accounting Review*, 9(1): 53–80.

Andrew, B., Gul, F., Guthrie, J., & Teoh, H. 1989. A Note on Corporate Social Disclosure Practices in Developing Countries: The Case of Malaysia and Singapore. *British Accounting Review*, 21(4): 371–376.

Belal, A. 2000. Environmental Reporting in Developing Countries: Empirical Evidence from Bangladesh. *Eco-Management and Auditing*, 7(3): 114–121.

Belal, A. 2001. A Study of Corporate Social Disclosures in Bangladesh. *Managerial Auditing Journal*, 16(5): 274–289.

Belal, A. R. 2002. Stakeholder accountability or stakeholder management: a review of UK firms' social and ethical accounting, auditing and reporting (SEAAR). *Corporate Social Responsibility and Environmental Management*, 9(1): 8–25.

Belal, A. R., & Owen, D. 2007. The Views of Corporate Managers on the Current State of, and Future Prospects for, Social Reporting in Bangladesh: An Engagement Based Study. *Accounting, Auditing & Accountability Journal*, 20(3): 472–494.

Deegan, C., & Gordon, B. 1996. A study of environmental disclosure practices of Australian corporations. *Accounting and Business Research*, 26(3): 187–199.

Deegan, C., Rankin, M., & Tobin, J. 2002. An examination of the corporate social and environmental disclosures of BHP from 1983–1997: A test of legitimacy theory. *Accounting, Auditing and Accountability Journal*, 15(3): 312–343.

Gray, R. 2000. Current Developments and Trends in Social and Environmental Auditing, Reporting and Attestation: A Reveiw and Comment. *International Journal of Auditing*, 4: 247–268.

Gray, R. 2001. Thirty years of social accounting, reporting and auditing: What (if anything) have we learnt? *Business Ethics: A European Review*, 10(1): 9–15.

Gray, R., Javad, M., Power, D. M., & Sinclair, C. D. 2001. Social and Environmental Disclosure and Corporate Characteristics: A Research Note and Extension. *Journal of Business Finance and Accountancy*, 28(3–4): 327–356.

Gray, R., Kouhy, R., & Lavers, S. 1995a. Constructing a Research Database of Social and Environmental Reporting by UK Companies. *Accounting, Auditing and Accountability Journal*, 8(2): 78–101.

Gray, R., Kouhy, R., & Lavers, S. 1995b. Corporate Social and Environmental Reporting: A Review of the Literature and a Longitudinal Study of UK Disclosure. *Accounting, Auditing and Accountability Journal*, 8(2): 47–77.

Gray, R., Owen, D., & Adams, C. 1996. *Accounting and Accountability: Changes and Challenges in Corporate Social and Environmental Reporting*. Hemel Hempstead: Prentice Hall.

GRI. 2006. Sustainability Reporting Guidelines [G3]. Amsterdam: Global Reporting Initiative (GRI).

Harte, G., & Owen, D. 1991. Environmental Disclosure in the Annual Reports of British Companies: A Research Note. *Accounting, Auditing and Accountability Journal*, 4(3): 51–61.

KPMG. 2005. KPMG International Survey of Corporate Responsibility Reporting 2005. Amsterdam: KPMG.

Krippendorff, N. 1980. *Content Analysis: An Introduction to its Methodology*. New York: Sage.

Milne, M., & Chan, C. 1999. Narrative Corporate Social Disclosures: How much of difference do they make to investment decision-making?. *British Accounting Review*, 31: 439–457.

O'Dwyer, B., & Owen, D. L. 2005. Assurance statement practice in environmental, social and sustainability reporting: a critical evaluation. *The British Accounting Review*, 37(2): 205–229.

Owen, D. 2004. Adventures in Social and Environmental Accounting and Auditing Research: A Personal Reflection. In C. Humphrey, & W. Lee (Eds.), *The Real Life Guide to Accounting Research*: 23–36. Oxford: Elsevier.

Singh, D., & Ahuja, J. 1983. Corporate Social Reporting in India. *International Journal of Accounting*, 18(2): 151–169.

Tsang, E. 1998. A Longitudinal Study of Corporate Social Reporting in Singapore. *Accounting, Auditing and Accountability Journal*, 11(5): 624–635.

Unerman, J. 2000. *Assessing Theoretical Explanations of Corporate Social Reporting: Evidence From The Early Years of Shell, 1897 to 1914*. Paper presented at the Interdisciplinary Perspectives on Accounting, Manchester.

Wilson, D., & Purushothaman, R. 2003. Dreaming with BRICs: The Path to 2050. Newyork: Goldman Sachs.

Zeghal, D., & Ahmed, S. 1990. Comparison of Social Responsibility Disclosure Media Used by Canadian Firms. *Accounting, Auditing and Accountability Journal*, 3(1): 38–53.

Part II
East Asia

Chapter 9
People's Republic of China

Richard Welford and Peter Hills[1]

Abstract CSR in a Chinese context is still driven mainly by the leading Western brands and a few locally based (indeed, more often Hong Kong based) companies that have a brand and image to protect. However, the government is now also promoting CSR as the private sector's contribution to a 'harmonious society'. Supply chain pressure and local government initiatives are now encouraging domestic companies to adopt environmental and social initiatives. Three key areas for CSR in China, namely the environment, labour and supply chain issues are discussed. Obstacles to the adoption of CSR are also examined along with the policies the government is using to try to encourage better CSR practices.

9.1 Introduction

Since the launch of the "Open Door" policy in 1978, China's economic growth has averaged around 10 per cent per year. China now has the fourth largest economy in the world (World Bank 2007) and this has meant that large numbers of people have moved from poverty to consumption-oriented lifestyles. Living standards have improved dramatically with life expectancy increasing from 35 in 1949 to 73 in 2005.

This growth has largely been as a result of the private sector investing in plants to supply thousands of Western companies seeking to source goods and profit from the cheap labour in China. The shift away from agriculture to manufacturing as the dominant source of domestic product has created wealth and reduced much poverty. Moreover, we are now seeing even more growth associated with new service sector companies also competing on the global stage. However, this rapid growth rate, coupled with large-scale urbanization, has generated significant pressures on the environment, natural resources, human health, workers, human rights and local

[1]The authors wish to acknowledge the support of the Hong Kong Research Grants Council for funding work forming parts of this paper under Grant Numbers 7305/03H and 7288/04H.

communities. These pressures are increasingly shaping corporate social responsibility (CSR) in the country.

The losses from pollution and ecological damage range from 7 per cent to 20 per cent of the GDP per year for the last two decades. Sixteen of the world's 20 most polluted cities are to be found in China. The impact on human health has been particularly severe. About 300,000 deaths a year have been attributed to problems of air quality alone. Most recently, we have seen local communities campaigning and protesting about local environmental damage and in some cases opposing new power plants and other infrastructure developments (Ho and Welford 2006).

The Chinese government is well-aware of the deterioration of the environment and the impact upon its citizens and has begun to promote more balanced economic development, emphasizing a need for rural areas to play catch-up. The emphasis on the policy of creating a "harmonious society" has included planning both national and social development, including a new emphasis on environmental and natural resource management and a new role for business, in particular (Ho and Vermeer 2006). Senior figures in the Chinese government have promoted CSR as the private sector's contribution to the "harmonious society". Business is seen to have a role to play in ensuring that a more sustainable development of the country takes place.

The drivers for CSR come from a wide range of stakeholders, but some are more demanding than others (Studer et al. 2006). It is often assumed that consumers (particularly in the West) exert a tremendous amount of pressure on companies but in fact CSR managers do not experience that much pressure from consumers in a direct way. Whilst they want to be reassured that companies are not abusing workers, using child labour and the like, consumers rarely come directly to companies for that information. They tend to rely on second hand information mainly through the media, which is in turn strongly influenced by NGOs and trade unions (and sometimes, although not always, a coalition of the two).

In China, where there are still relatively few NGOs most information relating to supply chain issues come from Hong Kong organisations such as the Hong Kong Christian Industrial Committee (HKCIC), the Asia Monitor Resource Centre (AMRC) and CSR Asia. The Institute of Contemporary Observation (in Shenzhen) is one of a growing number of civil society organisations that are raising issues surrounding labour rights and, in particular, migrant labour rights.

Companies are clearly now experiencing a great deal of pressure from some of their shareholders, particularly those who are long term investors (e.g. pension funds and investment trusts) rather than short term speculators. Unit trust managers, pension fund managers, venture capital companies, the investment banking sector and others are all asking for more information about CSR practices and more assurances about how potential risks in China are being handled. Many of them realise that protecting reputation and brands are central to protecting their investments. It is also one of the reasons why some companies are expanding the number of brands in their portfolio rather than relying on one overarching brand name in the future.

However, Welford (2007) points out that such shareholder pressure is completely absent from many smaller companies that make up the bulk of suppliers in China because they are often family owned or in the hands of a small group of partners (who often have more than one small company). In some circumstances, the Chinese family business is naturally benevolent and wants to see the staff treated as an extended family, but this is not always the case and poor employment practices, environmental damage and safety failures (and even deaths) are common and often relatively easy to conceal in Chinese companies.

When discussing CSR in a Chinese context most of the best practices come from the activities of companies from the leading Western brands and those of a few locally based (indeed, more often Hong Kong based) companies that have a brand and image to protect. In this paper we examine the three key areas for CSR in China, namely the environment, labour and supply chain issues. Companies wishing to be socially responsible in China would do well to prioritise those three areas.

But in a paper about CSR in China it is also important to examine the obstacles to the adoption of CSR, policies the government are using to try to encourage better CSR practices and the future shape of CSR in the country.

9.2 The Environment

Pollution in China is amongst the worst in the world. Air pollution continues to damage health, at least a third of all water resources are severely polluted, energy use is highly inefficient, desertification continues and biodiversity loss is alarming (Liu and Diamond 2005). China is building a new coal-fired power station every 12 days. In 2006, alone it added 70,000 megawatts of new power generation.

The pollution, energy, water and material intensities of the Chinese economy remain high. There are major opportunities for efficiency programmes and the introduction of new technologies in all these areas. China generates significantly more pollution and consumes more resources per unit of GDP than the OECD averages. Moreover, there is a very high rate of environment-related accidents and deaths. If the Chinese government is to achieve its target of quadrupling GDP over the next 20 years then this requires a dramatic increase in the efforts and resources put into environmental management.

China's economic miracle could soon be halted because of the pressures on the environment and resources. Acid rain affects on third of the country. Half the water in the seven largest rivers in China is heavily polluted and unable to be used. A quarter of the population does not have access to clean drinking water. Less that 20% of all solid waste is treated. Iron ore prices have risen to all time highs in 2006 because of demand for steel in China. Although, it has the greatest coal reserves compared to any country in the world, China still has to import coal because it cannot get of it out of the ground quickly enough. Highly hazardous and, at times, illegal coal mining activity killed around 6,000 workers in 2006 alone.

The government's State Environmental Protection Agency (SEPA) has released several regulations aimed at improving the environmental performance of firms and on corporate disclosure and reporting. The government is keen to see the private sector as part of its plans to deliver sustainable development. Indeed, the government has released much stricter laws and regulations on corporate environmental behaviour in response to growing public concern over environmental problems caused by enterprises. Such pressures are increasingly forcing Chinese enterprises and foreign investors to improve their environmental performance. Many are realizing that this can be linked to cost savings, subsequent improved financial performance and reputation and brand benefits.

Subject to the Constitution of the People's Republic of China (PRC), the legal provisions related to the environment of China consists of laws, provisions, regulations, ministerial and local regulations, all of which are based on the Environmental Protection Act of the PRC. The legal system requires enterprises to report to the government when they produce any pollutant, where their projects have negative environmental impacts, or where any operating change occurs that affects the environment. However, these laws and regulations are very general and open to significant interpretation. Such interpretation and re-interpretation feed into corruption and bribery (Ma and Ortolano 2000).

Whilst the Chinese government has committed itself to a new environmental focus and has introduced tough new requirements, what really matters is how those new policies and procedures are implemented on the ground (Welford et al. 2006). At the local level where the salaries of officials are linked to economic growth there is often an incentive to attract inward investment, even if it is highly environmentally damaging.

But some local governments have also released a number of additional regulations and companies that want to demonstrate good environmental performance need to make sure they are aware of those local regulations or local variations of national regulations.

Increasingly, a common strategy at the local level seems to be to play a game of 'name and shame'. The public disclosure of good and bad corporate environmental performance and the use of rating systems by local environmental protection bureaus have been widely used over the past few years. For example, China's Green Watch Program in Zhenjiang City of Jiangsu Province used a rating system dividing firms' environmental performance into five categories, with two (black and red) denoting inferior performance; one (yellow) denoting compliance with national regulations but failure to comply with stricter local requirements; and two ratings (blue, green) denoting superior performance (see Table 9.1).

Good environmental performance and associated disclosure is now becoming both more common and more important. Sustainable development is an important national strategy. Central government is requiring all government bureaucracies, including the environmental administration system, to be more transparent and disclose more information to the public. In response to this requirement, daily reports of air quality condition, monthly reports of water quality of selected rivers, an annual report on the national environment and "Black Lists" of polluting companies have all been produced. The China Securities Regulatory Commission (CSRC) is promoting corporate environmental performance and information disclosure is going to be an important requirement in the future.

Table 9.1 Zhenjiang's 5-Colour Rating Scheme for Polluters

Compliance status	Level	Performance criteria
Non-compliance	Black	Greatly exceeds pollutant emissions standards set by SEPA and causes serious damage.
	Red	Efforts don't meet pollution emissions standards set by SEPA, or have a record of serious pollution incidents.
Warning	Yellow	Meets pollutant emissions standards set by SEPA, but fails to meet local Environmental Protection Bureau standards.
Compliance	Blue	Exceeds all emissions standards set by SEPA and the local Environmental Protection Bureau; demonstrates superior environmental management.
	Green	Meets all requirements for Blue, plus satisfaction of ISO 14000 environmental standards; extensive use of clean technology.

Source: Public rating of industry's environmental performance: China's Green Watch Program, 2004.

Leading companies are taking these provisions seriously but there is still much to be achieved. The environmental situation facing China is nothing short of a crisis. The degradation of the environment caused by economic growth and a shortage of many basic resources are constraining further growth as well as creating huge hidden costs associated with health, an inability to do business (e.g. at times of water shortages) and transboundary impacts. There are real risks associated with China's continued degradation of the environment, for the country itself, for the Asian region and for the global environment. Not the least of it all, China is set to become the biggest contributor to the greenhouse gas emissions whilst having no real commitment to their reduction.

Nevertheless, the Chinese government is aware of the environmental problems associated with rapid growth and has a stated commitment to reversing some of the worst trends. This will provide huge opportunities for environmental services, consultancy and environmental technologies. Moreover, inward investment in technologies and systems capable of reducing greenhouse gas emissions, have the potential to be hugely profitable in the context of carbon offsetting.

There is little doubt that China's growth will soon be constrained by a lack of resources (including water). But again this leads to huge opportunities for those companies with the knowledge and know-how relating to resource efficiency. And with such inefficient industry across the whole country, the potential efficiency improvements are both achievable and relatively easy given experiences and lessons learned from more developed countries.

9.3 Labour

According to the International Labour Organisation labour rights should be at the heart of any debate on CSR in China because so many migrant workers in the country are denied their rights and are at significant risk of exploitation. The Chinese government agrees and has also made labour rights a key issue in recent years and is expecting companies to abide by comprehensive labour laws. In particular, the government has expressed severe concerns about the treatment of migrant workers, the payment of at least minimum wages and wages paid late (common practice in some sectors). Therefore, in the view of many CSR experts in China, labour issues are as important as price, quality and delivery (Welford and Frost 2006).

There are 40 million migrant workers in China's southern Guangdong province alone. Of Shenzhen's population of 13 million, 12 million are migrant workers. Most have low educational achievements and are often the subject of abuses (Chan 2001). Many businesses are making a significant contribution to society simply by developing (or just often implementing) sound laws and frameworks that provide a good degree of credibility and assurance for those engaged with CSR. However, in China although there are very clear laws on employment, working hours, minimum wages, overtime payments and health and safety, there is a lack of implementation of these laws.

China has a comprehensive legislation covering hours and wages (with the exception of the Hong Kong Special Administrative Region). In China, the maximum working week is 40 hours with an additional 36 hours per month permitted as overtime. However, at the local level such national laws can be amended by the local government such that commonly workers can work 40 hours per week in a regular work and 20 hours of overtime per week. However, as mentioned above, the issue is not a lack of law, but the failure to implement it. The key problems around these issues involve employees working longer hours than permitted, paid rates lower than the minimum wages and receiving incorrect (or often no) compensation for overtime.

Ensuring that workers in factories work to legal limits and are paid correctly (particularly for overtime) is proving to be near impossible, particularly in high seasons. The downward pressure on prices in many sectors, along with shorter lead times and the increasingly shorter periods between the release of new models (or fashions) has increased pressure along the supply chain to the factory floor. Rising wages in the Pearl River Delta (around 30 per cent in some cities per year), for instance, has been welcomed by most labour activists but not by some investors who have already moved to cheaper neighbourhood provinces or to other countries (most notably Vietnam).

There is also an issue surrounding workers not getting paid on time. Many factories do not pay the full monthly salary or delay payment – a three month delay is not uncommon. This is partly a response to cash flow problems but it is clearly also being used as a strategy to retain workers. Workers who are owed three months salaries are a lot less likely to give up their job.

Freedom of association is a fundamental human right as stated in the United Nations Universal Declaration on Human Rights and ILO Conventions 87 and 98. Increasingly, collective action is on the rise and workers are beginning to find their feet and we have seen an increase in the number of labour disputes in a number of different parts of China. CSR managers may not want to see more workers going on strike but it is true that they want to see workers being empowered to recognise their own rights and insist that they are respected. If that is done in a well managed way (e.g. through training worker representatives how to chair meetings with co-workers, interpret important points of the law, and negotiate with management) then it may actually help companies committed to CSR to achieve their own objectives.

But the right of workers and employers to form and join organizations of their own choosing is sometimes forbidden and in many other cases actively curtailed in China (Chan and Senser 1997). Workers can join the All-China Federation of Trade Unions but no other union and the ACFTU is linked to the Communist Party. Moreover the head of the union in factories is often a manager rather than a worker and it is widely suggested that it rarely works in the interest of protecting the rights of the workers. Therefore, brands that have a stated commitment to upholding freedom of association and encouraging collective bargaining and proper worker representation have problems in upholding this in China. Many have experimented with parallel ways of worker representation. Others have gone even further in developing mechanisms through which workers can make direct complaints to the brands through various types of phone call related services.

The majority of workers in China are migrants from rural areas and pose particular challenges for companies committed to CSR. Migrants face specific problems due to lack of family and community networks. Often housed in dormitories, they face a unique set of issues including finances (remittances home), relationships (a lack of partners or places for intimacy), and boredom (often confined to the factory compound or quarters for long periods).

Working practices in many factories have improved over the last few years, in part, due to a shortage of migrant workers (in some places) and the need for companies to retain workers, making sure they return to work after holiday periods. Here, increased levels of trust between workers and the factories and improvements in the way the workforce is treated have led to win-win outcomes. Many Chinese factory owners are for the first time being forced to consider how they might attract and retain a workforce. In an attempt to retain workers, some companies are now paying long service bonuses to staff returning to the factory for another year, for example. Labour shortages may have helped to combat the existence of sweatshops in China more than factory inspections ever did.

One particular concern in China relates to the treatment of young female migrant workers. Many responsible companies have introduced educational programmes aimed at personal skills development but the young women are often so timid and so tired that they did not seem very interested. They are under pressure to send as much money home as possible. But where educational programmes have been put in place workers have often benefited from, for example, learning IT skills, learning about their own health and gaining in confidence through practising better communications.

The amount of harassment of female employees by male managers (and sometimes co-workers) is something that many companies are also trying to tackle. But when gender differences and not gender equality are deeply engrained in a culture then it is difficult to empower women to speak out or begin to tackle this issue. It is also difficult to get male managers to take this issue seriously.

9.4 Supply Chains

Of course many of the labour issues discussed above are related to the extensive supply chains to be found in Chain. China is increasingly the manufacturing workshop of the world. It alone produces 80 per cent of the world's toys, 70 per cent of kitchen appliances, 75 per cent of all shoes and 50 per cent of all garments. However, it also has a rapidly growing service sector, in turn serving supply chains and including a range of IT firms, call centers and other service oriented provision for clients. One of the main focuses of CSR in China is therefore on the supply chains that make products for the leading brands as well as more generic goods to be found on the shelves of the world's budget supermarkets. In many cases the real process of these products (and services) have been falling over the last decade as competition amongst retailers increases and people seem ever more desirous of cheap bargain products.

China has long been associated with the accusation that many products are being made in sweatshop conditions that exploit people and damage the environment (Chan 1998). It is true that factories can be found in China where this is the case but those factories are normally producing low-priced generic goods, often for domestic consumption. They disregard the law, cheat their staff, bribe officials and pay little regard to their impact on local communities.

Decent workplace conditions are part of the challenge to building the government's concept of the "harmonious society". Labour is interested in opportunities for work that is productive and delivers a fair income in a safe and healthy environment. Despite under-reporting in many jurisdictions, deaths and injuries from occupational accidents or work-related diseases across China are rising. Over the last 2 years there is increasing evidence that child labour is increasing. Discrimination in the workplace is widespread on the basis of gender, health, political and religious beliefs, sexuality, ethnicity and other criteria. In Chinese factories, however, that discrimination is often against men because women workers are often preferred. Of course such discrimination is based on stereotypical assumptions around the better behaviour of women, their willingness to follow orders and them being less likely to protest or go on strike.

But for the world's leading brands, compliance with local laws, regulations and norms is not an option (Schmitz and Knorringa 2000). Chinese companies supplying to foreign clients understand that unless they can act in accordance with comprehensive codes of conduct, they are unlikely to get repeat orders. However, full compliance in the supply chain remains elusive and we have seen many cases where systems have failed leading to scandals over child labour, poor health and safety records and the need for product recalls.

Many companies sourcing from Chinese supply chains now have their own codes of conduct, most are based on a mix of relevant local laws and international norms and standards (such as those codified in the International Labour Organization's Core Conventions). Many procurement contracts now contain key elements from these codes of conduct and factories are expected to comply with these obligations in the same manner as other contractual requirements (Welford and Frost 2006).

Codes of conduct have to be enforced and this has been the reason that we have seen a massive growth in the auditing and inspection industry in China. Social and environmental audits may have been an optional extra a decade ago but now they are standard practices and for a big factory supplying a number of well known brands they may have to go through many audits in 1 year.

Codes of conduct designed for workplaces in low-wage locations stick to legal standards such as minimum wages, hours of work, health and safety, forced and child labour, dormitory accommodation and environmental protection. Interestingly, in China CSR via codes of conduct has often become an exercise in seeking compliance with local law than moving beyond it. Whether obeying the law can be seen as a good CSR practice remains questionable, of course, but on the other hand if companies obeyed all labour laws in China, employment practices would be much better, in general.

Companies working in partnership with overseas manufacturing plants expect their local partners to adhere to these codes. Different companies adopt different practices with regard to non-compliance, but they range from the outright cutting of contracts to long term programmes to rectify non-compliance issues. Some companies adopt a "three strikes and you are out" approach meaning that after three written warnings about non-compliance with a code of conduct, the contract will be severed. Others will work for years on remediation before finally severing relations. CSR or compliance managers working for the brands often talk of the difficult task of cutting contracts with suppliers when they know it will inevitably lead to job losses. Nevertheless, in order to make the code of conduct credible this sometimes needs to be done. Many however, feel that active engagement at an early stage can prevent the need for the severing of links although there are clear resource implications to such interventions.

Many suppliers run highly efficient, responsible factories where workers are paid well and where health and safety is seen as a priority. They have few problems when the auditors come to visit. But others struggle to pass audits and here we often see a good degree of cheating going on. Factory owners and managers often keep duplicate books in order to comply with stipulations over working hours in codes of conduct. Protective equipment is often issued when auditors are in the factory and taken back subsequently. Environmentally damaging processes may be turned off. Workers are often coached to give auditors the answers that they want to hear.

Companies are aware that some suppliers are cheating and many suppliers know that their customers know. Some of the things that they do in breach of codes of conduct are short cuts and not terribly serious, but where there is systematic cheating and dishonesty CSR managers are forced to intervene in a strong and clear way. Whilst most codes of conduct are practicable and workable, getting some suppliers to recognise that is a real battle. Most CSR managers see ILO conventions and guidelines as aspirations to work towards but most doubt that they can fully comply with many of them throughout all supply chains and this is seen as a challenge for the future. Many companies no longer expect full compliance to the code and instead work on a rough guide of 70 to 80 per cent compliance and the expectation that the supplier demonstrates a willingness to engage on the remaining

20 to 30 per cent (which are in most cases the very hard issues of remuneration for overtime and hours worked).

Although factory audits and inspections are now mandatory for any company seeking to protect brand, reputation and market position, their quality is variable leading to accusations that auditors are sometimes complicit in the cheating. Moreover, market forces have driven audit prices and quality down leading to uneven results across the industry. The increasingly sophisticated cheating by manufacturers and some poor quality auditing has led to growing distrust of audit results that has further diminished their effectiveness. Clients sourcing from factories require reliable information on workplace practices, environmental performance and product safety, but in the absence of such reliable data new approaches are needed.

With high rates of non-compliance, the question nowadays is not whether factories are complying, but whether it's possible for them to comply in a purchasing system that expects more performance for less money. Factory owners and managers repeatedly complain that they are expected to put expensive pollution control measures in place, buy expensive safety devices, provide better dormitory accommodation, keep working hours within legal requirements and increase wages. Yet at the same time as they are being asked to put their own CSR practices in place, big customers are asking for bigger and bigger reductions in price. Moreover, customers often change orders with little notice, requiring them to be delivered on a timescale that forces factories into illegal levels of overtime. Factories are often criticized for not paying workers on time, yet many brands do not pay their bills on time.

Whilst many CSR managers see their role as fire-fighting and dealing with endless incidences of non-compliance, it would be wrong to suggest that all suppliers create problems. Many local Chinese companies are now realising the benefits of adopting good CSR practices and a number of factories and other suppliers have exemplary practices themselves when it comes to labour issues. Many are doing impressive things to improve their environmental impact and they often find this saves them money. Some suppliers are excellent employers with generous packages for workers, including above minimum wage basic salaries, overtime paid at a premium and regular bonus payments on top of that. Some suppliers are even stipulating social and environmental requirements for their own suppliers to follow.

But CSR managers in China often complain about a lack of resources and insufficient personnel to inspect factories. Many say that they are forced to use third party inspectors and auditors but have not been satisfied by the quality of what they do or their own internal quality assurance mechanisms. Competition in the auditing business has seen prices for audits plummet as smaller and local companies enter the market with cut price terms. In the Pearl River Delta in China, for instance, audits are being offered for prices under US$300. As a consequence, audits are done more quickly and with little attention to quality. Staff are under trained, turnover is high, and a number of auditors are now as exploited as the workers in factories they are auditing for exploitative practices.

It is clear that in many companies codes of conduct are seen as a nuisance and that appearing to be in compliance with them was often seen as a better alternative than actually being in compliance with them. There is therefore a culture of cheating in many local companies. However, that is not to suggest that SME managers and owners are inherently dishonest. The fact is that many of them perceive that they cannot do business and make a profit and at the same time adhere to all rules, regulations and codes of conduct.

An example of this relates to working hours. Many codes of conduct do not allow workers to work more than 60 hours per week and require them to have at least one day off a week. But many factory managers are of the view that it they adhered strictly to that requirement they could not meet their orders and could not operate profitably. They get around this requirement in codes of conduct by falsifying records and mis-recording hours worked above the maximum in a different way (e.g. by giving staff two different work cards for recording hours worked at different times). However, other factories allow workers to work longer than 60 hours at their own request. Many workers prefer to work double shift and earn more money than sitting around playing cards or sleeping. But although workers may want to work long hours, attention to their health and safety makes this an unwise practice.

It is no surprise, therefore, that many companies are now working towards building trusting relationships with fewer rather than more factories. Where factories cannot do as they are asked then the termination of contracts becomes inevitable. There is also a desire to move to factories where shared values, skills development, adequate training and capacity building ultimately means that there is no need for an audit and inspection process. Many companies talk about building a "world class supply chain" rather than policing it; a fundamental shift from auditing to consulting.

Smaller suppliers often find it more difficult to comply with codes of conduct than larger organisations. A move towards consolidating supply chains with fewer (and therefore larger) factories in fewer locations could therefore impact more on smaller suppliers. There is a relatively urgent need to help the SME sector develop the skills to maintain their existing contracts and position themselves so as to be attractive suppliers based on high CSR standards. If this is not done it is highly likely that many SMEs will be forced to close and those that remain will be sourcing for companies that care only about price and little about any other aspect of CSR.

Many brands will now openly admit that codes of conduct are not working well and that full compliance with them is actually quite rare. The whole approach to auditing and inspection is increasingly being seen as necessary but not sufficient in getting factories to comply with codes of conduct. One of the problems is that the codes of conduct are often seen as a nuisance rather then something that can actually help with better management of a factory, motivation for staff and a way to avoid run-ins with regulators. Therefore, integrating audits into a holistic program that includes skills training for management, workers and civil society organisations is crucial for the long term sustainability of outsourced production.

Whilst auditing and inspections in the supply chain will remain the backbone of any compliance program, there is now a widespread realization that these alone will not ensure better workplace practices or increased product safety. Building skills in supply chains (for employees and managers) and capacity in civil society are now seen as key ingredients in the compliance mix. Capacity building is now very much at the cutting edge of good CSR practices. Such capacity building is about building skills and knowledge through training that facilitates compliance through hands-on techniques that make business sense.

9.5 Obstacles to CSR in China

The vast majority of CSR initiatives taking place in China are being done by the leading Western brands sourcing from supply chains there. It is clear that most domestic companies have limited awareness of what CSR is or of the external drivers that are pushing CSR along supply chains. Although they are often faced with codes of conduct from customers they often tend to see these as a nuisance and regard them as no more than an instrument of compliance. Local managers and owners often do not fully understand the demand coming from the stakeholders of their customers and therefore do not fully recognize the importance of CSR to them.

In particular, there is a significant lack of awareness of the benefits that can be derived from good CSR practices. For example, many managers (but not all) remain to be convinced that CSR can reduce staff turnover. Chinese companies seem to want to see the "proof" that CSR is really going to be beneficial to their business. Moreover, there are so many competing demands on managers that CSR often becomes a low priority unless they are mandated to do something (often through a buyer's code of conduct).

Since CSR is often seen by local Chinese companies as a compliance issue, the absolute minimum is done to adhere to codes of conduct (or to cover up noncompliance) and managers and owners see this compliance as costly. Therefore to go beyond anything that is mandated in codes of conduct is seen as something that will only add to costs.

Managers and owners repeatedly point out that they face tighter and tighter margins with rising wages, material and energy costs, in particular. They complain that their customers' put even more demands on them to improve workplace practices, health and safety, environmental performance, but at the same time are constantly looking for lower and lower prices for their orders. They complain of a mismatch between the demands of CSR departments and those of procurement managers.

Linked to the issue of costs is the lack of human resources that local Chinese companies can devote to CSR practices. They tend to perceive that they cannot devote too much of their management time to CSR issues. But one of the problems here is that management styles in many Chinese companies are more oriented around problem solving and "fire-fighting" than the building of good systems and procedures.

Many factories in the supply chain are still using outdated, inefficient production lines. They are of the view that it is simply cheaper to hire more workers than invest in better and more efficient technology. But in many cases there is even a lack of awareness relating to even what technology exists in order to update production systems. In the apparel sector, for example, inefficiencies are sometimes so great that some orders result in a 10 per cent rejection rate. Lack of communication within and between different departments, poorly designed production lines, and a lack of communication between management and staff all contribute to these inefficiencies.

The reality is that many local companies are managed badly and there is often a lack of a systems approach to management. This might be related to a lack of qualified personnel or simply the lack of recognition about the benefits of moving towards a properly structured management system. Many management systems in place in Chinese companies are simply inefficient, unproductive and wasteful of human resources.

But even those managers more aware of CSR find that their own second-line managers lack the skills and training to be able to engage with CSR issues or even understand why they should be engaging in such practices. In China there is a lack of trained, qualified and aware staff who would be able to lead and develop CSR initiatives in companies. There is a lack of skills development in this area by most educational systems (and particularly at university level).

It is not only the human resources within the factory setting that are lacking but also in many areas there is a real lack of consultancy expertise as well. There are simply not enough adequately trained experts in areas such as lean manufacturing, human resource management, the environment, health and safety. Skills development and building expertise in all the various CSR areas is therefore a priority for the region and this implies a significant emphasis on training and education initiatives at all levels. But there is also a role for training relatively senior managers to try to tackle inefficient management systems.

Many managers see CSR as just one more thing to do. They complain that they already have to deal with quality issues (and in some cases compliance to quality standards), health and safety requirements and a whole host of other legally mandated requirements. They point out the need to spend large amounts of time preparing for audits and inspections. Many managers express frustration with many of these requirements and in some cases there is a good deal of evidence to suggest a degree of burnout as well. Doing even more than they are already doing is therefore seen as unfeasible.

9.6 International CSR Standards in the Chinese Context

Globally a number of standards have been developed in order to help companies address various aspects of CSR. These have included the ISO14000 series for environmental management systems and related aspects, ISO18000 for health and safety, SA8000 and WRAP (Worldwide Responsible Apparel Production) for labour standards and the AA1000 assurance standard with its emphasis on stakeholder engagement. Regionally, there have also been some interesting developments, with perhaps the most important one recently being China's home-grown social responsibility standard for the apparel sector, CSC9000T.

The major standards for workplace conditions found in Chinese supply chains are SA8000 (from Social Accountability International and for use in any manufacturing sector, but not recognised by the Chinese government), WRAP (for apparel), the ICTI COBP (for toys), and a number of initiatives based on a membership model such as the Fair Labour Association (FLA, for apparel), Worker Rights Consortium (WRC, with membership based on US colleges and universities in a range of manufacturing sectors but mainly apparel), the Clean Clothes Campaign (CCC, a European NGO based on apparel production), and the Fair Wear Foundation (FWF, based in the Netherlands and targeting apparel). There are also a number of multi-stakeholder initiatives including the Ethical Trading Initiative (based in London and with member companies across a number of sectors, particularly retailers), the AVE/BSCI (the German Retailers Association/ Business Social Compliance Initiative). All of these initiatives are founded on a base code of conduct that is in turn based on international workplace norms outlined in the ILO conventions and the UN's Universal Declaration of Human Rights and the Convention on Rights of the Child.

The interesting addition to the standards above is China's home-grown social responsibility standard for the apparel sector launched in May 2005. Similar to SA8000 (i.e. a management systems approach), CSC9000T was developed and administered by the China National Textile and Apparel Council (CNTAC), a national non-profit organisation of all textile-related industries set up to help modernise China's textile industry. It is based on the relevant Chinese laws and international standards, but does not call for freedom of association and collective bargaining (and simply notes that the ACFTU is the legal representative of workers in China).

It is clear that China is reluctant to adopt international standards that are in conflict with the government's other agendas. But what we are seeing is the development of new standards that can accommodate Chinese idiosyncrasies. At the local level many local and regional governments are also progressing from the environmental initiatives outlined above into the development of their own CSR instructions, guidelines and standards. Stock exchanges have been examining various policy measures to encourage reporting and other aspects of CSR in listed companies as well (Chan and Welford 2005).

9.7 The Future of CSR in China

The main challenge for China for the future is in moving away from an inspection and auditing mentality towards capacity building on the ground and creating longer term trusting relationships down the supply chain. That is not going to be easy and it will need the cooperation of a range of agencies, NGOs and business throughout the supply chain. Unfortunately in China it is very difficult to find local partners that have the ability, knowledge and know-how to help. One multi-stakeholder initiative in southern China that started an occupational health and safety (OHS) pilot project in late 2005 could only find enough local NGO staff to provide training in four small factories (with less than 1,000 workers). The initiative had originally hoped to work in eight factories.

Nevertheless, we have seen that when workers are aware of their own rights, and the laws applicable to them, and are empowered to take steps to protect themselves, outcomes can be positive. The next big challenge is to identify how best to build this sort of capacity, with whom and when. Many experts recognise that this is the struggle now confronting companies. There is a lot of rhetoric about capacity building but very few big companies or funding agencies are willing to invest the money required. It is no exaggeration that the big brands sourcing from China are crying out for local groups with capacity. Much of the focus so far has been on OHS, but issues such as dispute resolution, mediation and other aspects of worker empowerment are also needed.

Further training is the key to improving CSR in China. There is a need to both raise the awareness of managers about CSR issues and to develop the capacity to begin to implement CSR practices within companies. This must involve managers in identifying priorities for their country, sector and company as well as developing effective skills in putting ideas into practice. One starting point here is to develop training programmes that are accessible to Chinese managers.

Such programmes need to be developed in areas where there is already little capacity and will therefore need to have the support of organizations and agencies that are able to bring expertise to the table. Local government officials with particular responsibilities for specific factory issues, the small but growing NGO community, academics, consultants and experienced CSR managers need to be brought together in a programme of information sharing and skills development.

However, a serious problem exists within China and that revolves around a lack of people to lead such training events with sufficient expertise and experience to provide a meaningful introduction to CSR. In such circumstances there needs to be 'training the trainers' programmes put in place in advance of launching training programmes.

But training programmes, should, in time be extended beyond just factory managers. There is a need to build capacity within workforces and within national and local government, NGOs and local communities. Training programmes can also be targeted at particular issues (e.g. health and safety, employment law, environmental protection, wages) or at particular groups (e.g. women workers, migrant workers, NGOs, the media, etc.). It may well be that business associations can be a focal point for training initiatives in many locations.

9.8 Conclusions

This paper has shown that most CSR activities in China are led by the large Western brands keen to protect their image and reputation and avoid accusations of making products in sweatshops. Amongst the majority of local Chinese companies there is much less happening although it should be noted that the pace of change on these issues is very rapid indeed.

The government has been increasingly intervening in order to promote policies associated with the "harmonious society", sustainable development, environmental protection and labour rights. Some of its initiatives on the environment are innovative and we have seen pockets of significant success in some cities. But implementation of the law and other initiatives to promote CSR are often highly dependent on the actions and activities of local governments. Some of those areas provide opportunities for the corrupt activities of some officials rather than to progress toward better CSR practices.

The picture is very mixed but there is evidence to suggest that CSR will grow in importance over the coming years. With government encouragement, pressures from the brands, growing community protests and an increasingly vocal workforce we are seeing a new breed of Chinese workplace where owners and managers have experienced the benefits of CSR programmes through improvements in productivity and a reduction in staff turnover.

The picture may be mixed but there are some important conclusions. Firstly, unlike in the West, CSR in China is often seen as getting companies to obey local laws rather than necessarily exceed them. Secondly, although international standards influence Chinese supply chains, it will be the new Chinese standards that will shape the behaviour of the Chinese private sector in the short to medium term. To date, it has tended to be large buyers who have insisted on the implementation of labour laws rather than government regulators. But large buyers cannot indefinitely enforce local labour laws in their supply chains by voluntary methods. They have neither the money, capacity nor the legal backing to do so. In any case, codes of conduct have had only limited success.

Many local Chinese companies barely understand the relevant laws or importance of CSR standards that exist. Moreover, their employment practices, manufacturing processes and management systems are inconsistent with a move towards more corporate social responsibility. The challenge lies in the need for capacity building. But as noted previously, the capacity to build capacity is also lacking. One solution lies in developing coalitions and partnerships to train trainers and in turn to convince Chinese factories that CSR can be good for business.

References

Chan, A. (1998) Labor Standards and Human Rights: The Case of Chinese Workers Under Market Socialism, Human Rights Quarterly, 20(4), 886–904

Chan, A. (2001) China's Workers under Assault: The Exploitation of Labor in a Globalizing Economy, M. E. Sharp, New York

Chan, A. and Senser, R. A. (1997) China's Troubled Waters, Foreign Affairs, 76(2), 524–550

Chan, J. C. and Welford, R. J. (2005) Assessing Corporate Environmental Risk in China: An Evaluation of Reporting Activities of Hong Kong Listed Enterprises, Corporate Social Responsibility and Environmental Management, 12, 88–104

Ho, M. and Welford, R. J. (2006) Power, Protests and the Police: The Shootings at Shanwei, Corporate Social Responsibility and Environmental Management, 13, 233–237

Ho, P. and Vermeer, E. B. (2006) China's Limits to Growth: Greening State and Society, Blackwell, Oxford

Liu, J. and Diamond, J. (2005) China's environment in a globalizing world, Nature, 435, 1179–1186

Ma, X. and Ortolano, L. (2000) Environmental Regulation in China: Institutions, Enforcement, and Compliance, Lanham, Maryland

Schmitz, H. and Knorringa, P. (2000) Learning from Global Buyers, Journal of Development Studies, 37(2), 177–205

Studer, S., Welford, R. J., and Hills, P. H. (2006) Engaging Hong Kong Businesses in Environmental Change: Drivers and Barriers, Business Strategy and the Environment, 15, 416–431

Welford, R. J. and Frost, S. D. (2006) Corporate Social Responsibility in Asian Supply Chains, Corporate Social Responsibility and Environmental Management, 13, 166–176

Welford, R. J., Hills, P., and Lam, J. (2006) Environmental Reform, Technology Policy and Transboundary Pollution in Hong Kong, in Ho, P. and Vermeer, E. B. (eds.) China's Limits to Growth: Greening State and Society, Blackwell, Oxford

Welford, R. J. (2007) Corporate Governance and Corporate Social Responsibility: Issues for Asia, Corporate Social Responsibility and Environmental Management, 14, 42–51

World Bank (2007) World Development Report 2007: Development and the Next Generation, World Bank, Washington

Chapter 10
Malaysia: Value Relevance of Accounting Numbers

Mazurina Mohd Ali, Muhd Kamil Ibrahim, Rashidah Mohammad, Mustaffa M. Zain, and Mohd Rashidee Alwi

Abstract The increasing demands placed on businesses to fulfill its social responsibilities have heightened interests in corporate donations. Corporate donations exist when a corporation donates a portion of its resources to a societal cause. In addition, corporations have developed a wide array of charitable vehicles, namely, foundations, non-profit and association umbrella groups, as well as community outreach programs. Studies on this particular topic have been carried out in other markets such as the United States and the United Kingdom as well as in Europe. Being the first research in Malaysia, the goals of this study were (1) to examine whether stakeholders especially investors consider corporate donations when they determine the value of the firm, (2) to test empirically the determinants (i.e., leverage, firm's size, and profitability) of corporate donations made by 774 Malaysian Public Listed Companies of the Main Board. Three of the firms' specific characteristics were derived from agency and stakeholder theories. Firstly, multiple regression analysis was conducted in order to examine the perception of the stakeholders, especially investors, on the corporate donations. Secondly, a logistic regression analysis was conducted in order to examine the determinants of corporate donations made by the Public Listed Companies in Malaysian market. The results revealed that there is a positive relationship between corporate donations and the market value of equity. This study also revealed that there is no significant relationship between the leverage and the corporate donations. This result contradicts the findings of some other researches. However, the study provides evidence that the company size and profitability are important determinants of companies that are more likely to contribute to the society.

10.1 Introduction

Currently, corporate donations to charitable and community service organizations have recorded a remarkable increase. This has been proven by a number of studies that have been carried out in Western countries over the last two decades

(Dabson 1991; Logan 1993; Simon 1995; Pharoah 1996; Willsher 1996; Bennett 1997), even though till now the reasons underlying this event have not been thoroughly assessed. The studies on this topic have mainly been made in the United Kingdom, the United States, Europe, China, Korea, and Hong Kong, but as far as we are aware, none has been carried out in Malaysia.

Bae and Cameron (2006) reported that corporations have made an intensive attempt to donate money to valuable social causes since the late 1990s. Importantly, along with the increasing media coverage on issues of corporate donations, companies themselves are also taking direct and visible steps to communicate their corporate donations initiatives to various stakeholders. The reason for such socially responsible activity is generally connected with rising positive community perceptions of contributor corporations. Conversely, some researchers have questioned whether donations are always directly linked to better business. This is because the public frequently perceives donations as self-serving activities, and such cynicism by the public can weaken the future reputation of the corporations.

Also, depending on previous corporate reputation, the public may observe corporate donation messages in a different way. If a company has a good prior reputation, its donation messages are interpreted as an evenly useful activity rather than being perceived as a self-serving action. The latter will have an effect on public attitudes toward the company.

Bae and Cameron (2006) further supported this view when they expressed that the market showed a positive attitude toward the company when they inferred the company had a philanthropic purpose for charitable giving. On the other hand, they found that the market showed a negative attitude toward the company when they inferred the company had a self-serving intention for charitable giving. Adams and Hardwick (1998), on the other hand, examined the characteristics of firms that are associated with corporate donations in the UK. They have established a model that comprises the firm determinants including leverage, company size, and profitability. Ever since, the determinants of corporate donations to social causes have become an interesting and researchable topic area.

As mentioned earlier, studies on this particular topic have been done in overseas markets such as the US and the UK as well as in Europe. There is a likely need to have similar research carried out on Malaysian markets. It is worth noting that this would be the first research to examine whether the market takes corporate donations into consideration when they determine the value of a company. Further, it is also to examine whether the factors attributed affect the amount of corporate donations made by the Public Listed Companies of the Main Board of Bursa Malaysia. If corporate donations could be analyzed, this could contribute to the accounting literature and specifically to the behavioral aspects of the firms. Additionally, it will be interesting to study whether the situations exist for firms operating in developing countries like Malaysia similar to those in developed countries.

This study attempts to verify whether investors perceive and respond toward corporate donations and take it into considerations when they determine the value of a Malaysian company. This study also attempts to verify the factors that can contribute and affect the donations made by the company. Therefore, the main point of this study is to provide empirical evidence of the determinants of corporate donations in the Malaysian perspective.

10.2 Literature Review

The increasing demands placed on business to fulfil its social responsibilities have heightened the interest in corporate donations. Corporate donations take place when a corporation donates a portion of its resources to a societal cause. This is in accordance with the announcement made by Andrew Carnegie, the founder of Carnegie Steel (currently known as U.S. Steel) in 1889 that the rich had a moral obligation to give away their fortunes (Syverson 2006). Since then, corporations have developed a wide array of charitable vehicles, namely, foundations, non-profit and association umbrella groups, as well as community outreach programs.

According to Cogill and Harry (1991), corporations nowadays face increasing demands on their time, their energy, as well as their finances. Given the increasing complexity of business today, most businesses concur that they share an economic responsibility to support and promote the social and cultural well-being of the communities in which they carry out their businesses. The need for donation reflects one's consciousness that donation is necessary for helping the poor. It appears to contribute to the intention to donate money (Diamond and Kashyap 1997).

After all, the quality of life should be the highest priority. For that reason, any risk to the quality of life such as failure of the education system, the lack of appropriate health services, and poor support for families should be the main concern to business people. Besides, corporate donations can play a major role in improving these problems in addition to overcoming the crisis of the welfare condition. Corporate donations also allow a company to communicate its values or its opinion of what is essential, ethical, and beautiful.

Most importantly, a corporate donation differs from commercial sponsorship because it supposedly involves donations made without any expectation of direct commercial reward (Bennet 1998). According to McAlister and Ferrel (2002), philanthropy is located at the most voluntary and discretionary element of corporate responsibility and has not always been related to profits or the ethical culture of the firm. Instead, sponsorships involve money and in-kind gifts in return for appreciation and recognition with a particular cause or event.

In addition to these charitable donations, companies also make community contributions, including gifts in kind, loans of equipment and/or employees to organizations, the provision of facilities and professional advice, advertising in charity magazines and brochures, and non-commercial sponsorship. When charitable and community donations were combined, the U.K. corporate philanthropy was worth approximately £366 million in 1995 representing between 5 and 8% of the total revenues of the voluntary sector (Aagaard 1996). Casson (1995) found that, on average, community contributions were 1.85 times higher than a philanthropic company's straight charitable donations. Dabson (1991) similarly described substantial rises in corporate giving in Belgium, Germany, and France during the 1980s, although with a change in emphasis (as in the UK) away from direct charitable donation towards community projects.

Casson (1991) attributed the rise in European companies giving since 1980 to (1) high levels of takeover and merger activity, resulting in larger businesses with more resources to donate to charity; (2) record company profits; (3) increased sophistication in the manners in which charities appealed to companies; and (4) government pressures on firms to contribute to community needs.

In making corporate donations, a company is recognizing its accountability to its stakeholders[1], including employees, suppliers, customers, and the public at large: i.e., all the groups that give any company a "conditional license to operate". There is no company that operates solely in isolation from the society around them even though much of sustaining that license involves turning a profit.

According to Cogill and Harry (1991), to a certain extent corporations must respond to the broad range of values, needs, and expectations of the society that supports it. Researchers in the US and the UK suggest that corporations make contributions for a large number of reasons. These include, among others, increased customer loyalty, enhanced company reputation and strengthened employee commitment, and productivity (Business for Social Responsibility 1999). Other than that, the reasons for corporate donations include an active attempt to influence society, to seek public acceptance and applause, to increase their name recognition among consumers, to develop a better public image, to achieve greater consumer loyalty, and to improve community relations (Syverson 2006).

Smith (1994) addressed this potential corporate philanthropy, stating confidently that:

> Philanthropic and business units have joined forces to develop giving strategies that increase their name recognition among consumers, boost employee productivity, reduce research and development costs, overcome regulatory obstacles and foster synergy among business units...

On the basis of the above reasoning, the objectives for corporate donations increasingly appear to be more towards corporate strategy. In fact, as highlighted in the existing literature (e.g., Ricks Jr 2005), corporate donations range from altruistic to strategic.

As mentioned, most of the prior studies were concerned with corporate donations for the firms operating in developed countries such as the UK and the US. Even though corporate donations are depicted as a common, realistic, and socially significant, as well as an ordinary behavioral pattern in both Western and Asian countries, it has not been critically discussed for lack of research, especially in Malaysia. It is interesting to compare whether the situation is similar for firms operating in developing countries such as Malaysia. For that reason, the focus of this article is on the firm-specific giving practices and evaluates both an agency theory and stakeholder

---

[1] The term stakeholders refer to groups of constituents who have a legitimate claim on the firm (Freeman 1984).

theory, which postulates that managers and board members increase their own utility through corporate donations. On the basis of the theories, testable hypotheses regarding whether corporate donations create value to the firm, and the determinants of corporate donations, including leverage, company, size and profitability, are generated.

10.2.1 Motivations for Corporate Donations

In modern times, the motivation for corporate managers to make discretionary donations has turned out to be a prominent issue. In fact, corporate donations are not recognized within a short period of time. It is like a habit that requires a practice, which needs to be completed over and over again. Also, to make it a habit, corporate donations do not just link it to a matter of time but also the culture of a society itself. For example, past donation behavior is an important determinant of future donation. According to Bandura (1986), past donation behavior provides a critical learning experience based on social cognitive theory.

Moreover, there are many causes that lead to corporate donations to happen. For example, the existing literature has focused on three rationales for corporate philanthropy: through-the-firm giving, corporate statesmanship, and profit-motivated giving. In addition to that, only a few empirical studies deal with the underlying debate regarding whether corporate donations enhance firm value (Brown et al. 2006).

Corporate donations are normally treated as discretionary activities above and beyond the required daily activities (Waddock and Graves 1997). Therefore, corporate donations can be an excellent mechanism through which to observe and analyze the interface between stakeholders and corporate strategy. Most importantly, corporate donations can be used as a means by corporations to develop their competitive advantage. This is the quality of the business environment, principally in the location where they operate in, and it benefits the communities where people live and work. That is, having been granted the right by society to operate within a community, corporations have an implied social responsibility towards the community (Carroll 1991). This responsibility requires that business help to improve the quality of life in the community.

According to Bae and Cameron (2006), managing the corporate prospect platform and safety nets that instigate the external eye of beholders should be the main role of the companies. This is because good corporate reputation brings several tangible and intangible benefits to corporate business environments such as favorable media coverage (Fombrun et al. 2000).

Corporate donations can be divided into two particular types. First, altruistic donations are considered as unconditional in which the donations are not linked to revenue-producing transactions with the firm. This unconditional donation has no strings attached, except that the cause must often agree to the use of its name and logo by the firm in announcing the donation to the public (Dean 2003).

Second, there are conditional corporate donations in which there is a linkage of a firm's contribution to a charitable cause to revenue-producing transactions with the firm (Varadarajan and Menon 1998).

Siegfried et al. (1983) believe that many corporations view their contributions as a form of investment rather than classic philanthropy, specifically pure gifts. This view is supported by Bennett (1997) from the perspective that a corporate donation is a product that can be marketed to the public. Therefore, in his view corporate donations must be treated as investments whether in cash or in kind and should be efficiently managed with returns that are eventually beneficial to the donating firm.

On the other hand, financial stakeholders are recognized as a potential influence on charitable contributions in much of the recent literature (see Adams and Hardwick 1998; Navarro 1988). Their impact on charitable donations will depend on their preferences and influences within the company. Incidentally, Bartkus et al. (2002) provide evidence that active, powerful investors may perceive corporate donations as too much and act to limit it.

However, elements of the existing literature advocate that corporate donations may have significant implications for corporate performance (Hillman and Keim 2001; Navarro 1988). Hillman and Keim (2001) argue that corporate social performance can play an important role in generating and developing value-creating relationships with primary stakeholders. In other words, first and foremost, corporate donations are considered to be motivated by profit considerations. This is also known as *through-the-firm giving* in the literature (Manne and Wallich 1972). A study done by Fry et al. (1982) examine the profit motivation by determining the relationship between giving and advertising expenditures. They found that contributions are motivated by profit considerations that influence both advertising expenditures and corporate giving.

Conversely, Norton (1991) and Lee (1996) have insisted that a genuine donation lies at the heart of the majority of corporate donations. Managers who are involved in the corporate donations may feel good because they can help someone in need and this leads to the positive feelings inside them (Williamson and Clark 1989). According to Luks (1988), these feelings include a sense of calmness, physical sensations of warmth, enhanced feelings of self-worth, and other pleasurable emotions. Furthermore, corporate donations create opportunities to develop social contacts among key opinion formers and to impress shareholders and important people in public life (Aagaard 1996). Another way of viewing such activities is as a form of compensation by companies for their abuses of monopoly power and as a way, therefore, of buying social peace.

However, there is an important question on whether stakeholders will perceive corporate donations as self-interest and exploitation of charity rather than altruism. If so, this perception could backfire and result in a loss of goodwill toward the company. A study done by Dean (2003) explores the effects of company reputation by the type of donations. He found that by pursuing an unconditional donation, the average firm could enhance its image; however, a conditional donation did not damage the firm's image. Perception of the scrupulous firm was little changed after unconditional donations, but a scrupulous firm suffered a loss of favor by pursuing a conditional donation. It is concluded that the average firm does not risk a loss of public goodwill when using conditional donations.

10.2.2 Malaysian Scenario

Traditionally, the main concern of Malaysian businesses is to make profit. Their main objective is to serve the shareholders by maximizing the shareholders wealth. To achieve this they exercise whatever means and ways they can for as long as they are within the ambit of the law. In the last several decades, companies are forced to reconsider their objectives. This is in response to issues such as the oil crisis, environmental degradation, human rights, labor issues, and natural disasters. Instead of just trying to maximize profit and please their shareholders, many corporations now are beginning to understand that they now have a broad spectrum of stakeholders. This includes investors, creditors, employees, governments, nongovernmental organizations (NGOs), and the various communities in which they operate. Businesses have to satisfy all these stakeholders' needs, and hence have an additional role and purpose. Consequently, the term *corporate social responsibility* (CSR) was born.

CSR is about the rules for proper conduct for business enterprises. Corporations need to embrace "corporate citizenship" and run their affairs according to the need of the different arrays of "stakeholders", so as to promote the goal of "sustainable development". This goal supposedly has three dimensions: economic, social, and environmental. Companies should aim to meet the "triple bottom line" Profit, People and Planet, rather than focusing on profitability alone.

CSR focus in Malaysia is more towards the second "P" i.e., people. In the last three decades Malaysian businesses have emphasized more on human resource or employees (See Teoh and Thong 1984; Foo and Tan 1988; Andrew et al. 1989; Mohamed Zain 2004). Though donations and other philanthropic activities are not new in Malaysia, the last decade saw a significant increase. Corporations have an invisible social contract with the community. In order to succeed, corporations must have the "license to operate". This license is normally approved by the society if the corporation is seen as socially responsible. Malaysian companies have been very generous in lending a helping hand. Recently, the major flood in Southern Malaysian Peninsular saw many companies coming forward to contribute and participate in the "Disaster Response Team". Similarly, companies' involvement in helping the victim of the Tsunami in Acheh in 2004 and the earthquake in Jogjakarta is commendable.

What actually motivates Malaysian corporations to give donations and participate in community work? Apart from the genuine concern for the community, accountability, and "feeling good", Mohamed Zain (2004) found that the driving force for charity work is indirect government pressure. This is particularly true for government-linked companies. The introduction of Vision 2020 and the Caring Society, for example, has influenced a number of companies to focus more on the community.

Mohamed Zain (2004) also identifies the capital market playing a vital role in the development of the Malaysian economy. Even though Malaysian investors are not as sophisticated as their counterparts in the Western world, they are moving towards that. Significantly, the annual report and other mass media serve as public advertising documents. Enhancing the corporate image in order to take advantage of market opportunities is also a major factor in companies participating in charitable activities. This was predominant during the 2004 Acheh Tsunami and the 2006 South Malaysia flood, when CSR activities were highlighted daily by the mass media.

An (Association of Chartered Certified Accountants) ACCA (2004) survey looked at all the listed companies on the Bursa Malaysia. It found an increase, compared to a previous survey, in the number of companies reporting on social activities. The findings, published in ACCA Malaysia's study "State of Corporate Environmental and Social Reporting in Malaysia 2004", reported that 43% of the companies reviewed reported to some extent on their social performance. For many Malaysian companies, commitment to CSR is expressed in terms of charitable giving. The major drivers for this increased activities were (in addition to growing awareness) "business case" issues such as reputation/brand enhancement, promoting shareholder value, reducing risk, and complying with legislation/regulation in Malaysia (and abroad).

10.2.3 Studies in Value Relevance

Accounting numbers are defined as "value relevant" if they have a predicted association with equity market values. One way in which accounting numbers can be assessed is to see how they relate to stock returns. Accounting numbers that update the market's beliefs will generate a change in returns. The technique for measuring the market impact of accounting numbers was developed primarily by Ball and Brown (1968) and was called the *Abnormal Performance Index*.

Basically, there are three objectives of studying the value relevance of the accounting numbers. First, it is intended to test the relevance and reliability of accounting numbers as reflected in equity values. Second, a research on value relevance of accounting numbers can help in assessing how well the accounting numbers reflect information used by equity investors. Finally, the conclusions derived from such studies can be used as inputs for those involved in the setting and monitoring of Accounting Standards.

Value relevance is defined as the power of specific financial statement variables to explain changes in equity values. The greater the explanatory power of the specific financial statement variables, the greater the value relevance (Hasan and Asokan 2003). In other words, value relevance is understood as the ability of financial statement information to summarize or capture information that affects share values and empirically tested as a statistical association between market values and accounting values (Hellstrom 2005).

According to Francis et al. (2004), value relevance is one of the basic attributes of accounting quality. High-quality accounting information is a precondition for well-functioning capital markets and economy as a whole and as such should be of importance to investors, companies, and accounting standard setters. Investors rely on accounting information in their valuation of shares, and companies that provide good-quality information therefore have an advantage in a lower cost of capital.

Traditionally, earnings and book values are stated to contribute to value relevance (Ohlson 1995). Researchers have proved a high degree of association between changes in earnings and book values as well as a combination of both with changes in equity values. The intrinsic assumption is that earnings and book values have information content to investors. This information is then reflected positively or negatively in stock prices.

Investors demand value-relevant information from financial statements and financial information. For example, earnings per share show a high association with market values or price returns indicates value relevance. More importantly, it is to evaluate the relevance of accounting numbers for investors in their investment.

Value relevance research assesses how well accounting numbers reflect information used by equity investors. As stated in the work by Ronen (2001), one of the studies carried out by Raman (2001) employs a "value-relevance" methodology, which finds associations between prices or measures derived there from and accounting numbers based on alternative treatments in an attempt to derive implication for accounting policy formulation. According to Ronen (2001), the reason underlying these value relevance studies is that prices are the best available reflection of fundamental value; accounting treatments that generate numbers more closely associated with prices are superior to accounting treatments that generate numbers less closely associated with prices.

Studies of the long-term association between stock returns and accounting numbers value the information in financial statements against that in stock prices. The association studies do not assume that investors use only accounting data in their investment decisions. Pritchard (2002) refers to study by Dumontier and Raffournier (2002) and suggests that accounting data are value relevant if they are good summary measures of the events incorporated in security prices because their use might provide a value of the firm that is close to its market value. Therefore, association studies test whether accounting numbers provide a good summary measure of the value-relevant events that have been incorporated in stock prices during the reporting period: in other words, test whether and how quickly accounting measures capture changes in the information set that is reflected in security returns over a given period (Kothari 2001).

Basically, on the basis of past studies that examine the association between accounting numbers (i.e., earnings and book values) and stock prices show that, generally, the association between accounting information and stock prices has been declining over time. These findings have been interpreted to be the result of a decline in the value relevance of accounting. The literature has also found that the value relevance of book values has been increasing; however, results are mixed on whether the increase in the relevance of book value has offset the decrease observed in earnings. The literature posits that one of the reasons for the observed decrease in value relevance is conservatism in accounting.

Numerous studies in the US have recognized that the value relevance of earnings has declined over the last few decades as measured by the extent of association between either share price or share returns and accounting earnings, but they offer different reasons for this decline (Goodwin and Ahmed 2006). In one instance, a study by Lev and Zarowin (1999) attribute this decline to the lack of proper recognition of intangibles in the financial statements by U.S. companies.

Nevertheless, the situation is different when similar research on the value relevance of the accounting numbers are undertaken in the Malaysian context. There are various but limited number of researches undertaken by Malaysian academicians to examine the value relevance of the accounting numbers. Most, if not all, of the research found that the accounting numbers provided by the financial statements prepared by corporations are still relevant and useful for the purpose of decision making among Malaysian investors.

A research carried out by Ibrahim et al. (2003a) examined the value relevance of accounting numbers by looking specifically on the purchased goodwill. The study seeks to investigate empirically the association between goodwill and market value and to describe the relationship between purchased goodwill and other assets of the firms operating in Malaysia. It was found that goodwill numbers are of value relevance to investors. The analysis also confirms that goodwill is an asset of considerable magnitude and is valued at least as equal to other assets, and the results also indicate that investors do use information in the balance sheet when making an economic decision.

Another empirical research performed by Ibrahim et al. (2003b) found that Malaysian investors do take into consideration the balance sheet numbers when determining the market value of companies. Specifically, the study investigates the association between the book value of equity and the value placed on the firm by the stock market. This study examined the top 100 firms for a period of eight years. The findings are consistent with the notion that the market incorporates the information on accounting numbers in the balance sheet in the valuation of a firm and support the existing findings on the usefulness of reported balance sheet numbers to investor decisions.

In another viewpoint, Ibrahim et al. (2004a) studied the value relevance of accounting numbers in predicting the financial health of distressed firms in Malaysia. The main finding shows that some of the accounting ratios have predictive ability in forecasting the financial health of Malaysian firms. This result also confirms that the book value of assets is a value-relevant item for both distressed and healthy firms. However, the earnings figure is value relevant only for healthy firms.

Ibrahim et al. (2004b) went one notch higher in their research with a study on the relative value relevance of earnings and book value in explaining market value of equity in Malaysia and Singapore. Results of the study indicate that the relative value relevance of book value is greater than earnings in both the countries under study. From the sensitivity analysis, factors such as the earnings sign, firm size, and macroeconomic events affect the relative value relevance of earnings and book value in the two countries. However, the results seem to be driven by large firms and firms reporting negative earnings only.

In conclusion, there has been a plethora of studies examining the association of financial statement numbers with equity values, which has been popularly referred to as *value relevance*. However, the research findings in two different environments (i.e., Western countries and Malaysia) has been mixed, whereas in Malaysia, most, if not all, of the research performed in studying the value relevance of the accounting numbers have shown evidence of supporting the relevance of such numbers to the investors.

10.3 Research Methodology

The purpose of this study is twofold. On the one hand, this study tries to examine whether the market or the investors tend to focus on corporate donations when valuing firms. On the other, this study is to find out whether the factors of leverage, firm's size, and profitability do influence the determinants of corporate donations by Public Listed Companies of the Main Board of Bursa Malaysia. Previous studies in developed countries provide evidence on these relationships, in which the association of corporate donations and the factors are based on the agency theory and stakeholder theory. This particular section explains the hypotheses of the study as well as research design, sample selection, data collection, and data analysis.

10.3.1 Value Relevance and Corporate Donations

The first research question to be addressed in this study is whether corporate donations should be considered as an important element when determining a firm's market value. Ball and Brown (1968) evaluated the informativeness of accounting numbers by looking at the stock market reaction to the release of accounting data.

This study particularly focuses on the value relevance of corporate donations on a firm's value in the Malaysian capital market. However, there is still a limited understanding of whether corporate donations affect the market value of the firm. Certainly, as stated in Luo and Bhattacharya (2006), Brown and Dacin (1997) immediately call for research on "how socially oriented activities might bring about positive outcomes for the firm". In the context of broader CSR, a study done by Luo and Bhattacharya (2006) found that CSR affects market value partly through a mediator of customer satisfaction. However, in this study the focus is on one aspect of CSR: corporate donations. It is considered that if market (i.e., investors) places value on the corporate donations of a firm, then the value of the contributor firm will increase. Hence, corporate donations should be significant and positively related to the firm's market value. Therefore, the first hypothesis of this study is

H1: *Ceteris paribus*, corporate donations are positively related to the firm's market value.

10.3.2 Determinants of Corporate Donations

The second research question in this study looks at the linkages between the level of donations and the characteristics of Malaysian public listed companies. Extensive empirical work relating firm-specific characteristics to the level of corporate donations have been done on the basis of a number of theoretical arguments that include stakeholder theory and agency theory.

In particular, the hypotheses in this study are developed on the basis of the hypotheses suggested by Adams and Hardwick (1998) and Brammer and Millington (2004). The area of interest revolves around the impact of a firm's characteristics such as leverage, company size, and profitability. Brammer and Millington (2004) have classified these characteristics into two non-mutually exclusive categories: size of the firm (size) and the role of financial constraints on corporate decision makers (profit, leverage).

10.3.3 Leverage

The agency theory suggests that companies with high corporate leverage (high debt to equity ratio) are regularly associated with increased contracting cost including liquidity and bankruptcy cost. For example, debt contracts could impose liquidity tests, unscheduled audit, investment restrictions, and sinking-fund requirement, in addition to establishing the pre-emptive claims of debt holders in the event of bankruptcy (Booth 1992).

Creditors, including debt holders and those individuals and organizations that would bear the financial cost in the event of bankruptcy, may also be expected to be influential. Debt holders have an interest in ensuring that debt is serviced and repaid, while government and the local community will wish to minimize the risk of bankruptcy and its attendant costs (Cornell and Shapiro 1987).

Also, managers may also come under pressure to reduce discretionary expenditures from other stakeholders who have an interest in the survival of the company such as employees, government, and the local community (Cornell and Shapiro 1987). Stakeholder theory holds that companies must not satisfy the explicit contractual rights of parties such as debt holders to receive a satisfactory return on their capital only. They need to fulfill the implicit claims of other constituencies such as government to avoid financial risks. In other words, a low level of corporate leverage could ensure that the firms continue to satisfy the implicit claims of external constituencies by means of charitable corporate contributions. McGuire et al. (1987) share this view when they argue that if a company has a low percentage of total debt to total assets, it may also have high social responsibility.

Moreover, agency costs are higher for firms with proportionally more debt in their capital structures since potential wealth transfers, from debt holders to shareholders and managers, increase with leverage. Thus, the agency theory posits that where debts are high, managers may act to minimize discretionary payments that are not central to the continuation of the company in order to service debt and ensure the continuing support of creditors (Adams and Hardwick 1998).

Financial stakeholders are recognized as a potential influence on charitable contributions in much of the recent literature (e.g. Adams and Hardwick 1998; Navarro 1988). Their impact on charitable contributions will depend on their preferences and influence within the company. Shareholders are assumed to be concerned with the maximization of shareholder wealth and act, and therefore as a restraint on discretionary activities by management (Navarro 1988). In contrast, debt holders will monitor the corporate donations made by the company and they come out to restrain the giving. This is because firms with higher debts are usually under greater scrutiny by creditors to ensure that the firms are not breaching debt covenants. The management is restrained by shareholders and debt holders, and faces the pressure of paying dividend and debt. This shows that firms with more debt give less.

However, recent evidence emphasizes the growing importance of ethical investment. Corporate social performance is coming under increasing scrutiny from both ethical investment research services and fund managers. Plus, earlier studies provide support for a negative relationship between debt, usually expressed as leverage (debt to assets or equity ratio), and charitable contributions (Adams and Hardwick 1998; Navarro 1988). Therefore, the second hypothesis is that:

H2: *Ceteris paribus*, lowly leveraged companies will tend to make larger donations than highly leveraged companies. Therefore, there is a negative association between corporate donations and the leverage.

10.3.4 Company Size

Company size has been identified in a number of studies as an important feature that could proxy corporate characteristics. Meznar and Nigh (1995) argue that organizational size is a good measure of organizational power and that powerful organizations are better able to resist external pressure. Differences in corporate donations based on organizational size have been observed in previous studies. There are many reasons why large companies might contribute more than the others. According to Brammer and Millington (2003), assessment of the relationship between corporate size and corporate contributions suggests that overall corporate giving is highly concentrated among the largest givers.

Large companies are likely to be more complex since they are more likely to be multiproduct based and operate in a number of geographical areas (Cooke 1989, 1991; Meek et al. 1995). Several studies have found evidence that company size has a strong influence on the corporate donations (Siegfried et al. 1983, Adams and Hardwick 1998; Brammer and Millington 2004, 2006). It has been argued that large firms, as compared to smaller firms, will be more motivated to provide corporate donations.

Larger firms are also subject to more political cost (Roberts 1992). Jensen and Meckling (1976) have suggested that some citizens may lobby elected officials for nationalization, expropriation, or the break-up of the entity or industry. Political lobbying may also be undertaken to increase the extent of regulation in a particular industry.

Prior studies by Roberts (1992) states that corporate size would be positively related to social activities because large companies are more likely to be subject to inspection from the general public and government bodies than small companies. Large companies could increase corporate donations to charities, the local community, and other bodies, in order to alleviate the risk that government agencies might impose additional cost (e.g., higher taxation and regulatory compliance costs) on them if they do not act in a socially responsible manner. Therefore, companies may invest in charitable contributions in order to improve external perceptions of the company, influence external decision makers, and reduce the risk of regulatory activity that may limit management discretion, or reduce the value of the firm (Roberts 1992; Watts and Zimmerman 1978). This reasoning suggests that a stakeholder analysis for corporate donation is theoretically consistent with the political cost framework proposed by Watts and Zimmerman (1978).

On the other hand, large organizations are likely to have a greater availability of extra financial and other resources. For that reason, large organizations may have a degree of discretion in determining their social responsiveness strategy that is denied to smaller, less powerful organizations.

Much of the empirical literature on corporate donations have found a strongly positive correlation between company size and corporate donations (Adams and Hardwick 1998; Brammer and Millington 2004, 2006) and they have highlighted the position of company size on philanthropic expenditures (McElroy and Siegfried 1985; Adams and Hardwick 1998). Therefore, the third hypothesis is that:

H3: *Ceteris paribus*, large companies will tend to make larger donations than small companies. Therefore, there is a positive association between the corporate donations and the company's size.

10.3.5 Profitability

Profitable and well-run firms have the inducement to differentiate themselves from less profitable firms in order to raise capital on the best available terms. It is expected that the greater the profitability of a firm, the greater the level of corporate donations. Previous researchers such as Ullmann (1985), McGuire and Schneeweis (1988), and Roberts (1992) among others have debated that financial performance could influence corporate social behavior. The positive linkage between profitability and CSR has also been acknowledged by Alexander and Buchholz (1978).

According to Navarro (1988), charitable contributions may have significant implications for corporate performance. Empirical evidence supporting a direct relation between the amount of money donated by companies and profitability is also reported in the U.S. study of Siegfried et al. (1983). Cochran and Wood (1984) have reported that there is a direct relationship between corporate donations and profitability. When profits are high, managers possess a pool of funds from which to resource discretionary activities and respond to stakeholder demands (Adams and Hardwick 1998). On the contrary, low levels of profit constrain discretionary behavior as managers seek to satisfy creditors and shareholders. Recent results provide convincing support to the view that a positive relationship exists between corporate donations and profitability (Adams and Hardwick 1998; Navarro 1988). Therefore, the fourth hypothesis is that:

H4: *Ceteris paribus*, profitable companies will tend to make larger donations than less profitable companies. Therefore, there is a positive association between the corporate donations and the company's profitability.

10.4 Research Design

10.4.1 Basic Model

As explained earlier, the main objective of this study is twofold. To examine the first objective, a multivariate regression was conducted using the basic model of market value predictions for the year 2003 and 2005, which are estimated as follows:

For the first objective, a linear regression analysis undertaken on SPSS (Statistical Package for Social Sciences) was used based on the basic model of market value predictions for the year 2003 and 2005. The empirical model is:

$$MVE_{jt} = \beta_0 + \beta_1 BVNA_{jt} + \beta_2 DON_{jt} + \varepsilon_{jt}$$

where

MVE_{jt} is market value of shareholders equity in firm j, year t,
$BVNA_{jt}$ is the book value of net assets in firm j, year t,
DON_{jt} is a dummy variable taking the value unity if the company is making corporate donations, otherwise coded zero for firm j in year t, and
ε_{jt} is an error term in firm j, year t.

The model adopted in this study has been used in prior studies in determining the market value of companies. The several studies include the pension fund property rights by Landsman (1986) and a study done by Jennings et al. (1996) on whether purchased goodwill is reflected in the distribution of equity values. In particular, this study has adopted the model from the work of Ibrahim et al. (1999, 2003a, b, c, 2004a, b) to test the market's perception of a firm's assets and liabilities.

In this study, the regression was conducted separately for each year. If the theoretical model is correct, then the empirical value of β_0 should be zero. The market value of shareholder's equity is defined as the total number of shares outstanding, multiplied by the share prices at the year's end. The book value of net assets ($BVNA$) is used as a proxy for the market value, as the latter is not observable. On the other hand, if β_2 is significant, it implies that investors take into consideration the value of corporate donations when valuing firms.

10.4.2 Logit Model

For the second objective, the model used to test empirically whether the corporate donation is related to the factors attribute is based on the previous model of Adams and Hardwick (1998). On the basis of their studies, a multivariate logit regression model is developed. Basically, logit regression is a form of regression that is used when the dependent is a dichotomy. In logistic regression, besides predicting the value of a variable Y from a predictor variable X or several predictor variables (X_k), the probability of Y occurring given known values of X (or X_k) is also predicted. In mathematics, probabilities always lie between 0 and 1. An impossible event has a probability of 0 and a certain event has a probability of 1.

In general, logit model takes the form

$$Logit(p) = \log\left(\frac{p}{1-p}\right) = \log(p) - \log(1-p) \tag{10.1}$$

or

$$Logit(p) = \ln\left(\frac{p}{1-p}\right) = a_0 + a_1X_1 + a_2X_2 + \cdots a_kX_k \tag{10.2}$$

Fundamentally, if p is a probability then $\frac{p}{1-p}$ is the corresponding odds, and the logit[2] of the probability is the logarithm of the odds. Similarly, the difference between the logits of two probabilities is the logarithm of the odds ratio, thus providing an additive mechanism for combining odds ratios.[3]

Moreover, by looking at the equation (10.2), the logarithm of the odds of the outcome is modeled as a linear function of the independent variables, X_k and is equivalent to multiple regression equation with log of the odds as the dependent variable. Also, equation (10.2) is usually referred to as multiple logistic regressions. Subsequent discussions provide further explanation for referring to the equation (10.2) as logistic regression.

For simplicity, when there is only one predictor variable, X_1, the logistics regression equation from which the probability of Y occurring, $P(Y)$, predicted is given as

$$P(Y) = \frac{1}{1 + e - (a_0 + a_1X_1)} \tag{10.3}$$

On the other hand, when several predictors are included into the equation, the equation becomes

$$P(Y) = \frac{1}{1+e} - Z$$
$$Z = a_0 + a_1X_1 + a_2X_2 + \cdots a_nX_n + d_{ii} \tag{10.4}$$

---

[2] Gujarati, D.N. (2003). Basic Econometrics. Fourth Edition, McGraw-Hill.

[3] The explanation on logistic regression is taken from http://en.wikipedia.org/wiki/Logit as well as from Gujarati (2003).

In this particular study, $P(Y)$ is the probability of the firms making corporate donations and X_n are the measurement of firm attributes. Meanwhile, a_n is the parameter estimates. The independent variables used in this study are more or less the same as in the work of Adams and Hardwick (1998). The model to be estimated is expressed as follows:

$$DON_{jt} = \beta_0 + \beta_1 LEV_{jt} + \beta_2 InSIZE_{jt} + \beta_3 PROF_{jt} + \varepsilon_{jt}$$

where

DON_{jt} is a dummy variable taking the value 1 if the company is making corporate donations, otherwise coded 0, for firm j in year t,

LEV_{jt} is the total debt/total assets for firm j in year t,

$InSIZE_{jt}$ is measured by the natural log of total assets of firm j in year t,

$PROF_{jt}$ is the earnings per share (EPS) for firm j in year t, and

ε_{jt} is the error term for firm j in year t.

The selection of corporate donations as a dependent variable is derived from a dichotomous measure whereby this variable takes a value of 1 if the company is making corporate donations; otherwise it is assigned a value 0. Since there is a dichotomous dependent variable, linear regression is not suitable for estimating the parameters (Theil 1971; Hagerman and Zmijewski 1979). The rationale is that one of the assumptions of linear regression is that there must exist linear relationship between variables. In this case, since there is a dichotomy dependent variable, the assumption might be violated.

As a result, logit regression analysis is selected, as it applies the maximum likelihood estimating procedure, which is logarithmic transformation of the dependent into a logit variable (the natural log of the odds of the dependent occurring or not). According to Adams and Hardwick (1998), logarithmic transformations also alleviate the likelihood of the empirical results that may be confounded by extreme values in the data set. Besides, logit regression overcomes the problem of violating the assumption of linearity since the logit regression does not assume linearity of relationship between the independent and the dependent variables.

10.4.3 Independent Variables

The independent variables to be included in this study are based on the variables used in previous research that has significant explanations in the past regression model. Also, the selection of these variables is based on the availability of the financial data and their relevance to the factors that will be tested in relation to the determinants of corporate donations by Public Listed Companies of the Main Board of Bursa Malaysia. Hence, only specific related variables are chosen. The organization's characteristics chosen were leverage, company size, and profitability.

Table 10.1 Independent variable definitions and summary of hypotheses

Variable	Measurement	Symbol	Expected sign
Leverage	Ratio of total debt to the total value of assets (Brammer and Millington 2004)	*LEV*	–
Company size	Natural logarithm (ln) of total value of assets of the firm (Brammer and Millington 2004)	*SIZE*	+
Profitability	Measured by the earnings per share (EPS)	*PROF*	+

On the basis of the above, the independent variables are defined as follows:

Leverage: In this study, leverage is measured by a variable *LEV* that is defined as the ratio of total debt to total assets (Brammer and Millington 2004). Earlier researchers such as Adams and Hardwick in their study defined leverage as the ratio of total long-term debt at book value plus prior charge capital (e.g., preference shares) to the total value of assets.

Company size: Following Adams and Hardwick (1998) and Lenway and Rehbein (1991), size is measured by total value of assets. According to Adams and Hardwick (1998) and Brammer and Millington (2004), in order to minimize and reduce the impact of heteroscedasticity and extreme values, this variable is expressed in natural logarithms (ln). Therefore, this study employed the natural log value of total assets (Brammer and Millington 2004) to avoid those problems.

Profitability: Much of the accounting literature (e.g., Waddock and Graves 1997; Adams and Hardwick 1998) commonly measured profitability as the ratio of net profit before interest and taxation to turnover. In contrast, this study uses earnings per share (EPS) to measure the profitability of the company. This is due to the availability of the data and because it gives a contribution to this study as well. Thus, we expect the profitability to be positively related to the corporate donations by the Malaysian companies.

The independent variables (i.e., the determinants of corporate donations) are summarized in Table 10.1. The table also shows the expected signs of the independent variables in this study.

10.4.4 Sample Specification

In order to carry out this study, the 2003 and 2005 annual reports were obtained for the sample from Public Listed Companies of the Main Board of Bursa Malaysia. The 2003 sample consisted of companies with year-end between January 1, 2003 and December 31, 2003. Similarly, the 2005 sample consisted of companies with year-end between January 1, 2005 and December 31, 2005. The annual reports were downloaded primarily from the Bursa Malaysia Website.[4]

---

[4] http://www.bursamalaysia.com/website/bm/listed_companies/company_announcements/annual_reports/index.jsp

Table 10.2 Description of the sampling procedures

Sample selection	2003	2005	Total
Total number of companies listed on Bursa Malaysia Website as in March 2007	656	656	1,312
Banking/Financial Services Companies	(46)	(46)	(92)
Missing data/variables	(227)	(219)	(446)
Number of companies available	383	391	774

The first stage in shaping the sample was by taking all companies listed in the Main Board of Bursa Malaysia. A list of all companies listed in the Main Board was obtained from the Bursa Malaysia Website. Until March 2007, there were 656 publicly traded companies listed on Bursa Malaysia Main Board.

A sample selection was prepared on the basis of the subsequent criterion: First, full samples of companies listed in the Main Board of Bursa Malaysia were included except for the finance sector. The finance sector was excluded because of its exclusive features and business activities including the fact that they were governed by the Banking and Financial Institutions Act 1989. This means that they would have different regulations compared to other sectors. Second, all the variables of interest must be available for a company for both 2003 and 2005. The variables of interest included in both models in the study were (1) the basic model that includes variables such as share prices, total number of shares, total assets, and total liabilities; (2) corporate donations model that includes, among others, total debt, total assets, and earnings per share. Specifically, for the variable corporate donations (DON) that are used in both of the models, only companies that make donations will be considered as 1. Any companies that do not make donations or otherwise make sponsorship will not be considered as donations. Therefore, this will be considered as zero.

After fulfilling all the above requirements, there were 383 and 391 companies available for 2003 and 2005, respectively. A description of the sampling procedures is presented in Table 10.2.

The financial statement data for the study, including the data on earnings per share, long-term assets, current assets, current liabilities, long-term liabilities, and total number of shares issued, were collected from the financial statement section of annual reports. The information of whether the company was making corporate donations was obtained from the Corporate Events Section. Finally, share prices data were obtained from the DataStream.

10.5 Data Analysis and Findings

A summary of the final sample used in this study is presented in Table 10.3. The table also outlines the number of companies making corporate donations and those not making corporate donations. The final sample of this study is

Table 10.3 Summary of the sample

Decision	Years		N	% (Overall)
	2003	2005		
1 = Donate	144	98	242	31.27
0 = Not Donate	239	293	532	68.73
Total	383	391	774	100.00

774 firm-years. The corporate donations model is estimated on the basis of the dichotomous dependent variable whereby firms making donations are coded as 1, otherwise coded 0. Table 4.1 shows that only 31.27%, which is equivalent to 242 companies, of the total sample making corporate donations.

10.5.1 Correlation Matrix of Variables

A Pearson product moment coefficient of correlation (r) was computed to examine the correlation between the independent variables as well as to have some approximate idea relating to the multicollinearity[5] problem. According to Keller and Warrack (2000), multicollinearity exists in almost all multiple regression models. In actual fact, to find two totally uncorrelated variables is uncommon. In this study, the results of Pearson correlation indicated the existence of significant correlation between certain variables. The correlation matrix of variables was tested for both models.

10.5.2 Basic Model

By referring to the Table 10.4 and Table 10.5, as expected, the market value of equity (*MVE*) is significantly correlated with the book value of net assets (*BVNA*) and the level of corporate donations (*DON*). At the 0.01 significance level, *BVNA* was correlated with the level of corporate donations, as the coefficient of correlation was 0.253 for the year 2003. For the year 2005, there is no evidence that the two independent variables are significantly correlated. Overall, the effect of multicollinearity does not suggest any problems as the coefficient of correlation between *BVNA* and *DON* was with only 0.104 at the 0.01 significance level.

---

[5] In accounting terms, multicollinearity refers to the condition that exists when independent variables are highly correlated with each other. In the presence of multicollinearity, the estimated Regression Coefficients may be unreliable. The presence of multicollinearity can be tested by investigating the correlation (r) between the independent variables.

Table 10.4 Estimated correlation matrix of variables

Year	Variables	MVE	BVNA	DON
	MVE	1.000	0.309[b]	0.203[b]
2003	BVNA		1.000	0.253[b]
	DON			1.000
	MVE	1.000	0.117[a]	0.226[b]
2005	BVNA		1.000	0.046
	DON			1.000

[a]Correlation is significant at the 0.05 level (two-tailed).

[b]Correlation is significant at the 0.01 level (two-tailed)

10.5.3 Corporate Donations Model

Table 10.6 reports correlation coefficients for variables used in a logit regression model for the year 2003 and 2005. Table 10.9 shows the overall correlations of corporate donations and the independent variables, which are leverage (*LEV*), firm's size (*InSIZE*), and profitability (*PROF*). As expected, there is a significant correlation between corporate donations with the leverage (*LEV*), company size (*InSIZE*), and the profitability (*PROF*).

Table 10.7 reveals statistically significant r statistics between the following independent variables: leverage and the company size (0.313, $p < 0.01$), and company size and profitability (0.143 $p < 0.01$). Hossain et al. (1995) refer to study done by Gujarati (1988), which suggests that the correlation below absolute 0.80 should not be deemed harmful with regard to multicollinearity.

Turning to the correlation coefficients of the determinants of the variables, as expected, the level of corporate donations (*DON*) is positively and significantly correlated with the company size (*InSIZE*) and the profitability (*PROF*). There is also evidence of significant positive correlation between level of corporate donations (*DON*) and the leverage (*LEV*), which is contrary to our hypotheses.

Table 10.5 Overall estimated correlation matrix of variables

N = 774	MVE	BVNA	DON
MVE	1.000	0.144[a]	0.200[a]
BVNA		1.000	0.104[a]
DON			1.000

[a]Correlation is significant at the 0.01 level (2-tailed).

Table 10.6 Correlation coefficient matrix

Year	Variables	DON	LEV	SIZE	PROF
	DON	1.000	0.100[a]	0.301[b]	0.129[a]
2003	LEV		1.000	0.253[b]	−0.079
	SIZE			1.000	0.102[a]
	PROF				1.000
	DON	1.000	0.124[a]	0.391[b]	0.245[b]
2005	LEV		1.000	0.303[b]	0.059
	SIZE			1.000	0.265[b]
	PROF				1.000

[a]Correlation is significant at the 0.05 level (two-tailed).
[b]Correlation is significant at the 0.01 level (two-tailed).

10.5.4 Corporate Donations and Market Value

To test whether the market, especially investors perceive corporate donations as an important variable in the determination of the value of a company, a multiple regression analysis was undertaken on SPSS. Table 10.6 presents the results of the regression analysis for the year 2003 and 2005, which have defined the market value of shareholders' equity (*MVE*) as the share price at year-end times the total number of shares. As mentioned, β_1 and β_2 are the slope coefficients for book value of net assets and corporate donations respectively. If the investor places value on the book value of net assets, then β_1 should be positively related to a firm's market value. Likewise, if the investor places value on the corporate donations of a firm, then β_2 should be positively related to a firm's market value.

As shown in the Table 10.8, the basic model reported the F-value of 23.905 and 12.908 (both are significant at the 0.01 level) for the year 2003 and 2005, respectively. This basic model was highly significant.

The value of the beta coefficient was used to measure how sensitive of market value of equity to the changes in all independent variables. The bigger the value of coefficient beta, the stronger the effect of the independent variables on the market value of equity. The +/− sign of the coefficient beta indicates the positive or negative relationship between the market value of equity and the independent variables.

Table 10.7 Correlation coefficient matrix (Overall)

N = 774	DON	LEV	SIZE	PROF
DON	1.000	0.131[b]	0.367[b]	0.154[b]
LEV		1.000	0.313[b]	−0.027[a]
SIZE			1.000	0.143[b]
PROF				1.000

[a]Correlation is significant at the 0.05 level (two-tailed).
[b]Correlation is significant at the 0.01 level (two-tailed).

Table 10.8 Market value predictions (Basic Model)

Predicted Sign	β_0 ?	β_1+	β_2+	R^2	Adjusted R^2	F Value	N
2003	331546911.2	0.275	0.133	0.112	0.107	23.905[b]	383
T-statistic		3.73	5.501	2.659			
p-value		0.000[b]	0.000[b]	0.008[b]			
2005	547676206.7	0.107	0.221	0.062	0.058	12.908[b]	391
T-statistic		4.349	2.183	4.484			
p-value		0.000[b]	0.030[a]	0.000[b]			

[a]Significant at the 0.05 level.
[b]Significant at the 0.01 level.

$$Model: MVE_{jt} = \beta_0 + \beta_1 BVNA_{jt} + \beta_2 DON_{jt} + \varepsilon_{jt}$$

where: MVE_{jt} Market value of shareholders equity in firm j, year t; $BVNA_{jt}$ Book value of net assets in firm j, year t; DON_{jt} A dummy variable taking the value one (1) if the company is making corporate donations, otherwise coded zero (0), for firm j in year t; ε_{jt} Error term in firm j, year t.

A positive relationship implies that the market value of equity will increase if the independent variables increase; and a negative relationship indicates that the market value of equity will decrease if the independent variables increase.

Out of the two variables used in the model, both were found significant. For the book value of net assets ($BVNA_{jt}$), it is found to have coefficients of the correct sign. As book value of net assets was calculated by deducting the total liabilities from the total assets, it is obvious that this finding is consistent with the premise that book assets and book liabilities carried at historical cost may systematically understate or overstate the values of the theoretical variables owing to economic factors (Kane and Unal 1990). The estimated coefficients for $BVNA_{jt}$ are significant at the 1% level and 5% level for years under study. Thus, these findings confirm that the investors were taking into consideration the accounting book value of net assets in determining the market value of the firms. These findings support the findings of most prior research (e.g., Ibrahim et al. 1999).

However, the major concentration of this study is on β_2, which is the slope coefficient for corporate donations (DON_{jt}). In order to determine whether the company involves in corporate donations or vice versa, p-value for dummy variable was checked to ascertain its significance. DON, which is a dummy variable, indicates whether the company is making corporate donations or not. If the markets, especially investors, place value on the reported corporate donations of a company, then the corporate donations should be significant and positively correlated with the firm's market value. In this study, the β_2 coefficient for corporate donations was found to be significant at the 0.01 level for the year 2003 and 2005. This can be assumed that, from the investors' point of view, corporate donations are one of the criteria that they looked into when they evaluate the company. The positive sign of β_2, the slope coefficient of the corporate donations (DON_{jt}), also suggests that the market value of the company making corporate donations are higher as compared to the companies not involved in this social activity. As a result, these findings are

Table 10.9 Corporate donations model logistic regression summary statistic

Predicted Sign	β_0 ?	β_1-	β_2+	β_3+	Pseudo $-R2$	N
2003	−10.835	0.362	0.497	0.42	0.101	
T-ratio	−5.554	0.794	5.071	1.867		383
p-value	0.000	0.428	0.000^c	0.062^a		
2005	−13.83	−0.029	0.641	1.282	0.171	
T-ratio	−6.833	−0.054	6.047	2.203		391
P-value	0.000	0.957	0.000^c	0.028^b		

[a]Significant at the 0.10 level.
[b]Significant at the 0.05 level.
[c]Significant at the 0.01 level.

$$Model: DON_{jt} = \beta_0 + \beta_1 LEV_{jt} + \beta_2 InSIZE_{jt} + \beta_3 PROF_{jt} + \varepsilon_{jt}$$

where: DON_{jt} A dummy variable taking the value one (1) if the company is making corporate donations, otherwise coded zero (0), for firm j in year t; LEV_{jt} Total debt/total assets for firm j in year t; $InSIZE_{jt}$ Measured by the natural log of total assets by firm j in year t; $PROF_{jt}$ Earnings per share (EPS) for firm j in year t; ε_{jt} Error term for firm j in year t.

consistent with our first hypotheses that corporate donations are positively related to the firm's market value.

10.5.5 Determinants of Corporate Donations

Given a dichotomous dependent variable, ordinary least square (OLS) regression is not appropriate for estimating the parameters (Theil 1971, Hagerman and Zmijewski 1979). This is because the assumptions of OLS will be violated when using a binary response variable. As a result, logit regression analysis was selected since this is the maximum likelihood estimating procedure, where it applies a logarithmic transformation to the dependent variable.

The hypotheses H2, H3, and H4 were tested using a logistic regression. The logit model helps to eliminate the heteroscedasticity problems associated with OLS regression using a dichotomous dependent variable by transforming the dependent into a logit variable. In order to test the significant of each of the independent variables, logistic regression was implemented for the year 2003 and 2005.

This particular logit model examines whether corporate donations by the Public Listed Companies in Malaysia are associated with the firm's characteristics, namely, leverage, company size, and profitability. Therefore, to measure the relationship of the leverage, company size, and profitability with the corporate donations, as mentioned earlier, logit regression analysis was performed separately for the year 2003 and 2005. Table 10.9 lists the summary statistics of determinants of corporate donations for each year.

The estimate of the coefficient of leverage (LEV), β_1, was not significantly different from zero at the level at least 0.10 in which the t-ratio is 0.794 and −0.054

for the year 2003 and 2005, respectively. This finding is contrary to the expectation of agency theory, and therefore does not support our second hypotheses that there is a negative correlation between a company's leverage and the level of corporate donations. This finding contradicts the finding of previous researchers such as Barton et al. (1989), Adams and Hardwick (1998) and Brown et al. (2006), who argue that corporate donations are linked to a company's capital structure and leverage.

Statistically, the estimate of the coefficient of company size (*InSIZE*), β_2, is significant and positively related to the corporate donations at the 0.01 level. Therefore, it was found that there is clear support for the view where larger companies are more likely engage in charitable corporate donations as compared to the smaller firms. Thus, our results support our third hypotheses. This is consistent with the view of Adams and Hardwick (1998), Brammer and Millington (2004), and Brown et al. (2006).

Finally, the estimate of the profitability (*PROF*), β_3, is positive, as expected, and is statistically significant at the 0.10 level or better for the year 2003 and 2005. This supports our fourth hypotheses that more profitable companies are more able and more likely to make larger corporate donations than less profitable companies. Thus, this result is consistent with the views of Roberts (1992), Adams and Hardwick (1998), and Brammer and Millington (2004).

Generally, these overall findings are consistent with earlier works by Adams and Hardwick (1998) as well as Brammer and Millington (2004). Size and profitability were both found to be significant, at the 10% level or better, with the expected signs. However, the finding for leverage was not consistent with the previous research. It is assumed that this situation occurs because the Public Listed Companies in Malaysia engage in the corporate donation activities regardless of their situation of leverage. It is believed this happens because due to the low leverage, companies do not want to lose their reputation in the eyes of the public.

10.6 Summary and Conclusion

The purpose of this study was to increase the general understanding on the issues regarding corporate donations. Corporate donations will never become an exact science, but they are inherently an act of judgment and faith in the pursuit of long-term goals. Specifically, the goals of this study were to examine whether investors perceive corporate donations when they determine the value of the firm and to test empirically the determinants of corporate donations made by 774 Malaysian Public Listed Companies of the Main Board. The three firms' specific characteristics (i.e., leverage, firm's size, and profitability) were derived from the agency and stakeholder theory.

This study used the sample of 774 companies in Malaysia which was listed on the Main Board of Bursa Malaysia for the year 2003 and 2005. The final full sample was tested with regards to all types of firms. The missing data was excluded and the final full sample was tested by using the SPSS software. Descriptive statistics and correlation analysis were carried out for all the variables under study to obtain important statistical results and the correlation matrix among the variables.

Firstly, multiple regression analysis was conducted in order to examine the perception of the investors on the corporate donations by the company as to whether they take the corporate donations into consideration when they determine the value of the company. The results for the first hypotheses (H1) revealed that there is a positive relationship between corporate donations and market value of equity. This has been proven by checking p-value of the dummy variable (*DON*), which denotes the firms making and not making corporate donations. At the 1% significance level, the p-value of 0.008 and 0.000 was significant for the year 2003 and 2005, respectively. The findings show that the corporate donation is relevant for investors in valuing a firm's equity. Therefore, it can be concluded that the companies involved in the corporate donations will have higher market value of equity as compared to the companies that do not undertake such social responsibilities. This is consistent with Mohamed Zain (2004), who identifies that participating and reporting charitable and philanthropic activities is an image-enhancing exercise which is profit motivated (see also Hillman and Keim 2001; Navarro 1988). In the context of broader CSR, this study is consistent with Luo and Bhattacharya (2006), who found that CSR affects market value partly through a mediator of customer satisfaction. Therefore, we can conclude that taking advantage of market opportunities through CSR, particularly donations, adds value to the corporations.

Secondly, logistic regression analysis was conducted in order to examine the determinants of corporate donations made by the Public Listed Companies in Malaysian market. This paper looks at the company's characteristics, specifically leverage, company size, and profitability, that might relate to the company's contribution of corporate donations. The empirical evidence in this study supports the hypotheses (i.e., H3 and H4) from the previous researches especially in the UK except for the second hypotheses (H2), which is on the variable leverage (*LEV*). In this study, it was found that there is no significant relationship between the leverage and the corporate donations. This result contradicts the findings of other research.

Basically, our corporate donations model was able to provide evidence that company size and profitability are important determinants to consider the companies that are more likely to contribute to the society. But of course, the bigger the company, the more able and the more generous the company will be to provide donations. The public expects bigger corporations to provide more. As explained by Roberts (1992) and Watts and Zimmerman (1978), bigger companies may invest in charitable contributions in order to improve external perceptions of the company, influence external decision makers, and reduce the risk of regulatory activity that may limit management discretion, or reduce the value of the firm. On the profitability front, our study concurs with Navarro (1988), who states that charitable contributions may have significant implications for corporate performance.

Several factors in this study limit the generality of the results. First, the set of data for the sample includes only Public Listed Companies of the Main Board of Bursa Malaysia. Additionally, the results are specific to the years 2003 and 2005 and may not be relevant to prior or future years. Further, there are other possible quantitative and qualitative factors that could explain the determinants of corporate donations by the Malaysian market, which is not being tested in this study. Therefore, it is not possible to generalize the findings beyond these areas.

Second, thus far we could not find (through literature review) any study ever attempting to investigate whether investors perceive corporate donations when they determine the value of a company of the Malaysian market. This is also the first study that investigates the determinants of the corporate donations by the Malaysian companies. Since this study used the data in the Malaysian context, the results are limited and could not be generalized to other corporate donations market.

Third, this study used the logistic regression analysis in determining whether the independent variables can be associated with the corporate donations. Therefore, the implication is that we are just able to demonstrate an association, not a causal relationship. Moreover, any interference about cause of the changes in the dependent variable must be justified by a reasonable theoretical relationship. As far as it is concerned, the logistic regression analysis can only show that a statistical relationship exists, and therefore we cannot infer that one variable causes another (Keller and Warrack 2000).

The idea of CSR has caught on. Many corporations have embraced CSR. They have participated in a lot of CSR activities. However, corporations can do more by incorporating CSR in their business philosophies, values, and objectives. Hence corporations should set their CSR objectives, measure their performance, and have that performance independently audited. This has been endorsed by a substantial and growing number of businesses, especially multinational enterprises, academics and commentators, NGOs, investment institutions, consultants, and international agencies. However, CSR in Malaysia still has a long way to go and definitely needs new ways to promote it. It begins with human resources and proceeds to giving back to the community through donations and charitable activities. However, taking care of the community or society does not only mean charitable contribution or philanthropy, but more importantly the ongoing participation in community development and improving the quality of lives.

References

Aagaard, P. (1996). Finding common ground. *Hollis Sponsorship and Donations Yearbook (Fourth Edition)*, Hollis Directories Ltd, London, pp. 295–96.

ACCA (2004). State of Corporate Environmental and Social Reporting in Malaysia 2004, ACCA Malaysia.

Adams, M. and Hardwick, P. (1998). An analysis of corporate donations: United Kingdom evidence. *Journal of Management Studies*, 35 (5), pp. 641–654.

Alexander, G. J. and Buchholz, R. A. (1978). Corporate social responsibility and stock market performance. *Academy of Management Journal*, 22 (3), pp. 479–486.

Andrew, B. H., Gul, F. A., Guthrie, J. E., and Teoh, H. Y. (1989). 'A note on corporate social disclosure practices in developing countries: the case of Malaysia and Singapore'. *British Accounting Review*. Vol. 21, pp. 377–380.

Bae, J. and Cameron, G. T. (2006). Conditioning effect of prior reputation on perception of corporate giving. *Public Relations Review,* 32, pp. 144–150.

Ball and Brown (1968). An empirical evaluation of accounting income numbers. *Journal of Accounting Research,* Autumn.

Bandura, A. (1986). Social foundations of thought and action: A social cognitive theory. Englewood Cliffs, NJ: Prentice-Hall.

Bartkus, B., Morris, S., and Seifert, B. (2002, September). Governance and corporate philanthropy. *Business and Society,* 41, pp. 319–344.

Barton, S. L. N. C. and Sundaram, S. (1989). An empirical test of stakeholder theory predictions of capital structure. *Financial Management,* 18, 1, pp. 36–44.

Bennet, R. (1998). Corporate philanthropy in France, Germany and the UK International comparisons of commercial orientation towards company giving in European nations. *International Marketing Review,* 15 (6), pp. 458–475.

Bennett, R. (1997). Corporate philanthropy in the United Kingdom: Altruistic giving or marketing communications weapon, 3 (2), pp. 88–110.

Booth, J. R. (1992). Contract costs, bank loans and the cross-monitoring hypothesis. *Journal of Financial Economics,* 31, 1, pp. 25–41.

Brammer, S. and Millington, A. (2003). The evolution of corporate charitable contributions in the UK between 1989 and 1999: industry culture and stakeholder influences. *Journal of Business Ethics: A European Review,* 12 (3), pp. 216–228.

Brammer, S. and Millington, A. (2004). The development of corporate charitable contributions in the UK: A stakeholder analysis. *Journal of Management Studies,* 41 (8), pp. 1411–1434.

Brammer, S. and Millington, A. (2006). Firm size, organizational visibility and corporate philanthropy: an empirical analysis. *Business Ethics: A European Review,* 15, 1, pp. 6–18.

Brown, W. O., Helland, E., and Smith, J. K. (2006). Corporate philanthropic practices. *Journal of Corporate Finance,* Vol. 12 (5), pp. 855–877.

Brown, T. J. and Dacin, P. A. (1997). Corporate Branding, identity and corporate response. *Journal of the Academy of Marketing Science,* Vol. 34(2), pp. 95–98.

Bursa Malaysia. Retrieved December 20, 2007, from http://www.bursamalaysia.com/website/bm/listed_companies/company_announcements/annual_reports/index.jsp.

Business for Social Responsibility (BSR) (1999). Introduction to corporate social responsibility, San Francisco, CA. Retrieved March 6, 2007, from www.bsr.org.

Carroll, A. (1991). The pyramid of social responsibility. *Business Horizons,* 34 (July/August), pp. 39–48.

Casson, D. (1991). The major companies guide, *Directory of Social Change,* London.

Casson, D. (1995). A guide to company giving 1995/96, *Directory of Social Change,* London.

Cochran, P. L. and Wood, R. A. (1984). Corporate social responsibility and financial performance. *Academy of Management Journal,* 27, 1, pp. 42–56.

Cogill, Harry, J. (1991). Sponsorships and corporate contributions. *Canadian Business Review,* 18 (3).

Cooke, T. E. (1991). "An Assessment of Voluntary Disclosure in the Annual Reports of Japanese Corporations" *The International Journal of Accounting,* 26, 3, pp. 174–189.

Cooke, T. E. (1989). "Voluntary Disclosure by Swedish Companies" *Journal of International Financial Management and Accounting,* Vol. 1, No. 2, pp. 1–25, Summer.

Cornell, B. and Shapiro, A. C. (1987). Corporate stakeholders and corporate finance. *Financial Management,* 16 (1), pp. 5–14.

Dabson, B. (Ed.) (1991). Company giving in Europe, *Directory of Social Change,* London.

Dean, D. H. (2003). Consumer perception of corporate donations Effects of company reputation for social responsibility and type of donation. *Journal of Advertising,* 52 (4), pp. 91–102.

Diamond, W. D., & Kashyap, R. K. (1997). Extending models of prosocial behavior to explain university alumni contributions. *Journal of Applied Social Psychology,* 27, pp. 915–928.

Dumontier, P. and Raffournier, B. (2002). Accounting and Capital Markets: A survey of the European Evidence. *The European Accounting Review,* Vol. 11(1), pp. 119–152.

Eastwood, M. (1993). A guide to company giving, *The Directory of Social Change,* London.

Fombrun, C. J., Gardberg, N. A., & Barnett, M. L. (2000). Opportunity platforms and safety nets: Corporate citizenship and reputational risk. *Business and Society Review*, 105(1), pp. 85–106.

Foo, S. L., and Tan, M. S. (1988). "Comparative Study of Social Responsibility Reporting in Malaysia and Singapore", *Singapore Accountant*, August 1988: 12–15.

Francis, J., LaFond, R., Olsson, P. & Schipper, K. (2004). Costs of equity and earnings attributes, *Accounting Review*, 79(4), pp. 967–1010.

Freeman, E. (1984). Strategic management: A stakeholder approach. Boston: Pitman Press.

Fry, L. W., Keim, G. D. and Meiners, R. E. (1982). Corporate contributions: altruistic or for-profit? *Academy of Management Journal*, 25 (1), pp. 94–107.

Goodwin, J. and Ahmed, K. (2006). Longitudinal value relevance of earnings and intangible assets: Evidence from Australian firms. *Journal of International Accounting, Auditing and Taxation*, Vol. 15, pp. 72–91.

Gujarati, D. N. (2003). Basic Econometrics. Fourth Edition, McGraw-Hill.

Hagerman, R. L. and Zmijewski, M. E. (1979). Some economic determinants of accounting policy choice. *Journal of Accounting and Economics*, pp. 141–161.

Hasan, I. and Asokan Anandarajan (October 2003). Transparency and value relevance: the experience of some MENA countries. Preliminary Version.

Hellström, K. (2005). The Value Relevance of Financial Accounting Information in a Transitional Economy: The Case of the Czech Republic. SSE/EFI Working Paper Series in Business Administration No 2005:10.

Hillman, A. J. and Keim, G. D. (2001). Shareholder value, stakeholder management and social issues: What's the bottom line? *Strategic Management Journal*, 22, pp. 125–139.

Hossain, M., Perera, M. H. B., and Rahman, A. R. (1995). Voluntary disclosure in the annual reports of New Zealand Companies. *Journal of International Financial Management and Accounting*, 6 (1), pp. 69–87.

Ibrahim, M. K., McLeay, S., and Neal, David. (1999). Market value, book value and goodwill, *British Accounting Association Conference* (proceeding), Glasgow, United Kingdom.

Ibrahim, M. K. M., Marzita, M. S., Radziah, A. L., and Zaleha, A. S. (2003a). Value-relevance of Accounting Numbers: An empirical Investigation of Purchased Goodwill, *Malaysian Accounting Review*, Kuala Lumpur, Malaysia.

Ibrahim, M. K. M., Raudah, D., Haslinda, Y., and Normahiran, M. Y. (2003b). Market Value and Balance Sheet Numbers: Evidence from Malaysia. *Asian Accounting Review*, Australia.

Ibrahim, M. K., Wan Ismail, W. A. and Kamarudin, K. A. (2003 c). Income smoothing and market perception of accounting numbers: An empirical investigation of extraordinary items. *Capital Market Review*, Kuala Lumpur, Malaysia.

Ibrahim, M. K. M., Khairul, A. K., Wan, A. (2004 a). Value Relevance of Accounting Numbers in Predicting Financial Health: Evidence from Distressed Firms in Malaysia, Seminar CSSR, Kuching, Sarawak, Malaysia.

Ibrahim, M. K., Dalilawati, Khairul, Anuar, Jagjit (2004 b). The Relative Value Relevance of Earnings and Book Value in Malaysia and Singapore, *Discussion Paper 2/2004*, UiTM-ACCA Financial Reporting Research Centre, Shah Alam, Malaysia.

Jennings, Ross, Robinson, John, Thompson, Robert, B., II, and Duvall., Linda, (1996). The relation between accounting goodwill numbers and equity. *The Journal of Business Finance Accounting*, 23 (4).

Jensen, M. C. and Meckling, W. H. (1976). Theory of the firm: managerial behavior, agency costs and ownership structure. *Journal of Financial Economics*. 3 (4), pp. 305–360.

Keller, G. and Warrack, B. (2000). Statistics for management and economics, Fifth Edition, Duxbury.

Kothari, S. P. (2001). Capital markets research in accounting, *Journal of Accounting and Economics*, 31, pp. 105–231.

Landsman, W. (1986). An empirical investigation of pension fund property rights. *The Accounting Review*, 61 (4), pp. 662–691.

Lee, S. (1996). *Philanthropy still has its place. Hollis Sponsorship and Donations Yearbook (Fourth Edition).* Hollis Directories Ltd, London, pp. 293–4.

Lenway, S. A. and Rehbein, K. (1991). 'Leaders, followers and free riders: an empirical test of variation in corporate political involvement'. *Academy of Management Review*, 34, pp. 893–905.

Lev, B. and Zarowin, P. (1999 Autumn). The boundaries of financial reporting and how to extend them. *Journal of Accounting Research*, Vol. 37, pp. 353–385.

Logan, D. (1993). Transnational Giving: An Introduction to the Corporate Citizenship Activity of International Companies in Europe, Directory of Social Change, London.

Luks, A. (1988, October). Helper's high. *Psychology Today*, pp. 39–40.

Manne, H. and Wallich, H. (1972). The modern corporation and social responsibility. Washington, D.C: American Enterprise Institute.

Mann Hyung Hur (2006). Exploring the motivation factors of charitable giving and their value structure: a case study of Seoul, Korea. *Social Behaviour and Personality*, 34(6), pp. 661–680.

McAlister, D. T. and Ferrel, L. (2002). The role of strategic philanthropy in marketing strategy. *European Journal of Marketing*, 36 (5/6), pp. 689–705.

McElroy, K. M. and Siegfried, J. J. (1995). The Effect of Firm size on corporate philanthropy. *Quarterly Review of Economics and Business*, Vol. 25(2), pp. 18–26.

McGuire, J. B., Sundgren, A., and Schneeweis, T. (1988). Corporate social responsibility and firm financial performance. *Academy of Management Journal*, 31, 4, pp. 857–872.

Meek, G. K., Gray, S. J., and Roberts, C. B. (1995) "Factors Influencing Voluntary Annual Report Disclosures by U.S., U.K., and Continental European Multinational Corporations" *Journal of International Business Studies*, Third Quarter, pp. 555–572.

Meznar, M. B. and Nigh, D. (1995). 'Buffer or bridge? Environmental and organizational determinants of public affairs activities in American firms'. *Academy of Management Journal*, 38:4, pp. 975–996.

Mohamed Zain, M. (2004). "The Driving Forces Behind Malaysian Corporate Social Reporting", *The National Accounting research Journal*, Vol. 2, No. 1. pp. 89–111.

Navarro, P. (1988). Why do corporations give to charity? *Journal of Business*, 61 (1), pp. 65–93.

Norton, M. (1991). Raising money from industry, Directory of Social Change, London.

Ohlson, J. A., (1995). Earnings, book values, and dividends in equity valuation. *Contemporary Accounting Research*, Vol. 11 (Spring), pp. 661–687.

Pharoah, C. (Ed.) (1996). *Dimensions of the voluntary sector (Second Edition)*. Charities Aid Foundation, London.

Pritchard, N. J. (2002). The Relationship between Accounting Numbers and Returns in the Baltic Stock Markets, *Discussion Paper 2002/06*.

Ricks Jr, J. M. (2005). An assessment of strategic corporate philanthropy on perceptions of brand equity variables. *Journal of Consumer Marketing*, 22, 3, pp. 121–134.

Roberts, R. W. (1992). Determinants of corporate social responsibility disclosure: an application of stakeholder theory. *Accounting Organizations and Society*, 17:6, pp. 595–612.

Ronen, J. (2001). On R&D Capitalization and Value Relevance: a Commentary. New York University.

Sargeant, A., West, D. C., and Ford, J. B. (2004). Does perception matter?: an empirical analysis of donor behaviour. *The Service Industries Journal*, 24, 6, pp. 19–36.

Siegfried, J. J., McElroy, K. M. and Biernot-Fawkes, D. (1983). The management of corporate contributions. *Research in Corporate Performance and Policy*, 5, pp. 87–102.

Simon, F. L. (1995). "Global corporate philanthropy: a strategic framework", *International Marketing Review*, Vol. 12 No. 4, pp. 20–37.

Smith, C. N. (1994). The new corporate philanthropy. *Harvard Business Review*, 72(3), pp. 105–116.

Suchman, M. C. (1995). Managing legitimacy: Strategic and institutional approaches. *Academy of Management Journal*, 20 (3), pp. 571–610.

Syverson, N. (2006). Corporate Philanthropy in America: Better to Give Than Receive. *IMPO Magazine*, pp. 22–25.

Theil, H. (1971). Principles of Econometrics. Wiley.

Teoh, H. Y. and Thong, G. (1984). 'Another look at corporate social responsibility and reporting: an empirical study in a developing country', *Accounting, Organisation and Society*, Vol. 9, No. 2, pp. 189–206.

Ullmann, A. A. (1985). Data in search of a theory: a critical examination of the relationship among social performance, social disclosure and economic performance. *Academy of Management Review*, 10 (1–2), pp. 540–557.

Varadarajan, P., Rajan, and Anil Menon (1988). Cause-related marketing: A coalignment of marketing strategy and corporate philanthropy. *Journal of marketing*, 52, pp. 58–74.

Waddock, S. A. and Graves, S. B. (1997). The corporate social performance-financial performance link. *Strategic Management Journal*, 18 (4), pp. 112–134.

Watts, R. L. and Zimmerman, J. L. (1978). Towards a positive theory of determination of accounting standards. *The Accounting Review*, 53 (1), pp. 112–134.

Williamson, G. M. and Clark, M. S. (1989). Providing help and desired relationship type as determinants of changes in mood and self-evaluations. *Journal of Personality and Social Psychology*, 56 (5), pp. 722–34.

Willsher, R. (1996). "Trends in corporate giving", *CBI European Business Handbook*, Kogan Page, London, pp. 7–13.

Xueming Luo and Bhattacharya, C. B. (2006). Corporate Social Responsibility, Customer Satisfaction and Market Value. *Journal of Marketing*, 70, pp. 1–18.

Part III
The Americas

Chapter 11
United States of America: Internal Commitments and External Pressures

Jennifer J. Griffin and Ben Vivari

Abstract With the varied definitions of corporate social responsibility (CSR) we examine the motivation for firms' CSR activities, how firms credibly demonstrate CSR, and firms' CSR reporting. These three topics, i.e., why firms participate, how firms participate, and CSR reporting rubrics, help describe and explain the core question of this chapter: what is the practice of CSR in the United States (US)? We argue that the practice of CSR in the US is evolving and accelerating at an uneven pace across industries and within firms because of differences in beliefs in CSR, leadership, employee pressures, government demands, and community input.

This chapter suggests examining specific stakeholder relations and how firms co-create value that leads to a more nuanced view of CSR. The practice of CSR in the US continues to be a matter of choice within a market-driven economy. This freedom to choose underlies many CSR activities. CSR for consumers may include better, safer, and quality products. For employees, CSR is about pride, retention, and being an employer of choice. CSR is a differentiator from rival firms – especially in fiercely competitive markets. For policy makers, CSR is about building trust, credibility, and repetitive access. For suppliers, CSR is about being the partner of choice. And for communities, CSR is about pride, sponsorships, and inclusion. CSR in U.S. firms is the sum of these stakeholder systems plus the innovative creativity resulting in new product/markets to serve shifting social demands.

11.1 Introduction

One topic closely tied to current questions on corporate responsibility in the United States (US) and worldwide is global warming (Kolk and Hoffmann, 2007). While the U.S. government has not imposed mandates or proposed comprehensive regulations, many American-based companies have been trying to join the "green" movement and promote themselves as environmentally responsible.

Dell Inc., wanting to be part of the green movement, launched their "Plant a Tree for Me" program in 2007. Partnering with The Conservation Fund and Carbonfund.org, Dell's program was announced at the annual Consumer Electronics Show in Las Vegas. Dell's customers can donate between $2 and $6 to a tree-planting program to offset the carbon emissions of their computer purchase and its lifetime of electricity use. Dell's new green website, www.dell.com/earth, highlights this program among its other environmental initiatives.

Not lost on the green community, however, is that Dell's "Plant a Tree for Me" program is not exactly a financial burden on Dell. EcoGeek, an online green technology website, wrote, "The system has absolutely no drawbacks for Dell, as customers aren't required to pay, and Dell has basically handed off responsibility for the devices carbon footprint to the consumer" (www.ecogeek.org/content/view/424/). Dell's shareholders, in other words, were not going to see any of their investments supporting the new program. With its "Plant a Tree for Me program" Dell creatively answered a key corporate social responsibility (CSR) question discussed in many U.S. corporate boardrooms: Are CSR activities financially viable?

While general consensus among green advocates is that Dell's program is a positive step forward, many questions still remain for Dell and CSR practices in the US more generally. How did this program come about? How was the partnership between Dell and the two NGOs formed? Why did Dell decide to start this program – was it a sense of responsibility, a new marketing strategy, a response to specific stakeholder pressures, a competitive pressure, or something else entirely?

Using Dell and other examples, this chapter highlights learnings from the varied practices of corporate responsibility initiatives in America. Asking corporate executives about the importance of CSR lends itself toward many different answers depending on whom you ask. The vague and often differently understood idea of CSR in the US continues to be negotiated, changed, debated, and explored among American society, corporations and their supply chains, citizens, and the government (Carroll, 1999). For some firms and citizens, CSR is not a negotiable idea (Wood, 1991). For others, CSR is a passing fad or a pseudonym traditionally tied to philanthropy (Porter & Kramer, 2002; Sharfman, 1994; Smith, 1994).

In this chapter, we explore why American companies participate in CSR activities, how firms credibly demonstrate CSR, and what activities are included in CSR reporting. These three topics, i.e., why firms participate, how firms participate, and CSR reporting rubrics, help describe and explain the practice of CSR in the US.

We argue that the practice of CSR in the US is evolving and accelerating at an uneven pace across industries and within firms because of differences in leadership, beliefs, employee pressures, economic incentives, government demands, and community input. We suggest that examining specific stakeholder relations and industry-level pressures, as well as examining how firms co-create value within its stakeholder system, leads to a more nuanced view of CSR.

Each stakeholder views CSR differently. CSR for consumers means better, safer, and quality products. For employees, CSR is about pride, retention of employees, and being an employer of choice. CSR is a differentiator from rival firms – especially in fiercely competitive markets. For policy makers, CSR is about building trust, credibility, and repetitive access. For suppliers, CSR is about being the partner of choice. And for communities, CSR is about pride, sponsorships, and inclusion. Taken altogether, CSR is the sum of these stakeholder relations as well as the innovative creativity from creating new product/markets that meet shifting social demands.

11.2 Why CSR? Moving beyond the Business Case

CSR discussions in America have been traditionally and predominantly focused on the financial returns of CSR initiatives. While three decades of research suggests no clear-cut answer on a direct and unassailable link between profitability and CSR initiatives (Griffin, 1997; Margolis, 2001; Orlitzsky et al., 2003; Barnett, 2007), the range of corporate CSR initiatives continues to expand and penetrate deeper into organizational routines (Bies et al., 2007; Fort, 2007). The business case for the CSR question is becoming clouded by more nuanced, insightful questions such as: Are CSR activities indications of good management for modern organizations? (The Economist, 2005; Frooman, 1997); Are these initiatives in the best interest of the firm to avoid externalities and potentially egregious governmental action? (Friedman, 1970; Jensen, 2001); and, Are there missed opportunities in the CSR initiatives for new organizations and new product markets for the innovative firm and entrepreneur, particularly in overseas expansion? (Kolk, & van Tulder, 2002; Prahalad, 2005).

CSR in the US has traditionally been understood as philanthropy. More recent insights have both broadened and narrowed the definition of CSR. In its broadest form, CSR is nominally understood as "corporate citizenship" and reflects the position and placement of corporations in a society and how the firm interacts with governments, special interest groups, civil society, and other corporations (Waddock, 2006; Logsdon & Wood, 2002, 2005). More narrow conceptualizations of CSR focus on communications, outreach, corporate community involvement, and corporate community investment initiatives (Allen, 2007). Still other scholars suggest that CSR reflects only those voluntary activities that furthers some perceived social good and is beyond legal requirements (McWilliams & Siegel, 2001). In this chapter we include all social-oriented activities that are directed towards, or impact, a firm's stakeholders. CSR includes both economic and non-economic outcomes (e.g., reputation, community building, trust, goodwill, resource dependence, mutual dependency, and power imbalances) for a firm's value-creating systems.

Below, we look at some of the internal driving forces motivating many U.S. companies' CSR efforts including leadership, employees, marketing/public relations, and competitive advantage/rivalry.

Leadership. CSR, oft times, starts at the top. Early moving CSR-conscious CEOs have built their corporation around CSR principles. From the UK, Anita Roddick's Body Shoppe and Ben & Jerry's Ice Cream Shoppe are oft-cited yet controversial examples of entrepreneurial CEOs combining a social and economic mission (Frederick, 2006). Socially driven CEOs will tie socially responsible practices into the very fabric of their companies, explicitly citing CSR aspirations into mission statements (e.g., Marriott Corporation, Johnson & Johnson, Levi Strauss & Co.), creating departments around CSR, and reporting on CSR initiatives in their annual financial reports (Zadek, 2004; Porter & Kramer, 2006).

Organizations and publicly traded corporations building an identity around CSR are proliferating (e.g., Patagonia, Whole Foods). These identity-based organizations are creating niche markets, innovative products, and new market opportunities (Whetten & Mackey, 2002; Rowley & Moldoveanu, 2003; Reason, 2005).

On the other hand, CEOs who are not socially responsible can cast a pall over their entire company. CEO compensation is a highly controversial topic that is often associated with social responsibility. When Home Depot's Robert Nardelli walked away with $210 million after being fired, he fueled a populist backlash drawing the attention of NGOs, the media, and even the White House (International Herald Tribune, 2007).

Employees. Employees wear many hats when it comes to CSR. Employees can be a motivator for firms' choices of CSR initiatives, a means for firms engages in CSR, and/or beneficiaries of CSR. Employees are a motivator for CSR engagement since being a socially responsible company can improve employee morale, which in turn can increase productivity and profitability. Being "an employer of choice" is important for maintaining, recruiting, and hiring employees (Greening and Turban, 2000; Lawrence, 2002). CSR activities are often featured in recruiting brochures.

Employees can be a means for engaging in CSR because they provide manpower for CSR programs, particularly volunteer programs. Corporate volunteerism has grown exponentially over the past decade (Jones, 2007; Houghton et al., 2007). Many companies encourage employees to volunteer in the community rather than come to work for a certain number of days each year by coordinating projects or paying regular salaries for independent projects.

Employees benefit from CSR initiatives because treating employees well – with competitive pay, good benefits, etc.– is seen as a socially responsible thing to do. *Fortune's* annual "Best Companies to Work For" list is just one place where employee-based CSR programs receive recognition (Szwajkowski & Figlewicz, 1999). Google, the 2007 winner of *Fortune's* "Best Company to Work For" award included free meals, a swimming spa, free doctors onsite, and numerous other healthcare services. Employee-based CSR innovations from 10 years ago including babysitting services, food deliveries, and dry cleaning services are now provided by many companies.

Marketing/Public Relations. Another reason companies engage in CSR activities is the positive image it can create (Fombrun & Shanley, 1990) and the positive impacts on the firm's reputation (Clarkson, 1995). Whether it is a news story about a philanthropic act, positive reporting by watchdog groups, or having a logo attached to a positive program, the positive publicity resulting from CSR initiatives can improve the image of a company in the minds of customers and investors alike (Kotler, 2007). Because of the immediate uptick in positive goodwill, companies often use CSR as a way to repair their corporate image after disasters (Epstein & Schnietz, 2002; Schnietz & Epstein, 2003) or build insurance via philanthropic giving (Godfrey, 2005). Some firms' leading lists of best CSR practices, or most admired companies, come from companies that have been highlighted as irresponsible corporations such as Nike, McDonalds, and Hewlett-Packard (Zadek, 2004, Frooman 1999).

CSR done for PR reasons is problematic since it may reveal deeper problems once the initial crisis blows over. Just because a company sponsors a gala, donates to a charity, or runs awareness promotions, does not mean the firm is active on behind-the-scene issues like human rights, poverty alleviation, homelessness, human dignity, or climate change (Levy and Kolk, 2002). The recent scandals at Enron, World-Com, Royal Ahold, Parmalat, and other companies have led the American public to be skeptical of these bolted-on approaches to CSR (Grayson & Hodges, 2004) that decouple corporate rhetoric from corporate action (Weaver et al., 1999).

Competitive Advantage and Rivalry. CSR can also be used as a competitive advantage to differentiate a firm and its products from those of its rivals. Innovative, socially responsible firms are offering consumers fair-trade coffee, organic foods, carpeting, energy-efficient light bulbs, hybrid cars, and LEED (Leadership in Energy and Environmental Design) buildings. As consumers demand more green and socially responsible products and practices, innovative companies are responding. Some companies have built reputations as socially responsible companies by being consistently responsive to a variety of social issues (e.g., homelessness, disease prevention, poverty alleviation). American companies using CSR as a competitive advantage include Ben & Jerry's, Whole Foods, Interface Carpets, and Patagonia.

11.3 CSR and External Outreach

Financial Analysts and Institutional Investors. Over the last decade, socially responsible investing has grown exponentially in the US (Social Investment Forum, 2006). According to the Social Investment Forum, as of 2005 almost 1 in every 10 dollars under professional management was involved in socially responsible investing. Calvert is one of the nation's largest socially responsible mutual fund firms with approximately $14 billion in assets under management. Companies participate in CSR to gain access to investors of socially responsible investment (SRI) funds and to qualify for credit lines from banks requiring social investment data.

Socially Responsible Investing in the US • 1995-2005						
(In Billions)	1995	1997	1999	2001	2003	2005
Social Screening[1]	$162	$529	$1,497	$2,010	$2,143	$1,685
Shareholder Advocacy	$473	$736	$922	$897	$448	$703
Screening and Shareholder[2]	N/A	($84)	($265)	($592)	($441)	($117)
Community Investing	$4	$4	$5	$8	$14	$20
Total	**$639**	**$1,185**	**$2,159**	**$2,323**	**$2,164**	**$2,290**

SOURCE: Social Investment Forum Foundation
1. Social Screening includes mutual funds and separate accounts. Since 2003, SRI mutual fund assets have increased (see Section II) while separate account assets have declined (see Section III) as single issue screening has waned and shareholder advocacy increased on the part of institutional investors.
2. Assets involved in Screening and Shareholder Advocacy are subtracted to avoid double counting. Tracking Screening and Shareholder Advocacy only began in 1997, so there is no datum for 1995.

Mitigating, preventing, or responding to shareholder advocacy efforts such as shareholder resolutions can be a motivating factor for firms to build CSR policies. Calvert introduced ten shareholder resolutions and co-filed an additional six in 2006 (CSRwire, 2007) on climate change, board diversity, corporate governance, and human rights. In addition to resolutions, Calvert teamed with CERES (Coalition for Environmentally Responsible Economies) to commission a report analyzing climate risk disclosure among S&P 500 companies. The Carbon Disclosure Project report was very critical of U.S. companies' disclosure practices and emissions management.

Non-Governmental Organization (NGO) Pressures. Some NGOs exert pressure on a corporation to initiate CSR practices, while others provide an avenue for CSR to develop. Others participate in both of these activities. As an example, consider CERES and UNEP (United Nations Environmental Programme), which introduced the Global Reporting Initiative, an international standard for reporting on CSR performance. UNEP and CERES not only pressures groups to participate in CSR-related topics like climate change when it issues critical reports, but also provides a way for corporations to measure and publish their performance. In 2006, a CERES report on climate change policy applauded British Petroleum's (BP's) approach toward climate change (Cogan, 2006). Immediately after the report was released, BP's U.S. division trumpeted their recognition (British Petroleum, 2006).

Other NGOs, however, stick to one type of engagement or the other. Watchdog groups like Human Rights Watch, Corporate Watch, or Greenpeace continue to pressure corporations to become better corporate citizens. Meanwhile, charities provide opportunities for corporations to partner and engage in CSR activities.

NGOs can also attack a CSR issue from every possible angle. Consider the plight of the companies involved in one of the most controversial industries in the world – tobacco. NGOs affect them on many different issues, and on many different levels. They can be global organizations like the World Health Organization, national anti-smoking campaigns like the Campaign for Tobacco-Free Kids, and even local groups like the Iowa Tobacco Prevention Alliance. Some exist in multiple facets – for example, the American Cancer Society works on a national level, but has over 3,400 local chapters that work within their municipalities.

Government Mandate – Prevent, Respond, or Forestall. There is no government-wide mandate for corporate social responsibility in the US (GAO, 2005). Choices abound for participation in CSR activities. Without CSR standards mandated by the federal government, CSR behavior varies from industry to industry and within industries. Governmental mandates regulate specific practices within certain firms and industries. Financial disclosure regulations set by the Securities and Exchange Commission (SEC), international trade requirements set by the Department of Justice of the Federal Trade Commission, or environmental regulations set by the Environmental Protection Agency (EPA) can affect firms in multiple industries. Government mandates can also empower others to create their own influence on CSR activities. For example, the shareholder resolutions discussed earlier were made possible by an SEC rule that required companies to allow the resolutions to be put to a vote.

Other Stakeholder Pressures – Supply Chains, Customers, and Communities. CSR in the US is often the result of pressures from various stakeholders such as unions, competitors, supply chains, customers, and communities which the corporation affects. While the concept that "the business of business is business" is still prevalent in America, corporations are finding it more and more difficult to create business value without addressing the needs of their stakeholders. See Table for examples of CSR stakeholder engagement activities stemming from various internal and external pressures.

Just as there are many reasons for CSR to emerge in a U.S. corporation, there are also many outlets for CSR activities and impacts. How a corporation credibly and genuinely manifests its CSR beliefs – which road it eventually travels down – is in part affected by the motivations, conditions, and aspirations of the corporation. Often, the why and how of CSR are closely related. But the why and how are not necessarily tied together, nor does it mean that the whys dictate the how or vice versa. The lack of an explicit and consistently widespread link between the why and how in practice contradicts CSR theoretical development (Wood, 1991).

In the next section we discuss some of the espoused drivers, and identify some of the many outlets and outcomes stemming from the practice of CSR in the US. We focus on three broad types of CSR practices: business/industry-led activity, government-led activity and civil society/NGO-led activity.

11.4 How Do Firms Credibly Demonstrate CSR?

Overall, three broad types of CSR activities are examined below. We focus on the three broad sectors: business, government, and civil society, and discuss their leadership in various CSR initiatives.

Table 11.1 Examples of internal and external motivators for CSR activities

Motivation	Company	Industry	Issue	Outcome
Internal				
PR/Marketing	Sprint/Nextel and Motorola	Telecommunications	AIDS in Africa	Pledged to donate $17 from the sale of each RED MOTORAZR V3m phone to the (RED) campaign
Employees	Philip Morris	Tobacco/groceries	Employee morale	PM21, a program which – among other things – worked to improve morale by reshaping the company's image and participating in corporate responsibility programs
Executives	Whole foods	Grocery	CEO pay	CEO John Mackey reduced his own salary to $1 a year
Competitive advantage	Patagonia	Sporting goods	Sustainability	Since 1996 Patagonia has give 1% of total sales to environmental causes. They use organic cotton, and have extensive recycling programs. In 1989 Patagonia co-founded The Conservation Alliance, which encourages other companies to act similarly
External				
Stakeholder pressures	Wal-Mart	Retail	Competition	Wal-Mart has faced criticism from the press, NGO's, and union groups because of its effect on small business. Wal-Mart is able to drive out smaller businesses with lower prices and better selection, leading many family-owned businesses to close their doors
Shareholder pressures	Great Plains Energy Inc.	Utility	Carbon disclosures	In 2006, agreed to address their CO_2 disclosure position before a resolution went to a vote before shareholders
NGO pressures	Nike	Apparel	Sweatshops in Asia	NGO's including Global Exchange and the Worker's Rights Consortium publicized the conditions in Nike's factory and led to more oversight by Nike and by the U.S. Government
Government mandate	All	All	Corporate accounting	The Sarbanes–Oxley Act was passed in 2002, requiring more disclosure on the part of American corporations, and setting minimum disclosure and oversight (e.g., audit committees)

Business/Industry-Led Activity. In many cases, CSR activity is led by the corporation itself. The reasons for this are clear – they are able to set the parameters of their engagement; they can report on it however they see fit; and they maintain control of the activity.

Business-led CSR activity often affects many organizations – for-profit, not-for-profit, and coalitions of organizations. Large, multinational businesses can impact entire supply chains by re-writing contracts, sharing best practices, providing oversight, demanding accountability, and giving management training to suppliers, wholesalers, and retailers throughout their value chain. Consider Whole Foods (see Table 11.1); while they act in a socially responsible manner, their presence creates CSR activity in other businesses (Reason, 2005).

- Whole Foods' marketing and promotion of organic foods has had an effect on the entire supermarket industry. Safeway, which has seen Whole Foods move into many of their markets, has introduced their own line of organic foods to compete with Whole Foods.
- Whole Foods has been able to work with their suppliers to improve animal treatment at their farms, and improve the quality of the meat that they offer at their stores.
- Whole Foods does business with over 2,400 independent farms promoting local agriculture both promotionally and financially.

By thinking creatively and engaging stakeholders, Whole Foods has been able to drive CSR not just within their own organization but also in the organizations that surround them.

Range of U.S. Government Activities Related to Global CSR

Source: GAO illustration based on World Bank report. GAO Report, 2005.
www.gao.gov/cgi-bin/getrpt?GAO-05-744.

Government-Led Activity. In the market-driven U.S. economy, the government generally takes a passive role in its policies regarding U.S. corporations and this is true for CSR activities as well. A 2005 Government Accountability Office (GAO) report found that there was no "broad federal mandate" related to CSR. However, numerous CSR-related activities are being led by the government. One of the reasons that CSR is not mandated by the government is because there are so many definitions of what CSR is – in fact, this issue was a major problem when the GAO created their report because they had trouble getting all parties to agree on what, exactly, they were looking for (GAO, 2005) Table 11.2.

Table 11.2 Examples of CSR programs at the environmental protection agency

Endorsing	National environmental performance track	Recognizes "top environmental performance" through congratulatory letters to elected officials, listings on EPA website, awards, and more
Facilitating	Climate leaders	An EPA industry-government partnership that works with companies to develop long-term comprehensive climate change strategies. Partners set a corporate-wide greenhouse gas (GHG) reduction goal and inventory their emissions to measure progress
Partnering	Energy star	A joint program with the Department of Energy that places labels on energy efficient products. Over 8,000 organizations have partnered with the EPA on this project
Mandating	Clean air mercury rule	Permanently caps and reduces mercury emissions from coal-fired power plants

Source: GAO Report, 2005.

Government-led CSR generally occurs at the agency level or state level rather than via coordination by the federal government with a systematic, overarching policy and regulatory system. The few federal government-led CSR initiatives generally address a specific issue, and isolate this issue from a comprehensive concept of a socially responsible company. For example, the popular CSR issue of climate change falls under the jurisdiction of the EPA. And, as Table 11.2 shows, EPA has a number of policies that aim to reduce emissions and/or recognize compa-

Table 11.3 Varying types of corporate commitments with habitat for humanity

Company	Type of commitment	Details
Whirlpool	Partnership program	The Whirlpool Building Blocks Project built ten new homes in Nashville, TN, in a span of a week. Workers included Whirlpool employees and Habitat volunteers, and homes were outfitted with Whirlpool products. Whirlpool also donates a refrigerator and range to every new Habitat home
Lowes	Donation	The "Homes for the Holidays" program allowed Lowe's customers to add a donation to their checkout at Lowe's during the 2006 holiday season
General Mills	Sponsorship	The General Mills Gulf Coast Student Building Project pays for students to visit the Gulf Coast and help in Habitat for Humanity's hurricane recovery program
Pella	Product donation	Pella, a window and door manufacturing firm, committed nearly $1M of products to Habitat to Humanity for use in Habitat's homes

nies that have done well in their efforts to combat climate change. These programs span the wide range of government participation in CSR activities recognized by the GAO.

NGO/Civil Sector-Led Activity. Just as NGOs are organized around a wide variety of topics, the CSR activity they lead comes in all shapes and sizes as well. NGO-led impacts can be as far-reaching as worldwide impacts (e.g., Environmental Defense), or as small as only affecting a specific community (e.g., Arlington for a Clean Environment). NGO-led activity may focus on a particular corporation or hone in on a specific action or cause. Corporations, in turn, can take part in these activities on a variety of commitment levels, including partnering, sponsoring, or simply donating to the NGOs. In Table 11.3 we examine a single charitable organization – Habitat for Humanity – and identify the varying levels of corporate participation with Habitat for Humanity.

11.5 How Do Firms Report CSR Activities?

The prominence of CSR reporting in the US has been rising over the past decade, as it has across the globe, and has been growing exponentially over the last few years. Many of the largest companies in the US have just begun issuing CSR reports, including the media conglomerate Time Warner (first issued in 2005) and General Electric (also in 2005). However, despite the expanding focus on CSR issues, some companies, according to a 2006, report do almost no reporting (SIRAN, 2006). A particularly poor industry when it comes to CSR reporting is the financial services sector. Within the S&P 100, financial services corporations American Express, U.S. Bancorp, Hartford Financial Services, and Lehman Brothers do no CSR reporting whatsoever, Tables 11.4 and 11.5.

Comparing U.S. companies with companies from other countries in terms of CSR reporting, the US is sixth out of seven Organisation for Economic Development and Co-operation (OECD) countries. The US is on the lower end of the reporting scale when compared to European countries such as France, Germany, and the UK as well as other OECD countries like Japan, Canada, and Australia. Unlike the majority of the countries included in the survey, there was a decline in the percentage of the top 100 U.S. companies reporting their CSR activities from 2002 to 2005, from 36 to 32%, respectively.

Table 11.4 CSR reporting: S&P 100 index companies

	2006	2005
Companies that issue annual CSR reports	43	39
Companies with CSR websites	79	59
Companies whose CSR reports are based on GRI Guidelines	34	25

Table 11.5 Percentage of nation's 100 largest companies with CSR reports, 2005

Country	%
Japan	80
UK	71
Canada	41
France	40
Germany	36
USA	32
Australia	23

Source: KPMG, 2005.

A recent trend in CSR reporting is assurance of claims within CSR reports. Only 1 of the 32 reports from U.S. companies was assured, as was the case in 2002 when only 1 of the 36 U.S. CSR reports was assured. This compares very poorly to the percentage of reports that are assured in the UK (53%), Japan (31%), Italy (71%), and France (40%). Despite the new emphasis on third-party assurances mandated by the U.S. Sarbanes–Oxley Act of 2002, it is unclear if assurance of non-financial reporting will become a widespread business opportunity in the US.

11.6 Findings: What is CSR in the US?

As we have seen, CSR in the US can take many different forms, come from many different sources, and have very different results. As a result, it is very difficult to pigeonhole CSR in America with any strict definition of activities, beliefs, or outcomes. What we can do instead is recognize a couple of traits of CSR initiatives in the US For example:

- *CSR that originates in the US can reach to all corners of the globe.* We have seen this in the aforementioned cases of Nike (human rights in Asia) and Sprint (AIDS in Africa). As the world moves to a "global economy," US-based companies are increasingly multinational corporations with impacts felt through financial performance. Nike has come face to face with issues of human rights and child labor practices in Asia, while Sprint faced new questions regarding AIDS medications in Africa. As companies grow internationally, CSR efforts are less likely to be isolated within a certain region, geography, or country. Coordinated and global, or more likely, multidomestic CSR initiatives are expected
- *U.S. companies often use partnerships for their CSR efforts.* Partnerships are prevalent in CSR initiatives: e.g., partnering with other corporations, NGOs, or the government or creating new public–private–NGO associations to tackle complex social problems including the U.S. Climate Action Partnership's (US CAP) initiatives to urge timely and viable policy on global climate change. The benefits

and ability to partner vary as do the stories of doomed partnerships. Partnering with groups having seemingly little connection with the company itself are increasingly rare. For example, General Mills teamed up with Habitat for Humanity for the Gulf Coast Student Building Project. Partnering can build numerous win-win benefits: no one firm bears the brunt of organizing a CSR program, facilitation is shared, and once the project is finished a wider audience is reached in publicizing its impacts.

- *U.S. companies use market mechanisms for CSR initiatives.* With no over-riding guidance from federal government initiatives, firms as well as local and state municipalities are actively engaged in defining how they approach CSR initiatives – if they approach it at all. A number of different stakeholders can and do exert pressure on a company with direct as well as indirect impacts. Innovation, creation of new markets, development of new trading tools, additional micro-financing projects, as well as consumer demands for safe products with investors' stringent disclosure requirements are likely to drive CSR initiatives. More nuanced activities and innovations in processes and sourcing are likely to drive U.S. CSR activities in the future.

So what does this mean for CSR in the US? With divergent CSR beliefs and practices, CSR practice in America might best be described as schizophrenic. For some firms, U.S. companies are long-established leaders in CSR. On the other hand, other U.S. companies blatantly disregard the laws, regulations, and social commitments of their communities. Ignoring customer, employee, shareholder, and community demands, their CSR initiatives are negligible. Not surprisingly, credible CSR practices are unevenly applied across countries, across industries, and within companies.

For example, consider Fannie Mae, a quasigovernmental mortgage finance company that is the fourth largest company in the US in terms of assets. Fannie Mae is very active in CSR and corporate citizenship. Focusing on helping first-time buyers achieve home ownership, they have a highly regarded diversity program called "Diversity Works at Fannie Mae." Fannie Mae has won numerous awards including being listed in the "40 Best Companies for Minorities" June 2007, "Hispanic Corporate 100" February 2007, *Fortune's* "America's Most Admired Companies," and listed as the best of the "100 Best Corporate Citizens" list in 2004 by *Business Ethics*.

After years of extensive accolades, Fannie Mae was charged with engaging in "extensive financial fraud" over a period of 6 years in the late 1990s and early 2000s (Day, 2006). Allegedly, the financial fraud allowed Fannie Mae executives to collect significant bonuses each year. An SEC investigation revealed that Fannie Mae had a "weak" board of directors, lacked basic internal controls, and allowed executives to dominate the company. The same report said the behavior of the Fannie Mae executives was "inconsistent with the values of responsibility, accountability, and integrity." Results from investigating Fannie Mae were a far cry from the awards the company was winning at the same time. Interestingly, the role of Fannie Mae in the 2007 mortgage banking and the U.S. housing credit crunch remains unknown.

The stark contrast between the CSR performance in one area of the company versus the complete lack of "responsibility, accountability and integrity" in another is an extreme example of the uneven application of CSR in the US, but a telling one nonetheless. We have seen CSR grow in the US over the past decade, thanks to NGO involvement, awards and recognition, stakeholder engagement, and other pressures.

Overall, managerial discretion plays a large and increasingly important part in deciding the future of CSR in America. Innovative managers are creatively designing new products, new processes, and new structures that incorporate socially responsible initiatives as an integral part of the business. Other managers are purposefully ignoring CSR-based markets and produce in potentially an irresponsible way. The practice of CSR in the US continues to be a matter of choice within a market-driven economy. This freedom to choose underlies many CSR activities. Co-creating value, by design, via CSR requires examining CSR systems with a more nuanced, action-based perspective. Examining stakeholder relations, on a one-by-one basis, as well as an aggregate system is needed to better understand the specific nuances underlying CSR outcomes in America.

Acknowledgments

Support from the George Washington University Institute for Corporate Responsibility (ICR) for help in creating time to write this chapter is deeply appreciated. Additional thanks are due to Chuck Koerber, Samuel Idowu, the editor, and anonymous reviewers for comments on earlier drafts. Deep appreciation of all GW students engaging in Global CSR conversations in SS05, SS06, and SS07 is gratefully acknowledged.

References

Allen, G. 2007. Corporate Community Investment in Australia, Melbourne, Australia: Centre for Corporate Public Affairs.

Barnett, Michael L. 2007. Stakeholder influence capacity and the variability of financial returns to corporate social responsibility. Academy of Management Review, 32(3): 794.

Bies, Robert J., Bartunek, Jean, Fort, Timothy L., and Zald, Meyer. 2007. Corporations as social change agents: Individual, interpersonal, institutional, and environmental dynamics. Academy of Management Review, 32(3): 788–793.

British Petroleum. 2006. 'BP has come out on top in a new CERES report on how 100 leading companies are addressing the growing financial risks and opportunities from climate change.' www.bp.com/genericarticle.do?categoryId = 9006198&contentId = 7016310, March 21, 2006.

Carroll, Archie B. 1999. Corporate social responsibility: Evolution of a definitional construct. Business & Society, 38(3): 268–295.

Clarkson, Max B. E. 1995. A stakeholder framework for analyzing and evaluating corporate social performance. Academy of Management Review, 20(1): 92–117.

Cogan, David G. 2006. Corporate Governance and Climate Change: Making the Connection. Washington, DC: Investor Responsibility Reporting Center, Inc.

CSRwire. 2007. Calvert Seeks Progress Through Shareholder Activism, January 11. www.csrwire.com/PressRelease.php?id = 7233.

Day, Kathleen. 2006. Study Finds 'Extensive' Fraud at Fannie Mae: Bonuses Allegedly Drove the Scheme. Washington Post, May 24, 2006; Page A01.

Epstein, Marc J., & Schnietz, Karen E. 2002. Measuring the cost of environmental and labor protests to globalization: An event study of the failed 1999 Seattle WTO talks. International Trade Journal, 15: 129–160.

Fombrun, Charles & Shanley, Marc. 1990. What's in a name? Reputation building and corporate strategy. Academy of Management Journal, 33(2): 233–258.

Fort, Timothy L. 2007. The corporate contribution to one planet living in global peace and security: Introduction. The Journal of Corporate Citizenship, Issue 26: 20–24.

Frederick, William C. 2006. Corporation, Be Good! The Story of Corporate Social Responsibility. Dog Ear Publishing.

Frooman, Jeffrey. 1997. Socially irresponsible and illegal behavior and shareholder wealth: A meta-analysis of event studies. Business & Society, 36(3): 221–249.

Friedman, M. 1970. Social responsibility of business. The New York Times Magazine. September 13, 33: 122–126.

GAO. 2005. Globalization: Numerous Federal Activities Complement U.S. Business's Global corporate Social Responsibility Efforts. Washington, DC: Government Accountability Organization Report #: GAO-05–744 Global CSR.

Godfrey, Paul C. 2005. The relationship between corporate philanthropy and shareholder wealth: A risk management perspective. Academy of Management Review, 30(4): 777–798.

Grayson, David and Hodges, Adrian. 2004. Corporate Social Opportunity: Seven Steps to make Corporate Social Responsibility work for your business. London: Greenleaf.

Greening, Daniel W. and Turban, D. B. 2000. Corporate social performance as a competitive advantage in attracting a quality workforce. Business & Society, 39(3): 254–280.

Griffin, Jennifer J. & Mahon, John F. 1997. The corporate social performance and corporate financial performance debate: Twenty-five years of incomparable research. Business & Society, 36(1): 5–31.

Houghton, S., Gabel, Joan T. A., & Williams, David W. 2007. Connecting Two Faces of CSR: Does Employee Volunteerism Improve Compliance Behavior? Presented at the Annual Academy of Management Meetings, Social Issues in Management Division, August 2007, Philadelphia, PA.

International Herald Tribune. 2007. Letter from Washington: As U.S. rich-poor gap grows, so does public outcry. February 18, 2007.

Jensen, M. C. 2001. Value maximization, stakeholder theory, and the corporate objective function. Journal of Applied Corporate Finance, 14(3): 8–21.

Jones, David A. 2007. Corporate Volunteer Programs & Employee Responses: How Serving the Community Also Serves the Company. Presented at the Annual Academy of Management Meetings, Social Issues in Management Division, August 2007, Philadelphia, PA.

Kolk, Ans and Hoffmann, Volker 2007. Business, climate change and emissions trading: Taking stock and looking ahead. European Management Journal, 25(6): 411–414.

Kolk, A., & van Tulder, R. 2002. The effectiveness of self-regulation: Corporate codes of conduct and child labour. European Management Journal, 20(3): 260–271.

Kotler, P. 2007. What is the relation between company profits, company reputation and corporate giving? Robert P. Maxton Lecture at the George Washington University School of Business, April.

Lawrence, Anne T. 2002. The drivers of stakeholder engagement: Reflections on the case of Royal Dutch/Shell. Journal of Corporate Citizenship, 6: 71–85.

Levy, David L., & Kolk, Ans 2002. Strategic responses to global climate change: Conflicting pressures on multinationals in the oil industry. Business and Politics, 4(3): 275–300.

Logsdon, J. M. and Wood, D. J. 2005. Global Business citizenship and voluntary codes of ethical conduct. Journal of Business Ethics 59: 55–67.

Logsdon, J. M., & Wood, D. J. 2002. Business citizenship: From domestic to global level of analysis. Business Ethics Quarterly, 12(2): 155–187.

Margolis, Joshua D. and Walsh, James P. 2001. People and Profits? The Search for a Link Between a Company's Social and Financial Performance. Mahwah, NJ: Lawrence Erlbaum Associates.

McWilliams, A. & Siegel, D. 2001. Corporate social responsibility: A theory of the firm perspective. Academy of Management Review, 26(1): 117–127.

Orlitzky, Marc, Schmidt, F. L., and Rynes, Sara. L. 2003. Corporate social and financial performance: A meta-analysis. Organization Studies, 24(3): 403–441.

Porter, Michael E. & Kramer, Marc R. 2002. The competitive advantage of corporate philanthropy, Harvard Business Review, 80(12, December): 56–68.

Porter, Michael E. & Kramer, Marc R. 2006. Strategy & Society: The link between competitive strategy and corporate social responsibility. Harvard Business Review, 84 (12, December): 78–92.

Prahalad, C. K. 2005. The Fortune at the Bottom of the Pyramid: Eradicating Poverty through Profits. Upper Saddle River, NJ: Wharton School Publishing.

Reason. 2005. Rethinking the Social Responsibility of Business: A Reason debate featuring Milton Friedman, Whole Foods' John Mackey, and Cypress Semiconductor's T.J. Rodgers, October 2005.

Rowley, T. J. and Moldoveanu, M. 2003. When will stakeholder groups act? An interest- and identity-based model of stakeholder group mobilization. Academy of Management Review, 28(2): 204–219.

Schnietz, Karen. E. and Epstein, Marc. J. 2003. The Crisis Value of a Rreputation for Corporate Social Responsibility: Evidence from the 1999 Seattle WTO Meeting. Presented at the Sixth Annual International Conference on Corporate Reputation, Boston, MA, May 2002.

Sharfman, M. 1994. Changing institutional rules: The evolution of corporate philanthropy, 1883–1953. Business & Society, 33(3): 236–269.

SIRAN. 2006. Social Investment Research Analysts Network Report 2006, http://www.siran.org/pdfs/csrreportingpr2006.pdf

Smith, C. 1994. The new corporate philanthropy. Harvard Business Review, (May/June), 72(3): 105–116.

Social Investment Forum. 2006. 2005 Report on Socially Responsible Investment Trends in the United States: Ten year Review. Washington, DC: Social Investment Forum.

Szwajkowski, Eugene and Raymond E. Figlewicz. 1999. Evaluating corporate performance: A comparison of the fortune reputation survey and the Socrates social dating database. Journal of Managerial Issues, 11: 137–154.

The Economist. 2005. "The good company: Companies today are exhorted to be 'socially responsible'. What, exactly, does this mean?" January 22, page 11.

Waddock, S.A. 2006. Leading Corporate Citizens: Vision, Values, Value Added, 2nd edition. New York, NY: McGraw-Hill.

Weaver, G. D., Trevino, L. K. and Cochran, P. L. 1999. Integrated and decoupled corporate social performance: Management commitments, external pressures, and corporate ethics practices. Academy of Management Journal, 42(5): 539–552.

Whetten, D. A. and Mackey, A. 2002. A social actor conception of organizational identity and its implications for the study of organizational reputation, Business & Society, 41(4), 393–414.

Wood, Donna J. 1991. Corporate social performance revisited. Academy of Management Review, 16(4): 691–718.

Zadek, Simon. 2004. The path to corporate responsibility. Harvard Business Review, 82(12 December): 125.

Chapter 12
United States of America: A Snapshot of US' Practices

Adam Lindgreen, Valérie Swaen, and Wesley J. Johnston

Abstract Organizations increasingly are embracing the concept of corporate social responsibility (CSR). In this study CSR refers to actions that further some social good, beyond the interests of the firm and that which is required by law (McWilliams et al., 2006). Specifically, CSR consists of economic citizenship, legal citizenship, ethical citizenship, and discretionary citizenship (Maignan, 1997; Maignan and Ferrell, 2001; Maignan et al., 1999). Despite the fact that CSR is popular, with its theoretical underpinnings having been the topic of frequent discussions, empirical studies often involve only limited aspects. This state of affair implies that theory may not be congruent with actual practices, which again may impede our understanding and further development of CSR. We examine actual CSR practices that relate to five different stakeholder groups; subsequently, we develop an instrument to measure those CSR practices and apply it to a survey of 401 U.S. organizations. We identify four different clusters of organizations, depending on the CSR practice focus. The distinctive features of each cluster relate to organizational demographics, perceived influence of stakeholders, managers' perceptions of the influence of CSR on performance, and organizational performance.

12.1 Introduction

The high ranking of corporate social responsibility (CSR) on research agendas is reflected by theoretical debates in academic journals and books, as well as practitioner discussions that argue, "not only is doing good the right thing to do, but it also leads to doing better" (Bhattacharya and Sen, 2004, p. 9). Many consider it an absolute necessity that organizations define their roles in society and apply social, ethical, legal, and responsible standards to their businesses (Lichtenstein et al., 2004). Examples of organizations pursuing CSR objectives include Patagonia, Starbucks, and The Body Shop.

S. O. Idowu and W. L. Filho (eds.), *Global Practices of Corporate Social Responsibility*   251
© Springer-Verlag Berlin Heidelberg 2009

However, despite the well-accepted belief that CSR is important for organizations to meet their stakeholder obligations, various unresolved issues exist in the literature, including an incomplete picture of the type of CSR that organizations practice. For example, empirical studies tend to focus only on limited aspects of CSR. There is therefore an urgent need for studies to start examining organizations' actual CSR practices.

First, no studies address how organizations might emphasize different aspects of CSR. This issue has remained largely unexplored in the literature (e.g., Bhattacharya and Sen, 2004; Maignan and Ferrell, 2001; Matten et al., 2003). For example, how do different stakeholder groups influence the adoption of certain CSR practices? To address this research gap, we identify CSR practices, the combinations of CSR practices that different organizations pursue, and the influence of different stakeholder groups on CSR practices.

Second, we respond to the need to measure the returns to CSR programs (e.g., Aupperle et al., 1985; Bhattacharya and Sen, 2004; Griffin and Mahon, 1997). The issue of insufficient measures is exacerbated by the complex correlation between CSR and performance outcomes, which is not as straightforward as some seem to believe. By reporting on how 401 organizations' chosen CSR practices, we address this critical issue and thereby contribute to ensuring better congruence between CSR theory and practice.

We structure the remainder of this article as follows: First, we provide a brief literature review about CSR practices, which we use to develop a survey to gather descriptive data about how organizations practice CSR. Second, we describe the methodology we use, and third, we present and discuss the results of our survey of 401 U.S. organizations and their CSR practices. Fourth and finally, we identify our study's contributions and managerial implications, as well as some limitations, and suggest avenues for further research.

12.2 Literature Review and Theoretical Framework

In this section, we consider three topics: the background of CSR, the influence of different stakeholder groups on CSR practices, and the performance outcomes of CSR practices.

12.2.1 CSR Background

The CSR concept relates closely to corporate citizenship, corporate social responsiveness, corporate social performance, and stakeholder management. Common to these concepts is the idea that organizations should be not only concerned about making a profit but also engaged in "actions that appear to further some social good, beyond the interests of the firm and that which is required by law" (McWilliams et al., 2006, p. 1).

Table 12.1 Conceptualizations of CSR

CSR is "the firm's consideration of, and response to, issues beyond the narrow economic, technical, and legal requirements of the firm [...] to accomplish social benefits along with the traditional economic gains which the firm seeks" (Davis, 1973, p. 313)

"Corporate social responsibility implies bringing corporate behavior up to a level where it is congruent with the prevailing social norms, values, and expectations" (Sethi, 1975, p. 62)

CSR is defined as activities that "protect and improve both the welfare of society as a whole and the interest of the organization" (Davis and Blomstrom, 1975, p. 5)

"Corporate responsibility is the notion that corporations have an obligation to constituent groups in society other than stockholders and beyond that prescribed by law or union contract" (Jones, 1980, p. 59)

"Corporate citizenship is concerned with the relationship between companies and society – both the local community, which surrounds a business and whose members interact with its employees, and the wider and increasingly worldwide community, which touches every business through its products, supply chain, dealer network, and its advertising, among other things" (McIntosh et al., 1998, p. 20)

"Good corporate citizenship can be defined as understanding and managing a company's wider influences on society for the benefit of the company and society as a whole" (Marsden and Andriof, 1998, qtd. in Andriof and Marsden, 2000, p. 2)

According to the World Business Council for Sustainable Development, "Corporate Social Responsibility is the continuing commitment by business to behave ethically and contribute to economic development while improving the quality of life of the workforce and their families as well as of the local community and society at large" (Holmes and Watts, 1999, qtd. in Chand, 2006, p. 240)

In this sense, CSR generally refers to business decision making related to ethical values, compliance with legal requirements, and respect for people, communities, and the environment. However, as we indicate in Table 12.1, though the term "CSR" gets used often, multiple conceptualizations of it exist, and a single definition has yet to be agreed on. The earliest conceptualizations of CSR, developed in the 1950s, pertained to business responsibility (Bowen, 1953). A quarter of a century later, Carroll (1979, p. 500) specified that organizations' obligations must "encompass the economic, legal, ethical, and discretionary expectations that society has of organizations at a given point in time."

Building on Carroll's (1979) work, Maignan developed an instrument to measure CSR practices, and validated the instrument in France and the United States (Maignan, 1997; Maignan and Ferrell, 2001; Maignan et al., 1999). Her conceptualization of CSR consists of four dimensions: (1) organizations should be productive and profitable and meet the needs of consumers (economic citizenship), (2) they are compelled to work within existing legal frameworks (legal citizenship), (3) organizations must follow socially established moral standards (ethical citizenship), and (4) their voluntary corporate activities must attempt to help other people and contribute to the well-being of society (discretionary citizenship).

Questions still remain. For example, Maignan and Ferrell (2001) consider only employees, customers, and public stakeholders, though they acknowledge that other stakeholder groups exist. We extend Maignan and Ferrell's (2001) research by including a wider variety of stakeholder groups, in line with Clarkson's (1995, p. 106) suggestion that stakeholders include the "persons or groups that have, or claim, ownership, rights, or interests in a corporation and its activities, past, present, or future". In so doing, our study provides a more accurate picture of CSR.

12.2.2 The Influence of Stakeholder Groups on CSR Practices

Organizations must take into account the responsibilities in which their stakeholders are interested. Consumers, investors, and business leaders demand that organizations "remember their obligations to the employees, communities, and environment" (Martin, 2002, p. 69) and employees look for help dealing with myriad complex and pressing social and economic issues. In return, these stakeholders supply the elements necessary for the organization to function, such as human, financial, and technical resources. The availability of these resources determines the organization's ability to survive.

Consumer stakeholders may exercise pressure on an organization if they believe it is not acting in a "desirable" way, especially because their access to instant and free information, as well as a multitude of alternative providers, has become even easier. Therefore, these stakeholders come to expect more of organizations in terms of corporate citizenship (McIntosh et al., 1998; Pinkston and Carrol, 1994).

In the supply chain, partners with CSR policies may require suppliers to document that their raw materials, components, or services meet environmental and ethical standards. Therefore, the pressure for better social and environmental performance moves upstream through the value chain (Warhurst, 2001). In some cases, especially when the stakeholder is a large, powerful organization, this influence represents a formidable force that can effectively exclude suppliers from the marketplace if they appear socially irresponsible. Within this context, the use of child labor and social diversity protections represent some of the most important issues.

Managers inside the organization constitute a third group of stakeholders. They have access to, or are themselves, the people in charge of decision making related to CSR, so they have the ability to assess the relevance and importance of stakeholder issues, select which issues should be considered, and participate in implementing the decisions. Managers also play important roles in orienting the organization and its decisions and actions (Deshpandé and Webster, 1989). The level of commitment managers hold to issues of public interest – measured in terms of the time they spend on these issues – correlates positively with the development of management structures concentrated on social issues inside the organization (Greening and Gray, 1994). Top management support for environmental and social initiatives, as well as the presence of policy entrepreneurs (i.e., managers who bring these issues to the forefront), positively influence an organization's CSR orientation. In this sense, managers have considerable influence over the organization's CSR involvement; for example, Anita Roddick has been instrumental in developing the CSR visions of The Body Shop.

In summary, organizations exist within larger networks that consist of various stakeholder groups that exert pressure on them. A good corporate citizen must address the concerns and satisfy (some of) the demands of stakeholders who, whether

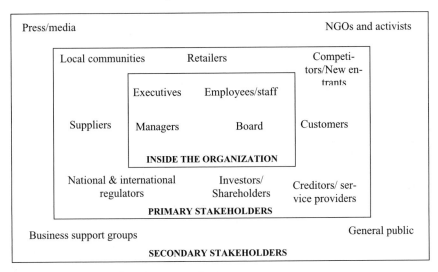

Fig. 12.1 Stakeholders influencing an organization

directly or indirectly, can affect or be affected by the organization's activities (Fig. 12.1).

12.2.3 The Performance Outcomes of CSR Practices

Several studies consider the performance outcomes that result from an organization's investment in CSR, but none has established any clear relationship between CSR and economic performance (Aupperle et al., 1985; Griffin and Mahon, 1997). The most commonly identified positive relationship suggests that CSR offers organizations the potential to increase sales and reduce costs. However, prior research also indicates a negative relationship with performance because of the costs involved to invest in CSR. Yet another group of studies suggests no relationship between CSR and performance. We refer to Lindgreen and Swaen (2004).

Research also addresses the impact of CSR practices on stakeholders' attitudes and behaviors toward an organization, though it remains poorly developed. In general, CSR appears to influence an organization's attractiveness to a potential employee (Turban and Greening, 1997) and the degree of current employees' commitment (Maignan and Ferrell, 2001; Maignan et al., 1999). In a survey conducted by the Conference Board, executives reported that volunteer programs improved employee productivity and morale, fostered teamwork, and built skills (Leonard,, 1997). Another survey indicates that 84% of managers believe that achieving a responsible image in the community is important for employee morale (*Business Ethics*, 1997a). Thus, CSR initiatives may help establish a bond between the organization and its employees (Leonard, 1997).

Awareness of CSR policies and practices also seems to have a positive influence on consumers' evaluations of product attributes (Brown and Dacin, 1997) and attitudes toward the organization (Brown and Dacin, 1997). Through customer satisfaction, CSR also affects market value (Luo and Bhattacharya, 2006). Finally, CSR practices positively influence the organization's corporate reputation (Fombrun and Shanley, 1990) and customer loyalty (Maignan et al., 1999).

12.3 Research Questions

From our literature review, we derive several research questions to guide our study. Insights into these questions help us develop the CSR concept further.

> (a) What current types of CSR are currently practiced by U.S. organizations? and (b) What relative emphasis do different organizations place on different aspects of CSR?
>
> How are different stakeholders perceived to influence organizations' CSR practices?
>
> How are different CSR practices perceived to relate to different performance outcomes?

Because CSR has been conceptualized in so many ways, the answer to the first question will contribute to a better understanding of CSR, in particular by providing empirical evidence of current CSR practices. Also, our first research question clarifies how different organizations choose to emphasize different aspects of CSR. In addition, by answering the second question, we gain a better understanding of how different stakeholders are perceived to influence organizations in choosing different CSR practices. Finally, previous studies fail to agree whether practicing CSR affects performance outcomes, so an answer to the third research question contributes to existing research by identifying organizational perceptions about the relationship between their CSR investments and performance outcomes; furthermore, using measures of organizations' real performance, independent of the perceived impact of CSR, we can determine whether a correlation exists between CSR investments and real performance.

12.4 Methodology

12.4.1 Survey Instrument: Questionnaire

We collected data through a survey questionnaire (that will be mailed to readers requesting it). The questionnaire first asks respondents to provide details about their organizations. The second part of the survey relates to the organizations' CSR practices, developed on the basis of an extensive review of academic and business literature to identify activities commonly considered representative of CSR (Beltz et al., 1997; Maignan et al., 1999; Swaen, 2004; Swaen et al., 2003). In the third section of the survey, we ask for details about sales revenue and return on investment, as well as an evaluation of the organizations' performance relative to its main competitor(s) on these two measures. Respondents also evaluated their organizations' performance relative to expectations with regard to improving relations with different stakeholders; the influence of different stakeholders; improving the social and economic health of their society; attaining desired profitability; improving their corporate reputation; and gaining national and international visibility. For this part of the survey, we measure both respondents' perceptions of the effect(s) of CSR on different performance criteria, as well as how the organization has performed over time relative to expectations. Finally, the last part of the survey requests respondents to describe themselves in terms of their position in the organization, the length of time they had held their current position, as well as their gender and age.

12.4.2 Data Collection: Sampling Procedure

We collected data through a nationwide survey of managers of U.S. organizations, whom we contacted through e-Rewards, a Dallas-based online sample provider that has built its own consumer, business, and specialty panels with a total of 1.5 million members. We specified that our sample should cover a broad range of organizations in terms of type of business activities, amount of sales revenues, number of employees, and sales revenue generated by sales to export markets. Of the functional roles captured by e-Rewards, we identify executives/owners, marketing/advertising personnel, and general management as particularly appropriate for our study purpose. We also consider five additional roles as appropriate: communication/public relations, market research, customer service, sales/business development, and administration.

e-Rewards contacted all respondents via e-mail with an invitation to participate in the survey, to which they would respond online, which enabled us to capture the completion time and date the questionnaire was returned. Respondents from 523 different U.S. organizations completed the survey and answered all the survey's questions. However, because preliminary tests showed that respondents would need at least 10 min to answer the survey, we exclude questionnaires from respondents who spent less than 10 min filling out the survey. We therefore retained 401 organizations in our study.

12.5 Results and Discussion

12.5.1 Respondent Demographics

The age of the respondents averages 45 years (SD = 10.7 years), as we indicate in Table 12.2. The majority of respondents hold upper (64.7%) or middle (28.0%)

Table 12.2 Respondent demographics

Demographic variable	Number	Percentage
Level of job position		
Upper management	257	64.7
Middle management	111	28.0
Lower management	29	7.3
Missing	4	
Number of months in current job position		
Less than 36 months	106	26.4
36 months, but less than 72 months	119	29.7
72 months, but less than 120 months	68	17.0
120 months or more	108	26.9
Gender		
Male	399	99.5
Female	2	0.5
Age		
35 years old or younger	85	21.2
Older than 35 years old, but not more than 45 years old	116	28.9
Older than 45 years old, but not more than 55 years old	130	32.4
More than 55 years old	70	17.5

management positions. On average, the respondents have spent 7.6 years in their current position (SD = 7.3 years).

12.5.1.1 Organization Demographics

As we indicate in Table 12.3, the sample represents a variety of organizations, with 45.5% in business-to-business and 44.3% in business-to-consumer organizations; 10.2% of organizations operate in both markets. The products that the organizations offer are distributed as follows: physical goods (37.0%), services (57.5%), and physical goods combined with services (5.5%). In terms of duration, 29.3% of the organizations were established less than 10 years ago. The number of employees ranges from less than 20 (38.0%) to 1,000 or more (29.5%), with the remaining organizations (32.5%) employing between 20 and 1,000 persons.

Also as we indicate in Table 12.3, 71.3% of the organizations generate 10% or less of their sales revenue through sales to export markets. The 2004 sales revenues of 52.5% of the organizations were $10 million or less, and 18.6% enjoyed more than $1,000 million in sales revenue. Furthermore, 29.0% of the organizations consider their 2004 sales growth level comparable to that of their primary competitor, and 57.5% believe that their sales growth in 2004 was better that that of their primary competitor.

Table 12.3 Organization demographics and performance outcomes

Demographic or performance outcome variable	Number	Percentage
Types of goods and services		
Business-to-business	155	45.5
Business-to-consumer	151	44.3
Both business-to-business and business-to-consumer	35	10.2
Missing	60	
Types of products		
Physical goods	126	37.0
Services	196	57.5
Both physical goods and services	19	5.5
Missing	60	
Establishment of organization		
Less than 10 years ago	115	29.3
10 years ago, but less than 30 years ago	134	34.1
30 years ago or more	144	36.6
Missing	8	
Number of employees		
Less than 20 employees	151	38.0
20 employees, but less than 100 employees	60	15.1
100 employees, but less than 1,000 employees	69	17.4
1,000 employees or more	117	29.5
Missing	4	
Proportion of sales generated by sales to export markets		
10% or less	249	71.3
More than 10%	100	28.7
Missing	52	
Sales revenue		
US$ 10 million or less	192	52.5
More than US$ 10 million	174	47.5
Missing	35	
	Mean	SD
Growth in sales revenue relative to competitors[a]	3.72	1.13
Return on investment relative to competitors[a]	3.64	1.12
Performance relative to expectations[a]		
Improving relations with customers	3.82	0.92
Improving relations with employees	3.55	1.02
Improving relations with local community	3.35	0.86
Improving social health of local community	3.31	0.89
Improving economic health of local community	3.29	0.88
Improving stakeholder relations in general	3.44	0.90
Attaining desired profitability	3.58	1.11
Improving corporate image/reputation	3.68	0.93
Gaining national and international visibility	3.38	1.03

[a]Scale used was [min 1; max 5]

12.6 CSR Practices and Relationships to Stakeholders

In 15.0% of the organizations, a CSR department deals with social, environmental, and ethical issues. Employees in another 31.2% of organizations regularly allocate some time for these issues. The remaining 53.9% of organizations do not possess a CSR department or employees who regularly allocate their time to such issues.

Using factorial analysis with Varimax rotation, and as depicted in Table 12.4 with means and standard deviations, we identify five reliable dimensions of CSR practices that relate to customers and suppliers, employees, financial investors, philanthropy, and the environment. On a seven-point scale, respondents indicate that their organizations have adopted specific CSR practices relating to employees, customers and suppliers, and financial investors. To a lesser extent, they also apply CSR practices related to philanthropy and the environment.

Table 12.4 Organizations' CSR practices and relationship to identified stakeholder(s)

CSR Practices	Identified Stakeholder(s)	Score	
		Mean	SD
Practice[a]			
Provide all customers with the information needed to make sound purchasing decisions	Customers and suppliers	5.54	1.51
Satisfy the complaints of our customers about products or services	Customers and suppliers	5.65	1.42
Incorporate the interests of our customers in our business decisions	Customers and suppliers	5.48	1.37
Treat suppliers, regardless of their size and location, fairly and respectfully	Customers and suppliers	5.35	1.50
Incorporate the interests of our suppliers in our business decisions	Customers and suppliers	4.77	1.61
Inform our suppliers about organizational changes affecting our purchasing decisions	Customers and suppliers	4.76	1.62
Average ($\alpha = 0.912$)	Market_CSR	5.26	1.22
Support our employees who want to pursue further education	Employees	5.22	1.72
Provide procedures that help to insure the health and safety of our employees	Employees	5.55	1.52
Treat our employees fairly and respectfully, regardless of gender or ethnic background	Employees	5.81	1.56
Help our employees balance their private and professional lives	Employees	5.02	1.75
Incorporate the interests of our employees in our business decisions	Employees	4.98	1.69
Provide our employees with salaries that properly and fairly reward them for their work	Employees	5.16	1.67
Average ($\alpha = 0.924$)	Empl_CSR	5.29	1.38
Provide our investors with full and accurate financial information about the organization	Financial investors	5.29	1.77
Incorporate the interests of our investors in business decisions	Financial investors	5.19	1.71
Inform our investors of changes in corporate policy	Financial investors	5.09	1.76
Average ($\alpha = 0.941$)	Invest_CSR	5.19	1.64
Incorporate the interests of the communities, where we operate, in our business decisions	Philanthropy	4.82	1.66

(Cont.)

Table 12.4 Continued

CSR Practices	Identified Stakeholder(s)	Score	
		Mean	SD
Financially support education in the communities where we operate	Philanthropy	4.45	1.88
Stimulate the economic development in the communities where we operate	Philanthropy	4.64	1.76
Help improve the quality of life in the communities where we operate	Philanthropy	4.83	1.73
Give money to charities in the communities where we operate	Philanthropy	4.89	1.81
Financially support activities (arts, culture, sports) in the communities where we operate	Philanthropy	4.57	1.86
Average ($\alpha = 0.938$)	Philan_CSR	4.70	1.53
Voluntarily exceed government-imposed environmental regulations	Environment	4.81	1.69
Incorporate environmental concerns in our business decisions	Environment	4.92	1.64
Incorporate environmental performance objectives in our organizational plans	Environment	4.73	1.72
Financially support environmental initiatives	Environment	4.26	1.77
Measure our organization's environmental performance	Environment	4.31	1.82
Minimize the environmental impact of all our organization's activities	Environment	4.54	1.77
Average ($\alpha = 0.941$)	Envir_CSR	4.60	1.50
Organization's standing relative to that of competitors[b]			
Social policies and practices		3.57	1.02
Environmental policies and practices		3.43	0.98
Ethical policies and practices		3.93	1.02
Perceived effect of social, environmental, and ethical practices[b]			
Corporate image/reputation		3.68	1.18
Financial performance		3.47	1.16
Morale of its employees		3.68	1.10
Satisfaction of its customers		3.81	1.09
Satisfaction of other groups, for example employees, suppliers, and local community		3.54	1.05
The well-being of people in general ('social welfare')		3.36	1.09
National and international visibility		2.98	1.32
Support from the government		2.75	1.33

[a]Scale used was [min 1; max 7]
[b]Scale used was [min 1; max 5]

Again, using factorial analysis with Varimax rotation, we next distinguish four groups of stakeholders that were perceived as influencing the organization. These stakeholders are listed in Table 12.5: owners, CEOs, and boards of directors; internal stakeholders; market stakeholders; and governmental and other pressure groups. Using a five-point scale, respondents evaluated the influence of each group of stakeholders (see Table 12.5 for means) as 3.97, 3.34, 3.01, and 2.63, respectively. In other words, respondents perceive the influence of owners, CEOs, boards of

Table 12.5 Stakeholder influence

Stakeholder[a]	Relates to...	Mean	SD
Employees	Workers	3.33	1.17
Middle-level managers	Workers	3.34	1.18
Average ($\alpha = 0.845$)	Workers	3.34	1.09
Chief executive officer	Directors and owners	4.35	0.98
Board of directors	Directors and owners	3.70	1.43
Owners/shareholders	Directors and owners	3.86	1.23
Average ($\alpha = 0.658$)	Directors and owners	3.97	0.94
Customers	Market stakeholders	3.47	1.15
Suppliers	Market stakeholders	2.78	1.18
Competitors	Market stakeholders	2.79	1.20
Average ($\alpha = 0.771$)	Market stakeholders	3.01	0.97
Trade unions	Government and pressure groups	2.14	1.25
Local communities	Government and pressure groups	2.87	1.23
Press/media	Government and pressure groups	2.78	1.26
National regulators	Government and pressure groups	2.98	1.33
International regulators	Government and pressure groups	2.38	1.34
Average ($\alpha = 0.846$)	Government and pressure groups	2.63	1.01

[a]Scale used was [min 1; max 5].

directors, and internal stakeholders as relatively high, whereas that of governmental and other pressure groups and regulators is relatively low.

Finally, the following two paragraphs answer partially our third research question. Respondents rated the perceived effect of their CSR policies and practices (five-point scale) in terms of various noneconomic and financial performance criteria (Table 12.4). The CSR policies and practices reportedly are perceived to have some effect, with the highest score for customer satisfaction (mean = 3.81; SD = 1.09) and the lowest for governmental support (mean = 2.75; SD = 1.33). Our finding that CSR is perceived to have a positive effect on customer satisfaction, corporate image/reputation, and employee morale matches previous research, which suggests CSR plays an important role in building and maintaining corporate image (Fombrun and Shanley, 1990; Menon and Menon, 1997), offers a way to create bonds with customers (Kennedy et al., 2001; Swaen, 2004), and motivates employees at work (*Business Ethics,*, 1997b; Leonard,, 1997; Maignan et al., 1999).

Our managerial respondents also declared that CSR practices could have a slightly positive impact on financial performance. Only 7.7% of the surveyed organizations believe CSR practices have no effect on financial performance, 47.9% indicate "some effect," and 20.9% believe it has a "very high effect."

12.6.1 Cluster Analysis

To determine the possibility of identifying meaningful groups of organizations in terms of their CSR practices, we perform a cluster analysis on the construct scores. For specific details of analysis, readers are welcome to contact the authors.

Table 12.6 K-means four-clusters solution (solution from Ward's method)

Clusters	Variables	N	Minimum	Maximum	SD	Mean	Conclusion
Organizations focus on CSR activities related to customers, suppliers, and employees	Market_CSR	95	1.67	7	1.27	5.19	High
	Empl_CSR		1	7	1.58	5.08	High
	Invest_CSR		1	6.67	1.70	3.50	Low
	Philan_CSR		1	7	1.59	4.47	Medium
	Envir_CSR		1	7	1.60	4.50	Medium
Organizations focus on CSR activities related to customers, suppliers, employees, and financial investors	Market_CSR	99	2.83	7	1.06	5.40	High
	Empl_CSR		2.33	7	1.17	5.39	High
	Invest_CSR		3.33	7	1.02	5.93	High
	Philan_CSR		1.33	6.67	1.39	3.98	Low
	Envir_CSR		1.50	7	1.29	4.92	Medium
Organizations focus on CSR activities related to customers, suppliers, employees, financial investors, and philanthropy	Market_CSR	135	2.50	7	1.06	5.58	High
	Empl_CSR		1.83	7	1.18	5.67	High
	Invest_CSR		2.33	7	1.13	5.85	High
	Philan_CSR		1.17	7	1.48	5.08	High
	Envir_CSR		1	6.83	1.48	4.03	Medium
Organizations focus on CSR activities related to investors, natural environment, and philanthropy	Market_CSR	72	1	7	1.33	4.54	Medium
	Empl_CSR		1	7	1.46	4.71	Medium
	Invest_CSR		1	7	1.45	5.16	High
	Philan_CSR		1	7	1.31	5.28	High
	Envir_CSR		2.17	7	1.24	5.34	High

Notes: The thresholds applied are as follows: Low < 4, Medium [4;5], and High > 5

In terms of organizational profiles, as we show in Table 12.6, the identified four different clusters focus on issues related to (1) employees, customers, and suppliers; (2) employees, customers, suppliers, and financial investors; (3) employees, customers, suppliers, financial investors, and philanthropy; and (4) financial investors, the environment, and philanthropy. The inclusion of customers in three clusters should not be surprising, because customers represent an extremely important stakeholder group (Bhattacharya and Sen, 2004).

We find that organizations combine different CSR practices into hybrid configurations, most often by relating their CSR activities to different core stakeholders (i.e., employees, customers, suppliers, and financial investors). Indeed, our results imply a kind of a continuum for the first three clusters, with the first and third at the extremes and the second in between. The fourth cluster exists in addition to this continuum. At one end of the continuum, organizations invest in CSR activities that relate directly to their primary stakeholders (customers, employees, and suppliers), then include another group of stakeholders (financial investors), before eventually adding peripheral activities related to the general public (philanthropy). In the fourth cluster, CSR appears linked to management/ownership philosophy, not the organization's core activities. That is, CSR activities among organizations in the fourth cluster focus on sustainable development rather than activities designed to satisfy customers, suppliers, or employees.

In addition, we suggest that the first and second clusters refer to a traditional model of managerial capitalism, in which the organization pertains only to suppliers, employees, and financial investors, which provide basic resources that the organization employs to offer goods and services to customers (Crane and Matten, 2004). In contrast, the third and fourth clusters take a stakeholder view of the organization, in which financial investors represent only one among several groups of stakeholders (including the general public) affected by the organization's activities (Crane and Matten, 2004).

In summary, by considering current CSR practices, their relationships with stakeholders, and the relative emphasis of different organizations on different aspects of CSR, we derive a four-cluster segmentation in which each cluster emphasizes different aspects of CSR. That is, CSR implementation involves various methods, not just one, which offers a response to our first research question.

12.6.2 Differences across Clusters

Organizational demographics. As we indicate in Table 12.7, we find significant differences across the different clusters in terms of the organizations' age and number of employees. Organizations in the fourth cluster are significantly older – 50.7% of them were established more than 30 years ago, and only 17.4% were established less than 10 years ago. In comparison, 25.5% or more of the organizations in the other clusters had been established less than 10 years ago. In addition, the fourth cluster contains larger organizations, with 53.5% of them employing 1,000 or more persons; in the other clusters, this size exists in a maximum of 26.5% of the organizations. Previous studies report that larger organizations invest more in CSR (Greening and Gray, 1994; Stanwick and Stanwick, 1998). Because of their greater visibility, larger organizations tend to attract more attention from the media, pressure groups, and other stakeholders, but they also have greater resources and skills to change the context in which they find themselves and to meet environmental and social pressures. As a result, such organizations generally are inclined to pay special attention to their corporate image.

We also uncover some significant differences between clusters depending on whether employees work on CSR activities. Most organizations in the fourth cluster dedicate employees (34.7%) or even a department (31.9%) to social issues. In contrast, in the other clusters, between 51.9% and 72.6% of organizations commit no employees to dealing with such issues.

However, we do not identify any significant differences across clusters in terms of industry, that is, whether the organizations represents a business-to-business or business-to-consumer effort or offers physical goods or services.

Table 12.7 Differences across clusters (chi-square analyses)

Variables	Cluster 1 N (% within the cluster)	Cluster 2 N (% within the cluster)	Cluster 3 N (% within the cluster)	Cluster 4 N (% within the cluster)	Chi-square	p-values
Organization age					15.834	0.015
Less than 10 years	31 (33.3%)	25 (25.5%)	47 (35.3%)	12 (17.4%)		
Between 11 and 30 years	30 (32.3%)	31 (31.6%)	51 (38.3%)	22 (31.9%)		
More than 30 years	32 (34.4%)	42 (42.9%)	35 (26.3%)	35 (50.7%)		
Organization size					43.462	0.0001
Less than 20 employees	50 (53.2%)	30 (30.6%)	59 (44.0%)	12 (16.9%)		
Between 20 and 99	11 (11.7%)	15 (15.3%)	24 (17.9%)	10 (14.1%)		
Between 100 and 999	13 (13.8%)	27 (27.6%)	18 (13.4%)	11 (15.5%)		
1000 or more	20 (21.3%)	26 (26.5%)	33 (24.6%)	38 (53.5%)		
CSR department?					38.702	0.0001
A separate department	11 (11.6%)	12 (12.1%)	14 (10.4%)	23 (31.9%)		
Employees	15 (15.8%)	34 (34.3%)	51 (37.8%)	25 (34.7%)		
Neither	69 (72.6%)	53 (53.5%)	70 (51.9%)	24 (33.3%)		
Sales revenue in 2004					28.746	0.0001
10 million or less	56 (65.9%)	40 (45.5%)	78 (61.4%)	18 (27.3%)		
More than 10 million	29 (34.1%)	48 (54.5%)	49 (38.6%)	48 (72.7%)		
Business-to-business or business-to-consumer?					5.985	0.112
Business-to-business	35 (51.5%)	30 (39.5%)	52 (49.1%)	34 (60.7%)		
Business-to-consumers	33 (48.5%)	46 (60.5%)	54 (50.9%)	22 (39.3%)		
Goods or services?					3.602	0.308
Goods	27 (38.0%)	38 (46.3%)	38 (33.3%)	23 (41.8%)		
Services	44 (62.0%)	44 (53.7%)	76 (66.7%)	32 (58.2%)		

12.6.2.1 Perceived Influence of Stakeholders

The perceived influence of different stakeholders varies across the four clusters. For example, in the first cluster, CEO influence is lower than in the third cluster, the influence of the board of directors is lower than in any other cluster, and that of owners and shareholders is less than in the second or third clusters. Thus, these results confirm the role of investors and top managers in implementing more developed CSR practices, in that the personal involvement of the CEO or directors in social and environmental issues appears to influence the extent of CSR an organization embraces (Drumwright, 1994).

The influence of competitors is greater in the fourth cluster than in the second cluster, possibly because more intense competition requires organizations to depend on their external environment in terms of relationships and corporate image (Khireche-Oldache, 1998). To attract new customers, the organization must distinguish its corporate image from those of competing organizations (McStravic, 2000), and CSR may offer a way to do so (McWilliams and Siegel, 2001) by, for example, redefining its relationships with stakeholders and the wider community or creating greater value (Andriof, 2000).

Finally, the influence of trade unions, local communities, press/media, and national and international regulators is greatest in the fourth cluster. All else being equal, larger organizations (compared to the other clusters, the fourth cluster represents more such organizations) experience greater visibility and therefore tend to be the subjects of public scrutiny. As a result, these organizations must act in a responsible manner, in this case by investing in CSR.

These combined results thus provide comprehensive answers to our second research question regarding the influence of various stakeholders on organizations' CSR practices.

12.6.2.2 Managers' Perceptions of the Influence of CSR on Performance

When organizations invest in CSR, its impact on various noneconomic performance aspects appears positive to our respondents. However, we find differences among the clusters in terms of the size of these perceived positive effects. For example, organizations in the third cluster believe CSR has a greater impact on employee morale than those in the first cluster. For the fourth cluster, the impact of CSR on national and international visibility is greater than that perceived in the first cluster, and the impact of CSR on governmental support is greater than in the first or third clusters. Again, because organizations in the fourth cluster tend to be bigger, they are relatively more concerned about their national and international visibility than are organizations in the other clusters. As a result, if CSR is perceived to influence positively national and international visibility, as well as governmental support, then organizations will invest in CSR. In the third and fourth clusters, the impact of CSR on people's well-being appears greater than for those in the first cluster, which may be congruent with the greater and more diversified CSR investments

Table 12.8 Differences across clusters (ANOVA analyses)

Variables	Cluster 1 mean	Cluster 2 mean	Cluster 3 mean	Cluster 4 mean	Fisher	p-values
Stakeholders' influence						
Employees	3.27	3.31	3.42	3.28	0.407	0.748
Middle-level managers	3.04	3.46	3.44	3.38	2.097	0.102
Chief executive officer	4.13	4.41	4.53	4.21	3.855	0.018
Board of directors	3.17	3.94	3.85	3.78	6.131	0.002
Owners/shareholders	3.52	4.08	4.01	3.72	4.646	0.007
Customers	3.38	3.41	3.59	3.47	0.732	0.533
Suppliers	2.61	2.78	2.88	2.82	1.017	0.385
Competitors	2.65	2.58	2.88	3.08	3.220	0.023
Retailers	2.36	2.21	2.59	2.88	5.000	0.001
Trade unions	2.02	2.02	2.07	2.58	3.830	0.010
Local communities	2.65	2.67	2.90	3.38	6.181	0.0001
Press/media	2.58	2.58	2.79	3.31	6.070	0.0001
National regulators	2.66	2.95	2.92	2.56	6.735	0.0001
International regulators	2.12	2.26	2.36	2.94	5.992	0.001
Perceived CSR impact on …						
Corporate image/reputation	3.49	3.74	3.71	3.76	1.015	0.386
Financial performance	3.22	3.49	3.54	3.61	1.997	0.114
Employee morale	3.44	3.64	3.83	3.75	2.479	0.099
Customer satisfaction	3.78	3.77	3.90	3.75	0.428	0.733
The satisfaction of other groups, for example employees, suppliers, and local community	3.56	3.42	3.70	3.64	2.614	0.060
The well-being of people in general ("social welfare")	3.11	3.25	3.53	3.51	3.766	0.011
National/international visibility	2.66	2.94	3.05	3.32	3.642	0.013
Support from the government	2.55	2.80	2.65	3.15	3.283	0.015
Performance relative to expectations over 2004 in terms of…						
Customer relations	3.77	3.73	3.94	3.79	1.223	0.301
Employee relations	3.57	3.47	3.67	3.41	1.199	0.310
Environment relations	3.40	3.29	3.28	3.51	1.354	0.257
Social health of the local community	3.29	3.10	3.36	3.51	3.159	0.015
Economic health of the local community	3.30	3.07	3.33	3.50	3.395	0.008
Relations with stakeholders in general	3.25	3.46	3.53	3.49	1.759	0.155
Profitability	3.54	3.44	3.61	3.75	1.148	0.329
Corporate image/reputation	3.61	3.51	3.85	3.68	2.845	0.038
National and international visibility	3.32	3.30	3.41	3.51	0.654	0.581

by organizations in the third and fourth clusters. Generally speaking, organizations from the first cluster – those least involved in CSR – seem less convinced of the potential benefits of CSR activities, which may explain why they do not invest as heavily in CSR practices. Another explanation, however, could be that organizations from the first cluster do not perceive any positive effects of CSR practices because they do not invest much in CSR.

12.6.2.3 Organizational Performance

In Table 12.7, we show that sales revenue is significantly higher for organizations in the fourth cluster (72.7% earn more than US$10 million) compared with organizations in other clusters (34.1–54.5% earn more than US$10 million). This finding is logical, because we already know that organizations in the fourth cluster are larger and have been established for longer than organizations in the other clusters.

The results in Table 12.8 also indicate some significant differences between clusters in terms of levels of performance relative to expectations about improving corporate image/reputation, social health, and the economic health of the local community. Organizations in the third and fourth clusters, with their more developed CSR, appear to perform better than organizations in the first and second clusters in terms of corporate image and impact on social and economic health. This result matches previous research that supports a positive link between CSR investments and corporate image (Fombrun and Shanley, 1990). Thus, we offer a response to our third research question regarding the connections between different CSR practices and various performance outcomes.

12.7 Conclusions

Overall, our findings demonstrate that CSR is not the result of episodic and unrelated CSR activities but rather that many organizations systematically monitor and address different stakeholder groups' demands. We expand on this finding in this section.

First, there is not one way to act responsibly. To build an image of social responsibility, organizations pursue, at a minimum, four different types of CSR practices that target different stakeholder groups. The four clusters imply a continuum of CSR practices and indicate that the use of particular practices depends on the type of stakeholders the organization considers important.

Second, only the third and fourth clusters refer to the stakeholder view of the organization; the first and second clusters are closer to a traditional model of managerial capitalism. This interesting finding speaks to the frequent claim that organizations increasingly are investing heavily in broad-scale CSR. Our study indicates instead that different organizations emphasize different aspects of CSR, which may reflect the different power of stakeholders versus the organization. We also note that organizations in the fourth cluster are relatively old. Newer organizations may be more inclined to consider, first and foremost, their short-term financial performance objectives and activities, then at a later stage address their long-term survival, in which arena CSR can play an important part.

Third, our study examines the embeddedness of CSR within organizations. The extent of CSR formalization may depend on whether the organization assigns a department or, at a minimum, some employees to work specifically on CSR-related issues. In some cases, an organization might, of course, need to develop CSR first and then as a result require employees to deal with CSR issues.

Fourth, the size of the organization and its initial economic performance may help explain the development of CSR practices. Larger organizations have more resources to monitor social demands, address them, and communicate the organization's efforts to develop and address its CSR practices (Greening and Gray, 1994; Stanwick and Stanwick, 1998).

Fifth and finally, our findings suggest that managers have a relatively positive perception of CSR practices as improving, or at least not harming, business performance. For example, CSR is perceived to have a positive impact on corporate image and customers' and other stakeholders' (e.g., employees, suppliers, local communities) satisfaction. Furthermore, the more organizations invest in CSR (which moves them along our continuum of clusters), the more they realize the benefits associated with CSR with respect to national and international visibility, support from the government, and the well-being of people (social welfare). These "softer" benefits may be translated into "hard" benefits (e.g., profits, sales returns) in the long run and also give the organization legitimacy.

References

Andriof, J.: 2000, 'Mapping the Research within Corporate Citizenship: Concepts, Evidence, and Implications', working paper.

Andriof, J. and C. Marsden: 2000, 'Corporate Citizenship: What Is It and How to Assess It?' in M. McIntosh and A. Warhurst (eds.), *Third Annual Warwick Corporate Citizenship Unit Conference* (University of Warwick, Coventry).

Aupperle, K.E., A.B. Carroll, and J.D. Hatfield: 1985, 'An Empirical Examination of the Relationship Between Corporate Social Responsibility and Profitability', *Academy of Management Journal* **28**(2), 446–463.

Beltz, F., M.-P. Kestemont, and L. Strannegard: 1997, *International Business Environmental Barometer* (Cappelen Akademisk Forlag, Copenhagen).

Bhattacharya, C.B. and S. Sen: 2004, 'Doing Better at Doing Good: When, Why, and How Consumers Respond to Corporate Social Initiatives', *California Management Review*, **47**(1), 9–24.

Bowen, H.R: 1953, *Social Responsibilities of the Businessman* (Harper-Row, New York).

Brown, T.J. and P.A. Dacin: 1997, 'The Company and the Product: Corporate Associations and Consumer Product Responses', *Journal of Marketing* **61**(1), 68–84.

Business Ethics: 1997a, 'Does It Pay to be Ethical?' (March/April), 15.

Business Ethics: 1997b, 'NLC Names Corporate Names in Sweatshop Reports', (January–February), 9.

Carroll, A.B.: 1979, 'A Three-dimensional Conceptual Model of Corporate Performance', *Academy of Management Review* **4**(4), 497–505.

Chand, M.: 2006, 'The Relationship between Corporate Social Performance and Corporate Financial Performance: Industry Type as a Boundary Condition', *The Business Review*, **5**(1), 240–245.

Clarkson, M.B.E: 1995, 'A Stakeholder Framework for Analyzing and Evaluating Corporate Social Performance', *Academy of Management Review*, **20**(1), 92–117.

Cone Corporate Citizenship Study: 2004, http://www.mybizwarehouse.com/2ndbusiness/2004ConeCorporateCitizenshipStudy.pdf.

Crane, A., and D. Matten: 2004, *Business Ethics: A European Perspective* (Oxford University Press, Oxford).

Davis, K.: 1973 , 'The Case For and Against Business Assumption of Social Responsibilities', *Academy of Management Journal* **16**(3), 312–22.

Davis, K. and R.L. Blomstrom: 1975, *Business and Society: Environment and Responsibility* (McGraw-Hill, New York).

Deshpandé, R. and F.E. Webster: 1989, 'Organizational Culture and Marketing: Defining the Research Agenda', *Journal of Marketing* **53**(1), 3–15.

Drumwright, M.E.: 1994, 'Socially Responsible Organizational Buying: Environmental Concern as a Noneconomic Buying Criterion', *Journal of Marketing* **58**(3), 1–19.

Fombrun, C. and M. Shanley: 1990, 'What's in a Name? Reputation Building and Corporate Strategy', *Academy of Management Journal* **33**(2), 233–258.

Greening, D.W. and B. Gray: 1994, 'Testing a Model of Organizational Response to Social and Political Issues', *Academy of Management Journal* **37**(3), 467–498.

Griffin, J.J. and J.F. Mahon: 1997, 'The Corporate Social Performance and Corporate Financial Performance Debate', *Business and Society* **36**(1), 5–31.

Hair, J.F., R.E. Anderson, R.L. Tatham, and W.C. Black: 1998, *Multivariate Data Analysis*, 5th ed. (Prentice-Hall International, Upper Saddle River, NJ).

Holmes, Lord and R. Watts: 1999, 'Making Good Business Sense', in The World Business Council for Sustainable Development, Conches-Geneva.

Jones, T.M.: 1980, 'Corporate Social Responsibility Revisited, Redefined', *California Management Review*, **22**(3), 59–67.

Kennedy, M.S., L.K. Ferrell, and D.T. LeClair: 2001, 'Consumers' Trust of Salesperson and Manufacturer: An Empirical Study', *Journal of Business Research* **51**(1), 73–86.

Khireche-Oldache, B.: 1998, 'L'entreprise citoyenne, une approche par les normes environnementales', *Cahier de Recherche* 1998–10, Grefige-Université Nancy 2, Nance.

Leonard, M.: 1997, 'Count on Them in. Corporate America Is Eager to Volunteer Help to the Needy. The Reason Is the Bottom-line', *The Boston Globe*, (April 20), F1.

Lichtenstein, D.R., M.E. Drumwright, and B.M. Braig: 2004, 'The Effect of Corporate Social Responsibility on Customer Donations to Corporate-supported Nonprofits', *Journal of Marketing* **68**(4), 16–32.

Lindgreen, A. and V. Swaen: 2004, 'Corporate Citizenship: Let not Relationship Marketing Escape the Management Toolbox', *Corporate Reputation Review* **7**(4), 346–363.

Luo, X. and C.B. Bhattacharya: 2006, 'Corporate Social Responsibility, Customer Satisfaction, and Market Value', *Journal of Marketing* **70**(4), 1–18.

Maignan, I.: 1997 , *Antecedents and Benefits of Corporate Citizenship: A Comparison of U.S. and French Businesses*, unpublished PhD thesis (University of Memphis at Tampa, TN).

Maignan, I. and O.C. Ferrell: 2001, 'Antecedents and Benefits of Corporate Citizenship: An Investigation of French businesses', *Journal of Business Research* **51**(1), 37–51.

Maignan, I., O.C. Ferrell, and T. Hult: 1999, 'Corporate Citizenship: Cultural Antecedents and Business Benefits', *Journal of the Academy of Marketing Science* **27**(4), 455–469.

Maignan, I. and V. Swaen: 2004, 'La Responsabilité Sociale d'une Organisation: Intégration des Perspectives Marketing et Manageriale', *Revue Française du Marketing* **200**(5), 51–66.

Marsden, C. and J. Andriof: 1998, 'Towards an Understanding of Corporate Citizenship and How to Influence It', *Citizenship Studies* **2**(2), 329–352.

Martin, R.L.: 2002, 'The Virtue Matrix: Calculating the Return on Corporate Responsibility', *Harvard Business Review* **80**(3), 68–75.

McIntosh, M., D. Leipziger, K. Jones, and G. Coleman: 1998, *Corporate Citizenship: Successful Strategies for Responsible Companies* (Pitman Publishing, London).

McStravic, S.: 2000, 'Strategic Differentiation becoming "Watchword" for Health Care Organizations', *Health Care Strategic Management* **18**(8), 15–18.

McWilliams, A. and D. Siegel: 2001, 'Corporate Social Responsibility: A Theory of the Firm Perspective', *The Academy of Management Review* **26**(1), 117–127.

McWilliams, A., D.S. Siegel, and P.M. Wright: 2006, 'Corporate Social Responsibility: Strategic Implications', *Journal of Management Studies* **43**(1), 1–18.

McWilliams, A., D.D. Van Fleet, and K. Cory: 2002, 'Raising Rivals' Costs Through Political Strategy: An Extension of the Resource-based Theory', *Journal of Management Studies* **39**(5), 707–723.

Menon, A. and A. Menon: 1997, 'Enviropreneurial Marketing Strategy: The Emergence of Corporate Environmentalism as Marketing Strategy', *Journal of Marketing* **61**(1), 51–67.

Pinkston, T.S. and A.B. Carroll: 1994, 'Corporate Citizenship Perspectives and Foreign Direct Investment in the US, *Journal of Business Ethics* **13**(2), 157–169.

Pinkston, T.S. and A.B. Carroll: 1996, 'A Retrospective Examination of CSR Orientations: Have They Changed?' *Journal of Business Ethics* **15**(2), 199–206.

Sethi, S.P.: 1975, 'Dimensions of Corporate Social Performance: An Analytical Framework', *California Management Review* **17**(3), 58–64.

Snider, J., R.P. Hill, and D. Martin: 2003, 'Corporate Social Responsibility in the 21st Century: A View from the World's Most Successful Firms', *Journal of Business Ethics* **48**(2), 175–187.

Stanwick, S.D. and P.A. Stanwick: 1998, 'Corporate Social Responsiveness: an Empirical Examination Using the Environmental Disclosure Index', *International Journal of Commerce and Management* **8**(3/4), 26–40.

Swaen, V. (2004), *Etude des perceptions et des réactions des consommateurs face aux activités citoyennes des entreprises: Application à deux catégories de produits*, Université catholique de Louvain, Louvain-la-Neuve.

Swaen, V., R. Chumpitaz, E. Bigné, and L. Andreu: 2003, 'Being a Socially Responsible Company: What does it Mean for European Young Consumers? Analysis of the Impact of Perceived Environment, Culture and Values', *Proceedings of the European Marketing Academy Conference*, May 20–22, University of Strathclyde, Glasgow.

Turban, D.B. and D.W. Greening: 1997, 'Corporate Social Performance and Organizational Attractiveness to Prospective Employees', *Academy of Management Journal* **40**(3), 658–672.

Warhurst, A.: 2001, 'Corporate Citizenship and Corporate Social Investment: Drivers of Tri-Sector Partnerships', *Journal of Corporate Citizenship* **1**(Spring), 57–73

Chapter 13
Mexico: An Overview of CSR Programmes

Velázquez Luis, Marín Amina, Zavala Andrea, Bustamante Claudia,
Esquer Javier, and Munguía Nora

Abstract *Corporate Social Responsibility (CSR) is a concept that has been present in the literature for more than a decade. This concept encourages corporations to make substantial commitments to society by taking into account their social, environmental and economic impacts on the environment and society. At a first glance, CSR programmmes would benefit both the corporation and society; however, this could be an oversimplification and inaccurate depiction of Mexican CSR programmes. The findings in this study have revealed some important and at the same time disturbing insights. CSR benefits seem to be blurred by a lack of information and access to information; as a consequence, the field of Corporate Social Responsibility is still not well known in Mexico. This has adversely affected Mexicans' ability to understand and support corporations with social responsibility programmes. Although Mexicans would like to participate in charitable programmes promoted by corporations; some Mexicans hesitate to participate because they are suspicious about the corporations' genuine social concerns.*

13.1 Introduction

This chapter seeks to explore the acceptance of Corporate Social Responsibility (CSR) in Mexico. At a glance, a CSR programme would be good enough for both corporations and society; however, this could be an oversimplified and inaccurate depiction of Mexican CSR programmes.

Looking for better opportunities, many Mexicans have illegally migrated to the United States. By 2004, there were 5.9 millions of illegal immigrants from Mexico living in the USA (Passel 2005). On the other hand, the Fortune Magazine has just published that a Mexican is the richest man in the world (2007).

Although the Mexican government has the obligation to put in place several social projects, it is obvious that being CSR active is a necessity for the country. In the literature, there are several definitions of Corporate Social Responsibility

(United Nation 2000), (World Business Council on Sustainable Development 2000), (European Commission 2001) and (Centro Mexicano para la filantropía 2007); however, most of them agree that the field encompasses common topics, such as: ethics, sustainability, environment, and human rights among others. The European Green Book divides these topics in to two dimensions: internals and externals (European Commission 2001).

According to the CEPAL, the concept of Corporate Social Responsibility has evolved from a philanthropic approach to a new way for doing business taking into account social, environmental and economic aspects (2004).

For the purposes of this study, Corporate Social Responsibility is concerned with what the World Business Council for Sustainable Developments (WBCSD) describes in its definition of the field as "the continuing commitment by business to contribute to economic development while improving the quality of life of the workforce and their families as well as of the community and society at large."

13.2 Overall Strategy

In order to fulfill the study's goal, the authors have integrated multiple method-ologies and data sources. This method is known as multiple triangulation and is very useful when there is little prior knowledge (Pranee 1999). This approach was deemed essential to the success of the study, due to our serious concerns about lack of information about the topic. A thorough review of corporations' websites, a sur-veillance of national television commercials, and a survey were the methods of data collection used in this research.

13.2.1 Corporations' Websites Review

The identification of CSR Programmes operated by Mexican companies and/or transnational companies located in Mexico, commenced by searching on Google with the following key words in Spanish; Social Corporations, Corporate Social Responsibility Programmes, Social Companies, Corporate Social Responsibility in Mexico, and other synonymous terms and combinations thereof.

The CSR Seal award (described in later sections) was the foundation for the analysis of corporations' websites. In 2006, 174 organizations were awarded CSR seals. For determining the sample size, researchers used the (13.1). This is used for estimating proportions; where the population size [N] was 174, the level of confi-dence was 95%, the proportion [p] was 2% and the sampling error [e] was 5%.

$$n = \frac{Np(1-p)}{\frac{(N-1)e^2}{4} + p(1-p)},$$

(13.1)

where

$$n = \frac{174 \times 0.96(0.04)}{\frac{(174-1) \times 0.05^2}{4} + 0.96(0.04)} = 45.6$$

Forty six corporations' websites were scrutinized for further CSR information. The following parameters were used:

1. Does the organization have a CSR link on its website?
2. Does the organization have a CSR manual on its website?
3. Does the organization have a CSR report on its website?
4. Does the organization have a CSR definition on its website?
5. Does the organization have a CSR programme on its website?

13.2.2 National Commercial Television Surveillance

The second data source for identifying CSR programmes was a surveillance of commercials broadcasted on Mexican open television. This task was performed in order to identify specific social corporate efforts. The surveillance was conducted in the city of Hermosillo, Sonora from May 7, 2007 to May 20, 2007 and from 6:00 to 24:00 h on channels, 7, 13, 2, and 5, belonging to the two most important Mexican television stations: TV Azteca and Televisa.

13.2.3 SCR Survey

After the researchers had identified CSR programmes in Mexico, they were interested in knowing Mexican-consumers' perceptions these programmes. For that reason, an interviewee-administered questionnaire was developed for analyzing the consumers' perceptions. The questionnaire was made up of eight questions divided on three categories, see Appendix. The first part aims at collecting information about interviewers' knowledge of CSR in Mexico. The second part asks about interviewees' support of corporations with social responsibility programmes and activities, and in the last part; interviewees were asked about their acceptance of three CSR programmes in Mexico; the round up programme, the Teleton programme and the Movimiento Azteca programme. The round up programme is used by several corporations in Mexico. Basically, corporations engage customers to voluntarily round up their bill to an even peso (a bill of 5.95 becomes 6.00). The extra money goes to charitable initiatives. The Teletón and the Movimiento Azteca programmes are operated by the more powerful TV station in Mexico; they ask customers for donations to enable corporations and the general public fund charitable initiatives.

The questionnaire was administered on two different populations; the first survey subjects were adult consumers buying from eight larger retail stores in the cities of Hermosillo and Sonora. The questionnaire was also administered on professors in the University of Sonora. Simple random sampling was the sampling design. Equation (13.1) was used to determine the sample size of professors and (13.2) was used to determinate the sample size of adult consumers.

$$n = \frac{1403 \times 0.38(0.62)}{\frac{(1403-1)\times 0.05^2}{4} + 0.38(0.62)} = 88.75$$

The population of professors in the University of Sonora [N] is 1,403, the level of confidence was 95%, the proportion [p] was 38% and the sampling error [e] was 5%. The sampling size was 89 professors. The statistical software "mini tab 15" was used to randomly select professors.

In the case of adult consumers, it was assumed that it is a larger and unknown population; therefore, (13.1) becomes (13.2) where the level of confidence was 95%, the proportion [p] was 20%, and the sampling error [e] was 5%. The sample size of adult consumers surveyed was 243. A systematized approach was used to select adult consumers; that is one in five of consumers out all consumers buying in the retail store. This was a sampling with replacement. Statistical analysis for both adult consumers and faculty survey was conducted in SPSS v.15 (SPSS Inc., Chicago, IL).

$$n = \frac{4p(1-p)}{e^2},$$

where

$$n = \frac{4 \times 0.2(0.8)}{0.05^2} = 243$$

13.3 Results

13.3.1 Corporations' Websites Review

The search on the internet was useful to generate several insights into CSR programmes; however, the most important finding was the identification of the Mexican for Philanthropy (Centro Mexicano para la Filantropia, CEMEFI). According to its internet site, this is an organization created to promote philanthropic and social responsibility matters in Mexico and strengthen the organized participation of society (2007).

This organization grants an annual award, called CSR Seal, to companies that implement CSR programmes in Mexico. There are four spheres in which companies can implement initiatives; they are: the quality of life within the company, commitments in the World Pact (human rights, labour conditions, environment, transparency and anti-corruption), care for and preserve of the environment, and links between the company and the community.

Fourty-six corporations that were awarded the CSR Seal in 2006 were selected to be scrutinized. This is 26% of all corporations that were awarded the Seals. Forty-three percent these corporations are owned by Mexicans, 20% by Americans (from

Table 13.1 CSR information access through awarded corporations' websites

Parameter	Total	Percentage
Awarded corporations (CSR Seal 2006)	174	100
Sample size (awarded corporations)	46	26
Mexican awarded corporations	20	43
American awarded corporations	9	20
Corporations from other countries awarded	16	37
Awarded corporations with website	25	54
Awarded corporations defining a SCR concept on their website	13	28
CSR reports or manuals on websites	6	13
Awarded corporations claimed to operate a CSR programme on their website	10	22
Awarded corporations posting a CSR program on their website	9	20

the United States), and 37% of them are from other parts of the world. Twenty-five out of the 46 corporations have a website. Only 13 of the corporations with a website have defined Corporate Social Responsibility on these websites. These researchers were able find electronic CSR reports or some sort of manuals only in six of the websites scrutinized. Ten of the corporations with websites claim to have implemented CSR programmes, but only nine have their programmes posted on it. Table 13.1 summarizes the results found.

13.3.2 National Commercial Television Surveillance

Nine corporations that practice social responsibility were identified through television surveillance. Once identified, the corporations' websites, if there was evidence that they have it, were reviewed following the instructions in the Corporations' websites review section.

As shown in Table 13.2, five corporations are Mexican owned, three are owned by Americans, and one is owned by a corporation from another country. Six of the corporations identified on TV have a website. Two of them have a definition of Corporate Social Responsibility and one corporation has a report on internet. Four corporations claim to have a CSR programme, but only three corporations had posted their programmes on the internet.

13.3.3 CSR Survey

13.3.3.1 Professors at the University of Sonora

Eighty-nine professors at the University of Sonora were surveyed, only 36% out of the total claimed to understand the concept of social corporate responsibility;

Table 13.2 SCR information access through corporations' websites identified on TV

Parameter	Total	Percentage
Corporations with Social Responsibility Identified on TV	9	100
Mexican Awarded Corporations	5	56
American Awarded Corporations	3	33
Other countries awarded corporations	1	11
Awarded corporations with website	6	67
Awarded corporations defining a CSR concept on their website	2	22
CSR Reports or manual on websites	1	11
Awarded corporations which claim to operate a CSR programme on their websites	4	44
Awarded corporations posting a CSR programme on their website	3	33

19% of them cannot identify corporations with social responsibility and 38% of the professors are claiming to know the concept cannot identify any corporate social responsibility programmes. The other 62% of the professors claimed to know that CSR programmes are designed to improve conditions of health, education, and environment. Table 13.3 summarizes this information.

As shown in Table 13.4, 69% of the professors who know the concept prefer to buy products from corporations that are socially responsible, but only 44% would buy their products if they are more expensive than products from corporations, which are not socially responsible.

Table 13.5 shows that only 67% of the professors have participated in round up CSR programmes, 72% on the Teletón programme, and 64% on the Movimiento Azteca programme. Forty percent of these professors have

Table 13.3 Professors' knowledge of SCR

Questions	Attribute	Professors	Percentage
Do you know the CSR concept?	Yes	32	36
	No	57	64
	Total	89	100
Do you know any corporations with social responsibility programmes?	Yes	26	81
	No	6	19
	Total	32	100
Do you know what CSR programmes entail?	Yes	20	62
	No	12	38
	Total	32	100
Can you identify some CSR issues?	Health	6	30
	Education	7	35
	Environment	7	35
	Total	20	100

Table 13.4 Professors' support to corporations with social responsibility?

Questions	Attribute	Professors	Percentage
Do you prefer to buy products of corporations,	Yes	22	69
which are socially responsible?	No	10	31
	Total	32	100
Would you pay more for products of corporations	Yes	14	44
with social responsibility?	No	17	56
	Total	32	100

participated in CSR programmes in order to help people in need – philanthropic CSR.

13.3.4 Adult consumers at Retail Stores

As observed in Table 13.6, 243 adult consumers were interviewed, only 19% out of the total claimed to know the concept of corporate social responsibility, but 28% of them are unaware of corporations with social responsibility activities. Seventy percent out of the adult consumers claimed to know the concept but are unsure of corporate social responsibility programmes.

Table 13.7 shows that only 48% of the adult consumers know the concept and would prefer to buy products from corporations, which are socially responsible and 74% are not willing to buy their products if they are more expensive than products from corporations without social responsibility.

Seventy percent of the consumers surveyed agreed in participating on round up programmes, 85% on the teletón programme, and 71% in the Movimiento Azteca programme. This is summarized in Table 13.8.

Table 13.5 Professors' support to SCR programs?

Questions	Attribute	Professors	Percentage
Have you participated in a round up programme?	Yes	60	67
	No	29	33
	Total	89	100
Have you participated in the Teleton programme?	Yes	64	72
	No	25	28
	Total	89	100
Have you participated in a Movimiento Azteca programme?	Yes	57	64
	No	32	36
	Total	89	100

Table 13.6 Consumers' knowledge of SCR

Questions	Attribute	Consumers	Percentage
Do you know the CSR concept?	Yes	46	19
	No	197	81
	Total	243	100
Do you know corporations with social responsibility?	Yes	33	72
	No	13	28
	Total	46	100
Do you know CSR programmes	Yes	14	30
	No	32	70
	Total	46	100
What kind of CSR programmes do you know?	Health	6	43
	Education	6	43
	Environment	2	14
	Total	14	100

Table 13.7 Consumers' support to corporations with social responsibility

Questions	Attribute	Consumers	Percentage
Do you prefer to buy products from corporations with social responsibility?	Yes	22	48
	No	24	52
	Total	46	100
Would you pay more for products of corporations with social responsibility?	Yes	12	26
	No	34	74
	Total	46	100

Table 13.8 Consumers' support to SCR programs

Questions	Attribute	Consumers	Percentage
Have you participated in a round up program?	Yes	171	70
	No	72	30
	Total	243	100
Have you participated in the Teleton program?	Yes	206	85
	No	37	15
	Total	243	100
Have you participated in a Movimiento Azteca program?	Yes	172	71
	No	71	29
	Total	243	100

13.4 Discussion

This study has revealed some important and at the same time disturbing findings. The most important is that the Corporate Social Responsibility concept is not well known in Mexico. Although CSR is increasingly found in business and engineering literature still, most respondents are unfamiliar with the concept. In fact, even some people in academia are unfamiliar with the concept. This asseveration brings some implications to debate. First of all, this raises the question of why is an overwhelming majority of respondents ignorant of the concept.

This can be explained by the lack of information about it. As revealed by the corporations' websites review, information access about CSR programmes is difficult; this is severely impacting society's ability to understand and support corporations with social responsibility activities because the concept remains blurred. If society cannot understand it, how can they value it?

Transparent public information is not common as it should be expected in corporations with social responsibility; society relies on corporate data to evaluate their social performance. Therefore, there is evidence of hesitation on the part of Mexicans to support corporations about the issue of CSR.

The CSR survey revealed that most of the adult consumers who are familiar with the concept would not pay more to buy a product from corporations with social responsibility if these products are more expensive than similar products from corporations without social responsibility. A high percent of professors share this perspective.

Despite their hesitation, more than half of respondents are happy to participate in charitable programmes through a corporation's CSR programmes. Usually in Mexico, CSR initiatives are aimed at improving the environment, education, or/and health.

On the other hand, the commonest reasons – 65%, for refusal to participate in a CSR programme are suspicion and distrust. These respondents believe that Mexican companies use their privileged position to exploit poor and medium class Mexicans; therefore, their social concerns are not genuine or authentic. There were also a few comments from people, 5%, that link CSR programmes with tax evasion and some fraudulent activities.

Identifying driving forces to implement and maintain CSR programmes might vary from one corporation to another; however, improving their corporate image is often used as a strong driving force.

13.5 Conclusions

Lack of transparency and access to information about Mexican companies' Corporate Social Responsibility Programmes are findings of this research that challenge some of the theoretical concepts that have been discussed during the last few decades in the literature.

Theoretically, implementing Corporate Social Responsibility initiatives should result in increased productivity and a better image; however, this could not be possible in Mexico because Mexicans are unfamiliar with the concept of Corporate Social Responsibility. Therefore, they cannot appreciate the enormous benefits that could emanate from its practice.

Mexicans are happy to participate in corporate charitable programmes promoted basically for altruistic reasons; however, some Mexicans hesitate to participate because they are suspicious about corporations' genuine social concerns.

Very often some corporations, mainly transnational, have been under fire over allegations of environmental pollutions and poor labour conditions. Helping their society is a useful tool for improving their image; however, corporations need to be aware that society requires to be certain of their intentions. Lack of transparency and difficult access to information are causing a major hindrance to the authenticity of Corporate Social Responsibility Programmes and are adversely affecting the image of corporations that are implementing CSR policies in Mexico.

Appendix

Corporate Social Responsibility Survey

This survey has been designed to reveal the knowledge and support of the respondents to Corporate Social Responsibility Programmes. Thank you for your anonymous participation.

1. **Do you know the CSR concept?**
   ☐ Yes ☐ No
2. **Do you know Corporations, which practice Social Responsibility?**
   ☐ Yes ☐ No
   If yes, list them _____
3. **Do you know CSR some programmes?**
   ☐ Yes ☐ No
   If yes, list them _____
4. **What activities fall under CSR programmes as far as you are aware?**
   ☐ Health ☐ Poverty ☐ Environment ☐ Other
5. **Do you prefer to buy products from corporations with Social Responsibility?**
   ☐ Yes ☐ No
   Why? _____
6. **Would you pay more for products of corporations with Social Responsibility?**
   ☐ Yes ☐ No
   Why? _____
7. **Have you ever participated in a round up programme before?**
   ☐Yes ☐ No
   Why? _____

8. **Have you participated in the Teleton programme?**
   ☐ **Yes** ☐ **No**
   Why? _____
9. **Have you participated in a Movimiento Azteca programme?**
   ☐ **Yes** ☐ **No**
   Why? _____

References

Centro Mexicano para la filantropía (Cemefi), 2007. El Cemefi y AliaRSE entregaron el Distintivo ESR 2007 a 174 empresas [online] available from: http://www.cemefi.org/spanish/index.php?option = com_content&task = view&id = 1175&Itemid = 64 [cited 13 august 2007]

CEPAL, 2004. Responsabilidad social corporativa en América Latina: una visión empresarial. (Serie: Medo ambiente y desarrollo No. 85)

European Commission, 2001. Promoting a European framework for corporate social responsibility Green Paper [Internet] available from: http://www.jussemper.org/Resources/Corporate%20Activity/Resources/greenpaper_en.pdf [cited 13 august 2007]

Fortune, 2007 CNNMoney.com [online] 13 august available at: http://money.cnn.com/2007/08/03/news/international/carlosslim.fortune/[accessed on 13 august 2007]

Passel, Jeffrey, S., 2005 "Estimates of the Size and Characteristics of the Undocumented Population". Pew Hispanic Center, 2005

Pranee Liamputtong, R. and Douglas, E., 1999. *Qualitative Research Methods: a health focus*, Oxford, NY: Oxford University Press.

United Nation, 2000. Global compact [Internet] available from: http://www.unglobalcompact.org/AboutTheGC/index.html [cited 13 august 2007]

World Business Council on Sustainable Development (WBCSD), 2000. Corporate Social Responsibility [Internet] available from: http://www.wbcsd.org/DocRoot/hbdf19Txhmk3kDxBQDWW/CSRmeeting.pdf [cited 13 august 2007]

Chapter 14
Costa Rica

Elizabeth Hogan

Abstract The article begins by exploring the different approaches to CSR between domestic businesses and subsidiaries of large multinational corporations within Costa Rica. The attempt to initiate CSR in Costa Rican businesses is viewed in the context of the pending Central America Free Trade Agreement (CAFTA) legislation and the effect it is anticipated to have on smaller businesses. After examining efforts made by the domestic business community, the article examines current practices of Corporate Social Responsibility (CSR) by two multinational companies (MNCs) in the technology sector operating in Costa Rica and examines both aspects of what they are currently doing in the interests of CSR and whether those actions are appropriate for both their goals as a private enterprise and for the well-being of the country for which they are intended. Looking specifically at Microsoft, Oracle, and Intel, the study then goes on to examine the incentives behind CSR and whether those goals are best met by the current practices. It also discusses the scalability of CSR via the origins of the programs currently being conducted by MNCs operating in Costa Rica, and how those practices can be emulated by corporate entities of varying sizes and resources. Lastly, it looks at the need for both operational integration and specificity in CSR in order for the practice to function as intended; the integration of socially and environmentally sound business and production practices, and specificity of local solutions to address particular areas of concern based on the actual needs of a given location rather than a one-size-fits-all blanket approach mandated from a head office in another country. Ultimately, CSR is growing as a practice and becoming increasingly effective, but is still in the early stages both as a concept and a methodology, and needs to develop in scalability and diversification to reach its full potential.

14.1 Introduction

> "CSR centers on the idea that a corporation may be held socially and ethically account-
> able by an expansive array of stakeholders such as customers, employees, governments,
> communities, NGOs, investors, supply chain members, unions, regulators, and media.... to
> define a model that extended corporate performance beyond traditional economic and legal
> considerations to include ethical and discretionary responsibilities."
>
> ~ Michael Maloni and Michael Brown

The phrase "Corporate Social Responsibility" has in recent years become one of
the most popular corporate catchphrases used throughout the global marketplace to
distinguish the virtues of one company from another. While many definitions could
be provided, the generally accepted concept of CSR is that which is provided by
the World Business Council for Sustainable Development: "The ethical behavior of
a company towards society – acting responsibly in its relationships with all stakeholders who have a legitimate interest in the business, not just the shareholders"
(World Business Council for Sustainable Development, 1998). The popularity of
the practice has grown in sync with public awareness of and standards for corporate
operational conduct and practices. Where the end product or service and the price at
which it is sold were previously the only standards for which the buying public held
a company accountable, greater media exposure of large business practices, particularly those of multinational corporations (MNCs), has led to rising expectations of
these wealthy and resourceful entities.

In lieu of philanthropy, CSR applies to the actual practices of a company's day to
day business operations, rather than a separate endeavor attributable solely to charitable donations. The idea that a company is in fact a member of the surrounding
community whose obligations extend beyond their own four walls is not new in itself, but the rising expectations of the public, the media, and the NGO community
in recent years have created a new impetus among the business community to raise
their standards of citizenship. While the expectations of governments do not appear
to have risen in tandem with other stakeholders in the form of legislative obligation,
a "soft" network of standards and accountability is beginning to take shape in the
form of corporate and industry codes, stakeholder initiatives, and private standard-
setting bodies such as the Global Reporting Initiative, the Equator Principles, or
ISO 26000 (Vogel, 2005). Partnerships between non-profit organizations and corporations such as the United States Climate Action Partnership embody this new
regime in that their very existence shifts the strategy of corporate responsibility
from defensive to offensive in nature. Rather than react to public criticism from the
NGO community, or pre-empt negative publicity by instituting the simplest policy
changes in order to appease the "name and shame" advocates, companies are now
adopting more progressive strategies in turning directly to NGOs for guidance and
expertise, as well as joining forces with these former opponents to lobby for stricter
legal standards in order to level the commercial playing field. Likewise, the rapid
growth of socially responsible investment firms, such as KLD or Innovest, is bridg-
ing the gap between corporations, the media, and a more socially conscious public.
Heightened public awareness of corporate behavior and the resulting demands for

greater degrees of transparency have affected not only investment behavior, but the very means by which the prospects of a corporation are evaluated.

The relative novelty of CSR as a practice leaves open many possible paths for growth. In which directions will the practice evolve? Perhaps more importantly, in which of these directions will the newfound efforts of CSR be able to do the greatest amount of good, both for the companies which initiate them and the communities in which they operate? In order to address these questions, it is also necessary to examine the driving forces behind CSR: what incentives exist to change the status quo? Costa Rica presents an excellent lens through which to view these questions as their economy is currently split between hundreds of subsidiaries of multinational corporations (MNCs) setting up shop and a growing domestic economy with a highly educated workforce and greater purchasing power than any of their neighbors. Is Costa Rica then any more or less susceptible to those incentives than other countries? And ultimately, will the CSR practices initiated by the subsidiaries of multinational corporations reflect the values of the host country, in this case Costa Rica, or the home country of the company in question? How then do MNCs influence business practices such as CSR on the regional and domestic levels?

14.2 Methodology

The methodology utilized for this chapter is comprised of three separate components, divided into a study of MNC behavior, a separate study focused on domestic Costa Rican businesses, and a literature review of the subject for contextual purposes. Initially, I utilized firsthand case studies and interviews in order to address the MNC sector. The objective was to observe individually held approaches, methodologies, and standards within the private sector by investigating the already established corporate social responsibility programs of three powerful multinational companies. In addition to a three-week case study conducted with the Community Relations group at Microsoft Costa Rica, I also participated in a conference on "Institutional Innovation and Corporate Social Responsibility" sponsored by Intel Corporation and INCAE Business School of Costa Rica, addressing the incorporation of CSR into all elements of Costa Rican business operations, based on the practices of Intel. I also procured interviews with David Stangis, Global Director of Corporate Responsibility of Intel, and Richard D'Amato, former Executive Director of Corporate Philanthropy at America Online. Comparing their responses to those of the Microsoft staff was particularly useful in that I was able to evaluate the approaches of three multinational corporations (MNCs) within the same industry. Similar answers to identical questions have provided visible patterns within the relationship between corporate responsibility and the profitability of the company itself; the end result of this interconnectivity being the incentive to operate in a socially sustainable manner.

Also included in the interview process were two independent analysts of CSR, Paul Hilton, Director of Institutional and SRI [Socially Responsible Investing]

Marketing with The Calvert Group and Deborah Wissel, Manager of Business Development with Innovest. Both firms evaluate future business performance of publicly traded companies based not only on their financial data but on their inclusion of social and environmental factors in their business operations and conduct and base all financial assessments on these factors in recommending – or not – the stock of any given corporation.

Secondly, in order to contrast the CSR initiatives of such vast and well-resourced multinational corporations with domestic Costa Rican businesses, I conducted a three month study with the Cámara de Industrias de Costa Rica, the Costa Rican Chamber of Industries (CICR). The purpose of the CICR, which is a private organization representing the entrepreneurial and industrial sectors of the country, is to enhance the competitiveness of Costa Rican businesses via the establishment of standards of behavior across six different categories; two of the six being social and environmental. The terms of measurement are established through a CICR-developed set of standards collectively known as the Program for Excellence (PPE). From working with the CICR for three months, I was able to observe the efforts being made by domestic Costa Rican businesses in the interests of CSR, as well as the methods being used to guide them in these efforts to establish and maintain both socially sustainable practices and economic competitiveness.

Thirdly, I conducted a literature review of the subject, inclusive of several academic journal articles and books from both developed and developing country perspectives. This review focused on standards held throughout the private sector, both self-imposed and maintained via an internal checks-and-balances system existing within various industries, according to the client demands and operational necessities of their specific marketplace. The theories put forth in this collection of literature were evaluated in the context of current events in the field of CSR as reported by mainstream media.

To balance the literature review, I also utilized multiple documented case studies. These case studies examined new business practices adopted by different companies in order to compare differing, current efforts to address this relatively new component of business strategy. As will be demonstrated, the cases focused on context-appropriate measures for the companies in question and primarily attempted to distinguish between legitimate efforts at improving citizenship as opposed to minimal efforts for the sake of marketing or public relations purposes. In these instances, a greater contrast between Costa Rican domestic businesses and MNCs is clearly visible given that publicity of corporate behavior is not as rampant or as consequential for smaller and lesser-known companies.

14.3 Different Incentives Driving CSR in the Global Marketplace

At present, the growth of the practice of CSR is still dependent upon the realization that effective CSR will mutually benefit both society *and* the company. The most difficult element to ascertain is one of the most basic to the field: how can the impact of corporate responsibility be quantified? In order to be able to promote corporate responsibility, it must first be demonstrated that it does have a positive impact on the profitability of the company. However, the return on the investment (ROI) depends entirely on the type of CSR that they choose to invest in.

14.3.1 Operational Efficiency

In some cases, CSR is purely a matter of business sense: efficiency equals profit. More companies are discovering that in exercising socially and environmentally-friendly practices within their standard operating processes, they are able to improve their efficiency in a number of areas: enhanced safety measures reduce compensation and insurance payments and paperwork, minimization of waste produced eases local community relations as well as disposal fees and effort, or streamlining the input required per unit of product eases procurement budgets and resource exploitation. Such improvements translate to money saved for the company. Thus the decision to participate in CSR in such cases serves as both financial and marketing strategy; profit and sustainability complement rather than contradict one another. CSR then becomes an active component of the business rather than an addition to it.

14.3.2 Strategic Positioning

Other companies have chosen to incorporate CSR directly as a component of their product line. Rather than change their means of production, they are actually changing *what* they produce in order to meet a potential new demand in their market sector. One prominent example is General Electric, which has approached CSR as a means of establishing their brand as the leading producer in a new and growing market for environmentally sustainable products, such as energy efficient light bulbs and recyclable photovoltaic roofing tiles. They are also basing their product lines on anticipated future strictures, via either government regulation or shortages. Thus in establishing GE as a leading producer of alternative fuel sources and household products which meet higher emissions standards, the company stands to gain financially.

In other situations, what is termed "CSR" is merely meeting the demands of the marketplace. The decision of GE to dedicate $1.5 billion annually to clean technology research and to reduce their emissions of greenhouse gases by 1% by 2012 – an effort which simultaneously prevents what would have been an estimated GHG increase of 40% in that same time period – is used liberally in their brand marketing (Ignatius, 2005). But GE also does business in the European Union, whose members all ratified the Kyoto Protocol. Emissions standards for GE plants operating in the EU are thus stricter than in other countries, including the United States. In applying the European standards to all of their plants, GE can standardize their operations across the globe, simplifying their own operational needs, and put forth a brand image of being environmentally conscious in the United States because their emissions standards are stricter than those of most U.S. companies.

14.3.3 Consumer Perception

MNCs are also driven toward socially responsible behavior by the opportunity to gain both publicity and market positioning within their own industry. When products such as light bulbs and gasoline are virtually identical, being able to distinguish your brand from another is a vital advantage. With the rise in visibility of CSR, companies within the same industry sectors are in a position of pushing each other to raise their operating standards as a means of standing out and achieving customer loyalty in sectors where products have small degrees of distinction; "raising the bar for and with each other", according to David Stangis, Global Director of Corporate Responsibility for Intel (Stangis, 2006). If, for example, a consumer can buy the same fuel for their car from either Shell or BP, or ibuprofen from Merck or Pfizer or GlaxoSmithKline, the label of being socially and environmentally responsible serves as a means of branding where there is no other means of distinguishing one version of a product from another. Such a tactic is seen as "offensive" positioning within the marketplace (Vogel, 2005).

Another purpose to this offensive stance on CSR is employee satisfaction. Employee loyalty is a significant factor in cost savings for MNCs because higher retention rates mean less money spent on recruiting, Human Resources staffing, employee training, and administrative resources. Additionally, many MNCs have reported that their participation in CSR has a significant impact on their ability to hire and retain top talent, and offer less compensation. According to a 2004 survey of over 800 MBA students in North America and Europe, 97% would be willing to sacrifice an average of 14% of their anticipated earnings in order to "work with an organization with a better reputation for corporate social responsibility and ethics" (Vogel, 2005). After Merck established a reputation as a solid corporate citizen for their development of a drug which cured river blindness and their distribution of the drug free of charge, CEO Roy Vagalos declared that"We could hire almost anybody we wanted to for 10 years" (Vogel, 2005). Conversely, Nike reported great difficulty in attracting employees after reports of child labor and sweatshop conditions were broadly publicized in 2004. Despite the fact that the negative publicity had almost no effect on Nike sales or their share price, the internal pressure from employees had an effect on company policy as many executives reported that their subordinates were ashamed to tell acquaintances where they worked (Vogel, 2005).

Cases like that of Nike have led to "defensive" branding, which is primarily driven by fear of the activist community and the "naming and shaming" tactics they typically employ, i.e. aggressive negative publicity and organized consumer boycotts. In contrast with offensive branding, which attempts to establish their brand name as responsible and then target a welfare-conscious consumer base, risk-averse firms act responsibly merely to avoid being distinguished within their industry as *not* responsible in order to avoid negative publicity. In other words, their social initiative is reactive as opposed to being proactive. Rather than creating any new paradigm or benchmark for CSR within the scope of their industry, they will meet the most fundamental of standards already in place in order to sidestep a competitive disadvantage (Vogel, 2005).

14.3.4 Investor Awareness

A significant component of the business strategy for any publicly traded multinational corporation is not only the ability to sell their product, but also the ability to sell their stock. "Green" or socially responsible investing (SRI) focuses on portfolios consisting only of companies which have been evaluated as having sustainable practices. SRI has yet to gain enough momentum in the investment market to force an overhaul in corporate behavior by itself, making up less than 10% of mutual funds (Logan, 1998). However, a new industry has grown in response to rising investor demand for corporate accountability and interest in sustainable investing. Leading Wall Street brokerage firms such as Goldman Sachs, Deutsche Bank Securities, UBS, Citigroup, Morgan Stanley, and others now have entire divisions dedicated solely to the evaluation of company performance in areas such as climate change, social contribution, reporting transparency, and corporate governance (Engardio, 2007). In addition to the growth of these new teams in "old guard" financial firms, new firms have begun to emerge which base their investor assessments entirely on a new method of corporate evaluation, focused not merely on financial performance but on the overall health of a company predicting long-term growth and future success based on what is becoming known as the "triple bottom line", that is, the assessment of economic, social, and environmental impacts all considered in equal measure. Firms such as KLD, Innovest, and ISS base their clients' financial futures on sustainable business practices. Innovest includes 120 different factors including energy use, health and safety records, litigation history, and employee practices to rate company stock selections. According to Paul Hilton of the Calvert Group, a judge for the '100 Most Responsible Companies' list published by *Business Ethics* magazine, the ability of a company to meet financial, social, and environmental standards simultaneously serves as an indicator of innovation and farsightedness, both key factors in the long-term success of any multinational business, and thus a sounder investment (Hilton, 2006). The ability of a company to accurately understand, anticipate, and respond to consumer trends and demands within their industry constitutes a powerful competitive edge and demonstrates their capacity for long-term growth. Thus for a Wall Street analyst to evaluate a company based on more well-rounded criteria is actually a safer bet for their clients in an era where innovation and adaptability are prized by the marketplace.

14.3.5 Social Returns

The lack of direct correlation between reputation and net profit is not deterring the rapid expansion of CSR as a practice across multiple industries. There are multiple reasons for this trend, both offensive and defensive in nature. Some companies may have CEOs who truly have altruistic motives at the heart of their decision making. Younger CEOs in particular have attended business school in an era where transparency, ethics, and corporate philanthropy are emphasized not only as sound business practice in an era of Enron and media spotlights on corporate behavior, but also as a holistic economic philosophy. According to Lenny Mendonca, chairman of the economic research firm McKinsey Global Institute, "sustainability is [now] right at the top of the agendas" of more CEOs, particularly the younger and more recently appointed (Engardio, 2007).

Whether or not CSR is employed by any given company and the manner in which it is incorporated into standard operations is ultimately a decision made by individuals within upper management. And the decisions that are made by individual managers are as different as the people within these positions, all of whom have differing ideas and experiences regarding CSR and how it is likely to affect their company. The majority of top management personnel currently charged with the operations of these companies attended business school and gained their formative experience in an era prior to the incorporation of social values into business practices; therefore they are operating in largely uncharted territory (Margolis and Joshua, 2003). Thus many of the choices being made in this field at present are being made in a trial-and-error context as each MNC determines which path of CSR best meets both their needs and the needs of their stakeholders. While each company is unique, with individual philosophies, resources, cultures, and circumstances, an overwhelming number of MNCs share an interest in improving their contributions to and interactions with their stakeholders. As these entities realize the potential of their role as corporate citizens with global reach, their response to a growing shift in perspective on corporate social responsibility has the capacity to improve the wellbeing of their fellow citizens around the world.

For their article "Perceptions of Socially Responsible Activities and Attitudes: A Comparison of Business School Deans and Corporate Chief Executives", Robert Ford and Frank McLaughlin conducted a survey sent to 700 chief executive officers in the United States as far back as 1984 – long before "CSR" became a corporate catchphrase. Over 77% of the CEOs agreed with the statement: "A business that wishes to capture a favorable public image will have to demonstrate that it is socially responsible". In that same survey, 55% of the CEOs also stated that CSR needed to be factored into their business strategy in order to avoid facing larger social problems in the future which would prevent their company from achieving its primary business goals. In other words, CSR is a component to fundamental long-term business strategy. While this data demonstrates that CSR is gradually becoming a part of business rather than an accessory to business, it also demonstrates a fairly split field. Not all managers view CSR the same way, thus their decisions and actions will be equally diverse. In another study, profiled in the article "Misery Loves

Companies: Rethinking Social Initiatives by Business", Joshua D. Margolis and James P. Walsh compiled CSR data over a 30 year span consisting of 127 different studies of the correlation between financial performance and corporate social conduct. Their data demonstrated that in 54 of the assembled reports, a positive correlation existed between CSR and financial success. Yet a far greater ratio of companies is currently practicing some element of CSR in their business practice today. Such a discrepancy could be interpreted as a willingness to contribute to the greater good of society regardless of the effect that such action has on the bottom line.

14.3.6 Relevance to Costa Rica

This is the current face of the marketplace that Costa Rica is anxious to join. As the wealthiest country in the Central American region, Costa Rica's economy is dependent on external trading partners and the ability to attract foreign direct investment. As of 2006, the GDP purchasing power parity of Costa Rica was over (US) $50 billion, while those of its two closest neighbors, Nicaragua and Panama, were (US) $17.33 billion and (US) $26 billion respectively. Rising import prices combined with the inability of their immediate neighbors to provide their economy with a profitable foreign trade drives the Costa Rican economy to enhance the ability of their businesses to compete globally. In order to accomplish this, Costa Rican businesses must adhere to the changing global market standards. These standards now include the adoption of socially responsible corporate practices.

14.4 Organizations Promoting CSR in Costa Rica

A few organizations have risen to the relatively newfound mandate of promoting CSR in Costa Rica. The following three organizations have played the most significant role in advancing responsible business practices in multinational and domestic businesses alike:

- The Chamber of Industries of Costa Rica (CICR)
- The Costa Rican Investment Promotion Agency (CINDE)
- The Ministry of Environment and Energy (MINAE)

The Chamber of Industries of Costa Rica (CICR) is charged with the task of maintaining the highest possible level of "competencia" among Costa Rican firms across all industry sectors. CICR is a private organization representing the entrepreneurial and industrial sectors of the country, and their purpose is to enhance the competitiveness of Costa Rican businesses via the establishment of standards of behavior across multiple categories. In addition to producing publications and holding conferences to address the evolving standards of the global marketplace, CICR runs a program known as the Programa para la Excelencia (PPE) which specifically addresses the areas in which each participating company must improve in order to maintain competitiveness; including corporate social responsibility.

The goal of the Costa Rican Investment Promotion Agency (CINDE) is to promote foreign direct investment in Costa Rica and in doing so "advance the country's social and economic development" (www.cinde.org). CINDE is a non-profit organization which, though technically considered independent from the government, was confirmed in 1984 to be "of public interest". Their statement of vision describes an ambition to achieve not only growth, but specifically "*sustainable* growth in areas that have proven to be competitive in Costa Rica". In attempting to achieve sustainable growth for the Costa Rican economy, CINDE repeatedly emphasizes the need for quality in all of their endeavors. Given the need for effective supply chain management and subsidiary oversight in developing countries in order to meet the expectations of ever more socially conscious investors and consumers, MNCs are now more than ever drawn by a location which will provide socially acceptable labor and environmental practices (Williams 2002, and Singh et al., 2005).

Active participation in influencing more socially responsible business practices in a host country indicates that an MNC is taking an additional step to fully utilize their purchasing power in order to influence the operational practices of their suppliers, and thereby spreading socially conscious production. According to Michael Maloni and Michael Brown, whose comprehensive study of CSR in the form of Supply Chain Logistics included industry-specific implications, "a corporation's supply chain may be generally defined as the series of companies, including suppliers, customers, and logistics providers that work together to deliver a value package of goods and services to the end customer." Therefore, CINDE is approaching their mission to position Costa Rica as an attractive investment and subsidiary location by shaping the Costa Rican business community into a community that will be able to meet these requirements.

The Ministry of Environment and Energy (MINAE) is the department of the Costa Rican government which is designated with the responsibility of "guaranteeing the constitutional right of all Costa Ricans to a healthy environment........ and to conserve important natural resources" (www.minae.go.cr). The second of the four objectives listed on their website is "to identify, promote, facilitate and elaborate strategies for technical cooperation.......... in support of national environmental priorities." Among the values listed in their Department of Investment and Physical Infrastructure are efficiency, transparency, and "ecotouristic vision". The symbol of MINAE, a handprint in which the palm of the hand is represented by a leaf, is well known throughout Costa Rica as it often appears as a symbol of government approval granted upon an environmentally sound business. The very fact that all planning for Costa Rican infrastructure takes place within the purview of the Ministry of Environment and Energy serves as an indicator that concepts of sustainability and responsibility have become strategic components of development and economic growth. Tourism has steadily remained the primary source of foreign exchange in Costa Rica, as well as the largest economic sector and employer in the country. Therefore, protection of the very assets which draw this form of income – biodiversity and a pristine environment – is of paramount importance and thus carries a significantly high level of government support in the form of MINAE.

14.5 Domestic Businesses in Costa Rica

While heightened expectations of responsible behavior for companies in the "developed" world are keeping competitors within each industry sector in check, pushing each other for ever more prominent displays of responsible behavior, smaller businesses in the "developing" world have yet to face those same pressures, but are beginning to recognize that CSR is a component of the global marketplace which they must embrace in order to join. To that end, the Cámara de Industrias de Costa Rica (CICR) has become the de facto scorekeeper of socially responsible business initiatives within Costa Rica. The role of this organization has become even more poignant since the introduction of the Central American Free Trade Agreement (CAFTA) into the local economy (Fig. 14.1).

Given the generation of net exports under a free trade regime, and the extent to which it caters to the needs of those multinational corporations providing foreign direct investment for Costa Rica, CAFTA is receiving tremendous support from the government and the majority of the business sector alike. Both CICR and CINDE fully endorse the ratification of CAFTA and support the free trade agreement among their member companies.

At present, the overwhelming political support for CAFTA in the interest of raising the standards of Costa Rican products in order to compete in the global marketplace has brought the role of corporate responsibility to the forefront of the larger-scale business practices in this country. However, small-business owners are conversely left with the concern of competing with lower priced mass-produced goods from the United States as a result of a ratified Free Trade Agreement. For

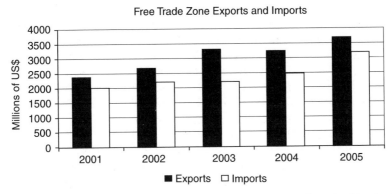

Fig. 14.1 Impact of the free trade zone regime within Costa Rica (as determined by the Costa Rican Investment Promotion Agency)

small and medium sized businesses (PYMES) in particular, the prospect of being undercut by cheaper imports in their local marketplace makes the promise of efficiency – as well as the opportunity to declare themselves to be environmentally compliant – greatly attractive; thereby raising their willingness to comply with environmental and social guidance from the Cámara. Environmental responsibility is deemed of particular importance in Costa Rica, where the explosion of ecotourism is responsible for the relatively high local standard of living throughout the country and the single largest contributor to the GDP, as well as a significant source of foreign currency.

At present, the CICR is relying in part on self-evaluation in the form of surveys to their members in order to assess areas of environmental and social improvement. However, the Centro Nacional para la Producción más Limpia, (National Center for Clean Production, or CNP+L) regularly provides environmental consultants to evaluate current conditions and make recommendations. Additionally, the surveys which are utilized in this assessment provide valuable baseline data from which to measure progress and define goals. Unfortunately, the lack of updated infrastructure in Costa Rica represents an obstacle to environmental practices, particularly in the management of waste water and trash disposal. Furthermore, the practice of utilities supply management as a form of CSR is severely limited in that utilities are monopolized by the state, thus companies are unable to ensure that their providers of water, electric power, or telephone service are operating in sustainable manners because they have no alternative sources for any of these basic necessities. The very existence of competition in the market ultimately compels efficiency, but in the case of a monopoly there is no such pressure and the potential influence of a large client is lost.

The driving incentives for the local and national businesses to participate in cleaner technologies, socially progressive hiring practices, fair trade, and other fundamental components of CSR are fairly straightforward – these are the areas which have been identified as essential for their business to compete on the global market. The eagerness of Costa Rica to comply with rising operating standards is greatly driven by the fact that Costa Rica is significantly wealthier than its immediate neighbors. Higher wage rates in Costa Rica mean that their closest neighbors cannot afford their products. Hence incentives to participate in CSR in the smaller domestic components of the economy are based on a very simple economic game plan: meet the growing global standards of CSR in order to be able to export and trade with the top industrialized countries. This strategy not only augments the Costa Rican economy directly via trade, but also establishes a pro-business infrastructure which will attract ever more foreign direct investment (FDI) in the form of subsidiaries from multinational corporations.

The CICR is attempting to assist Costa Rican businesses compete in the global market by raising their standards across a myriad of categories, including Leadership & Strategic Planning, Client Satisfaction, Human Resources, Processes, Innovation & Technology, and the Environment. One of the primary steps toward this goal is a program known as the *Programa para la Excelencia* (PPE), offered across all industries and in each of the six categories mentioned above (Fig. 14.2).

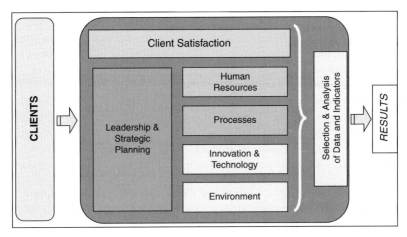

Fig. 14.2 Process of the *Programa para la Excelencia* of the Chamber of Industries of Costa Rica*

Companies become eligible for the *Premio* (Award) *a la Excelencia* by attaining a particular score in each area of the program; the score being based on their performance against a written set of questions in each category. All participating companies are assessed against only these prescribed questions by various consultants at the Camara. However, one category which is far behind the others is that of the environment. Not a single Costa Rican company has won the Premio a la Excelencia in this category for the past 3 years, and only three have ever won it in the history of the program. However, in establishing environmental business standards and incorporating them into the program, the hope is that leading businesses in Costa Rica will adapt their corporate behavior to a more environmentally sustainable model, and that as leaders in their industry they will be able to influence others to emulate their example.

As a relatively new practice, the current efforts of CSR prevailing amongst domestic companies in Costa Rica are primarily directed at identification of current detrimental environmental practices and more efficient processes. Establishing baseline data for comparative purposes, projected growth rates, and setting benchmark goals and plans for reaching them are the current requirements. Analysis and processes are the current indicators of social responsibility rather than progress against statistics. Results can be seen in the response rate to surveys for environmental data. According to Luisa Díaz Sánchez, Chief Assessor of Competitiveness and the Environment at CICR, the typical response rate in accumulating environmental data across member businesses nationwide is over 30% of the more than seven hundred companies to which they are distributed (Díaz Sánchez, 2006). The aim of the survey is to determine current environmental and social practices by local businesses in order to locate patterns of environmental damage that can be targeted for correction within a given industry, as well as to gain an idea as to their current levels of sustainability regarding their practices of waste disposal, recycling, water use and treatment, emissions, and pollution of water, soil, and air. Additionally, comparative data for these same indicators within the surrounding community as well as averages across the industry in question is required. The surveys provide crucial updated data; thus establishing actionable environmental indicators from which to base future benchmarks.

With data and national averages established, the PPE is now able to focus on processes to improve upon, for each participating business. As they are currently written, the standards for the Environmental category are extremely vague and do not specifically address particular environmental concerns; rather the category is focused on establishing a means to identify, track, and improve upon the relevant indicators for each industry. Qualifying standards within this category include the

- Has the organization identified clear and measurable environmental goals?
- Are proactive systems in place to anticipate any possible negative environmental impact derived from their processes, products, or services?
- Does the organization analyze and effectively utilize environmental data in their daily planning and performance?
- Does the company regularly evaluate their data collecting processes in order to maintain consistency?
- Is their environmental impact data shared with relevant organizations?

One of the fundamental strengths of the *Programa para la Excelencia* program at CICR has been their ability to convert social and environmental responsibility from a luxury or an inconvenience into a positive goal sought by many leading Costa Rican businesses. The prestige and positive public relations affiliated with the program (and the awards) have enticed business leaders to participate, which in turn allows them to see that initial investment in sustainability is not only good for their image but that it can actually help their business both by improving efficiency, stimulating innovation, and saving money. Conversely, a weakness of the program is that there is no means of enforcement, and political maneuvering can often prevent progress. While many attempts have been made to encourage MINAE and the Ministry of Economy, Industry, and Commerce to convert many of the processes and practices outlined in the PPE program into law, the government is reluctant to impose changes which could be deemed unfavorable by wealthy business leaders.

The primary drawback to the Programa para la Excelencia as run by CICR is the current inability to divide the participating businesses into industry sectors and to evaluate their progress in the program against their peers by standards pertaining specifically to the operational reality of a given industry. Thus the Award for Business Excellence, given out to those businesses which successfully complete the PPE at a certain success standard, is skewed toward less damaging industries. However, the organization is attempting to change this crucial disadvantage via their survey data and the environmental analyses conducted by the CNP+L. Once baselines per sector are established in the environmental categories (and broken down further by the already existing category of business size), standards will be in place to compel more sustainable business practices, and through the ever increasing pressures of publicity and competition, those standards will consistently increase. Ultimately,

Table 14.1 Success of Costa Rican versus foreign-owned companies

Winners of the CICR award for business excellence 2005–2006	
Domestic Costa Rican Businesses	*Foreign-Owned Subsidiaries*
Grupo Café Britt	Western Union
BAC San José	Coca Cola
Etiquetas Impresas Etipres S.A.	Alamo
Proquinal Costa Rica	Eaton Electrical, S.A.
Servicios Públicos de Heredia	Novartis Consumer Health
Fomento Urbano, S.A.	Roma Prince, S.A.
Demasa	Metalco, S.A.
Rex Internacional	Alienware (Dell, Inc.)
BN Valores	Sykes

the desire and the intent amongst domestic Costa Rican companies to join in the race for sustainability are there, yet the actual practice of these behaviors is still to come.

Hence an important item to note is that the majority of these companies were actually subsidiary branches of foreign-owned MNCs, such as Roma Prince and Western Union, the two most successful ones. And in the environmental category for 2005, not a single company reached the 80% qualification benchmark for the environmental Excellence Award in the small or medium sized categories. According to Martha Castillo, Executive Director of CICR, approximately 5–10% of their member companies, eligible to participate in the PPE are foreign-owned subsidiaries; yet they constitute 50% of the winners of this endeavor to improve business operations and standards within Costa Rica (Castillo, 2006) (Table 14.1).

While an initial interpretation of this data could indicate that CSR remains a "luxury" afforded by businesses originating in the Global North, the alternative perspective is that the growing presence of multinational businesses in Costa Rica and the corresponding rising standards of socially responsible business conduct are gradually proliferating throughout their Costa Rican suppliers, counterparts, and rivals to fulfill the objectives of both the CICR and CINDE: the increased competitiveness of Costa Rican products in the global marketplace and the enhanced attractiveness of Costa Rica to foreign investors.

14.6 Multinational Corporations Operating in Costa Rica

By virtue of readily available funds, in addition to their relative independence from government bureaucracy, a MNC has greater purchasing power than almost any other global entity. Furthermore, their vast human and technological resources in addition to financial capital, and considerable freedom in how they are utilized, create an unrivaled capacity for these entities to contribute significantly to the societies where they are located. Therefore, the ability to compel an MNC to conduct their business in a more sustainable manner has the potential for far-reaching beneficial consequences.

In looking at MNCs, Costa Rica has upheld higher standards in what they require of those MNCs wishing to set up shop within their borders. Potential damage to their landscape, pollution, emissions, training and hiring standards, corporate giving, and impact on local communities are all assessed by the Costa Rican Investment Promotion Agency (CINDE), The Ministry of Environment and Energy (MINAE), and the Costa Rican legislature before a foreign-owned subsidiary is established. The arrival of Intel in 1998 was something of a turning point for Costa Rica in their visibility as a contender for hosting subsidiaries in high-tech industries. Microsoft and Oracle have since established their presence in the country as well. Surprisingly, these three multinational corporations, within the same industry sector, operating in the same host country, and facing similar levels of scrutiny have chosen to approach CSR in vastly different ways.

Oracle has not responded to the challenge of local social responsibility that either of their industry colleagues has posed. The company has demonstrated little interest in local initiatives in Costa Rica. While Oracle does follow an environmental agenda and energy-saving practices focusing on packaging reduction and utilization of renewable energy sources, such efforts are vastly concentrated in the United States, and their social involvement in Costa Rican communities remains minimal and unreported.

14.6.1 Case Study: Microsoft Costa Rica

Microsoft has initiated two programs in all of their locations worldwide, Partners In Learning (PIL) and Potencial Sin Limites. Both are education oriented, providing tools and instruction in information technology. Hardware, software, training, and support & maintenance are provided to schools in every country where Microsoft operates, in regions where the financial need is greatest in order to enable entire communities via access to computers and instruction in their use. The total expenditure for these programs worldwide in 2006 was $US253 million. The expected reach in Costa Rica alone is 3.2 million students (Leiva, 2006).

The altruistic purpose of these ventures is to provide both learning opportunities and a necessary skill to people who would otherwise not have access to them; as well as to prepare a future generation for the technological demands of the workforce to further develop the economy of the country. In this manner, the programs address personal needs of individual Costa Rican citizens as well as the holistic economic welfare and collective growth of the country. Furthermore, it makes use of a large product which has previously been extremely difficult to recycle or dispose of in a sustainable manner, at what would be the end of its lifecycle, and recycles it for further use. The means of refurbishing these computers is a component of an additional social program, "Computadoras para Educar". The refurbishing is done by convicted prisoners in order to teach them job skills which can be used upon their release, while simultaneously recycling the hardware and providing schools with necessary educational tools.

However, Microsoft is not gaining from the amount of positive public relations that would presumably accompany such an outwardly generous contribution to society. In the case of Microsoft Costa Rica, very little is ever publicly mentioned of their investment in the local education system. While one contention is that the Ministry of Education has a poor public relations department, another possibility is that the government of Costa Rica does not want to appear to be unable to provide for their own children and thus dependent on a wealthy foreign business to do it for them; therefore any publicity is intentionally avoided. An estimate from the Public Relations Department of Microsoft Costa Rica was that the program received coverage in the local press approximately three times throughout 2006, none of them prominently (Leiva, 2006).

The most difficult element to ascertain is the most basic to the field: how can the impact of corporate responsibility be quantified? In order to be able to promote corporate responsibility, it must first be demonstrated that social and environmental responsibility do make a positive difference to the profitability of the company. Ultimately, a multinational company is a for-profit business with a responsibility to their investors to maintain the largest possible profit margin. Any venture that detracts from that profitability must be justified to the public, and that justification must demonstrate a positive impact on the bottom line. That being the case, no multinational company is likely to invest in any social or environmental endeavor without an expected return on their investment.

14.6.2 Case Study: Intel

Intel in particular maintains that corporate responsibility is not an addition to their business operations, but is instead a requisite constant that shapes the foundation of those very operations, forming a crucial component of each element of the business. In keeping with this premise, Intel has attempted to establish CSR in areas such as Government Relations, Investor Relations, Human Resources, Manufacturing, Facilities, and Supply Chain Management & Procurement.

In addressing the efficiency of their production of microchips, Intel has reduced intensive water use and eliminated a high percentage of waste by-product. In keeping with the standards of clients whom they supply, Intel was also able to revise their production methodology to utilize less energy as well as to decrease the quantity of heat that was originally given off in the manufacturing process (Cohen, 2007). These environmental efficiencies also served to reduce production costs by reducing the amount of water utilized and waste disposal volume (Cohen, 2007).

Intel also has extremely high reporting standards and levels of transparency, which impacts both their investor and government relations. The type of data that is fully disclosed to the public and the amount and level of detail of that data, literally raises the standard within the industry; the premise being that if Intel is capable of tracking, analyzing, and reporting such matters as volume of waste water produced per unit of product, or progress measured against baseline greenhouse gas emission goals, then a competitor within the industry is capable of reporting this as well. Once reported, businesses can be measured against one another and more sustainable practices can then be rewarded by consumers and investors (Stangis, 2006).

By investing in advanced worker safety equipment and training, Intel is able to keep their insurance premiums and compensation outlay extremely low by industry standards (Stangis, 2006). This investment in worker safety can also be recovered in time-to-market advantages, because permit acquisitions take less time and products reach the shelves faster as a result (Stangis, 2006). Was this particular form of CSR selected because Intel is concerned in the safe working conditions of their employees, or because it represented an advantage to the bottom line? Once again, the two are sufficiently intertwined that the original incentive is obscured; both financial and social objectives are met. This adjustment in labor standards represents a dual advantage to Intel; by adopting more stringent measures and investing in the best and safest equipment, they are reducing their insurance premiums, reducing their outlay of workers compensation by minimizing risk, and caring for their employees which in turn lowers turnover rates and training expenses while enhancing loyalty (Stangis, 2006). The results point to employee loyalty and retention as one of the more prominent fundamental benefits of a socially progressive business practice.

As was first determined in Costa Rica, these measures likewise benefit the local population. Once the higher labor conditions and safety standards had been initiated and applied with local contracting teams and construction firms for the opening of the Intel facility in Belén, the host country unions had the ability to require them from domestic companies as well and a higher standard, such as mandatory use of fall protection equipment, is now established across all Intel facilities globally (Stangis, 2006). Furthermore, in requiring that certain safety standards and equipment be utilized for the local contractors hired by Intel, the improved standards were adopted by the Costa Rican Ministry of Labor and proliferated throughout the country. Rather than take advantage of lower costs and bureaucratic ease associated with less stringent safety requirements, Intel utilized the difference as an opportunity to educate the industry and made the changing of high-risk labor practices a condition of their foreign direct investment in the host country.

14.7 Case Studies in Contrast

Despite their shared industry sector and host country, the CSR programs of Microsoft and Intel are quite different. In the case of Microsoft this vision of responsibility is dictated from corporate headquarters. Clearly, the programs receive support from the local offices, but that support is not reflective of a given host country's particular needs or interest. Leiva and her team at Microsoft Costa Rica have no voice in determining the means by which Microsoft interacts with the communities where their employees and customers live; their role is to carry out the nuances of these two programs as directed from the office in Redmond. At no point is a stakeholder analysis conducted or local concerns considered. The programs are "cookie-cutter" in that they are operated in identical fashion in every location in the world where Microsoft conducts business.

A key difference in the internal organization of Intel and Microsoft is that the people charged with running their local social programs and those charged with converting those efforts into positive marketing for the company and their products are one and the same in the case of Microsoft, and have little to do with each other in the case of Intel. Intel does not factor the Environmental, Health and Safety Program (EHS) into their marketing efforts or utilize it in promoting brand name recognition. When asked how the EHS program was utilized in marketing or PR purposes, Intel did not know and had no recollection of being directly involved in such efforts (Stangis, 2006). Leiva, on the other hand, has a joint role in both the execution of the social programs as well as managing the publicity and the impact of that publicity on marketing efforts (Leiva, 2006). Marketing and CSR in this case are one and the same. The construct of the program is such that the company is putting their product in front of what they hope is their future market. In donating their software and creating means with which more people can access it, Microsoft is creating brand recognition and a certain degree of dependence on their product (Leiva, 2006). This program is centrally designed, in conjunction with Marketing, to apply universally in all countries where Microsoft operates regardless of cultural or economic differences. Such uniformity limits the potential of corporate responsibility in that it fails to address actual social needs. A CSR approach which targets specific needs of individual communities has significant opportunity for long-term benefits to all stakeholders, including the company in question.

14.8 Incentive and Responsibility: Mutually Beneficial

After two weeks of interviews with multiple Microsoft and Intel employees, all including the question "What does your investment in corporate responsibility actually buy?" each employee promptly offered the same response: corporate responsibility buys a good image, thus improving their brand name. In the case of Microsoft, the follow-up question of "In the event that all social programs were eliminated tomorrow, what would be the effect on the company profit margin?" produced responses that were almost identical: little to no effect. Clients would continue to buy Microsoft products regardless of their publicly perceived level of corporate responsibility (Leiva, 2006). Thus the mere reputation of being a "good corporate citizen" appears to offer no immediate financial benefit that is not the direct result of operational efficiency with a positive environmental impact. That being the case, what is the investment in corporate responsibility paying for?

In the specific case of Microsoft Costa Rica, the answer did not lie in public relations or increased sales, but rather in the relationship maintained between the company and the local government. The money invested in the local communities procures the time and attention of legislative decision makers who have the capacity to engage the company (or not) for lucrative government projects, enact (or not) favorable business legislation (including the enforcement of anti-piracy laws which do affect sales), and agree to support the use of the product in the school systems, thus creating brand recognition throughout their future marketplace. Thus the intangible influence of corporate responsibility actually functions as a down payment for conducting overseas business, manifesting itself in multiple positive results:

- Additional motivation to accept the MNC-favorable Tratado de Libre Comercio (Free Trade Act)
- Government project contracts
- Favorable (pro-business) legislation
- Stricter enforcement of anti-piracy legislation
- Adoption of Microsoft software in the Costa Rican education system, which both creates a current clientele through the school and university systems, as well as serves as a future market by means of familiarization of the next generation with the product

While interviews with representatives of CSR departments in three different MNCs within the technology sector – Patricia Leiva of Microsoft, David Stangis of Intel, and Rich D'Amato of America OnLine – produced some differing answers on best practices of CSR, one area where all three concurred was in the intangible payoff for government influence and the significance of the connection between CSR efforts and company-government relations. D'Amato, former Executive Director of Corporate Philanthropy at AOL, including AOL Latin America, revealed that while he recalled meeting with marketing personnel once or twice per year throughout his tenure with the company, he worked with the government relations office on a weekly basis (D'Amato, 2007). According to Stangis, the site selection process for an MNC to start operations in a new location takes an average of 2 years, during which time the company is in constant communication and negotiation with the government of the host country. Furthermore, the government of a potential host site country is typically anxious to encourage the arrival of a new source of employment. Therefore multiple incentives, such as tax breaks, free imports of equipment, low-cost leases for property, work/hire programs with the top universities for employees, etc. are offered. Such interest from the host country leaves the MNC in a powerful bargaining position, and that typically results in the ability to influence policy such as higher labor safety standards in the case of Intel, or favorable business legislation such as stricter anti-piracy laws in the case of Microsoft.

14.9 Lessons Learnt: How Other MNCs Can Benefit

The most important element of the triple bottom line concept – and what Stangis was quick to point to – is the transferability of this approach to CSR to other companies.

There is very little in the Intel approach that is specific to their individual company or industry sector. The intricacies of production in regard to their product, i.e. the water saving methodologies that have been developed, pertain to their own production techniques, but in all other respects their approach can be applied to any MNC.

When asked what first step he would recommend to another company that wanted to establish responsible behavior, including SMEs (Small and Medium-sized Enterprises) which may not have the budgetary or resource capacities to establish large-scale programs, Stangis' immediate response was "reporting". Transparent reporting is scalable to the scope and size of any company, across all industry sectors. It also serves as an indicator to the public and to the financial markets that the company has determined where their actions are impacting their stakeholders and is dedicating the time and resources to monitoring and improving those impacts. As such, it sets benchmarks that the MNC must be prepared to meet.

Facilities accommodations, from the smallest changes such as energy-saving light bulbs to retrofitting an entire production line to utilize steam traps as an energy source, can be researched and applied. Human Resources can encourage the hiring and promotion of local residents in order to familiarize a multinational corporation with local needs and concerns. Where efficiency, safety, or environmental best practices have been developed, these can be applied in subsidiary locations and proliferated amongst other contractors, distributors, or suppliers as a condition of investment. Community welfare can be a component of any business as long as the appropriate research is dedicated to the endeavor beforehand. Each component of the private sector has the ability to make some contribution to the well-being of their local stakeholders. By incorporating CSR as fundamental to their operations, that ability can be converted into both social welfare and a successful business.

14.10 Conclusion

At present, corporate social responsibility is still emerging as both a concept and a practice. Companies are still beginning to determine which forms of Corporate Social Responsibility will work most effectively for their particular circumstances and determining their means of engagement in and execution for these initiatives.– Multinational businesses must learn the management of Internal versus external practices, proactive versus reactive approaches and determine how they can best engage in CSR. But the primary lesson which is rapidly becoming clearer across multiple industries and countries is that social wellbeing and corporate profit are not mutually exclusive. In looking at all of the different incentives for CSR which were explored – those of a small domestic company or those of a large multinational corporation – all are able to be combined with altruistic aims for a better society. Specific approaches which fit both business and stakeholder needs in Costa Rica do exist, and are able to benefit both parties. Such specificity demonstrates a dedication to responsibility which can pay dividends for stakeholders and business alike. Gradually, through the growth of company-community interaction and individualized developmental approaches, corporate presence in a community can become an indicator of wellbeing rather than exploitation. Such an approach can make the difference between CSR being a burden on the business or a means to optimal performance on all fronts.

Ultimately, Costa Rica is facing a growth pattern very similar to the rest of the world in terms of CSR; wealthy multinational corporations are taking the lead over domestic businesses due to more readily available funds and technological access. With time, and with global commercial opportunities presented via CAFTA, larger regional and domestic business will progress and meet the gradually rising social standards in order to compete. To that end, Costa Rican businesses appear more than willing to adopt demonstrated best practices from MNCs in order to further develop their own industries and enhance their ability to participate in the global marketplace. However, Costa Rica has one significant advantage over other countries of similar economic size in that the significant reliance of their economy on ecotourism is likely to compel much stricter standards and overseeing. Costa Rica, marketing itself to the rest of the world as an ecological paradise, cannot afford to jeopardize their environment or even the appearance of hypocrisy in this regard. Ultimately, the approach to CSR in Costa Rica is a reflection of their desire for economic growth which caters to the protection of their greatest economic asset.

Thus the concept that stakeholder benefit and corporate benefit are not mutually exclusive and can in fact be achieved simultaneously and through similar channels is finally being recognized in Costa Rica, and business entities there are learning to utilize these channels to contribute to their own growth as well as the growth of a better world.

References

Cohen, Stephen D; Multinational Corporations and Foreign Direct Investment; Oxford University Press: New York, NY; 2007

La Coalición Costarricense de Iniciativas de Desarrollo/The Costa Rican Investment Promotion Agency, CINDE (CINDE); http://www.cinde.org/esp-cinde.shtml

Engardio, Peter; "Beyond the Green Corporation"; *Business Week*; The McGraw-Hill Companies; January 29, 2007

Ford, Robert and McLaughlin, Frank; "Perceptions of Socially Responsible Activities and Attitudes: A Comparison of Business School Deans and Corporate Chief Executives"; The Academy of Management Journal; Vol. 27, No.3; September 1984

Ignatius, David; "Corporate Green"; *The Washington Post*; May 11, 2005

Logan, David; "Corporate Citizenship in the Global Age"; The Corporate Citizenship Company; The Royal Society; London, UK; 1998

Maloni, Michael and Brown, Michael; "Corporate Social Responsibility in the Supply Chain"; *Journal of Business Ethics*: Springer; 2006

Margolis, Joshua D. and Walsh, James P.; "Misery Loves Companies: Rethinking Social Initiatives by Business"; Administrative Science Quarterly, Vol. 8, No.2; June 2003

Ministerio de Ambiente y Energía de Costa Rica/Ministry of Environment and Energy of Costa Rica (MINAE); http://www.minae.go.cr/mn/despacho_ministerial.htm

Programa para la Excelencia; Calificaciones de Categoría 6, Cámara de Industrias de Costa Rica, 2006

Singh, Anupama, Kundu, Sudarshana, and Foster, William; "Corporate Social Responsibility Through the Supply Chain"; The World Bank Institute and Columbia University; May 11, 2005

Vogel, David; The Market for Virtue; Brookings Institution Press: Washington DC; 2005

Williams, Dean; "Weaving Ethics into Corporate Culture"; *Communication World*; Vol.19 No.4; 2002.

World Business Council for Sustainable Development, "Meeting Changing Expectations: Corporate Social Responsibility" Geneva, Switzerland: WBCSD, 1998.

Interviews

Castillo, Martha; Executive Director; Chamber of Industries of Costa Rica; Interview conducted on June 2, 2006

D'Amato, Richard; former Director of Corporate Philanthropy, America Online, Inc; Interview conducted on June 8, 2007

Díaz Sánchez, Luisa; Assessor of Competitiveness and the Environment, Chamber of Industries of Costa Rica; Interview conducted on July 20, 2006

Hilton, Paul; Director of Institutional and SRI Marketing, The Calvert Group; Interview conducted on July 19, 2006

Leiva, Patricia; Director of Public Relations, Microsoft Costa Rica; Interview conducted on August 14, 2006

Stangis, David; Global Director of Corporate Social Responsibility; Intel Corporation; Interview conducted on August 21, 2006

Wissel, Deborah; Manager of Business Development; Innovest; Interview conducted on July 19, 2006

Chapter 15
Brazil: CSR Under Construction

Mariana Lima Bandeira and Fernando Lopez Parra

Abstract The discourse of social responsibility invades and becomes institutionalized in contemporary society – and not only in Brazil – creating different forms and instruments through which the negative effects of modernity and capitalism can be minimized. One of these instruments legitimizes itself by its legal character – a group of laws, norms, and juridical means that regulate corporate responsibility. Within this perspective, the concept of social responsibility would be restricted to the concept of regulated responsibility. Thus, it can be observed that in the literature the innumerable "faces" presented as social responsibility, indicating a difference in terms of the concept: many meanings, interpretations, and possibilities. Since there is not much clarity, many actions can be classified as social ones. However, the truth is that they tend to be more regulated actions or another component of management.

Briefly, this paper aims to identify and provide understanding to the discursive practices about social responsibility in Brazil. The idea was to analyze the institutionalized practices and how the discourse is configured in that country.

In Brazil, one could observe the different approaches taken about the field of corporate social responsibility. During the 1960s, the attitude taken by Brazilian corporate entities was that "the problem didn't exist"; by the 1970s, there was a general acceptance that "the problem exists, but it is not mine"; by the 1980s the view changes to that of, "the problem exists, and I know how to solve it"... and today, with all the social problems in the country and pressures from various sources, Brazilian companies are concerned about the problem and how to solve it from its very source. In this sense, one can argue that Brazilian society is more participative and more pro-active about the subject of CSR than ever before.

Presently, the configuration of corporate social responsibility in Brazil is changing as a result of the sustainability discourse, there are many critical positive aspects of CRS, especially those concerning social and philanthropic actions. The main argument is that taking a social action does not necessarily mean being socially responsible, since the action is simply philanthropic and does not produce sustainability.

S. O. Idowu and W. L. Filho (eds.), *Global Practices of Corporate Social Responsibility*   309
© Springer-Verlag Berlin Heidelberg 2009

Finally, one can conclude that social responsibility in Brazil is a discourse that is under construction. Therefore, there is an opportunity to reflect and to learn more about it. Nowadays, social responsibility is shared among social actors and Brazilian civil society is more concerned about the need for sustainable development. Brazilians are more conscious of irresponsible social practices and would put pressure on the government, corporate entities, and individuals in order to produce sustainable development. In this sense, we concur with José Gabriel López, from Ford Foundation, who pointed out the need to develop new models for development that promote equity, social justice and sound environmental stewardship. It is a challenge for everyone, regardless of whether Brazilians or some other nationals.

15.1 Introduction

This paper aims to present a general view about social responsibility in Brazil, its evolution and present configuration. López and Bandeira (2004), argue that the social responsibility movement in Brazil was just under construction. In addition, they stated that the social responsibility discourse assumes the role of one of the justifications of Boltanski and Chiapello (2002). Three years after that, López and Bandeira (2004) argument is still valid, but now the concept of construction is considered under a Derrida's perspective. In fact, the social responsibility discourse is always under construction, because mistakes allow opportunities for learning.

In this sense, this paper is based on bibliographic and documental research and it is organized in the following way: first of all, we present the concept of discourse and the general social responsibility discourse; secondly, we indicate the evolution of the social responsibility discourse in Brazil and finally, how this discourse is presently constructed.

15.2 The Corporate Social Responsibility Discourse: About the Discourse

"Discourse" has been commonly associated with linguistics. In the linguistic tradition associated with the work of Saussure[1], the constitutive elements of language are concept and sound image (Ballalai, 1989). Language is understood as a social fact while speech is considered an individual aspect; discourse is understood as the result of the combination of the language and speech.

Dubois et al. (1995) defines discourse as a conjunction of manifestations of a given social condition in a specific time and space, that is: the combination of language elements with institutionalised social practices at a given historical moment.

---

[1] Saussure provides a structuralist analysis of language as a signifying system. The language or signifying system is a close union between the sound image (SIGNIFIER) and the concept (SIGNIFIED). The sound image is not the physical sound, but rather the psychological imprint of the sound, the impression it makes in one's mind.

Foucault (1979), states that the social subjects who produce and reproduce the discourses are not set apart from the process of construction of the discourse itself; subjects are also constructed by it. Therefore, subjects are at the same time the vehicle and product of discourse.

Chan (2000) suggests that the discourse constructs the internal limits of the individual, as well as creates her/his values and aspirations. According to him, 'excellence', 'learning organizations' and 'corporate culture' are all manifestations of subjectivation (Chan, 2000: 1060). So is 'social responsibility'.

According to Fairclough (2001), Foucault has a huge contribution for the "social theory of discourse": he stated the need of a social-historical analysis of the discursive formation[2], as the discursive and non-discursive elements interact with a social practice, defined for specific historical facts of a determined time.

According to this perspective, discourse analysis could have the responsibility to articulate a set of texts and practices of a social group in such a context. However, to understand this continuous construction it is necessary to accept the discourse dialogical dynamics, in which two or more 'voices' are in permanent confrontation, construction, de-construction and re-construction[3]. In this sense, the discursive formation concept seems to be more adjusted in this work, because it allows for the inter-textualities[4] and inter-discursivities[5] present (Spink, 2000).

The discourse of social responsibility invades and becomes institutionalized in contemporary society – and not only in Brazil – creating different forms and instruments through which the negative effects of modernity and capitalism can be minimized. One of these instruments legitimizes itself by its legal character – a group of laws, norms, and juridical means that regulate corporate responsibility. Within this perspective, the concept of social responsibility would be restricted to the concept of regulated responsibility. Thus, it can be observed that in the literature the innumerable "faces" presented as social responsibility, indicating a difference in terms of the concept: many meanings, interpretations, and possibilities. Since there is not

---

[2] According to Foucault (1979, p. 153), the discursive formation is "a set of anonymous rules, historical ones, always determined by time and space. Each discursive formation give an identity to a specify time and to a given context" (Foucault, 1979, p. 153). Daudi (1986: 141–145) remember that Foucault preferred the expression "discursive formation" because of it suggests a theory or a science which is never finished or developed. Doing so, it is possible understanding the discursive formation as a process in permanent developing and construction and, based on dispersive speeches in a relationship, they constitute a discourse.

[3] Deconstruction is used here in the same sense as Derrida (Spink, 2000).

[4] The word "intertextuality" was created by Kristeva at the end of sixties, based on the Bakhtin's work, who understood the present texts as a set of *'past and post texts'*. We mean: the past texts reflect the historical moments that influence the present texts; the future texts are the anticipated answers that are observed in present texts, as a projection.

[5] "Interdiscursivity", according to Spink (1995), consists in the interface of two forces: in one hand, the content that is present in the organizational context; on the other hand, the pressure which is result from the interpersonal relationship and the pressures of the collectivity identity. In order to understand this concept, it is essential to recognize the relevance of symbolic universe and its meanings (Fairclough, 2001). Foucault (1972, p. 98) completes: "there is no speech that doesn't bring up to date other speeches".

much clarity, many actions can be classified as social ones. However, the truth is that they tend to be more regulated actions or another component of management.

In brief, this paper aims to identify and provide an understanding on the discursive practices of social responsibility in Brazil. The idea was to analyze the institutionalized practices and how the discourse is configured in the country.

15.3 Exploring the Concept of Social Responsibility

One of the many versions regarding the appearance of the term "social responsibility" draws on a manifesto written by 120 industrial Englishmen at the end of the eighteenth century. The document defines the responsibility of a company's head as that of searching for and the maintaining of an equilibrium between the interests of the public, consumers, employees, stockholders, and thus reaching the largest possible contributions to the wellbeing of the nation as a whole.

With this stated, the first concrete manifestation of this idea developed at the beginning of the twentieth century with the Americans: Charles Elliot (1906), John Clark (1916), and in 1923 with the Englishman Oliver Sheldon as cited in Carroll 1999. Despite their defense of the inclusion of the social question between the concerns of the companies in addition to the profit of stockholders, their time periods did not grant them acceptance and their questioning was put to the side. CSR was not generally accepted until 1953, when Howard Bowen in the USA released his book "Responsibilities of the Businessman". Several authors including Carroll (1999) have described Bowen's book of 1993 as the initial point in the study and debate of social responsibility.

In the early 1960s, the debate on CSR started in Brazil. The events and social transformations characterized the socio-economic problems, and in a certain way, prepared the acceptance of the idea. In the seventies, the topic won amplitude, and in the eighties it came to be considered as part of corporate ethics and quality of life in the workplace.

In these times, social responsibility has come to be discussed more largely by diverse sectors of society, becoming relevant in that it looked to better the understanding of the role of the State in current society, further questioning which social and economic objectives should be pursued by companies.

Although its importance is recognized, there has not been a consensus in order to define the term social responsibility and that has caused a series of different interpretations. If, for some, the term means legal responsibility or social obligation, for others it signifies socially responsible behavior in which ethics or mere contributions of charity can be observed in companies. There are also those that argue that social responsibility is only an obligation to pay employees well and ensuring the compliance of labor rights. There are still even those that believe that social responsibility is an evasive "battle" for contemporary capitalism. This lack of consensus probably denotes how many values and motivations are behind the movement, which becomes many times more dominant in the capitalist discourse.

According to Carroll (1999), the first systematization of the term social responsibility came about during the decades of the thirties and forties, with the most important references of that period being the works of Barnard (1938), Clark (1939) and Kreps (1940). Bowen's "Social Responsibility of Businessmen" (Bowen *apud* Carroll, 1999) is considered a mark in the beginning of modern literature on this topic as already indicated.

The social responsibility of businessmen can be defined as "obligations of businessmen to pursue politics, make decisions or follow the lines of action that are beneficial in terms of objectives and values in society" (Bowen[1] *apud* Carroll, 1999). Bowen's work had as a base the belief that the large companies were vital centers of power and decision-making and that their actions affected many aspects in the lives of citizens.

Besides that study, McGuire (1963) and Elbing & Elbing (1967) also contribute to reinforce the ideas defended by Bowen, in the way in which they affirmed that companies should accept social obligations and current responsibilities from "prominent and powerful positions in society" (Litz, 1996).

Therefore, the liberal focus counts on the opposition of a more conservative current. The neoclassic economy argues that the objectives of companies should restrain themselves to the efficient allocation of scarce resources in the production and distribution of products or services in the free market. Thus, according to the most expressive authors, businessmen practice actions of social responsibility to profitably administer their companies (Tomei, 1984).

The authors who are most characteristic of this current were Levitt and Friedman. According to Levitt (1960), the efforts to increase social responsibilities of companies result in the destruction of the capitalist system. It can be observed that this positioning is very much the opposite of Boltanski and Chiapello (2002), which justly argues the contrary: that the movement of social responsibility presents itself as the necessary justification to manage capitalism.

In his terms, Friedman (1962) argues that social responsibility of the company should only be based on the profitable use of resources and in the environment of activities conducive to the increase of profitability, always following "the rules of the game". This author used the idea of Adam Smith, in the sense that the company should only look for profit, since an "invisible hand" will try to do the rest (Oliveira, 1984).

Even in the era of Chamberlain (Oliveira, 1984) it was believed that social responsibility could be satisfied by the good pledge of obligations for individuals, in particular, and not for society as with all. Krautz (Oliveira, 1984) also followed the same line of thought in terms that the companies should concern themselves with being productive and with generating profit, since only in that way will they be responsible to society.

Under this perspective, the beginning of the market would be the support of society, independent of the harm that could be caused. Corporate responsibility would be restricted to maintaining a functional system as long as capital would be accumulated.

In this sense Henderson (2000) argues that assuming a socially responsible attitude by part of the company is an enticement since behind the discourse of social responsibility there is an incessant search for the maximization of profit. Thus, the discourse can be understood to serve for capitalistic purposes even if not clearly defined. Henderson (2000) considers social responsibility to be an idiom which is incapable of understanding the rationality of capitalism. Furthermore, a socially responsible stance is never free and once it provokes costs for the company it can bring the consequences of raising prices.

On this aspect Carroll (1999) assures that the costs of socially responsible actions are at times more relevant than the behavior by itself or the qualitative results created by the decision. In this case what is really important is the cost-benefit relationship as opposed to the ethical process. The subjacent values at reach are completely instrumental.

Paradoxically, it was Samuelson, an American economist in the age of Levitt and Friedman who elaborated the concept of social responsibility (Carroll 1999). For him companies cannot just assume responsibility for the consequences of their decisions and actions for society. From this idea new theoretical constructs were proposed. Among them, the work of Davis distinguished itself as the concept of social responsibility referred to as "the considerations and answers by the company to questions that go further than strict economic, technical, or legal demands" (Davis *apud* Carroll, 1999). Davis even proposed the known "law of responsibility", according to which the company is a social institution that should utilize its power in a responsible form because if it fails to do this, then society can take the power from its hand (Litz, 1996).

Among the defenders of social responsibility in the heart of the corporate world, Frederick (*apud* Oliveira, 1984) indicated that social responsibility was a concern of companies with expectations from the public. Afterwards, this would have as a base the use of human, fiscal, and economic resources for ample social ends and not simply just to satisfy the interests of particular people or organizations.

There are also conceptual contradictions that arise and are accentuated from the basis of the social responsibility movement. This discourse is permeated by the historical movements which constructed them and mixed them with the perception of the authors who classified them. Whether social responsibility assumes a role as a representative of capitalism or as a means to build citizenship, the fact is that the discourse finds itself being crossed by many other discourses and presents rationales that at first hand may seem conflictive.

Some authors tried to identify the fundamental principals, the processes, and the results that embrace the study of business and society in such a way that it integrates the approaches. Depending on their intentions, the authors were not always successful.

In Brazil, Neto and Froes (1999) also refer to these two dimensions. – the internal and the external – upon affirming that the leant support for community development and the preservation of the environment are not sufficient to attribute to a socially responsible company's condition. It would never be necessary to invest in the well being of its employees, dependents, and in a healthy work environment, besides promoting clear communication, giving a return to stockholders and assuring synergy among the various third parties and guaranteeing the satisfaction of clients and consumers.

Neto and Froes (1999) argue, however, that the company should offer something to society in exchange for what was usurped by the company. Thus, social responsibility would be seen as: "a compromise from the company in relation to society and humanity in general and as a way to give back what was based on the appropriation and use of resources that did not originally belong to it" (Neto and Froes, 1999, p. 84).

According to Ferrel et al. (2001), social responsibility also takes the form of an obligation assumed by the company with regards to "maximizing its positive impact on stakeholders (clients, proprietors, employees, community, consultants, and governments) and to minimize the negative impact" on society (Ferrel et al., 2001, p. 68).

In terms of social objectives, there is a very instrumental relationship in these concepts. Offering something in exchange, obligations to maximize positive impact and to reduce the negative for stockholders, giving satisfaction to clients and a return to stockholders are the terms that denote an instrumentality behind the concept. Supposedly what is most important is not the values, ethical ideas or ethical processes.

Moreira (2001) agreed that the ethical-social functions of the business world do not become reduced by actions of corporate social responsibility. The author mentioned defines several criteria which designate an action of socio-economic responsibility: complying with social rights with regards to society, respecting the environment, complying with laws and regulations such as payment of taxes and social contributions. Besides this, Moreira argues that pure corporate responsibility counts on the responsibility of public agents as well as central and local administrations. The author even argues for a freer exercise by all citizens, whose actions or lack of action are based on socially responsible behavior.

From Moreira (2001), it can be noted that there are a series of regulations, criteria, and norms that give organizations the title of 'socially responsible'. Ashley (2002) understands that other obligations, which aren't just those defined by law, should be assumed by the organization in such a way that they contribute to the quality of societal life. For Ashley (2002, p. 6):

"social responsibility can be defined as a compromise which an organization should have with society, expressed by means of its acts and attitudes that positively affect it or a community in a specific manner, promoting proactive behavior for its specific role in society and its accounting for it."

Even Ashley (2002) refers to the moral dimension, being vague in what is understood as "positively ", "behaving proactively", and what will be "accounting for" society.

Rego (2002) includes another variable, the compromising of the members of organizations. The author calls attention to the fact that organizations only function efficiently if the people that make up part of them do more than just what is only required by their jobs. For this to happen it is necessary that they believe that something besides the accumulation of capital matters, as Boltanski and Chiapello (2002) argue. In this sense, there exists a necessity to introduce justifications that make them compromise with the spirit of capitalism. One of these justifications, as earlier mentioned, is the discourse of social responsibility and even its correlations as the corporate volunteering with respect to social questions.

Santos (2002) argues that neoliberal globalization, the bearer of social exclusion, of the precariousness of work, the decline of public politics, the destruction of the environment and biodiversity, unemployment, the violation of human rights, pandemics and ethical prejudice, is about to be confronted by another type of globalization which is alternative and counter-hegemonic in addition to being organized from the bottom to the top of society. One of the arms of this new form of globalization is precisely the movement that has been generated in social terms.

Tenorio (2000) views this position favorably, affirming that in a society marked by scientific-technological evolution and by the globalization of the economy, the value of citizenship arises as a means to promote a new organizational paradigm based on management which involves dialogue and participation. Tenorio and Fernando Guilherme (2002) adds that the epistemological basis of social management should be the intersubjectivity based on dialogue. Only this way can citizenship be solidified in the private sphere and in front of the most involved management of human resources.

This idea goes to the sources of the definition of social responsibility as introduced by the Commission of European Communities (2001) in which dialogical social management becomes a part of the internal dimensions of social behavior in companies. According to the Green Book, "the social responsibility of companies is essentially a concept according to which companies decide on a voluntary basis to contribute to being fairer to society and a cleaner environment" (p. 9). In this way, being socially responsible does not restrict itself to legal obligations, implying going beyond and including a "larger investment" in human capital, environment and in relation to communities in general.

In Brazil, we could observe different approaches about corporate social responsibility (Kishiname and Others, 2007): until the 1960s, "the problem didn't exist" was the common answer of companies; in the 1970s, we could see that it was "the problem exists, but it is not mine"; in the 1980s it became, "the problem exists, and I know how to solve it"... and in the present, with all the social pressures, the companies are concerned about the problem and how to solve it in its origins. In this sense, we can state that the society is more participative and more pro-active about the subject.

15.4 Capitalism and Corporate Social Responsibility in Brazil

In Brazil, we were included very late in the dynamic of capitalism. It was just in the beginnings of the twentieth century that our country was inserted into the global economy, leaving very slowly its condition as a Portuguese colony. Consequently, the Social Responsibility Discourse has only been recently discussed in both professional and academic contexts. In fact, it is possible to find some books, articles and research before 1960, but that subject was not really included in corporate, social or governmental agendas at that time.

In 1981, the sociologist Herbert de Souza, known as Betinho, founded the Brazilian Institute of Social and Economic Analyses (Ibase). It has the status of a federal nonprofit charitable organization, with no links to any religious institution or political party. In 1996, IBASE promoted a campaign in favor of Social Responsibility with the support of Gazeta Mercantil (a newspaper in Brazil). The main objective was stimulating managers and corporative directors to be committed to organizational strategies and actions with social impacts. At the same time, the State could not continue to support all the social demands, and there was a strong need to share responsibilities with other social actors. So, the number of non-governmental organizations increased and some companies became more concerned about the social consequences of their decisions. Since that time, the social responsibility discourse assumed a new configuration in this context.

As Cohen (2000) points out, companies in Brazil are becoming more concerned about social responsibility at the present time. According to his research, 56% of Brazilian and multinational companies are investing in social actions and this number is increasing.

The Institute of Economic and Applied Research, IPEA, developed a study in 1998 which reveals that 95% of big companies located at south east of Brazil practice social actions and only 62% of micro companies invest in social actions.

Oliveira (2003) also verified that publishing social information is a common practice in Brazil, especially among big companies. Probably it happens because of Brazilian taxes, which increase the costs of a micro organization. Some particular segments appear to be more committed to social actions, such as electricity, derivatives of petroleum and chemical products. On the other hand, others sectors are not concerned about it, such as the food industry for example (Oliveira, 2003).

Despite these results, some authors (Oliveira, 2003; Passador, 2002) (Portugal) recognize that there is no consensus on the concept of social responsibility. This situation appears very clear in the research of Oliveira (2003), who analyzed the social information published by 500 non-financial companies. His results confirmed that there is some confusion about what is included in social balance. Additionally, these social actions refer to external and internal aspects of social responsibility regulated by Law.

The reasons behind (or beyond) this movement could consist of many aspects: strategy, image, profits, institutional legitimacy, ethical process, fulfillment of legal devices, and so on. Anyway, we can observe that the social responsibility discourse is growing among Brazilian companies, especially the big ones, following a global movement. These practices also appear as a partnership among Society, State and Private Sector. Despite this new social and economic configuration of modernity, the divergence of *what* could be considered a social action from *who* is responsible for *what*, i.e., which role each actor ought to play in this scenery, is evident. The great challenge, we suggest, is to extend social responsibility practices and improve the critical discussion about it among all social actors.

15.5 CSR as a Sustainability Dimension

The configuration of corporate social responsibility in Brazil is changing. Because of the sustainability discourse, there are many critical assets about the CSR, especially concerning social and philanthropic actions. The main argument is that social action does not mean being socially responsible. Many times, social action is just philanthropic; which does not produce sustainability.

According to the United Nations World Commission on Environment and Development, the definition of sustainable development is one which "meets the needs of the present without compromising the ability of future generations to meet their own needs". This concept is the most widely used definition, as stated by Pearce et al. (1989).

The understanding of these *needs* is beyond common sense: poverty and the unequal distribution of resources are identified as major causes of environmental degradation (Carter, 2001).

Temple and Old Issue (1992) affirms that the concept of sustainability means, at the same time, "everything" and "nothing" as it is used without comprehension of its meaning.

The research of Claro, (2005) aimed at identifying the meanings that individuals give to the term sustainability, considering its three dimensions: economic, social and environmental. Their findings indicated that the way the individuals interpret 'sustainability' is strongly influenced by the educational level and amount of information they had received from their companies.

According to Carter (2001), most typologies of sustainability were identified in academic literature, in search of showing the 'weak' and 'strong' sides of sustainable development. One of these studies, developed by O'Riordan et al. (1996), distinguished between levels of sustainability according to the way human and environmental resources are valued along a continuum from techno-centrism to eco-centrism, as follows:

1. Very weak sustainability: the stock of human and natural capital remains constant over time and it allows for infinite substitution among the other kinds of capital.
2. Weak sustainability: there are some critical natural processes that are crucial to life (ozone, for instance) and need for protection, but it allows for substitution among other types of natural capital.
3. Strong sustainability: the use of natural resources must be compensated with processes such as reforestation.
4. Very strong sustainability: it is the most radical form of ecologism and it has some of socialist values (as redistribution of property rights).

The principles of sustainable development were organized during the 1992 Earth Summit in Rio de Janeiro, Brazil, creating the *Agenda 21*. This document outlined a 'global partnership for sustainable development', reinvigorating the commitment to sustainability, which must be extended far beyond government into the world of business and civil society. In other words, each social actor is socially responsible for the development and, of course, for the sustainability.

The basic principles of sustainable development are: equity and social justice, democracy, political integration and the planning. The first principle states that the environmental problems are related to the social and economic inequity. Democracy is important for solving these problems in a more participative way. The need of political integration is essential for including the three important dimensions of sustainability: social, economic and environmental.

In Brazil, the work of Camargo et al. (2007) explored seven issues central to the debate on sustainable development in Brazil: biodiversity and ecosystems; agriculture; urban environment; water; energy; production and consumption; and corporate social responsibility. Their findings pointed to good news: there have been significant advances in the legal structure and within the society on the vital importance of the environment. Nevertheless, although the participation of civil society had improved, there is a great need of more social commitment on this subject.

As evident, the term of Sustainable Development has become very popular and most times does not mean the real sustainability: there is a strong dimension of politics that is sometimes an obstacle for the implementation of its proposals. As Carter (2001) shows, the concept was first concerned with ecological sustainability, or the conservation of living resources, and directed little attention to wider political, economic or social issues.

The shift observed in this debate, from a traditional view of protection, to the notion of sustainability, requires a much more complex discussion. Carter (2001) indicates that the set of meanings is not simply an exercise in academic or practical clarification but it reflects a political process to conciliate different interests of the social actors.

In the last few years, there is a change in the attitude of mistrust among business, government and civil society. As pointed by Camargo et al. (2007), this has come about through recognition of the negative social-environmental impacts resulting from many corporate practices and led to the search for sustainable alternatives and to the implementation of social and environmental projects by companies – either independently or in partnership.

Kishiname and Others (2007) established some critical factors to the social and environmental sustainability of the companies:

– Establishing commitment among the different social actors
– Making social and political pressures, in order to construct legitimacy and transparency in the "power game"
– Opening to new opportunities for social and environmental "business"
– Improving the transparency of companies' activity

Although we have observed some advances related to sustainable development in Brazil, there are still many challenges to overcome, as José Gabriel López affirms: "Brazilian society is increasingly aware of the need to address the negative effects of environmental degradation on quality of life for current and future generations and of the urgent need to develop new models for development that promote equity, social justice and sound environmental stewardship" (Camargo et al., 2007, p.7).

References

Ashley, Patricia Almeida (Org.) (2002) Ètica e Responsabilidade Social nos negócios. 01 Ed. São Paulo: Saraiva.

Ballalai, Roberto (1989) Notas e subsídios para a análise do discurso: uma contribuição à leitura do discurso da administração. *Forum educ.*, Rio de Janeiro, v. 13, n.1–2, p. 56–80, 1°/2° trim. fev./mai.

Barnard, Chester (1939) The functions of the executive. Cambridge, MA: Harvard University Press.

Boltanski, L. & Chiapello, Ève. (2002) *El nuevo espíritu del capitalismo.*Madrid, Espanha: Editorial Akal.

Bowen, Howard, R. (1953) Social Responsibilities of the Businessman. Harper Brothers, New York.

Camargo, Aspásia; João Paulo Ribeiro Capobianco & José Antonio Puppim de Oliveira (2007). The state of Brazilian environment 1992–2002: a view from civil society. Rio de Janeiro: CIDS/EBAPE/FGV/ISA.

Carroll, A. B. (1999) Corporate Social Responsibility: Evolution of a Definitional Construct, Business & Society, Vol. 38(3), pp. 268–295.

Carter, Neil (2001). The politics of the environment. London: Cambridge University Press.

Chan, Andrew. (2000) Redirecting critique in postmodern organization studies: the perspective of Foucault. Organization Studies, 21(6), p.1059–1075.

Clark, J. M. (1939) Social control of business, McGraw-Hill, New York.

Claro, Priscila Borin de Oliveira; Claro, Danny Pimentel & Amâncio, Robson, (2005). Entendemos Sustentabilidade em sua Plenitude? Análise de Fatores que Influenciam a Interpretação do Conceito. ANPAD.

Cohen, David (2000) Empresa e sociedade: pressão social e relações com a comunidade e o meio ambiente. Revista Exame, vol.

Commission of European Communities (2001) Definition of CSR: http://ec.europa.eu/enterprise/csr/index_en.htm first accessed in 2001.

Daudi, P. (1986). *Power in the Organisation: The Discourse of Power in Managerial Praxis.* Oxford: Basil Blackwell.

Davis, K. (1960). Can business afford to ignore social responsibilities? California Management Review, Spring, Vol. 2, pp. 70–76.

Dubois, J. et al. (1995) *Dicionário de Lingüística*. São Paulo: Cultrix.

Elbing, A. and Elbing, C. (1967). The value issue of business, McGraw-Hill, New York.

Fairclough, Norman (2001). *Discurso e mudança social*. Brasília: Editora UnB.

Ferrell, O. C., Fraedrich, J. & Ferrell, L. (2001). Ética empresarial: dilemas, tomadas de decisões e casos. 4.ed. Rio de Janeiro : Reichmann & Affonso Editores. (Translated by Ruy Jungmann; technical review by Maria Cecilia Coutinho de Arruda).

Foucault, Michel. (1979) Microfísica do poder. Rio: Edições Graal (11a reimpressão).

Frederick, W. C. (1960). The growing concern over business responsibility, California Management Review, Spring, Vol. 2, pp. 54–61.

Gil, Antonio Carlos. *Métodos e técnicas de pesquisa social*. São Paulo: Ed. Atlas, 1991.

Gomes, Â. C. A política brasileira em busca da modernidade: na fronteira entre o público e o privado. In SCHWARCZ, L.M. *et Al. História da vida privada no Brasil - contrastes da intimidade contemporânea*. São Paulo: Companhia das Letras, 1994.

Henderson, H. (2000). Alem da globalizacao: modelando uma economia global sustentavel, Traducao de Maria Jose Scarpa, Editora Cultrix Sao Paulo.

Kishiname, Roberto; Oded Grajew, Paulo Itacarambi e Carmen Weingrill. Artigo-base sobre responsabilidade socioambiental das empresas. In: CAMARGO, A. e outros (org.) Meio ambiente Brasil: avanços e obstáculos pós Rio-92. Rio de Janeiro: Estação Liberdade, 2007.

Kreps, T. J. (1940). Measurement of the social performance of business in 'An investigation of concentration of economic power for temporary national economic committee (Monograph No. 7), Washington DC, US Government Printing Office.

Levitt, Theodore. Marketing Myopia. *Harvard Business Review (HBR)*, 1960.

López-Parra, M. F. and Bandeira, M. L. (2004). Social responsibility in Brazil under construction, in Social responsibility World of RecordPedia, Penang, Ansted Service Center, Malaysia.

Litz, R. A. (1996). A resource based view of the socially responsible firm: stakeholder interdependence, ethical awareness and issue responsiveness as strategic assets, Journal of Business Ethics, Vol. 15(12), pp. 1355–1363.

McGuire, S. L. W. (1963). Business and Society, McGraw-Hill, New York.

Moreira, S. L. A., (2001). Liga Nacionalista de Sao Paulo: ideologia e atuacao. Dissertacao de mestrado, Depto de Hisoria FFLCH-USP, mimeo.

Neto, Francisco P. de Melo. & FROES, César. Responsabilidade social e cidadania: a administração do Terceiro Setor. Rio de Janeiro: Qualitymark, 1999.

Neto, Francisco Paulo de Melo; FROES, César. *Gestão da responsabilidade social corporativa: o caso brasileiro*. Rio de Janeiro: Qualitymark, 2001.

Neto, Sydenham Lourenço. Marchas e contra-marchas da intervenção estatal. Estado, empresariado e burocracia na política siderúrgica brasileira. Tese de doutorado apresentada ao Instituto de Pesquisa do Rio de Janeiro 2000.

Oliveira, Francisco (1984) "O Surgimento do Antivalor: Capital, Força de Trabalho e Fundo.

Oliveira, José Antônio Puppim de. Um balanço dos balanços sociais das 500 maiores empresas S.A. não-financeiras do Brasil. In: XXVII ENCONTRO NACIONAL DOS PROGRAMAS DE PÓS-GRADUAÇÃO EM ADMINISTRAÇÃO – ENANPAD (2003: Atibaia, SP). Anais . . . Rio de Janeiro: Associação Nacional de Programas de Pós-Graduação em Administração, 2003 (Texto Integral em CD-ROM dos Anais do 24° ENANPAD).

O'Riordan, Timothy, and Jäger, Jill (Eds.). Politics of climate change in Europe: a European perspective. London: Routledge, 1996.

Passador, Cláudia Souza. A responsabilidade social no Brasil: uma questão em andamento. In: VII Congreso Internacional del CLAD sobre la Reforma Del Estado y de la Administración Pública (2002, Lisboa, Portugal), p. 8–11, Oct. 2002.

Pearce, David, Anil Markandya and Edward Barbier. Blueprint for a Green Economy. United Kingdom, Earthscan Publications Ltd., 1989.

Rego, M. L. (2002). A responsabilidade social como resposta do sistema S ao ambienete institucional brasileiro pos-decada de 1990: o caso SESC Rio de Janeiro: Escola Brasileira de Administracao Publica e de Empresas, Centro de Formacao Academica e Pesquisa, (Tese de doutorado).

Santos, Boaventura de Sousa. *Democratizar a Democracia: os caminhos da democracia participativa*. Rio de Janeiro: Civilização Brasileira, 2002.

Spink, Mary Jane (org.) (2000) Práticas discursivas e produção de sentidos no cotidiano: aproximações teóricas e metodológicas. 2ª ed. São Paulo: Cortez.

Sucupira, João. A responsabilidade social. Boletim IBASE, 20 de maio de 2000.

Temple, S. Old Issue, New Urgency? In Wisconsin Environmental Dimension, Spring Issue, vol. 1, nr: 1, 1992.

Tenorio, Fernando Guilherme. Flexibilização Organizacional: mito ou realidade? Rio de Janeiro: FGV, 2000.

Tenorio, Fernando Guilherme. *Tem razão a Administração?* Ijuí: Unijuí, 2002.

Tomei, P. A. (1984). Responsabilidade social de empresa: analise qualtativa da opiniao do empressariado nacional. Revista de Administracao de Empresas, Rio de Janeiro, 24(4): 189–202, out./dez.

Part IV
Middle East & Africa

Chapter 16
Egypt: Social Responsibility Disclosure Practices

Aly Salama

Abstract This paper offers updated evidence on social disclosure trends in Egypt. It examines whether Egyptian companies care about the community as an important stakeholder in their Internet social reporting. In doing so, the paper employs content analysis to measure and explore the social responsibility self-disclosure practices of major Egyptian companies in their online annual reports and/or Websites. The analysis shows that although there are good examples of corporate social responsibility practices in some Egyptian companies working in the telecommunication and construction industries, the extent of social disclosure in other Egyptian companies working in other industries is inadequate and there is still a long way to go. There is evidence to suggest that these companies' social disclosure is still below the expectations of the community of stakeholder groups.

16.1 Introduction

The growth in global awareness of corporate social responsibility has increased substantially. Consequently, the academic interest in voluntary disclosures of social responsibility information in corporate annual reports has been raised to a large extent. In other words, there has been a rise in empirical studies on reporting practices in recent years, which provide insights into the number of companies disclosing such information, the subject matter included in these disclosures, the trend in overall disclosure over time and the general relationship between corporate characteristics and the tendency to disclose social responsibility initiative information.

However, much of the literature to date has focused on the experience of companies in the industrialized developed countries, mostly of Europe, the USA, Australia and New Zealand. No study has examined the corporate social disclosure practices in the Egyptian context. Within Egypt there are no requirements, legislative or professional requirements, for firms to disclose social initiatives undertaken. Yet, in a

S. O. Idowu and W. L. Filho (eds.), *Global Practices of Corporate Social Responsibility*   325
© Springer-Verlag Berlin Heidelberg 2009

developing country like Egypt, which has been experiencing great political reforms and speedy economic growth in recent years, there has been an increased societal demand for corporate social responsibility initiatives.

During my period of study as a PhD candidate in corporate environmental disclosures, I considered applying my research in the Egyptian context by contacting some Egyptian companies to obtain their most recent annual reports in order to look for corporate social and environmental disclosures. It was very difficult to obtain copies of these reports at that time. However, I was able to obtain four annual reports, but, unfortunately, there was no such disclosure, the Egyptian companies only provided their financial statements along with the auditor's report.

Nonetheless, during the past few years there has been a growing public and media awareness of the role of corporations in the Egyptian society. For example, a new ministry of State for Egyptian Environmental Affairs has been established and has focused, in close collaboration with the national and international development partners, on defining environmental policies, setting priorities and implementing initiatives within a context of sustainable development.

Therefore, after more than 6 years from my first attempt, I thought it was a good idea, to re-examine what major Egyptian companies are doing in terms of caring about the community as an important stakeholder in their corporate social reporting via exploring the social responsibility self-disclosure practices of major Egyptian companies in their annual reports and/or Websites. The remainder of this paper is organized as follows. The first section discusses Stakeholder Theory. The research method applied to examine the data is outlined in the methodology section. Section four presents data analysis. Finally, section five presents brief conclusions and implications.

16.2 The Stakeholder Theory

The Stakeholder Theory arises from a rejection of the idea that the corporation should strive to maximize the benefits of a single set of stakeholders, the shareholders (Wijnberg, 2000). Freeman in his 1984 seminal work, *Strategic Management: a Stakeholder Approach* explains the relationship between the business and its behaviour within its external environment. Every corporation has complex involvements with stakeholders who have an interest in its actions and outputs and, therefore, they are a critical factor in determining the success or failure of a modern business corporation. Stakeholder Theory has two categories (Gray et al., 1996; Deegan, 2000). The first relates to the managerial branch and the second relates to the ethical (or normative) branch.

The managerial branch argues that organizations tend to satisfy the information demands of those stakeholders who are important to the organization's ongoing survival and who have voting or political power (i.e. shareholders and governments). According to Ullmann (1985), the more critical the stakeholder resources

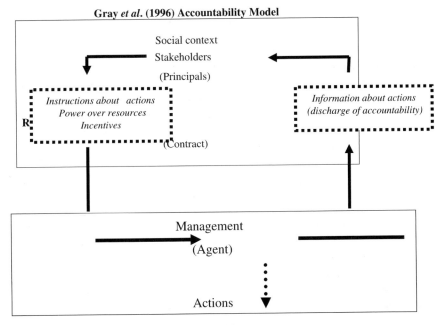

Fig. 16.1 Gray et al. (1996) Accountability model
Source: adapted from: Gray et al. (1996, p. 39).

are to the continued viability and success of the organization, the more powerful the stakeholders and the greater the probability that the stakeholder demands will be incorporated within the organization's operations. From this perspective, various activities undertaken by organizations, including social responsibility reporting, will be directly related to the expectations of particular stakeholder groups (Deegan, 2000).

On the other hand, the ethical view argues that all stakeholders, regardless of their power, have a right to be provided with information about how the corporation is impacting on them, even if they choose to ignore the information provided, and even if they have no direct impact on the survival of the organization (Deegan, 2000). It is therefore appropriate to consider Gray et al's (1996) view of accountability: the managers' responsibility to manage financial and non-financial resources assigned to them by the stakeholders and the responsibility to provide an account (by no means necessarily a financial account) of those responsibilities. They created a model of a simple socially grounded two-way relationship between the management of an organization and its stakeholders. The model can be expressed as follows (see Fig. 16.1):

Applying the accountability model to corporate social reporting, the role of a corporate annual report is to inform stakeholders (the principal) about the extent to which the actions for which a management (the agent) is supposed to be responsible have been fulfilled (Gray et al., 1991).

16.3 Methodology

This section presents the methodology adopted in the conduct of the research for this paper. It considers the background of the environment in which the Egyptian companies operate, the sample population and sources of data, the definition of corporate social disclosure and the measurement of such disclosure.

16.3.1 Egypt – Background

Egypt is probably the world's oldest civilization that dates back to 700,000 years.

Egypt is located in the north east of Africa, bordered by the Mediterranean Sea to the north, Palestine, Israel and the Red Sea to the east, Sudan to the south, and Libya to the west. Cairo is the capital and the commercial centre of Egypt. The population of Egypt (2007 estimate) is about 80 million. Almost 99% of its population lives within the Nile Valley and Delta, which constitutes less than 4% of Egypt's total area. Islam is the official religion and Arabic is the official language.

Parliamentary life began in Egypt in 1866. The Parliament authorizes laws, approves the general policy of the country, and monitors the government's practices. There have been great economic, social, cultural and political reforms in Egypt. Authority is represented in an elected president who can appoint a vice president, a prime minister and governors. In addition to the ruling National Democratic Party, there are many opposition parties who make their views public and represent their constituents at various levels in the political system.

The Egyptian economy depends principally on tourism, agriculture, petroleum exports and traffic that go through the Suez Canal. Egypt has a developed energy market based on coal, oil and natural gas. There is substantial strategic coal reserves located in the north-east of Sinai. Oil and gas are produced in the western desert regions, the Suez Gulf and the Nile Delta. Egypt has huge reserves of gas which has been exported to many countries. Also, the Egyptian telecom sector is one of the healthiest and fastest growing sectors, with a consistent high performance level. It is also perhaps the most liberalised, competitive and dynamic sector in Egypt.

Economic conditions have started to improve significantly in Egypt after the increasing of revenues from both tourism and the stock market. Egypt has been recently rated by the International Monetary Fund as one of the top countries in the world undertaking economic reforms. Egypt's economic reform programs began in 1991 and has led the country into becoming one of the world's outstanding emerging markets. The Egyptian Government announced that there are no restrictions on investment in Egypt and continues to provide incentives and facilities (e.g. 10 years tax break) for all investments undertaken in ambitious investment projects.

16.3.2 Sample Population and Sources of Data

The initial sample population chosen is based on the 50 Most Active Companies in Cairo & Alexandria Stock Exchange (CASE), available from the Disclosure Book (June: 2006, 3rd Issue). An important justification for choosing CASE 50 is that they cover a broad range of industrial and commercial activities and account for a significant proportion of the Egyptian economic output (80% of the trading volume). Also, the CASE 50 are considered as the most active companies in terms of fulfilling their corporate social and environmental responsibilities. The initial sample is presented in Table 16.1.

Information is communicated by companies in a number of ways. The main disclosure vehicle is the annual report. In addition, companies may use other means such as Internet home pages, as a part of the accountability-discharge activity, to reach the stakeholders (Zeghal and Ahmed, 1990; Marston and Shrives, 1991; Gray et al., 1995b). Internet reporting is an activity that been increased in recent years and a growing number of companies around the world are using the Internet to communicate corporate information. Internet reporting has the advantages of low cost, wider reach, frequency and speed. In spite of the enormous benefits that the Internet provides, there is an apparent need of effort to conceptualize the Internet use for corporate social disclosure (Isenmann and Lenz, 2001). This is echoed by Ashbaugh et al. (1999) who noted that little is known about how firms use the Internet to disseminate corporate information.

This paper fills the gap in existing literature by studying the Internet social disclosure practices, as a proxy for social responsibility activities of Egyptian companies rather than using hard copy annual reports. In particular, the purpose of this study is to examine empirically the nature, location, extent, and quality of Internet social disclosures of major Egyptian companies. The Companies' Web Sites were accessed to search for corporate social disclosures and the most recently published annual reports downloaded from Web Sites were subsequently printed to allow for the relevant analysis to be effected. The following criteria were used in the selection of the final sample:

1. The company must still be alive
2. The company must have a "*working*" (active) Web Site

Applying the selection criteria reduced the final sample to only 16 companies. Table 16.2 shows the sample selection procedures.

16.3.3 Defining Corporate Social Disclosure

Empirical research has indicated an increase in the amount of social responsibility information disclosed by companies over the past few decades (Gray et al. 1996). Such disclosures are seen by some as a mechanism that corporations utilize in order to enhance their status, provide information to stakeholders and discharge the

Table 16.1 The 50 most active Egyptian companies – June 2006

Company Name	Industry	Website
EL EZZ ALDEKHELA STEEL-ALEXANDRIA	Building Materials & Construction	N/A
EL EZZ PORCELAIN (GEMMA)	Building Materials & Construction	N/A
EL EZZ STEEL REBARS	Building Materials & Construction	N/A
MISR BENI SUEF CEMENT	Building Materials & Construction	N/A
MISR CEMENT (QENA)	Building Materials & Construction	N/A
NATIONAL CEMENT	Building Materials & Construction	N/A
ORASCOM CONSTRUCTION INDUSTRIES (OCI)	Building Materials & Construction	www.orascomci.com
SINAI CEMENT	Building Materials & Construction	N/A
SUEZ CEMENT	Building Materials & Construction	www.suezcem.com
TORAH CEMENT	Building Materials & Construction	N/A
ABO KIR FERTILIZERS	Chemicals	www.abuqir.com
EGYPTIAN FINANCIAL & INDUSTRIAL	Chemicals	N/A
MISR CHEMICAL INDUSTRIES	Chemicals	N/A
PAINT&CHEMICALS INDUSTRIES (PACHIN)	Chemicals	www.pachin.com
SIDI KERIR PETROCHEMICALS	Chemicals	N/A
EGYPTIAN COMPANY FOR MOBILE SERVICES (MOBINIL)	Communication	www.mobinil.com
ORASCOM TELECOM HOLDING (OTH)	Communication	www.orascomtelecom.com
VODAFONE EGYPT TELECOMMUNICATIONS	Communication	www.vodafone.com.eg
EGYPTIAN ELECTRICAL CABLES (ECE)	Electrical Equipment & Engineering	www.ece.com.eg
EGYPTIAN FOR TOURISM RESORTS	Entertainment	www.sahlhasheesh.com
ORASCOM HOTELS & DEVELOPMENTS	Entertainment	http://www.orascomhd.com/
COMMERCIAL INTERNATIONAL BANK (CIB) (EGYPT)	Financial Services	www.cibeg.com
EGYPTIAN AMERICAN BANK (EAB)	Financial Services	www.eab-online.com
EL AHLI INVESTMENT & DEVELOPMENT	Financial Services	www.adi-alahly.com
ELWATANY BANK OF EGYPT	Financial Services	N/A
EXPORT DEVELOPMENT BANK OF EGYPT (EDBE)	Financial Services	N/A
MISR INTERNATIONAL BANK (MIBANK)	Financial Services	www.mibank.com.eg
NATIONAL SOCIETE GENERALE BANK (NSGB)	Financial Services	www.nsgb.com.eg

Table 16.1 *Continued*

Company Name	Industry	Website
OLYMPIC GROUP FINANCIAL INVESTMENTS	Financial Services	N/A
SUEZ CANAL BANK	Financial Services	N/A
DELTA SUGAR	Food & Beverage	N/A
EASTERN TOBACCO	Food & Beverage	N/A
AMOUN	Health & Pharmaceuticals	N/A
EGYPTIAN INTERNATIONAL PHARMACEUTICALS (EIPICO)	Health & Pharmaceuticals	www.eipico.com.eg
EGYPTIAN FINANCIAL GROU-HERMES HOLDING COMPANY	Holding Companies	www.efg-hermes.com
EI KAHERA HOUSING	Housing & Real Estate	N/A
MEDINET NASR HOUSING	Housing & Real Estate	N/A
SIX OF OCTOBER DEVELOPMENT&INVESTMENT (SODIC)	Housing & Real Estate	www.sodic.org
UNITED HOUSING & DEVELOPMENT	Housing & Real Estate	N/A
RAYA HOLDING FOR TECHNOLOGY& COMMUNICATIONS	Information Technology	www.rayacorp.com
EGYPTIAN MEDIA PRODUCTION CITY	Media	www.empc.com.eg
EAST DELTA FLOUR MILLS	Mills & Storage	N/A
UPPER EGYPT FLOUR MILLS	Mills & Storage	N/A
ALEXANDRIA MINERAL OILS COMPANY	Mining & Gas	N/A
ARAB COTTON GINNING	Textiles & Closing	N/A
ARAB POLVARA SPINNING & WEAVING CO.	Textiles & Closing	N/A
ELNASR CLOTHES & TEXTILES (KABO)	Textiles & Closing	N/A
NILE COTTON GINNING	Textiles & Closing	N/A
ORIENTAL WEAVERS	Textiles & Closing	www.orientalweavers.com
CANAL SHIPPING AGENCIES	Utilities	N/A

social contract between the entity and the relevant public (Gray et al., 1988). Guthrie and Parker (1990) stated that these disclosures "appeared to reflect public social priorities, respond to government pressure, accommodate environmental pressures and sectional interests and protect corporate prerogatives and projected corporate images" (pp. 171–172).

Generally speaking, disclosure is the presentation of information necessary for the efficient operation of capital markets (Hendriksen, 1982). Corporate social disclosure has been defined by many researchers. For example, it can include, among other things, disclosure relating to the interaction between a corporation and its physical and social environment inclusive of disclosures relating to

Table 16.2 Summary of sample selection procedures

Initial sample		50 companies
Excluded:		
• Companies without web sites	29	
• Companies with under-construction web sites	4	
• Dead/takeover companies	1	
Final sample		16 companies

human resources, community involvement, the natural environment, energy, and product safety (Deegan and Rankin, 1996). Mathews (1984, p. 204) defined it as: "voluntary disclosure of information, both qualitative and quantitative, made by organizations to inform or influence a range of audiences. The quantitative disclosures may be in financial or non- financial terms". Gray et al. (1987, p. ix) defined corporate social disclosure as: '.... the process of communicating to the social and environmental the effects of the organizations' economic actions to particular interest groups within society and to society at large. As such, it involves extending the accountability of organizations (particularly companies), beyond the traditional role of providing a financial account to the owners of capital, in particular, shareholders. Such an extension is predicated upon the assumption that companies do have wider responsibilities than simply to make money for their shareholders'.

Environmental disclosures, which constitute part of social responsibility disclosures, may be defined as the preparation and provision of information, by management, on the impacts corporation economic activities have on the physical or natural environment in which they operate, for the use of relevant stakeholders in assessing their relationship with the reporting entity. This involves the environmental aspects of production, covering such activities as pollution control in the conduct of business operations (i.e., installation of environmentally friendly machinery), prevention or repair of damage to the environment resulting from processing of natural resources (i.e., undertaking site rehabilitation), recycling of waste materials, conservation of natural resources, incurrence of fines relating to environmental misdemeanours, and the like (Ingram, 1978; Abbott and Monsen, 1979; Deegan and Rankin, 1996; Wilmshurst and Frost, 2000).

16.3.4 Content Analysis – An Appropriate Measure of Social Disclosures

The accounting literature has accumulated a substantial number of studies which seek to measure corporate social disclosures (e.g. Bowman and Haire, 1976; Abbot and Monsen, 1979; Ingram and Frazier, 1980; Wiseman, 1982; Guthrie and Mathews, 1985; Cowen et al., 1987; Belkaoui and Karpik, 1989; Guthrie and Parker, 1990; Zeghal and Ahmed, 1990; Patten, 1991, 1992; Gibson and Guthrie, 1995; Gray et al., 1995a, b; Deegan and Rankin, 1996; Deegan and Rankin, 1996; Hackston and Milne, 1996; Burritt and Welch, 1997; Walden and Schwartz, 1997; Neu et al., 1998; Cormier and Magnan, 1999; Toms, 2000; Gray et al., 2001). One research method that has been widely adopted in the majority of such literature is the content analysis which quantitative criteria distinguish it from other forms of textual analysis (Ingram and Frazier, 1980). As with previous studies, this paper employs content analysis to measure the level of the Internet social disclosure practices.

Berelson (1952; p. 18) defined content analysis as "a research technique for the objective, systematic and quantitative description of the manifest content of communication". Abbott and Monsen (1979; p. 504) defined content analysis as "a technique for gathering data that consists of codifying qualitative information in anecdotal and literary form into categories in order to derive quantitative scales of varying levels of complexity". Krippendorff (1980) is critical of Berelson's definition because several of Berelson's definitional requirements are either unclear or too restrictive. To exclude these deficiencies, Krippendorff (1980; p. 21) defined content analysis as, "a research technique for making replicable and valid inferences from data to their context". The requirement of a content analysis to be "replicable" means that when other researchers, at different times under different circumstances, apply the same technique to the same data, the results must be the same (Krippendorff, 1980).

The preferred units of analysis in written communications tend to be pages, words or sentences (Gray et al., 1995b). In this paper, the number of sentences related to the social themes was chosen as the most appropriate measure of the amount of the Internet social disclosure. Ingram and Frazier (1980) used sentences as the unit of analysis. They (p. 617) chose this method stating, "The sentence was selected as the unit of analysis for the final research since a sentence is easily identified, is less subject to inter-judge variation than phrases, clauses, or themes, and has been evaluated as an appropriate unit in previous research". Sentences overcome the problems of allocation of portions of pages and remove the need to account for, or standardize, the number of words (Hackston and Milne, 1996). Furthermore, sentences are a more natural unit of written English to count than words (Hughes and Anderson, 1995, cited in Hackston and Milne, 1996).

16.4 Research Findings

The aim of this section is to provide a realistic account of the current state of social responsibility disclosure practices of Egyptian companies. It starts with general noteworthy points and then provides some examples of the Egyptian companies' best practices.

16.4.1 General Analysis

The key findings of the content analysis of corporate social disclosures on the Internet along with the industry membership and total assets of each company are presented in Table 16.3.

The analysis of Table 16.3 reveals that nine companies chose not to disclose social responsibility information on their Web Sites or in their online annual reports. Only seven companies (about 44% of the final sample) disclosed a total of 231 social responsibility sentences, representing an average of 33 sentences disclosed by any single company. Of the whole social responsibility sentences disclosed, declarative and monetary good news sentences clearly dominate. In contrast, and not surprisingly, no company chose to disclose bad news This asserts the fact, concluded in prior literature, that social responsibility information is most often provided in a positive way (Guthrie and Parker, 1990; Deegan and Rankin, 1996).

There are some possible explanations for the lack of disclosure of negative social responsibility information. One possible explanation that managers are willing to disclose positive information is to enhance corporate image, credibility and trustworthiness with a wide range of stakeholders. The more weight managers place on maximising current firm value, the greater their incentive to disclose positive environmental information (Lang and Lundholm, 1993).

Corporate size is the variable most consistently reported as significant in studies examining differences across firms in their disclosure policy (Foster, 1986). Similarly, Trotman and Bradley (1981), Belkaoui and Karpik (1989) and Hackston and Milne (1996) all concluded that social disclosure is a function of firm size. However, the noteworthy and surprising finding in this study is that corporate size, as measured by total assets, is not correlated to Internet social disclosures. This is evidenced by Fig. 16.2.

Table 16.3 Disclosing companies (making at least one disclosure)

Company name	Industry	Total assets (2005) (EGP)	Number of disclosed sentences (amount)	Disclosed sentences (as a % of all disclosed sentences)
OTH	Communication	38,274,231	2	0.9
ECE	Electrical Equipment & Engineering	594,192	4	1.7
EIPICO	Health & Pharmaceuticals	1,363,861	8	3.5
CIB- EGYPT	Financial Services	30,389,544	28	12.1
OCI	Building Materials & Construction	17,809,889	40	17.3
VODAFONE	Communication	7,702,000	67	29
MOBINIL	Communication	6,445,091	82	35.5
Total			231	100.00

Note 1: Total sample of companies = 16; all disclosing companies = 7.
2: EGP (Egyptian Pound): 1 EGP = 0.18 U.S. dollars (October: 2007).

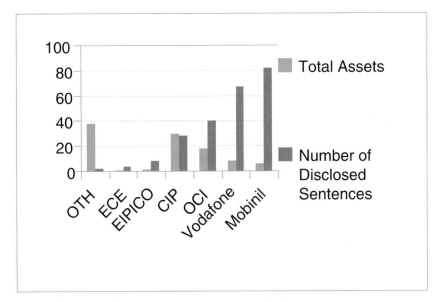

Fig. 16.2 The relationship between total assets and social disclosures

16.4.2 Disclosing Companies – Examples of Good Practice

16.4.2.1 OTH's Internet Disclosures

Social disclosures were noticed in only one occasion in the 2006's online corporate annual report under "Corporate Social Responsibility" section:

> "Stemming from its belief of its role in society, Masrawy.com proudly declares its sole and exclusive online responsibility towards the Children@ Risk Program initiated by Cilantro/ Nahdet El Mahrousa. Masrawy.com is taking the responsibility of spreading online awareness of the program through covering all issues of concern related to the problem of homeless children" (p. 29).

It is my view that the above OTH's social disclosures are considered as general rhetoric or general statements of commitment to the society.

16.4.2.2 ECE's Internet Disclosures

Environmental disclosures were noticed in only one occasion on the Web Site:

> "ECE depends on the strictest quality standards to produce its products. In addition, the strictest measures are enforced to ensure environment-friendly operation. The company grounds are spread over a large area, with plenty of green spaces. The company is situated far from any populated areas and no pollutants are emitted into the environment".

Again, the above environmental disclosures could be defined as general rhetoric or just general statements of commitment to the environment.

16.4.2.3 EIPICO's Internet Disclosures

Environmental Disclosures were noticed in only one occasion on the company's Web Site:

Realizing the Importance of environmental protection for safe environment for the present and future generations, EIPICO is committed to:

- Providing safe and effective pharmaceutical products according to GMP with continual reduction of impacts.
- Compliance with legal regulations and other requirements.
- Prevention of pollution and conservation of resources.
- Continuous enhancement of the performance, competence and awareness of EIPICO's employees.
- Therefore, EIPICO has established, implemented and maintained integrated management systems for Quality Environment satisfying the requirements of both ISO 9001 and ISO 14001.

Unlike OTH and ECE, there is some evidence of effort or responsibility towards the environment. In other words, the company is committed to a programme of continuous improvement to reduce its impact on the environment. This has been evidenced by environmental responsibility initiatives specifically tied to the firm and its operating environment and also evidenced by the ISO 14001 and ISO 9001 certificates.

16.4.2.4 CIB-Egypt's Internet Disclosures

Social disclosures were noticed on many occasions in the 2006's online corporate annual report on the "Board of Director's Report" and also in the "Corporate Social Responsibility Section". Here are some examples:

"For the fourth consecutive year CIB pursued its role as a valued corporate citizen in 2006 by making significant positive contributions to numerous community development programs. The Bank's involvement included donations to various charitable causes in addition to active sponsorships of cultural and social events inside and outside Egypt. CIB is increasing its role in the community and across Egyptian society by supporting fundraising for charitable organizations in Egypt. The service has demonstrated its effectiveness as the number of organizations that joined the Bank has increased from three since the launch in 2003 to 26 organizations; we expanded the service to attract both local and regional donations. Our service is covering various types of charitable organizations classified into three major fields: Health Care, Educational and Social Support & Commitment" (p. 11).

"CIB organized the Egyptian food Bank event during 2006 whereby total collected funds during the event reached approximately EGP 1.6 Million" (p. 11).

There is some evidence here of positive contribution to the community. It is clear that CIB has implemented and monitored a programme of social responsibility initiatives including health care, educational and social support programmes. The bank also provided information about funds they have allocated to charity.

16.4.2.5 OCI's Internet Disclosures

Social and environmental disclosures were noticed in a number of occasions in the 2006's online corporate annual report in many locations including the "Corporate Social Responsibility section". Here are some examples:

> "All of our cement plants utilize the latest dry process manufacturing technologies and production control systems from ThyssenKrupp Polysius and FL Smidth, the two leading European equipment suppliers, to ensure that they are among the most cost efficient and environmentally friendly plants in the world" (P. 7).

> "We believe strongly in protecting and supporting the local communities in which we operate. Through our activities, we contribute to the economic and social well-being of our stakeholders" (p. 34).

> "What we do and how we do it can have an impact on the lives of every one of our shareholders, employees, customers, business partners and those in the communities where we operate. We recognize that we have a social responsibility to our stakeholders and are committed to acting in accordance with international best practices for corporate governance, corporate citizenship and sustainable development. OCI, its subsidiaries and affiliates demand that all their employees conduct themselves in accordance with the highest standard of professional conduct and ethics" (p. 34).

> "Payments for charitable purposes made by the Company during the year ended 31 December 2006 amounted to LE 7.8 million (2005, LE 1.6 million). The primary beneficiaries of these charitable donations were public sector institutions and qualified nongovernmental organizations for social development projects" (p. 39).

As we can see, there is a strong evidence of positive contributions of OCI to both of the environment and society. It is clear that OCI has implemented and monitored a programme of social and environmental responsibility initiatives including using environmentally friendly machinery and supporting social programmes. Also, some detailed information about donations OCI has allocated to charitable programmes had been reported.

16.4.2.6 Vodafone's Internet Disclosures

Social disclosures were noticed on the company's Web Site in two main sections: "Community Development" – Human Development, Millennium Competition, and Safety Driving Campaign and "Charity" – Lost Children, Upper Egypt Schools, Back to School, Charity Caravan and Charity Tent. Here are a few examples:

> "Vodafone Egypt launched mobile usage and safe driving awareness raising campaign. The campaign aims to acquaint car drivers and the public in general with the most important behaviours and safe driving tips while using mobile phones. Special booklets have been prepared including information and instructions on safe driving and the right way to use mobile phones, especially on high ways and during travelling. A dedicated Vodafone Egypt exists in some of Egypt's high ways during peak hours to give these booklets out to the public as well as familiarize drivers with key safe driving tips while using mobile phones. The Vodafone team makes sure car drivers have earphones and gives them tokens for their safe usage of mobiles on highways. Throughout the past few years, Vodafone Egypt has initiated mobile usage and safe driving awareness raising campaign concurrently at the beginning of

vacation seasons when travelling escalates on highways, especially to the North Coast and Alexandria. This campaign has been well received by the public and highly appreciated by the concerned authorities and societies. Also Vodafone Egypt has earlier launched a campaign raising the awareness of the importance of using earphones while driving under the motto: "thanks for using the earphone while driving." These awareness raising campaigns come about as part of Vodafone Egypt's corporate social responsibility program. Vodafone Egypt undertakes such initiatives out of its concern for the world around us and in turn providing its customers and the public in general with all available information related to safe driving within its interest in their security. It is worth mentioning that Vodafone Egypt covers most of high ways in Egypt. Its concern to reach its customers wherever they are increases their feelings of security and gives them the chance to communicate and make phone calls while travelling. The company considers customers' safety on highways a top priority. Vodafone Egypt even covered most highways with low traffic density, despite the high cost of installing networks in these areas. The company has announced its full commitment to cover highways and the facilitation of services to provide safety to travelers and commuters".

"Vodafone Egypt's "Push to Talk" technology plays a vital role in combating the phenomenon of lost children in Gamasa and Ras El-Bar cities during the summer season. To do so, Vodafone Egypt has established 18 meeting points in a form of equipped small camps to host the lost children until their parents show up. Present at these camps experienced baby sitters, toys and all the necessities that children might need. "Push to Talk" service also enables the camps' supervisors to be in continuous contact with each other so that the parents would be able to find their lost children easily. It is known that Gamasa and Ras El-Bar are two of the most popular Mediterranean beaches in Egypt; the thing that heightens the occurrence of this phenomenon. Vodafone Egypt offers this service in the framework of its concern to solving the public problems. Also, it comes in view of its commitment towards supporting the community in resolving this critical problem in Gamasa and Ras El-Bar".

"In the framework of its commitment to the CSR principles, Vodafone Egypt continues its intensive social program through its launching of the "Charity Campaign" and the "Vodafone's Charity Caravan" project. The campaign was kicked off during the first week of Ramadan 2006 and is continued after the Lesser Bairam. It involves several governorates in the Coastal Zone of Egypt, Upper Egypt and Cairo. The campaign aims at supporting more than 300 civil societies and charitable institutions that are interested in orphans, the aged and people with special needs to supply them with Ramadan essentials and winter provisions. Moreover, gifts and toys were distributed over the children during the feast to share with them its happiness. A team of Vodafone Egypt's personnel takes part in this campaign by visiting civil societies and institutions to help around in distributing those supplies. This reflects the keenness of Vodafone Egypt's personnel on participating in voluntary work stressing the meaning of humanitarian communication between citizens, which effectively contribute in developing society".

Again, there is a strong evidence of Vodafone's positive contributions to both of the community and charity programmes through implementing and monitoring a programme of social responsibility initiatives.

16.4.2.7 MOBINIL's Internet Disclosures

Social and environmental disclosures were noticed on a number of occasions in the 2006's online corporate annual report in many locations. These include:"Mission Statement", "Commitment to the Community", "Environment", and "Corporate Social Responsibility" sections. Here are few examples:

"We understand our business principles clearly and we believe in the responsibility we owe to our community. We have a responsibility to balance the needs of our stakeholders with our social, ethical and environmental obligations. This means ensuring that we have clear principles of corporate social responsibility, which is an integral part of our strategic planning and daily activities" (p. 10).

"Our employees are our most valued asset. Our ability to succeed depends on the integrity, knowledge, skills, diversity, and teamwork of our employees. We are shaping a challenging, fair, firm, and productive work environment, which emphasizes mutual respect and team-work. We strive to reward high performance and we promise to be responsive to the needs of our employees. The company is committed to providing equitable compensation, excellent working conditions, and a fair atmosphere with great opportunities for professional growth" (p. 27).

"Mobinil is an equal opportunity employer and we pride ourselves with the Equal Em-ployment Opportunity policy (EEO). All employment applications are considered without regard to age, gender, religion, disability, or marital status" (p. 27).

"Mobinil plays a leadership role in serving the community in which it operates. We have sponsored many charitable events to aid the disabled and disadvantaged, and funded a num-ber of social activities including sports events to support public interest. We will continue to make contributions toward development programs in Egypt" (p. 30).

"We will work to understand people's concerns about the environment and health. We are committed to responsibly managing and minimizing our impact on the environment. We are committed to the ISO 14001 standards by establishing, implementing, and maintaining an environmental management system that complies with its requirements. We are keen to provide maximum environmental protection for the local community, and we consider it one of our main responsibilities" (p. 30).

It could be argued that MOBINIL is committed to a programme of continuous improvement to reduce its impact on the environment, although there is not much evidence on the environmental responsibility initiatives. Compared with other com-panies, MOBINIL has achieved the highest social and environmental disclosure per-centage. Although interesting, the social disclosures do not give us much of the story of the MOBINIL's social commitments and hence could be classified as gen-eral rhetoric disclosures or just general statements of commitment to the society and the environment. Therefore, the emerging question which should be addressed seri-ously is: should managers care about the quantity or the quality of social and envi-ronmental disclosures? The answer to such a crucial question would have important implications on the stakeholders and the overall quality of corporate reporting.

16.5 Conclusion

Over the last few years, corporate social responsibility in Egypt has become the focus of increasing attention and concern. Many managers have developed social and environmental management systems and increasingly adopted social disclosure within the annual reports.

This study has documented the nature, location, extent, and quality of Internet social and environmental disclosures of major Egyptian companies. The Compa-nies' Web Sites were accessed to search for such disclosures and the most recently published annual reports downloaded from Web Sites were subsequently printed out to allow for the relevant analysis to take place.

Content analysis was used to provide a detailed measure of community involvement disclosure contents for the sample firms. The data derived from the content analysis were used to analyze the disclosure practices made by Egyptian companies in order to provide evidence on such practices.

The response of Egyptian companies to the demands of stakeholders and to the absence of regulation, since there is no Egyptian legislation requiring social disclosure in the annual reports, has been to provide non-standardized information on the matter. Therefore, corporate social responsibility information has fundamentally taken the form of voluntary disclosure. The social information disclosed is essentially qualitative, positive to enhance the company's image, credibility and trustworthiness with a broad range of stakeholders. The amount of social disclosure made by any individual Egyptian company on average is about thirty three sentences.

Taken together, this analysis offers updated evidence on social disclosure trends in Egypt. The good news is that corporate social responsibility disclosures on the Web Sites and annual reports in the 2007 are much better than when the author first examined these in the 1999. However, the general message is that the extent of social disclosure in the Egyptian companies is inadequate and there is still a long way to go. It is probably below the expectations of community stakeholders.

The results in this paper may have implications for managers of Egyptian companies. As the stakeholder demands for social responsibility information increase it is becoming more evident that a company's social responsibility reporting activities should be considered more seriously by those managers as a strategic issue. This means that corporate social responsibility decisions need to be integrated within the wider organizational decision-making processes. Managers have to learn how to communicate successfully and effectively with a wide range of stakeholders who want firms to provide them with explicit and good quality information about their responsibilities towards social and environmental issues.

Acknowledgments

The author also acknowledges the assistance of Mrs Mona Saleh, Mr. Amir Iskander and Mr. Tarek AbdElFattah in the data collection process.

References

Abbott, W.F. and Monsen, R.J. (1979). 'On the measurement of corporate social responsibility: self reported disclosures as a method of measuring corporate social involvement', *Academy of Management Journal*, 22(3), pp. 501–515.

Ashbaugh, H., Johnstone, K.M., and Warfield, T.D. (1999). 'Corporate reporting on the internet', *Accounting Horizons*, 13(3), pp. 241–258.

Belkaoui, A. and Karpik, P.G. (1989). 'Determinants of the corporate decision to disclose social information', *Accounting, Auditing and Accountability Journal*, 2(1), pp. 36–51.

Berelson, B. (1952). *Content analysis in communications research*, New York: Free Press.

Bowman, E.H. and Haire, M.A. (1976). 'Social impact disclosure and corporate annual reports', *Accounting, Organizations and Society*, 1(1), pp. 11–21.

Burritt, R.L. and Welch, S. (1997). 'Accountability for environmental performance of the Australian Commonwealth public sector', *Accounting, Auditing and Accountability Journal*, 10(4), pp. 532–561.

Cairo and Alexandria Stock Exchanges, Disclosure Book, 3rd issue-June 2006.

Cormier, D. and Magnan, M. (1999). 'Corporate environmental disclosure strategies: Determinants, costs and benefits', *Journal of Accounting, Auditing and Finance*, 14(4), pp. 429–451.

Cowen, S.S., Ferreri, L.B. and Parker, L.D. (1987). 'The impact of corporate characteristics on social responsibility disclosure: A typology and frequency- based analysis', *Accounting Organizations and Society*, 12(2), pp. 111–122.

Deegan, C. (2000). *Financial accounting theory*, Australia: The McGraw- Hill Companies, Inc.

Deegan, C. and Gordon, B. (1996). 'A study of the environmental disclosure practices of Australian corporations', *Accounting and Business Research*, 26(3), pp. 187–199.

Deegan, C. and Rankin, M. (1996). 'Do Australian companies report environmental news objectively? An analysis of environmental disclosures by firms prosecuted successfully by the environmental protection authority', *Accounting, Auditing and Accountability Journal*, 9(2), 50–67.

Foster, G. (1986). *Financial Statement Analysis*, USA: Prentice- Hall International.

Freeman, R.E. (1984). *Strategic management: A stakeholder approach*, Boston: Pitman.

Gibson, R. and Guthrie, J. (1995). 'Recent environmental disclosures in annual reports of Australian public and private sector organizations', *Accounting Forum*, 19(2/3), 111–127.

Gray, R.H., Javad, M., Power, D.M., and Sinclair, C.D. (2001). 'Social and environmental disclosure and corporate characteristics: A research note and extension', *Journal of Business Finance and Accounting*, 28(3&4), pp. 327–356.

Gray, R.H., Kouhy, R., and Lavers, S. (1995a). 'Corporate social and environmental reporting: A review of the literature and a longitudinal study of UK disclosure', *Accounting, Auditing and Accountability Journal*, 8(2), pp. 47–77.

Gray, R.H., Kouhy, R., and Lavers, S. (1995b). 'Methodological themes: Constructing a research database of social and environmental reporting by UK companies', *Accounting, Auditing and Accountability Journal*, 8(2), pp. 78–101.

Gray, R.H., Owen, D.L., and Adams, C. (1996). *Accounting and accountability: Changes and challenges in corporate social and environmental reporting*, London: Prentice hall.

Gray, R.H., Owen, D.L., and Maunders, K.T. (1987). *Corporate social reporting: Accounting and accountability*, London: Prentice Hall.

Gray, R.H., Owen, D.L., and Maunders, K.T. (1988). 'Corporate social reporting: Emerging trends in accountability and the social contract', *Accounting, Auditing and Accountability Journal*, 1(1), pp. 6–20.

Gray, R.H., Owen, D.L., and Maunders, K.T. (1991). 'Accountability, corporate social reporting and the external social audits', *Advances in Public Interest Accounting*, 4, pp. 1–21.

Guthrie, J. and Mathews, M.R. (1985). 'Corporate social accounting in Australia', in Preston, L.E. (Ed.), *Research in Corporate Social Performance and Policy*, 7, pp. 251–277.

Guthrie, J. and Parker, L.D. (1990). 'Corporate social disclosure practice: A comparative international analysis', *Advances in Public Interest Accounting*, 3, pp. 159–176.

Hackston, D. and Milne, M.J. (1996). 'Some determinants of social and environmental disclosures in New Zealand companies', *Accounting, Auditing and Accountability Journal*, 9(1), pp. 77–108.

Hendriksen, E.S. (1982). *Accounting Theory*, Illinois: Richard D. Irwin, Inc.

Hughes, S.B. and Anderson, A. (1995). '*Some determinants of social and environmental disclosures in New Zealand companies*', Paper Presented at the First Asian Pacific Interdisciplinary Research in Accounting Conference, Sydney, Australia.

Ingram, R.W. (1978). 'An investigation of the information content of (certain) social responsibility disclosures', *Journal of Accounting Research*, 16(2), pp. 270–285.

Ingram, R.W. and Frazier, K. (1980). 'Environmental performance and corporate disclosure', *Journal of Accounting Research*, 18(4), pp. 614–622.

Isenmann, R. and Lenz, C. (2001). 'Customized corporate environmental reporting by internet-based push and pull technologies', *Eco-Management and Auditing*, 8(2), 100–110.

Krippendorff, K. (1980). *Content analysis: An introduction to its methodology*, London: Sage Publications.

Lang, M. and Lundholm, R. (1993). 'Cross- sectional determinants of analyst ratings of corporate disclosures', *Journal of Accounting Research*, 31(2), pp. 246–271.

Marston, C.L. and Shrives, P.J. (1991). 'The use of disclosure indices in accounting research: A review article', *British Accounting Review*, 23, pp. 195–210.

Mathews, M.R. (1984). 'A suggested classification for social accounting research', *Journal of Accounting and Public Policy*, 3, pp. 199–221.

Neu, D., Warsame, H., and Pedwell, K. (1998). 'Managing public impressions: Environmental disclosures in annual reports', *Accounting, Organizations and Society*, 23(3), pp. 265–282.

Patten, D.M. (1991). 'Exposure, legitimacy, and social disclosure', *Journal of Accounting and Public Policy*, 10, pp.297–308.

Patten, D.M. (1992). 'Intra- industry environmental disclosures in response to the Alaskan oil spill: A note on legitimacy theory', *Accounting Organizations and Society*, 17(5), pp. 471–475.

Toms, J.S. (2000). *Environmental management, environmental accounting and financial performance*, London: CIMA.

Trotman, K. and Bradley, G.W. (1981). 'Associations between social responsibility disclosure and characteristics of companies', *Accounting, Organizations and Society*, 6(4), pp. 355–362.

Ullmann, A.A. (1985). 'Data in search of a theory: A critical examination of the relationships among social performance, social disclosure, and economic performance of U.S. Firms', *Academy of Management Review*, 10(3), pp. 540–557.

Walden, W.D. and Schwartz, B.N. (1997). 'Environmental disclosures and public policy pressure', *Journal of Accounting and Public Policy*, 16, pp. 125–154.

Wijnberg, N.M. (2000). 'Normative stakeholder theory and Aristotle: The link between ethics and politics', *Journal of Business Ethics*, 25, pp. 329–342.

Wilmshurst, T.D. and Frost, G.R. (2000). 'Corporate environmental reporting: A test of legitimacy theory', *Accounting, Auditing and Accountability Journal*, 13(1), pp. 10–26.

Wiseman, J. (1982). 'An evaluation of environmental disclosures made in corporate annual reports', *Accounting Organizations and Society*, 7(1), pp. 53–63.

Zeghal, D. and Ahmed, S.A. (1990). 'Comparison of social responsibility information disclosure media used by Canadian firms', *Accounting, Auditing and Accountability Journal*, 3(1), pp. 38–53.

Chapter 17
Turkey: Civil Society Practices

Topal, R. Ş. and Gurdag, H.

Abstract This chapter discusses the evolution of the concept and practice of CSR in Turkey. It addresses the political, economic and social developments of CSR from Turkish's perspective. It provides an overview on the roles of public and private sector organizations and non-governmental organizations (NGOs) as well as the way in which Turkish culture in terms of philanthropy compliments the practice of CSR. The chapter also provides some concrete examples of the practice of CSR in corporate Turkey with some concluding remarks on the concept's current status in Turkey.

17.1 Introduction

The European Commission Green Paper "Promoting a European Framework for Corporate Social Responsibility (2001)", defines CSR as: "a concept whereby companies integrate social and environmental concerns in their business operations and in their interaction with their stakeholders on a voluntary basis" (Michael and Öhlund 2005). CSR is about acknowledging that sustainable competitive advantage requires companies to be economically viable, environmentally sound, and socially responsible. Rapid political, economic, and technological developments have led to an ever more complex operating environment for business, governments, and society. The importance of building alliances and partnership has also increased. There is a growing awareness of the need to develop new types of consultation and partnership between companies and their secondary stakeholders-communities, governments, non-governmental organizations (NGOs), and the general public. Governments are no longer able to deal with developmental challenges and achieve "sustainable" development on their own. In seeking to raise the country's socio-economic status, there is consensus that other sectors such as the private sector and the NGOs have a role to assume in developmental activities. International organizations and institutions (the UN, UNDP; World Bank, EU) are all emphasizing a wider role for business and are encouraging them to include CSR in their agenda.

17.2 Civil Conceptualization and Implications of CSR in Turkey

The evolution of the concept of good business practice in Western countries alongside the principles encompassed in human rights and environmental protection standards is now evident in corporate Turkey. It may well be said that, in the case of Turkey, attempts to meet the needs of NGOs, which have provided the necessary foundation for civil society in the West, were initiated by the state itself during the presidency of the Ataturk. He did not only maintain the trend towards modernization that had begun late in the Ottoman era, but also accelerated it, moving rapidly towards Western ideology in numerous fronts. As a result, the civil society appeared to have been developing rapidly, at least in form if not in function, by means of the regulatory initiatives of the state in the early years following the founding of the Republic. The institution of a civil society can, perhaps, accurately be said to have started, at least in a nominal sense, after the founding of the Republic (Karaman and Aras, 2000).

The institution of Turkish civil society has gained momentum with the establishment of multi-party politics. This was a critical turning point – a watershed in Turkish history. However, this development was insufficient for the development of civil society in its most modern, functional, and democratic form. Labour unions serve as a particularly good example of the way in which NGOs in Turkish civil society have failed to meet the criteria of civil society. According to Gramsci, the private labor organizations of civil society that have emerged in the West represent fully independent organizations of the working class, and they exist outside of the state structure. In Turkey, however, they are established only within restricted areas with pre-determined boundaries (Karaman and Aras, 2000).

While it is true that the 1980 military intervention "set out to destroy the institutions of civil society," paradoxically, it "helped to strengthen the commitment to civilian politics, consensus-building, civil rights, and issue – oriented associational activities". It can easily be observed that the revitalization of civil society has not been restricted to intellectual circles only, but has spread throughout different segments of society through the blossoming activity of numerous associations. According to recent data, "at present, there are 54,987 non-governmental associations in Turkey that are active". What is more, this plethora of organizations in civil society embraces almost all segments of the society, incorporating people from all walks of life, with widely disparate world views, while, at the same time, these organizations have become increasingly issue oriented, as distinct from the ideological orientations that characterized the organizations of the 1970s (Karaman and Aras, 2000).

Turkey's declared foreign policy focus since the mid-1980s has been the achievement of full EU membership. In its long march for integration with Europe, Turkey has made substantial improvements in achieving macroeconomic stability through restructuring and monitoring of the financial industry, establishing the independence of the Central Bank, implementing a tight fiscal policy, dramatically reducing inflation, deregulating the monopolized sectors, and generally reducing the role of the state in the economy. This improvement has been backed up by substantial reforms in accounting and financial reporting standards, audit practices, and disclosure regulations (Ararat and Göcenoğlu 2006).

According to Ararat and Ugur (2003) the role of state in Turkey's history is as follows: "... *the state's heavy involvement in the economy has led to two undesirable consequences. On the one hand, it fostered a political culture in which the legitimacy of the state is a function of the 'rents' that the government could distribute rather than its ability to provide 'public goods' such as stable macroeconomic environment, a transparent regulatory system, and social conflict resolution mechanisms, etc. On the other hand, the state's heavy involvement increased 'private risks'. Therefore, it induced private economic agents to pressure the government of the day to compensate at least part of their risks – irrespective of whether or not such risks have been due to government action or the private actors' own actions. This second tendency combined with the first led to persistent favouritism, corrupt practices, opacity, etc. – all of which have their own path dependencies*".

One of the multipliers of this problem is considered to be the existence of a powerful and highly monopolized media with strong political and commercial affiliations (Ararat and Göcenoğlu, 2006).

Perhaps because of the special circumstances behind the development of Turkey's private sector, entrepreneurs have always been almost apologetic about their wealth and felt diffident about the legitimacy of their ventures. This psychology materializes in a strong discourse of social purpose and value of private enterprise. Hence shareholder value is a relatively new concept for Turkey and it is weakly pronounced except by business schools. Highly concentrated family ownership does not help to mitigate the timidity about shareholder value. As one of the strongest business organizations in Europe, the Turkish Businessmen and Industrialists' Association (TUSIAD), follows suit with a mission to establish the social role of Turkish private enterprise, rather than to protect the interests of its member companies. Consequently, corporate philanthropy is strong in Turkey; most companies that are organized into business groups (diversified conglomerates) have provisions in their articles of association to donate a percentage of their net profits to foundations set up by their founding families. The drivers behind this phenomenon can be related to the need for gaining legitimacy and social acceptance for the relatively new wealth in a country where the disparity in income levels is disturbing (Ararat and Göcenoğlu, 2006).

17.3 The Trend in CSR Activities in Turkey Today

Turkey is going through a major transformation. In the 1990s the role of private and public sectors and NGOs began to be redefined. Turkey also began to debate the efficiency of a strong central state, a widening role for the private sector, and more space for NGOs as actors of social development. Recently, the process of accession to the EU fuelled the development and importance of civil society organizations. EU funding created a platform for capacity building of civil society organizations (CSOs). The CSO Training and Research Centre of some universities and the Civil Society Development Programme are examples of these processes. In a nutshell, the state's (including the military's) dominant role in the economic and political scene is being gradually balanced with that of the private sector and the civil society – a process exacerbated by the desire to join the EU and an acceptance of the alignment of societal values and norms with those of European Union member countries (Ararat and Göcenoğlu, 2006).

17.3.1 Society, Culture, and Leadership Behaviour in the Turkish Case

Society's expectations of business are influenced by many factors. In a global study conducted in 2001 by Environics International (*www.environics.com*), it was found that Turkish consumers valued business ethics, labour practices, environmental impacts, and demonstrable social responsibility far less than brand quality when forming an impression of a company. The same study found that in low to mid-income level countries, the perception of companies as socially responsible is based on reasons which are not CSR related. Society predominantly expects economic performance (jobs) from business in those countries, which is consistent with the findings in Turkey. Society's expectations from business can be articulated by CSOs, and CSO activism may be a good indicator of society's monitoring capacity. During the recent past, limitations imposed upon Turkey's CSOs, coupled with a highly monopolized and censored media and a tradition of opacity, had exacerbated the information asymmetry between society on one hand and the state and the private sector on the other – a picture that is changing rapidly; however, the cultural characteristics do not change fast. Turkey's societal culture is defined by large power distance, strong collectivism (low individualism), strong uncertainty avoidance, and femininity. As per the values underpinning these dimensions, note that Turkey is ranked above average in values of conservatism, hierarchy, and harmony. A more recent study of Turkish culture was conducted as a part of the GLOBE study, which highlighted in-group collectivism and power distance as two predominant characteristics of Turkey. Among the 62 cultures surveyed by Kabasakal and Bodur (1998), Turkey ranks below average on gender egalitarianism (56th), uncertainty avoidance (49th), performance orientation (45th), societal collectivism (42nd), humane orientation (37th), and future orientation (36th), whereas it ranks higher in terms of in-group collectivism (4th), power distance (10th), and assertiveness (12th). Future orientation, which is tested as a cultural variable in the study, is related to having long-term perspectives in society and hence can be considered as a proxy of that society's commitment to sustainability (Kabasakal and Dastmalchian, 2001).

The debate of whether effective leadership processes reflect the culture in which they are found continues. As described by Rodrigues in 1990, there exist four leadership styles: *directive, supportive, achievement, and participative.* He concludes that participative leadership style can work everywhere except in those societies with a combination of high power distance, strong collectivism, and high uncertainty avoidance – a combination that applies to Turkey and its neighbours. Among the studies of culture-specific leader attributes, "consultation" and "participation" require further attention, as they are related to the concept of stakeholder involvement. Also, Pasa et al. (2001) found that leaders in Turkey use participation to induce feelings of belonging to the group, rather than to reach consensus or improve the quality of decisions, whereas Ozen (1998) notes a case where consultation emerges as a dominant leadership attribute in a Turkish business organization which is known to adopt Islamic values. Fikret Pasa, Kabasakal, and Bodur (2001) conclude that a leader in the Turkish context emerges as a parent who takes care of the followers' feelings of belonging to the family. One manifestation of this is the "regionalism" fed by local businesses in Turkey. Local businesses seek competitive advantage and legitimacy by involving in and financing community activities (e.g., funding the local soccer team). Fikret-Pasa et al. (2001) further reports that culture-specific behaviour is more dominant in the leadership behaviour of Turkish organizations relative to the universally influenced behaviour of rationalizing and legitimizing (Ararat and Göcenoğlu 2006).

17.3.2 The Tradition of Philanthropy in Turkey

Turkey has a rich and significant philanthropic history. In the Ottoman era, the "waqf" (foundation) was the premier institutional mechanism for philanthropic provision of public services. Waqfs are the common form of philanthropy in the Islamic tradition. Most family-owned conglomerates in Turkey have associated Waqfs. Subsidiaries of parent holdings allocate a percentage of their profits to the foundation for redistribution to social causes. Educational institutions, hospitals, and arts/cultural centres are among the most popular beneficiaries.

Despite the longstanding culture of giving, legal and fiscal frameworks that support corporate philanthropy in Turkey are relatively weak. Maximum 5% (10% for designated foundations in underdeveloped regions) of a company's annual income can be allocated to donations, whereas the average in Europe is around 10%. Furthermore, tax exemption can be granted only for donations made to organizations that are given the "public good" status. Organizations can be granted such status by the Cabinet only if they focus on one of the four areas: *education, health, scientific research, and arts and culture.* Birkmen's (2003) determined that about 200 foundations out of approximately 3,500 private foundations have been classified as serving "public good" in those four areas. Donations made to non-exempt CSOs are not tax deductible. An additional obstacle to corporate philanthropy is the minimum endowment required for establishing a foundation (approximately 200,000 USD). Furthermore, the registration process is complicated and approval takes a long time. These factors serve to deter smaller companies from setting up foundations (Ararat and Göcenoğlu, 2006).

17.4 The Role of Civil Society Gaining Prominence on CSR and Some Samples of Civil Society Activities in Turkey

This situation has led to an increasing demand for the functions of the individual, in addition to that of the state and groups of individuals – and therefore for the functions of NGOs. It has also led to the emergence of individuals and NGOs as more active players in the international arena (TESEV, 2001).

These developments make people living in various countries and in the world at large to be more interested in what is happening in international relations and in foreign policy, and whether the events are close to home or far from it. The major international changes and changes in the global balance have also concentrated on projects and initiatives that will enable the individual and civil society in Turkey to actively participate in these changes. The evolution of concepts such as good business practices in Western countries alongside the development of human rights and environmental protection standards as well as the pressures of international competition brought on by globalizing forces have brought the issue to the agenda in Turkey as well. Tax payment, ILO standards, ISO quality standard, EU consensus application studies, and environmental impact evaluation reports are being adopted in accordance with current national laws. The adoption of these principles can, in turn, be a factor contributing to business competitiveness. For, as companies begin to take on wider social responsibilities, they change their profiles and increase their marketability. This widening responsibility context was pointed out that joint initiatives should be created to facilitate cooperation between the state, the private sector, and the NGO sector and this needs a platform as a mediator from Turkish Volunteers. Under the heading, "Transparency, accountability, and corporate social responsibility", in order for the three sectors to enter into a productive cooperative relationship, transparency and accountability need to be adopted. Currently, even though some Turkish businesses are working to gain the trust of the consumer through improving their corporate image, they do not display an obvious preference for accountability and transparency. The year 2001 witnessed the acceleration of this vocation. We have realized an intensive programme of activities in order to contribute to the public's understanding of major developments and to provide vision and direction based on mainly understanding ethics and political preferences. So must be initiated a project that monitors companies according to the criteria of CSR. Therefore, many organizations and NGOs in Turkey, as well as some universities, have partnered with international and local civil society organizations in numerous joint projects. An overview of this perception demonstrates that they have taken determined steps forward to promote and embody a new understanding of responsibility and social service and are strongly committed to developing this understanding in the coming years (TESEV 2001, 2002a, b).

17.5 EU – Turkey Relations on the Issue of CSR in Turkey

During the December 2004 negotiations between Turkey and the EU, a number of commentators noted that Turkish companies could work more constructively with other organizations such as the government, civil society groups, and even other business actors such as the labour unions and their own suppliers. The 2004 *Regular Report on Turkey's Progress Toward Accession* notes that while Turkey has been doing much to pass the laws needed for her to join the common market "*Turkey needs to address a number of shortcomings in the transposition of some Directives*". In non-bureaucratic language, the "shortcomings in the transposition" refers to the way Turkey companies treat their employees as well as relate to government and the trade unions. Such shortcomings are not simply a Turkish problem, but have been longstanding for other European countries as well. Corporate Social Responsibility – the term under which firms are encouraged to consider the interests of other stakeholders instead of simply shareholders – has become increasingly important. Section 1.13 of the *Acquis Communautaire* relating to social policy and employment evaluates Turkish law (and thus Turkish company compliance) with labour law, equal treatment of women and men, health and safety at work, social dialogue (coordination between government trade union confederations, employers' unions, and the civil servant union), public health, employment policy, social inclusion, social protection, and antidiscrimination (Michael and Öhlund 2005).

From the side of EU Requirements of CSR Perspective, it is known that the European Union's 380 million potential consumers with their €8.5 trillion worth of market demand will represent an important customer base for Turkish companies. Many indications suggest that Turkish companies can compete successfully in this market. The recently released Business Competitiveness Index from the World Economic Forum ranks Turkey as 52nd out of 103 countries. While Turkey ranks below, for example, the Czech Republic (35th) and Hungary (42nd), Turkish businesses are still more competitive than many accession countries such as Romania (56th place), Poland (57th place), or Bulgaria (75th place). A European Commission Green Paper stresses that CSR is important in increasing competitiveness by stating that, "*the experience with investment in environmentally responsible technologies and business practice suggests that going beyond legal compliance can contribute to a company's competitiveness.*" CSR will not only be helpful but will also be necessary. Turkey is working on increasingly harmonizing its legislation in preparation for EU accession. Part of this harmonization entails the adoption of the *Acquis Communautaire* – the legislation that all EU members must share as members of a political and economic union. Yet, according to highly visible groups such as Greenpeace (the international environmental NGO), "*in order to make sense of it and to make it credible to the public, the CSR process itself – even when being voluntary for companies – must go beyond the Acquis Communautaire and other existing national legislation in the EU.*" Also, if Turkey wants to compete in EU markets, it should eventually comply with three types of European Union activities pertaining to CSR (see Table 17.1).

As seen from the table, the first type of activity deals with promoting CSR and encompassing activities such as raising awareness and research. The second type of activity ensures transparency. Environmental labels and certification are examples of such an activity. The third type of activity aims at developing CSR-supportive policies.

Compliance with international conventions represents another important way that both Turkish business and government can consider their stakeholder groups. The Organization of Economic Co-operation and Development (OECD) Guidelines for International Investment and Multinational Enterprises provide concrete operating guidelines for OECD member countries (of which Turkey is one) covering investors (the principle on disclosure), employees (the principle on employment and industrial relations), social and environmental issues (principles on consumer interest and environment), other businesses (principles on competition and science and technology), and the government (principles on taxation and combating bribery). The UN Global Compact provides the guiding framework for company operations within the four areas of human rights, labour, environment, and anti-corruption. The respect of human rights continues to be a point of contention not only between the Turkish government and Brussels, but remains problematic for Turkish businesses who are perceived abroad to gain competitive advantage by not respecting human rights. Turkish labour practice also continues to be a point of contention (Michael and Öhlund 2005).

The Global Compact principles on labour – which are identical to the ILO Declaration on Fundamental Principles and Rights at Work – cover four areas. These areas are freedom of association and right to collective bargaining, elimination of forced and compulsory labour, abolition of child labour, and elimination of discrimination at the workplace. Turkish business, especially in the textile, food, and carpet-making sector, has been widely perceived as violating all four of these elements. Anti-corruption will be a key element of the Global Compact and potential EU accession for Turkey. As given, the main obligations will be compliance with the Copenhagen Criteria, which mandated that accession countries must reduce corruption. The Criteria require *"institutions guaranteeing democracy [and] the rule of law"* and policies that help secure a *"functioning market economy."* More specific guidance on reducing corruption for these countries is given by the *Acquis Communautaire*, which requires the adoption of a number of international conventions making bribery a civil and/or criminal offence in domestic legislation. Compliance with these international requirements can only be done by the Boards of Directors of Turkish companies. Only Turkish directors will have the connections and influence needed to work with high-ranking government officials on a CSR-friendly regulatory environment. And these Boards of Directors will have to know where Turkey is today in order to adopt these requirements (Michael and Öhlund 2005).

CSR is important for business in Europe as shown in Fig. 17.1; human rights issues top the list of issues that companies must respect. Labour rights, as reflected

Table 17.1 CSR Activities in the European Union[a]

Activity	Examples of Countries Engaging in Activity
Promoting CSR	
Awareness raising	Belgium organised a big European conference on CSR in 2001.
Research	The Danish Institute of Social Research monitors CSR developments until 2006 and will publish an annual yearbook with results from the study.
Public-private partnerships	The German Federal Citizenship Responsibility Network promotes co-operation between NGOs, companies and federal governments.
Business incentives	An annual award is given to enterprises promoting health and security at work from the Greek Institute of Hygiene and Security at Work.
Management tools	The Ministry of Labour and Social Affairs in Spain has a programme promoting equal opportunities as a good management strategy for companies, by constructing and implementing action plans.
Ensuring transparency	
Codes	Austrian ministries and enterprises have collaborated in developing a code of conduct for the protection of children from sexual exploitation in travel and tourism.
Reporting	More than 300 Dutch companies are required to submit reports on their environmental performance to the government and the general public.
Labels	NGOs, academics and public officials in the Italian region Emilia Romagna are developing a social quality label which includes responsible production criteria.
Socially responsible investment	The Swedish Public Pension Funds Act requires national pension funds to describe how environmental and ethical considerations are taken into account in their investment activities.
Advertising	Belgian law prohibits misleading advertising concerning effects on the environment.
Developing CSR-supporting policies	
Sustainable development	The German business community has voluntarily signed an agreement with the government promising to follow the Kyoto Protocol guidelines.
Social policies	The Training Place Developer programme aims at increasing opportunities for eastern German companies to provide training.
Environmental policies	Swedish government agencies must integrate environmental management systems and report annually on their progress.
Public procurement	The Belgian government has introduced a social clause for certain federal public procurements, favouring the inclusion of disadvantaged groups.
Fiscal policies	Spain gives tax benefits to NGOs and enterprises which contribute to public interest goals and activities.
Trade and export policies	Most EU countries, including Belgium, France, Germany, and the Netherlands, follow the OECD trade guidelines and inform the business sector about these guidelines.
Development policies	Dutch Ministry of Development Co-operation supports NGOs who aims at raising CSR awareness in developing countries.

[a] As given by Michael and Öhlund (2005) and declared as main source: European Union (2004). Corporate Social Responsibility: National Public Policies in the European Union available at: http://eu.greenpeace.org/downloads/corplia/Green8PosPaperOnCSR.pdf

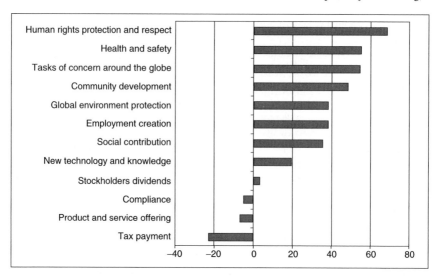

Fig. 17.1 Relative importance of CSR activities in Europe versus non-European countries (*Note*: Non-European countries here apply to Japan and USA. These data take the difference between the percentages of European firms claiming that a particular CSR issue was important from the percentage of non-European firms claiming the issues was important).

by health and safety issues, are considered to be the second most important issue. Moreover, a number of empirical studies suggest that there is a positive correlation between the implementation of CSR activities and firm value.

As indicated earlier, there is a positive and strongly significant correlation between the creation of shareholder wealth and good relations with stakeholders. Companies with good relations with their stakeholders – and companies with CSR activities – create more wealth for their shareholders. Contrary to these, the picture of Turkish CSR is mixed as shown in Table 17.2.

This table shows Turkey's ranking according to several "proxy" CSR measures. The first is the political rights and civil liberties index, which is the CSR measure and in which Turkey has the lowest performance when compared with other countries that have recently acceded into the EU, as well as other EU candidate countries. Turkey is the only country that is regarded as "partly free". The second measure is labour standards, where Turkey also gets the lowest score among the surveyed countries. The third measure, environmental concerns, measured by carbon dioxide emissions per capita, contributes slightly to improve the picture of CSR performance of Turkish business. Turkey has almost the lowest carbon dioxide per capita but not the least of the included countries. Within the Turkish context, the data suggest a qualitative relationship between attention to corporate social responsibility and firm performance.

Attention to CSR could be a signal about managerial quality or about the strength of the relation between the firm and its stakeholders. For example, according to the December 1995 issue of *Capital* magazine, the five Turkish companies with the best reputations – Arçelik, Vestel, Türkcell, Koç/Sabanci, Garanti Bankasi, and

Table 17.2 Turkey's ranking in three CSR measures

	Freedom House PR and CL status	ILO Labour Standards (percentage compliance score for each country)	Carbon dioxide emissions (metric tonnes per capita)
Turkey	Partly tree	59.9%	3.3
Bulgaria	Free	n/a	5.2
Cyprus	Free	n/a	8.5
Czech Republic	Free	84.8%	11.6
Estonia	Free	n/a	11.7
Hungary	Free	90.6%	5.4
Malta	Free	n/a	7.2
Latvia	Free	n/a	2.5
Lithuania	Free	n/a	3.4
Poland	Free	81.7%	7.8
Romania	Free	n/a	3.8
Slovakia	Free	n/a	6.6
Slovenia	Free	n/a	7.3

Source: Freedom House, ILO and UNDP as referred by Michael and Öhlund (2005).

Coca-Cola (Turkish affiliate) – all have some form of CSR programmes. Some scholars argue that CSR promotes "reputational capital" and trust which sustains long-term relationships. Yet, common sense argues that firms that treat workers well get employees who stay longer and ask for lower wages because they get other benefits. Turkish CSR performance with respect to corruption (another key factor of CSR) seems relatively more promising. According to one of the best known indicators, the Transparency International (2004) Corruption Perceptions Index, Turkey is 77th among 145 ranking places in the Index. In comparison to other European countries (a comparison which is important as it represents a yardstick for thinking about Turkish competitive performance in EU markets), Turkish CSR has made important first steps. Human rights, while still worry many, have become much better. Labour standards have improved and environmental protection – while needing further improvement – holds the promise of making the major cities' streets clean. Anti-corruption is being embraced, though business must work with government. Turkish businesses that want to "do CSR" can engage in a number of activities (see Table 17.3). Training represents possibly the most important activity that Turkish directors can undertake to promote CSR. So adoptions of CSR certifications and engagement in socially responsible investment require training, and are the main determined necessities. Turkish business will not respond to CSR unless given incentives by the government. The Turkish parliament will need to play an important role in passing CSR-friendly legislation, and Turkish political parties will need to place the issue on the table. In modern Turkey, NGOs will have a key role to play. Many foreign NGOs are already partnering with Turkish partners to engage in CSR – and some Turkish NGOs have organized activities. Larger membership organizations such as TUSIAD and TOBB (the Union of Chambers and Commodity

Exchanges of Turkey) have sponsored dialogues on CSR, while universities have increasingly worked on merging the academic and policy debates on CSR. Table 17.3 gives further suggestions on the roles of NGOs in improving Turkish companies' competitiveness through CSR.

For presenting the main findings from a survey of the top 50 Turkish companies on the extent to which they evaluate human resources, Turkish NGO involvement will be particularly important as in the EU since the civil sector plays a large role in CSR. NGOs play a large role because people trust NGOs more than other organizations. These NGOs bring CSR issues to the attention of businesses and policymakers by organizing national workshops, policy committees, public–private partnerships, and facilitating donor funding of innovative CSR practices. Without tackling corruption, much of the CSR activity will be either ineffective or less credible. On the anti-corruption aspect of CSR, several measures also have to be taken within Turkish companies. In a countrywide survey by TESEV in 2001, 22% of business people responded that "bribery and corruption" is the most pressing problem in Turkey today. There are two key measures that have to be taken to decrease corruption in Turkish companies. The first measure is cooperation among the corporate sector, the government, and NGOs. Business activity can, for example, be strengthened by increasing the role of TOBB and TUSIAD members in promising not to engage in corruption and reporting corruption when they find it. The second measure will be comprehensive deregulation. Turkey has embarked on a programme of deregulation outside the public sector covering sectors such as telecommunications, banking, gas, and infrastructure as well as increased competition and market openness. Training will also be an important element in any anti-corruption programme. Training programmes for employees on how to comply with international laws that prohibit bribes are a first step. Turkish companies must also implement long-term training strategies to stop corruption and bribery if they want to compete on the European market. Currently, Turkish companies have already started thinking about CSR broadly. While Turkish Boards already have complied with much of the legislation required by the *Acquis Communautaire*, they will need to continue work on provisions regarding environmental protection, customer safety, workers' rights, competition policy, and anti-corruption. Also, such responsibility will involve the way that Turkish companies implement programmes such as triple bottom line reporting, limited stakeholder boards, and consultative bodies with the government, in order to work more responsibly in their business environment (Michael and Öhlund 2005).

In a work on dimensions of CSR policies and practices by Akgeyik (2005), five human resources management (HRM) dimensions of CSR were analyzed: *"To what extent do the companies see the role of HRM in their CSR policies and practices? How do the companies communicate their CSR policies to their stakeholders? To what extent do the companies view the influence of CSR policies and practices on the HRM functions? To what extent do the companies consider the HRM practices from their CSR perspective? What kind of incentives do the companies offer to employees to get involved in CSR activities?"* The sample, including 50 companies, for the survey was drawn from the ICI Annual List of Turkey's 500 Major Industrial

Table 17.3 CSR activities for businesses and key stakeholders of CSR activities for businesses CSR activities for policy makers CSR activities for civil society[a]

CSR Activities for Businesses	CSR Activities for Policy Makers	CSR Activities for Civil Society
Training – companies can learn how to incorporate CSR into strategy, finance, operations, marketing, and human resource management.	**Introduce CSR to main political parties** like AKP, CHP, DYP and HHP. Smaller parties – SP or ANAP – may try to use CSR to get votes!	**Organise fora on CSR** – help government by organising fora and making concrete proposals to parliamentarians and ministers.
Join a CSR membership organisation – Company membership organisations like the Copenhagen Centre or the Business Social Responsibility allow business to "outsource" CSR to an organisation which is competent.	**Vote for tax breaks for CSR activity** – which tax breaks may go against important fiscal policy objectives to raise tax revenue and compliance, they internalise externalities.	**Provide training to companies** – academics and specialists removed from the grind of daily business can provide training and present examples from EU countries.
Adoption of certifications – certifications show potential consumers, investors and others that the company is serious about the communities in which they work. Some examples include the ISO 9000/14000 standards, the Global Reporting Initiative (GRI) guidelines, the Social Accountability 8000 (SA 8000) standard and the AcountAbility 1000 standard.	**"Talk up CSR"** – since Kemal Ataturk, the Turkish government has always been a progressive role in educating the public and preparing it for integration in the world economy. Parliamentarians can educate their constituencies directly and can mandate that the central government provides educational materials,	**Collect data and case studies** – in the EU, NGOs conduct surveys and watch business and government.

Triple Bottom Line Reporting – companies should report not only the financial, but also the social and environmental impacts of their work. In some EU countries, this is becoming a legal obligation.

Stakeholder board committees – putting people such as suppliers, key customers, and evens prominent members of the local community of the Board of Directors can be a way to increase the flow of information to the company.

Socially responsible investment – these companies can refrain from investing in high polluting technologies or in companies which do not respect workers' rights.

Participate in multi-national fora – the EU as a multi-stakeholder forum for CSR and the UN, OECD, World Bank and other organisations are becoming increased involved in CSR.

Establish a department in an existing ministry to work on CSR and/or mandate a CSR ministerial post.

Provide funds to the national governments for CSR grants and rewards to innovative companies.

Host a National CSR norkskop inviting all stakeholders to contribute ideas toward a Turiash CRS law

Source: [as given by Michael and Öhlund (2005), Michael, B., J. Riedmann, and S. Dinler. (2005): Implementing CSR Programmes in Turkish, from 5 European Union (2004). Regular Report on Turkey's progress towards accession; available at: http://europa.eu.int/comm/enlargement/report_2004/pdf/rr_tr_2004_en.pd [a For more on Turkish deregulation, see the *OECD Reviews of Regulatory Reform. Turkey: Crucial Support for Economic Recovery* (Paris: OECD 2002). *http://users.ox.ac.uk/~scat1663/Publications/Turkish%20Insight.pdf*].

Enterprises by revenue as ranked by the Istanbul Chamber of Industry (ICI 2002). The respondent companies ranged in size from having 30 employees to 4,000 employees. The majority of companies were classified as small or medium, with one-quarter having more than 500 employees. Some companies in the sample (35%) have operations in more than one country. Procedure of this survey involved the use of a pre-designed a questionnaire, focus group discussions, and observations. The questionnaire was developed to examine the extent and nature of CSR among the respondent companies. Some of the questions in the research were adapted from various surveys (as given in Zappala and Cronin, 2002).

The questionnaire included 33 questions comprising three sections. The survey was conducted through e-mail. The respondents were assured that there were no right or wrong answers and that the best answer was their own personal opinion. The first section of the questionnaire comprised background questions (e.g., the multinational status of respondents, sectors they operate in, and the primary status of person who completed the questionnaire). While the second section asked questions on the CSR profile of the respondents, the last included a series of questions on the HRM dimensions of CSR.

From the stakeholder approach, if companies are "citizens" then they also have rights, duties, and responsibilities to their stakeholders. In this study, the companies indicate similar reasons. For example, loans, medical care, pension funds, maternity, and safety programmes are CSR activities for the internal stakeholders. The external CSR mainly consists of investment in community outreach, good employee relations, creation and maintenance of employment, environmental stewardship, financial performance, etc.

The findings from the survey present that the companies consult at least one stakeholder when deciding the projects on CSR. In the survey, cooperation with stakeholders in determining the CSR policy is one way that companies can increase acceptance and receptiveness of their CSR practices, and help facilitate their success, when CSR activities are used as a marketing means especially. In the survey, the respondents were asked two questions about the role of HRM on the CSR activities. First, they were asked on the responsibility of HRM in managing and coordinating their CSR projects. The HRM department mostly is the key coordinator unit with respect to the CSR (45%). This was not surprising since the role and influence of HRM has increased especially since the second part of 1990s in Turkish firms. Besides developing and implementing the HRM functions, the department is also responsible for coordinating social activities in the company. It seems that the companies perceive the CSR programs as a sort of social activity. In 30% of the companies, the responsible unit is the public relations department which mostly manages external affairs. Some of the firms see their CSR activities as a part of the marketing function (5%), while in the small companies the primary responsibility rests with the CEO's office. Secondly, the companies were asked about the job description of the professional responsible for the CSR activities in the relevant unit. They mostly indicate that the duties on CSR activities are listed in the formal job description of the responsible professional(s). This shows that they pay attention to their CSR activities. The professional responsible is expected to implement and coordinate the CSR activities. Communicating with employees is a critical issue to improve the performance of the CSR mission.

Another important aspect of an integrated stakeholder approach to CSR is that this communication allows a company to gain additional benefits from their investment including improving their public image, increasing employee morale, and support from the community (Zappala and Cronin, 2002). That is why almost all companies (97%) state that they communicate their CSR policies and activities to their employees. There are several mechanisms of communicating with employees, e.g., e-mail, company newsletters, regular staff meetings, and posters. The fastest way of communication especially in large organizations is through e-mail. The findings of the survey are consistent with that. The main mechanisms are e-mails (65%) and company newsletters (55%). On the other hand, in 45% of firms face-to-face communication is still seen to be a popular and effective form of employee communication. A small number of them use the traditional mechanisms such as posters (25%). In the survey, the respondents were asked to evaluate the HRM functions such as recruitment and training from the CSR perspective. The CSR may increase attractiveness to current and prospective employees. In this survey, the respondents identified CSR as the distinction criterion in their selection process. Sixty-five percent say that the candidates who get involved in CSR activities have an advantage over others *ceteris paribus* (all other things being equal). This perspective is very important since the firms prefer candidates who have participated in CSR programmes, which may lead people to introduce the concept of CSR before entering the labour market. Secondly, the relationship between CSR and training function is a strategic issue, which is confirmed by 70% of the respondents in this survey. In particular, employees are more likely to respond if training programmes incorporate policies, procedures, and systems used in the workplace on how to meet the CSR objectives. The respondents do this mostly for the new employees. During the orientation period, 85% of them train new recruits on their CSR policy and projects. In this way, the new employees perceive the importance of CSR policy in the first stage. On the other hand, data show that the companies also ask their new recruits about their interests on the CSR (70%), and whether they prefer to take part in volunteer activities (90%). In this way, the firms use the orientation programme to analyse the CSR profile of new staff (Akgeyik 2005).

However, seeing CSR projects as a way to improve their public image and reputation, the companies largely (75%) identify the public opinion as the most important source in formulating their CSR policy. There are some evaluation methods. Mostly benchmarking, social auditing, and self-reporting are used by companies. Another aspect of evaluating CSR activities is whether companies measure the effectiveness of CSR for the particular stakeholder groups (Zappala and Cronin, 2002). In their research, the results suggest that 80% of the respondents indicate as having a formal policy for evaluating the effectiveness of CSR activities. According to the data, the companies, assessing their CSR activities, utilize the methods of public image survey, customer satisfaction survey, and return on investment (ROI). As a result, the firms mostly consider that the impacts of CSR activities are more easily monitored by the external stakeholders such as community and customers.

In the survey, the respondent companies were asked to list the types of their CSR activities. Sponsorships and student scholarships are the most popular CSR projects. Since for companies the main motivation of CSR is to improve their public image, it is not surprising that most CSR activities are sponsorship projects. Secondly, there has always been a strong tradition of charity in the Turkish society, which contributes to a solid foundation of volunteerism. Most foundations and institutions provide funds for students. The results of this survey are consistent with that. It may be concluded that the companies, measuring the effectiveness of CSR activities, place more importance on them. Evaluating CSR practices allow companies to assess the costs and benefits of any CSR program, which is a critical indicator for expansion by the respondent companies as the most popular second CSR activity (65%). Also another important aspect of the charitable tradition is the strong relationship between companies and the NGOs. It is known that in Turkey there are many charitable organizations managing their activities by the donations of corporations. One of these organizations is the Private Sector Volunteers Association (OSGD) that was formed in 2002 to bring together concerned companies and professionals interested in CSR activities.

Overall, the community expectations, changing social values, and public opinion are the basic causes of engaging in CSR activities. The building of good relationship with the surrounding community and employees is another motivation for the CSR programmes. Consequently, 95% of the respondents point out that financial benefit is not the primary reason for the CSR programs, which means that they consider the long-term advantages instead of the short-term financial gains. In Turkey (mainly in Istanbul) art festivals are mostly organized through the sponsorship of the private sector. Also, during the past years there has been a growing tendency among the Turkish companies to increase their sponsorship (Akgeyik, 2005).

Responsible organizations consider social and environmental activities as priority actions and therefore contributing to their economic success with documented and CSR database. Businesses are taking steps to answer to the needs of their workers, suppliers, and the society that they are a part of and making a positive impact more seriously, while they provide for their customers as a part of their activities. Today, CSR activities are defined as the positive contribution business will have on the society and stakeholders in the context of "corporate citizenship" rather than the change in an activity or a product. The main component of this initiative is to support Turkish business organizations that practice CSR activities and encourage others in a similar framework. It aims at widening the CSR implementation by raising public awareness and showing what can be accomplished by new working methods in order to establish CSR cooperations between the business world and stakeholders. The database aims to share the success stories and best practices in order to support the Turkish business in complying with the EU environmental *Acquis* by promoting environmentally friendly management/production methods. The database will be using an on-line data entry platform made up of various questions in order to allow businesses to share their responsible practices and projects. On the other hand, users will be able to search the database for projects, businesses, and/or CSR activities. The information on the database will be systematically shared with other stakeholders in order to develop a feeling of responsibility of the business world concerning urgent environmental issues (governments, NGOs, etc.) of the country. With the permission of the businesses, the responsible practices and/or CSR projects will be systematically shared with the media in order to promote these businesses. This will be an inspiration for other businesses to start implementing CSR activities.

Also, Ararat and Göcenoğlu (2006) worked on summarizing the roles of economy, state, and the society in Turkey with respect to the society's attitude toward business, and attempted to explore how cultural characteristics of the society may have an impact on corporate behaviour. Their argument was that the cultural characteristics combined with the economic fundamentals of Turkey did not encourage the socially responsible behaviour of corporations as demonstrated by opacity and corrupt practices. They further explained that the EU accession process and macroeconomic stability achieved under IMF conditionality opened up Turkey to intensified interaction with global institutions perpetuating international values and practices. They also concluded that the drivers for CSR in Turkey and in countries with similar cultural characteristics and economic fundamentals would be exogenous and institutional rather than endogenous and cultural. In the summary of this study, 68% of the companies did not recognize any of the stakeholders explicitly mentioned by the CMB. These findings can be cross-checked by the companies' disclosed method of stakeholder involvement, and these were as follows: six companies declare that no methods or instruments are used for stakeholder involvement; five companies refer to "law" as providing the framework for stakeholder involvement; and three companies mention departmental meetings as a means to encourage stakeholder participation. These findings suggest that recognition of a "stakeholder" does not necessarily imply acceptance of stakeholders' involvement in company affairs, supporting our argument that the concept of stakeholder is not well understood by Turkish companies. The high level of ownership concentration in Turkey positions the controlling shareholders as the "owners" of the companies. The concept of shareholder is usually associated with minority shareholders. The fact that none of the other companies mentions shareholders as a stakeholder demonstrates the insignificance of the role minority shareholders and institutional investors play in the market. Hofstede's work reveals similarities between cultural dimensions of the Middle Eastern countries as given by researchers. In his studies of 53 countries, Turkey, Arab countries (Egypt, Lebanon, Libya, Kuwait, Iraq, Saudi Arabia, and UAE), and Iran score comparably, whereas Israel deviates in two dimensions from the others. Hofstede formulates the value dimensions in three matrices: (1) *Power distance versus individualism*, (2) *Power distance versus uncertainty avoidance*, (3) *Uncertainty avoidance versus masculinity*. Turkey, Iran, and Arab countries are positioned in the same quadrant in all three matrices with high Power Distance Index (PDI), low Individualism Index (IDV), low Masculinity Index (MAS), and high Uncertainty Avoidance Index (UAI) values compared to other countries in Tables 17.4 and 17.5 (Ararat and Göcenoğlu 2006).

As can be seen from the list, none of the projects that was recognized by the jury was related to the actual business of the corporations. They can all be categorized as philanthropy or corporate giving at best and they fall under the public

Table 17.4 Comparative scores[a] of PDI, IDV, MAS, UAI and LTOI rank

Country	Power Distance Index(PDI)	Individualism Index(IDV)	Masculinity Index(MAS)	Uncertainty Avoidance Index(UAI)	Long Term Orientation Index(LTOI)
Arab Countrie	80 (7)	38 (26)	53 (23)	68 (27)	
Turkey	66 (18)	37 (28)	45 (32)	85 (16)	(36)
Iran	58 (29)	41 (24)	43 (35)	59 (31)	
Israel	13 (52)	54 (19)	47 (29)	81 (19)	

[a]Scores of PDI, IDV, MAS and UAI (out of 100) and rank (out of 53), constructed from Hofstede (1991)), LTOI rank out of 62 from Kabasakal and Bodur (1998).

Table 17.5 Registered CSOs' area of activity[a,b]

Activity Area	Number of CSOs
Clubs	952
Rights and Freedom	162
Human Rights	138
Special interest and solidarity	21618
Turkish Aeronautical Association	575
Sports	9372
Environment	1355
Religious Support	14364
Agriculture	761
Human Rights	138

[a]*Source Civil Society Development Program's Web site (www.stgp.org) as given by Ararat and Göcenoğlu (2006).*

[b]*Some of the CSR awards given by a business magazine explain the focus and nature of CSR initiatives in Turkey. The top 10 CSR projects that were recognized by a jury composed of business representatives, experts, academicians, and the press in 2005 were as follows (Ararat and Göcenoğlu (2006) :*

1. *Eczacibasi Group pioneered establishment of a "Modern Art Museum" in Istanbul, the very first in Turkey*
2. *Kagider (Women Entrepreneurs Association) has set up a fund to finance small enterprises and civil society organizations initiated by Anatolian women*
3. *Show TV, a privately owned TV channel, has sponsored a project to build schools in rural areas and provide scholarships to students*
4. *TOBB (Turkish Chambers of Industry and Commerce) set up a foundation which established a modern University in Ankara*
5. *Yapi Kredi Pension Fun sponsored a project to protect genetic sources of and commercial cultivation of Turkish saffron plant*
6. *Mercedes-Benz Turk, initiated and sponsored a project to financially support girls' vocational education in less developed regions of Turkey*
7. *Garanti Bank, in cooperation with the World Wildlife Foundation, sponsored a project to protect the wild life in Kure Mountains*
8. *Procter & Gamble sponsored a project to help children with puberty problems*
9. *Turkish Banking Association financed procurement of medical equipment by health centres that are used in health care of premature babies*
10. *Pfizer sponsored a project called "Social Teams" to support civil society initiatives*

relations activities regardless of the decision makers' motives. The fact that supporting education seems to be the preferred choice of the corporations, one may conclude that the Turkish society expects the corporations to support education and these projects contribute more to the brand value. Other stakeholder-based views of CSR abound, such as Professor Michael Hopkins' which defines CSR as "*concerned with treating the stakeholders of the firm ethically or in a socially responsible manner*". Stakeholders exist both within a firm and outside. A number of Turkish companies are already practicing some form of CSR. Through Turkcell's programme – "Contemporary Girls of Contemporary Turkey" – which provides scholarships to girls in Eastern Anatolia, Türkcell seeks to alleviate the budgetary burden on local government, improve the welfare of future generations, and contribute to the wider business community through a more educated workforce. Ülker's contribution to the "10 Billion Oak Tree Campaign" considers stakeholders such as local communities and the environment itself. Often, these programmes work in collaboration with the current government. Government is one of the most important stakeholders – especially in the Turkish context, and participation is through quasi-public institutions, such as business associations and the trade. While these interactions have sometimes been nurturing, sometimes they have involved the solicitation of "the use of public power for private gain" (corruption). Corruption "is one of the most serious obstacles to Turkey's accession" according to an unnamed official at Transparency International, an international NGO dedicated to fighting corruption. Some of these examples of corruption are summarized in the following for clearly pointing to broader problems with the systems by which Turkish companies are responsible to their stakeholders (including the government). Such responsibility entails more than philanthropic contributions – which Turkish firms do make. Instead, such responsibility will involve the way that Turkish companies implement programmes such as triple bottom line reporting, limited stakeholder boards, and consultative bodies with the government, in order to work more responsibly in their business environment. The Turkish government will need to pass through parliament legislations providing positive incentives for the CSR work undertaken by Turkish business. Turkish NGOs will need to conduct surveys, present CSR projects, and monitor both government and business responses to these initiatives. Therefore, the urge to provide higher standards of living, while preserving the profitability of the corporation, for its stakeholders both within and outside the corporation appears to be the main important handicap for its applications (Michael and Öhlund 2005).

17.6 Legal and Regulatory Instruments

A credible government's attempt to promote CSR was undertaken by the Capital Markets Board of Turkey (CMBT) by recognizing stakeholders as legitimate parties in the governance of companies as stipulated in its Corporate Governance Guidelines (OECD 2003). A stakeholder is defined as "*any person, entity or party who has an interest in the operations of the company and achievement of its targets*".

The guidelines list *"employees, creditors, customers, suppliers, trade unions, various non-governmental organizations and potential investors"* as examples of stakeholders. Listed companies in the ISE are mandated to implement the principles listed in the guidelines or explain in their annual reports why they have not complied and what measures they have taken to improve their compliance. The guidelines suggest companies to recognize that *"cooperation with the stakeholders will be advantageous for the companies in the long term"* and include a "Stakeholders" section with recommendations under seven headings (Ararat and Göcenoğlu 2006):

1. *Protecting the interests of the stakeholders and respecting their legal rights*

The corporate governance practices of the company must protect and guarantee the rights of the stakeholders, whether they are safeguarded by legislation or not.

2. *Participation of stakeholders in company management*

Mechanisms and models that are supportive of the participation of stakeholders, mainly of the company employees, in the company management, must be encouraged.

3. *Protection of company assets*
4. *Human Resources Policy*

Measures must be taken to prevent race, religion, language, and sex discrimination among the employees, to respect the human rights, and to protect the employees against physical, spiritual and emotional mistreatments. Furthermore, in order to ensure a participative working environment, informative meetings must be organized with the employees on the subjects like the company's financial opportunities, wage, career, training, and health where opinions can be exchanged.

5. *Customers and suppliers*

All measures must be taken to ensure customer satisfaction in marketing and sales of goods and services.

6. *Code of ethics*

Operations of the company must be executed within the framework of ethical rules, which are developed by the Board of Directors, announced and approved in the general shareholders meeting, and disclosed to the public. Practices regarding how these rules are implemented must also be publicly disclosed.

7. *Social responsibility*

The company must be sensitive towards its social responsibilities: compliance with the regulations and ethical rules regarding the environment, consumer protection, and public health, and disclosure of its policies to public (Ararat and Göcenoğlu 2006).

17.7 Some Practices of CSR in Turkey

CSR is high on the agenda for major foreign corporations with a presence in Turkey. At least a dozen different companies continuously donate funds and supplies, provide volunteers and more for the environment, education, and the arts as well as provide critical support during times of crisis in Turkey.

17.7.1 TESEV's Project Activities on CSR

During the first year of operation in 2000, TESEV set a project and agenda for the public opinion, which aroused a great deal of interest and contributed to the process of public policy making. The project was designed to be completed in three phases. Its purpose, on one hand, was to understand the inter-relationships between corruption and households, businesses and the public sector; and on the other, to analyze corruption in each of these arenas separately. The Corruption Project was prepared under modules that would take into account Turkey's special conditions and which would take appropriate procedures for each of the three phases. Thus, this research differs from similar projects conducted by the World Bank in several countries. The first phase was a field survey based on a sample representing the urban voting population. The second phase examined one representing a sample of business actors. In the third phase the objective is to understand the place of bureaucracy within corrupt networks – an analysis that will be conducted with the aid of the findings of the first two surveys (TESEV 2001). The European Commission meeting at Lisbon, in March 2000, saw the designation of a strategic goal for the European Union in the same direction: to create the most competitive and dynamic information society in the globe, which would create more and better job opportunities for the employees, and being capable of sustainable economic development that will contribute to social integration. After this call to companies to be sensitive to social issues, the Commission published a Green Paper, on July 18, 2001, in order to open a debate on the concept of CSR, a cause deemed to be in accordance with the objectives of the European Union (TESEV 2001).

According to the household first phase of the survey, which had face-to-face interviews with 3,021 people representing the Turkish population over 18 years old living within municipal limits across around Turkey, the results were publicized on February 27, 2001 (www.TESEV.org.tr). The second phase of research concerning the private sector was conducted through face-to-face interviews with business owners or top executives of 1,220 companies active in six sectors (industry, construction, trade, transport and communication, finance, self-employment, and services). In the coming years TESEV is to spearhead a project monitoring the performance of public administration policies regarding corruption. For this purpose the TESEV-led Corruption Watch Committee – with the participation of DİSK, Hak-İş, Arı Group, TÜSİAD, and TOBB – has begun its work. TESEV intends to contribute through annual public opinion surveys to be conducted, once again, with the support of

World Bank. With regard to the third scheduled phase of research, field research with members of the bureaucracy will continue with the full permission and cooperation of the government. Meanwhile, the project team has begun its work for this third phase.

The first step of the project was a brainstorming meeting that saw wide participation from NGOs, trade unions, business people, and experts. The wider responsibilities of the private sector and partnership between sectors were discussed (TESEV 2001).

17.7.2 Some of the Other Related Projects

The most important other samples of these applications are given below by using documents of TAIK (2007):

BP Turkey. BP Turkey, which received a Chairman's Commendation Award for its initiatives during the earthquake in 1999, has a long history of social investment in Turkey. BP Turkey, in cooperation with the Photography Societies Work Group, published a photo album titled "Turkey 1992" in memory of the master photographer Sami Güler. The album, which contains the works of 132 Turkish photographers, also contributed to the promotion of Turkey in foreign countries. In cooperation with the Plastic Arts Society, BP Turkey ensured the participation of Hülya Botasagun from Turkey along with 12 artists from Europe in the "Public Art Project" held in 1993 in Spain. As part of this project, the artists created permanent works of art in an open area in Castellon, Spain. In terms of environmental activities, BP Turkey helped in the protection of crested pelicans that are becoming extinct in Turkey, in 1994. In the same year, the company assisted Young Turkish and Azeri Artists. In the following year, as a new year's gift, BP Turkey planted 30,000 saplings in Sile Green Valley, which is one of the fire-eaten forests of Turkey, in cooperation with the Foundation for the Protection and Promotion of the Environmental and Cultural Heritage (ÇEKÜL), for which it received many domestic and foreign awards. BP Turkey presented wheelchairs to handicapped children with the guidance of the Turkish Confederation of the Handicapped. BP made a step towards ensuring child safety in traffic by giving support to the "Traffic Training Program" of the Education Volunteers Foundation of Turkey aimed at primary school children. In that context, training CD-ROMs were prepared for primary school students. In 1998, BP Turkey in cooperation with the Police Headquarters Traffic Services Department set up a mobile theatre team to teach traffic rules through entertainment to 180,000 students in more than 500 primary schools. The children's play that taught traffic rules to students in all tent cities following the earthquake disaster on August 17, 1999 was organized in Izmir, Aydin, and Mersin as well as in Istanbul. The play on road safety continues to teach traffic rules to the first and second grade primary school students in Istanbul. In 2000, BP Turkey decided to give support to an important social issue following the earthquake disaster by building a primary school in the earthquake zone in cooperation with the Society for Supporting Modern Life.

The Düzce Cumhuriyet primary school which will educate 1,500 students is the first steel structure built in the earthquake area. BP Turkey became a sponsor for the education campaign held by the Education Volunteers Foundation of Turkey and NTV, MSNBC and provided 1 trillion TL financial resources for the educational activities of the foundation. BP Turkey, in cooperation with the Society for the Protection of Natural Life, incorporated photographs of bulbed plants in 2002 calendars to promote these plants in the society and to help prevent their extinction.

Coca-Cola. The Coca-Cola system in Turkey supported the "All Girls Go to School (Haydi Kizlar Okula)" campaign launched by the Ministry of Education and UNICEF in 2003. The company donated $250,000 for school materials for girls in 10 provinces and utilized the *Rock'n Coke Festival* as a platform to raise additional funds. During 2002 and 2003, Coca-Cola Turkey donated 80,000 books and libraries to 400 schools. Following the earthquake of August 1999, the Coca-Cola Company joined with many others to provide relief. Among the Company's initiatives was the rebuilding of Sakarya University Vocational Training School, which reopened in November 2001. In Turkey, local townspeople and emergency-relief workers recovering from the devastating earthquake in Izmit received bottled water, blankets, and other supplies through Coca-Cola delivery trucks. The Coca-Cola system's plant in Ankara, Turkey, is playing a central role in helping to bring European Union funds to the country. The project was created by Turkey's Ministry of Labour to improve the health conditions and safety standards in the country's workplaces. Under the programme, 21 laboratories would help train workers in order to decrease the large number of workplace accidents. For example, there were 74,847 job-related accidents in 2000 around the country. The Turkish government provided 10% of the funds for the project. Then the Minister of Labour, Yasar Okuyan, appealed to Brussels – the seat of the European Union – for the additional funds. When the EU experts asked for a workplace in Turkey that could be shown as a model, the ministry officials pointed out Coca-Cola's Ankara plant as a success story. EU officials who toured the Ankara plant were so impressed that they decided to provide 7 million euros, or just over $7 million – well above the project's goal. The plant is one of 36 in the company's system worldwide that has received the Coca-Cola Quality Systems award. Four of the five plants in Turkey have received this award, making Turkey the country with the most awards in the world. *The Quality Systems awards program*, started in 1998, promotes greater productivity, lower costs, and constant increases in quality guarantees at Coca-Cola plants worldwide. The EU's decision and the high-quality work are a great source of pride to the Operations Director of Coca-Cola Bottlers of Turkey. They explained their policy as follows: "We owe our success to teamwork and the commitment of our employees to quality at all levels."

Lafarge Turkey. Lafarge Turkey provided help in the Izmit earthquake area with their vehicles, equipment, and employee support, all coordinated by the Lafarge Turkey Crisis Committee. Aid teams reached more than 1,100 children in these places, where "the life units" provided by Lafarge were put into use at local hospitals and other institutions. Moreover, Lafarge contributed to the construction of the Gölcük Hospital and the Düzce Student Dormitory. Alongside these activities, Lafarge Turkey participated in the preparation of a children's book giving necessary and useful information on earthquakes. Lafarge Turkey also provided aid to employees who suffered damage to their homes, to Lokman Hekim Saglik Vakfi (Healthcare Foundation), for a special crisis dispatch center, and for the repairs to the Lafarge Aslan Cimento Technical High School, and contributed to the building of a primary school in Akyazi, a village of prefabricated houses in Degirmendere. After the earthquake disaster in Turkey in 1999, the help provided (including a financial donation of US$ 250,000, among others) contributed to the restoration and the recovery of the country after this natural disaster. On its 10th anniversary, Lafarge Turkey built a memorial forest near Gebze, where more than 4,000 trees were planted. The project aims to protect the natural environment, in cooperation with the Regional Forestry Department. It is also a way for Lafarge to develop national and regional stakeholder relationships by emphasizing its environmental commitment. It also wishes to increase the environmental awareness and motivation of the employees by involving them in the planting activities. Lafarge Turkey planted 4,000 trees. All employees (around 1,500 people) were granted with a certificate symbolizing a planted tree. With other plantation programmes in and around the plants and other areas in cooperation with local institutions and schools, more than 15,000 trees have been planted in order to improve environmental awareness. A sum of €15,000 was awarded to the Fethiye Friends of Animals Association from Turkey. The organization provided a proposal relating to mass "neuter and return" programs for dogs. Such schemes have demonstrated value in reducing and controlling stray dogs, improving the general health of the dogs, and changing the attitudes of municipal authorities and people within local communities toward the management and treatment of stray dog popuations.

Proctor & Gamble (P&G). P&G co-sponsored Turkey's first Sustainable Development Congress for the Business World, in cooperation with TEMA (the Turkish Foundation for Combating Soil Erosion, for Reforestation and the Protection of Natural Habitats) and TOBB. The Congress was aimed at accelerating sustainable development action initiated by the Turkish business community and providing understanding that allows the business community to broaden its activity. In addition to speakers from P&G, TEMA, and TOBB, there were speakers from the State Planning Organization DPT, the United Nations Development Program, the World Business Council for Sustainable Development, Shell, the Turkish LP gas company Aygaz, the European Commission, the World Bank, and the Turkish Ethical Values Center. In the audience were local and national regulatory officials, academicians, and NGOs. P&G made two presentations at the Congress, one on the role of business in the twenty-first century in sustainable development, and another giving examples of P&G Turkey's local sustainability projects. P&G also participated in a panel discussion on the future of sustainable development in Turkey and what needs to be done. Procter & Gamble the giant of the Fast Moving Consumer Goods sector, has to date distributed more than 500 million litres of clean drinking water in ten countries within the scope of its Children's Safe Drinking Water corporate social responsibility project. Over the last 20 years, The Body Shop has collected around five million signatures to protest against the use of animals in experimental tests (Fırat 2007).

RWE Thames Water. RWE Thames Water in Turkey is actively involved in education, arts, sports, healthy living and public awareness. The company works with local schools and higher education institutions to promote key skills development and foster learning. In a city where education has become a luxury, especially after the devastating 1999 earthquake, RWE Thames Water and its local partner Izmit Su funded scholarships for 20 university students. In addition, cultural activities being very important to the local community, the company seeks to reflect their diverse interests by supporting a wide range of local arts activities. RWE Thames Water gives financial support to the Kocaeli Municipality Conservatories, which supports local arts and artists, and has contributed to the Izmit and Anatolian Turkish Theatres. The company also actively works with local communities to promote a healthy lifestyle and sponsors the Yuvacik Female Athletics team. With the help of Thames' support, the team has won many national awards and is now competing in international tournaments. In the aftermath of the earthquake, statutory funding was limited for sporting activities, so Thames increased its support of local teams, in particular the Kocaeli National Soccer team.

GAP sells T-shirts made from African cotton and it sends half of the revenue from each T-shirt to charity helping Africans suffering from AIDS. When it comes to Turkey, there are tens of companies that are aware of the concept of social responsibility and are working on this subject actively. By investing 6.6 million euros in this field, SabancıHolding is one of them. The holding has been chosen the best in Turkey in the field of social responsibility by the survey "The leaders of social responsibility in Turkey" (Fırat 2007).

Some holdings as well as Koç, Sabanci, Eczacibasi, etc., or some Turkish Banks and other sectional organizations, and also NGOs (e.g., No-GMO's Platform, TUKODER, KIZILAY) are still active in some of national CSR applications. We have given some samples of these activities.

17.8 Conclusion

Solidarity is a key factor in Turkish culture. Individual actions of responsibility have always existed in the daily life of Turkish people such as the concepts of friendly neighborhood and citizenry. However, an organized and systematic activism has not been quite well established. It was not well organized as large-scale social applications should. Aside from the governmental efforts on social responsibility and some distinctive exceptions, a network of civil society, NGOs and corporate-based organizations are new concepts for Turkey.

Traditionally, Turkish culture is based on the concept of "mass behaviour", which eliminates individualism and enables people to take action for others out of concern. In that sense, with the ongoing impact of religion and traditions on Turkish people's daily life, the interest to the less fortunate ones, or a loss of balance in social or economic relations has become a centre of attention. Also, personal applications are well established on an individual scale, but institutional and social performance is not well established yet. The main reason of this structural difference is the incomplete dialogues between the governmental side and NGOs and also the weak interactive relations. Also, Turkey has long been characterized by a duality and/or gap between the civil society on the one hand, and the state on the other. The crucial point here is that state control limits the full functionality of the civil society, and, therefore, one could argue that an arbitrary state control renders the very existence of a civil society less functional. There is a direct correlation, from a liberal perspective, between the weakness of a civil society, on the one hand, and the continuing progress towards democracy in Turkey on the other. In other words, state interference in the civil society would be limited only to the resolution of conflicts that arise within civil society, thereby safeguarding the existence and integrity of the civil society.

NGO activities in Turkey face internal and external limitations. In general, Turkish NGOs do not have a leadership model and need assistance in developing management capacity. In addition to this, the most important internal challenge is management quality. The Education Volunteers initially lacked a defined and systematic format, but efforts to professionalize have resulted in significant improvement in the group's performance. According to other basic points, NGOs must have links to outside resources, but they must also be independent in certain areas. Furthermore, existing laws impede cooperation between NGOs. To devote a full life for voluntary work in NGOs is to improve the quality of life in communities in a local, national, and global sense for feeling CSR. Article 18 of the U.N. Declaration on Human Rights Defenders 45 states: "*Individuals, groups, institutions and non-governmental organizations have an important role to play and a responsibility in safeguarding democracy, promoting human rights and fundamental freedoms and contributing to the promotion and advancement of democratic societies, institutions and processes. Individuals, groups, institutions and non-governmental organizations also have an important role and a responsibility in contributing, as appropriate, to the promotion of the right of everyone to a social and international order in which the rights and freedoms set forth in the Universal Declaration of Human Rights and other human rights instruments can be fully realized.*" The alternative voice raised by civil society is not yet fully accepted as legitimate in Turkey. According to "Accession Partnership Recommendation of NGOs" "*the constructive function of NGOs in raising human rights awareness should be encouraged and there should be closer cooperation and communication with them,*" but these documents make no explicit provisions for public government. NGOs must negotiate a formidable succession of legal obstacles to their activities (Anon. 1998).

In Turkey, the organization of civil society has traditionally lagged far behind the official governmental organization – ever since the imperial period – in terms of the interests expressed, the functions carried out, and even the timing involved in the appearance of organizations. The main reason why civil society has not developed to a level of full functionality is that there is a noteworthy lack of Turkish businesses that have taken a leadership role in promoting better business practices. Nevertheless, the pressures of international competition, brought about by globalizing forces, have brought the issue to the agenda in Turkey as well. The adoption of these principles can be, in turn, a factor in contributing to business competitiveness. For, as companies begin to take on wider social responsibilities, they change their profiles and increase their marketability (Karaman and Aras 2000).

From a management perspective it can be concluded that if one compares the private sector, the state, and NGOs, it is apparent that the state is not yet prepared to embark on what promises to be a long road to cooperation among the three sectors. In effect, the organizational culture needs to change. Greater self-awareness and clearer understanding of purpose could make the road shorter. In addition *"owner-ship of corporate shares is not widespread with most Turkish companies still under family control. With newly emerging institutionalization, companies do not have a tradition of giving an account of themselves to their stakeholders. As corollary, those that are influenced by the companies lack the tradition of holding them accountable for performance and /or non-performance on social issues."* (TESEV 2003)

But now it is growing well and better than before. The most important examples of growing CSR applications in Turkey started in the recent past. Currently we are experiencing a very remarkable example of a mass movement in "Walks for the Republic" series, which may be considered as an awakening movement for some authorities as organized by only civic initiative. The most interesting point here is the cosmopolitan character – as a mosaic – of these movements. People from very different backgrounds, ages, organizations, and from different political perspectives with very different areas of concern come together to protest against the present government for a better administration and claiming the Republic's basic units and also Ataturk's principles as before. These protests were really the biggest and the most meaningful social responsibility performance example since "independence war" and "establishment of Turkish Republic period (1918–1922)".

The participation of civil the society in decision-making mechanisms has increased tremendously in parallel with the rising importance of social responsibility policies in the international arena in the last decades. European Union, too, develops and implements policies to engage NGOs in different levels of the decision-making processes with the EU mechanisms and those of its member countries. In addition, it fosters candidate countries to strengthen civil society involvement in policymaking.

As a consequence of Turkey's becoming an applicant country, EU has set forth its expectations from Turkey on the issue and therefore Turkey has gone into a complicated search of identity on issues to improve the engagement with social responsibility projects. In fact, this search need not be so complicated. We are headed towards a global role and must therefore accept the responsibilities involved. Turkey will need to engage in some CSR activity if it hopes to successfully compete in EU markets. However, Turkey should not simply follow EU laws or react to international trends in CSR. Turkey has already demonstrated leadership in some areas of CSR and can provide the EU the best practice if it can coordinate its own business, government, and NGOs (Midillili 2000).

In order for the three sectors (the government, NGOs, and corporations) to enter into a productive cooperative relationship, transparency and accountability need to be adopted. In the context of this widening responsibility, a platform for joint initiatives should be created to facilitate cooperation between the state, the private sector, and the NGO sector. In modern Turkey, NGOs will have a key role to play in bringing CSR issues to the attention of businesses and policymakers. Moreover, the reforms need to be tailored for each country in view of their specific conditions. The point remains, nevertheless, that change is both desirable and necessary. The region has enormous potential, but this cannot be realized without a concerted and cooperative reform effort by all by ensuring the active support of participants so that the project might succeed in its goal of showing the Turkish society that the future lies is in its own hands and that all initiatives cannot be expected to come from the state (TESEV 2001).

References

Akgeyik T. 2005. "The human resource management dimensions of corporate social responsibility in Turkey: a survey". *Journal of the Academy of Business and Economics, Jan, 1, 2005.* [Business enterprises, Corporate social responsibility (- Surveys). Product: Venture Analysis: Turkey Saturday, January 1; 2005.] *http://www.allbusiness.com/management-companies-enterprises/ 1186166–10.html, http://www.allbusiness.com/management-companies-enterprises/1186166– 1.html* 20. Turkey Social Responsibility in A State-Dependent Business System

Anon. 1998. *Milliyet* newspaper, 14 May 1998. *http://www.milliyet.com.tr. arsiv.htm*

Ararat M, and Göcenoğlu C. 2006. "Drivers for Sustainable Corporate Responsibility, Case of Turkey" (April 2006). Available at SSRN: Sabanci University – Corporate Governance Forum April 2006. *http://ssrn.com/abstract = 965136, http://papers.ssrn.com/sol3/ papers.cfm?abstract_id = 965136*

Ararat M, and Ugur M. 2003. Corporate governance in Turkey: an overview and some policy recommendations. Corporate Governance; 3, (1) 58 – 75. ISSN: 1472–0701. Pub. by MCB UP Ltd.

Birkmen, F. 2003. Corporate philanthropy in Turkey: Building on Tradition, Adapting to Change, www.tusev.org

Fikret Pasa, [1]Department of Management, Bogaziçi University, Istanbul, Turkey S., Kabasakal, [1]Department of Management, Bogaziçi University, Istanbul, TurkeyH. and Bodur, [1]Department of Management, Bogaziçi University, Istanbul, TurkeyM. (2001). Society, Organisations, and Leadership in Turkey, Applied Psychology 50 (4), 559–589

Fırat E. 2007. "The Leaders in Social Responsibility in Turkey". Capital, 1 Nisan 2007. *http://www.capital.com.tr/haber.aspx?HBR_KOD = 4120*

ICI, 2002. ICI Annual List of Turkey's 500 Major Industrial Enterprises by revenue as ranked by the Istanbul Chamber of Industry. *http://kutuphane.iso.org.tr/web/catalog/results.php?lst = 1*

Kabasakal H, and Bodur M. 1998. "Leadership, values and institutions: the case of Turkey", paper presented at Western Academy of Management Conference, Bogazici University, Istanbul, research paper. *www.emeraldinsight.com/ . . . /published/emeraldfulltextarticle/ pdf/0500220302_ref.html*

Karaman ML, and Aras B. 2000. "The Crisis of Civil Society in Turkey. "*Journal of Economic and Social Research 2, (2),* 45–50.

Michael B, and Öhlund E. 2005. The Role of Social Responsibility in Turkey's EU Accession. *Appearing in Insight Turkey.* Oxford Business Knowledge, *January–March.*

Michael B, Riedmann J, Dinler S. 2005. "Implementing CSR programmes in Turkish companies: how to do it and why". *Eldis Document Store,* "Corporate Social Responsibility in Turkey". *http://www.tesev.org.tr/temmuz/jul3.html, http://findarticles.com/p/articles/ mi_m0OGT/is_1_5/ai_n16619645*

Midillili A. 2000. "Governance In Search Of An Identity" *http://www.elegans.com.tr/arsiv/ 51/sonbahar2000/html/036.htm*, *http://www.csrturkey.org/*, *http://www.c-s-p.org/Flyers/ Globalization-and-Social-Responsibility.html*

OECD, 2003. Survey of Corporate Governance Developments in OECD Countries. 10-Dec-2003. *www.oecd.org/document/49/0,3343,en_2649_37439.*

Ozen, C. 1998. Neo-functionalism and the change in Dynamism Turkey-European Union Relations, Perceptions: *Journal of International Affairs*, September–November 1998, Vol. III, No. 3, pp. 34–57.

TAIK, 2007. Focus On Corporate Social Responsibility in Turkey. TAIK- Turkish – U.S. Business Council (Türk- Amerikan IŞ Konseyi). *http://www.turkey-now.org/default.aspx?pgID = 401*

TESEV, 2001. *Turkish Economic and Social Studies Foundation.* (Türkiye Ekonomik ve Sosyal Etüdler Vakfı) *http://www.tesev.org.tr/ekim01/e3.html*), (*http://www.tesev.org.tr/ ekim01/e4.html*), *http://www.worldbank.org/mdf/mdf4/presspdf/presscurtain.pdf*).

TESEV, 2002a. "Corporate Social Responsibility" workshop) in October 6–9, 2002, Amman, Jordan. *(http://www.worldbank.org/mdf/mdf4/special/3-corporate.html*

TESEV, 2002b. Corporate Social Responsibility *Session Leader: Monday, October 7, 2002.* (*http://www.tesev.org.tr*).

TESEV, 2003. "Corporate Social Responsibility in Turkey". *http://www.tesev.org.tr/ temmuz/jul3.html*

Zappala, G. and Cronin, C. 2002. The Employee Dimensions of Corporate Community Involvement in Australia: Trends and Prospects, Paper Presented at the 6th ANZTSR Conference, 27–29 November, 2002, Auckland, New Zealand, pp. 1–24.

Chapter 18
Turkey: CSR in Practice

S. Burak Arzova

Abstract Companies which use societal resources in order to provide goods and services and consequently improve their financial performance are now being required by society to account for their actions. Several smaller businesses are growing into larger companies and changing their status from family owned business into a formal and well organized structure. This rapid change in structure is transforming companies into becoming more transparent, accountable, fair and credible. The governance of these entities which is often confused with the corporate social responsibility is the system adopted by those at the helm of their affairs to effect the entities' proper management, it also involves an application of the rule of law, accounting standards and ethics necessary to obtain social trust and improve the methods and techniques applicable in running the affairs of these companies (Di Piazza and Eccles, 2002). In this chapter, after a short definition of CSR, we propose to demonstrate what Turkish companies believe corporate social responsibility entails and how these entities apply the concept of CSR in their day to day operations.

18.1 Introduction

The need for companies to behave in a socially responsible manner has been discussed extensively in the literature and has been a topic of academic studies for decades (Heald, 1957; Ullman, 1985; Moir, 2001). Gray et al., (2003) noted that investors do care about social disclosure and social performance but only in so far as it will affect the financial performance of their companies. The relationship between corporate disclosure and improved social responsibility is unclear. Arguably, the amount of corporate disclosure is greater now than has been without any clear corresponding increase in social responsibility (Shaoul, 1998).

Besides the attention companies have given to social responsibility, most people would agree that corporate social responsibility is concerned with what is (or

S. O. Idowu and W. L. Filho (eds.), *Global Practices of Corporate Social Responsibility*   373
© Springer-Verlag Berlin Heidelberg 2009

should be) the relationship between the company and its stakeholders such as customers, employees, government and citizens. Unfortunately, it is the corporate focus on profit and the creation of shareholders value (with concomitant increase in share price) which has caused both bad publicity and public concern about corporate behavior (Caliyurt and Crowther, 2004).

Freeman's classic definition of a stakeholder is "any group or individual who can affect or is affected by the achievement of the organization's objectives" (Freeman, 1984; Moir, 2001). The term 'stakeholder' is widely used in the accounting literature too. Indeed, post-1945 company law, government and professional reports and accounting textbooks are all prefaced with the need to provide relevant and useful accounting information for a range of users (Shaoul, 1998). However, stakeholder accountability arises only "if an organization has a social responsibility-otherwise there is no (stakeholder) accountability to discharge" (Gray et al., 1996).

According to the "green paper" launched by the European Commission: 'Business Respect Issue: 9', dated 28th July, 2001, CSR has been defined as "the voluntary contribution of companies to a better society and a cleaner environment". On 22 March 2006, the European Commission launched its Second Communication on Corporate Social Responsibility. Following the Appeals on CSR by Jacques Delors in 1995 and the European Heads of State in 2000, and building on the first EC Communication on CSR in 2002, this communication brings a new dimension to the role of enterprises in the European Strategy for Growth and Jobs, through the announcement of a European Alliance on CSR.

This Alliance takes a new EU political approach which aims to make Europe "a pole of excellence on CSR". To help achieve the objectives of Europe's strategy for Growth and Jobs, the Alliance highlights that:

> Europe needs a public climate where entrepreneurs are appreciated not just for their wealth creation but also for addressing the challenges of promoting global competition, demographic trends and a sustainable future.

> While enterprises are the primary actors in CSR, dialogue and engagement with relevant stakeholders are essential as they can encourage companies to anticipate and deal with social and environmental issues which may affect future competitiveness.

As such, CSR has become an increasingly important concept both globally and within the EU, and is part of the debate about globalization, competitiveness and sustainability. In Europe, promoting CSR reflects the need to defend common values and increase the sense of solidarity and cohesion (The European Alliance for CSR, 2007) (Table 18.1).

Seen in this light, two significantly different approaches to researching CSR have emerged in the literature. First, CSR may be treated as an addendum to conventional accounting activity and *researched* with the same assumptions and preconceptions which inform much of mainstream accounting research. The second places CSR as a core concept in social and environmental reporting in any dialogue between organization and society when examining the role of information (Gray et al., 1995).

Table 18.1 CSR activities in the European Union

Activity	Examples of countries engaging in activity
Promoting CSR	
Awareness raising research	Belgium organized a big European conference on CSR in 2001
Public-private partnerships business incentives	The Danish Institute of Social Research monitors CSR developments until 2006 and will publish an annual yearbook with results from the study
Management tools	The German Federal Citizenship Responsibility Network promotes co-operation between NGOs, companies and federal governments
	An annual award is given to enterprises promoting health and security at work from the Greek Institute of Hygiene and Security at Work
	The Ministry of Labor and Social Affairs in Spain has a program promoting equal opportunities as a good management strategy for companies, by constructing and implementing action plans
Ensuring transparency	
Codes	Austrian ministries and enterprises have collaborated in developing a code of conduct for the protection of children from sexual exploitation in travel and tourism
Reporting labels	More than 300 Dutch companies are required to submit reports on their environmental performance to the government and the general public
	NGOs, academics and public officials in the Italian region Emilia Romagna are developing a social quality label which includes responsible production criteria
Socially responsible investment	The Swedish Public Pension Funds Act requires national pension funds to describe how environmental and ethical considerations are taken into account in their investment activities
Advertising	Belgian law prohibits misleading advertising concerning effects on the environment
	(Cont.)

Table 18.1 *Continued*

Activity	Examples of countries engaging in activity
Developing CSR-supporting policies	
Sustainable development	The German business community has voluntarily signed an agreement with the government promising to follow the Kyoto Protocol guidelines
Social policies	The Training Place Developer program aims at increasing opportunities for eastern German companies to provide training
Environmental policies	Swedish government agencies must integrate environmental management systems and report annually on their progress.
Public procurement	The Belgian government has introduced a social clause for certain federal public procurements, favoring the inclusion of disadvantaged groups
Fiscal policies	Spain gives tax benefits to NGOs and enterprises which contribute to public interest goals and activities
Trade and export policies	Most EU countries, including Belgium, France, Germany, and the Netherlands, follow the OECD trade guidelines and inform the business sector about these guidelines
Development policies	Dutch Ministry of Development Co-operation supports NGOs which aims to raising CSR awareness in developing countries

Source: European Union (2004). Corporate Social Responsibility: National Public Policies in the European Union cited in (Michael and Öhlund, 2005)

Ethical concern is an important topic in today's global business world. Cross-cultural differences within the business environment are compounded when the topic of business ethics is considered. For developing and under-developed countries, the need to behave ethically is considered as one of the most important virtues in attracting investments into developing markets. This is reflected by an increasing number of studies that have provided empirical evidence to show the influence of culture on various dependent variables including professional ethics Patel (2000). Holme and Watts (2000) define CSR as "the continuing commitment by business to behave ethically and contribute to economic development while improving the quality of life of the workforce and their families as well as of the local community and society at large."

In September 2004 a Working Group was established within ISO, to develop an International Standard which provides guidelines for social responsibility (SR). The objective was to produce a guidance document, written in plain language that is understandable and usable by non-specialists and not a specification document intended for a third party certification.

The work was intended to add value to, and not replace, existing inter-governmental agreements with relevance to social responsibility, such as the United Nations Universal Declaration of Human Rights, and those adopted by the International Labor Organization (ILO). The standard should be usable by organizations of all sizes, in all countries at any stage of development.

ISO is taking action to ensure that the standard will benefit from broad input by all those with a serious interest in social responsibility. This is being achieved by a balanced representation in the working group, of six designated stakeholder categories: industry, government, labor, consumers, nongovernmental organizations and others, in addition to geographical and gender-based balance.

The designation of the standard is ISO 26000 and the target date for publication is November 2009 (ISO, 2007a).

According to the new proposal the standard (ISO, 2007b) should:

1. Assist organizations in addressing their social responsibilities while respecting cultural, societal, environmental and legal differences and economic development conditions
2. Provide practical guidance related to operationalizing social responsibility, identifying and engaging with stakeholders, and enhancing credibility of reports and claims made about social responsibility
3. Emphasize performance results and improvement
4. Increase confidence and satisfaction in organizations among their customers and other stakeholders
5. Be consistent with and not in conflict with existing documents, international treaties and conventions and existing ISO standards
6. Not be intended to reduce government's authority to address the social responsibility of organizations
7. Promote common terminology in the social responsibility field
8. Broaden awareness of social responsibility.

18.2 Corporate Social Responsibility Practices in Turkey

Although there seems to be a growing demand for social responsibility information, up to the time of this study, there is no legislation in Turkey, enforcing companies to disclose information on their CSR activities. Companies are given the freedom to voluntarily choose to demonstrate their social consciousness through their disclosure of CSR information. The general practice in Turkey is for companies to disclose information in financial reports about their CSR activities.

In Turkey, the government is an important driver of CSR through its new laws and regulations such as Corporate Governance Codes, disclosure and reporting requirements. The Ministry of Environment and Forestry: Forestry, the Ministry of Finance: Corporate Governance, the Ministry of Trade and Industry: Standards and the Ministry of Labor and Social Security: Labor Issues are the government bodies which are directly or indirectly related with CSR applications in Turkey (UNDP, 2007).

Corporate social responsibility is high on the agenda of major foreign corporations operating in Turkey. At least a dozen companies continuously donate funds, supplies, provide volunteers and many more resources for the improvement of the environment, education and the arts as well as providing critical support during the time of crisis in Turkey.

Ascigil (2003), in her unpublished survey conducted for TESEV explored management attitudes towards CSR in Turkey. Using Caroll's (1979) and Aupperle's (1984) contextualized questionnaires, Aşçıgil (2004) found that 75% of managers included in the survey give priority to economic criteria when making decisions about CSR whereas 19.11% gives priority to ethical criteria and only 6% gives priority to legal criteria. Ascigil notes that Turkish managers do not differentiate between legal and ethical responsibilities as evidenced by the structural analysis of the responses. Furthermore, the study shows that customers are considered to be the most important stakeholders by 75.8% of managers, employees being the second by 50.8% and society at large by only 24.3% (Ararat and Gocenoglu, 2006).

A number of Turkish companies are already practicing some form of CSR. Through Turkcell's (Cellular Phone Service Provider) program – *Contemporary Girls of Contemporary Turkey* – which provides scholarships to girls in Eastern Anatolia, Turkcell seeks to alleviate the budgetary burden on the local government, improve the welfare of future generation, and contribute to the wider business community through a more educated workforce. Ülker's contributions to the *10 Billion Oak Tree Campaign* considers stakeholders such as local communities and the environment itself. Often, these programs work in collaboration with the government Michael and Öhlund (2005).

Turkish businesses will not respond to CSR unless given incentives by the Turkish government. The Turkish government has already collaborated with the United Nation's Global Compact, the OECD Guidelines for Multinational Enterprises and has endorsed the ILO Declaration on the Fundamental Principles and Rights at Work. The Turkish parliament will need to play an important role in passing CSR-friendly legislations and Turkish political parties will also need to put the issue on the table. Table 18.2 lists a few components of the law which Turkish

Table 18.2 Working toward a CSR law for Turkey

a. *Introduce CSR to main political parties* like AKP, CHP, MHP and DYP. Smaller parties – SP or ANAP – may try to use CSR to get votes!

b. *Host a National CSR workshop* inviting all stakeholders to contribute ideas toward a Turkish CSR law

c. *Talk up CSR* – since Kemal Ataturk, the Turkish government has always played a progressive role in educating the public and preparing it for integration in the world economy. Parliamentarians can educate their constituencies directly and can mandate that the central government provides educational materials

d. *Participate in multi-national fora* – the EU as a multi-stakeholder forum for CSR and the UN, OECD, World Bank and other organisations are becoming increased involved in CSR

e. *Establish a department* in an existing ministry to work on CSR and/or mandate a CSR ministerial post

f. *Provide funds* to the national governments for CSR grants and rewards to innovative companies

g. *Vote for tax breaks for CSR activity* – while tax breaks may go against important fiscal policy objectives to raise tax revenue and compliance, they internalize externalities

Source: Michael B.; Riedmann J. and Dinler S. (2005) "Implementing CSR Programmes in Turkish Companies: How to Do it and Why" http://www.eldis.org/fulltext/Implementing_CSR_Programmes_in_Turkish_Companies.doc (Accessed October 23, 2007).

parliamentarians can pass in order to help provide an environment where CSR can flourish in corporate Turkey Michael et al. (2005).

Below are some examples of what "Selected" Turkish Companies do in order to apply CSR (Focus on Corporate Social Responsibility in Turkey, 2007), (Topcuoglu, 2007) (Ülker, 2006 Annual Report), (Company History: Koc Holding A.S.), (Koc, 2006 Annual Report), (Sabanci, 2006 Annual Report)

18.2.1 CNN Turk

CNN Turk was created from a Time-Warner and Dogan Broadcasting Holding (DYH) partnership, CNN Turk is also an example of U.S. investments in the Turkish media. CNN Turk was the Time-Warner media giant's first broadcasting agreement outside its own country. Its motto says "Be the first to know" the company appears to have worked well in Turkey in line with this motto!

The biggest evidence of CNN Turk's localization is their social responsibility projects. In these projects, just as in their broadcasting approach, they are developing projects to solve both international problems and Turkey's local problems, with education, health and environment topping the list. Within this framework, to date, CNN Turk has supported education with the "Clean Future" project, street children with the "1 Million Wrist Bands" project, women with the "End Domestic Violence" project, and the environment with the "Clean Sea" campaign.

The basis of these social responsibility projects are bringing social problems to the television screen by getting support from institutions, accumulating knowledge on the designated subjects and reaching broad masses. The goal of these projects is to make people a part of the solution. One of the biggest projects was special broadcasting support in 2006 for the Nature Association's Target Zero Extinction, one for The Turkish Foundation for Combating Soil Erosion, for Reforestation and the Protection of Natural Habitats (TEMA) "Hands On" campaigns. Donations were collected for the campaign, which put serious environmental issues on the agenda.

The latest project on CNN Turk's agenda is organ donation, "Donate to Life," which has been coordinated with the Health Ministry since Jan. 25, 2007. Every year 8,000 patients are added to the list of 44,000 people in Turkey waiting for organ transplants. With only 143 organ donations being made to hospitals in 2006, 7,000 people lost their lives while waiting. In light of this, CNN Turk set out to put one of Turkey's least talked about, but most important health problems on the public agenda.

The "Donate to Life" project was born as a result of highlighting this problem on the television. This subject requires great attention to detail. They put the project in action after 3–4 months of discussions.

A special program is broadcast every Thursday at 10:00 p.m. within the framework of the campaign. Miscommunication and misinformation regarding organ donations and transplants are explained and experts answer questions on the subject. While only three people in Istanbul donated their organs from 2006 to January 2007, 16 families have donated organs after the campaign began.

Noting that "Donate to Life" has been very successful, they will continue the campaign until the end of the year.

18.2.2 Ülker Group

Ülker was established in a back street building of Eminönü, Istanbul in 1944. Sabri Ülker who is the founder of Ulker began production with just three employees and, in his first year, produced 75 tons of cookies. In 1948, Ülker opened its first factory in Istanbul's Topkapı district, tripling production capacity. In 1974 Ülker established its second plant in Istanbul, and began modern chocolate production. A Research & Development unit was established to make the company more competitive with international brands. In 1992, they diversified into margarine, vegetable oil and industrial fats segments. Ülker and Dan Cake established the Group's second joint-venture in 1995. In 1996, Ülker extended the company's production into dairy. In 2002, Ülker began producing carbonated beverages. In partnership with Hero of Switzerland, a facility was established to produce Turkey's first domestic baby food in Ankara in 2003. Ülker added ice-cream and Turkish coffee to its product range. Since the day it was founded, Ülker has worked to contribute to the economy of Turkey. Apart from the traditional social responsibility of entrepreneurs, the Group's comprehensive community service activities stretch from education, family counseling and environmental awareness to sponsorship of the arts, medical research and sports. Ülker is one of the corporations that pioneered the concept of sponsorship in Turkey. Three Big Football Clubs are sponsored by Ülker while Beikta F.C. is the main sponsored club with Cola Turka (a product similar to Coca-Cola of U.S) on his badge.

Ülker believes that enhancing the educational infrastructure is essential to Turkey's economic and social development. The Group has long been involved in the construction of schools and donation of libraries and computer laboratories to the Turkish Ministry of Education. All these facilities are built in strict compliance with laws and the Ministry's standards.

They include: The Ülker Primary School in Pursaklar, Ankara, with a capacity of 850 students; The Ali Ülker Primary School in Bayrampaa, Istanbul, named after the deceased son of Sabri Ülker, The Sabri Ülker Primary School, built in honor of the 75th anniversary of the Turkish Republic in Batman, Southeast Turkey, with a 600 student capacity, and fully equipped with a sports center and science laboratory, The Ülker Primary School in Alibeyköy, Istanbul, equipped with a science laboratory and library and a student dormitory in Erzurum.

Ülker continues to encourage the human factor in the Turkish educational system with a program called "Ülker Parents School" which assists parents in communication and learning to play a more effective role in their children's education. These parenting workshops involve leading figures in the fields of psychology and education. A second program called "Ülker Teacher Dialogues", initiated in October 1999 under the guidance of expert academics, help teachers to identify and discuss their problems. The third of the series, "Ülker Administrator Dialogues," is consisted of seminars with high-ranking education officials.

Mr. Sabri Ülker is one of the founding members of TEMA, the Turkish Foundation for Combating Soil Erosion for Reforestation and the Protection of Natural Habitats, and actively contributes to its programs, including the "10 Billion Oak Tree Campaign." The Foundation undertook a 3-year TEMA grassland rehabilitation project in the Village of Alatlı in Turkish Thrace in 2003.

Following the devastating earthquake of 1999, Ülker donated 40 prefabricated houses to the municipality of Izmit, the city most extensively damaged by the disaster.

In 1999 to mark the 55th anniversary of the group, 55 scholarships were established for the children of Turkish Military Men who died in the service of their country in collaboration with the Turkish Armed Forces Mehmetçik Foundation.

Ülker has a long history of supporting the development of Turkey's healthcare services. The Group has helped hospitals such as the Haseki Hospital in Istanbul, where Ülker built and equipped an operating theatre. The Group also contributes wings and floors to various hospitals in Turkey. The Group is now one of the founding members and an important supporter of the Istanbul Children's Foundation.

18.2.3 Koc Group

Koç (pronounced "coach") is a name immediately recognized in Turkey, but virtually unknown elsewhere. It is the name of several of Turkey's most prominent companies, including Koç Holding A.S., the largest industrial group in Turkey. Component companies are engaged in a variety of businesses, including automotive (the Tofas unit, Turkey's largest car manufacturer), supermarkets, appliances, and energy, as well as banking, construction, food production, and hospitality. The founder of the Koç group of companies was Vehbi Koç, the first Turkish businessman to gain national prominence. He was known as a generous philanthropist, he was also responsible for introducing a number of modern Western business practices in Turkey.

Vehbi Koç was a pioneer in countless areas in Turkey, the Koç Group has broken new grounds by establishing the country's first private philanthropic foundation, Vehbi Koç Foundation, which in turn has signed up to many "firsts" like the first privately operated museum, first industrial museum and first student dormitory.

Koç Holding carries out several projects all of which share the common aim of being an 'engine of change' in both economic and societal transformation by striving for excellence in all its activities and commitments. The Group's 80th anniversary provided an impetus to add new projects to complement and expand past efforts.

One of the Group's major corporate social responsibility projects which was initiated in 2006 aims to increase the attractiveness of vocational secondary schools. As a major employer of blue collar workers, Koç invests in their education from the secondary school level, thus bringing attention to the issue of the need for skilled workers on one hand and reducing the level of unemployment on the other. Thus it is envisioned that the project will support Turkey's bid for membership to the EU by triggering a structural change in the economy through productivity increases and enhanced value creation.

This project was developed to create awareness amongst the public and to set off a public debate among the private and academic circles about the needs for vocational education. Koç Holding has pledged to grant 8,000 students scholarships throughout their education, while providing internship opportunities and priority in employment.

The Vehbi Koç Building of the Faculty of Vocational and Technical Education in Adıyaman was opened on September 20, 2006. The Faculty will be the main pillar of a university to be established in this southeastern city. The foundation for the building was laid in 2005 by Koç Holding and Vehbi Koç Foundation and construction has been completed in 1 year at a cost of USD2 million. "Sizinkiler" Musical for Children, Limon and Zeytin, the characters of cartoonist Salih Memecan's popular Sizinkiler series, came to life in a children's musical performed by the BKM (Besiktas Culture Center) Players. Nearly 100,000 children saw the show, which was performed in Istanbul and then in 16 other cities in Turkey through the support of Koç Holding as part of its 80th anniversary celebrations.

As a tribute to its 80th anniversary, in 2006 the Group launched a grassroots effort to spread the practice social responsibility through its distribution network in 81 Turkish cities.

The projects encompassed a wide variety of ideas: 144 focused on repairing and equipping schools, 51 contributed to orphanages and rehabilitation centers, others dealt with specific social and environment problems. Dealers from Kahramanmara, for example, organized annual newspaper subscriptions to 185 families who did not receive newspapers; in Mersin a daycare center was opened to look after street children; and in Van employees of Migros and Tansa organized a clean-up of Lake Van together with local citizens.

Some projects initiated "For My Country Day" have become part of the way Turkish companies do business. For example, Divan collects and refrigerates the leftovers from industrial meals it serves and donates them to animal shelters. Thanks to this project, close to 3,000 homeless dogs are fed each week.

In 1969, Vehbi Koç founded the first private philanthropic foundation in Turkey. The Foundation has supported education, culture and healthcare for nearly 40 years. With an endowment of close to USD1 billion, Vehbi Koç Foundation is one of the largest foundations not only in Turkey but also in Europe. It operates The Koç School, a private elementary and high school, and Koç University in the area of education; American Hospital and MedAmerican Polyclinic in the field of healthcare; Sadberk Hanım Museum, Vehbi Koç and Ankara Research Center, Suna – nan Kıraç Mediterranean Civilizations Research Institute and Kaleiçi Museum in the field of culture. These organizations are among the most highly regarded in their fields in Turkey, serving hundreds of thousands of people every year.

Both Koç School and University give scholarships to promising low-income students over and above the legal thresholds set by the law. Koç University has succeeded in becoming a world-class institution of higher learning in a short period of time in terms of various criteria including student rankings, success of graduates in business and academic life and the number of publications per faculty member. In 2006, Koç University faculty members published a total of 412 articles, 24 books and received 11 patents. Of the published materials, 140 appeared in ICI attributed journals. The Scholarship Program, one of the most important activities since the establishment of the Foundation, gave over 5,000 scholarships during the academic year, 2006–2007. The Vehbi Koç Award, which was first presented in 2002, was given in the area of education in 2006 to the Governor of Sakarya for his leadership and exemplary efforts in the field of pre-school education.

Group supports the efforts of various key non-governmental organizations (NGOs) such as Turkish Volunteers for Education (TEGV), Foundation for Combating Soil Erosion, Reforestation and Protection of Natural Habitats (TEMA), Family Health and Planning Foundation (TAPV), and Turkish Maritime Environment Protection Association (TURMEPA).

With the support of the Ministry of National Education, Yapı Kredi and TURMEPA organized the Limitless Blue project to make primary, middle and high school students aware of the need to preserve natural resources. The program reached 3,000 teachers and 400,000 students in 2006.

Through the Green Road Project, Opet has planted 261,923 trees and other plants around 302 stations and in areas designated by city governments, taking care to choose plants suited to the region's climate and soil. This project won Golden Compass Awards from the Turkish Public Relations Association in the categories of Social Responsibility and Environment.

YapıKredi and The Educational Volunteers Foundation (TEGV) have organized "I am reading and learning Project", which is a multifaceted educational project to contribute to the personal and social development of primary school children. The project aims to develop the capacity of school-age children to think, research, question and analyze various educational activities relevant to their studies. With YapıKredi's support, the project will be implemented at TEGV's 11 Education Parks and 57 Teaching Units by volunteer teachers, including well-known academicians, until 2010 in order to instill the love of reading among 50,000 students.

Opet's Clean Toilet Campaign is one of the longest running social projects in Turkey. The project highlights the importance of cleanliness and hygiene in public restrooms. In cooperation with the Ministry of National Education, nearly 100,000 school children were educated. Furthermore, the restrooms in Opet gas stations were redressed for the disabled. Standards thus introduced were enforced in all stations. Animated films were prepared to instruct children and adults and these films were broadcast on television.

The Opet Clean Toilet Campaign was awarded first place in the International Public Relations Association (IPRA) Golden World Awards in 2004 in the Social Responsibility category as well as in the Golden Compass Award given by the Turkish Public Relations Association. Opet was ranked as one of the "Top Companies" in Turkey in the Social Responsibility category in an annual survey published by Nokta weekly magazine.

18.2.4 Sabanci Group

Haci Omer Sabanci Holdings A.S. is one of Turkey's largest companies, posting almost $6 billion in sales per year. Sabanci Group is owned by one of the richest families in Turkey. They are the main rival of the Koc Group which is owned by another of the richest families in Turkey.

The Sabanci family in addition to their business interests both in Turkey and other parts of the world are also famous for all their philanthropic acts. In 1999, the group opened its own private university, Sabanci University, promising low tuitions; under family head Sakip Sabanci, son of Haci Omer and company chairman, the group has also created the Sabanci Museum.

Based on the accepted core values of modesty, respect and proximity to people, the Sabanci Group regards basing all corporate conduct on the awareness of social responsibility as an unchangeable core component of its management approach. In Sabanci Group, the SA-Ethics program prepared and put into practice in accordance with the principles of Corporate Social Responsibility constitute a guide to their business operations.

The Group's CSR principles is stated on Sabanci Group Web Pages (http://www.sabanci.com.tr/En/st_sosyal_sorumluluk.asp). The basic principles of the social responsibility practice of Sabanci Group are as below:

1. We fulfill our social and environmental responsibilities toward society in all our places of operation, in close collaboration with our shareholders, employees, the public, non-governmental organizations and other stakeholders.

2. We regard our human resources as the most significant component in creating sustainable growth. We ensure that all employees take advantage of their personal rights as members of the Group, fully and accurately. We treat our employees with honesty and fairness; we are committed to creating a non-discriminatory, safe and healthy work environment. We undertake efforts to enable the personal development of all employees while pursuing a balance between their private and professional lives.

   a. Any discrimination within the organization based on race, religion, gender, age, political opinion, language, physical challenge or similar reasons are not tolerated.
   b. We strive to ensure that people of different beliefs, views and opinions work together in harmony by creating a positive and cordial work environment that supports cooperation and prevents conflict.
   c. We administer programs that contribute to preserving employee health that we accept as important to ensuring our employees' quality of life and success.
   d. As the SabancıGroup, we believe that all employees deserve to work in a healthy and secure work environment consistent with human dignity. Our employees are our most valuable assets and we strive to provide employee safety and security as our primary goal.

3. We manage the environmental impact of our activities with a sense of responsibility. All of our companies are required to identify and apply the necessary improvements and development activities that minimize or eliminate negative environmental impact. We require our companies, beyond their legal requirements, to apply the best environmental solutions to all they do and to support any initiative that will develop and deploy environment-friendly technology and enhance environmental awareness.
4. At the SabancıGroup, we struggle toward the improvement of society pursuant to our sense of corporate social responsibility. We encourage our employees to take part in social and societal volunteering.
5. We develop and implement strategies which ensure that all of our partners and particularly our suppliers act in accordance with the social responsibility standards of the Group.
6. We show sensitivity to the traditions and culture of Turkey and other countries in which we operate. We comply with all legal regulations currently in operation.
7. We encourage our Group companies to comply with international standards and ensure that their operations are certified.

18.2.5 Bp Turkey

BP Turkey received a Chairman Commendation Award for its initiatives during the earthquake in 1999. It has a long history of social investments in Turkey. BP Turkey, in cooperation with the Photography Society's Work Group, published a photo album titled 'Turkey 1992' in memory of the master photographer Sami Güler. The album that contains the works of 132 Turkish photographers also contributed to the promotion of Turkey in foreign countries. In cooperation with the Plastic Arts Society, BP Turkey ensured the participation of Hülya Botasagun from Turkey along with 12 artists from Europe in the 'Public Art Project' held in 1993 in Spain. As part of this project, artists created permanent works of art in the open area in Castellon, Spain.

In terms of environmental activities, BP Turkey also helped in the protection of crested pelicans that are becoming extinct in Turkey in1994. In the same year, the company assisted Young Turkish and Azeri Artists. The following year, as a new year's gift, BP Turkey planted 30,000 saplings in Sile Green Valley, which is one of the fire-eaten forests of Turkey, in cooperation with the Foundation for the Protection and Promotion of the Environmental and Cultural Heritage (CEKUL), for which it received many domestic and international awards.

BP Turkey has donated wheeled chairs to handicapped children with the guidance of Turkish Confederation of the Handicapped.

BP has also contributed towards ensuring child safety in traffic by giving support to the 'Traffic Training Program' of the Education Volunteers Foundation of Turkey aimed at primary school children. In that context, training CD-ROMs were prepared for primary school students. In 1998 BP Turkey in cooperation with the Police Headquarters Traffic Services Department, set up a mobile theatre team to teach traffic rules through entertainment to 180 thousand students in more than 500 primary schools since 1998. The children's play, taught traffic rules to students in all ten Turkish cities following the earthquake disaster of August 1999. This was organized in Izmir, Aydin and Mersin as well as in Istanbul. Child's play on Road Safety continues to teach traffic rules to the first and second grades primary school students in Istanbul.

In 2000, BP Turkey gave support to an important social issue following the earthquake disaster building a primary school in the earthquake zone in cooperation with the Society for Supporting Modern Life. Duzce Cumhuriyet, Primary School which educates 1,500 students, is the first steel construction structure built in the earthquake area.

BP Turkey became a sponsor for the education campaign held by the Education Volunteers Foundation of Turkey and NTV, Msnbc and provided 1 trillion TL (old Turkish Lira) – 1.000.000 YTL (New Turkish Lira) financial donations for educational activities of the foundation.

BP Turkey, in cooperation with the Society for the Protection of Natural Life, has incorporated photographs of bulbed plants in the 2002 calendars to promote these plants in Turkish society and to help prevent their extinction.

18.2.6 Coca-Cola

The Coca-Cola Corporation in Turkey supported the "All Girls Go To School (Haydi Kizlar Okula)" campaign launched by the Ministry of Education and UNICEF in

2003. The company donated $250,000 for school materials for girls in ten provinces and utilized the Rock'n Coke Festival as a platform to raise additional funds. During 2002 and 2003, Coca-Cola Turkey donated 80,000 books and libraries to 400 schools.

Following the earthquake of August 1999, The Coca-Cola Company joined with many others to provide relief. Among the Company's initiatives was the rebuilding of Sakarya University Vocational Training School, which opened in November 2001.

In Turkey, local townspeople and emergency-relief workers recovering from the devastating earthquake in Izmit received bottled water, blankets and other supplies from Coca-Cola delivery trucks.

The Coca-Cola system's plant in Ankara, Turkey, is playing a central role in helping to bring European Union funds to the country. The project was created by Turkey's Ministry of Labor to improve the health conditions and safety standards in the country's workplaces. Under the program, 21 laboratories would help train workers in order to decrease the large number of workplace accidents. For example, there were 74,847 job-related accidents in 2000 around the country. The Turkish government provided 10% of the funds for the project. The Minister of Labor, appealed to Brussels – the seat of the European Union – for additional funds. When the EU experts asked for a workplace in Turkey that could be shown as a model, ministry officials served up Coca-Cola's Ankara plant as a success story. EU officials who toured the Ankara plant were so impressed they donated 7 million Euros, or just over $7 million – well above the project's goal. The plant is one of 36 in the company's system worldwide that has received the Coca-Cola Quality Systems award. Four of the five plants in Turkey have received this award, making Turkey the country with the most awards in the world. The Quality Systems awards program, activated in 1998, promotes greater productivity, lower costs and constantly increasing quality guarantees at Coca-Cola plants worldwide. The EU's decision and the high-quality work are a great source of pride to Ali Huroglu, operations director of Coca-Cola Bottlers of Turkey. "We owe our success to teamwork and the commitment of our employees to quality at all levels," he said.

18.2.7 Lafarge Turkey

Lafarge Turkey companies provided help after the earthquake in the Izmit area with their vehicles, equipment and employee support, all coordinated by the Lafarge Turkey Crisis Committee. Aid teams reached more than 1,100 children in these places, where the life units provided by Lafarge were put into use at local hospitals and other institutions. Moreover, Lafarge contributed to the construction of the Gölcük Hospital and the Düzce Student Dormitory.

Alongside these activities, Lafarge Turkey participated in the preparation of a children's book giving necessary and useful information on earthquakes. Lafarge Turkey also provided aid to employees who suffered damage to their homes, to Lokman Hekim Saglik Vakfi (Healthcare Foundation), for a special crisis dispatch center, for the repairs to the Lafarge Aslan Cimento Technical High School, and contributed to the building of a primary school in Akyazi, a village of prefabricated houses in Degirmendere.

After the earthquake disaster in Turkey in 1999, the help provided (including a financial donation of US$ 250,000) among others contributed to the restoration and the recovery of the country after this natural disaster.

For its 10th anniversary, Lafarge Turkey built a memorial forest near Gebze, where more than 4,000 trees have been planted. The project aims to protect the natural environment, in cooperation with the Regional Forestry Department. It is also a way for Lafarge to develop national and regional stakeholder relationships by emphasizing its environmental commitments. It also wishes to increase the environmental awareness and motivation of the employees by involving them in the planting activities. Lafarge Turkey planted the 4,000 trees. All employees (around 1,500 people) were granted with a certificate symbolizing a planted tree. With other plantation programs in and around the plants and other areas in co-operation with local institutions and schools, more than 15,000 trees have been planted in order to improve environmental awareness.

A sum of €15,000 was awarded to the Fethiye Friends of Animals Association from Turkey. The organization provided a proposal relating to mass neuter and return programs for dogs. Such schemes have demonstrated value in reducing and controlling stray numbers, improving the general health of the dogs and in changing the attitudes of municipal authorities and people within local communities toward the management and treatment of stray dog populations.

18.2.8 Proctor & Gamble

P&G co-sponsored Turkey's first Sustainable Development Congress for the Business World, in cooperation with TEMA (the Turkish Foundation for Combating Soil Erosion, for Reforestation and the Protection of Natural Habitats) and TOBB (the Union of Chambers and Commodity Exchanges of Turkey). The Congress was aimed at accelerating sustainable development action initiated by the Turkish business community and providing understanding that allows the business community to broaden its activity. In addition to speakers from P&G, TEMA, and TOBB, there were speakers from the State Planning Organization DPT, the United Nations Development Program, the World Business Council for Sustainable Development, Shell, the Turkish LP gas company Aygaz, the European Commission, the World Bank, and the Turkish Ethical Values Center. In the audience were local and national regulatory officials, academicians, and NGOs. P&G made two presentations at the Congress, one on the twenty-first century role of business in sustainable development and another, giving examples of P&G Turkey's local sustainability projects. P&G also participated in a panel discussion on the future of sustainable development in Turkey and what needs to be done.

18.2.9 Rwe Thames Water

RWE Thames Water in Turkey is actively involved in education, arts, sports, healthy living and public awareness in Turkey. The company works with local schools and higher education institutions to promote key skills development and foster learning. In a city where education became a luxury, especially after the devastating 1999 earthquake, RWE Thames Water and its local partner Izmit Su funded scholarships for twenty university students.

In addition, cultural activities are very important to the local community and as such the company seeks to reflect the diverse interests by supporting a wide range of local arts activities. RWE Thames Water gives financial support to the Kocaeli Municipality Conservatory, which supports local arts and artists, and contributed to the Izmit and Anatolian Turkish Theatres.

The company also actively works with local communities to promote a healthy lifestyle and it sponsors the Yuvacik Female Athletics team. With the help of Thames' support, the team has won many national awards and is now competing in international tournaments. In the aftermath of the earthquake, statutory funding was limited for sporting activities so Thames increased its support of local teams in particular the Kocaeli National Soccer team.

Other companies actively supporting Turkey's environment, education, communities, arts and culture projects include TNT International Express and Veolia Water.

18.3 Conclusion

This chapter has taken a broad overview of what is meant by corporate responsibility and how Turkish companies perceive Corporate Social Responsibility and the applications of CSR by these companies. The chapter shows that the CSR applications in Turkey are significantly related to the leverage and size of the company. Listed companies use either annual reports or other channels (Media-Official Web Site, etc) to disclose information to their readers, in order that social auditing can be carried out. In the Turkish context, originally, a large number of citizens were unaware of CSR and its implications. However, things have started to change, citizens are gradually becoming more aware of the field and the landscape of CSR in corporate Turkey is quite different from what it used to be. As Turkey is still a country on the way to negotiate its E.U. admission, it is safe to suggest that the future of CSR in Turkey will be promising. We can conclude by quoting what the last Secretary General of the UN said:

> "...Globalization must mean more than creating bigger markets. The economic sphere cannot be separated from the more complex fabric of social and political life, and sent shooting off on its own trajectory. To survive and thrive, a global market economy must have a more solid foundation in shared values and institutional practices -it must have a broader, and more inclusive, social purpose."

Kofi Annan, "We the Peoples: The Role of the United Nations in the 21st Century"

The field of CSR is relatively new to corporate Turkey, a small number of academicians and practitioners have recently started working on this subject. The Corporate Social Responsibility Association has been established in Turkey in order to increase the social responsibility consciousness amongst early signers; for example the Turkish NGOs. A new web site has been set up by a private advertisement agency on March 24th, 2006 as the country's CSR Platform. Other NGOs related with CSR are: Business Association for Sustainable Development, TEMA, TUSIAD, Turkey's Ethical Values Center, Private Sector Volunteers Foundation, Third Sector Foundation of Turkey, the Turkish Society for Quality and Turkish Education Volunteers Foundation. Most often, CSR is confused with corporate Governance. Currently, there is no legal obligation on the part of companies to practice CSR, but there are several statements in the Turkish Constitution, Turkish Law for Consumer Protection, Public Procurement Environment, Bribery and Corruption and Labor Legislation which indirectly encourage CSR. It is the view of this author that Turkey requires some form of legislation on CSR. Having said this, it must be noted that Turkish Citizens and Companies are naturally charitable, thanks to the Cultural and Religious Roots of its citizens.

References

Annan, K. (2002), "We the People: The Role of the United Nations in 21st Century", http://www.worldbank.org/mdf/mdf4/special/3-corporate.html (accessed April 27, 2007).

Ararat, M. and Gocenoglu, C. (2006), *"Drivers for Sustainable Corporate Responsibility, Case of Turkey"*, Report for MDF 5, http://www.gocenoglu.net/CSRTurkeyMDF5.pdf (Accessed October 23, 2007).

Aşçıgil, S. (2004); *"TESEV research on CSR"*, unpublished.

Aupperle, K.E. (1984); "An empirical measure of corporate social orientation", *Research in Corporate Social Performance and Policy, 6*, pp.27–54.

Caliyurt, K.T. and Crowther, D. (2004), "Social responsibility effects on shareholder value: an analysis of the banking sector in Turkey"; *Proceedings of 2nd International Conference on Corporate Social Responsibility*; Penang, Malaysia.

Caroll, A.B. (1979), "A three dimensional conceptual model of corporate performance", *Academy of Management Review, 28 (2)*, pp.446–443.

Di Piazza, S.A. (2002), *"Building Public Trust-The Future of Corporate Reporting"*, John Wiley Sons, New York, p.47–52.

European Alliance for CSR (2007), "A New Political Approach on CSR", http://www. csreurope.org/whatwedo/alliance/ (accessed August 21, 2007).

European Union. (2004), *Corporate Social Responsibility: National Public Policies in the European Union.*

Freeman, R.E. (1984), *"Strategic Management: a Stakeholder Approach"*, Pitman Publishing, Boston, MA.

Gray, R., Bebbington, J. and Walters, D. (2003), *"Accounting for the environment"*, London, Paul Chapman, p. 21.

Gray, R., Kouhy, R. and Lavers, S. (1995), "Corporate Social and Environmental Reporting", *Accounting, Auditing and Accountability Journal*, Volume: 8, Issue: 2, pp.47–77.

Gray, R.H., Owen, D.L. and Maunders, K.T. (1996), *"Corporate Social Reporting: Changes and Challenges in Corporate Social and Environmental Reporting"*, Prentice-Hall, London. p.56.

Green Paper (2001), European Commission Business Respect, Issue: 9, 28th July.

Holme, R. and Watts, P. (2000), "Corporate Social Responsibility: Making Good Business Sense", January, http://www.wbcsd.org/web/publications/csr2000.pdf (accessed March 18, 2007).

Implementing The Partnership For Growth And Jobs: Making Europe A Pole Of Excellence On Corporate Social Responsibility (2006), Communication From The Commission To The European Parliament, The Council And The European Economic And Social Committee, Brussels, 22.3.2006 COM (2006), 136 final, pp. 1–13.

ISO (2007a), "About ISO SR", http://isotc.iso.org/livelink/livelink/fetch/2000/2122/830949/3934883/3935096/07_gen_info/about.html (accessed April 14, 2007).

ISO (2007b), "About the Standart", http://isotc.iso.org/livelink/livelink/fetch/2000/2122/830949/3934883/3935096/07_gen_info/aboutStd.html (accessed April 14, 2007).

Koc Group, "Kurumsal Sosyal Sorumluluk", http://www.koc.com.tr/tr-TR/SocialResponsibility/SocialProjects/ (accessed August 21, 2007).

Michael, B. and Öhlund, E. (2005). "The Role of Social Responsibility in Turkey's E.U. Accession", *Insight Turkey*, March, pp.1–10.

Michael, B. Riedmann, J. and Dinler, S. (2005) "Implementing CSR Programmes in Turkish Companies: How to Do it and Why" http://www.eldis.org/fulltext/Implementing_CSR_Programmes_in_Turkish_Companies.doc (Accessed October 23, 2007).

Moir, L. (2001), "What do we mean by corporate social responsibility", *Corporate Governance*, Vol: 1 Issue: 2, pp. 16–22.

O'Donovan, G. (2002), "The Social Bottom Line", *Australian CPA*, December, Volume: 72, Issue: 11, Accounting and Tax Periodicals.

Patel, C. (2000), 'A review of selected cross-cultural studies on accountants' values and judgments: Some theoretical and methodological suggestions', *Proceedings of the Emerging Issues in International Accounting Conference*, Niagara Falls, Canada.

Sabanci Group, "Corporate Social Responsibility Policy and Principles", http://www.sabanci.com.tr/En/st_sosyal_sorumluluk.asp (accessed 21.08.2007).

Shaoul, J. (1998), "Critical Financial Analysis and Accounting for Stakeholders", *Critical Perspectives on Accounting*, Number: 9, pp.235–249.

Topcuoglu, N. (2007), "US Media Giants Setting Up Shop in Turkish Television", Turkish Daily News, 23rd June, http://www.turkishdailynews.com.tr/article.php?enewsid=76518 (accessed August 21, 2007).

Transparency International. (2006). Global Corruption Report. http://www.globalcorruption-report.org/ (accessed June 13, 2007).

Turkish-U.S. Business Relations Council (2007), "Focus on Corporate Social Responsibility in Turkey", http://www.turkey-now.org/default.aspx?pgID=401 (accessed August 03, 2007).

Ulker Group, "Corporate Social Responsibility", http://www.ulker.com.tr/ulkerportal/kurumsal/sosyal_sorumluluk/ (accessed August 21, 2007).

Ulker, Annual Report (2006).

Ullman, A.A. (1985), "Data in search of a theory: a critical examination of the relationships and social performance, social disclosure, and economic performance of US firms", *Academy of Management Review*, Volume: 10, pp.540–57.

UNDP: United Nations Development Programme (2007); "Baseline Study on CSR Practices in the New E.U. Member States and Candidate Countries", pp.20–25.

Chapter 19
Nigeria: CSR as a Vehicle for Economic Development

Olatoye Ojo

Abstract It is generally believed that no matter how benevolent, a government alone cannot provide all the needs of its citizenry. The development of the economy of any nation is therefore perceived as the joint responsibility of the government, the citizenry, and corporate entities operating within its boundaries. This paper examines the corporate social responsibility (CSR) activities of corporate entities in Nigeria, with specific focus on six key sectors of the economy that operate principally for profit (oil and gas; food, beverages, and tobacco; banking; telecommunications; construction; and conglomerates) and two other sectors that are not-for-profit (churches and charitable organizations).

Primary data were obtained from corporate entities operating within the aforementioned sectors of the economy and duly analyzed. The study showed that corporate entities in Nigeria embrace CSR practices, with their activities being pronounced in varying degrees, in areas such as health care, manpower development and capacity building, football and sports, scholarship schemes and educational development, youth development schemes, staff welfare, provision of basic infrastructure, microcredit, business development, and economic empowerment. A major feature of these activities is that they are primarily focused on the geographical areas of operation of the respective organizations. The study also showed that rather than presenting stand-alone CSR reports, Nigerian corporate entities incorporate their CSR activities in their annual report and accounts and that the CSR philosophy of most companies is still based on the philanthropic model rather than business strategy. The study concluded that CSR activities could be a potent vehicle for economic development in Nigeria.

Drawing from the experiences of advanced countries (like the UK), the paper suggests that the government should encourage corporate entities to be more involved in CSR activities, so as to serve as a more effective vehicle for economic development in Nigeria through persuasion and appropriate legislation. The implication of this is that, with the appropriate legal and regulatory framework, corporate entities in Nigeria can meaningfully partner with the government in the development of the country's economy.

S. O. Idowu and W. L. Filho (eds.), *Global Practices of Corporate Social Responsibility*   393

19.1 Introduction

It is generally believed the world over that no matter how benevolent, a government alone cannot provide all the needs of its citizenry. The development of the economy of any nation is therefore perceived as the joint responsibility of the government, the citizenry, and corporate entities operating within its boundaries.

Currently, the various sectors of the Nigerian economy are virtually in a state of decadence and decay. The road system is in a terrible state of disrepair, while the rail system has been grounded over the years and all efforts to revamp it have not yielded any positive result. For example, the Ibadan-Lagos, Benin-Ore-Sagamu, and Ilesa-Akure expressways are typical examples of highways in the country that create untold hardships and nightmares for road travelers. Most government hospitals across the country do not have modern equipment or even drugs to dispense to patients. The situation in the country's secondary and tertiary public institutions is no different, where laboratory equipment and library books are outdated in most cases. The phenomenon of brain drain in the nation's tertiary institutions is just being reversed, especially with the establishment of privately owned universities.

The security situation in our urban centers and particularly in the Niger Delta (the home of the nation's oil industry) is now very worrisome and has consistently constituted a global concern that appears to defy solutions. The issue of corruption in governance by the political class (especially the past state chief executives, some of who are now on the run) as recorded in the print media (and revealed by Economic and Financial Crimes Commission) is now a major problem facing the nation's economy (Tell No. 41, October 8, 2007; Tell No. 42, October 15, 2007). The looting of government treasuries at various levels of governance has hampered the provision of essential infrastructure and other basic services that are necessary in moving the economy forward.

It is the contention of this paper that in spite of the failure of the government to provide necessary impetus for the sustenance of the various sectors of the economy as enumerated above, the CSR phenomenon, which is gradually gaining prominence globally, can serve as an avenue for improving the lot of the masses, especially the host communities where these organizations operate. It is reasoned that CSR activities can complement the market-oriented reform measures embarked upon by the government in the various sectors of the economy (such as energy, telecommunications, and banking) to bring about the much needed positive changes in the nation's economy. Some of these reform measures are expected to reduce waste, improve efficiency, and curb corruption in governance.

It is against the foregoing background that this paper examines the CSR activities of corporate entities in Nigeria as a way of complementing these market-oriented reform measures of the government, with specific focus on the oil and gas, food, beverages, and tobacco, banking, telecommunications, construction, and conglomerates sectors of the economy. While these six sectors operate principally for profit, the study also considered CSR activities of churches and charitable organizations that are not-for-profit. Based on the experience of advanced countries that have embraced CSR practices, the paper looks at the level of awareness of CSR, its philosophy, the mode of reporting, and the motivation behind involvement in CSR and related activities in Nigeria. Before presenting the concluding remarks, the paper highlights the major projects sponsored by the various organizations in the selected sectors of the economy. It is submitted in this paper that with the appropriate legal and regulatory framework (as present in advanced countries), coupled with a very conducive environment, CSR activities can be made to serve as a potent vehicle for socio-economic development in Nigeria.

19.2 Review of Literature

Although its practice could be traced back to such examples as the Quakers in the 17th and 18th centuries whose business philosophy was not primarily driven by profit maximization but by the need to add value to society at large, so that business was perceived as an integral part of society, the expression *corporate social responsibility* (CSR) was first used in 1953 by Bowen in his book "Social Responsibility for Businessmen", where he posited what responsibilities businessmen can be reasonably expected to assume. Drucker (1984) wrote about the imperative of turning social problems into economic opportunities.

As of today, many definitions of CSR have emerged. The World Business Council for Sustainable Development in its publication titled "Making Business Sense", authored by Lord Holme and Richard Watts, defined CSR as "the continuing commitment by business to behave ethically and contribute to economic development while improving the quality of life of the workforce and their families as well as of the local community and the society at large". The World Bank (2006) defined CSR as the "commitment of business to contribute to sustainable economic development, working with employees, their families, local community and society at large to improve the quality of life in ways that are both good for business and good for development". This World Bank definition appears flawed in that it does not put business under any obligation to do something if there is no enhancement in profit, which is considered the primary motive of business. The EU's (2001) Green Paper on CSR defined it as "a concept whereby companies integrate social and environmental concerns in their business operations and in their interaction with their stakeholders on a voluntary basis".

There are several other definitions of CSR by scholars and countries (UK Department of Trade and Industry, 2004; Industrial Canada, 2006; Bajpai, 2001; International Institute for Sustainable Development, 2007). Although there are variations in the definitions from the cited sources, they are all unanimous about the concept and ideology of CSR, which is broadly all about making life worthwhile for the stakeholders in all aspects of a company's operations. In other words, CSR is supposed to involve inculcating into the business strategy of organizations the voluntary execution of activities that are meant to improve the living standard of its stakeholders and, at the same time, enhancing the profit generation of the company. It also involves treating the stakeholder of the firm ethically or in a responsible manner. "Ethically" or "in a responsible manner" means treating stakeholders in a way considered acceptable in civilized societies. Stakeholders exist both within and outside a firm.

The scope of coverage of CSR stakeholders is wide and all-encompassing, and not limited to company shareholders and investors in a business enterprise. The following CSR stakeholders of an organization can be identified – the shareholders and potential investors, managers, employees, customers, business partners and contractors, the natural environment, the communities within which the company business operates, and the government at various levels. The main CSR activities and commitments that an organization will address normally center around the following issues – health and safety, environmental protection, human rights, human resources management practices, and corporate governance. Others include consumer protection, supplier relations, stakeholders' rights, community development, labor protection, and business ethics. These CSR activities (as applicable) are reported either on a stand-alone basis or embedded in the annual reports of such organizations. For example, a typical CSR report of a UK company will give information on its relevant activities during the year that has just ended, under four main headings: environment, community, marketplace, and workplace.

The philosophy of CSR activities is based on two models, namely the philanthropic or US model and the European model (Ekpu, 2007). Under the philanthropic model (which is prevalent in the US), companies are expected to make profits and then pay taxes to the appropriate authorities, as well as donate a certain portion of the profits to charity. The European model, on the other hand, is more focused on operating the core business in a socially responsible manner, complemented by investment in communities for solid business case reasons. The advantage of the European model is that social responsibility will be an integral part of the wealth creation process that can enhance the competitiveness of business and enhance the value of wealth creation to society at large. In such a situation, the incentive to practice CSR will remain unhampered whatever happens.

According to Ekpu (2007), there has been a clamor by civil society and the media for a more regulated business environment, especially with respect to environmental and human rights and general transparency. This clamor has led to the establishment of the Extractive Industries Transparency Initiative (EITI), which has been embraced by many governments (including Nigeria), the Good Neighborhood Agreements (GNAs), and many other protocols aimed at bringing business in line with human rights, labor rights, transparency and environmental concerns.

Ralph (2004) identified some reasons as the driving force behind the involvement of organizations in CSR and related activities. These include the government's role in shirking responsibility, demand for greater disclosure, increased customer interest, competitive labor markets, growing investor pressure, and supplier relations. In an earlier UK study (Idowu, 2005) that was designed to elicit the motivation behind UK companies' involvement in CSR and its related activities, the following reasons were adduced: to inform their stakeholders, to inform the public at large, in response to competitors' action on best practice reporting, and for positive public relations benefits. Other reasons stated were to satisfy disclosure requirements of institutional investors, to demonstrate open management style in compliance with government directives, to demonstrate to stakeholders that non-financial matters are equally important to them, and in response to questionnaires to be completed for tenders and for government departments. It should be noted that the concept of CSR is now firmly rooted on the global business agenda.

The practice of CSR and its related activities in different countries of the world is now being documented in literature and unpublished works. For example, the European Foundation (2002) sponsored a study on the practice of CSR in enterprises in the UK, France, Germany, and Hungary. Similar studies on the practice of CSR in enterprises in Canada, Japan, and India (http://strategic.ic.gl, 2006; Bajpai, 2001) have also been undertaken by different scholars, groups, and organizations. This further confirms that CSR is firmly rooted on the global agenda. As this paper is on CSR in Nigeria, it is reasoned that discussions of outcomes of CSR studies in the various countries mentioned are not necessary here.

However, in an earlier study on CSR in Nigeria by Amaeshi et al. (2006), it was found that indigenous firms perceive and practice CSR as corporate philanthropy aimed at addressing socio-economic development challenges in Nigeria, thus confirming that CSR is a localized and socio-culturally embedded construct. The study also acknowledged the meager literature on CSR in developing economies and that the Nigerian corporate governance framework still essentially reflects the shareholder supremacy, where companies are viewed as private actors to be run exclusively in the interests of shareholders. This view is also followed by the Nigerian courts. While the study shows that the understanding and practice of CSR in Nigeria is still largely philanthropic and altruistic, the finding is in many ways at variance with the current understanding and practice of CSR in Western economies, where CSR is argued to have "advanced" beyond philanthropy. It is hoped that this paper, like its predecessors, will be a contribution to the study of CSR and its related activities in Nigeria.

19.3 Methodology

The study population for this work was drawn from six key sectors of the country's economy that operate principally for profit, and two other sectors that are not-for-profit (see Appendix). The samples adopted for each of the eight sectors were generated from the records of the Corporate Affairs Commission and are as indicated in Table 19.1

- Oil and Gas (6)
- Food, beverages, and tobacco (3)
- Banking (6)
- Telecommunications (3)

Table 19.1 Sectoral distribution of organizations studied

Sector	No	Percentage
Oil and gas	6	22.22
Food, beverages, and tobacco	3	11.11
Banking	6	22.22
Telecommunications	3	11.11
Construction	2	7.41
Conglomerates	2	7.41
Churches (not-for-profit)	2	7.41
Charitable Organizations (not-for-profit)	3	11.11
Total	27	100

Source: Author's Field Survey, 2007.

– Construction (2)
– Conglomerates (2)
– Churches (2) – not-for-profit
– Charitable (3) – not-for-profit

The CSR and other related activities of 27 organizations in Nigeria have been studied and analyzed in this work. Primary data were obtained from the 27 organizations operating within the aforementioned sectors with the aid of a combination of structured questionnaires, personal interviews, and CSR web reporting of the studied organizations (where applicable), which were duly analyzed. The administered questionnaire was structured to elicit information from the respondent organizations on issues such as awareness of CSR, involvement in CSR practices, mode of CSR reporting, CSR philosophy, motivation behind CSR activities embarked upon, and CSR projects sponsored by the organizations studied.

Personal interviews were held with top management staff of the organizations studied, especially their managers in charge of CSR activities. Information was also obtained from CSR web reporting of the studied organizations. Secondary data for the work were obtained from review of existing published works on CSR and its related activities across the globe. Data collection was between March and August 2007.

19.4 Results and Discussion

The results of analysis of data obtained on the organizations studied in this work are contained in Tables 19.1–19.7. Table 19.1 shows the sectoral distribution of organizations studied. As indicated earlier, the first six sectors, (oil and gas; food, beverages, and tobacco; banking; telecommunications; construction; and conglomerates) operate principally for profit, while the two other sectors (churches and charitable organizations) are not established for profit motives. The first sector in the first category, oil and gas, is very central to the country's economy because petroleum

Table 19.2 Awareness of CSR concept

Opinion	No	Percentage
Aware	27	100
Not aware	–	0
TOTAL	27	100

Source: Author's Field Survey, 2007.

Table 19.3 Involvement in CSR practice

Opinion	No	Percentage
Involved	27	100
Not Involved	–	0
TOTAL	27	100

Source: Author's Field Survey, 2007.

Table 19.4 Mode of CSR reporting

Opinion*	No	Percentage
Stand-alone	–	0
Embedded in annual report & accounts	22	100
TOTAL	22	100

Source: Author's Field Survey, 2007.
*Five of the respondents did not answer this question.

Table 19.5 CSR philosophy

Opinion	No	Percentage
Philanthropic model	20	74.1
Business strategy (European Model)	2	7.4
Others (religious and humanitarian)	5	18.5
TOTAL	27	100

Source: Author's Field Survey, 2007.

Table 19.6 Drivers of CSR activities by the studied organizations

S/N	Motivation behind CSR Activities embarked upon	Percentage*
1	Community relations (identify with needs of local communities where they operate)	100
2	Complement government efforts	100
3	Proof of being socially responsible	81
4	Proof of organization's success	55
5	Public relations and business promotion	81
6	Global trend influence	22
7	Religious and societal persuasion	19

Source: Author's Field Survey, 2007.
*Respondent organizations gave multiple answers.

Table 19.7 CSR projects sponsored by the organizations studied

S/N	Project description
1	Health care
2	Manpower development and capacity building
3	Football and sports
4	Scholarship schemes and educational development
5	Youth development schemes
6	Microcredit, business development, and economic empowerment schemes
7	Basic infrastructure
8	Staff welfare
9	Legal aid, human rights protection, and support for the less privileged
10	Conservation and protection of the environment

Source: Author's Field Survey, 2007.

accounts for about 40% of the GDP. Nigeria is the 12th largest world producer and 8th largest exporter and has the 10th largest proven reserves of crude oil. The five other sectors are also very important, and they contribute significantly to the development and growth of the nation's economy in one form or another, as will be further enumerated later in this paper. Also, the contributions of the organizations studied in the second category, namely churches and charitable organizations, will be discussed later in the paper. The study includes 22 organizations in the six sectors of the first category (for profit motives) and 5 organizations in the two sectors of the second category (not-for-profit), giving a total of 27 organizations altogether.

Table 19.2 provides information on the awareness of the CSR concept by the organizations studied. It shows that all the organizations are conversant with the CSR concept. Table 19.3 documents the involvement of the studied organizations in the practice of CSR and its related activities. It shows that all the studied organizations are involved in CSR and its related activities in one form or another, an indication that they are socially responsible corporate entities or citizens. Some of the specific CSR activities of these organizations will be presented in this paper. This result also corroborates that of Table 19.2 above, that all the organizations are aware of the CSR concept and have in fact gone ahead to get involved in it.

Table 19.4 provides information on the mode of CSR reporting in the studied organizations. While 5 of the organizations (in the second category) did not supply information on this aspect, all the remaining 22 respondent organizations have their CSR activities embedded in their annual report and accounts. It is reasoned that these organizations see this mode of CSR reporting as a more effective means of disclosing their CSR and related activities to their shareholders, stakeholders, and the public at large. In fact, in addition to the annual reports and accounts being sent directly to shareholders in Nigeria, many companies publish these in reputable national newspapers. The stand-alone mode of CSR reporting is yet to be embraced, except reports carried as news items in print and electronic media, highlighting such CSR activities to present the affected organizations to the public as socially responsible corporate entities or citizens.

Results of the analysis of the CSR philosophy of organizations studied are contained in Table 19.5. Information was elicited within three main contexts: philanthropic model, business strategy (European model), and others (religious and humanitarian). The 74.1% of the studied organizations based their CSR philosophy on the philanthropic model. This is anchored in their perceived obligation to plow part of their profits back into society and, particularly, promote the well-being of people in the communities that fall within their areas of operations and contributing to their sustainable development. 18.5% based their CSR philosophy on religious and humanitarian considerations. This is anchored in religious beliefs and the need to help the less privileged. The remaining 7.4% based their CSR philosophy on business strategy (European model), which is anchored more in economic, legal, and ethical responsibilities, over and above philanthropic considerations.

Table 19.6 documents drivers of or motivations behind CSR and its related activities among the studied organizations. All the organizations (100%) see their CSR activities as being motivated by community relations (identifying with the needs of local communities where they operate) and the need to complement government efforts in the socio-economic development of the country. Eighty-five per cent embark on CSR activities to prove that they are responsible corporate citizens and for public relations and business promotion purposes respectively. Fifty-five per cent are driven by the need to prove their organizations' success. Community relations, which are aimed at identifying the socio-economic needs of the host communities where these organizations operate, attracted 30% of the response rate. Twenty-two per cent adduced influence of the global trend and debate on the CSR concept as the driving force behind their involvement, while religious and societal persuasion accounts for 19% of the response rate.

The categories of CSR projects sponsored by the organizations studied are presented in Table 19.7. These include health care, manpower development and capacity building, football and sports, scholarship schemes and educational development, and youth development schemes. Others are microcredit, business development and economic empowerment schemes, and basic infrastructure. Also included are staff welfare, legal aid, human rights protection and support for the less privileged, and conservation and protection of the environment. The next section of this paper will discuss, in detail, the specific CSR projects and related activities embarked upon by the studied organizations in the various sectors of the economy.

19.5 CSR Activities of Studied Organizations in Nigeria

This section documents CSR and its related activities of the organizations studied in the various sectors of the country's economy.

19.5.1 Oil and Gas Sector

19.5.1.1 Shell Nigeria

Shell Nigeria places great importance on making a difference to the environment in which people live and work, fostering and maintaining relationships with communities, taking care to be a good neighbor, and contributing to sustainable development initiatives. The company's community development program in the Niger Delta region is based on the principles of sustainable development and best global practice. The scope of Shell Nigeria's CSR activities covers health care, the Shell Intensive Training Program (SITP, designed to develop the skills of young Nigerian graduates and technicians to prepare them for employment in the oil industry), and youth development schemes (basically aimed at reducing unemployment among youths and bringing them up as responsible citizens through its Citizenship Education, Youth Links Program, and Peace Education Program. In the area of health care, Shell Nigeria's giant strides, especially in the communities within its areas of operation, include provision of 14 cottage hospitals, 13 health centers, Land and Swamp mobile clinics, many health posts, as well as supply of equipment and drugs through a revolving scheme. These are in addition to immunization schemes and collaborative efforts with the National Advisory Council on AIDS (NACA) through the Nigerian Business Coalition against AIDS (NUBICAA) for stopping the spread of HIV/AIDS in the country.

In the area of football and sports, Shell Nigeria instituted the Shell Cup to ensure that talented youths are able to combine education with developing their football skills and career. Over 3,000 schools across the country take part in each edition of the competition. Shell Nigeria invests about NGN 30 million yearly in sponsoring the event. As regards scholarship schemes, capacity building, manpower and educational development, the company offers scholarships at various levels. Competition for its undergraduate scholarship scheme (which is open only to first year students) is in two categories – the National Merit Award (NM), open to all Nigerian undergraduates and Areas of Operation Merit Award (AOM) for students from communities in which Shell Nigeria operates.

There is also the Shell Centenary Scholarship Fund, which was established as a registered charity in 1997 for postgraduate studies at the Masters level, for students from developing countries to gain skills that will enable them to make long-term contributions to the further development of their countries. At the secondary level, there is the Shell Nigeria Secondary School Scholarship scheme, specifically designed for host communities in Abia, Akwa Ibom, Bayelsa, Delta, Edo, Imo, and Rivers states. An average of 2,600 scholarships are awarded in the seven states under this scheme annually and this has made it a welcome feature of educational development, especially in the Niger Delta region of Nigeria.

In addition to laudable staff welfare schemes, Shell Nigeria's CSR activities are also quite noticeable in the areas of microcredit, business development, and economic empowerment initiatives. The company's Micro-Credit and Business Development Program, which was launched to promote Micro, Small, and Medium Enterprises (MSMEs), has as its major components microcredit, the Live Wire Nigeria Program, and Women in Development. These initiatives are part of Shell Nigeria's efforts at ensuring the economic empowerment of host communities and enhancing their contribution to the socio-economic development of Nigeria.

19.5.1.2 Total Nigeria

Building partnerships for sustainable development is part of Total Nigeria's corporate philosophy. Over the years, Total Nigeria has seen itself as part of the people and the environment in which it operates by identifying positively with their aspirations – economically, socially and culturally. Total Nigeria's development activities are identified via community categories, namely host communities, ethnic communities, coastline communities, and pipeline communities. Host communities are those on whose land the company has been producing oil and gas and has wells and/or oil and gas production facilities, office or housing facilities, as well as communities that are on the coastline and that are near the company's offshore operational facilities. Such communities are spread across Delta, Rivers, and Lagos states.

Ethnic communities are those which are of the same ethnic nationalities as their host communities, but which have none of Total Nigeria's facilities on their land, nor are they affected by the company's offshore operations. An example is the Egi Ethnic Communities (non-producing). The coastline communities are those considered and selected on the basis that the company's offshore operations (including movement of boats) could have a direct impact on their ecological environment. They are either directly on the coastline or have tidal rivers within their shores. They are found in Rivers and Akwa Ibom states. The pipeline communities are those where the trunk lines pass.

The scope of Total Nigeria's CSR activities covers provision of basic infrastructure, health care, scholarship schemes and educational development, staff welfare, manpower development and capacity building, as well as microcredit, business development, and economic empowerment schemes. In 2003, Total Nigeria devoted some USD 17 million to its program of socio-economic initiatives in Nigeria. Total Upstream is engaged in bringing the basic necessities of modern life – energy, water supply, roads, and electricity – to people throughout the country as well as developing important community infrastructure such as modern markets and civic centers.

The Egi electrification project is perhaps the most ambitious and comprehensive community development embarked upon by Total Nigeria, with the objective of supplying an effective and uninterrupted electricity supply to all communities (over 20 towns and villages) within the Egi kingdom in Rivers state. The project, whose cost is estimated at over NGN 800 million, has brought along with it other ancillary benefits, such as improvement in quality of life in the rural communities of Egi kingdom, eradication of power outage within the kingdom, and encouragement of the growth of small industries due to constant power supply. Under its basic infrastructure commitment, the company provides potable pipe-borne water for its communities through water schemes that are centrally located at Akabuka, Akabta, Amah, Erema, Ibewa/Obukegi, Obagi, Obite, and Obiyebe. To ensure steady water supply, all the water schemes are operated and maintained through local contractors.

The objective of the road component of Total Nigeria's basic infrastructure program is to open the communities to further development and economic empowerment. The road network, which is asphalted and executed in three phases, covers a distance of 70 km and is valued at more than USD 2.4 million (approximately NGN 308 million). In order to boost trade and commerce in the communities, the company has constructed a number of modern markets. In addition, civic centers and community halls are built for community use and provided with libraries, postal agencies, guest rooms, beauty saloons, and large halls for social gatherings, town meetings, educational meetings, and other purposes for public good.

In the area of health care, Total Nigeria's CSR activities involve contributions to building renovations and equipment for community hospitals, donation of ambulances and medications, sponsorship of free community health care programs and local campaigns against AIDS. For example, the company undertook the renovation and equipping of the Erema hospital in Rivers state and the Ikot-Idaha Health Center in Akwa Ibom state, the two projects costing over NGN 45 million. A new hospital at Obagi Community in Rivers state, valued at about NGN 58 million, is under construction. There is also the donation of two ambulances to the Delta Manna Foundation near Warri and to the Erema hospital, for emergency health care delivery. In 2002, the company organized the Great Aids Walk in Onelga in collaboration with the Rivers State Ministry of Health, and over five thousand people from 42 communities participated in the rally against HIV/AIDS.

As regards scholarship schemes and educational development, the company has taken a number of giant strides as well. Scholarships at all levels of education have been awarded to over 15,000 Nigerian students, along with provision of educational infrastructure and computer equipment to over 90 educational institutions in the Niger Delta and donations to endowment funds in universities and colleges. Recently, the company established an Institute of Petroleum Studies (IPS) at the University of Port Harcourt in conjunction with the French Petroleum Institute (IFP) in Paris with a view to providing high-level training for Nigerians in Petroleum Engineering and Management-related studies. In 2005, the company provided an E-library and an electricity generating set to the Rivers State Polytechnic, Bori. In the same year, it provided VSAT and internet facilities to the Rivers State University of Science and Technology, Port Harcourt.

In the area of staff welfare, the organization carries out staff development assistance at departmental, divisional, and company levels, complemented by infrastructure facilities when necessary. The company's CSR activities in the areas of manpower development and capacity building, youth development, microcredit, business development, and economic empowerment are implemented through a number of initiatives. The company pursues a deliberate policy that guarantees the award of contracts to skilled and qualified contractors, and the employment of indigenes of host communities. To this end, all contracts for community projects are reserved exclusively for qualified community contractors. Currently, a program called Development of the Potentials of Proven Talents is being run by the company in partnership with the French Embassy to identify young talent in Nigeria and expose these future professionals to modern laboratories, methods, and techniques in French Universities, up to Ph.D. level.

About 1,200 youths from Akwa Ibom, Delta, and Rivers states have benefited from the company's Skills Development program, which teaches them a wide range of trades, such as welding and fabrication, carpentry, hairdressing, fashion and design, among others. This initiative aims at preparing youths to contribute meaningfully to the growth and development of their respective communities through gainful self-employment in their various trades, to employ others and, in the long-term, to pass on their knowledge to others. Other economic empowerment schemes being executed by the company in this regard include the Agricultural and Micro-Credit program and the community business initiative and talent trading programs. All these community development strategies or initiatives are aimed at empowering the host communities and creating conditions that would enable them to achieve sustainable development.

19.5.1.3 Oando Group

The Oando Group's interest has matured from core business operations to include issues relating to corporate social responsibility, with the main objective of making a positive impact on the lives of people that reside in communities where the organization operates. Besides staff welfare schemes, Oando Plc's current CSR activities focus mainly on scholarship schemes, educational development, and sports development, which are pursued through a number of initiatives.

In April 2007, the company initiated the Adopt-A-School project to serve as an avenue to contribute toward the growth of education in communities where it operates. The project involves contribution toward the development of the schools for the duration of the "adoption" through the renovation of facilities, provision of teaching aids, books, and the like. The maiden beneficiary of the project is the Government Primary School, Ekorinim, Calabar, Cross Rivers state, which was "adopted" on 28th June 2007. The school has over 500 pupils and six classrooms, and is in need of structural renovation and assistance. The company has decided to improve the quality of education in Nigeria through its CSR initiative, with 90% of its CSR budget being geared toward empowering youths through education.

In 2005, the company initiated its Post Primary School Children's Scholarship project, which is awarded annually to indigent students of host communities, who are identified and recommended by the communities based on financial and other special needs. The project, so far, provides scholarships to ten children collectively in the Bundu and Onne communities in Rivers state. The aim of the company's scholarship and educational development projects is to promote education of youths in Nigeria, with special focus on primary and secondary schooling for less privileged children in the communities where it operates.

In addition to sponsoring various children's competitions, programs, and activities, Oando Plc has been sponsoring a young and talented golfer, Mohammed Muazu, since 2005. He was discovered in 2005 at the Ikoyi Club, where he was nursing the dream of becoming a professional golfer. Oando has supported him through sponsorship of matches, golf kits, and pre-university examinations. Oando Plc's support of Mohammed Muazu is part of the company's strategic stance on CSR initiatives.

19.5.1.4 Nigeria LNG

In helping to put out gas flares in Nigeria, Nigeria LNG (NLNG), through its community relations management, is also serving the interest of the communities in which it operates. Community development emphasis is geared toward self-reliance and sustainability. The scope of NLNG's CSR activities covers provision of basic infrastructure, health care, manpower development and capacity building, scholarship schemes, and educational development. Other CSR activities are youth development schemes, staff welfare and microcredit, business development, and economic empowerment.

The aforementioned CSR activities are aimed at enabling the community to develop the appropriate mindset for self-reliance and development independent of outsiders, as well as ensuring the development or refurbishment of existing physical infrastructure. On the whole, the company has so far executed no fewer than 50 community projects on Bonny Island and about 200 self-help projects in its pipeline communities. On these projects, NLNG expends more than USD 7 million annually.

The company's CSR activities on provision of basic infrastructure cover the following components: road construction/rehabilitation; provision of potable water; power generation, distribution, and maintenance; and other social amenities. Some of the projects executed under the road construction/ rehabilitation initiative include the construction of the Coal Beach roundabout and Bonny Sandy Road. In addition, the following roads have been rehabilitated: Court Road, Park Road, King Perukele Road, Lecox/Isowari Road, New Layout, and King Jaja Road, among others. The Joint Industry Committee (JIC) – with NLNG having 50% participation and Mobil and Shell having 30% and 20%, respectively – established the Bonny Utilities Company (BUC) for the management, operation, and maintenance of utilities on Bonny Island, and the company has provided Bonny communities with approximately 95% uninterrupted power supply since its inception.

Some of the JIC's executed projects include the 2.7 km link road along the existing embankment to Abalamibie, the 2.7 km Bonny by-pass road, provision of a higher capacity power distribution network, the Bonny town water scheme, the Abalamibie water extension, and production of a Master Plan for Bonny. Besides the JIC projects, NLNG has contributed to the provision of potable water to its host communities with the construction of a gigantic water borehole in Ubeta and being responsible for the operation and distribution of water supply in Finima town and many parts of Bonny.

In the area of health care, several CSR health projects sponsored by the company were completed in Ogba, Emohua, Ekpeye, and Abuja kingdoms, prior to 2002. In addition, the following projects have been undertaken: renovation of health staff quarters in the Bakana and Isaka Health Centers, provision of health center equipment at Omoku, completion of the Ohali-Elu Health Center, and refurbishment of Okposi and Ebogoro water extension in the Obite Health Center.

As regards scholarship schemes and educational development, in 1998 NLNG established a community scholarship scheme designed for the sons and daughters of the company's host communities. The scheme, which covers post primary and tertiary education, kicked off in 1998 with 35 awardees/recipients. The number rose to 240 during academic year 1999/2000, and by 2000/2001 more than 632 candidates had benefited. So far, over 2,400 students from among NLNG's host communities in Bonny and GTS have benefited from the scholarship scheme. The scholarship scheme has now been extended to merit students from other parts of Rivers state and Nigeria.

In addition to staff welfare, the company also instituted a number of CSR programs to address projects/issues related to manpower development and capacity building, youth development, microcredit, business development, and economic empowerment, all to the advantage of its host communities. Specifically, the company's Business and Human Development programs have a number of components that address the aforementioned issues, such as award of pipelines, right-of-way surveillance and inspection contracts, and asset maintenance contracts to serve as encouragement to indigenous contractors. Other initiatives include provision of employment opportunities to skilled and unskilled members of its host communities, as well as provision of micro credit.

The Bonny Education Endowment Fund was established in 1997 to "top up" Bonny teachers' salaries. Since then, the company has spent over NGN 43 million on the project. The Fund is an incentive to encourage teachers to remain in the classroom rather than drifting to construction sites, where the pay is more attractive. The Fund also serves other beneficial purposes, such as provision of text/exercise books and school desks, rehabilitation of schools, and supply of science equipment.

The Bonny Vocational Center (an educational establishment) is an NLNG/Bonny Kingdom partnership project designed to promote vocational/entrepreneurial skills acquisition, development of technical competencies, and self-reliance in youths in the Bonny community in particular and Rivers state in general. The Youth Empowerment Scheme (YES) is a sustainable development initiative of NLNG, which targets youths in the host communities and is designed to encourage them to acquire skills through technical training. It was launched in 2004 to promote self-employment, small-scale businesses, and economic empowerment. Trainees are given a monthly allowance for transportation and sundry needs and the program is open to unemployed youths between 18 and 25 years of age. Under the just-concluded first phase of the micro-credit scheme, more than NGN 110 million was disbursed to 248 groups, out of which NGN 67 million (representing 78% of due loans) has been recovered.

19.5.1.5 Addax Petroleum

At Addax Petroleum, being a good corporate citizen – giving back to the community, caring about the health and safety of its employees, protecting the environment of its host communities, and conducting business with integrity and accountability – is seen as a critical part of building a dynamic and profitable company. The company's good reputation with stakeholders rests on three pillars: (a) the Community Relations Program (b) Health, Safety, and Environment Programs and (c) the Code of Conduct.

The scope of the company's CSR activities covers health care, manpower development and capacity building, scholarship schemes and educational development, staff welfare, and provision of basic infrastructure. These various projects, which are executed through the company's community relations program, involve the financing of road construction and improvements like road upgrading in Ndioko and Ugbele villages. The company has supplied and installed water and power systems in a number of other communities. The company also delivers financial support for a range of education and training projects that provide real and immediate benefits to the people.

Under the company's Health, Safety, and Environment (HSE) initiative, Addax Petroleum sees as key priorities the creation of a safe and healthy workplace for employees, contractors, and the public, and the practice of responsible stewardship of the environment in its activities. The company instituted the Training and Safe Operations initiative, under which employees and contractors' staff are trained in the company's HSE policy and work procedures. Under this initiative, the company conducts regular safety training sessions and emergency response drills. Task Risk Assessments of activities are conducted regularly and control measures instituted to eliminate or mitigate HSE impact.

In order to encourage employees to report unsafe conditions and practices, the company adopted a "No Blame" approach to responding to accidents and near-misses under its Incident Reporting and Investigation initiative. The "No Blame" approach has ensured that there is excellent two-way communication between employees and management on health and safety issues. Environmental protection and conservation are a fundamental part of the company's operations and this is pursued under the company's initiative on the environment. The company ensures that all new projects comply with the relevant standards and regulations, while its existing facilities are upgraded. The company's waste management policy promotes minimization and recycling. The Leadership and

Commitment Company (which is another initiative of Addax) conducts, through its management, regular safety tours of facilities and also sponsors and promotes health and safety programs. On the whole, the company focuses on developing strong local relationships and on aligning its priorities with those of its host communities.

19.5.1.6 Zenon Petroleum and Gas Ltd

The belief at Zenon is that success is unachievable without the highest standards of social responsibility. Commitment to corporate responsibility constitutes the driving force of the organization, and it aims at continuing to build upon its value-driven ideals by supporting value-driven initiatives in its host communities.

The scope of Zenon's CSR activities covers health care, staff welfare scholarship schemes and educational development, as well as sports. With its commitment to CSR activities as outlined above, the company seeks to positively impact the lives of people in its host communities through donations to NGOs and charitable organizations and sponsorship of various events. In pursuit of its CSR activities, Zenon provides support to the following organizations: (a) the Children's Developmental Center – a service oriented, non-profit organization providing a broad range of educational support services for disabled children and their families within the host communities and (b) the Family Care Association – a locally-based humanitarian missionary organization dedicated to the goal of helping those in need through various medical and educational projects throughout the country. In the area of sports, Zenon has sponsored the 2004 Ladies Open Golf Championship, Abuja, Nigeria, and the 2004 Lagos Polo tournament, where the company served as the major sponsor of the event's HIV/AIDS Awareness Fund.

19.5.2 Food, Beverages and Tobacco Sector

19.5.2.1 Cadbury Nigeria Plc

Cadbury Nigeria's CSR philosophy is based on the recognition that, as a manufacturer and marketer of various consumer products and as a corporate citizen, it must articulate and pursue its obligations to society at large. To this end, its social responsibility is not limited to a concern with welfare schemes, charity work, or the occasional support for health, education, and sports, but includes being socially responsible at all times and in all its activities, maintaining high standards of integrity in its methods and practices of doing business. Cadbury's philosophy of social responsibility is predicated on three main elements: corporate responsibility to stakeholders, supporting society's important activities, and social development. According to Cadbury's erstwhile Managing Director and CEO, Mr. Bunmi Oni, the company's commitment to growing community value is an integral part of Cadbury's business and it will remain firmly on its agenda into the future.

The scope of Cadbury Nigeria's CSR activities covers health care, manpower development and capacity building, football and sports, scholarship schemes and educational development, youth development schemes, staff welfare, and provision of basic infrastructure. Through these CSR activities, Cadbury has, for the past four decades, supported local community projects and initiatives. This heritage of caring has been the underlying principle that governs the company's relationships with consumers, customers, shareholders, suppliers, employees, and society at large. The company's policies also span respect for the environment, corporate governance, ethical trading, human rights, safety at work, diversity, and include equal opportunity employment practices.

In the area of health care, Cadbury Nigeria has been at the vanguard of the promotion of healthy lifestyles for the overall benefit of society. The company was the first to offer a quality guarantee on its brands as a clear statement of its commitment to the safety of consumers. The company partnered with UNICEF to develop Vitamin A supplements for Bournvita as a result of widespread deficiency of that vitamin, especially among children. Cadbury Nigeria is also involved in health advocacy on HIV/AIDS awareness and has partnered with the Genotype Foundation and C.O.P.E. to raise awareness on sickle cell disease and breast cancer, respectively. Mr. Bunmi Oni, the company's erstwhile CEO, is on the Board of Trustees of the Nigerian Heart Foundation, while the company has sponsored individuals who required plastic surgery, kidney transplants, and prostheses. Cadbury Nigeria has also sponsored seminars and workshops organized by health institutions.

Many initiatives are in place for Cadbury's CSR activities related to scholarship schemes and educational development. One of them is the Bournvita Children's Magic Flight, which is an annual event that seeks to develop leadership capabilities in children by exposing them to different geographies and scenarios in order to broaden their mental frontiers. Since its inception in 1998, the initiative has taken children from all over Nigeria to Abuja, Ghana, the UK (twice), Paris, South Africa, and to Kenya in 2003. The initiative has created new friendships across countries and built harmonious relationships amongst children, adults, companies, and countries. In 2002, Cadbury Nigeria instituted the Bournvita Teachers Awards for promoting and rewarding excellence amongst teachers, in acknowledgement of their unique role in national development. There is also the Bournvita Brainmatch initiative, which is an interschool quiz and debate competition designed to foster healthy rivalry and raise standards. In addition, the company awards scholarships and donates equipment, such as computers, to schools. It also partners with credible and relevant organizations such as APCON and JAN to add value to education.

Cadbury Nigeria has recorded giant strides in its CSR activities in football and sports development. Starting from the 1970s, when the company sponsored the broadcast of Brazilian soccer on television, through the 1980s, with its involvement in table tennis and the Bournvita Soccer Awards, to the 1990s, with the Bournvita Football League and the Cadbury Cup Golf Tournament, Cadbury Nigeria has established an unrivalled track record in sports sponsorships in Nigeria.

The Bournvita Professional League pioneered by Cadbury Nigeria provided the solid foundation that subsequently produced world-class stars such as Kanu Nwankwo, Jay Jay Okocha, Wilson Oruma, and several others. The Bournvita Table Tennis Classic also brought some of the best players in the world to Nigeria to conduct coaching clinics for budding Nigerian players. Cadbury's Tom Tom sponsors chess competitions and the very popular Cadbury Cup Golf Tournament, the only inter-club match-play competition, regarded as the most prestigious golf tournament in Nigeria. The company also sponsors inter-house sports competitions in many schools throughout Nigeria.

In the area of manpower development and capacity building, Cadbury is involved in a number of CSR initiatives. A unique feature of the company's activity in this area is its involvement in the development and promotion of the arts, focusing on two genres: literary arts and fine arts. In 1995, Cadbury Nigeria sponsored the "Hope" Art Exhibition, which featured Idowu Akinrolabu, a physically challenged but talented artist who is today a celebrated painter. The company also supports the prestigious Cadbury/ANA poetry award, a joint initiative with the Association of Nigerian Authors (ANA). Poets within and outside Nigeria annually compete for this prize, and past winners included Professor Niyi Osundare and Professor Chimalum Nwankwo of the University of North Carolina.

Concern for the environment occupies top priority on Cadbury Nigeria's CSR agenda. The company proactively manages environmental issues associated with the supply of raw materials, manufacturing processes and facilities, as well as the distribution, sales, and consumption of its products. The company's effluent plant remains a reference point in the country's manufacturing industry, ensuring that all discharges meet or even exceed the standards stipulated by the regulatory environmental protection agencies. In addition, Cadbury Nigeria also promotes environmental awareness by sponsoring workshops and seminars in conjunction with credible and established NGOs such as the Nigerian People & Environment and the Nigerian Conservation Foundation (NCF).

Cadbury Nigeria has proved itself to be a highly responsible and caring corporate citizen among its neighbors in the area of provision of basic infrastructure. The Agidingbi community in Ikeja, where the company's head office is located, has, for the past 40 years, enjoyed regular and wholesome pipe-borne water from Cadbury Nigeria. From the foregoing discussion of the various activities of Cadbury Nigeria, it is clear that the company's corporate social responsibility goes beyond traditional corporate philanthropy. The company recognizes society as a whole as the stakeholder whose interest must always be protected. It embraces such issues with regard to people, the community, and the environment, and avoids the instinct for immediate profit maximization, thereby operating its business in a way that meets or exceeds the ethical, legal, commercial, and public expectations.

19.5.2.2 Nigeria Bottling Company Plc

Nigeria Bottling Company Plc (NBC) provides extensive support in Nigeria for community programs. The scope of NBC's CSR activities covers health care, football and sports, scholarship schemes and educational development, youth development, staff welfare, and provision of basic infrastructure. Under its CSR health care activity, NBC supports HOPE Worldwide Nigeria, an NGO that calls attention to the plight of children orphaned by AIDS or vulnerable to this disease that is ravaging Africa.

NBC has a long-standing tradition of sports development through its sponsorship of sporting activities. In the area of lawn tennis, NBC's relationship with the Lagos-based Ikoyi Club 1938 is a long-standing one. The club's annual competition, the Coca-Cola Lawn Tennis Tournament, is sponsored by NBC, and trophies and cash donations are given to the winners. Free refreshments, T-shirts, and caps are provided to all participants during the week-long event.

NBC has exclusive sponsorship rights to the Football Association Cup and the national teams (in the various categories) for which Coca-Cola is the official beverage. The Football Association's "FA Cup", better known as the Coca-Cola FA Cup, is the country's most inclusive and largest annual football competition. The company is also the major sponsor of the Coca-Cola/Hilton ProAm Golf Tournament. NBC provides golf attire for the players and uniforms for the caddies, and it also furnishes complimentary beverages during the four-day tournament.

NBC's concern for the environment as a responsible corporate citizen is displayed and pursued through its being a key sponsor of the NCF, an NGO focused on conserving natural resources and improving the quality of human life. The company also sponsors the Flora/Fauna Fancy Dress Competition in conjunction with NCF to mark World Environment Day. The competition features Lagos schoolchildren who dress up to depict an aspect of the natural environment. In the area of educational development, the Fanta National Schools Art and Essay Competition is a CSR initiative for which NBC has been solely responsible for more than 5 years. The competition seeks to instill a high level of environmental awareness in students who are 5–18 years of age, studying full-time. The overall first place winners in the Art and Essay categories receive all-expense-paid trips to a Nigerian forest/game reserve.

The company's CSR activities are also pronounced in the areas of manpower development and capacity building, as well as in the provision of basic infrastructure. NBC Plc., through its Port Harcourt plant, donated computer equipment to the local community of Oginigba in an attempt to provide support for socio-educational development in the region. The company also provided street lights in areas leading to the female residence halls at the headquarters of the National Association of Nigerian Students, furnished the Students' Union offices (including computers and a color printer), and installed cable TV at the Coke Village, a recreational on-campus facility built by NBC.

19.5.2.3 British American Tobacco Nigeria

British American Tobacco Nigeria (BAT Nigeria) is determined to demonstrate that a tobacco company can not only be socially responsible, but could equally set high standards of good corporate conduct. The company recognizes that by running its business well, it helps to drive the engine of economic development, which in turn helps to achieve social and environmental development. The company believes that high standards of CSR should be promoted within the tobacco industry, in which it has set standards by providing social amenities to the communities in which it operates.

The scope of BAT Nigeria's CSR activities covers environment, health and safety matters, rural agricultural development activities, afforestation programs, and provision of basic infrastructure. Their other CSR activities are manpower development and capacity building, scholarship schemes and educational development, staff welfare, poverty reduction, and economic empowerment. The various activities are pursued through a number of initiatives. As a responsible organization, BAT Nigeria recognizes that effective management of environmental, health, and safety (EHS) issues is an integral part of its business. The company has demonstrated this by working in partnership with relevant organizations to impart additional knowledge about environment, health, and safety measures to all its employees. The company's environmental management systems conform to international standards such as ISO 14001, while in safety management it has a zero target for accidents across its operations and is developing occupational health management (OHM) from a sound framework that is already in place.

BAT Nigeria is committed to the conservation of the environment and the sustainability of natural resources. The company is involved in the afforestation program of the Federal Government of Nigeria, and has also taken the initiative of nurturing its own conservation area located alongside its new Ibadan factory. BAT Nigeria has sponsored and promoted the planting of managed, renewable woodlands in Iseyin in addition to providing seedlings for afforestation purposes to the Federal Government of Nigeria. OHM occupies a prominent place on BAT Nigeria'S CSR health care agenda. Under its OHM program, the company ensures that none of its staff is exposed to any major causes of occupational health hazards. The company has on-site clinics that provide health services for factory workers in Zaria and Ibadan. It also provides workplace health education programs, basically to serve as a means of teaching its staff members how to protect themselves from contracting major diseases such as HIV/AIDS, tuberculosis, and malaria.

Two other major initiatives of BAT Nigeria that effectively address its CSR activities are BAT Iseyin Agronomy Limited (BATIA Ltd) and the BAT Nigeria Foundation. BATIA Ltd was incorporated in June 2003 as a wholly owned subsidiary of BAT Nigeria, with core responsibility for all tobacco growing operations and rural agricultural development activities. The specific activities of the initiative cover tobacco growing, crop financing, technical assistance, banking literacy, and mechanization schemes that promote timely land preparation, which is an essential ingredient for successful crop production. BATIA has put in place business opportunities to interested transporters by way of farm input and tobacco transportation. In the 2004 crop season alone, close to NGN 5 million and NGN 22 million was spent on transporting inputs and tobacco leaf, respectively.

The British American Tobacco Nigeria Foundation is another major initiative through which many of BAT Nigeria's CSR activities are pursued. The Foundation is an independent charitable organization incorporated in Nigeria in 2002 as a company limited by guarantee, in fulfillment of the Memorandum of Understanding (MOU) signed between the BAT Group and the Federal Government of Nigeria in 2001. The main objectives of the foundation are provision of potable water, agricultural development, poverty reduction, environmental protection, health care and immunization delivery, education, and disaster relief. The Foundation works closely with the Corporate Social Responsibility Team of BAT Nigeria to respond to stakeholder expectations.

Some of the major CSR projects executed by the Foundation include:

1. Supply of potable water to two communities each in Kano, Adamawa, and Sokoto states and one community in Kogi state.
2. Agricultural development project within the Ago-Are community, benefiting some farmers.
3. Introduction of watermelon production to farmers in Ago-Are with a view to assisting them in the production of a mid-season crop that will serve as a source of extra income to the farmers.
4. A poverty reduction project that focuses on empowering young adults to be self-employed and has so far been executed in three stages.

In 2004, a scholarship scheme was instituted by BATIA Ltd. The BATIA/BATN Scholarship provides educational sponsorship for Nigerians in tertiary institutions. Since inception, 25 undergraduates studying Agriculture/Agronomy in Universities and Polytechnics have been sponsored under the scheme. Through these various initiatives, BAT Nigeria, in conjunction with its subsidiaries, has proved itself a responsible corporate citizen committed to the socio-economic development of Nigeria.

19.5.3 Banking Sector

19.5.3.1 Zenith Bank Plc

Zenith Bank's CSR philosophy is evidently based on the philanthropic model, as the bank has, since inception, aggressively pursued a corporate policy geared toward giving back to the communities in which it operates. In pursuance of this policy, the bank set up Zenith Philanthropy, a fully functional department responsible for identifying areas, sectors, and causes deserving of philanthropic aid. These areas include the less privileged and needy members of society, victims of natural and manmade disasters, and other charitable causes. The bank sees giving something back to society as a serious and passionate cause, and this vision is carried out efficiently and professionally.

Zenith Bank's philanthropic activities are anchored in the premise of ensuring that the host communities and society at large receive something back for providing the bank with an environment that is conducive enough for the pursuit of enterprise and the creation of wealth. It is the bank's way of saying "thank you". The bank's strategic philanthropic objective is achieved by disbursing budgeted funds toward charitable causes and pooled funds from donations, on behalf of the benevolent public who desire to give to charitable causes through a trusted and reliable medium.

The scope of the bank's CSR activities covers health care, scholarship schemes and educational development, staff welfare, and economic empowerment schemes. The bank executes sustainable projects in the aforementioned areas of activities in selected communities, with special emphasis on education, information and communication technology, and health, in collaboration with its partners, reputable NGOs, and development agencies. The bank also gives direct assistance to individuals deserving of such aid. Zenith Philanthropy's track record includes the donation of an impressive NGN 68,084,811 to charitable causes in the financial year 2002. Some notable beneficiaries of Zenith Philanthropy assistance include, among numerous others, Lagos bomb blast victims, Childcare Trust, Nigeria Internet Group, Kanu Heart Foundation, Pediatric Center, Miss Anuoluwapo Oseni Heart Surgery, and Delta Manna Foundation. Other beneficiaries are the Ijaw Education Foundation, Lagos State University (LASU), University of Lagos Students Union ICT Center, the United Nations Development Program (UNDP), and the United Nations Development Fund for Women (UNIFEM).

19.5.3.2 Afribank Nigeria Plc

Afribank's CSR philosophy is based on the philanthropic model. As a good corporate citizen, the bank believes in plowing back some of its earnings to society, to enhance growth and sustainable development. The scope of the bank's CSR activities covers scholarship schemes and educational development, sports, safety, and staff welfare.

The bank's CSR initiatives in the area of scholarship schemes and educational development constitute giant strides. Afribank is the first financial institution in Nigeria to sponsor a Chair in Banking and Finance at the University of Ibadan. Soon after, the bank endowed funds for research at the University of Nigeria (Energy Studies) and at the Ahmadu Bello University (Agriculture). The bank has instituted awards for academic excellence in Finance/Banking in 13 Federal Universities in Nigeria. Afribank also sponsors the annual awards of the three best candidates in the University Matriculation Examination (UME) conducted by the Joint Admissions and Matriculation Board (JAMB).

In the area of sports, the bank has established a strong presence through the IBWA Football Club. It has been involved in lawn tennis through the sponsorship of the annual Afribank/Lagos Lawn Tennis Club's Masters Tournament. The bank also sponsors the NICON HILTON Pro-AM Golf Tournament. The bank is committed to staff welfare. In the area of safety, Afribank is the sponsor of the first independent road safety campaign tagged "Your Life in your Hands".

19.5.3.3 Union Bank of Nigeria Plc

Union Bank demonstrates its commitment as a socially responsible corporate citizen in various ways, by identifying with worthy causes in the host communities where it does business. In this regard, the bank renders financial and moral assistance to a number of social and community-based activities. The bank's CSR philosophy is based on the philanthropic model, while the scope of its CSR activities include health care, scholarship schemes and educational development, staff welfare, sports, microcredit, business development, and economic empowerment schemes.

In the aforementioned areas of CSR activities, the bank made donations of NGN 19,251,954 and NGN 30,720,286 in 2005 and 2006, respectively. In the area of health care, Union Bank made a donation of NGN 5,000,000 toward the sponsorship of the International Conference on AIDS and Sexually Transmitted Infections and another NGN 1,000,000 toward the Silver Anniversary celebrations of the College of Medicine, University of Ibadan. As regards educational development, the bank donated computer equipment worth NGN 16, 244 750 to the University of Maiduguri, the University of Port Harcourt, Nnamdi Azikwe University, and the Yaba College of Technology. The bank also sponsored the sinking of a borehole worth NGN 1 million at the Yaba College of Technology.

Regarding sports development, the bank's CSR initiatives include donations of NGN 1 million each toward the sponsorship of the Nigerian Cup Golf Tournament 2005 and the Hard Court Tennis Championship. The bank also made contributions to the Enugu Sports Club and toward the sponsorship of the Lagos Country Club Annual Tennis Tournament. In the area of microcredit, business development, and economic empowerment, the bank's contribution also needs acknowledgement. It donated NGN 1,975,536 to the World Economic Forum and NGN 3 million toward the sponsorship of the International Year of Microcredit in Nigeria. As a responsible corporate citizen, the bank made a contribution toward the hosting of the Commonwealth Heads of Government Meeting (CHOGM) in Nigeria. It also made a donation of NGN 500,000 toward the Chartered Institute of Bankers of Nigeria Library Project.

19.5.3.4 Platinum Habib Bank Plc

The social philosophy at Platinum Habib Bank Plc (Bank PHB) is based on the belief that the bank's involvement in CSR is directly proportional to its success as a financial institution. This philosophy is what has led the bank into sponsoring several projects that are aimed at reducing the economic challenges faced by the average Nigerian. The scope of the bank's CSR activities covers scholarship schemes and educational development, sports development, and staff welfare.

A major initiative of the bank's CSR activity in the area of scholarship schemes and educational development is the Bank PHB National Scholars Scheme. The scheme focuses on the proactive orientation and training of the coming generation as the basis for change, and also celebrates the few who continue to stick to the positive values that build a society. The scheme has three facets: motivational series, mind development, and mentoring scheme. The scheme was officially launched in February 2004 with 100 indigent students of five secondary schools as beneficiaries. For these students, the bank pays all levies and examination fees, provides them with textbooks, uniforms, sandals, and school bags, in addition to monthly stipends to ensure that they are not distracted from academic pursuit due to unavailable finances. Modern libraries, each with a seating capacity of over 70 students, have been reconstructed in each of the five schools benefiting from the pilot scheme, and equipped with relevant books in all the key subjects. A noteworthy beneficiary of the Bank PHB National Scholars Scheme is Issa Wasiu, who is studying Engineering at the University of Ilorin on a 5-year scholarship under the scheme.

In the area of sports development, the bank has put in place a number of CSR initiatives. The first is the Kaduna Golf Championship. The former Habib Nigeria Bank Plc started sponsoring the Kaduna Golf Club tournaments in 1989 and sustained the sponsorship until the bank merged its operations with Platinum Bank Plc. Bank PHB, which emerged from the merger, is now the sponsor of the Championship. Second, Bank PHB was one of the three major sponsors of (and the only bank that sponsored) the live broadcast (in Nigeria) of the 2006 World Cup competition.

19.5.3.5 Diamond Bank Plc

Diamond Bank Plc's CSR philosophy is based on the philanthropic model. The bank's policy on CSR is essentially driven by the imperative to directly and positively touch the lives of its stakeholders, with special emphasis on the indigent section of society. As a responsible corporate citizen, the bank is determined to continue its contributions in various areas of national life. The scope of the bank's CSR activities covers health care, manpower development and capacity building, football and sports development, scholarship schemes, and educational development. It also covers youth development, staff welfare, microcredit, business development, and economic empowerment schemes.

In the area of health care, Diamond Bank has been at the vanguard of the struggle for the elimination of all forms of avoidable blindness. Part of the bank's initiative under this advocacy is the Diamond Bank's and the Eye Foundation's annual Free Eye Expedition Program, which is a flagship project in this policy thrust. The maiden edition kicked off in 1999 at Emakuku near Owerri, and outings have since been held in other parts of the country: Epe, Awo-Omanna, Wagalada, and Abaka-liki. In 2002 alone, the bank spent more than NGN 5 million on eye surgeries, in addition to provision of free eyeglasses to patients. The Free Eye Expedition in Damaturu, Yobe state, in October 2005 was undertaken as a pilot scheme. The bank plans to expand the scope of the project, which serves as its contribution toward the Vision 2020 project that aims at reducing the incidence of blindness by half. In relation to health care, the bank also bolstered its fight against the HIV/AIDS scourge through support to the Nigerian Business Coalition Against AIDS (NIBUCAA), an NGO made up of companies that are committed to providing lead-ership in advancing the national response to the pandemic.

The bank has executed a number of projects under several initiatives in other areas of its highlighted CSR activities. The bank spent NGN 6 million for the con-struction of a special dormitory for the Madonna School for handicapped children in Okpanam near Asaba, and thereafter furnished the building. In the area of ed-ucational development, the bank wholly funded the NGN 10 million Imo State University Computer Center by providing a building, computers, and other in-formation technology support for the project, which was officially commissioned in July 2003. The bank also provided NGN 15 million toward the establishment of the Lagos Business School (LBS) Center for Entrepreneurial Studies of the Pan-African University. The motivation behind this gesture is to assist in deep-ening the culture of enterprise and thereby the wealth creation process in the country.

A number of laudable initiatives of the bank can be identified in the areas of sports and youth development, capacity building, and economic empowerment. The bank contributed toward the sponsorship of the maiden edition of the West African Universities Games (WUGA), the annual India Golf Cup, and the travel expenses of the swimming team of Saint Gloria School, Merry Island, Lagos, to a swimming competition in the United States, among others. The bank donated a brand new coaster bus each to the Sports Council of the University of Lagos and the authori-ties of The Nnamdi Azikwe University, Awka. The bank is involved in community development through sports, in partnership with British Council Nigeria. The bank also donated computers and ICT facilities to authorities of the Federal University of Technology, Owerri. Another laudable initiative of the bank is the inauguration of the Bright Ideas Campaign aimed at bringing creative business ideas to life.

19.5.3.6 Wema Bank Plc

Wema Bank's CSR philosophy is based on the philanthropic model. The bank has a consistent policy of ensuring that it remains socially responsible by plowing back part of its income into the community by way of community-based projects. The bank supports a number of charitable causes and community projects with its avail-able resources.

The scope of the bank's CSR activities is mainly in the area of donations and charitable gifts. Beneficiaries of the bank's philanthropic gestures in the year 2005, amounting to a total sum of NGN 2,105,000, were the Chartered Institute of Bankers of Nigeria (NGN 250,000), the 10th Nigeria Economic Summit (NGN 500,000), the Nigeria Police Force (NGN 15,000) and the Chartered Institute of Bankers of Nigeria Library Project (NGN 1,000,000). The following bodies also benefited: the Institute of Chartered Accounts of Nigeria (NGN 120,000), the Red Cross (NGN 100,000), the Rotary Club of Abeokuta (NGN 100,000), and Saint Agnes Catholic Church (NGN 20,000).

19.5.4 Telecommunications Sector

19.5.4.1 MTN Nigeria

MTN Nigeria's CSR philosophy is based on the philanthropic model. The company, which commenced business in Nigeria in 2001 (as a member of the MTN Group), has as its vision the aspiration to be the leading provider of telecommunication services in Nigeria. Its overriding mission is to be a catalyst for Nigeria's economic growth and development, helping to unleash Nigeria's strong developmental potential not only through the provision of word-class communications, but also through innovative and sustainable corporate social responsibility initiatives. Like Unilever Nigeria, which discharges all its CSR initiatives centrally through UACP, MTN Nigeria pursues its CSR initiatives through the MTN Foundation.

The MTN Foundation is established by the MTN Group in different countries of operation and, through it, each operation manages its CSR projects, which are embarked upon based on developmental priorities in the respective countries. The scope of MTN Nigeria's CSR activities covers health care, football and sports, scholarship schemes and educational development, staff welfare, and economic empowerment. In the area of health care, the MTN Foundation deploys resources to improve the health challenges facing the country through strategic partnerships with both public and private organizations. In 2006, the Foundation launched the first of its six targeted HIV/AIDS Voluntary Counseling and Testing (VCT) centers in Kogi state. The VCT center was built, equipped, and donated as part of the company's focus on health care-related community programs.

In relation to health care, the MTN Foundation has undertaken a number of other giant strides. It donated two Cyflow machines, valued at USD 60,000, to the University Teaching Hospitals at Jos and Ibadan, respectively, due to which the cost for obtaining white blood cell count in patients on drug therapy for AIDS has been reduced from NGN 5,000 to NGN 500! The company empowered the Family Care Association, an NGO focusing on rural health care, with a Hilux truck, to enable the organization to traverse local communities, administering health assistance. The company also donated a state-of-the-art ambulance to the Lagos state government to enable it to offer quick response to accident victims.

In the area of football and sports development, the MTN Foundation is involved in a number of laudable initiatives. These include contributions toward the sponsorship of the Confederation of African Football (CAF), the 2006 and 2008 Africa Cup of Nations, and the Africa Soccer Show, televised in five African countries, involving sponsorship of football associations in Cameroon and Swaziland and three clubs in South Africa. The CAF Champion League is sponsored by MTN in partnership with CAF and named the MTN CAF Champion League. In addition to the glory of being known as Africa's best club team, the tournament carries cash prizes of USD 1 million for the winners and USD 750 thousand for the other finalist. In 2005, the MTN Group announced the sponsorship of Africa's biggest football website, mtnfootball.com, a website dedicated to coverage of the game on the continent, especially the MTN Africa Cup of Nations and the MTN CAF African Champion League.

The company's CSR initiatives in the areas of scholarship schemes and educational development constitute giant strides. These initiatives include the Child Friendly School Initiative and MTN Schools Connect in Lagos, Enugu, and Kaduna, the last of which has benefited nearly 50,000 learners and more than 2,000 teachers to date. MTN Nigeria (in partnership with the Education Tax Fund and other agencies) launched the Book Aid Program in 2002, under which educational aids and books on mathematics and the sciences were donated to 10,000 junior secondary schools in the country. The company sponsored two students of Architecture from the University of Lagos on an educational tour of six European countries, tagged "Euro 2004", with a view to broadening their horizons in this field and coming back to pass on knowledge gained to their peers at home. The company also endowed a Chair in one of the tertiary institutions in Cross Rivers state for the research of Digital Wireless Telecommunications Technology and Systems.

The CSR initiatives of the MTN Foundation on economic empowerment focus on improving the economy of the country by empowering Nigerians to improve their individual well-being through poverty alleviation programs, business support, venture capital funding, micro lending, capacity building, employment creation, technical skills transfer, agricultural development/food security, entrepreneurship, and housing. Since 2005, the company has been running a rural phone project (in partnership with Growing Business Foundation – GBF, an NGO, on a revolving loan basis) whereby women are empowered with communication tools, trained, and equipped with skills and equipment needed to start a call center in their communities. The scheme, which started with 65 women in Enugu, Akwa Ibom, and Edo states, has spread to other parts of the country. The company donated 150 activated phones, including airtime, to the Lagos state government, to assist in the rescue operations following the bomb blast on 27th January 2006. The company also donated relief items to needy women of Akabo in Imo state, victims of the Okobaba fire disaster in Lagos, and victims of the ethno-religious crisis in Nassarawa, Kano, and Bauchi states.

19.5.4.2 Celtel Nigeria

Celtel Nigeria commenced its telecommunications business in Nigeria in 2001, when the company was originally known as Econet Wireless Nigeria, and later as V-mobile until 2006, when it took on its present name. The CSR philosophy of Celtel Nigeria is based on the philanthropic model. The overriding vision and commitment that drives the company is "making life better" for its customers, employees, shareholders, and the communities in which it operates. The company perceives and positions itself as an integral part of society, which must be socially responsible at all times in all its dealings, maintaining high ethical standards and compliance with the rules and regulations in its methods and practices of doing business. Like its counterpart, MTN, Celtel Nigeria pursues its CSR activities through the Celtel Foundation.

The scope of Celtel Nigeria's CSR activities covers health care, sports, provision of basic infrastructure, staff welfare, and donations to charity and other worthy causes. In the area of health care, Celtel Nigeria supports the National Action Committee Against Aids (NACA) through the sponsorship of its HIV/AIDS awareness campaign and the broadcast of messages through SMS. In support of the fight against breast cancer, Celtel Nigeria has donated a toll-free line (together with accessories) to an NGO, the Bloom, which is in the forefront of the campaign for guidance and counseling on breast cancer awareness. In the area of sports, the company is involved in the sponsorship of the first season of the Premier Basketball League.

Celtel Nigeria's CSR initiative on basic infrastructure involves the provision of over 500 boreholes to needy communities across the six geopolitical zones of the country. The completed ones, which are located at Ketu, Esa-Oke, Modakeke, Iloro-Ekiti, Iyin-Ekiti, Eruwa, Ilorin, Abeokuta and Ibadan, among other places, are named Celtel community boreholes and have since been handed over to the respective communities. As a responsible corporate citizen, the company has been making donations to charitable organizations, homes for the handicapped and the less privileged, and other worthy causes. In 2003, Celtel Nigeria donated NGN 50 million, SIM cards and recharge cards in support of the Commonwealth Heads of Government Meeting that was held at Abuja. The company donates free SIM cards and phones to the security apparatus of every state where it launches service.

In pursuit of its philanthropic gesture as a responsible corporate citizen, Celtel Nigeria donated materials (food items, children beddings, instructional materials, toys and other consumables, among others) worth over NGN 1 million to the Motherless Babies Home, Katsana state. Similar gestures have been extended to no less than six orphanages across the country between November and December 2006 alone. Beneficiaries of the company's gesture include Motherless Babies Home, Yemetu, Ibadan, Stella Obasanjo Children's Home, Abeokuta, Jaleyemi Orphanage, Osogbo, School for the Physically Handicapped, Ido-Ekiti, and Kwara State School for the Handicapped, Ilorin.

19.5.4.3 Glo Mobile

Glo Mobile Service was launched in Nigeria in August 2003 and the company has since brought about revolutionary changes in the GSM sector of the economy. The scope of Glo Mobile's CSR activities covers health care, football and sports, and staff welfare. In 2005, Glo Mobile sponsored some Nigerian qualified doctors' visits to four African countries (Ghana, Uganda, Zimbabwe, and Sierra Leone) with a view to rendering health support to those countries and, at the same time, enabling the medical consultants to acquire addition practical knowledge through the exposure. The company also sponsors a broadcast program, LIM Africa, on HIV/AIDS awareness campaigns. In the area of sports, Glo Mobile contributes toward the sponsorship of the African Football (CAF) Award and the Nigeria Premier League (i.e., Globacom League).

19.5.5 Construction Sector

19.5.5.1 Julius Berger Plc

The company's vision is to develop long-lasting cooperation in a spirit of partnership with its clients by adding value in fulfilling its objectives based on its performance, while its mission is to be the most capable and trustworthy indigenous multi-service construction company in Nigeria, for the benefit of the nation. Julius Berger Plc's reputation is based on its capability to plan, design, construct, and maintain a variety of civil engineering and building projects to the satisfaction of its clients. Its ability and experience in executing projects in Nigeria in record time (supported by the commitment and strength of its personnel and a large fleet of modern construction equipment) to the satisfaction of its clients adjudges the company as a responsible corporate citizen.

The scope to the company's CSR activities covers health care, staff welfare, commitment to the observance of health, safety, and environment requirements in accordance with international standards and best practice, as well as commitment to clients' satisfaction. In the area of health care, the company renders assistance by working in close cooperation with the government in the fight and campaign against HIV/AIDS. The company offers innovative and cost-effective solutions to its clients in the areas of engineering, design, procurement, construction, and long-term maintenance. Julius Berger Plc employs the services of external consultants for the training of its workers as a capacity building strategy.

The company has, over the years, been able to establish and sustain its reputation as a major key player in the nation's construction industry. This is quite evident from the diverse scope of engineering and construction activities it has undertaken in Nigeria. The company has built many roads and bridges across the country (e.g., in Lagos and Abuja). Its other construction activities cover sporting facilities (e.g., the National Stadium Main Bowl and IBB International Golf

Course, both at Abuja, and the Golf Course, Bonny Island), residential facilities (e.g., Army Barracks at Abuja, LNG Residential project at Bonny Island), and railways (e.g., Ajaokuta-Warri and Itakpe-Ajaokuta rail lines). Others are airports (e.g., Nnamdi Azikwe Airport at Abuja, and Yola Airport) and dams and water supply schemes (e.g., Challawa Gorge Dam and Ilorin water supply scheme).

19.5.5.2 Cappa and D' Alberto Plc

Cappa and D' Alberto Plc operates principally as a building and civil engineering contracting firm in Nigeria. The scope of the company's CSR activities covers staff welfare and commitment to clients' satisfaction, best practice and international standards in the discharge of its contractual obligations. The company discharges its obligations to its clients as a responsible corporate citizen by charging them low and affordable rates. Some of the projects handled by the company include the refurbishment of Lagos Island Maternity Hospital, the United Nations sponsored school at Kuje, and the waste-water treatment plant for the Nigeria Breweries Plc. at Ibadan.

Credit Risk Monitor, a sub-unit of Cappa and D' Alberto Plc, is an initiative that is worth mentioning here. It is a worldwide leading provider of real-time financial information analysis and news, created specifically for the corporate credit professional. It provides an innovative financial information service to busy senior finance executives and credit professionals to save them time.

19.5.6 Conglomerates Sector

19.5.6.1 UAC of Nigeria

The CSR philosophy of UAC of Nigeria (UACN Plc) is based on the philanthropic model. As a socially responsible corporate citizen, UACN assists communities, institutions, and charitable organizations and also awards scholarships at various levels of education.

The scope of the company's CSR activities covers manpower development and capacity building, scholarship schemes and educational development, youth development, and staff welfare. The company has a number of CSR initiatives in the areas of scholarship schemes and educational development, youth development, and staff welfare. For example, the company awards scholarships to students and undergraduates in Nigerian secondary schools and universities, respectively. As part of its CSR initiative on staff welfare, the company introduced a Secondary School Scholarship Scheme in 1948, which is open to children of both serving and retired employees of the company.

In the area of manpower development and capacity building, the company's contributions have been quite noticeable. Most of the company's divisions and businesses offer vacation jobs and industrial attachment to students in higher institutions of learning, enabling them to obtain practical experience in a wide range of business and technical skills. A CSR initiative of the company, which focuses on youth development, is the Goodness League, aimed at touching the lives of the nation's young children. The executional platform of this initiative is anchored in support (infrastructure and coaching) to legacy schools in Nigeria. UACN's initiatives have led to the execution of the Schools Support Program, which seeks to boost infrastructure and enhance facilities in schools across the country.

19.5.6.2 Unilever Nigeria Plc

Unilever Nigeria is committed to raising the quality of life of people in its operating environment through the quality of its brands and through contributions to the communities in which it operates. The company is committed to managing its social and environmental impacts responsibly, working in partnership with its stakeholders, addressing social and environmental challenges, and contributing to sustainable development. In order to ensure maximum impact of its CSR program, all the initiatives of the company are pooled under one umbrella, the Unilever Community Assistance Program (UACP). The company's strategy is to partner with reputable NGOs and other organizations that have technical expertise and infrastructure, to raise the quality of life of people in its operating environment.

The company's partners cut across NGOs, governments at three levels, and across communities. Some of these partners include UNICEF, WaterAid, Sight Savers International (SSI), and Liverpool Associates in Tropical health (LATH). Also included are Positive Action for Treatment Access (PATA), National Action Committee on AIDS (NACA), Nigerian Business Coalition Against AIDS (NIBU-CAA), professional associations of the medical and nursing professions, ministries of health and education at the federal and state levels, and the federal, state, and local governments, as well as the host communities.

The scope of the company's CSR activities covers health care, manpower development and capacity building, scholarship schemes and educational development, basic infrastructure, staff welfare, quality, and consumer safety. All these activities are geared toward raising the quality of life in the company's operating environment.

19.5.7 Churches (Not-For-Profit)

19.5.7.1 The Catholic Church

Churches are not-for-profit organizations that are primarily concerned with spiritual transformation and the general well-being of their members in the communities where they operate. This primary concern notwithstanding, some churches appreciate and are committed to meeting the needs of their members in other areas of human endeavor. The Roman Catholic Church in Nigeria is involved in a number of CSR activities that are pursued through a number of initiatives. The CSR philosophy and motivation are based on religious persuasions and humanitarian considerations. The Catholic Church's scope of CSR activities covers health care, rural development, women empowerment and youth development, human rights and good governance, and charity.

To be socially responsible, the Church established the Justice, Development, and Peace Movement (JDPM), which is an NGO with branches in all the dioceses. The various CSR activities of the Church are pursued through the four operational departments of this outfit: (a) Rural Development, (b) Women's Empowerment and Youth Development, (c) Human Rights and Good Governance (HRGG), and (d). The JDPM is a faith-based, non-governmental, non-political, not-for-profit, charity organization established as a social arm of the Church, propelled by the message of Christ and guided by the Church's social teaching to carry out the prophetic mission of the Catholic Church in society, without any bias of race, gender, religion, tongue, and color, by acting as the voice of the voiceless and the light of the world.

The Rural Development department focuses on sustaining farming systems (through soil and water conservation and soil fertility improvement measures, afforestation, tree crops management, and animal integration), post harvesting management (storage, processing, and marketing), farmers' groups initiatives (such as credit and savings schemes, exchange visits, and farmers' forums,) and community self-help initiatives (such as access roads, electricity, and potable water) This department works in collaboration with Primary Health Care (PHC), the Catholic Community Self-Help Association (CCSA), NGOs, and government institutions. This department is also involved in the campaign against HIV/AIDS and other health awareness campaign programs, as well as extension programs for small- and medium-scale farmers.

The main thrust of activities of the Women Empowerment and Youth Development department is on capacity building, business development, and economic empowerment. The department supports individuals and families with very low incomes by providing technical backup through training and re-orientation that ensure attitudinal change and improve their income-base and general life management.

The HRGG department gives political and human rights education to the general public. This is with a view to promoting respect for human rights and values, as well as ensuring popular and active participation of the masses in governance. Through the activities of this department, the Church instills rights order in society, and builds human capacity to know and do what is right, noble, good, enduring, and beneficial to the majority.

The Caritas (charity) department attends with Christ-like compassion to emergency situations that tend to rubbish human dignity and worth. The main thrust of the activities of this department is to give immediate succor, comfort, and hope to those in hopeless, distressing, or sub-human circumstances, in order to restore their human dignity and self-worth. The specific charitable activities of this department include welfare of prison inmates and refugees, assistance to indigent students, support to stranded persons, help to the sick, aged, or handicapped, as well as response to victims of communal violence or natural disasters. Through this department, the Osogbo Catholic Diocese runs an orphanage at Our Lady of Fatima Catholic Hospital, Jaleyemi, Osogbo and a Rehabilitation Center for the handicapped and the destitute at Ipetumodu.

19.5.7.2 Deeper Life Bible Church

The Deeper Life Christian Ministry was formally established in 1983 by Pastor W.F. Kumuyi after having operated earlier for 10 years as a bible study group at the University of Lagos, where the founder worked as a Mathematics lecturer. The Church has members in over 60 countries of the world including the UK, the USA, Canada, France, and Germany. The Church constitution provides for the establishment of Christian charity projects for the rehabilitation of refugees, the poor, the aged, the handicapped, and those in similar circumstances. It also provides for the Church's involvement in nation building projects such as agriculture, schools, well-equipped maternity homes in rural areas, and provision of Christian medical personnel in needy areas. The Church encourages its members to become involved in charitable giving and caring for each other. This is why charitable giving, scholarship awards (in form of sponsorship), and material donations for the needy have become ways of life among members of the Church in its various districts and regions across the globe.

The scope of the Deeper Life Bible Church's CSR activities covers health care, capacity building, youth development, economic empowerment, charity, and caring. The CSR philosophy and motivation, which are spirit-inspired, are based on religious persuasions and humanitarian considerations. Within an established structure, the Church's various activities are carried out at district and regional levels. These activities are carried out through the following units: Deeper Life Campus Fellowship (DLCF), Deeper Life Students Outreach (DLSO), Deeper Life Children Outreach (DLCO), Deeper Life World Mission, International Bile Training College (IBTC), Youth Fellowship, Prisons Outreach, Hospital Fellowship, and House Caring Fellowship. Others are Forces Ministry, Deeper Life Church Aid Ministry (DLCAM), and the Women's Ministry.

19.5.8 Charitable Organizations (Not-For-Profit)

19.5.8.1 Constitutional Rights Project

The Constitutional Rights Project (CRP) is a charitable organization that provides free legal assistance to victims of human rights abuses and promotes peaceful coexistence among communities, as well as the sanctity of the rule of law. CRP pursues its CSR activities through a number of initiatives. CRP's Outreach initiative involves publications in newspapers and through billboards, which are designed to sensitize the public on human rights issues. Under this initiative, the outfit also produces T-shirts, stickers, posters, and pamphlets, all of which seek to promote a greater awareness of human rights among Nigerians. Under its legislative advocacy initiative, the outfit, through its legislative agenda, intends to have a frequent and positive impact on the National Assembly in the discharge of its constitutional role and duties.

CRP's Research and Publications initiative involves the carrying out of investigations and preparation of analytic reports on various issues of concern in Nigeria. Such reports recommend the legal and institutional changes and improvements necessary for the full realization of human rights in Nigeria. The Women and Children initiative of the outfit was instrumental in the development of the text for human rights teaching in schools. In consonance with its human rights education program, CRP developed this text as a tool to facilitate the teaching of human rights at the tertiary level. As part of women's rights protection, CRP organized a seminar in 2000, entitled "The Place of Women Under Sharia", in response to the adoption of the Islamic Sharia legal code by some states in the northern part of the country. Thereafter, the outfit organized another training session on Sharia for Alkhali court judges, imploring them to consider progressive interpretations of Sharia that favor the upholding of human rights, especially the rights of women.

CRP's Peace Building and Conflicts Resolution initiative is aimed at promoting peaceful coexistence between communities and respect for the rule of law and human dignity in Nigeria. Through this initiative, CRP has thus far promoted peace building, using community leaders, women leaders, and youths in southeast and southwest Nigeria, as well as members of the Nigerian Police Force. CRP has organized a number of workshops on peace building and conflict resolution. These include the Training of Trainers (TOT), organized in 2000 and designed to promote the involvement of women in conflict resolution and peace building at the community level in Ondo and Osun states, and a similar workshop organized for community leaders in the southeastern geopolitical zone in April 2001. TOT workshops on Police Reform and Conflict Transformation for police officers were held at Enugu in February 2003 and Jos in August 2003, respectively.

19.5.8.2 KPMG Foundation

The KPMG Foundation is a charitable organization in Nigeria, but has its base in the UK. Although funded by KPMG (UK), it is a completely separate and distinct entity. The focus of the Foundation is on education and social projects for the disadvantaged and less privileged, with a special emphasis on unlocking the potential of children and young people up to 30 years of age who, for primary social reasons, have been unable to develop their educational potential.

The four groups that fall within the Foundation's definition of "disadvantaged" are: (a) refugees, (b) young offenders, (c) children and young people who have been in care, and (d) children and young people with literacy difficulties. The Foundation's donation policy focuses on community and environment, particularly through education, to help enhance social inclusion for individuals and communities and to support charities that maintain and enhance biodiversity. During 2005 and 2006, the Foundation made nearly 1,400 charitable donations.

19.5.8.3 Nigeria Conservation Foundation

The Nigeria Conservation Foundation (NCF) was established in 1990 with the main aim of conserving nature in Nigeria, and its operations have spread from Lagos to eastern and northern parts of the country. Lekki Conservation Center (LCC), is the premier nature center in Nigeria and serves as the headquarters of NCF in Nigeria. The LCC also serves the purpose of education and enjoyment for Nigerians and over 60,000 school children from over 1,200 schools are said to have visited the Center. The Foundation has just printed an activity manual for Nigerian youth on the environment as a tool for youth action on the environment.

NCF conceived a participatory Renewable Natural Resource Management project in 1995 for Buru village and Laminga village in Taraba and Plateau states, respectively. The main objectives of the two projects are to: (a) improve the well-being of rural dwellers, especially the poorest segment of society that depend on renewable natural resources, (b) maintain the management of such renewable natural resources toward sustainability in key biodiversity sites and maintain their biodiversity, (c) improve Nigeria's NGO capacity to manage, fundraise, and sustain such projects and to share lessons learnt from these projects to benefit other key sites and their local communities, and (d) use Nigeria's Important Bird Area (IBA) survey as the database for the biodiversity index.

NCF activities in Buru village involve working with members of the community on resource use and management plans through a Central Buru Development Committee that works on specific issues through sub-committees such as Education, Agriculture, Health, and Conservation. With impressive commitment from the local communities, the Buru project has opened ground for a few initiatives, such as establishment and registration of a cooperative society as well as a joint planning effort toward the survey of biodiversity in Taraba state. This project offers an excellent example of people's realization of the potentials of natural resources in their area, and their willingness and determination to take active part in its planning and management. The NCF project site at Laminga is also centered on people as active participants. The current level of commitment and attention to the project is an indication that involving people in programs and actions that concern their livelihood is not only an option, but is also a better choice for biodiversity conservation and integrated rural development.

Against a background of problems, such as invasion and displacement of the vibrant coastal host mangrove vegetation by nipa palms, NCF instituted the Nipa Palm Utilization project to reverse the dangerous trend due to of the threat and damage posed to the coastal ecosystem in the southeastern part of the country, especially Cross River and Akwa-Ibom states. The Nipa Palm (control by utilization) project was established by NCP in Akwa-Ibom state in 1996 with three components: (a) awareness of and education on the threat posed by the nipa palm to the coastal ecosystem, (b) training, skill development, and capacity building of local community people to utilize nipa in the production of domestic and commercial products, and (c) ecological rehabilitation, through a pilot program involving replanting of mangrove seedlings in plots originally invaded by nipa palms.

In executing the three components of this initiative, NCF has established a craft workshop on the use of nipa as a raw material for the production of craft items, and domestic materials such as roofing sheets. The Foundation is also involved in ecological studies on nipa and the rehabilitation of mangroves, with an experimentation site established at the riverbank in Oron, Akwa-Ibom state. Awareness workshops and seminars on the significance of the control of nipa are conducted periodically for people in the coastal areas. On the whole, the Foundation is contributing its quota to the development of the nation's economy, especially in the areas of natural resources conservation and management, ecology, and rural development.

19.6 Summary and Concluding Remarks

This paper has examined CSR and CSR-related activities of 22 organizations that operate principally for profit in six key sectors of the economy(oil and gas; food, beverages and tobacco; banking; telecommunications; construction; and conglomerates) and those of five organizations in two sectors that are not-for-profit (churches and charitable organizations). This is against the background that features of decadence and decay are quite noticeable in various sectors of the nation's economy (such as infrastructure, education, and health, among others), and that no matter how benevolent, the government alone cannot provide all the needs of its citizenry. The proposition advocated and canvassed in this paper is that, in view of its great potential, and if backed up with appropriate legal and regulatory framework (as present in advanced countries) coupled with a very conducive environment for operation, the CSR activities of corporate entities can be made to complement the efforts of the government at all levels, as a vehicle or catalyst for socio-economic development in Nigeria.

The study revealed that CSR and CSR-related activities of the organizations studied are in the areas of health care, occupational health and safety, manpower development and capacity building, football and sports. Others are scholarship schemes and educational development, youth development schemes, microcredit, business development, and economic empowerment. Also included are provision of basic infrastructure, staff welfare, legal aid, human rights protection and support for the less privileged, and conservation and protection of the environment. In the opinion of this author, the very diverse scope of CSR and its related activities undertaken by the organizations studied, as enumerated above, all of which aim at sustainable socio-economic development of society at large (although with special concentration on their geographical areas of operation), lends credence to the proposition advocated and canvassed in this paper: that CSR can be made to complement government efforts, to serve as a catalyst or vehicle for socio-economic development in Nigeria through persuasion, enabling a conducive environment and the appropriate legal and regulatory framework.

It was revealed in the study that all the organizations studied are aware of the CSR concept and are, in fact, involved in its practice in one form or another, although in varying degrees and with varying scope of involvement, while they focus primarily on their geographical areas of operation. Rather than report their CSR activities on a stand-alone basis, the studied organizations embed these activities in their annual report and accounts, although some of these activities are carried as news items in the print and electronic media to present and portray the affected organizations to the general public as socially responsible corporate citizens. While most of the organizations studied based their CSR philosophy on the philanthropic model, the reasons they gave as drivers of their CSR activities include community relations, complementing government efforts, proof of success and being socially responsible, public relations and business promotion, global trend influence, and religious and societal persuasion. It is striking that they all gave community relations and complementing government efforts as motivations behind their CSR activities, which again lends credence to the proposition advocated and canvassed in this paper.

Although no comparative quantitative analysis of the involvement of the organizations studied was carried out, going by the scope of their respective activities, it can be reasonably deduced from this work that the oil and gas sector occupies the foremost position in CSR and its related activities in Nigeria. The vantage position of this sector to the nation's economy (which has been virtually monolithically oil-based) could reasonably explain the sector's great commitment to CSR and its related activities, especially in the Niger Delta region. By reason of the duration of their operations in Nigeria and their commitment to ethics, best practice, and to the CSR philosophy itself, the studied organizations in the food, beverages, and tobacco sector also have landmark and laudable initiatives on CSR and its related activities.

As a matter of fact, all the organizations studied under the various sectors are commendable ambassadors of the CSR concept in Nigeria, notwithstanding the fact that their degree and scope of involvement varies. It is appreciated that the size and strength of each organization will determine the degree and scope of its involvement in CSR and its related activities. Interestingly, there appears to be an emerging trend of competition amongst corporate entities in Nigeria in the sponsorship of CSR activities, with the organizations designing unique initiatives in their areas of core operations, which are also aimed at promoting their brands (products) in some cases (as with Bournvita branded CSR initiatives by Cadbury Nigeria Plc and Coca-Cola branded CSR initiatives by Nigerian Bottling Company Plc). On the whole, all the organizations studied have fared well, as they all embraced CSR activities and are, in fact, involved in one form or another although there will always be room for improvement.

In order to give effect to and actualize the proposition advocated and canvassed in this work, namely, that CSR and its related activities should complement government efforts as a vehicle or catalyst for socio-economic development in Nigeria, the following specific recommendations are made. First, the government should put in place an appropriate legal and regulatory framework (based on the experience of countries like the UK, the US, Canada, France, Japan, and India) that will serve as a catalyst for the effective promotion of CSR and its related activities in Nigeria, and that will also capture and address the interest and responsibilities of all stakeholders and key players. Such a framework should have, as a major component, the establishment of a national CSR performance indicator that would make the various organizations more responsive to CSR. Second, pending the time that a Ministry will be created for CSR in Nigeria (as the UK did in 2000 by appointing a Minister for CSR), a Directorate of CSR should be established at the federal and state levels in the Ministry of Environment or the Ministry of Industry. The author is aware of the existence of some government agencies in Nigeria that oversee the development of the environment and operations thereon, such as the Federal Environmental Protection Agency, their state counterparts, and planning authorities, but the scope of CSR activities goes beyond what these agencies are statutorily established to do.

Third, the organized private sector (OPS), Manufacturers Association of Nigeria (MAN), Business Council for Sustainable Development, Nigeria (BCSDN), the Nigerian Extractive Industries Transparency Initiative (NEITI), and other major stakeholders should jointly work toward the establishment of CSR Nigeria as a not-for-profit organization that would pursue objectives similar to those of CSR Europe. Specifically, within the Nigerian context, CSR Nigeria should be established (as was CSR Europe) to help companies achieve profitability and sustainable growth, and to place CSR in the mainstream of business practice. It should aim at having working relationships with CSR Europe and similar organizations in other parts of the world in order to ensure its steady growth.

Fourth, the Nigerian Stock Exchange should henceforth compel listed companies in the country to provide information on their CSR activities as is done in other countries like the UK, France, and South Africa, among others. Fifth, the National Universities Commission (NUC) should encourage the universities in the country to mount CSR programs. Finally, the National Assembly should pass a bill on CSR to give it the force of the law.

Appendix

Organizations covered in the study

S/N	Organization	Sector
1	Shell Nigeria	Oil and gas
2	Total Nigeria	Oil and gas
3	Oando Group	Oil and gas
4	Nigeria LNG	Oil and gas
5	Addax Petroleum	Oil and gas
6	Zenon Petroleum & Gas	Oil and gas
7	Cadbury Nigeria Plc	Food, beverages, and tobacco
8	Nigeria Bottling Co. Plc	Food, beverages, and tobacco
9	British American Tobacco Nigeria	Food, beverages, and tobacco
10	Zenith Bank Plc	Banking
11	Afribank Plc	Banking
12	Union Bank of Nigeria Plc	Banking
13	Bank PHB Plc	Banking
14	Diamond Bank Plc	Banking
15	Wema Bank Plc	Banking
16	MTN Nigeria	Telecommunications
17	Celtel Nigeria	Telecommunications
18	Glo Mobile	Telecommunications
19	Julius Berger	Construction
20	Cappa and Dalberto Plc	Construction
21	UACN Plc	Conglomerates
22	Unilever Plc	Conglomerates
23	Catholic Church	Church (not-for-profit)
24	Deeper Life Bible Church	Church (not-for-profit)
25	Constitutional Rights Project (CRP)	Charitable Organization (not-for-profit)
26	KPMG Foundation	Charitable Organization (not-for-profit)
27	Nigeria Conservation Foundation – (NCF)	Charitable Organization (not-for-profit)

References

Addax Posted on http://www.addaxpetroleum.com/corporatexitizenship.htm

Adu, C.A. (2007) "Corporate Social Responsibility Activities as a vehicle for economic development in Nigeria: Experience from Telecommunications and Construction sectors". Seminar Paper Submitted to the Department of Estate Management, Obafemi Awolowo University, Ile-Ife. Nigeria.

Afribank Posted on http://www.afribank.com/afribankcares.htm

Amaeshi, K.M, Adi, "Corporate Social Responsibility (CSR) in Nigeria: Western B.C., Ogbechie, C and mimicry or indigenous practices?" *Journal of Corporate* Amao, O.O. (2006);. *Citizenship*, December, 2006.

Bank PHB Posted on http://www.bankphb.com/live/corporate citizenship.asp

Bajpai, G.N. (2001) *"Corporate Social Responsibility in India and Europe: Cross Cultural perspective"*. New Delhi.

British American Posted on http://www.batnigeria.com. Tobacco Nigeri.

Cadbury Nigeria Plc Posted on http://www.cadburynigeria.com/csr.php

Diamond Bank Posted on http://www.diamondbank.com/public/aboutus/community_inv.html

Drucker, P. (1984). The new meaning of corporate social responsibility, *California Management Review*, Vol. 26, pp. 53–63.

Ekpu, R. (2007) "Corporate Social Responsibility and peace in Nigeria's oil communities". Nigerian Tribune No. 14, 227, Tuesday 21 August, 2007. pp 40 & 24.

European Union (EU), (2001) Green Paper on promoting a European framework for corporate social responsibility.

European Foundation, (2002) Corporate social responsibility in France, Germany, Hungary and the United Kingdom.

Glo Mobile Posted on http://www.gloworld.com

Idowu, S.O. (2005) Corporate Social Responsibility What's it really about? *Accountancy Ireland*, 37(4), August 2005, pp. 86–88.

Industry Canada (2006) Corporate Social Responsibility.

International Institute of Sustainable Development, (2007) Corporate Social Responsibilty: An Implementation Guide for Business.

Julius Berger Posted on http://www.julius-berger-nigeria.com

MTN Group Limited Posted on http://www.mtnonline.com

Nigeria Posted on http://www.infoplease.com/ipa/A0107847.html

Nigeria Posted on http://en.wikipedia.org/wiki/Nigeria

Nigerian Bottling Company Plc Posted on http://www.coca-colahbc.com/country/files/en/nigeria/community.html

NLNG Posted on http://www.nlng.com/NLNGnew/community/Community+Projects.htm

Oando Group Posted on http://www.oandoplc.com/social_responsibility.htm

Ralph, H. (2004) Corporate Social Responsibility: An issues paper, World Commission on the Social Dimension of Globalization.

Shell Nigeria Posted on http://www.shell.com/home/content/nigeria/society environment/dir community environment.html

Tell No. 41, October 8, 2007 pp 18–23.

Tell No. 42, October 15, 2007 pp 18–22.

Total Nigeria Posted on http://www.ng.total.com/03 total nigeria commitments/0304 corporate social.htm

UACN Plc Posted on http://www.uacnplc.com/company/csr/index.htm

UK Department of Trade And Industry Corporate Social Responsibility. A Government Update (2004).

Unilever Plc Posted on http://www.unilevernigeria.com/ourvalues/environmentandsociety/default.asp

Union Bank Posted on http://www.unionbankng.com/socialares.htm

Wema Bank Posted on http://www.wemabank.com/philanthropy.htm

World Bank (2006) World Development Project.

World Fact Book Posted on http://www.cia.gov/library/publications/the-world-factbook/geos/ni.html

Zenith Bank Posted on http://www.zenithbank.com/philanthropy.cfm

Zenon Posted on http://www.zenonpetroleumng.com/corporate.htm

Chapter 20
South Africa: The Role of History, Government, and Local Context

Ralph Hamann

Abstract This chapter discusses the context and practices of corporate social responsibility (CSR) in South Africa. It argues that the country's complex and painful history has significant implications for how CSR is understood and implemented. On the one hand, big business has been implicated in human rights abuses committed under apartheid; on the other hand, the apartheid history gave rise to early manifestations of voluntary initiatives to contribute to government policy changes and social development. The chapter describes the historical progression of the CSR discourse and practices in South Africa from an emphasis on corporate social investment – philanthropic initiatives especially in education and health – to a more integrated approach focused on sustainable development and linked to collaborative governance initiatives and partnerships. It also discusses the emerging market-based drivers for the increasing prominence of CSR in South Africa, though it also emphasizes the key role played by the government, in particular, in terms of its black economic empowerment (BEE) policies. The second argument of this chapter, therefore, is that in a country like South Africa, CSR cannot be defined purely as voluntary initiatives (as in Europe, for instance) and arguably there are no clear distinctions or divisions between voluntary business actions and state-led interventions. The third and final argument of this chapter is that CSR-related performance assessments and rankings play an important role – and the chapter considers one such assessment in some detail – but they often adopt a relatively superficial perspective on the interactions between companies and their socio-economic and natural environments. In particular, there is a need for more context-specific assessments that take into consideration the complexities of sustainable development at the local level, and this is illustrated by means of a brief discussion of mining companies' CSR policies and practices in the Rustenburg area.

S. O. Idowu and W. L. Filho (eds.), *Global Practices of Corporate Social Responsibility*   435
© Springer-Verlag Berlin Heidelberg 2009

20.1 The Historical Context and Emergence of CSR

In South Africa, the context and definition of CSR has been significantly influenced by the legacy of colonialism and apartheid, with big business having been implicated in this history. Though there is much debate about the extent and manner of this involvement (for contrasting perspectives, see Lipton, 1985; Yudelman, 1984), it is clear, for instance, that mining companies played a role in initiating important aspects of the colonial and subsequent apartheid system, predicated upon their need for cheap, relatively unskilled labor for the mining of deep, low-grade ores (Moodie and Ndatshe, 1994). This resulted in the development of core elements of the South African state's racist policies, including the taxation of rural blacks in order to force them into wage labor (Jones, 1995: 16–17) and the establishment of a rigorous system of migrant labor recruitment and housing in military-inspired single sex compounds (Turrell, 1987; Crush et al., 1991; Moodie with Ndatsche, 1994). This system remained largely unchanged for much of the twentieth century, providing cheap labor to the mines and contributing to the steady impoverishment of rural areas (Crush et al., 1991). In summary, the Truth and Reconciliation Commission (set up after the transition to democracy in 1994 to uncover human rights abuses under apartheid) concluded in its final report, "The blueprint for 'grand apartheid' was provided by the mines and was not an Afrikaner state innovation" (TRC, 2003: 150).

At the same time, some South African companies tried to ameliorate some of the worst elements of the apartheid state, and also played an important role in the transition to democracy. During the 1970s, rising popular resentment about the state's classification of blacks as "informal sojourners" in urban areas, the absence of state investment in informal townships, and violent implementation of pass laws culminated in the Soweto uprising in 1976. In a bid to stabilize conditions in the townships, a number of corporations, led by Harry Oppenheimer of Anglo American (mining) and Anton Rupert of Rembrandt (alcohol and tobacco), set up the Urban Foundation, which would provide private sector support to urban development issues. The Director of the Foundation, Judge Steyn, wrote, "as the arm and voice of the private sector, the Urban Foundation is now applying its resources to help achieve the growth, prosperity, peace, and stability that all South Africans seek," while the *Financial Mail* saw its aim as "preserving an economy endangered by African revolt against conditions in the townships" (Pallister et al., 1987: 69).

With a membership of over 350 companies and having raised comparatively large amounts of money, the Foundation implemented and funded numerous urban development and education projects, particularly in Soweto. Towards the end of the apartheid era, business efforts such as the Urban Foundation went beyond contributions to education or housing, in order to lobby politically against the harshest elements of the apartheid state's policies. In this sense, it was in many ways the predecessor of the various collective private sector efforts that emerged in the 1980s and 1990s. These include the Consultative Business Movement, which emerged from the Urban Foundation in 1988 following the declaration of state of emergency in 1986, with the aim of establishing dialogue "across political and economic boundaries" (Whittaker, 2003: 20), and which contributed to the establishment of the CODESA process that led to the interim constitution in 1993. They also include the National Business Initiative (NBI), which was established after the first elections in 1994 through a merger of the Urban Foundation and the Consultative Business Movement merged to form the National Business Initiative in 1995. Over and above its contributions to initiatives such as teacher training and support to the criminal justice system, the NBI plays a key role as an advocate for CSR in South Africa, whereby this includes its role as the national chapter of the World Business Council for Sustainable Development and as the national focal point for the United Nations Global Compact.

Over and above these collective efforts, there was an increase in philanthropic initiatives also by individual companies towards the end of the apartheid regime. These commonly entailed grants and managerial structures set up to facilitate development projects, primarily in education (Alperson, 1995). These will be discussed in more detail in a subsequent section later.

Parallel to these philanthropic and public policy related efforts, the term CSR was formally raised for the first time in 1972. Feldberg (1972) argued that business was not responsible for the apartheid system, but it should take responsibility for social issues for its own long-term interests (see also Alperson, 1995; Bezuidenhout et al., 2007). In the late 1970s, the term CSR became prominent in the debates surrounding the question of whether foreign multinational corporations should disinvest from South Africa in connection with the apartheid system. The argument by many of these companies, which is common also in contemporary debates on business and human rights, was that companies could improve social standards within their business activities and by "constructive engagement" (Marzullo, 1987) with civil society and state interests. This was formalized by the Sullivan Principles, a set of principles focused on nondiscrimination in the workplace targeted especially at US-based companies. The Sullivan Principles were the important precursors of the growing importance of CSR in the international discourse in the subsequent decades (Sethi and Falbe, 1987). Their significance at the time can be seen in their concern for core business activities, whereas initiatives such as the Urban Foundation were primarily engaged at the philanthropic level. They also illustrate the obvious centrality of race discrimination in any consideration of CSR in South Africa, a theme that is still pertinent today in a different format. Alperson (1995: 5) describes the Sullivan Principles as a "turning point" in the "vocabulary" of CSR in South Africa. Yet they also met with considerable resistance or criticism, which emphasized that only a few corporations effectively adopted the principles. A prominent concern was that the principles were meant to accommodate the mounting pressures to disinvest (Orkin, 1989), thus preventing more significant pressure being exerted on the apartheid government (Bezuidenhout et al., 2007).

In summary, historical CSR efforts existed as part of a double-edged sword: the philanthropic gestures and political maneuvers characteristic of the Urban Foundation, though contributing no doubt to social development and perhaps a softening of the harshest elements of the apartheid government's policies, occurred side by side with continued exploitation of black labor, as well as low occupational health, safety, and environmental standards.

20.2 From Corporate Social Investment to Sustainable Development and Collaborative Governance

Until relatively recently, a dominant interpretation of CSR in South Africa has been in terms of corporate social investment (CSI), or strategic philanthropy with an emphasis on education and health projects either nationally or in communities surrounding companies' operations. This interpretation has its historical origins in initiatives such as the Urban Foundation, considered earlier. Of particular significance in this respect is the widespread notion that the emphasis on CSI is a peculiarly South African characteristic.

Corporate social investment is a... South African term, which actually means corporate social or community relations. The South Africans' understanding was that they were going beyond their responsibility of paying tax, saying that it is an investment in the community. But the problem was that there was no measure of what the social returns would be, because it was not an integral part of the business. While it was called an investment, in actual fact it was corporate philanthropy or charity. But it sounded better – in this sector there are always interesting phrases (Moshoeshoe, quoted in Bezuidenhout et al., 2007: 37).

National surveys of corporate social investments have been common, but their methodologies have been of varying rigor and they have been constrained by the uncertain definition of what constitutes CSI. Furthermore, companies have made little effort to account for their CSI expenditures in a comparable manner. For instance, the total CSI funding by listed corporate grant makers was estimated at just over R2 billion in 2001, though the total contribution "could be as much as double R2 billion when one accounts for... noncash contributions" (Rockey, 2001: 2). In 2003, the total CSI spend was estimated R2.35 billion, 6.8% higher than that in 2002, and the average company level spend among the largest 100 companies was estimated at R13 million (Rockey, 2004). This trend of inflation related increases has generally been upheld, though there are likely to be more significant recent increases due to the inclusion of CSI related issues in the Black Economic Empowerment (BEE) scorecard discussed in more detail later and summarized in Table 20.3.

Significantly, a large proportion of the total CSI spending comes from a relatively small group of large companies, with a predominant role played by the mining and finance companies. Anglo American, in particular, is a prominent recipient of CSI awards and recognition (see, for instance, Rockey, 2001, 2004). This dominant role of the large companies in CSI (as well as the broader CSR field) also needs to be seen in the context of the concentration of the South African economy in relatively few companies, especially in the mining and finance sectors, though this concentration has decreased somewhat since the transition to democracy in 1994.

The emphasis on philanthropic activities in the name of CSR in South Africa (and indeed in much of the rest of Africa, as well) is interpreted by Wayne Visser as a fundamental reorientation of the CSR definition in terms of Carroll's well-known pyramid model. According to Carroll, CSR encompasses the economic, legal, ethical, and discretionary – or philanthropic – expectations that society has of organizations, and the economic and legal responsibilities are described in terms of what is *required*, the ethical ones as what is *expected*, and the philanthropic ones as what is *desired* (Carroll, 2004). Visser argues that Carroll's model requires substantial revision if adapted to the (South) African context, suggesting that the dominant interpretation of CSR in terms of philanthropic activities means that discretionary aspects of CSR are often more important even than the legal and ethical ones. This, he argues, is because the socio-economic development needs in many parts of Africa are "so great that philanthropy is an expected norm," and also because CSR in general "is still in an early stage of maturity." In contrast, legal responsibilities are seen to represent "far less of a pressure for good conduct," because the legal infrastructure is often poorly developed and "many African countries are also behind the developed world in terms of incorporating human rights and other issues relevant to CSR into their legislation" (Visser, 2006).

Visser's critique is not itself backed by empirical research, though empirical studies discussed in more detail later provide important support to his argument. However, though Carroll's model may not be fully accurate in *descriptive* terms in the South African context – and arguably it is becoming increasingly more accurate in line with more recent developments discussed later – it is still an important *normative* model of what CSR *should* mean, also in the South African context. Perhaps a more significant critique of Carroll's pyramid in the South African context is that it does not adequately deal with the significant tensions between economic, legal, ethical, and discretionary aspects of CSR. Visser highlights this point with an example especially pertinent in South Africa:

> In an African context, such conflicts and contradictions [between the four levels in Carroll's pyramid] tend to be the norm, rather than the exception – how to reconcile job creation and environmental protection, short term profitability and Aids treatment costs, oppressive regimes and transparent governance, economic empowerment and social investment? And in reality, the interconnections between Carroll's four levels are so blurred as to seem artificial or even irrelevant. For example, is the issue of Aids treatment primarily an economic responsibility (given the medium to long term effects on the workforce and economy), or is it ethical (because Aids sufferers have basic human rights), or is it philanthropic (it is not an occupational disease, so surely treatment amounts to charity)?

The fundamental concern with the South African emphasis on CSI in the name of CSR is that though CSI initiatives have no doubt been making important developmental contributions, they are easy to criticize with regard to their lack of integration with core business strategy. As noted by one CSI manager:

> The view that CSR is primarily CSI is a result of how things were structured, in the sense that businesses thought that they needed to pay what some people referred to as 'blood money', but it never needed to be part of the business processes. So in order to operate they needed to do some charity work or CSI, but it has never been core to their own business strategy ... What you're looking at [in terms of CSR] is business strategy, reputation assurance, the social licence to operate – this is what we call it (Joseph, interview).

This broader conception of CSR has been emerging in the South African discourse under various terms. One of the most prominent ones has been corporate citizenship.

Corporate citizenship…advocates that a company that behaves ethically and contributes and builds relationships with all stakeholders will improve its long-term growth
prospects…Corporate citizenship is more than just CSI. It includes a number of other
elements, such as business ethics and good corporate governance, workplace health and
safety, labour practices and environmental standards. CSI is a key part of a corporate citizenship programme, but it remains only one of the legs on which corporate citizenship
stands (Rockey, 2001: 109–110).

An important aspect of this broader conception of CSR has been internalizing the
social and environmental costs of doing business. In this regard, one of the first
issues to deserve committed attention from business leaders has been safety, health,
and environment (SHE). This has also been the result of regulation, including the
Mine Health and Safety Act of 1996 and the National Environmental Management
Act of 1998 (see further for an overview of national legislation pertinent to CSR).

The emphasis on environmental issues with regard to internalizing the externalities of mining operations evolved into the increasing use of sustainable development
as the dominant term of reference pertaining to CSR. Though it had been given formal status already in the 1996 constitution, the concept of sustainable development
became particularly prominent in the lead-up to the World Summit on Sustainable
Development (WSSD), which was held in Johannesburg in August and September
2002. Hence, for instance, Anglo American employed a Group Manager: Sustainable Development in mid-2001. Though some commented that this post was primarily a public relations exercise in the run-up to the WSSD, the incumbent, Karin
Ireton (interview), is adamant that she has been given a mandate for real change in
the organization: "The fact that, in a time when jobs are being shed, the company has
created a new post with significant resources and an ability to access the executives
is remarkable." Ireton characterized her role as follows: "I am a catalyst, facilitator,
to help people understand that many different pieces form the jigsaw puzzle called
sustainable development."

While SHE is commonly seen as "the foundation stone" (Ireton, interview) for
a company's sustainable development efforts, a more recent emphasis has been on
the social aspects of sustainable development. As argued by Michael Spicer, Anglo
American's former executive vice-president for corporate affairs,

Particularly for companies operating in developing countries, environmental impact studies must now be accompanied by community involvement studies. It's as unacceptable for
companies, when they move on to leave great holes in the earth and polluted rivers as it is
to leave disrupted or un-enriched communities (quoted in Anglo American, 2002: 3).

The largest mining companies in South Africa were the first to include issues such
as community involvement and human rights in their narratives. Hence, the BHP
Billiton 2000 *Health, Safety, Environment and Communities* report is the first to
make explicit the company's intention to "employ local people as far as possible
and to provide further training to enhance skills" (BHP Billiton, 2000: 24). During
2002, Anglo American adopted community engagement guidelines, with the expectation that "by the end of 2003, over 90% of our significant managed operations
will have Community Engagement plans in place" (Anglo American, 2002: 35).
These plans are to facilitate both effective community developments, in terms of, for

instance, affirmative procurement, as well as effective ways of dealing with community complaints, including the establishment of committed entry points for community members to communicate with the company at a sufficiently high level (Ireton, interview). A key remaining challenge is to implement suitable indicators for the management and reporting of social performance: "Tailings and environmental issues are probably well managed, because that's good engineering practice – they are much easier than the social, soft issues" (Linnell, interview).

Indeed, next to climate change, human rights are arguably at the forefront of the current CSR agenda in South Africa, particularly for those South African companies operating in other parts of Africa characterized by what the OECD calls "weak governance"[1]:

> A weak governance zone is defined as an investment environment in which governments are unable or unwilling to assume their responsibilities. These "government failures" lead to broader failures in political, economic and civic institutions that, in turn, create the conditions for endemic violence, crime and corruption and that block economic and social development. About 15 per cent of the world's people live in such areas, notably in sub-Saharan Africa . . . The broader institutional failures create situations which pose many ethical dilemmas and challenges for companies. As companies themselves often note, weak governance zones represent some of the world's most difficult investment environments. In addition to the usual financial and business risks encountered in all investment environments, weak governance zones pose ethical dilemmas and present risks that stem directly from government failure – e.g. widespread solicitation, extortion, endemic crime and violent conflict, abuses by security forces, forced labour and violations of the rule of law (OECD, 2006: 9, 11).

To respond to these challenges, a number of guidelines and tools have been developed recently, including, for instance, the Voluntary Principles on Security and Human Rights (see http://www.voluntaryprinciples.org) and the OECD Risk Awareness Tool for Multinational Enterprises in Weak Governance Zones (OECD, 2006). Other initiatives have focused on particular sectors or issues, whereby the Extractive Industries Transparency Initiative (see http://www.eitransparency.org) is a prominent effort to enhance the disclosure of information on payment of taxes and royalties by companies in the extractives industry. Another example is the Kimberley Process, which brings together governments and companies to eradicate so-called blood or conflict diamonds (see http://www.kimberleyprocess.com). The Kimberley Process is also notable for the direct role played by the South African government in its establishment (see Hamann and De Cleene, 2005).

Two inter-related features characterize these emerging trends in CSR. The first is that companies' engagement is focused on systemic issues underlying the sustainability issue or challenge. That is, the scale of analysis and engagement has increased from the level of the individual company to the value chain and the broader governance framework. This has required a different mode of engagement, whereby proactive companies seek to support "collaborative governance" initiatives

---

[1] Note that some commentators may include South Africa in this definition of weak governance zones, though there are obviously important differences between the governance challenges confronting companies in South Africa in comparison to, say, the Democratic Republic of the Congo (see, for instance, Kapelus et al., 2008).

that entail a shift in responsibility for policy-making, implementation, and the provision of social goods and services from government to a more diffuse constellation of social actors, with a special role for business. While some see collaborative governance initiatives or "partnerships" as "key [emerging] pathways for enabling international development and the delivery of public goods" (Zadek and Radovich, 2006: 1), others argue that their role "should only be a very limited one" (Martens, 2007: 6). This debate is the focus of a current research project coordinated by the author.

20.3 Emerging Market-based Drivers for CSR

The emergence of CSR in South Africa needs to be seen in the context of the structural changes in the economy since 1990. Previously, South African companies were to a large extent cut off from the global economy due to sanctions and trade restrictions. With the political changes in the 1990s, these restrictions diminished and South African companies became part of and exposed to the global economy, including the concept of CSR as it was emerging in the UK, in particular. As a result, the companies that have been featuring most prominently in the South African CSR discourse are the "depatriated" companies, i.e., formerly South African companies that have moved their registration and primary listing overseas (most commonly London) (Bezuidenhout et al., 2007). The first companies to do this included Anglo American (mining), SAB-Miller (beverages), and Old Mutual (finance). The move to one of the primary stock exchanges is widely seen to have created a strong impetus to establish CSR policies and enhance public reporting at minimum, because of the more comprehensive corporate governance and risk management requirements of the stock exchanges and greater stakeholder expectations and shareholder activism in "Northern" countries.

A number of important market-based drivers for CSR have been also emerging in South Africa in the last decade. The first is the publication in mid-2002 of the second *King Report on Corporate Governance for South Africa*, colloquially known as the King 2 Report (King Committee on Corporate Governance, 2002). It is significant in that it explicitly defines and motivates for concepts such as "corporate citizenship," "social responsibility," "triple bottom line" performance, and "sustainability reporting." For instance, it advocates an inclusive "stakeholder approach," which "recognizes that stakeholders such as the community in which the company operates, its customers, its employees and its suppliers amongst others need to be considered when developing the strategy of a company" (*op. cit.*: 98). It also makes explicit reference to the GRI guidelines and it requires that "every company should report at least annually on the nature and extent of its social, transformation [including BEE], ethical, safety, health, and environmental management policies and practices" (*op. cit.*: 35). The King 2 report notes that while its recommendations are not mandatory, conformance is "in the enlightened self-interest of every enterprise" and "can be encouraged in various ways" (*op. cit.*: 19). Indeed, the JSE Securities Exchange now requires listed companies to demonstrate compliance with parts of the King 2 Code, and this represents a powerful market based institutional driver for

CSR. The King 2 report has had significant influence on corporate governance and CSR debates internationally, especially in Africa (see, for instance, Rossouw, 2005).

A further market-based development relates to the role of investors in pushing the CSR agenda, a driver frequently mentioned by corporate managers, as illustrated earlier. The London and New York stock exchanges, in particular, have significant amounts of investment funds allocated to so-called socially responsible investments (SRI). Primary mechanisms for these are the Dow Jones Sustainability Index in New York and the FTSE4Good in London. In South Africa, however, SRI represents only about 1% of investments under management, and there is relatively little awareness of and support for SRI, though it is growing rapidly (Sonnenberg and Hamann, 2006).

To provide a benchmark for SRI investors, as well as an impetus for CSR more generally, the JSE Securities Exchange launched a sustainability index in 2004 called the JSE Socially Responsible Investment (SRI) Index. This made it the first bourse in an emerging market to develop a sustainability index. The Index is centered on a set of about 70 criteria or indicators (originally more than 90), grouped in terms of the four overarching categories of corporate governance, society, environment, and economy. The original criteria were based on the FTSE4Good model but were tailored to suit the South African context, and they are continuously modified. With regard to the impact of the Index in South Africa, Sonnenberg and Hamann (2006: 316) conclude as follows:

> There is no doubt that the Index has increased awareness of corporate citizenship among JSE listed companies. Its most significant effect has arguably been on those companies that otherwise would have had limited exposure to sustainability issues...For those companies unfamiliar with the triple bottom line, the Index has provided them with a deeper understanding of a range of sustainability issues...A further important contribution, both for companies and the broader stakeholder community has been that the Index has for the first time provided a set of criteria that defines the priorities for corporate citizenship in the South African context...However, despite the media coverage of the Index, as well as the interest expressed by a range of listed companies, the anticipated increase in the number of companies participating in the second round of the Index did not materialise. The reasons include questionnaire fatigue and uncertainty as to the benefits of participating in the Index.

Over and above the JSE SRI Index and the King 2 report, of course, there is a multitude of international CSR initiatives that have also had a diverse range of impacts in South Africa. Table 20.1 provides an overview of some of these initiatives and the nature and extent of their impacts in South Africa. The initiatives listed in Table 20.1 are generally focused on CSR or an aspect thereof. In addition, there are other initiatives that have some relevance to CSR and one of the most prominent of these is the New Partnership for Africa's Development (NEPAD) *African Peer Review Mechanism* (APRM). The APRM includes a number of requirements for participating countries to have their corporate governance frameworks – defined broadly to include issues such as "human rights, social responsibility and environmental sustainability" – assessed through peer review (see http://www.nepad.org/aprm). South Africa is one of five African countries that have undergone this process (see http://www.aprm.org.za), but arguably it has not had a very significant or lasting effect on CSR, or indeed corporate governance, in South Africa.

Table 20.1 Selected International CSR initiatives and their status in South Africa (Hanks et al., 2007)

CSR-related Initiative	Brief review of status in South Africa
United Nations Global Compact: This is the most prominent international CSR initiative. It was launched in 2000 by the then Secretary General Kofi Annan and there are now over 4,000 members comprising large corporations and small companies, as well as organizations from government and civil society. Members commit themselves for supporting ten principles based on international agreements on human rights, environment, labor rights, and anticorruption, as well as to "catalyze actions in support of UN goals," such as the Millennium Development Goals.	In 2000, a number of South African companies joined the UN Global Compact voluntarily on their own initiative, but since then it has been relatively dormant in South Africa. One reason often mentioned in this respect is the prevalence of national policies and legislation on issues such as BEE, which made the "added value" of the Global Compact unclear to companies. Nevertheless, as at March 2007, there were 21 South African organizations signed up to the UN Global Compact. Africa as a whole is relatively poorly represented, with a total of 154 business participants as compared with, for instance, 1,462 in Europe. In 2007, the National Business Initiative (NBI) became the national Focal Point for the Global Compact, and given the NBI's established membership and track record in CSR issues, it is expected to increase the Global Compact's profile in the country.
Global Reporting Initiative: The GRI is a "long-term, multi-stakeholder, international process whose mission it is to develop and disseminate globally applicable Sustainability Reporting Guidelines… for voluntary use by organizations for reporting on the economic, environmental, and social dimensions of their activities, products, and services."[2] The GRI seeks to provide a common framework for a number of different guidelines.	The GRI has enjoyed some prominence in South Africa, including a number of national workshops and conferences. Though only a few South African companies are currently reporting "in accordance" with the guidelines, as reported on the GRI website, most companies' public sustainable development reports make some reference to the GRI guidelines.
The Carbon Disclosure Project (CDP): Established in 2003, the CDP serves as the secretariat for the world's largest institutional investor collaboration on the business implications of climate change. Their website provides the largest registry of corporate greenhouse gas emissions in the world. Supported by a group of international investors representing assets under management of $40 trillion, the CDP issues a simple questionnaire annually to targeted companies, with questions on awareness and management of climate change issues.[3]	The CDP was launched in South Africa in 2007 at the initiative of Incite Sustainability, a Cape Town based consulting firm, in collaboration with the National Business Initiative. Over 75% of the top 40 JSE companies responded to the questionnaire, including also the state-owned electricity producer, Eskom. The responses were analyzed for the first South African CDP report, launched in November 2007 to significant political and media interest.

(Cont.)

---

[2] See GRI (2002):1. www.globalreporting.org.

[3] See www.cdproject.net.

Table 20.1 (*Continued*)

CSR-related Initiative	Brief review of status in South Africa
ISO 14000 series: The ISO 14000 series of standards focus on corporate environmental management systems, promoting continual improvement without specifying actual standards of performance. Social issues are not given much explicit consideration, though there is reference to stakeholder engagement.	The ISO 14000 series has played an important role for South African companies, many of which have become certified in connection with international supply chain and consumer expectations. Many companies' public reports indicate that they are either ISO 14000 certified or aspiring certification. South Africa has participated actively in the development of the standard since drafting commenced in the early 1990s.
ISO 26000: ISO 26000 (due for release in 2008 or 2009) is the designation of the future International Standard giving guidance on social responsibility. The guidance standard, which is not for use as a certification standard, is intended for use by organizations of all types, in both the public and private sectors, including companies, nongovernmental organizations and trade unions. It will not describe a formal management system, but will provide issue-specific guidance and guidance on addressing these issues in an organizational context.	South Africa has participated actively in the development and drafting of the standard since the initial inception work. A South African is the convenor of one of the three international drafting teams, and chair of the Liaison Task Force. The likely impact of this Guidance Standard for South African companies remains uncertain.
OECD Guidelines on Multinational Enterprises: Guidelines, first developed in 1976 and revised in 2000, pertain to the disclosure of information, employment relations, environmental management, bribery, competition, consumer interests, and science and technology diffusion. "They are the only multilaterally endorsed and comprehensive rules that governments have negotiated, in which they commit themselves to help solve problems arising in corporations."[4] Signatory governments commit themselves to establishing National Contact Points, which will investigate complaints referring to the Guidelines.	The Guidelines are especially important for formerly South African companies that have moved their domicile to a signatory country, such as the UK. Their relevance to South African domiciled companies remains limited, despite initiatives to raise their profile in South Africa (Hamann and de Cleene, 2005).
The OECD The *Forest Stewardship Council (FSC)* aims to promote more sustainable forestry practices through the certification of sustainable forestry practices	A number of the South African pulp and paper companies have forests certified in accordance with FSC requirements; several paper and packaging manufactures and distributors specifically make use of FSC certified products.
The *Kimberley Process Certification Scheme* (KPCS) is a process designed to certify the origin of diamonds from sources that are free of conflict.	The Kimberley Process is comprised of states and regional economic integration organizations (Participants) (*Cont.*)

---

[4] TUAC-OECD (2002); see also www.oecd.org.

Table 20.1 (*Continued*)

CSR-related Initiative	Brief review of status in South Africa
	who are eligible to trade in rough diamonds under the provisions of the KPCS. South Africa is a participating country.
The international chemical industry's *Responsible Care* program, which seeks to promote improved health, safety, and environmental performance within the chemical industry and its service providers.	The Chemical and Allied Industry's Association (CAIA) administers the Responsible Care program locally; there are currently 131 signatories to the Responsible Care initiative.
The finance sector's *Equator Principles* are a benchmark for the financial sector to manage social and environmental issues in project financing.	Only one of the South African banks (Nedbank) has signed up, although another (ABSA) has merged with a founder signatory to the Equator Principles (Barclays)
The *Principles for Responsible Investment (PRI)* provide a menu of possible actions for incorporating environmental, social, and governance issues into mainstream investment decision-making and ownership practices.	Current South African signatories include Government Employees Pension Fund, Advantage Asset Managers (Pty) Limited, Frater Asset Management, and Empowerdex (Pty) Ltd. Further research into its application in South Africa is currently being undertaken.
The *Human Rights Compliance Assessment Tool* is a diagnostic tool, designed to help companies detect potential human rights violations caused by the effect of their operations on employees, local residents, and all other stakeholders	Developed in Denmark, this assessment tool is being adapted to the South African context, although its prominence among South African companies is currently limited.
The *Extractive Industries Transparency Initiative* (EITII) supports improved governance in resource-rich countries through the verification and full publication of company payments and government revenues from oil, gas, and mining.	Although these initiatives are more focused on African countries with less established governance systems than South Africa (such as Angola), a number of South African mining companies operate in these regions.
There has also been an increasing emphasis on *fair trade and related certification systems*, particularly in the food and clothes sectors, but also in tourism.	One of the key areas of the impact of these codes is in the food, wine, and agricultural sector, amongst suppliers to European and North American retail food outlets.

20.4 The Role of the State and Black Economic Empowerment

Notwithstanding the common assumption that CSR is primarily about voluntary initiatives (see, for instance, European Commission, 2001) and market-based drivers, national legislation plays a crucial role in the development of South Africa's CSR agenda. For a start, there is typically a significant gap between stated policy and its implementation, with compliance in some instances becoming an issue of business voluntarism. In other words, CSR cannot be seen as being only about "beyond compliance," but needs to be seen as contributing "towards compliance," as well. For instance, with reference to mines' environmental remediation trust funds, which are required by the 1991 Minerals Act (RSA, 1991), it has been argued that "companies could be cutting corners due to government capacity constraints, but they are not – so it is an issue of both obligation and responsibility" (Kilani, interview). Limited government capacity has also been identified as a potential driver for CSR in South Africa, in that businesses take on developmental or regulatory responsibilities because the state is not fulfilling them.

Furthermore, the South African government has gone further than most other states to legislate on social issues. This is most clearly evident in legislation relating to BEE, as discussed later. More generally, however, the South African State has embarked on an ambitious law reform program since the inception of the country's democratic dispensation in 1994. Premised on a progressive constitution, there have been numerous legislative developments that are pertinent in shaping the country's CSR landscape (see Table 20.2 for an overview of selected laws).

As noted, a particularly prominent government initiative has been BEE. Though it has been an important feature of policy debates and negotiations between the government, established companies, and other role-players for some time already, it was defined more conclusively only in 2007 by means of a so-called balanced scorecard (DTI, 2007), as summarized in Table 20.3.

The transfer of ownership to black South Africans ("previously disadvantaged South Africans") has been the most prominent aspect of BEE in the national media in the last few years. This has led critics of BEE to argue that it is primarily about the creation of black elite, with little benefit to the poor and vulnerable. Defenders of BEE, and the state in particular, have however been at pains to describe BEE as "broad-based" and inclusive of issues pertaining to the needs and interests of the poor. Hence the transfer of ownership accounts for only 20% of a company's total BEE score in the scorecard (see Table 20.3). This is the same proportion as for skills development and preferential procurement. The latter is a key mechanism through which BEE requirements are extended throughout the economy, as large companies that have licensing requirements (e.g., in mining) or for which government is a crucial client (e.g., IT) will stipulate adherence to scorecard criteria among their suppliers.

Though there are important critiques of BEE and its implementation in South Africa (e.g., Ponte et al., 2007), it can be argued that the BEE charters established in sectors such as mining and finance have provided important targets and exerted significant pressure on companies to adapt their strategies and management systems. The mining charter, for instance, was the result of protracted and at times acrimonious negotiations between the government, established mining companies, labor unions, and others, but it resulted in the first sector-specific scorecard (in 2004) that balanced the ownership aspects of BEE, with explicit targets in employment equity, skills development, and socio-economic development (see http://www.dme.gov.za/minerals/pdf/scorecard.pdf). The state wielded a powerful

Table 20.2 Selected examples of national legislation of pertinence to CSR in South Africa

Legislation	Overview and pertinence to CSR
Companies Act No. 61 of 1973 and Closed Corporations Act No. 69 of 1984	Contain various provisions regarding company registration and conduct, including directors' fiduciary duties. They also include the potential for "lifting the corporate veil" and adjudicating personal liability for directors (particularly section 424 of the Companies Act), though this has been criticized as being difficult to implement.[5] Note that the Companies Act is currently undergoing revision.
Occupational Health and Safety Act No 85 of 1993 and Mine Health and Safety Act No. 29 of 1996	The former provides requirements for health and safety management systems and standards in the workplace. The latter is focused on the need to reduce the number of fatalities and injuries in the mining industry. It provides for tri-partite (labor, business, and government) structures at all levels of the industry for the purpose of implementing and monitoring health and safety management systems, as well as identifying causes of accidents. These acts are complemented by the Compensation for Occupational Injuries and Diseases Act No 130 of 1993 and the Occupational Diseases in Mines and Works Act No 78 of 1973, respectively.
Labor Relations Act No. 66 of 1995 and Basic Conditions of Employment Act No. 75 of 1997	Provide for basic conditions of employment, promote collective bargaining at workplace and sector level, and promote employee participation in company decision-making through workplace forums.
Constitution No. 108 of 1996	Contains the Bill of Rights, including the rights to equality, a clean and healthy environment access to information, administrative justice, and others; significantly, constitutional provisions and case law suggests that key elements of the Bill of Rights are of horizontal application; that is, they bind individuals and corporations, as well as the state.
National Water Act No. 36 of 1998[6]	Designates water as a national resource and requires water users to apply for licences from the state, with an allocation to a basic water right and a natural reserve, including stringent water pollution regulations.
Employment Equity Act No. 55 of 1998	Seeks to eliminate unfair discrimination in the workplace and implement affirmative action for "designated groups": black people, women, or people with disabilities.
Competition Act No. 89 of 1998 (amended in 2000)	Defines and makes provision for the prevention of anticompetitive behavior, and provides for the Competition Commission (administrative body), Competition Tribunal (adjudicates on matters such as mergers), and the Competition Appeals Court.

(Cont.)

---

[5] See King Committee on Corporate Governance (2002) *op. cit.*

[6] Similar laws on natural resource management, which place natural resources under the stewardship of the state, are the National Forests Act No. 84 of 1998 and the Marine Living Resources Act No. 18 of 1998.

Table 20.2 (*Continued*)

Legislation	Overview and pertinence to CSR
Skills Development Act No 97 of 1998	In combination with the Skills Development Levies Act No 9 of 1999, this act requires companies to contribute a percentage of their total payroll to the National Skills Fund, which is controlled by 25 Sector Education and Training Authorities (SETAs). The SETAs compensate companies for legitimate training and skills development programs.
National Environmental Management Act No. 107 of 1998	Promotes development that is socially, environmentally, and economically sustainable, seeks environmental justice and equitable access to environmental resources, promotes the precautionary principle, promotes public participation in environmental decision-making, protects "whistle-blowers," allows for public interest litigation, and provides for duty of care and remediation responsibilities – particularly for employers. Importantly it includes the possibility of directors' liability for environmental damages.
Promotion of Access to Information Act No. 2 of 2000	Promulgated to enforce the constitutional right to access to information that is pertinent to the Bill of Rights; it allows access to (almost) all information held by the state, as well as significant types of information held by private persons.
Promotion of Equality and Prevention of Unfair Discrimination Act No. 4 of 2000	This act seeks to prevent and prohibit unfair discrimination and harassment and to promote equality and eliminate unfair discrimination, in line with the constitutional right of equality and the exercise of democracy. While the ambit of the Employment Equity Act is limited to the workplace, this act's scope is without limit throughout the Republic.
Mineral and Petroleum Resources Development Act No. 28 of 2002	Vests all mining rights with the state and requires mining companies to reapply for mining permits, with preference given to black economic empowerment companies; companies need to demonstrate due diligence in social and environmental matters, and directors may be held liable for environmental damage.
National Black Economic Empowerment Act No. 53 of 2003	Sets out a national framework for the promotion of BEE. Establishes the Black Economic Empowerment Advisory Council; and empowers the Minister to issue codes of good practice on BEE, including a scorecard to measure achievement, and to promote sector-specific BEE Charters that are deemed to be in accordance with the objectives of the act.
National implementing legislation for international treaties	The South African government is a party to numerous international treaties and conventions that have a bearing on CSR issues. These include (but are not limited to) the core conventions of the International Labor Organization (ILO), the conventions and protocols relating to biodiversity, climate change, ozone depleting substances, the handling and transportation of hazardous waste, and the phasing out of persistent organic pollutants; various conventions and treaties relating to the protection of humans rights.

Table 20.3 An overview of the generic broad-based black economic empowerment scorecard (DTI, 2007)

Scorecard component	Focus areas
Ownership (20%)	This includes consideration (amongst other things) of the following issues: • The nature of the exercisable voting rights in the hands of black people • The nature of the economic interest of black people in the enterprise • The level of involvement of black people in ownership of the enterprise through employee ownership schemes, broad-based ownership schemes, and co-operatives
Management control (10%)	This includes consideration (amongst other things) of the following issues: • The nature of the exercisable voting rights of black Board members • The number of Black Executive Directors • The level of representation of black in senior top managemen • The number of black independent nonexecutive directors
Employment equity (10%)	This includes consideration (amongst other things) of the following issues: • The level of representation of black employees in senior, middle, and junior management • The number of black disabled employees as a percentage of all employees
Skills development (20%)	This includes consideration (amongst other things) of the following issues: • The level of skills development expenditure on specified learning programs for black employees • The number of black employees participating in defined learnerships as a percentage of total employees
Preferential procurement (20%)	This includes consideration (amongst other things) of the following issues: • The level of B-BBEE procurement spend from all recognized B-BBEE suppliers as a percentage of total procurement spend • The level of B-BBEE procurement spend on suppliers that are 50% black-owned and suppliers that are 30% black women owned as a percentage of total procurement spend
Enterprise Development (10%)	This includes consideration of the following issue: • The level of the average annual value of all enterprise development contributions and sector specific programs made by the enterprise as a percentage of a defined target relating to profit and turnover
Socio-Economic Development initiatives (10%)	This includes consideration of the following issue: • The level of the average annual value of all socio-economic development contributions made by the enterprise as a percentage of a defined target relating to profit and turnover

"stick" in these negotiations because it tied companies' performance on BEE to the issuing of new mining licenses according to the Mineral and Petroleum Resources Development Act of 2002. Despite this regulatory approach, the mining BEE score-card may be interpreted as a negotiated definition of what CSR means in practice to the mining industry in South Africa, though of course crucial sustainability issues, such as the natural environment, are excluded. Though sustainable development or CSR was not an explicit topic of discussion during the negotiations surrounding the BEE scorecard, the Minister of Minerals and Energy stated in 2003 that the BEE requirements should be considered crucial elements of sustainable development in South Africa (Mlambo-Ngcuka, 2003). This perspective is shared by some mining company leaders, who emphasize the link between BEE, sustainable development, and long-term benefits to business in South Africa. Anglo Gold's chief executive argued,

> What the Charter is turning out to be is a test of the social license. A business will only survive if it benefits all of its stakeholders over time – if people, the community, customers, employees and shareholders are left better off having an association with the company. I think it's a very good document and is going to make the South African industry more competitive, not less, and lead to greater wealth creation, not less. To draw on the gene pool of 100% of South Africa, not just white males, has got to be a good thing (Godsell, quoted in Anglo Gold, 2002: 9).

Hence even in the wake of severe acrimony, state imperatives are being adopted, at least in the rhetoric of some business leaders, as being in business's enlightened self-interest. South Africa's CSR agenda is increasingly being defined by the extent to which BEE will, indeed, benefit the poor, rather than contribute only to the establishment of new elite. This will depend not only on the state, but also on companies' implementation of BEE.

20.5 CSR Performance and the Need for Local-level Analyses and More Fundamental Indicators

In the international Dow Jones Sustainability Index (DJSI), only four companies domiciled in South Africa are listed: African Bank Investments, Investec, Nedbank, Bidvest Group. However, this index represents a limited sample as only companies also listed on the Dow Jones World Index are included. Another international ranking exercise with regard to CSR is the Innovest *The Global 100 Most Sustainable Corporations in the World*, whereby no South African companies are currently included on this list (see http://www.global100.org). The closest local equivalent to these international initiatives is the JSE SRI index, described earlier. It does not rank all of the constituent companies, but mentions the leaders in each of its three categories in terms of high, medium, or low environmental impact. The leaders in the 2006 index were Anglo American and Anglo Platinum (both mining) in the high impact category, Woolworths (retail) in the medium impact category, and Nedbank (finance) in the low impact category.

In addition to these regular rankings, a recent research project ranked the top 52 companies listed on the JSE on the basis of an established methodology called the Accountability Rating^{TM} (Financial Mail, 2006). The research systematically investigated the sample companies' publicly available information (including but not limited to their annual and sustainability reports) in order to assess performance in the following areas:

Strategic intent: that is, the extent to which sustainability issues are reflected in company strategy

Governance: including issues such as board oversight and responsibility for sustainability issues

Performance management: the degree to which sustainability objectives are institutionalized in day-to-day management

Stakeholder engagement: the manner and extent to which stakeholders are engaged in setting objectives and their implementation

Public disclosure: with emphasis on the quality and content of sustainability reporting

Assurance: the extent and manner in which companies' public disclosure on sustainability issues is audited or verified by independent assessors.

Table 20.4 provides the ranking of the top 52 companies. It illustrates, among other things, the leadership role of the mining sector with regard to CSR, as noted earlier. This is premised on this sector's long-standing engagement with environmental and community issues; its exposure to significant critique and monitoring by both civil society and government (including also particular attention in terms of black economic empowerment); as well as important international initiatives, such as those led by the International Council for Metals and Minerals. The second most advanced sector is finance; this sector is also characterized by strong links to the international debates and, most importantly, a dedicated BEE charter.

Though performance evaluations and rankings undoubtedly play an important role in fostering awareness and a competitive impulse among companies, they have important limitations. In a review of a range of such "nonfinancial performance metrics and associated surveys," Chatterji and Levine (2006: 30) argue that these often contribute to continued uncertainty and confusion, because many of them are plagued by low reliability of their data (due to nonresponse bias and other factors), low validity of their measurement constructs (because they do not relate directly to performance issues that are important to society), and lacking comparability between their methodologies. Furthermore, most of these studies are characterized by an emphasis on company policies and practices, rather than impacts on particular stakeholders or impacts "on the ground."

This distrust in CSR ratings is also prevalent in South Africa. A prominent example is the case of Anglo Platinum, which in 2006 was a "winner" in both the JSE SRI Index rating and the Accountability Rating, as mentioned earlier. At the same time, a prominent group of advocacy NGOs gave Anglo Platinum the "Grim Reaper Floating Trophy" award for worst corporate practice on environmental and human rights (with a focus on a particular controversy surrounding resettlement in one of

Table 20.4 "Accountability Rating[TM]" of the largest 52 South African listed companies (Financial Mail, 2006)

Rating 2006	Company	Score 2006	Sector
1	BHP Billiton Plc	78.6	Resources
2	Anglo Platinum Ltd	70.1	Resources
3	Anglo American Plc	69.4	Resources
4	Nedbank Group Ltd	67.4	Financials
5	Sasol Ltd	66.0	Oil & Gas
6	Sabmiller Plc	61.6	Industrials
7	Anglogold Ashanti Ltd	54.9	Resources
8	Santam Ltd	54.7	Financials
9	Barloworld Ltd	54.2	Industrials
10	Kumba Resources Ltd	53.8	Resources
11	Harmony Gold Mining Company Ltd	52.9	Resources
12	Massmart Holdings Ltd	51.3	Retail/Consumer Services
13	Aveng Ltd	49.1	Industrials
14	Sappi Ltd	48.9	Industrials
15	Impala Platinum Holdings Ltd	48.4	Resources
16	Telkom SA Limited	48.0	Technology, Electronics and Telecoms
17	Absa Group Ltd	46.6	Financials
18	Pick n Pay Stores Ltd	46.6	Retail/Consumer Services
19	Standard Bank Group Ltd	45.7	Financials
20	Woolworths Holdings Ltd	45.1	Retail/Consumer Services
21	MTN Group Ltd	43.0	Technology, Electronics and Telecoms
22	Bidvest Group Ltd (The)	41.7	Industrials
23	Gold Fields Ltd	41.7	Resources
24	Metropolitan Holdings[7]	41.1	Financials
25	Sanlam Ltd	40.1	Financials
26	Edgars Consolidated Stores Ltd	39.7	Retail/Consumer Services
27	Richemont Securities Ag	38.8	Industrials
28	Investec Ltd	38.1	Financials
29	Investec Plc	38.1	Financials
30	Unitrans Ltd	37.4	Retail/Consumer Services
31	Firstrand Ltd	37.0	Financials
32	AECI Ltd	36.4	Industrials
33	Allied Electronics Corporation Ltd	35.5	Industrials
34	Liberty Group Ltd	34.8	Financials
35	Network Healthcare Holdings Ltd[8]	32.5	Healthcare
36	Imperial Holdings Ltd	31.7	Industrials

(Cont.)

[7] Metropolitan Holdings is ranked 51 on the Financial Mail SA Giants list and would therefore be excluded from the top 50.

[8] Network Healthcare Holdings (Netcare) is ranked 52 on the Financial Mail SA Giants list and would therefore be excluded from the Top 50 Companies.

Table 20.4 (*Continued*)

Rating 2006	Company	Score 2006	Sector
37	JD Group Ltd	30.1	Retail/Consumer Services
38	Old Mutual Plc	25.2	Financials
39	Nampak Ltd	24.9	Industrials
40	Datatec Ltd	24.1	Technology, Electronics and Telecoms
41	Super Group Ltd	24.0	Industrials
42	Dimension Data Holdings Plc	22.6	Technology, Electronics and Telecoms
43	Shoprite Holdings Ltd	22.5	Retail/Consumer Services
44	Murray And Roberts Holdings Ltd	20.0	Industrials
45	New Clicks Holdings Ltd	19.3	Retail/Consumer Services
46	Steinhoff International Holdings Ltd	19.0	Industrials
47	Mittal Steel Limited	18.9	Industrials
48	The Spar Group Limited	16.9	Retail/Consumer Services
49	Naspers Ltd N	14.5	Technology, Electronics and Telecoms
50	Remgro Ltd	13.0	Financials
51	Tiger Brands Ltd	12.8	Industrials
52	Liberty Holdings Ltd	5.2	Financials

its projects).[9] Mentioning this contradiction is not to imply that Anglo Platinum has not made important progress in terms of CSR, generally speaking, but it illustrates the need for more detailed, nuanced, and, above all, local level analyses of corporate performance to augment the current emphasis on corporate policies and systems in most CSR assessments. To illustrate, the remainder of this section will consider the CSR practices of mining companies in a particular area.

The mining region surrounding the town of Rustenburg in the North West Province includes a range of mostly old and large platinum mines owned by Anglo Platinum, Impala, and Lonmin (respectively, the largest platinum companies in the world), a smaller platinum mine owned by Aquarius Platinum, and chrome mines owned by Samancor (a subsidiary of BHP Billiton at the time of the research) and Xstrata. In total, these mines employ between 70,000 and 80,000 workers, though this number fluctuates depending on industry and mine cycles.

In line with the previous discussion, the mining companies' dominant interpretation of CSR has been in terms of so-called corporate social investment: philanthropic initiatives in communities surrounding the mines or via national programs in education, health, welfare, or small business development. Though these initiatives have represented welcome development contributions, they have had little impact on the root causes of social problems surrounding the mines. Many of these root causes relate to core business practices of the mining companies, especially employee recruitment and housing. As conceded by one business manager, "Albeit we have the

---

[9] The so-called Corpse Awards were coordinated by an NGO called groundWork, see http://www.groundwork.org.za.

right intentions, we might not be getting at the root causes, or getting at those business activities that may be exacerbating the social problems."

These core business practices were framed by South Africa's colonial and apartheid history, and the detrimental social impacts of migrant labor and large single-sex hostels were acknowledged in the 1970s already (Flynn, 1992; Pallister et al., 1987). Even at the local level, it has been frequently pointed out that a root cause for many of the Rustenburg area's social problems is the mining companies' continued reliance on single-sex hostels (CRC, 2001; Plan Associates, 2001). This pertains especially to the growing informal settlements (squatter camps) around the mines, whose residents suffer deteriorating social conditions, including lacking services, crime, and disease. As argued by one mining company director:

> You don't have to be a genius to see what the real threats are [in the area]: unemployment, crime, the disrupted social fabric created by the migrant system, and the fact that you have a lot of single men living in hostels in proximity to your operations.

Despite this general acknowledgement of companies' contribution to deep-seated social problems in the area, the topic of employee recruitment and housing was largely ignored in most companies' public sustainability reports until as late as 2006. This gives some credence to the "greenwash" criticism of CSR, as it shows that the proactive engagement with the social challenges around company operations is not yet within the ambit of public CSR reporting and, some would argue, CSR itself.

Further indication of the gap between companies' CSR-related initiatives and the root causes of social problems around the mines can be found in the relevant organizational structures. CSR-related company departments and staff have generally, until recently, had no policy influence on companies' housing practices, for instance. Furthermore, operational management has rarely had significant organizational responsibility for social issues, as indicated in the general, continued absence of social criteria in mine managers' performance assessment (with some notable, quite recent exceptions).

However, over the last decade there has been a shift away from single-sex hostels amongst most companies in the case study area. There have been a variety of reasons for why such a shift was motivated by companies' enlightened self-interest, over and above continuous pressure from the state and the unions. These pertain primarily to the desire to decrease the spread of HIV/AIDS amongst the workforce, decrease the risk of labor unrest, increase productivity, and establish legitimacy. However, amongst many companies, the overarching and guiding framework under which this shift has occurred is the drive to focus on companies' core competencies, according to which the labor hostels were considered a tedious and inefficient distraction.

There is no inherent problem with this modernization motivation, except that it manifested itself without sufficient consideration to its social implications. Hence the shift away from single sex hostels has generally occurred separate, in terms of policy and organizational management, from companies' CSR considerations. An outcome of this has been that the shift away from hostels has further contributed to the growth of informal settlements surrounding the mines, partly because many hostel dwellers were compelled or motivated by the new policies to move into informal lodgings. This is instead of the potentially beneficial outcomes of a more considered policy on housing, within a broader, collaborative approach to deal with informal settlements in the area.

Finally, the companies' dominant approaches to CSR have not been able to respond effectively to the growing problem of informal settlements around the mines because of a lack of strategic collaboration between the mining companies and other key role-players in the area, especially the local municipality and traditional (tribal) authorities. Indeed, any practical solution for improving conditions in the informal settlements will need to involve multiple parties. For a start, much of the land occupied by informal settlers in the study area is owned by the traditional authority of the Bafokeng tribe, which has been reluctant to allow any formalization of the settlements. Agreements as to available land, compensation, and the necessary infrastructure investments will require all relevant parties to be involved, including the squatters. As noted by another Anglo Platinum manager, "We will only be able to deal with the informal settlements through a multi-stakeholder approach."

Most case study companies are currently undergoing a potentially important transformation with regard to the definition and management of CSR. This entails a broadening of the definition of CSR to include core business practices, as well as organizational changes that see CSR-related issues considered much higher in the management hierarchy than previously the case. There have also been increasing efforts to develop improved cross-sector collaboration in the area. The key driver of this shift has been the South African state's transformation agenda, encapsulated in the BEE scorecard discussed earlier.

The above discussion suggests the need for any assessment of companies' CSR policies and practices to be more cognizant of historical context and local complexities than is commonly the case in most existing assessments. Based on the above discussion, for instance, the following indicators ought to be considered in a more detailed appraisal of companies in the case study area:

- The extent to which CSR is integrated into core business decision-making, particularly with respect to issues such as labor recruitment, employee benefits, and housing.
- The extent to which the various CSR-related functions are coordinated within the company, with respect to organizational structures and their interaction.
- The extent to which external stakeholders are involved in the establishment and implementation of CSR policies. In particular, this includes the efforts being made towards multi-stakeholder collaboration, especially in terms of local government development planning.

Though such considerations ought to inform CSR assessments, they are arguably not prominent enough in many ranking exercises, such as those in stock exchange indices (e.g., FTSE4Good). They are also absent in many decision-makers' portrayals of what constitutes a socially responsible company, in South Africa and elsewhere. This is illustrated by means of a comparison of some of the companies operating in the Rustenburg area, premised on research undertaken in 2003 (Hamann, 2004). Anglo Platinum is generally seen as a market leader in terms of CSR, as indicated in the above mentioned ranking exercises. It is also perceived as a leader by most local and national stakeholders. Even Lonmin's Director of Corporate Affairs argued:

> We're a bit behind the Anglos in this type of thing, in terms of CSR generally...they are recognised as the leaders, both Anglo American and Anglo Platinum. They have a Chairman's Fund for example...We tend to be more regional in focus (Reilly, interview).

Anglo Platinum's reputation as a leader in CSR is arguably based to a large extent on its significant CSI spending and related promotional material. This is in contrast to numerous concerns regarding the extent to which CSR has been an issue in core business decision-making, in particular, in its housing policies, as noted earlier. (Note, however, that Anglo Platinum has made important progress in integrating CSR into its core strategies in recent years subsequent to this assessment.)

In contrast, Lonmin is less commonly highlighted in terms of CSR, but has adopted strategic approaches that deserve recognition. Most significantly, Lonmin was the first to consider CSR in a manner that proactively dealt with the socio-economic challenges surrounding the mines. For instance, this included the Marikana housing project in which the company adopted a holistic and collaborative approach to developing sustainable settlements in the area – this provided an important model that has since informed other initiatives in this and other areas. Another example pertains to the company's successful labor relations program, which also facilitates the establishment and effective implementation of context and location specific CSR approaches. Hence, CSR was arguable integrated into core business functions earlier in Lonmin than in the case of Anglo Platinum, despite prevailing perceptions of the latter's leadership role.

20.6 Conclusion

This chapter discussed the context and practices of corporate social responsibility (CSR) in South Africa. It made three overarching arguments. First, it argued that the country's complex and painful history has significant implications for how CSR is understood and implemented. Big business has been implicated in human rights abuses committed under apartheid and there is still much distrust of big business among some in government and civil society. On the contrary, the apartheid history also gave rise to early manifestations of voluntary initiatives to contribute to policy changes and social development, including the South African concept of "corporate social investment" (CSI) and the Sullivan Principles (which were focused on international companies operating in apartheid South Africa). There has been an important progression from this emphasis on CSI to a broader conception of CSR linked to sustainable development and collaborative governance, though these more recent trends are still hotly debated and in need of more detailed research.

The second argument of this chapter is that in a country like South Africa, CSR cannot be defined purely as voluntary initiatives, as it is often done in, say, the European context. The South African government has developed, partly by means of negotiation with big business and other role-players, a "balanced score-card" for "broad-based black economic empowerment" (BEE), together with sys-tematic means for encouraging or enforcing compliance by companies. BEE has been adopted, at least publicly, by most companies as a component of CSR and is characterized by some business leaders as being in their enlightened self-interest. Arguably there are no clear distinctions or divisions between voluntary business actions and state-led interventions.

The third and final argument of this chapter is that many conventional approaches to assessing or even ranking CSR performance adopt a relatively superficial perspec-tive on the interactions between companies and their socio-economic and natural environments. In particular, there is a need for more context-specific assessments that take into consideration the complexities of sustainable development at the lo-cal level. It may also require indicators that consider the extent to which companies integrate CSR into core business decision-making and the extent to which they are able to approach sustainable development challenges in a collaborative manner.

References

Anglo American, 2002. *Anglo American's Corporate Social Investment in South Africa*. London: Anglo American plc.

Anglo Gold, 2002. *Anglo Gold Annual Report 2002*. Johannesburg: Anglo Gold.

Alperson, M., 1995. *Foundations for a New Democracy: Corporate Social Investment in South Africa*. Johannesburg: Ravan.

Bezuidenhout, A., Fig, D., Hamann, R. and Omar, R., 2007. "A political economy of corporate social and environmental responsibility in South Africa" in D. Fig (ed.), *Staking their claim: corporate social and environmental responsibility in South Africa*. Pietermaritzburg: University of KwaZulu-Natal Press.

Billiton, B.H.P., 2000. *HSE and Communities annual report*. London: BHP Billiton.

Black Economic Empowerment Commission (BEECom), 2001. *Black Economic Empowerment Commission Report*. Johannesburg: Skotaville Press.

Carroll, A.B., 2004. Managing ethically with global stakeholders: A present and future challenge. *Academy of Management Executive*, 18(2): 114–120.

Chatterji, A. and Levine, D. 2006. Breaking Down the Wall of Codes: Evaluating Non-Financial Performance Measurement, *California Management Review*, 48(2): 29–51.

CRC (Conflict Resolution Consortium), 2001. Rustenburg/Anglo Platinum Conflict Stabilisation Project. Rustenburg: Conflict Resolution Consortium.

Crush, J., Jeeves, A., and Yudelman, D., 1991. *South Africa's Labour Empire: A History of Black Migrancy to the Gold Mines*. Cape Town: David Phillip.

DTI (Department of Trade & Industry), 2007. General Notice 112 of 2007 *Codes of Good Practice on Black Economic Empowerment Act* (9 February 2007).

European Commission, 2001. *Promoting a European framework for corporate social responsibil-ity – Green Paper*. Luxembourg: Office for Official Publications of the European Communities.

Feldberg, M., 1972. Business Profits and Social Responsibility. Inaugural Lecture as Professor of Business Administration, University of Cape Town.

Financial Mail, 2006. Special Report: Accountability Rating South Africa," October 27, 2006 (available online via http://free.financialmail.co.za/report06/account06/aacc.htm; accessed 11 February 2007).

Flynn, L., 1992. Studded with Diamonds and Paved with Gold: Miners, Mining Companies and Human Rights in Southern Africa. Bloomsbury, London.

Hamann, R., 2004. Corporate social responsibility, partnerships, and institutional change: The case of mining companies in South Africa. *Natural Resources Forum*, 28(4): 278–290.

Hamann, R. and De Cleene, S., 2005. Promoting South African companies' corporate responsibility in the rest of Africa. *South African Journal of International Affairs*, 12(2): 127–142.

Hanks, J., Hamann, R. and Sayers, V., 2007. Corporate Social Responsibility in South Africa: A description of the CSR landscape, a review of the challenges and some recommendations for the UN Global Compact. Unpublished report.

Jones, J.D.F., 1995. *Through Fortress and Rock: The Story of Gencor 1895–1995*. Johannesburg: Jonathan Ball Publishers.

Kapelus, P., Hamann, R. and O'Keefe, E., 2008. Doing business with integrity in weak governance zones: Learning from the experience of AngloGold Ashanti in the Democratic Republic of the Congo. *International Social Science Journal*, forthcoming.

King Committee on Corporate Governance, 2002. *King Report on Corporate Governance for South Africa 2002*. Johannesburg: Institute of Directors.

Lipton, M., 1985. *Capitalism and Apartheid: South Africa 1910–84*. Aldershot: Gower.

Martens, J., 2007. Multistakeholder partnerships – future models of multilateralism? Berlin: Friedrich-Ebert-Stiftung.

Marzullo, S.G., 1987. American Business in South Africa: The Hard Choices. In S.P. Sethi and C.M. Falbe (eds.), *Business and Society: Dimensions of Conflict and Cooperation*. Massachusetts: Lexington.

Moodie, T.D., Ndatshe, V., 1994. *Going for Gold: Men, Mines, and Migration*. Johannesburg: Witwatersrand University Press.

OECD (Organization for Economic Cooperation and Development), 2006. OECD Risk Awareness Tool for Multinational Enterprises in Weak Governance Zones, Paris: OECD (available via http://www.oecd.org/dataoecd/26/21/3688521.pdf)

Orkin, M. (ed.), 1989. *Sanctions against Apartheid*. Cape Town: David Philip.

Pallister, D., Stewart, S., and Leppper, I. 1987. South Africa Inc.; The Oppenheimer Empire. Johannesburg: Media House Publications in association with Lowry Publishers.

Plan Associates, 2001. Greater Rustenburg Informal Housing Strategy (compiled for the Housing Strategy Forum). Unpublished document.

Ponte, S., Roberts, S. and van Sittert, L., 2007. 'Black Economic Empowerment', Business and the State in South Africa. *Development and Change*, 38(5): 933–955.

Rockey, V., 2001. *The CSI Handbook 2001*. Cape Town: Trialogue.

Rockey, V., 2004. *The CSI Handbook 2003*. Cape Town: Trialogue.

Rossouw, G.J., 2005. Business ethics and corporate governance in Africa. *Business & Society*, 44(1): 94–106.

RSA (Republic of South Africa), 1991. *Minerals Act (No. 50 of 1991)*. Available via http://www.iucnrosa.org.zw/elisa/Environmental%20Law/south_africa/minerals_act.html (last accessed February 2004).

RSA (Republic of South Africa), 1996. *Mine Health and Safety Act*. Available via http://www.gov.za/gazette/acts/1996/a29–96.htm (last accessed February 2004).

RSA (Republic of South Africa), 2002. Mineral and Petroleum Resources Development Act (No. 28 of 2002), Pretoria: Republic of South Africa.

Sethi, S.P. and Falbe, C.M. (eds.), 1987. *Business and Society. Dimensions of Conflict and Cooperation*. Massachusetts: Lexington.

Sonnenberg, D. and Hamann, R., 2006. The JSE Socially Responsible Investment Index and the state of sustainability reporting in South Africa. *Development Southern Africa*, 23(2): 305–320.

Truth and Reconciliation Commission of South Africa, 2003. *Truth and Reconciliation Commission of South Africa Report, 21 March 2003*. Available via http://www.gov.za/reports/2003/trc/index.html (last accessed 12 October 2003).

Turrell, R.V., 1987. *Capital and Labour on the Kimberley Diamond Fields, 1871–1890*. Cambridge: Cambridge University Press.

Visser, W., 2006. "Revisiting Carroll's CSR Pyramid: An African perspective," in E.R. Pedersen and M. Huniche (eds.), *Corporate Citizenship in Developing Countries*. Copenhagen: Copenhagen Business School.

Whittaker, B., 2003. Business in Transition: South African experience of companies cooperating to support transition. Paper presented at the Conference on the role of the private sector in peace building, reconciliation and development, Kathmandu, 21 July 2003.

Yuldelman, D. 1984. The emergence of modern South Africa: state, capital, and the incorporation of organized labour on the South African gold fields, 1902–1939, Cape Town: David Philip.

Zadek, S. and Radovich, S., 2006. Governing collaborative governance: Enhancing development outcomes by improving partnership governance and accountability. (Working Paper No.23.) Cambridge, MA: John F. Kennedy School of Government, Harvard University.

Interviews

- Andre van der Bergh, BHP Billiton, Johannesburg, 19 November 2001
- Sean de Cleene, African Institute of Corporate Citizenship, Johannesburg, 9 November 2001
- John Groom, Anglo American, Johannesburg, 7 January 2002
- Henk de Hoop, BJM Securities Analysts, Johannesburg, 11 April 2003
- Karin Ireton, Anglo Platinum plc, Johannesburg, 27 November 2002
- Michael Joseph, Anglo Platinum, Johannesburg, 1 November 2001
- Richard Linnell, BHP Billiton, Johannesburg, 19 October 2001
- John Kilani, Chamber of Mines, Johannesburg, 14 November 2001
- Glen Mpufane and Eric Gcili Tshana, National Union of Mineworkers, Johannesburg, 29 October 2001
- Michelle Pressend and Doctor Mthetwa, Group for Environmental Monitoring, Johannesburg, 9 November 2001
- Markus Reichardt, Anglo Gold, Johannesburg, 15 March 2002
- Julie Stacey, Anglo American, 11 September 2001

Part V
Australasia

Chapter 21
Australia: Practices and Experiences

Royston Gustavson

Abstract The practice of CSR in Australia is a recent phenomenon; a decade ago, most of the current formal frameworks and supporting networks did not exist. Australia is a wealthy country with extensive government social support, including universal health care. Combined, this has resulted in a slow move to corporate social responsibility on the part of most organizations, although the best, such as Westpac and BHP Billiton, are world leaders in their industries, and as at 31 October 2007, twenty-one Australian companies were among the 318 listed on the DJSI World Index, placing Australia in eighth position for number of companies listed. Legal obligations and investor expectations make financial performance paramount, and two recent government enquiries have recommended not to amend the *Corporations Act* to require CSR. The move towards CSR is being primarily driven by its refocusing as risk management (such as the recent changes to the Australian Stock Exchange Corporate Governance Principles), and the long-term view taken by the ever-increasing influence of institutional investors.

21.1 Introduction

21.1.1 Definitions in Australian Sources

Any discussion of CSR in Australia must begin with the observation that there is no clear consensus in Australia of what CSR is. The Australian Parliamentary Joint Committee on Corporations and Financial Services, in its report on corporate responsibility, simply stated that 'the committee makes no attempt to reach a conclusive definition. Because of the sheer diversity of modern corporations . . . the concept of corporate responsibility can have a different meaning to different people and different organizations' (Chapman Report 2006: 5). The Prime Minister's Community Business Partnership is of the opinion that:

S. O. Idowu and W. L. Filho (eds.), *Global Practices of Corporate Social Responsibility*   463
© Springer-Verlag Berlin Heidelberg 2009

'It is not possible to define corporate social responsibility precisely. The language surrounding the concept of CSR is still evolving and can be confusing – especially when reduced to acronyms! For example, CSR is linked to (and in some cases used interchangeably with) related terms and ideas such as corporate sustainability (CS), corporate citizenship (CC), corporate social investment (CSI), the triple bottom line (TBL), socially responsible investment (SRI), business sustainability and corporate governance' (www.partnerships.gov.au/csr/).

The Australian Government's Corporations and Markets Advisory Committee moved closer to a definition stating that:

'In essence, the focus of the issue of corporate social responsibility is on the way in which the affairs of companies are conducted and the ends to which their activities are directed, with particular reference to the environmental and social impact of their conduct. A responsible company, like a responsible individual, is one that acknowledges and takes responsibility for its actions' (CAMAC 2006a: 15).

This definition, however, implies that CSR should be limited to consideration of and action towards reducing and/or compensating for externalities.

For the purposes of this paper, the most useful definition is that provided by Standards Australia, which through an MOU with the Australian Government is Australia's peak national standards body and which represents Australia at the ISO. It states that CSR is: 'A mechanism for entities to voluntarily integrate social and environmental concerns into their operations and their interaction with their stakeholders, which are over and above the entity's legal responsibilities' (AS8003 2003: 4). It includes: profitability, competitive practices and pricing, governance/ethics, corruption/bribery/political contributions, employee issues, supplier issues, health and safety, environmental impact, impacts on the host community, regulatory compliance systems, and identification of and discussions with stakeholders (pp. 12–13).

21.1.2 Historical Overview

CSR has a relatively recent history in Australia, and traditionally was seen as involving sponsorship (especially of cultural and sporting events and institutions) and other philanthropic acts, or cash donations. Batten and Birch found that 'there is considerable hesitation in funding long-term community involvement' (2005: 302), and Thomas and Nowak note that 'a common theme in the Australian literature is the need for corporations to move away from the 'pat-a-poor-person' philanthropic approach to CSR' (2006: 15).

A turning point in public opinion about CSR was the media coverage in 1994 of the environmental and social damage done by the Ok Tedi mine in Papua New Guinea, operated by Australia's largest company, BHP. The environmental impact of its operations, which included dumping 80,000 tonnes of waste a day into the Ok Tedi River since 1984, has resulted in dieback of 1,588 square kilometres of vegetation along the Ok Tedi and Fly rivers; it is estimated that this figure will eventually reach 3,000 square kilometres (www.oktedi.com). The pollution in the river killed fish and heavily affected the lives of 50,000 people living in 120 villages downstream of the mine. BHP (now BHP Billiton) has since, become one of Australia's leading companies in the practice and promotion of CSR.

Despite various Acts of Parliament to protect the environment, consumers, and workers, the Corporations Act 2001 made director's obligations to shareholders paramount. Zappalà noted in 2003 that 'existing Australian public policy in the area of corporate citizenship is minimal' (2003a: 20). That year, two non-Government bodies, Standards Australia and the Australian Stock Exchange, issued guidelines supporting, but not requiring, CSR.

An Australian Parliamentary Committee report noted in June 2006 that, 'Despite evidence that Australian companies have shown a greater engagement with the corporate responsibility agenda over the past decade, the committee also heard that by international standards, Australia lags in implementing and reporting on corporate responsibility' (Chapman 2006: xiii). The committee's view was that 'although it is not appropriate to mandate the consideration of stakeholder interests into directors' duties, or to mandate sustainability reporting, there is a need to seriously consider options to encourage greater uptake and disclosure of corporate responsibility activities' (p. xvi).

In 2007, the key CSR issues in the public mind are global warming and water, driven by Australia being in the grip of the worst drought on record, and by all of the largest cities experiencing water restrictions (for example, residents of Brisbane, pop. 1.77 million, with dams at only 20.24% capacity as at 15 November 2007, are restricted to 140 l of water per person per day for domestic use; see www.target140.com.au). This has focused the attention of the population on issues of environmental sustainability and the role of business within it. Nevertheless, for many years the Australian government was, with that of the USA, one of the only two governments in the OECD that refused to ratify the Kyoto Protocol.

Immanent change is, however, expected. After more than eleven years of the Howard liberal government, which had little interest in promoting CSR, the Rudd labor government was swept to power in the elections of 26 November 2007. On the day that his new government took office, Rudd 'signed the instrument of ratification of the Kyoto Protocol...[which was] the first official act of the new Australian Government' (Rudd 2007), and also created a new ministry for Climate Change and Water.

21.2 Formal Framework

Under s.51(20) of the *Australian Constitution*, the Federal Government has the power to make laws relating to 'Foreign corporations and trading or financial corporations formed within the limits of the Commonwealth'. The Australian government's practice has been not to regulate in the area of CSR, but to leave such decisions to market forces and to industry self-regulation. The then-Australian Government's attitude was clearly expressed to the UN Office of the High Commissioner for Human Rights, in its comments on the *Norms on the Responsibilities of Transnational Corporations and Other Business Enterprises with Regard to Human Rights*:

'The Australian Government is strongly committed to the principle that guidelines for Corporate Social Responsibility (CSR) should be made voluntary. The Norms represent a major shift away from voluntary adherence. The need for such a shift has not been demonstrated. . . . We believe the way to ensure a greater business contribution to social progress, is not through more norms and prescriptive regulations, but through encouraging awareness of societal values and concerns through voluntary initiatives' (Australian Permanent Mission to the UN 2004).

However, this has led to significant tension, with legislation mandating the primacy of the shareholder but industry bodies, including the Australian Stock Exchange,recognizing the importance of other stakeholders. Kerr (2004) examined the problems of the current approach with regard to the natural environment, and recommended legislative change.

21.2.1 Corporations Act 2001

A key document regulating CSR in Australia is the Corporations Act 2001. The Act does not specifically mention CSR, sustainability, or ethics. The section most relevant to these issues is 181(1), which states that 'A director or other officer of a corporation must exercise their powers and discharge their duties (a) in good faith in the best interests of the corporation; and (b) for a proper purpose'; contravention is a civic penalty provision, that is, a fine and/or disqualification from holding a company's directorship. Directors are given considerable scope in determining what is in a company's 'best interests' by the business judgment rule, which states that:

'A director or other officer of a corporation who makes a business judgment is taken to meet the requirements of subsection (1), and their equivalent duties at common law and in equity, with respect to the judgment if they: (a) make the judgment in good faith for a proper purpose; and (b) do not have a material personal interest in the subject matter of the judgment; and (c) inform themselves about the subject matter of the judgment to the extent they reasonably believe to be appropriate; and (d) rationally believe that the judgment is in the best interests of the corporation' (s.180(2)).

Henley (2005: 155) and Wilson (2005: 279) have both argued that, under the *Corporations Act*, 'sincere' acts of CSR, defined by Parkinson as 'voluntarily sacrificing profits . . . [or] incurring additional costs . . . in the belief that such behavior will have consequences superior to those flowing from a policy of pure profit maximization'(1993: 261), are illegal under current Australian law. Indeed, *Parke v The Daily News Ltd & Others* showed the 'potential for shareholders to take action to prevent an exercise of CSR as being in breach of director's duties' (Wilson 2005: 279). Sir Gerard Brennan, a former Chief Justice of Australia, has written that: 'However, modern legal writers suggest, and corporate practice accords with the suggestion, that it is permissible to donate corporate assets if the donation is likely to redound to the benefit of the corporation, but donations without the prospect of financial return are not authorized' (2002: 496). As such, CSR is legal only when it supports the economic aims of the corporation, but the business judgment rule gives the directors, considerable scope in justifying the link if they choose to practice CSR. The relationship between corporate governance and CSR in Australia has been further examined by Horrigan (2002; at the time of writing, arguably the clearest overview for directors of their duties relating to CSR in Australia is given by Baker and McKenzie 92007).

Shareholders may use s.249D and s.249N of the *Corporations Act* in an attempt to indicate to a corporation that it should exercise CSR. Under these sections, shareholders may either requisition an extraordinary general meeting, or use an annual general meeting, to propose resolutions. A prominent example involved a campaign by The Wilderness Society against Australia's largest woodchipper, Gunns Ltd; an EGM was called in 2003 to prohibit the company operating in old growth forests, and resolutions were proposed for AGMs of Australia's four largest banks to prevent them from investing in corporations logging old growth forests. None of these attempts by shareholders was successful, but the resolution at the Commonwealth Bank AGM received support of almost a quarter of the shareholders (www.wilderness.org.au/campaigns/corporate/gunns).

21.2.2 Other Legislation

In many areas, a corporation's social and environmental responsibilities have been determined by legislation and so, it may be argued, they have been moved from CSR to law; but it may also be argued that abiding by the law is part of an organizations CSR, and that the law simply codifies minimum CSR expectations. In Australia, Commonwealth legislation covers many areas, including:

- Discrimination in employment: *Racial Discrimination Act 1975; Sex Discrimination Act 1984; Disability Discrimination Act 1992*
- Privacy: *Privacy Amendment (Private Sector) Act 2000*
- Worker Safety: *Occupational Health and Safety Act 1991*
- Fair treatment of consumers: *Trade Practices Act 1984*
- Environment: *Environmental Protection and Biodiversity Conservation Act 1999*

In addition, many responsibilities are also covered by the legislation of Australia's six States and two mainland Territories. For example, each has enacted legislation relating to environmental protection.

21.2.3 Government CSR Inquiries

21.2.3.1 Cooney Report (1989)

In 1989, an Australian Senate committee reported on *Company Directors' Duties: Report on the Social and Fiduciary Obligations of Company Directors* (The 'Cooney Report'). The committee stated that: 'The corporate sector possesses most of Australia's assets, employs most of its workers, and is the sector most capable of injuring the environment. Given this, it is of vital concern to the community, and the community is entitled to impose appropriate restrictions on it' (s.2.40). Chapter 6 of the report is devoted to 'Director's wider duties–other 'outside' interests' including employees, gratuitous benefits, environmental issues, and consumers, concluding that:

'It is appropriate that matters external to the company be dealt with in separate and specific legislation, as has been suggested recently in New South Wales and South Australia. This is because companies legislation should deal only with corporate structure and organization and matters arising as and between the constituents of the corporate body.... The Committee recommends that matters such as the interests of consumers, or environmental protection, be dealt with not in companies legislation but in legislation aimed specifically at those matters' (ss.6.55–6.56).

This view has underpinned subsequent legislative development on CSR in Australia.

21.2.3.2 Chapman Report (2001)

In 2000, a *Corporate Code of Conduct* bill was tabled in the Australian committee and referred to a committee (see also Deva 2004). The bill provided that its objects were:

(a) To impose environmental, employment, health and safety and human rights standards on the conduct of Australian corporations or related corporations which employ more than 100 persons in a foreign country
(b) To require such corporations to report on their compliance with the standards imposed by this Act
(c) To provide for the enforcement of those standards (Chapman Report 2001: 3)

The committee recommended that the bill not be supported, stating that 'It is probable that the governments and number of citizens of foreign nations will...resent any attempt by Australia, to apply its laws extraterritorially within their jurisdictions' (s.4.49).

21.2.3.3 Mays Report (2003)

The Australian Government Department of Environment and Heritage commissioned the Mays Report, which was published in 2003. It found that:

- Sustainability behaviors add value to commercial endeavor and make for good business sense. A number of Australian companies are undertaking sustainability initiatives in their business, even in the absence of a formal sustainability policy.
- Sustainability is a particularly useful device for managing intangible assets such as brand and reputation. The case studies offer insight to different approaches at the company level. Benefits include human capital management, stakeholder management and product differentiation.
- The potential for capturing sustainability benefits hinges on a successful move toward a common understanding of sustainability principles. In the absence of this, companies are not articulating their sustainability behaviors as well they might, and in some cases value-adding sustainability behavior is undersold. Equally, Australian investors do not seem to have developed a discipline for considering sustainability principles. (p. 6).

21.2.3.4 Chapman Report (2006)

In 2005, the Parliamentary Joint Committee on Corporations and Financial Services was directed to inquire as to the extent to which organizational decision-makers have an existing regard/should have a regard for the interests of stakeholders other than shareholders, and the broader community; the impact of the current legal framework on this and whether revisions to the legal framework are required; any alternative mechanisms, including voluntary measures that may enhance consideration of stakeholder interests by incorporated entities and/or their directors; the appropriateness of reporting requirements associated with these issues; and whether regulatory, legislative or other policy approaches in other countries could be adopted or adapted for Australia (Chapman 2006: vii). The committee released its report *Corporate Responsibility: Managing Risk and Creating Value.* The title of the report signals a shift in thinking about CSR towards being a risk management tool.

This inquiry gives perhaps the clearest overview of current experiences of CSR in Australia: not only in the report itself, but some 800 pages of official committee Hansard, and 146 major public submissions in addition to the many form letters, all of which are available online (Chapman Inquiry 2005–2006a, 2005–2006b).

The report (see also s.22.1.2 above) noted that

'Corporate responsibility in Australia is still in its developmental stages, and over the course of the inquiry, the committee has been encouraged by the evidence of increasing engagement by Australian companies and Australian government agencies with sustainable practices and sustainability reporting. There is still much progress to be made.... The committee strongly supports further successful engagement in the voluntary development and wide adoptions of corporate responsibility. The committee has formed the view that mandatory approaches to regulating director's duties and to sustainability reporting are not appropriate. Consequent on the [29] recommendations of this report, the committee expects increasing engagement by corporations in corporate responsibility activities. This would obviate any future moves towards a mandatory approach' (p.xix).

The veiled threat in the final sentence may motivate companies to increase their commitment to and reporting on CSR.

21.2.3.5 CAMAC Report (2006)

The Australian Government's Corporations and Markets Advisory Committee issued a discussion paper in November 2005, and a report, *The Social Responsibility of Corporations*, in December 2006 (CAMAC 2006a); a summary of the 61 submissions (available in full at www.camac.gov.au) was published (CAMAC 2006b). The report did not support revision of the Corporations Act to 'require' or to 'clarify the extent to which directors may take into account the interests of specific classes of stakeholders or the broader community when making decisions' (CAMAC 2006a: 7), but recommended 'specific legislation directed to the problem area' (p. 8). On reporting, the committee states that 'governments may see a need on discrete public interest grounds to require businesses to report on a particular matter, whether relating to environmental, social or other concerns' (p. 147), recommending specific legislation, citing the *Energy Efficiency Opportunities Act 2006* as an example.

The committee was also asked 'Should Australian companies be encouraged to adopt socially and environmentally responsible business practices and if so, how?', responding that 'In the end, however, it is for companies themselves and those who run them to take responsibility for what they do and the decisions they take in the shifting market place of law, consumer preferences, employee views, investor sentiments, community attitudes and other pressures under which they operate' (p. 167), noting however that 'in general, it is in a company's own interests, in terms of enhancing its value or managing its risks over time, to take into account the environmental and social context in which it operates and the impact of its activities' (p. 168). It recommended a 'light touch' approach by the government, such as public agencies leading by example (p. 169) and 'involving industry and other groups in the development of voluntary industry codes or other guidelines' (p.170).

21.2.4 Australian Standards

Standards Australia, beginning in 2003, has published a series of standards on governance that assist companies in implementing best practice on a range of issues relating to CSR; the series includes:

- AS 8000 Good governance principles
- AS 8001 Fraud and corruption control
- AS 8002 Organizational codes of conduct

- AS 8003 Corporate social responsibility
- AS 8004 Whistleblower protection programs for entities

AS8003, approved on 23 May 2003, 'sets out essential elements for establishing, implementing and maintaining an effective Corporate Social Responsibility Program' for public and private entities, government departments, and non-for-profit organizations (p.4). The standard requires a range of CSR issues to be identified, as noted in s22.1.1 above; operating procedures being put in place and implemented, a feedback system, record-keeping, reporting, and review. Ongoing dialogue with a wide range of stakeholders is expected.

21.2.5 Australian Securities Exchange

The Australian Securities (formerly Stock) Exchange's Corporate Governance Council issued the first edition of its *Principles of Good Corporate Governance and Best Practice Recommendations* in 2003 (ASX 2003). Although the listed companies are not required to follow the recommendations, if any recommendations are not followed, the company must report on its reasons for not doing so. Principle 10, 'Recognize the legitimate interests of stakeholders', stated that:

'Companies have a number of legal and other obligations to non-shareholders and stakeholders such as employees, clients/customers and the community as a whole. There is growing acceptance of the view that organizations can create value by better managing natural, human, social and other forms of capital. Increasingly, the performance of companies is being scrutinized from a perspective that recognizes these other forms of capital. That being the case, it is important for companies to demonstrate their commitment to appropriate corporate practices' (p. 59).

In November 2006, the ASX issued a discussion paper on revision of these guidelines, and received 106 submissions (all were made available on the ASX website); it later published a response to these submissions as part of the revision process (ASX 2007b). Part B of the discussion paper related to reporting of material business risks and corporate responsibility/sustainability risks. In the second edition, *Corporate Governance Principles and Recommendations* (ASX 2007a), Principle 10 had been demoted from independent status and incorporated into Principle 7, 'Recognize and manage risk'. Under recommendation 7.1, it is noted that:

'A company should also consider the reasonable expectations of its stakeholders. Stakeholders can include: shareholders, employees, customers, suppliers, creditors, consumers and the broader community in which the company operates. Failure to consider the reasonable expectations of stakeholders can threaten a company's reputation and the success of its business operations. Effective risk management involves considering factors which bear upon the company's continued good standing with its stakeholders' (p. 33).

This signals a significant shift in the understanding of the role of CSR; this move towards seeing CSR as risk management, also is discernable in some of the industry submissions to the enquiries discussed in s.2.3. Others, such as that by Catherine Livingstone (2007:1), one of Australia's most prominent company directors, stated that:

'the most concerning aspect of the discussion on CR&S is its positioning as a risk. This relegation to the status of a 'risk to be managed' denies the reality that CR&S is fast becoming part of the core strategic intent of corporations. This is being driven in part by direct complementarity with business models (i.e. CS&R makes good business sense) and/or because of the expectations of the community.'

21.2.6 DEH

The Australian Government Department of The Environment and Water Resources (www.deh.gov.au) has a number of roles, including 'working with government, industry, community stakeholders and international forums to protect and conserve the environment, improve the sustainable management and efficient use of water resources, and implement an effective response to climate change' (*Annual Report 2006–07, p. 14); the Australian Greenhouse Office (www.greenhouse.gov.au) is located in the department. The Secretary to the Department has written that 'Increasingly, the department's remit is to develop a cohesive and strategic set of policies and programs that deliver environmental, social and economic outcomes' (Annual Report 2006–07, p. 2).

21.3 Supporting Network

There is a significant network in Australia supporting CSR, ranging from government bodies to industry and professional associations, from research centers to specialist consultancies, from events to serial publications; a selection of these is given in Table 21.1. Apart from the government bodies and industry and professional associations, the generalization that characterizes them is that, they have been driven by an individual or a small team with a strong belief in the importance of CSR and corporate sustainability. Although the organizations, events, or publications benefit from the passion and energy of these entrepreneurial individuals, the downside is a lack of co-ordination and a lack of succession planning. Indeed, the lack of structure or co-ordination makes it difficult for corporations to be aware of, much less understand, the breadth and strength of the network available to them in their push to behave more responsibly and more sustainably.

Table 21.1 demonstrates that until the mid-1990s, the supporting network for CSR was framed within the context of ethics, and consisted primarily of industry bodies or professional associations which covered a broad array of issues, one of which was CSR. It is only recently that bodies focusing on CSR have been formed, and there has been an acceleration of their proliferation since 1999. Notably, there

Table 21.1 Supporting network timeline

Year	Fm	Details
1952	PA	CPA Australia (ABN: 64 008 392 452; www.cpaaustralia.com.au), incorporated in 1952 and an Organizational Stakeholder member of the GRI since 2006, issued a policy on CSR in 2007, that 'The uptake of sustainability reporting as a basis of stakeholder engagement, risk management and continuous improvement should be actively promoted, because it is a key element in the evolving understanding of corporate social responsibility. The development of such non-financial reporting should be achieved through principles based on guidance rather than by way of regulatory direction' (CPA 2007: 1).
1960	IB	The Australian Shareholders Association (ABN: 40 000 625 669; www.asa.asn.au) was founded in 1960 as a not-for-profit organization 'to protect and advance the interests of investors'. Its report on CSR is discussed in s.22.7 below. In its policy statement *Shareholders Expect* (19 April 2005) it states that: 'Donations, sponsorships and similar expenditures of a recognizably charitable nature are matters for decision by directors, and executives to whom such decisions are delegated by directors. Nevertheless, shareholders expect to be informed of unusual or significant expenditures of this nature, both as they occur and in the annual report. Where directors have links with institutions to which such payments are made, the nature of the association and the payments should be disclosed as related-party transactions' (ASA 2005).
1983	IB	The Business Council of Australia (ABN 75 008 483 216; www.bca.com.au), founded in 1983, is an association of 100 CEOs of Australia's largest companies. Parts of its 'Passing on Prosperity Agenda' is 'Developing a better understanding of the scope and value of business investment in the community.' In was a partner organization in the study CCPA (2007).
1986	PC	Australian Ethical Investment Ltd (ABN: 47 003 188 930; www.austethical.com.au) is a listed company with a mission 'to provide those investors who share our social and environmental aims (as set out in our charter) with the means to earn a competitive return for a chosen risk whilst at the same time, contributing to a just and sustainable human society and the protection of the natural environment'.
1988	Ch	The St James Ethics Centre (ABN 83 637 740 533; www.ethics.org.au) is an independent not-for-profit organization providing 'an open forum for the promotion and exploration of ethical questions arising in contemporary society'. Although it undertakes activities in a wide range of practical and applied ethics, business ethics is a core activity. It provides training programs for organizations in 'Ethical Intelligence and Good Decision-Making', 'Business Ethics', and 'Requisites for a Sound Ethical Culture'. Two key activities that it hosts are the Vincent Fairfax Fellowships, which 'contribute to the development of a core group of Australian leaders who are committed to factoring the ethical dimension into their decision-making processes', with up to 15 fellowships per year; and the annual Corporate Responsibility Index (see s.22.6.2 below). See also 1991 S and 1995 E.
1989–95	E	The St James Ethics Centre held symposia before CSR became mainstream, but this task has been taken over by more recently-founded organizations; its symposia included *Ethics Management in the '90s: surviving the corporate era* (1989); *The Regulation of Conscience—key issues in business & professional ethics* (1993); and *Can we afford to be efficient? Competition and the changing face of Australia* (1995); there are published reports of each. See also 1988 Ch.

Table 21.1 *Continued*

Year	Fm	Details
1990	Ch	Volunteering Australia (ABN: 23 062 806 464; www.volunteeringaustralia.org) is a public benevolent institution which is Australia's peak body for volunteering. One of the areas it supports is corporate volunteering, 'a commitment by a commercial organization to encourage staff to volunteer in the not-for-profit sector. It ranges from individual volunteer effort through to team or whole-of-company involvement.' Volunteering Australia has an Award for Corporate Volunteering, a Corporate Volunteering Register, and publishes a Corporate Volunteering Toolkit.
1990	IB	The Australian Centre for Corporate Public Affairs (ABN 52 007 061 930; www.accpa.com.au) has membership available only to organizations, and aims 'to support, advance and research corporate public affairs as a management function, encompassing government, media and stakeholder relations, corporate social responsibility/corporate citizenship, issues management, internal communications and reputation management.' It has been involved in two key reports (CCPA 2000; 2007).
1990	PA	The Australian Institute of Company Directors (ABN: 11 008 484 197; www.companydirectors.com.au), founded with the merger of two earlier bodies, issued a policy on sustainability in 2002, stating that the: 'Australian Institute of Company Directors supports the generally accepted definition of sustainable development—meeting the needs of the present generation without compromising the ability of future generations to meet their own needs. Australian Institute of Company Directors believes that the definition of sustainability should not be limited to environmental goals. Australian Institute of Company Directors supports the integration of three elements—Economic, Environment and Social, commonly referred to as the Triple Bottom Line—as a model of sustainability.... The issue of sustainability should be viewed as a positive opportunity. Many organizations have adopted sustainability as a business goal and prospered as a result. Sustainability and the profit motive are complementary. Indeed, it is the recognition of the former that may guarantee the latter' (AICD 2002).
1991	S	*Living Ethics*, quarterly, includes non-CSR related material, http://www.ethics.org.au/about-ethics/ethics-centre-articles/living-ethics-newsletter/index.html.
1993	PA	The Australian Association for Professional and Applied Ethics (ABN: 91 541 307 476; www.arts.unsw.edu.au/aapae), a non-profit association, aims 'to encourage awareness of applied ethics as a significant area of concern, and to foster discussion of issues in applied ethics', including business ethics. It hosts annual conferences, and publishes the *Australian Journal of Professional and Applied Ethics*.
1995	S	*Journal of the Asia Pacific Centre for Environmental Accountability*, quarterly, 1995–2003 available online for free at www.accg1.mq.edu.au/apcea/pastissues.html.
1997	R	The Corporate Citizenship Research Unit, Deakin University (www.deakin.edu.au/arts/ccr, formerly www.accalliance.asn.au) has strategic priorities which include to: 'Conduct research into how companies understand, manage, position and develop themselves, as good corporate citizens in their relationships with the communities in which they operate'; and 'Demonstrate the potential that exists for companies to operate as valued citizens within society, and to better understand the relationship between commercial advantage and community benefits.' It publishes a quarterly journal, *The Corporate Citizen*. Although now out of date, it published a valuable *Directory of Resources Promoting Responsible and Sustainable Business and Society: Networks and Organizations in Australia and Overseas* (Birch 2003).

Table 21.1 *Continued*

Year	Fm	Details
1998	E	National Conferences on Corporate Citizenship were held in 1998, 2000, and 2003; there are published proceedings of each (www.deakin.edu.au/arts/ccr/menu/pastconferences.php).
1999	Go	The Prime Minister's Community Business Partnership (www.partnerships.gov.au) is 'a group of prominent Australians from the community and business sectors, appointed by the Prime Minister to advise and assist the Government on issues concerning individual and corporate social responsibility.' Its strategy streams are advocacy of the business case for CSR; facilitation including through publications, the internet, workshops, seminars and conferences; and recognition through awards. The Partnership is responsible for the annual Prime Minister's Awards for Excellence in Community Business Partnerships (founded 1999), Community Business Partnerships Week (founded 2002), and the annual Social Responsibility Writers Prize (founded 2004) for secondary and tertiary students.
1999	IB	The Responsible Investment Association Australasia (ABN 47 003 188 930; www.eia.org.au), which changed its name from the Ethical Investment Association of Australia in June 2007, was founded to promote the concept and practice of SRI. The Charter of the Society includes that: 'Business needs to be judged on environmental, social, ethical or governance performance, as well as their financial performance'; and 'We support the growth of the responsible investment sector and believe it can assist business to improve performance.'
1999	PA	The Australian Institute of Social and Ethical Accountability (ABN 51 660 967 954; www.accountability.org.au) has a vision 'to create a more sustainable Australian society built on organizations that are socially and ethically responsible and accountable for their impacts'. It is involved in education, research, and advocacy.
2000	G	The Australia Business Arts Foundation (ABN: 88 072 479 835; www.abaf.org.au) was founded by the Australian Government to promote private sector support for the arts by connecting business, the arts, donors, and foundations. It has three programs: partnering, volunteering, and giving which, in the 2006 financial year, added $6.3 million to the arts sector (Annual Report 2005–06, pp. 4–5). It hosts an Annual Awards, which receive prominent media coverage, 'to publicly acknowledge and celebrate best practice in private sector support for the arts and culture through partnering, volunteering and giving.'
2000	R	The Centre for Applied Philosophy and Public Ethics (www.cappe.edu.au), established as a Commonwealth Special Research Centre under the directorship of Professor Seumas Miller, 'constitutes the largest concentration of philosophers working on applied philosophy and public ethics in Australia, and one of the largest such concentrations in the international philosophical community'. A defined core of *Research Area 2: Business and Professional Ethics* is Corporate Responsibility for Economic and Ethical Sustainability.
2000	R	The Centre for Australian Ethical Research (ABN 95 101 201 905; www.caer.org.au) is a not-for-profit research organization 'established to provide independent social and environmental data on companies operating in Australia and the Asia-Pacific region.'
Ca 2000	R	The University of Technology Sydney Corporate Sustainability Project (www.csp.uts.edu.au), under the leadership of Distinguished Professor

Table 21.1 *Continued*

Year	Fm	Details
		Dexter Dunphy and Dr Suzanne Benn, 'aims to generate a cross-disciplinary understanding of how corporations can develop the skills, approaches and tools needed to better integrate environmental and social performance with key business objectives, and how to design and lead the change programs needed to make these shifts. It has two points of focus: looking at both the changes needed for corporate sustainability and the corporate change strategies that are required.'
2001	E	The Sustainable Business Forum (www.sbf.net.au), a non-profit organization, 'promotes the aims and practice of environmental and social sustainability by bringing together the people and ideas needed to action sustainability in the way we do business', and has held 19 forums since 2001 (listed at www.sbf.net.au/previous_forums.php).
2001	E	The invitation-only National Business Leaders Forum on Sustainable Development (ABN 47 104 612 259; no website) is held annually.
2001	S	*The Corporate Citizen*, quarterly, volume 2 onwards (lagged one year) available online for free at www.deakin.edu.au/arts/ccr/magazine/index.php.
2002	E	Community Business Partnerships Week, held annually; see 1999 Go.
2002	R	The Natural Edge Project (www.naturaledgeproject.net) was founded by Charlie Hargroves, Cheryl Desha, James Moody, and Michael Smith. Initially hosted by Engineers Australia, it has been co-hosted since 2007 by Griffith University and The Australian National University. Its mission is 'to contribute to and succinctly communicate leading research, case studies, tools, policy and strategies for achieving sustainable development across government, business and civil society'. It has produced several series of lectures (freely available on their website) and the book *The Natural Advantage of Nations* (Hargroves and Smith 2005).
2003	PC	Australian Centre for Corporate Social Responsibility (ABN: 71 007 029 610; www.accsr.com.au), founded by Leeora D Black, has a mission 'to help companies become more socially responsible'.
2003	PC	Orfeus Research (ABN: 45 535 521 2031; www.orfeusresearch.com.au), founded by Gianni Zappalà, has a vision 'for a society where all organizations, communities and individuals embrace the principles of sustainability and responsible citizenship'.
2003	R	Curtin Business School Governance & Corporate Social Responsibility Research Unit, founded by Professor Margaret Nowak and Professor Alma Whiteley, has members from a wide range of disciplinary units and publishes a series of working papers (www.cbs.curtin.edu.au/business/research/areas-of-research-focus/governance-and-corporate-social-responsibility).
2003	R	ARIES, The Australian Research Institute in Education for Sustainability (www.aries.mq.edu.au), founded under the leadership of Associate Professor Daniella Tilbury, undertakes 'research that informs policy and practice in Education for Sustainability across a range of sectors including: business and industry, school education, community education, further and higher education.... ARIES is concerned with how we inform, motivate and manage structural change towards sustainability.' Important reports include *Education About and For Sustainability in Australian Business Schools* (Tilbury et al. 2004) and *Shifting towards Sustainability* (Hunting and Tilbury 2006); the latter involved a study of ten major Australian corporate and government organizations.
2004	E	Social Responsibility Writers Prize for secondary and tertiary students is held annually; see 1999 Go.

Table 21.1 *Continued*

Year	Fm	Details
2004	PC	Social Compass Pty Ltd (ABN: 48953149370; www.socialcompass.com), founded by Jehan Loza, has a vision that 'a socially inclusive future can occur through partnership between the business, government, and community sectors'.
2004	R	The Australian National University Corporations, Governance and Society Research Group was founded by Associate Professor Greg Shailer, 'to promote development and cooperation across the disciplinary areas relevant to governance of the relationships between corporations and their stakeholders through markets and regulation' (corpgov.fec.anu.edu.au).
2005	E	The Corporate Social Responsibility Summit (www.csrsummit.com), held annually, has the aim of 'bringing together leading Australian and International CEOs along with CSR and Sustainability, taught leaders to shape the debate, challenge the status quo, cross fertilize ideas and inspire business and government to make strategic impact on the practice and policy of sustainable business'.
2005	PC	Models of Success and Sustainability (ABN 11 120 102 025; www.moss.org.au) was seeded as an initiative from the inaugural Corporate Social Responsibility Summit.
2005	S	*Business Community Intelligence*, quarterly, www.aicr.com.au.
2007	PA	The Australian Institute of Management (ABN: 56 004 525 017; www.aim.com.au), founded in 1941, expects to issue a policy on CSR in 2008. It 2007 it formed CSR Special Interest Groups in some States, including NSW (groups.google.com/group/aim-corporate-social-responsibility?hl = en) and the ACT (groups.google.com/group/aim-act-csr?hl = en).
2007	PC	Australian Institute for Corporate Responsibility (ACN/ABN: 24 094 608 705; www.aicr.com.au), founded by Deloitte, Our Community, and Shannon's Way, is a public company with the mission 'to provide cutting-edge corporate responsibility resources for large, medium and small business and community organizations'.
2007	R	The Australian National University Behavioural, Sustainability and Management Accounting Research Team was founded by Associate Professor Juliana Ng and Dr Sumit Lodhia (www.cbe.anu.edu.au/schools/abis/BSMART/default.asp)
2007	S	*Community Business Review*, quarterly, www.socialcompass.com/index.cfm/cbr/
2007	S	*MOSS News, Views, and Events*, bimonthly newsletter, available online at www.moss.org.au/home/index.php?option = com_content&task = view&id = 33&Itemid = 56

Abbreviations: *Fm* Form; *Ch* charity; *E* event; *Go* government body; *IB* industry body; *PA* professional association; *PC* for profit consultancy; *R* research body; *S* serial publication.

is a shift away from CSR as ethics to CSR as risk management and as a tool for driving profit.

Although much research is undertaken by government, industry, and professional bodies, the core of CSR research in Australia is undertaken at its 38 universities, a number of which have CSR research centers. Although the subject matter is wide-ranging, Australia has a particular strength in social accounting research (Deegan and Soltys 2007, which includes a bibliography covering 1995–2006).

21.4 Examples of What Companies are Doing

A good overview of the social dimension of CSR in Australia is given in two reports, *Corporate Community Involvement: Establishing a Business Case* (CCPA 2000) and a major update, *Corporate Community Investment in Australia* (CCPA 2007). Trends noted in the latter report include 'rising community expectations that companies will make a wider contribution to community wellbeing (especially in younger generations...)' (p. 1) and that companies 'use [of] programs and relationships as a differentiator and for competitive advantage will itself drive deeper engagement—a virtuous cycle' (p. 129). Küskü and Zarkada-Fraser have shown the influence of culture on CSR in Australia, noting that, by comparison to Turkish companies, Australian firms are 'more likely to obey the law' (2004: 66), but 'Turkish firms appear more likely to undertake voluntary activities that provide support to the local communities.... In the more collectivistic Turkish culture... these links are stronger than in individualistic Australia' (p. 68).

As noted earlier, corporate philanthropy is central to CSR in Australia; a detailed examination of Australian corporate philanthropy is given in Smith 2005. There is anecdotal evidence that the economic downturn in the early 1990s resulted in a decline in CSR activities in Australia (Moon 1995: 8), but, for example, in 2000/01, the Australian Bureau of Statistics examined the generosity of Australian business; in that year, business gave AU\$670 million in sponsorship; \$586 m in donations, and \$182 m in business-to-community projects; this represented 1.66% of operating profit before tax of businesses that gave. Of the total, \$480 m went to sports and recreation, and \$243 m to community services and welfare (ABS 2002: 3). By 2003/04, the total value of corporate giving was estimated at AU\$3.3 billion, with 67% of all Australian businesses contributing, with \$810 m in sponsorship, \$1,900 m in donations, and \$540 m in business-to-community projects (ACOSS 2005: 1). The motives for corporate giving are analyzed by Sargeant and Crissman (2006), and corporate interactions between corporations and three NGOs are examined by Phillips (2005). Australian SMEs have 'a general preference for giving in-kind goods, services, skills or capacity rather than cash' (Madden *et al.* 2006: 54). The business case is further set out in the report *A Capital Idea: Realising value form environmental and social performance* (Deni Greene 2001).

Some Australian companies are taking a very pro-active role in CSR, as seen in the studies of the ANZ Banking Group (Brown 2006), of Bendigo Bank (Stubbs and Cocklin 2007), of Westpac's employee volunteering program (Zappalà 2003b), of BHP Billiton (Black 2006), of Rio Tinto's partnerships with Australian indigenous communities (Hall 2002: 14–15); and of the latter two companies and labor management systems (Jones *et al.* 2007).

As at 31 October 2007, Australian companies were signatories to the following international agreements:

- UN Global Compact (www.unglobalcompact.org): a total of 27 Australian institutions, of which 16 are for-profit corporations

- Equator Principles (www.equator-principles.com): three of Australia's four largest banks (ANZ, National Australia Bank, and Westpac)
- GRI Register (www.corporateregister.com): a total of 145 reports from 67 Australian corporations were included in the register
- Principles for Responsible Investment (www.unpri.org): a total of 18 Asset owner signatories, 15 investment manager signatories, and 6 professional service partners

This, however, must be placed in the context that, as at 31 October 2007, there were 1,595 063 Australian companies registered with the Australian Securities and Investments Commission (ACSI 2007b), and as at 30 June 2007, the Australian Stock Exchange had 2090 listed companies, with a domestic market capitalization of AU$1.63 trillion (US$1.38 trillion) (ASX 2007c).

The mining giant BHP Billiton (www.bhpbilliton.com; market capitalization as at 30 June 2007: US$165 billion) has become an Australian leader in CSR. It divides its strategy into business and sustainability dimensions; of the latter, it states that:

'Our bottom line performance is, however, dependent upon ensuring access to resources and gaining and maintaining a license to operate and grow. Maximizing bottom line performance is about recognizing the value protection and value add to be achieved through performance in non-financial dimensions - or sustainability dimensions, such as:

- Aspiring towards Zero Harm to people, our host communities and the environment
- Ensuring that effective governance and risk management processes are in place, to ensure that a precautionary approach is taken to achieving business outcomes
- Recognizing the need to be socially responsible and contribute to sustainable community development
- Ensuring the broader economic contributions of our operations that are effectively injected into the regions where we operate' (BHP 2007)

Westpac (www.westpac.com; market capitalization as at 30 September 2007: AU$53.2 billion) is another example of an outstanding Australian corporate citizen. In 2006, it maintained its position as global banking sector leader in the Dow Jones Sustainability Index for the fifth year in a row, and was re-elected Chair of the Global Steering Committee for the United Nations Environment Program Finance Initiative. Its CSR activities are demonstrated in its *Stakeholder Impact Report* (Westpac 2006), which is prepared in accordance with the 2006 'G3' GRI Guidelines, but even in this report the link to the business case is not made explicit in quantitative terms. Like BHP, Westpac's position may have been driven by its past; in the years leading up to 1992, 'Westpac squandered billions of dollars of its shareholders' money in less than half a dozen years. How it did that is a story of hubris, greed, vision, arrogance, ambition, fear and incompetence. The bank turned 175 years of business leadership into unprecedented financial disaster that left its shareholders alienated and its customers disgusted' (Carew 1997).

Driven by Brisbane's serious water shortage, Coca-Cola Amatil's Richlands site in Brisbane 'has reduced water consumption by almost 20 per cent from 2004 to 2006, despite a production increase of 11 per cent. The team at Richlands has embraced a culture in which water saving is considered a necessity, not a luxury' (QWC 2007).

CSR is often driven from the top, and Birch and Littlewood (2004) found that there was a positive attitude towards corporate citizenship by Australian CEOs and senior executives invited to a conference on corporation citizenship. This, however, is in contrast to the attitudes evident in the CPA Australia report (see 22.7 below), suggesting that Birch and Littlewood's sample was not representative. Indeed, McLellan found that, in a study of 241 company directors between 2004 and 2006, 'when discussing the risks that are most likely to occasion strategic failure the directors in the research made no mention of: ethics or morality sustainability, environment or CSR . . . ' (2007: 459).

Zappala argues that corporate community involvement has an important role in, and should be more closely aligned with, HRM, but that 'the HRM function is not playing a significant role with respect to CCI decision-making and implementation among top companies in Australia' (2004:198–199). The complexity of stakeholder management has resulted in two Australian companies developing software to assist with the task (Houghes and Demetrious 2006). Acttiv developed *Active Community Engagement*; it has since been taken over by Jurat Canada and trades as Jurat Australia. Reputation Qest developed *Stakeholder Database*; it has since been taken over by GDH.

Actions, however, must not be uncritically assumed to be motivated by a belief in CSR. As noted in a Chamber of Commerce and Industry paper:

'Indeed, even giving public expression to disagreement with the prevailing acceptance of corporate social and environmental responsibility may invite a public outcry which could be harmful to the corporation. So a chief executive who took seriously the responsibility to maximize shareholder value wouldn't do it. There is clearly a paradox here. Business leaders committed to maximizing shareholder value are obliged by that very commitment to maintain a reputation for social and environmental responsibility and to keep quiet any reservations they might have. So dissenting business operators are largely absent from the debate on the merits of corporate social responsibility, triple bottom line accounting, and so on' (CCIWA 2002: 17).

21.5 Reporting on What Companies are Doing

There is no legal requirement in Australia for CSR reporting, other than under s.299(1) of the Corporations Act 2001 (introduced into the previous corporations act in 1999) which states that 'The director's report . . . must (f) if the entity's operations are subject to any particular and significant environmental regulation under law . . . give details of the entity's performance in relation to environmental regulation'; further information is given in ASIC 2007a, ss.68.72–68.75. The impact of this section on corporate environmental reporting has been examined by Frost (2007), who noted that it resulted in an increase in disclosure, but that there was a lack of consistency in how companies interpret the section (see also Burritt and Roger 2002: 393–395). However, Australian social and environmental NGOs 'very strongly advocate the introduction of legislation or standards requiring minimum disclosure levels' (Danastas and Gadenne 2006: 59).

The Chapman Report (2006) stated that 'it is premature to adopt the Global Reporting Initiative Framework as the voluntary Australian sustainability reporting framework; and that the Australian Government continue to monitor the acceptance and uptake of the Global Reporting Initiative Framework, both nationally and internationally, with a view to its suitability as the, or a basis for a, voluntary Australian sustainability reporting framework' (s.7.55). Reporting against the GRI in Australia is discussed in Frost *et al.* (2005) and Loftus and Purcell (2006a).

Studies of social and environmental disclosures in the 1980s and 1990s have been undertaken by Deegan *et al.* (2000, 2002). An important initiative to encourage voluntary disclosure was undertaken by Environment Australia through the Natural Heritage Trust, with the publication of *A Framework for Public Environmental Reporting* (National Heritage Trust 2000), and a subsequent study of *The State of Public Environmental Reporting in Corporate Australia* (CAER 2003). The latter included a section on the 'Benefits of Producing PERs', noting that the most commonly given reasons by companies for public environmental reporting were reputation enhancement (77%), gain confidence of investors, insurers, and financial institutions (65%), improved management of risks (62%), and operational and management improvements (59%) (p. 20).

Many companies now mention CSR in their annual reports, often in the Chairman's report where it is used as a marketing tool. Few Australian companies present good CSR/Sustainability reports; many of the best are found in the online library maintained by the Australian Government Department of the Environment and Water Resources; as at 2007 there are 400 reports from 122 organizations. (www.environment.gov.au/settlements/industry/corporate/reporting/reports/index. html). Guidelines with Australian examples, such as Suggett and Goodsir (2002), or guidelines specific to environmental reporting, such as Environment Australia (2003), have been developed to assist companies with their reporting. There is also an interim Australia standard on verification, validation, and assurance of environmental and sustainability reports (Standards Australia 2005). It was, however, noted in a recent report that 'the common observation is that good news is in the annual reports and bad news in the media' (Opinion Leaders 2007: 18).

KPMG (2005: 10) noted that reporting rates in Australia was comparatively low, with only 23% of the S&P/ASX100 reporting, compared to 71% in the UK. Roger Adams, technical director of ACCA, has stated that 'sustainability reporting on other countries has reached a point where Australia's half-hearted acceptance of the practice is becoming noticeable, and that a 'grudging approach' may lead to questions being asked of Australian companies' long-term

strategy for meeting their regulatory and corporate governance responsibilities'
(Kellerman 2005).

The situation, however, appears not to be so bleak. McMurtrie (2005) found that
in the companies he examined (although too small a sample), the Annual Report
contained less than 10% of the organizations' total corporate social disclosures, with
the internet being the preferred medium. Lodhia (2005, 2006a, b) has undertaken
detailed investigations of web-based dissemination of environmental information
by Australian mining companies.

21.5.1 Department of the Environment and Heritage Report

In 2005, the Centre for Australian Ethical Research, KPMG, and Deni Greene Consulting Services produced a report for the Australian Government on *The State of
Sustainability Reporting in Australia* (DEH 2005). Undertaken annually since 2003,
it looked at 'a broad range of non-financial reports' including triple bottom line reports, environment reports, and community reports. It found that, of the 486 companies covered by the survey, 24% produce a sustainability report. Of those that
produce reports, 55% are in the mining and manufacturing sectors (p. 3). Reports
are independently verified in 34% of cases, an increase from 28% in 2004. Reporting 'in accordance with' or 'with reference to' GRI Guidelines increased from 35%
in 2004 to 51% in 2005 (p. 9).

21.5.2 CPA Australia Report

CPA Australia's *Sustainability Reporting: Practices, Performance and Potential*
(CPA 2005a) found that:
'only a small proportion of listed entities prepare discrete reports on sustainabil-
ity/ TBL issues. These companies generally also provide disclosures about sustain-
ability/TBL issues in their annual reports and on their websites. The evidence of
low levels of sustainability reporting is contrasted with the growing global trend toward increasing corporate social responsibility. . . . The diversity of reporting scope
and format impedes comparison of environmental and social performance between
entities. . . . The inability or reluctance of organizations to modify or develop tools,
processes and frameworks through which they can report their direct and indirect
economic, social and environmental impacts to stakeholders provides a challenge
for the accounting profession and policymakers. In particular, there is a need to develop more accessible approaches and guidelines to enable entities to discharge a
broader accountability than that is currently reflected in reporting practices in the
public and private sectors in Australia' (p. 19).

CPA Australia has also published a study on regulatory and professional initiatives in sustainability reporting across the Asia Pacific (CPA 2005c).

21.5.3 ASX Report

The ASX reviews reporting by the listed companies. In its review of the 2005 reporting year, it noted that of 1,162 annual reports, 108 (including 43% of the Top 300 companies) included reporting which falls in the categories of corporate responsibility, corporate social responsibility, sustainability/environmental, community or people reporting; it was noted that reporting in a separate sustainability report or on a sustainability section of the company's website was not included in this analysis (ASX 2006: 13).

21.6 Evaluating and Rewarding CSR in Australia

Independent awards, evaluations, and rankings for CSR pay an important role in not only rewarding but also justifying CSR, and success is usually announced in press releases, displayed on websites, and featured in annual reports.

21.6.1 CSR Awards and Competitions

The ACCA Australia and New Zealand Awards for Sustainability Reporting (australia.accaglobal.com/australia/publicinterest/sustainability), begun by the ACCA in Britain in 1991, were introduced into Australia in 2002. In 2006, some 39 organizations competed. According to the criteria, 'An excellent sustainability report clearly acknowledges and explains the environmental and social impacts of an organization's operations and products. The report also demonstrates the organization's policies, targets and long-term objectives to reduce any adverse environmental and social impacts' (ACCA, 2006 p. 4) In the 2006 Judges' Comments, which provide an important overview of weaknesses in sustainability reporting in Australia, it is noted that the standard of sustainability reporting is not increasing, and it is suggested that Australian companies should look to Japan for models. It is also noted that 'too often, companies address trivial sustainability matters in their reports, without dealing with the bigger picture sustainability issues' (p. 11).

The Australasian Reporting Awards Inc. (ABN: 29 9232 99251; www.arawards.com.au), an independent not-for-profit organization, was founded in 1950 as the Annual Report Awards, with the aim of improving the standard of financial reporting in Australia by having companies benchmark their reports against the ARA criteria. In 1997, a Special Award for Excellence reporting on environmental matters was introduced, now renamed the Sustainability Reporting Award, the criteria for which focus on completeness, credibility (internal and external), and communication.

In 1995, the Australian Government established the Greenhouse Challenge, which in 2004 became the Greenhouse Challenge Plus (www.greenhouse.

gov.au/challenge), managed by the Australian Greenhouse Office as part of
the Australian Government's Department of the Environment and Water Resources. It aims to reduce greenhouse gas emissions, accelerate the uptake of energy efficiency, integrate greenhouse issues into business decision-
making, and provide more consistent reporting of greenhouse gas emissions
levels. Government also markets the challenge to business as a way to
'strengthen environmental credentials and demonstrate good corporate citizenship'
(www.greenhouse.gov.au/challenge/members/marketingtools.html). To date, some
700 businesses and industry bodies from throughout Australia and across industry sectors, have been involved. (www.greenhouse.gov.au/challenge/members/
pubs/list_of_challengers.pdf). Although originally, from 2006, totally voluntary
companies receiving fuel excise credits of more than $3 million, are required to
participate.

21.6.2 Indices

The Corporate Responsibility Index (www.corporate-responsibility.com.au), developed in the UK by Business in the Community (www.bitc.org.uk), was li-
censed without fee to the St. James Ethics Centre for use in Australia and, in
partnership with two leading daily newspapers, the *The Sydney Morning Herald* and Melbourne's *The Age*, was launched in Australia with the inaugural
awards, covering 2003, being made on 28 August 2004. The most recent awards,
made in 2007 and covering 2006, had 34 participating companies with a total
of 1.25 million employees; they included 14 of the ASX 50 (www.corporate-
responsibility.com.au/PDFs/cri_results_2006.pdf).

The Good Reputation Index was compiled between 2000 and 2002 by Reputation Management (now Reputex Australia Pacific, ABN 75 097 546 426;
www.reputationmeasurement.com.au), the rankings undertaken by a wide range of
organizations; for example, social impact was examined by a major Australian charity, The Smith Family (see Cronin *et al.* 2001b). The index was heavily criticized
by Johns (2003) and Johns (2005).

The National Stock Exchange of Australia (ABN: 11 000 902 063;
www.nsxa.com.au), which changed its name on 22 December 2006 from the Stock
Exchange of Newcastle, was 'established specifically for the listing of small to
medium sized companies'. Its Sustainability and Cleantech Investment Market,
which operates as a board promoted by the Financial and Energy Exchange Ltd
(FEX) (ABN: 20 122 086 284; www.fexclimate.com) launched by sustainability
campaigner and former US Vice-President Al Gore on 19 September 2007. Its vision is 'to help develop externality recognition in capital markets'.

Sustainable Asset Management Australia (ABN: 72 097 840 821), founded in
2001 as a wholly owned subsidiary of the Switzerland-based SAM Group Holding AG, launched the Australian SAM Sustainability Index (AuSSI) in February
2005 (see www.aussi.net.au). It 'tracks the performance of Australian companies

that lead their industry in terms of corporate sustainability. Based on a thorough assessment of economic, environmental and social criteria, the AuSSI comprises the top sustainability-driven companies from each of 21 industry clusters covering the entire Australian economy' (SAM 2006: 5). A cluster such as 'food, beverages, and tobacco' makes it clear that a product that some people may consider it to be socially irresponsible to sell, namely tobacco, may be included on the index, highlighting a difference between 'sustainability' and 'corporate social responsibility'.

The Dow Jones Sustainability Indexes (www.sustainability-indexes.com) identifies its sustainability leaders based on SAM Indices. Of the 318 companies on the DJSI World Index as at 31 October 2007, twenty-one were Australian companies: AGL Energy, AMP, ASX Ltd, Australian and New Zealand [ANZ] Banking Group, BHP Billiton, Bluescope Steel, Brambles, CFS Retail Property Trust, Coles Group (delisted from the ASX in November 2007 after takeover by Wesfarmers), Commonwealth Property Office Fund, GPT, Insurance Australia Group, Lend Lease Corp., National Australia Bank, Rio Tinto, Stockland, Tabcorp Holdings, Transurban Group, Wesfarmers, Westpac, and Woodside Petroleum. As such, Australia is ranked 8th in the world in terms of number of companies listed.

SustainAbility (www.sustainability.com), in its *The Global Reporters 2006 Survey of Corporate Sustainability Reporting*, listed four Australian companies in the Top 50: two mining companies, BHP Billiton (12) and Rio Tinto (19); and two banks: Westpac (20) and Mecu (41). Three of these are on the DJSI; Mecu is not as it is an unlisted co-operative.

The Global 100 (www.global100.org) in 2007 listed three Australian companies, all in the finance sector, among the world's 100 most sustainable corporations: Insurance Australia Group, Investa Property Group (purchased in September 2007 by Morgan Stanley Real Estate and delisted), and Westpac.

21.7 The Role of Investors

In *Investor Attitudes to Corporate Social Responsibility* (Opinion Leaders 2007), a survey of Australian shareholders, it was noted that individual investors have 'notions of altruism' but that institutional investors are focused on 'ensuring continuity of adequate returns' (p. 15); both groups therefore desire the same ends, but for different reasons. Three quarters of investors know about the CSR activities of some of at least some of the companies in which they invest (p. 21), however negative CSR has a bigger impact on investment decisions than positive CSR (p. 25). Investors also wished to avoid certain industry sectors, notable Gaming (65%), Defense supplies (37%), Alcohol (34%), and Tobacco (24%); no other industry was above 10% (p. 26).

Hanson and Tranter found that 'considerable proportions of shareholders have ethical concerns that influence their Shareholding'(2006: 31), but Vyvyan *et al.* found that 'financial performance is the most influential factor when it comes to investment decision-making. Our evidence suggests that this is even the case for those who indicate strong attitudes towards factors such as environmentalism' (2007: 379).

This latter finding consistent with the study *Do Australian Institutional Investors Aim to Influence the Human Resource Practices of Investee Companies*, which found that the studied institutional investors 'believe that companies that pursue "high commitment" human resource practices are more likely to produce long-term value for members than those that adopt poor human resource practices', and this was related 'to the broader risk management strategies of institutional investors. It was not conceived of in ethical terms' (**? ?**: 60). In 2006, the Australian Council of Super Investors signed the UN Principles of Responsible Investment, and stated that its 'engagement with companies will broaden to take account of material Environmental, Social and Governance (ESG) risks' (ACSI 2006: 2), and in a discussion paper noted that 'the availability of robust information on material CSR risks and rewards is a critical requirement to provide investment decision-makers with the confidence to integrate CSR criteria into investment, engagement and analytic strategies with the assurance that fiduciary responsibilities can be maintained' (ACSI 2005: 2). The rise of the institutional shareholder, especially as a result of Australia's compulsory superannuation, has seen increasing expectations on institutional investors taking a leading role in the drive towards corporate social responsibility.

Responsible investment is clearly growing: between 2004 and 2007, managed responsible investment portfolios grew from $4.5 billion to $17.1 billion, an increase of 380%, and in the 2006–07 financial year, core responsible investment (including managed portfolios, community finance, green loans and ethical portfolios of charities and clients of financial advisers) grew from $13.52 billion to $19.39 billion, an increase of 43% (RIAA 2007: 3). Clearly, many investors are not only prepared to put their money into socially responsible investments, but actually do. This should further encourage corporations to become socially responsible.

21.7.1 CPA Australia Report

It is clear from the CPA report that, to generalize, the public and shareholders want socially and environmentally responsible business, but the company directors, CEOs, and CFOs share this enthusiasm to a significantly lesser extent.

In 2005, CPA Australia's annual *Confidence in Corporate Reporting* (CPA 2005b) sampled 700 people on corporate social responsibility (the 2006 report focused on other issues and so is not discussed here). The results were published are aggregated into five groups, so that comparisons may be made: the public; shareholders; analysts, advisors and brokers; Directors/CEOs/CFOs; and Auditors.

Those seen as being 'very responsible' for a company meeting its environmental and social obligations, were the Board of Directors (67%), followed by the CEO (66%), the Government (58%); shareholders were not seen to have a high level of responsibility (15%) (pp. 2–3)

Stakeholders were seen as being above all shareholders (92%), followed by employees (85%), the local environment where the business operates (71%), creditors

(71%), customers (65%), local communities where the business operates (63%), future generations (45%), and the Australian public (44%). Of concern is that only 34% of the Directors/CEOs/CFOs believed that future generations were stakeholders, and 30% that the Australian public were stakeholders, whereas for shareholders the figures were 45% and 47%, respectively (p. 4).

The proportion of people who agreed to the following questions (percentage in brackets) paints a picture of a need for improvement in CSR by Australia companies, and of the disjuncture between the views of Directors/CEOs/CFOs (CD) and Shareholders (S) (pp. 6, 23):

- A company exists only to build shareholder value (49%, CD 58%, S 43%)
- Australian company directors adequately balance the financial performance of the company with its social and environmental concerns (51%, CD 58%, S 46%)
- Financial performance is more important than social and environmental concerns (43%, CD 53%, S 34%)
- The interests of the shareholders and other stakeholders should be of equal importance to the company (78%, CD 66%, S 87%)
- Australian company directors have adequate regard to the interests of all stakeholders (45%; CD 54%; S 31%)
- Institutional investors should encourage better social and environmental practices from companies on behalf of the Australian community (86%, CD 82%, S 89%)
- Companies' social and environmental reporting is just a public relations exercise (54%, CD 51%, S 60%)

The public is willing to make sacrifices for CSR: 68% of shareholders would be prepared to accept a lower investment return from a company with an excellent social reputation, and 72% would be prepared to accept lower returns from a company with an excellent environmental reputation (p. 14). Of the public, 57% would accept a lower wage/salary to work for a company with an excellent social and environmental reputation (p. 12). CSR also affects the public decision to purchase a company's products and services, with more than half being discouraged a lot by a poor environmental or social reputation.

21.8 Australia in an International Context

The other chapters in this volume provide a current and rich international context against which the reader can assess the current position and direction of CSR in Australia. As such, only a few brief observations will be made here and, owing to the availability of data, they are restricted to large companies.

A number of studies have made international comparisons using the FTSE All World Developed Index (AWDI), which over the period of these studies, consisted of almost 2000 companies in 23 countries. Australia ranks well above average with regard to quality of corporate codes of business ethics and for the system of implementing the ethics code (EIRIS 2005: 4–5). Australia performs only slightly above average with regard to SEE risk management grades (Tozer 2005: 8), which given the focus on CSR as risk management is perhaps surprising. It performs below average with regard to environmental management systems: the AWDI average for high environmental-impact companies having ISO14001 certified sites is 59.8%, but Australia has only 38.3%, ranking 20th of 23 countries (Maier and Vanstone 2005: 8). Australian companies perform extremely well on advanced adoption (3rd out of 21 countries) and reporting (2nd of 21 countries) on human rights in their operations in high risk countries (Gordon 2007: 41, 43), but perform poorly with regard to supply chain labor rights (47–48). Gordon ranks Australia 12th out of 23 countries for percentage of companies adopting community involvement strategies (2005: 67). Overall, he states that, with regard to environmental, social and governance challenges, 'Australian, New Zealand and Canadian companies do not perform exceptionally on any issues compared to their peers in other countries' (2005: 8).

With regard to reporting, a study by KPMG of the top 100 companies in each of 16 countries listed Australia as 11 out of 16 countries for production of separate corporate responsibility reports, and 14 out of 16 countries for production of a corporate responsibility report, either separately or as part of their Annual Report (2005: 10).

21.9 Conclusion

Australian companies increasingly see CSR as an important issue but, with a small number of notable exceptions including BHP Billiton and Westpac, are lagging behind other developed countries. The general public has a much more positive attitude to CSR than either the government or Directors/CEOs/CFOs. Although shareholders support CSR, in neither 2005/2006 nor 2006/2007 were there any shareholder resolutions relating to social or environmental responsibility, indicating a lack of shareholder activism on these issues (RIAA 2007: 4). It is expected that institutional shareholders, especially superannuation funds, will play an increasingly important role in ensuring that companies take a long term view of benefits, including risk reduction, of CSR.

The 2007 Mercer Quality of Living Survey placed all Australian cities with more than 1 million people among the world's best, ranging from Sydney in 9th position, to Brisbane at 31st (www.mercer.com). The GDP per capita, at US$33,300, ranks 22 in the world, higher than the UK, Germany, or Japan (CIA Factbook 2007). There is a generous social welfare system, and universal health coverage through Medicare. By land, Australia is the world's sixth largest country, but with a population of just over 21 million (ABS 2007), it is a sparsely populated country, and so dirty industries can be placed out of sight. Australia has vast reserves of coal, gas, and 30% of the world's known recoverable reserves of uranium. Further, the conservative Australian Government under John Howard (1996–2007) had little interest in developing legislative or other formal structures, or progressive networks, for the development of CSR, until the environment became a core issue in the lead-up to the Federal Election on 26 November 2007. That CSR, apart from issues relating to global warming and water, has not become a more prominent issue, is surely linked to former government's attitude to CSR, and to Australia's standard of living and strong social welfare system which reduce the social, if not the business, imperative for corporations to be socially responsible. Whether or not the labor Australian Government under Kevin Rudd, sworn in on 3 December 2007, leads a move towards CSR remains to be seen, but the ratification of the Kyoto Protocol as the first official act of his government is an auspicious start.

Acknowledgments

I would like to thank Sumit Lodhia, School of Accounting and Business Information Systems, The Australian National University, and two anonymous reviewers, for comments on a draft of this chapter.

References

ABS. (2002). Australian Bureau of Statistics. *Generosity of Australian Business 2000–01*. Report 8157.0. Canberra: Australian Bureau of Statistics.

ABS. (2007). *Australian Bureau of Statistics: Population Clock*. http://www.abs.gov.au/ausstats/abs%40.nsf/94713ad445ff1425ca25682000192af2/1647509ef7e25faaca2568a900154b63?Open Document. Accessed 10 December 2007.

ACCA Australia. (2006). Association of Chartered Certified Accountants Australia and New Zealand. *Report of the Judges*. http://australia.accaglobal.com/pubs/australia/publicinterest/sustainability/archive/au06_jud.pdf

ACOSS. (2005). Australian Council of Social Service. *Giving Australia: Research on Philanthropy in Australia. Survey of Business*. http://www.partnerships.gov.au/downloads/Survey%20of%20Business_final%20for%20online%20release.PDF

ACSI. (2005). Australian Council of Super Investors Inc. *Corporate Social Responsibility: Guidance for Investors. Executive Summary*. [Full paper not publicly available.] Prepared by [Ken Coghill, On Kit Tam, and Leeora Black]. Melbourne: ACSI. www.acsi.org.au/documents/CSR_Monash_Paper_(website).doc

ACSI. (2006). *Annual Activities Statement for the Financial Year Ended 30 June 2006*. Melbourne: ACSI. www.acsi.org.au/documents/ACSI_Annual_Report_2006_web.pdf

AICD. (2002). Australian Institute of Company Directors. *Policy: Sustainability*. http://www.companydirectors.com.au/Policy/Policies+And+Papers/2002/Sustainability.htm

Anderson, Helen, and Ingrid Landau. (2006). *Corporate Social Responsibility in Australia: A Review*. Corporate Law and Accountability Research Group, Monash University, Working Paper No. 4. http://www.buseco.monash.edu.au/blt/clarg/working-paper-4.pdf

ASA. (2005). Australian Shareholders Association. *Shareholders Expect*. http://www.asa.asn.au/PolicyStatements/ShareholdersExpect.pdf

ASIC. (2007a). Australian Securities and Investments Commission. *New Financial Reporting and Procedural Requirements*. Regulatory Guide 68. Sydney: Australian Securities and Investments Commission. http://www.asic.gov.au/asic/pdflib.nsf/lookupbyfilename/pn68.pdf/$file/pn68.pdf

ACSI. (2007b). '2007 Company Registration Statistics'. http://www.asic.gov.au/asic/asic.nsf/byheadline/2007+company+registration+statistics?openDocument. Accessed 16 November 2007.

ASX. (2003). Australian Stock Exchange. *Principles of Good Corporate Governance and Best Practice Recommendations.* Sydney: Australian Stock Exchange. http://www.shareholder.com/visitors/dynamicdoc/document.cfm?documentid=364&companyid=ASX

ASX. (2006). *2005 Analysis of corporate governance practice disclosure.* [Sydney]: Australian Stock Exchange.

ASX. (2007a). *Corporate Governance Principles and Recommendations.* 2nd edition. Sydney: ASX Corporate Governance Council. http://asx.ice4.interactiveinvestor.com.au/ASX0701/Corporate%20Governance%20Principles/EN/body.aspx?z=1&p=-1&v=1&uid=

ASX. (2007b). *Response to Submissions on Review of Corporate Governance Principles and Recommendations.* Sydney: ASX Corporate Governance Council. http://www.asx.com.au/supervision/pdf/corp_governance_response_to_submissions_aug07.pdf

ASX. (2007c). 'ASX at a glance'. http://www.asx.com.au/about/asx/index.htm. Accessed 16 November 2007.

Australian Permanent Mission to the UN. (2004). *Comments by Australia in respect of the report requested from the Office of the High Commissioner on Human Rights in its decision 2004/116 of 20 April 2004 on existing initiatives and standards relating to the responsibility of transnational corporations and related business enterprises with regard to human rights.* 8 September, received by OHCHR Registry 13 September. www2.ohchr.org/english/issues/globalization/business/docs/australia.pdf Accessed 6 December 2007.

Baker & McKenzie. (2007). *Corporate Responsibility: A Guide for Australian Directors.* Sydney: Baker & McKenzie. http://www.moss.org.au/home/images/stories/2007/bmcsaguideforaustraliandirectors.pdf

Batten, Jonathan A., and David Birch. (2005). 'Defining corporate citizenship: Evidence from Australia'. *Asia Pacific Business Review* 11(3): 293–308.

BHP. (2007). BHP Billiton Ltd. 'Our approach to sustainability'. http://www.bhpbilliton.com/bb/sustainableDevelopment/ourApproachToSustainability.jsp

Birch, David. (2003). *Directory of Resources Promoting Responsible and Sustainable Business and Society: Networks and Organisations in Australia and Overseas.* Deakin University Corporate Citizenship Research Unit. http://www.deakin.edu.au/arts/ccr/menu/directoryofsustainabilitywithwebsites1.pdf

Birch, David, and George Littlewood. (2004). 'Corporate Citizenship: Some perspectives from Australian CEOs'. *The Journal of Corporate Citizenship* 16: 61–69.

Black, Leeora D. (2006). 'Corporate Social Responsibility as Capability: The Case of BHP Billiton'. *The Journal of Corporate Citizenship* 23: 25–38.

Brennan, Gerard. (2002). 'Law, values and charity', *Australian Law Journal* 76: 492–498.

Brown, Gerard. (2006). 'Australia and New Zealand Banking Group (ANZ): Aligning community strategy with business strategy'. *The Journal of Corporate Citizenship* 22: 18–22.

Burritt, Roger. (2002). 'Environmental reporting in Australia: current practices and issues for the future'. *Business Strategy and the Environment* 11: 391–406.

CAMAC. (2006a). Australian Government Corporations and Markets Advisory Committee. *The Social Responsibility of Corporations: Report.* http://www.camac.gov.au/camac/camac.nsf/byHeadline/PDFFinal+Reports+2006/$file/CSR_Report.pdf

CAMAC. (2006b). Australian Government Corporations and Markets Advisory Committee. *The Social Responsibility of Corporations: Summary of Submissions.* http://www.camac.gov.au/camac/camac.nsf/byHeadline/PDFFinal+Reports+2006/$file/CSR_Summary_of_Submissions.pdf

CAER. (2003). Centre for Australian Ethical Research. *The State of Public Environmental Reporting in Corporate Australia.* http://www.environment.gov.au/settlements/industry/finance/publications/state-of-per/pubs/state-of-per.pdf

Carew, Edna. (1997). *Westpac: The Bank that Broke the Bank.* Sydney: Double Day.

CCIWA. (2002). Chamber of Commerce and Industry Western Australia. *Shareholders, Stakeholders, Ethics, and Social Responsibility: A Discussion of Views of Business Accountability.* http://www.sustainability.dpc.wa.gov.au/docs/submissions/CCIBusinessAccountability.pdf

CCPA. (2000). Centre for Corporate Public Affairs in conjunction with Business Council of Australia. *Corporate Community Involvement: Establishing a Business Case.* http://www.partnerships.gov.au/downloads/ccipart1.pdf and http://www.partnerships.gov.au/downloads/ccipart2.pdf

CCPA. (2007). The Centre for Corporate Public Affairs, Business Council of Australia, and Prime Minister's Community Business Partnership. *Corporate Community Investment in Australia.* http://www.partnerships.gov.au/downloads/cci_report_07.pdf

Chapman Inquiry. (2005–2006a). Parliamentary Joint Committee on Corporations and Financial Services Inquiry into Corporate Responsibility. *Public Hearings and Transcripts.* http://www.aph.gov.au/Senate/committee/corporations_ctte/corporate_responsibility/hearings/index.htm

Chapman Inquiry.(2005–2006b). Parliamentary Joint Committee on Corporations and Financial Services Inquiry into Corporate Responsibility. *Submissions Received by the Committee.* http://www.aph.gov.au/Senate/committee/corporations_ctte/corporate_responsibility/submissions/sublist.htm

Chapman Report. (2001). The Parliament of the Commonwealth of Australia Parliamentary Joint Statutory Committee on Corporations and Securities. *Report on the Corporate Code of Conduct Bill 2000.* www.aph.gov.au/Senate/Committee/corporations_ctte/completed_inquiries/1999–02/corp_code/report

Chapman Report. (2006). Parliamentary Joint Committee on Corporations and Financial Services. *Corporate responsibility: Managing risk and creating value.* http://www.aph.gov.au/Senate/committee/corporations_ctte/corporate_responsibility/report/report.pdf

Cooney Report. (1989). The Parliament of the Commonwealth of Australia Senate Standing Committee on Legal and Constitutional Affairs. *Company Director's Duties: Report on the Social and Fiduciary Duties and Obligations of Company Directors.* http://www.takeovers.gov.au/display.asp?ContentID=542

Corporations Act 2001. Commonwealth of Australia. http://www.austlii.edu.au/au/legis/cth/consol_act/ca2001172/

CPA Australia. (2005a). *Sustainability Reporting: Practices, Performance and Potential.* Melbourne: CPA Australia. http://www.cpaaustralia.com.au/cps/rde/xbcr/SID-3F57FECA-F54BD4AB/cpa/sustainability_report.pdf

CPA Australia. (2005b). *Confidence in Corporate Reporting 2005: Detailed Findings.* Melbourne: CPA Australia. http://www.cpaaustralia.com.au/cps/rde/xbcr/SID-3F57FECA-36953E3F/cpa/CICR.pdf

CPA Australia. (2005c). *Sustainability Reporting: Perspectives on Regulatory and Professional Initiatives across the Asia Pacific.* Melbourne: CPA Australia. http://www.cpaaustralia.com.au/cps/rde/xbcr/SID-3F57FECA-F4619D06/cpa/sustainability_reporting_asia_pacific.pdf

CPA Australia. (2007). *Policy Statement: Corporate Social Responsibility and Corporate Disclosure.* https://www.cpaaustralia.com.au/cps/rde/xbcr/SID-3F57FECA-0D7F4BF8/cpa/CSR_CD_policy_statement_2007.pdf

Cronin, Caitlin. (2001a). *Corporate Social Responsibility in Australia: A Select Review of the Literature.* The Smith Family Research & Social Policy Team Background Paper No. 3, 2001. Camperdown, N.S.W.: The Smith Family.

Cronin, Caitlin, Gianni Zappalà, and Melissa Clarkson. (2001b). *Measuring the social impact of companies in Australia: The Smith Family's participation in the Good Reputation Index.* The Smith Family Research and Social Policy Briefing Paper 1444–6383, No. 9. Camperdown NSW: The Smith Family.

Danastas, Lauren, and David Gadenne. (2006). 'Australian social and environmental NGOs: A study of their influencing activities on corporate social disclosure'. *The Journal of Corporate Citizenship* 23: 53–66.

Deegan, Craig, Michaela Rankin, and Peter Voght. (2000). 'Firms' disclosure reactions to major social incidents: Australian evidence.' *Accounting Forum* (Adelaide) 24(1): 101–130.

Deegan, Craig, Michaela Rankin, and John Tobin. (2002). 'An examination of corporate social environmental disclosures of BHP from 1983–1997.' *Accounting, Auditing & Accountability Journal* 15(3): 312–343.

Deegan, Craig, and Sharon Soltys. (2007). 'Social accounting research: An Australasian perspective'. *Accounting Forum* (Adelaide) 31: 73–89.

DEH. (2005). Australian Government Department of the Environment and Heritage. *The State of Sustainability Reporting in Australia 2005.* http://www.environment.gov.au/settlements/industry/corporate/reporting/pubs/survey2005.pdf

Deni Greene Consulting Services. (2001). *A capital idea: Realising value from environmental and social performance.* http://www.environment.gov.au/settlements/industry/finance/publications/pubs/capital-idea.pdf

Deva, Surya. (2004). 'Acting extraterritorially to tame multinational corporations for human rights violations: who should 'bell the cat'?' *Melbourne Journal of International Law* 5: 37–65.

EIRIS. (2005). Ethical Investment Research Services. *Corporate codes of business ethics: An international survey of bribery and ethical standards in companies.* London: EIRIS. http://www.eiris.org/files/research%20publications/corporatecodesofbusinessethicsep05.pdf

Environment Australia. (2003). *Triple Bottom Line Reporting in Australia: A Guide to Reporting against Environmental Indicators.* Australian Government Department of Environment and Heritage. http://www.environment.gov.au/settlements/industry/finance/publications/indicators/pubs/indicators.pdf

Frost, Geoff, Stewart Jones, Janice Loftus, and Sandra van der Laan. (2005). 'A survey of sustainability reporting practices of Australian reporting entities'. *Australian Accounting Review* 15(1): 89–96.

Frost, Geoffrey R. (2007). 'The introduction of mandatory environmental reporting guidelines: Australian evidence'. *Abacus* 43(2): 190–216.

Gordon, Bob. (2007). *The state of responsible business: Global corporate response to environmental, social and governance (ESG) challenges.* London: Ethical Investment Research Services. http://www.eiris.org/files/research%20publications/stateofrespbusinesssep07.pdf. Accessed 9 December 2007.

Hall, John. (2002). 'The social responsibility of corporations'. *Alternative Law Journal* 27(1): 12–15.

Hanson, Dallas, and Bruce Tranter. (2006). 'Who are the shareholders in Australia and what are their ethical opinions? An empirical analysis'. *Corporate Governance* 14(1): 23–32.

Hargroves, Karlson Charlie, and Michael H. Smith. (2005). *The Natural Advantage of Nations: Business Opportunities, Innovation and Governance in the 21st Century.* London: Earthscan.

Henley, Peter. (2005). 'Were corporate tsunami donations made legally?' *Alternative Law Journal* 30(4): 154–158.

Horrigan, Bryan. (2002). 'Fault lines in the intersection between corporate governance and social responsibility'. *University of New South Wales Law Journal* 25(2): 515–555.

Hughes, Patricia, and Kristin Demetrious. (2006). 'Engaging stakeholders or constructing them? Attitudes and assumptions in stakeholder software'. *Journal of Corporate Citizenship* 23: 93–101.

Hunting, Sally-Ann and Daniella Tilbury. (2006) *Shifting towards sustainability: Six insights into successful organisational change for sustainability.* Australian Research Institute in Education for Sustainability (ARIES) for the Australian Government Department of the Environment and Heritage, Sydney: ARIES. http://www.aries.mq.edu.au/pdf/InsightsBooklet.pdf

Johns, Gary. (2003). 'The Good Reputation Index: A tale of two strategies'. *IPA Backgrounder* 15(2). Melbourne: Institute of Public Affairs. http://www.ipa.org.au/files/IPABackgrounder 15-2.pdf

Johns, Gary. (2005). 'Deconstructing corporate social responsibility'. *Agenda* 12(4): 369–384. http://epress.anu.edu.au/agenda/012/04/12-4-NA-1.pdf

Jones, Meredith, Shelley Marshall, and Richard Mitchell. (2007). 'Corporate Social Responsibility and the Management of Labour in Two Australian Mining Industry Companies'. *Corporate Governance: An International Review* 15(1): 57–67.

Kellerman, Bernard. (2005) 'Strange Fruit'. *CFO Magazine* 1 June: 22. http://www.eia.org.au/html/s02_article/article_view.asp?id=309&nav_cat_id=280&nav_top_id=92&dsa=495#x

Kerr, Michael. (2004). *Greening our corporate law: A prerequisite for achieving sustainable development.* LLM Thesis, University of Sydney. http://www.aph.gov.au/Senate/committee/corporations_ctte/corporate_responsibility/submissions/sub07.pdf

KPMG. 2005. *KPMG International Survey of Corporate Social Responsibility Reporting.* http://www.kpmg.com/NR/rdonlyres/66422F7F-35AD-4256-9BF8-F36FACCA9164/0/KPMGIntlCRSurvey2005.pdf

Küskü, Fatma, and Anna Zarkada-Fraser. (2004). 'An empirical investigation of corporate citizenship in Australia and Turkey'. *British Journal of Management* 15: 57–72.

Livingstone, Catherine. (2007). 'ASX review of the Principles of Good Corporate Governance Part B of Consultation Paper: Response submission'. http://www.asx.com.au/supervision/governance/Submissions_on_review_of_principle.htm. Accessed 16 June 2007; not on website as at 31 October 2007.

Lodhia, Sumit. (2005). 'Legitimacy motives for World Wide Web environmental reporting: An exploratory study into present practices in the Australian minerals industry'. *Journal of Accounting and Finance* 4: 1–15.

Lodhia, Sumit (2006a). 'The World Wide Web and its potential for corporate environmental communication: A study into present practices in the Australian minerals industry'. *International Journal of Digital Accounting Research* 6(11): 65–94.

Lodhia, Sumit. (2006b). 'Corporate perceptions of Web based environmental communication: An exploratory study into companies in the Australian minerals industry'. *Journal of Accounting and Organizational Change* 2(1): 74–88.

Loftus, Janice A., and John A. Purcell. (2006a). 'Corporate Social Responsibility: Concepts, Approaches to Regulation and Public Sector Application of the GRI', *Financial Reporting, Regulation, and Governance* 5(1). http://www.cbs.curtin.edu.au/files/FRRaG_2006_5-1_professional_Loftus_Purcell.pdf

Loftus, Janice A., and John A. Purcell. (2006b). 'Regulatory developments in corporate social responsibility: Directors' and officers' duties and the role of reporting'. *Financial Reporting, Regulation, and Governance* 5(2). http://www.cbs.curtin.edu.au/files/FRRaG_2006_5-2_Professional_Purcell_Loftus.pdf

Loza, Jehan with Sarah Ogilvie. (2005). *Corporate Australia Building Trust and Stronger Communities? A Review of Current Trends and Themes.* Canberra: Department of Family and Community Services. http://www.partnerships.gov.au/downloads/Corporate%20Australia%20Building%20Trust%20and%20Stronger%20Communities.pdf

McLellan, Julie Garland. (2007). 'Directors' views of strategic risks'. *Keeping Good Companies* 59(8): 457–459. http://search.informit.com.au/fullText;dn=200710124;res=APAFT> Accessed 10 December 2007.

Madden, Kym, Wendy Scaife, and Kathryn Crissman. (2006). 'How and why small to medium size enterprises (SMEs) engage with their communities: An Australian study'. *International Journal of Nonprofit and Voluntary Sector Marketing* 11(1): 49-60.

Maier, Stephanie, and Kelly Vanstone. (2005). *Do good environmental management systems lead to good environmental performance?* London: Ethical Investment Research Services. http://www.eiris.org/files/research%20publications/emsperformanceoct05.pdf

Mays Report. (2003). Australian Govermnent Department of the Environment and Heritage and BT Financial Group (headed by Shaun Mays). *Corporate Sustainability: An Investor Perspective.* http://www.environment.gov.au/settlements/industry/finance/publications/mays-report/pubs/mays-report.pdf

McMurtrie, Tony. (2005). 'Factors influencing the publication of social performance information: An Australian case study'. *Corporate Social Responsibility and Environmental Management* 12: 129–143.

Moon, Jeremy. (1995). 'The firm as citizen? Social responsibility of business in Australia'. *Australian Journal of Political Science* 30: 1–17.

National Heritage Trust. (2000). *A Framework for Public Environmental Reporting: An Australian Approach.* Canberra: Environment Australia. http://www.environment.gov.au/settlements/industry/finance/publications/framework/pubs/perframework.pdf

NSX. (2007). National Stock Exchange of Australia. 'Press Release: Al Gore opens FEX SIM launch Wednesday, September 19, 2007'. http://www.nsxa.com.au/news_view.asp?id=150

Opinion Leaders. (2007). *Investor Attitudes to Corporate Social Responsibility: This extract has been specially prepared for ASA Members.* http://www.asa.asn.au/Miscellaneous/OpinionLeaderCSRSurveyResults.pdf

Parkinson, John. E. (1993). *Corporate Power and Responsibility: Issues in the Theory of Company Law.* Oxford: Clarendon.

Phillips, R. (2005). Australian NGOs: Current Experiences of Corporate Citizenship, *The Journal of Corporate Citizenship*, 17: 21–25

QWC. (2007). Queensland Water Commission. 'Business Leaders: Coca-Cola Amatil'. Press Release, 12 November 2007. http://www.qwc.qld.gov.au/tiki-read_article.php?articleId=181. Accessed 16 November 2007.

RIAA. (2007). Responsible Investment Association Australasia. *Responsible Investment 07: A Benchmark Report on Australia and New Zealand by the Responsible Investment Association Australasia.* http://www.eia.org.au/files/78RUBP9VVA/RIAA%20Benchmark%20Report%202007%20FINAL.pdf

Rudd, Kevin. (2007). 'Ratifying The Kyoto Protocol Media Statement—3rd December 2007'. http://www.alp.org.au/media/1207/mspm030.php. Accessed 5 December 2007.

SAM. (2006). *Australian SAM Sustainability Index Guide.* Version 3.0. http://www.aussi.net.au/aussi_pdf/AuSSI_publications/Guidebook/AuSSI_Guidebook_06.pdf

Sergeant, Adrian and Kathryn Crissman. (2006). 'Corporate giving in Australia: an analysis of motives and barriers'. *Australian Journal of Social Issues* 41(4): 477–492.

Smith, Dawn P. (2005). *The Management of Australian Corporate Philanthropy Perspectives of Donors and Managers: A Study of Motivations and Techniques.* Unpublished PhD thesis, Flinders University, South Australia. http://catalogue.flinders.edu.au/local/adt/public/adt-SFU20060523.132142/

Standards Australia. (2003). *Corporate social responsibility.* AS8003–2003. Sydney: Standards Australia.

Standards Australia. (2005). *General guidelines on the verification, validation and assurance of environmental and sustainability reports.* AS/NZS 5911(Int):2005. Sydney: Standards Australia.

Stubbs, Wendy, and Chris Cocklin. (2007). 'Cooperative, community-spirited *and* commercial: social sustainability at Bendigo Bank'. *Corporate Social Responsibility and Environmental Management* 14(5): 251–262.

Suggett, Dahle, and Ben Goodsir. (2002). *Triple Bottom Line Measurement and Reporting in Australia.* Melbourne: The Allen Consulting Group. http://www.allenconsult.com.au/resources/TBL_part1.pdf

SustainAbility. (2006). *Tomorrow's Value: The Global Reporters 2006 Survey of Corporate Sustainability Reporting.* London: SustainAbility. http://www.sustainability.com/downloads_public/insight_reports/tomorrowsvalue.pdf

Thomas, Gail, and Margaret Nowak. (2006). *Corporate Social Responsibility: A Definition.* GSB Working Paper No. 62. Perth, WA: Curtin University of Technology Graduate School of Business.

Tilbury, Daniella, Cathy Crawley, and Fiona Berry. (2004). *Education About and For Sustainability in Australian Business Schools.* Report prepared by the Australian Research Institute in Education for Sustainability and Arup Sustainability for the Australian Government Department of the Environment and Heritage. http://www.aries.mq.edu.au/pdf/MBA_Report.pdf

Tozer, David. (2005). *SEE risk management: A global analysis of its adoption by companies.* London: Ethical Investment Research Services. http://www.eiris.org/files/research%20publications/seeriskmanagementdec05.pdf

Vyvyan, Victoria, Chew Ng, and Mark Brimble. (2007). 'Socially responsible investing: The green attitudes and grey choices of Australian investors'. *Corporate Governance* 15(2): 370–381.

Westpac. (2006). *Westpac 2006 Stakeholder Impact Report.* http://www.westpac.com.au/manage/pdf.nsf/21F2EC3D9E013921CA25724200155A85/$File/SIR_2006.pdf?OpenElement

Wilson, Therese. (2005). 'The pursuit of profit at all costs: Corporate law as a barrier to corporate social responsibility'. *Alternative Law Journal* 30(6): 278–282.

Zappalà, Gianni. (2003a). *Corporate Citizenship and the Role of Government: The Public Policy Case.* Department of the Parliamentary Library Research Paper No. 4, 2003–04. Canberra: Information and Research Services, Department of the Parliamentary Library. http://wopared.parl.net/library/pubs/rp/2003-04/04rp04.pdf

Zappalà, Gianni. (2003b). *The motivations and benefits of employee volunteering: What do employees think?* Camperdown NSW: The Smith Family.

Zappalà, Gianni. (2004). 'Corporate citizenship and human resource management: A new tool or missed opportunity?' *Asia Pacific Journal of Human Resources* 42(2): 185–201.

Corporate Social Responsibility: Some Future Perspectives

Walter Leal Filho and Samuel O. Idowu

The subject matter of corporate social responsibility (CSR) is barely more than 20 years old. This interdisciplinary field has grown substantially since the late 1990s, and now generates a substantial amount of literature addressing a range of environmental, technical, political, economic, and policy issues within and across corporate boundaries. While most of the research efforts seen to date have been descriptive and normative, the understanding of institutional arrangements and practices has proven to be a new area of emphasis that is attracting greater scholarly attention. The impressive body of information and knowledge amassed in this book gives reason for optimism about the future perspectives of CSR and its related disciplines. First of all, in a world where projections about the future of mankind relate to population, water, food, energy, climate change, deforestation, biodiversity, and a host of other variables, the future prospect does not appear very optimistic in general terms; in fact, it looks bleak as some commentators would like to describe it. However, a serious attempt at installing the required CSR mechanisms on the part of corporate entities, governments, and international organizations will help to provide acceptable solutions that may assist mankind's efforts towards addressing these current environmental problems, as opposed to exacerbating them. All hands now appear to be on deck! Second, CSR allows companies to reassess their activities not only from merely an environmental perspective, but also from an integrated way and, concomitantly, catalyses a discussion on what can be done to achieve sustainable industry practices in both the industrialized and developing nations.

Furthermore, along the process of implementation of CSR policies, companies have the opportunity to interact with both their customers and suppliers to demonstrate their commitments, hence reaping the extra benefits in respect of marketing or even simply in improving their public image and reputation among the end users of their products or services and similarly amongst those they interact with, in their supply chains.

S. O. Idowu and W. L. Filho (eds.), *Global Practices of Corporate Social Responsibility*   497
© Springer-Verlag Berlin Heidelberg 2009

Equally, there are several reasons why we should all be concerned about the future of CSR. Industrialists and CSR experts alike all over the world believe that, although certain problems caused by some sectors of the industry will probably continue to level out due to increased corporate commitments to strategic CSR; unsound practices from some sector may create new socio-economic or environmental problems. Moreover, CSR commitments are likely to increase both qualitatively and quantitatively at a rate that keeps up with industrial growth, greater demands on time and resources, as well as other logistical issues may prevent a significant number of companies from engaging in CSR efforts. The reasons for this apparent dilemma are well known: CSR compels decision-makers in the business community to carefully balance productivity with resource use, bearing in mind important values such as ecological integrity and social cohesion. The key question as to whether material gains now will preclude material gains in the future is also a matter of continuous concern, along with those issues relating to consumer gratification and investor rewards.

A further problem is that, because of the various preconditions that need to be met in successfully implementing CSR practices, there is a risk that some enterprises in certain sectors of the economy may perhaps abandon corporate (social and sustainable development) goals as policy objectives (albeit some would still keep it as a conceptual framework) and resuscitate instead older, more narrow, and arguably less complicated goals of environmental protection that are perceived as being "easier" to pursue. The picture is a bit more complex in the case of multinational enterprises where all the factors pertaining to CSR have a moderate or considerable effect on financial performance and consequently shareholder value creation. Such a trend, which is potentially harmful, needs to be avoided by all means and replaced with appropriate mechanisms in order to ensure that companies pursuing CSR policies are adequately rewarded rather than being penalized, as a result of their socially responsible actions.

The main task of this book has been to document and report on current efforts in CSR across the globe. Future studies that may follow it should not only analyze the nature of the impending problems, but also suggests ways of solving them.

The future of CSR in both emerging and advanced economies appears to be promising; this is our view. Other indications also suggest it. The United Nations and some governments around the world are taking several commendable actions that are designed to ensure that our planet survives the test of time. Several actions taken by corporate entities in the quest for productivity and profitability in years past were without realizing their future consequences on both the environment and our natural resources; some of these consequences are gradually becoming apparent to us all. It is needless to say that, now is the time for actions by us all, wherever we are in the world. In the recently held Bali Climate Change Conference, Secretary General Ban Ki-moon of the United Nations rightly noted after the "Bali Roadmap" was adopted by the 187 countries present, when he referred to the agreement as "*A pivotal first step forward towards an agreement that can address the threat of climate change, 'the defining challenge of our time'*." That statement perhaps is a pointer to the future of CSR and its subsets, but only if we rise up to meet the challenge. Roadmap adoptions unbacked by actions by all nations, regardless of whether they are large or small, rich or poor, far or near, old or young might turn out to be a missed opportunity to avert an impending but preventable catastrophe on *mankind* and planet *Earth*.

About the Editors

Samuel O Idowu

Samuel O. Idowu is a senior lecturer at the city campus of London Metropolitan Business School, London Metropolitan University, where he was course organizer for Accounting Joint degrees and lately, the Course Leader/Personal Academic Adviser (PAA) for students taking Accounting Major/Minor and Accounting Joint degrees. He is a fellow member of the Institute of Chartered Secretaries and Administrators, a fellow of the Royal Society of Arts, a Liveryman of the Worshipful Company of Chartered Secretaries & Administrators and a named freeman of the City of London. Samuel has published about 31 articles in both professional and academic journals and contributed chapters in edited books. Samuel won one of the Highly Commended Emerald Literati Network Awards for Excellence in 2008. Samuel has been in academia for 20 years. He has examined for the following professional bodies: the Chartered Institute of Bankers (CIB) and the Chartered Institute of Marketing (CIM) and has marked examination papers for the Association of Chartered Certified Accountants (ACCA). His teaching career started in November 1987 at Merton College, Morden Surrey; he was a Lecturer/Senior Lecturer at North East Surrey College of Technology (Nescot) for 13 years, where he was the Course Leader for BA (Hons) Business Studies, ACCA and CIMA courses. He has also held visiting lectureship posts at Croydon College and Kingston University. He was a senior lecturer at London Guildhall University prior to its merger with the University of North London; when London Metropolitan University was created in August 2002. He is currently an External Examiner at the following Universities in the UK: Anglia Ruskin; in Chelmsford, Sunderland and Ulster in Belfast. Samuel is a Trustee and Treasurer of Age *Concern*, Hackney in East London and he is on the Editorial Advisory Board of the Management of Environmental Quality Journal. He has been researching in the field of CSR since 1983.

Walter Leal Filho

Professor Walter Leal Filho has a Ph.D. and a D.Sc. in environmental technology, plus a honorary doctorate (DL) in environmental information. He is the Head of the Research and Transfer Centre "Applications of Life Sciences" at the Hamburg University of Applied Sciences, where he is in charge of a number of European projects. He has authored, co-authored or edited over 40 books on the subjects of environment, technology and innovation and has in excess of 130 published papers to his credit.

Prof. Walter Leal Filho teaches environmental management at many European universities. He is also the editor of the Journal "Management of Environmental Quality" and founding editor of the "International Journal of Sustainability in Higher Education" and "Environment and Sustainable Development". He is a member of the editorial board of "Biomedical and Environmental Sciences", "Environmental Awareness", and "Sustainable Development and World Ecology". He is also the founding editor of the new "International Journal of Climate Strategies and Management" which will among other issues analyze the links between CSR and Climate Change. His work on CSR has primarily focused on the institutional aspects and tools for benchmarking within industry.

Index